Economics

Economics

Volume 5

Economic theory

GROLIER
EDUCATIONAL

Sherman Turnpike,
Danbury, Connecticut
06816

Published 2000 by Grolier Educational
Sherman Turnpike
Danbury, Connecticut 06816

© 2000 Brown Partworks Ltd

Set ISBN: 0-7172-9492-7
Volume ISBN: 0-7172-9570-2

Library of Congress Cataloging-in-Publication Data
Economics.
    p. cm.
    Includes index.
    Contents: v. 1 Money, banking, and finance — v. 2.
Business operations — v. 3. The citizen and the
economy — v. 4. The U.S. economy and the world —
v. 5. Economic theory — v. 6. History of economics
    ISBN 0-7172-9492-7 (set: alk. paper). — ISBN 0-7172-
9482-X (v. 1: alk. paper). — ISBN 0-7172-9483-8 (v. 2:
alk. paper). — ISBN 0-7172-9484-6 (v. 3: alk. paper). —
ISBN 0-7172-9485-4 (v. 4: alk. paper). — ISBN 0-7172-
9570-2 (v. 5: alk. paper). — ISBN 0-7172-9571-0 (v. 6:
alk. paper).
    1. Economics—Juvenile literature [1. Economics.] I.
Grolier Educational Corporation.

HB183. E26 2000
330—dc21   00-020414

For information address the publisher:
Grolier Educational, Sherman Turnpike,
Danbury, Connecticut 06816

FOR BROWN PARTWORKS LTD

Project editor:
Jane Lanigan
Editors: Tim Cooke, Julian
Flanders, Mike Janson,
Henry Russell
Editorial assistance:
Wendy Horobin,
Tim Mahoney,
Sally McEachern,
Chris Wiegand
Design: Tony Cohen,
Bradley Davis,
Matthew Greenfield
Picture research:
Helen Simm
Graphics: Mark Walker
Indexer: Kay Ollerenshaw

Project consultant: Robert
Pennington, Associate
Professor, College of
Business Administration,
University of Central
Florida
Text: John Andrew, Asatar
Bair, Sarah Culver,
Giuseppe Fontana, Amanda
Friedenberg, Rob Gayton,
Pura Granero-Gomez, Peter
Hess, Jane Lanigan, Henry
McCarl, Jack Morgan,
Dennis Muraoka, Adam
Potter, Alun Powell, Gary
Stone, Zuza Vrbova,
Jaejoon Woo

GROLIER
EDUCATIONAL

About this book

Economics is all around us. It covers almost
every aspect of life today, from how much
money you have in your pocket to the price of
real estate, from how much tax people pay to
the causes of wars in distant lands. In today's
world it is essential to understand how to manage your money, how to save wisely, and how
to shop around for good deals. It is also important to know the bigger picture: how financial
institutions work, how wealth is created and
distributed, how economics relates to politics,
and how the global economy works that ties
together everyone on the planet.

Economics places everyday financial
matters in the wider context of the sometimes
mysterious economic forces that shape our
lives, tracing the emergence of economic doc-
trines and explaining how economic systems
worked in the past and how they work now.

Each of the six books covers a particular area of economics, from personal finance to
the world economy. Five books are split into
chapters that explore their themes in depth.
Volume 5, Economic Theory, is arranged as an A-
Z encyclopedia of shorter articles about fundamental concepts in economics and can be used
as an accessible reference when reading the
rest of the set. At the end of every chapter or
article a See Also box refers you to related articles elsewhere in the set, allowing you to further investigate topics of particular interest.

The books contain many charts and
diagrams to explain important data clearly and
explain their significance. There are also special
boxes throughout the set that highlight particular subjects in greater detail. They might explain
how to fill out a check correctly, analyze the
theory proposed by a particular economist, or
tell a story that shows how economic theory
relates to events in our everyday lives.

If you are not sure where to find a
subject, look it up in the set index in each
volume. The index covers all six books, so it
will help you trace topics throughout the set.
There is also a glossary at the end of the book,
which provides a brief explanation of some of
the key words and phrases that occur throughout the volumes. The extensive Further Reading
list contains many of the most recent books
about different areas of economics to allow you
to do your own research. It also features a list
of useful web sites where you can find up-to-
date information and statistics.

Contents

Economic theory

Balance of payments

The U.S. balance of payments is a record of America's trade in goods, services, and financial assets with the rest of the world. A country's balance of payments is a good indication of the health of its economy, and data are reported quarterly in most developed countries.

The balance of payments comprises the current account—where the value of exports and imports is recorded—and the capital account—where the value of investment, saving, and borrowing is recorded. Together the current and the capital account must balance for any nation, with the money leaving the country equaling the money coming in. This is the same as with personal bank accounts—the money spent and saved must be the same as the money received and borrowed. However, different parts of the account need not balance. If the United States exports more than it imports, it can use the surplus to invest abroad. If imports are greater than exports, the country must pay for this by borrowing from abroad or selling financial assets or gold.

In the 1980s and early 1990s the U.S. balance of payments regularly made the news

ABOVE: *Logging is a lucrative source of foreign revenue for the U.S. economy. For the balance of payments to be in equilibrium, this foreign revenue coming into the country should equal money leaving the country.*

U.S. Balance of payments 1997 $ million	
CURRENT ACCOUNT	
Goods	
Exports	679,325
Imports	-877,279
Balance of trade	-197,954
Services	
Military transactions (net)	6,781
Travel and transportation (net)	22,670
Other services (net)	58,297
Investment income (net)	-5,318
Transfers (net)	-36,691
Balance on current account	**-155,215**
CAPITAL ACCOUNT	
Outflow of capital from U.S.	-477,492
Inflow of capital from overseas	733,441
Net capital inflow	255,949
Change in official reserves	-1,010
Balance on capital account	**254,939**
Statistical discrepancy or balancing item	**-99,724**

Note: a negative sign denotes a payment flow out of the United States
Source: Economic Report to the President, February 1999

with announcements of the latest trade deficit since imports into the country regularly exceeded exports out of it. As with an overdraft on your bank account, such a situation cannot be maintained indefinitely.

A country's balance of payments is always notionally regarded as being in perfect equilibrium. In practice, however, the difficulties involved in collating the statistics needed to determine this balance mean that it is never actually measured at all. Rather, since all data are actually statistical estimates of the true numbers, an adjustment has to be made, and the errors must be balanced. This is called the balancing item or statistical discrepancy and can be very large. For the United States in 1997, for instance, the balancing item needed to be $99.724 billion.

SEE ALSO:

• Volume 3, page 6: Government and the economy

• Volume 4, page 35: International trade and finance

• Volume 4, page 63: The world economy

The business cycle

The business cycle is a historically observed cycle of expanding real Gross Domestic Product (GDP), followed by negative GDP growth or a fall in output. The cycle has four phases: peak; recession—a decline in real output lasting 6 months or longer; trough—when output and employment bottom out; and recovery or expansion.

Although in the industrial world economies have tended to grow over time, the rate at which they grow is not constant. Periods of higher than average growth tend to be followed by periods of lower, zero, or negative growth. As growth accelerates, the economy starts to overheat, and inflationary pressure builds up (*see* Inflation and deflation, page 49). Growth continues until a peak is reached. Then real GDP begins to fall and continues to fall until inflationary pressure is eliminated. If there are at least two quarters—over six months—when real GDP growth is negative, this is known as a recession (*see* Recession and depression, page 91). As an economy falls into recession, the level of activity is low, and employment falls. Eventually this fall in output and employment begins to level out—this is known as the trough in the cycle. When the growth rate picks up again, it is known as the recovery or expansion stage. Real GDP continues to grow until inflation once again becomes a problem.

The U.S. economy has experienced periods of prosperity followed by periods of recession. However, GDP in the U.S. has grown overall at an average rate of around 3 percent per year since 1959.

Even though these periods of expanding and contracting output occur over and over again, the duration of business cycles and the rate at which GDP rises and falls can vary considerably. However, analysis of historic data for various economies has identified this cycle—i.e., the period between one peak and the next—as lasting approximately 10 years.

Graph 1 shows the growth rate of an economy over time. The economy expands, reaches a peak, then contracts and goes into a recession. Eventually the recession bottoms out, and the economy begins to recover and expand again. The overall trend is one of a slow rise in real GDP.

In addition to GDP there are other variables that move in a fairly regular manner over the business cycle. Leading indicators change

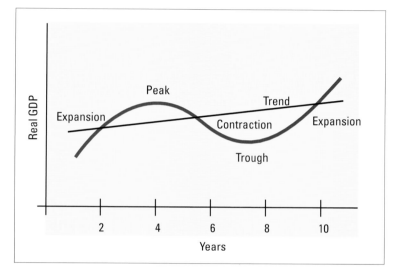

Graph 1 The business cycle. A typical business cycle contains four phases: a peak, which is the end of the expansion on the previous business cycle; a contraction or recession when real GDP is falling; a trough, as the recession bottoms out; and a new expansion (or boom) as real GDP starts to rise again. The trend indicates the tendency for economies to grow over time.

before real GDP and are thus used by economists to forecast changes in output. These include unemployment claims, which increase when an economy is about to go into a recession. Also, manufacturers' new orders, new building permits, and new plant and equipment orders will increase as the economy is about to start to recover and expand.

Some economists advocate government intervention to reduce the effects of the business cycle. For example, counteracting inflationary pressure—via fiscal or monetary policy—during an expansion or taking action to expand the economy and stimulate employment during a contraction (*see* Fiscal policy, page 40; Money: its supply and demand, page 72). Others believe that it is government intervention that causes, or at least exaggerates, the business cycle in the first place. An expansionary fiscal policy, with tax cuts and an increase in government expenditure, for example, might boost the economy artificially and make the subsequent contraction and recession all the more severe.

SEE ALSO:

• Volume 3, page 6: Government and the economy

• Volume 4, page 63: The world economy

• Volume 6, page 86: The West in the 20th century

Capital

Capital is a man-made resource. It is the machinery, tools and equipment, roads, factories, schools, and office buildings that people have produced in order to produce other goods and services. This capital is sometimes called physical capital to distinguish it from human capital. Financial capital refers to the funds used to purchase physical capital.

Circulating capital—otherwise known as working capital—comprises the stocks of raw materials, partly manufactured, and finished goods that are waiting to be sold. Fixed capital, on the other hand, is defined as the factory, machinery, and equipment of a business that will not be transformed into the final product.

All firms have at least one thing in common—they need capital both to start up in business and to continue to operate successfully. Increases or updates of capital stock—capital accumulation—by a firm or by a nation are known as investments (*see* Savings and investment, page 97). If an economy is going to grow and produce more and increasingly sophisticated goods and services, it needs to invest in capital and make more efficient use of existing capital (*see* Growth and development, page 46).

Sometimes you hear production described as capital-intensive or labor-intensive. These terms refer to the relative inputs of capital or labor into the production process. A high capital-to-labor ratio represents a capital-intensive production technique, while a high labor-to-capital ratio is a labor-intensive production technique. The chosen production technique in an industry tends to be governed by the relative prices of labor and capital. Industries in developed countries such as the United States, for instance, now face a steady increase in the relative price of labor and are moving toward greater capital intensity as a result, as for example, in car production. In developing countries, such as Brazil or Mexico, on the other hand, labor is relatively cheap, and production, of coffee, for example, therefore tends to be labor-intensive.

Capital accumulation, together with technological progress, e.g., the development of new and better ways of producing goods, will enable a firm or a nation to produce more goods and services in the future (*see* Production, page 86). However, there is a trade-off in

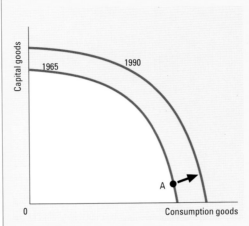

Figure 1 *Production possibility frontiers in the United States.*

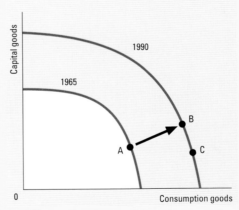

Figure 2 *Production possibility frontiers in Japan.*

In 1965 the U.S. production possibilities (Figure 1) were much greater than those in Japan (Figure 2). This can be seen in the relative positions of the two country's production possibility frontiers (PPFs) in 1965. However, the United States devoted only one-fifth of its reources to prod-ucing capital goods (point A on Figure 1), while Japan devoted one-third (point A on Figure 2). Japan's more rapid increase in capital resources resulted in its PPF shifting out more quickly than that of the United States so that by 1990 the two PPFs were similar. Japan then had the choice of producing at point B and continuing to grow more quickly than the United States, or increasing consumption, producing at point C, and reducing its growth rate.

the present. If a firm or a nation is to produce more goods and services in the future, it needs to devote fewer resources to the production of consumption goods—such as food, clothing, and housing—today. If it does this, it can devote more of its present resources to research, development, and building up its stock of capital, and so will have greater future capacity. This will have an effect on a country's rate of economic growth (*see* box).

SEE ALSO:

• Volume 2, page 6: Introduction to business

• Volume 6, page 54: Industrialization, urbanization, and modernization

Capitalist or free market economies

A capitalist, free market, or free enterprise economy is one in which market forces are dominant. Resources—such as workers, machines, factories, land, and natural resources—and all goods and services are allocated through the market mechanism.

By definition, a completely free market or capitalist economy will display all the following characteristics:

• Consumers, producers and the owners of factors of production—land, labor, and capital—are all motivated purely by self-interest. Consumers aim to maximize utility (*see* Utility and value, page 115); producers aim to maximize their profits; while the owners of land, labor, and capital aim to maximize rents, wages, interest, and profits.

• The factors of production are owned by private individuals, firms, and organizations, not by the government.

• People are free to set up their own businesses and to sell whatever they wish to sell. Consumers are free to use their money to buy whatever they wish to buy.

• Competition exists. Producers have to compete for consumers' spending on goods and services, and workers have to compete for the spending of producers on wages.

• There is no central body to allocate resources. On the contrary, decision-making is decentralized, and resources are allocated through the market via what Adam Smith called "Invisible Hand."

What, how, and for whom?

What is produced in a free market economy is determined by what it is most profitable to produce. A computer manufacturer, for example, may sell 1,000 computers each year. If this is not enough for the firm to make normal profits, it must either sell more computers or sell the same number of computers at a higher price. The owners or shareholders of the company will lose confidence in the firm if it continues to make a loss and will eventually move their money to other, more profitable firms or industries. The firm might have to go out of business altogether.

The market mechanism also encourages firms to produce output using the most efficient methods available; hence the free market results in productive efficiency (*see* Economic efficiency, page 28). If firms do not organize their production efficiently, keep up to date with changes in the technologies, and produce the type and quality of goods and services that people want to buy, then they lose out to rivals and are liable to go bankrupt.

Advantages and disadvantages

Output produced in a capitalist economy is allocated to those who can afford to pay for it. In simple terms it is easy to see that if you have no money, then you cannot afford to buy anything. If, on the other hand, you are a millionaire, then you can afford to buy large quantities of goods and services. This creates a wide gulf between the rich and the poor.

One of the clearest advantages of a free market or capitalist economy is that consumers will be provided with a wide range of choice.

ABOVE: In a capitalist or free market economy consumers have a great deal of choice of goods and services. Nonetheless, this choice is only available to those with the money to pay for it.

Competition also provides a strong incentive for producers to innovate and produce high-quality goods and services—if they don't, firms are likely to be driven out of the market by more innovative, efficient businesses.

However, in a free market or capitalist economy choice is available only to those consumers who have the money to pay for it. This, in the view of many, is its biggest disadvantage. Those on the lowest incomes will have the fewest options at their disposal. In addition, while competition may stimulate innovation and provide quality products in an economy, most markets are actually quite oligopolistic—in other words, they are dominated by a few producers who exploit their position and manipulate consumers through advertising, branding, and marketing campaigns (*see* Oligopoly and oligopolistic competition, page 78).

At the same time, in a purely free market economy there is no link at all between need and the allocation of resources. The sick can die from lack of access to health care, the unemployed can starve through having no income to buy food, and the homeless may be left to freeze to death on the streets.

Free markets in practice

Theoretically, in a purely free market system all resources, all goods, and all services will be allocated through the forces of demand and supply with no government intervention. In practice, however, this is not possible. Although most economies in the developed world are run on free market principles, they all—even those run by the most dedicated free marketeers—have at least some degree of government intervention in the economy.

Few people—no matter what their political viewpoint—would disagree that governments need to provide public goods, such as national defense, streetlighting, and law and order, and need to help in the provision of some mixed or merit goods, such as education, healthcare, public parks or museums (*see* Public sector, page 89). Furthermore, it is generally agreed that some government intervention is also necessary to deal with factors such as externalities and anticompetitive practices by firms (*see* Externalities and government policy, page 38; Market failure and anticompetitive practices, page 64; Regulation and antitrust laws, page 93).

Other government roles include issuing money, maintaining the value of the currency, keeping prices stable, and providing an ade-

quate legal framework to protect people's rights to private ownership. In addition, a successful modern society must allocate resources to provide for the role of government through taxation.

The free market in the United States

So, for example, even in the United States—which is by far the most important free market economy in the world today—the government still provides funds for spending on national defense, law and order, public highways, schooling, national parks, and so on. At the same time, there are state and federal laws to protect the environment, legislation to prevent firms colluding and fixing prices, and regulations protecting the rights of consumers. Spending by the U.S. government has actually increased significantly since the 1930s; government outlays now stand at roughly a third of GNP. Thus in the Land of the Free there clearly remains a significant degree of control.

Some economies, although run largely on free market principles, still have a quite considerable proportion of the economy's resources allocated through the government. These economies are referred to as mixed economies (*see* Mixed economies, page 68).

ABOVE: Although the United States is run largely on free market principles, the government will still intervene in the provision of certain public, mixed or merit goods, such as healthcare.

SEE ALSO:

• Volume 3, page 6: Government and the economy

• Volume 4, page 6: The U.S. government and world economics

• Volume 4, page 63: The world economy

• Volume 6, page 38: The Age of Reason and early industrialization

The circular flow of income and expenditure

The circular flow of income and expenditure refers to the circular nature of the flow of payments from firms to households and of expenditure from households to firms. A simple way to represent the basic relationship between income and expenditure is the circular-flow diagram.

The inner loop of Figure 1 shows a clockwise flow of productive resources in the form of labor from households to firms, and the flow of goods and services from firms to households. The outer loop represents the corresponding counterclockwise flow of monetary income, wages, from firms to households and of monetary expenditure on goods and services from households to firms.

Figure 1 can be made more realistic if saving, by households, and investment, by firms, are taken into account. Saving is a leakage from the system, whereas investment is an injection to the monetary flow from households to firms. The banking system—banks and other financial institutions—plays the essential role of collecting savings from households and passing them on to firms.

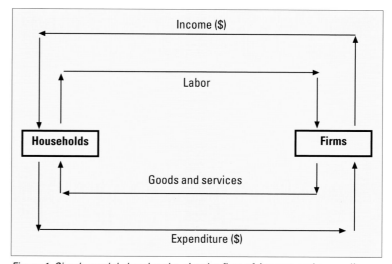

Figure 1 Simple model showing the circular flow of income and expenditure.

The next step is to introduce the government sector. In the United States this comprises the federal government plus the state and local governments. In this case taxation is a leakage from the system, whereas government spending is an injection to the monetary flow from households to firms.

Figure 2 illustrates the complete circular-flow diagram. This extended macroeconomic model confirms that Gross Domestic Product (GDP) is equivalent to the total expenditure by consumers, firms, and government on final goods and services. Both GDP and total expenditure are also equivalent to the total income received by the resources—the land, labor, capital, and entrepreneurship—used in the production of those final goods and services.

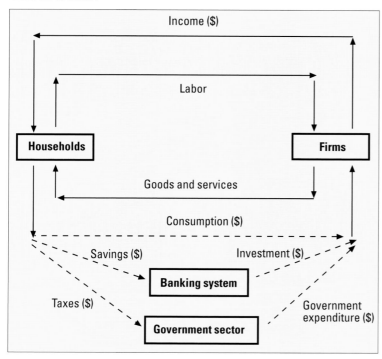

Figure 2 Complete circular flow model, including saving, investment, and the government sector.

SEE ALSO:

• Volume 3, page 6: Government and the economy

Comparative advantage

Comparative advantage is a term used to describe a situation in which a firm or country can produce a good at a lower opportunity cost than another firm or country. Although it might seem that comparative advantage benefits only those people or nations who enjoy it, it encourages specialization that benefits the whole marketplace and stimulates trade.

A producer—be it a business or a nation—is said to have a comparative advantage if it can produce a good at a lower cost in terms of other goods than another producer. In terms of international trade the law of comparative advantage states that as long as a country enjoys a comparative advantage in producing a particular good, then by specializing in production of that good and trading it, it creates a situation in which all countries benefit. This still holds true even if one country proves to be more efficient at producing all goods and services than other countries, that is, even if the country has an absolute advantage. As long as it concentrates on the product or products it is relatively better at producing, all countries will still benefit from specialization and trade.

Trade exists because people want something that other people produce and wish to sell surplus products they produce themselves. If the resources and economies of countries are very similar, then no country will enjoy a comparative advantage. However, some countries are at a clear advantage over others when it comes to producing certain goods and services. For example, a country may have valuable natural resources such as precious metals, deposits of fossil fuels, such as coal or oil, or useful metals such as copper, which other countries do not have. Or the climate in a particular country might be more suitable for growing certain types of crop.

Natural resources and climate are only one way a nation achieves a comparative advantage. Some countries or regions have workers who, over the years, have become particularly skilled at producing certain goods and services. Rich countries, meanwhile, are better able to

SEE ALSO:

• Volume 4, page 35: International trade and finance

• Volume 6, page 38: The Age of Reason and early industrialization

• Volume 6, page 106: Today and tomorrow

LEFT: *Beneficial conditions for agriculture, including flat, fertile plains and a temperate climate, give the Great Plains of the United States and Canada a comparative advantage in the production of cereal crops. Comparative advantage also lies, however, in the technology to produce efficient farm machinery and a financial system that allows investment in land, in crops, and in machinery.*

Understanding comparative advantage

To understand how comparative advantage works, it is useful to consider a world of just two countries, the United States and the United Kingdom, and to suppose that only two products are produced, bread and cloth. We will assume that the United States, with a workforce of 10 people, can produce either 600 loaves of bread or 40 bales of cloth. The United Kingdom, on the other hand, has a workforce of 8 people who can produce either 400 loaves or 80 bales of cloth. If both countries decide not to specialize and trade, production might be as follows, with half of each workforce producing bread and half producing cloth:

	United States	United Kingdom	Total
Bread	300	200	500
Cloth	20	40	60

The law of comparative advantage says that if each country were instead to produce the good it is relatively better at, then both countries would be better off. The relative efficiencies can be measured by looking at opportunity costs (*see* page 79). In the United States the opportunity cost of producing a bale of cloth is 15 loaves of bread; in the United Kingdom the opportunity cost of producing a bale of cloth is just 5 loaves. It follows then that the United States is relatively better at producing bread, and the United Kingdom is relatively better at producing cloth. If the United States concentrates on producing bread and the United Kingdom specializes in cloth, total production would rise to 600 loaves and 80 bales. The countries can then trade, and both will be better off than if they had continued to produce in isolation.

The same benefit can be seen even if one country has an absolute advantage in producing both products, meaning that it can produce more of both goods. Take a case in which the United States could produce either 600 loaves or 160 bales, but the United Kingdom could only produce 400 loaves or 80 bales. With both countries producing in isolation, the following might result:

	United States	United Kingdom	Total
Bread	300	200	500
Cloth	80	40	120

In this case the United States is relatively better at producing cloth. The opportunity cost of producing a bale of cloth would now be the lost production of 3.75 loaves of bread. In the United Kingdom the opportunity cost of producing a bale of cloth remains 5 loaves. Once again, specialization results in an increase in total production. The United States could produce 120 loaves of bread, using 2 workers, say, and 128 bales of cloth, using 8 workers. The United Kingdom, concentrating on bread production alone, could produce 400 loaves.

provide the finance for investment in the machinery that is needed for the production of sophisticated products. Poorer countries, on the other hand, might not have such a skilled workforce but can achieve comparative advantage in certain areas because this workforce is cheaper for the manufacture of less sophisticated products. History also plays a part in shaping comparative advantage. It may be that certain countries were able to build up a lead in an industry because they were among the first in the field, such as the German domination of the chemical industry in the late nineteenth century. In the twentieth century rapidly changing technology and cheaper workforces often turned an advantage around, however. Shipbuilding, which was traditionally dominated by western Europe and the United States, became the speciality of East Asian countries, for example.

Even if productive capability is spread more equally in global terms, the specialization and international trade stimulated by comparative advantage will still be beneficial to the world economy, as the example in the box above makes clear.

Competition and perfect competition

Competition is a process in which firms or the owners of factors of production offer goods or services for sale in the same market to the same customers. Perfect competition is a situation where there is a large number of buyers and sellers, all goods produced are identical, and there are no barriers to entry into or exit from the market. In such a situation it might also be assumed that it is possible to buy or sell any amount at the market price, that all buyers and sellers have perfect information about the market, and that sellers aim to maximize their profits.

The key feature of a perfectly competitive market is that all parties are "price-takers"—they base decisions on the predetermined market price and have no influence over this price. Under perfect competition it is assumed that it is possible to buy or sell any amount at this price. This produces a flat demand curve along which marginal revenue (MR)—the revenue gained by selling an extra unit of production—equals average revenue (AR)—the revenue received per unit sold (see Marginal analysis, page 62). Since sellers aim to maximize their profits, they produce where marginal cost (MC) equals marginal revenue (see Profits and profit maximization, page 88). As shown in Figure 1, this is at the foot of the average cost curve, where marginal cost equals average total cost (ATC). Average variable costs are represented by AVC (see Costs, page 21). The cost curves are u-shaped as a result of diminishing marginal returns (see Diminishing returns, page 27).

Under perfect competition, therefore:
MC = MR (profit maximization condition)
MC = AC (see below for explanation)

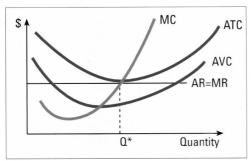

Figure 1 Long-run equilibrium.

AR = MR (flat demand curve)
MC = MR = ATC = AR (derived from above)

This is the long-run equilibrium position for a perfectly competitive market and gives a Pareto-efficient outcome—it is not possible to move to another quantity-produced and price combination that would make some sellers better off and no others worse off (see Economic efficiency, page 28). If ATC = AR, then sellers make only "normal profits." This is the consequence of them being "price-takers," as opposed to "price-makers" in other forms of competition.

The demand curve and perfect competition

It is important to distinguish between market demand and the demand curve faced by each individual seller. Under perfect competition market demand is unaffected by a buyer's or a seller's actions. Each seller faces a horizontal demand line at the current market price. Each seller is so small relative to the total market that any one seller's actions have no effect on market price in perfect competition. If the number of sellers decreases enough, the market supply will decrease, resulting in a higher market price. Each of the remaining perfectly competitive firms will expand production until MC equals the new, higher AR. An increase in the number of sellers will have the opposite effect.

Determining market price

The assumptions for perfect competition state that it is possible to buy or sell any amount at the market price, yet the level of the market price remains to be determined. If the demand

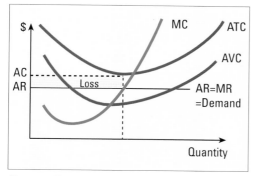

Figure 2 *Firms make a loss in the short-run.*

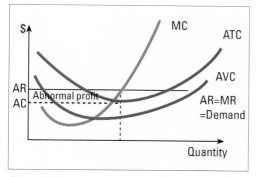

Figure 3 *Firms make short-run abnormal profits.*

curve (where AR=MR) falls below the low point of the ATC curve, where MC equals ATC, then average total cost is greater than average revenue, and the seller will make a loss (Figure 2). Sellers cannot afford to remain in business if their costs are greater than the money they make. Assuming no barriers to exit from the market, the seller will leave the market. The demand curve faced by each remaining seller will begin to rise. Traders will continue to leave the market until the individual demand curve moves back to the point where average total cost equals average revenue, and normal profits are made again by all sellers.

On the other hand, if the demand curve (market price) rises above where average cost was at its minimum, then sellers make above-normal profits (Figure 3). Assuming no barriers to entry, this attracts new sellers into the market. As more and more traders enter the market, each one faces a reduced demand. The individual demand curve shifts back down toward ATC = AR. In the long run, therefore, the demand curve for each seller will be at the point at which ATC = AR. Since AR = MR, and MC = MR, this is the point where ATC = MC.

The supply curve and perfect competition

In each scenario above, there is a short-run change in the level of production for each seller. At all times they wish to maximize profits where MC = MR. If MR rises or falls because of a change in the market equilibrium price, then the firm's production level will change until MC equals the new MR. The supply curve for any individual seller, therefore, follows the path of the MC curve. However, sellers will choose to leave the market in the long run if ATC is greater than AR, but produce in the short run if AVC is greater than AR. They will produce in the short run only if their losses are no larger than the fixed costs and will produce nothing if AR is less than AVC. The minimum of the AVC is the short-run shutdown point. Market price below the minimum of the ATC is the long-run exit signal. The individual supply curve is therefore the MC curve above the AVC curve. The market supply curve is the aggregate of all these individual curves.

Each scenario above represents a short-run shock away from the equilibrium position. The fact that the final outcome reverts to this position in both cases is confirmation that this is indeed the equilibrium point.

ABOVE: All firms in a perfectly competitive market face a market price for the goods and services they sell. However, perfect competition is very rare; firms in the real world will put on sales and cut prices to attract customers.

SEE ALSO:

• Volume 2, page 62: Competition, expansion, and growth

• Volume 2, page 80: How firms behave in the real world

• Volume 3, page 43: Government and business

Consumers and consumption

Consumption can be defined as the total expenditure by households on goods and services over a period of time. This definition excludes spending on savings and investment, where expenditure is allocated to future needs and wants.

Choices made by individual consumers are the bedrock of microeconomic theory—that is, the branch of economics that studies the decisions of individual households and firms, and the way in which individual markets work. In a competitive, free market system all economic activity is geared toward consumer satisfaction. In such a situation there is said to be consumer sovereignty—consumers tell producers what to produce, rather than producers dictating to consumers what they can and cannot buy.

In theory, all consumers act rationally and attempt to maximize their satisfaction with what they buy. Since all economic commodities are scarce, and resources are limited, consumers have to choose between alternative points of equal satisfaction or utility. Microeconomics assumes that each consumer has preferences—a list of goods and services they want and how these are valued compared to each other. These sorts of choices can be represented graphically as indifference curves (*see* Marginal analysis, page 62; Utility and value, page 115).

Consumers will buy a particular good until its marginal utility—the amount of satisfaction or use they get from buying one more unit of a good—is equal to its money price. Anyone who carries on buying beyond this point makes themselves worse off. In the real world few people are aware of these marginal calculations when they change what goods they choose to buy according to changes in prices and income. Even though people do not consciously make decisions on such calculations, their spending patterns actually do change in the way predicted by economic theory.

Total consumption in an economy is the sum of all these individual consumer choices.

ABOVE: Although they are usually unaware of the law of marginal utility, individual consumers actually make choices that follow this law quite closely. Economists can predict changes in consumer spending as a result.

There are a number of factors that determine how much a household consumes. The relationship between consumption and these factors is called the consumption function. The most important determinant of consumption is disposable income. The economist John Maynard Keynes (1883–1946) first popularized the idea that consumption was linked to income. If income increases, consumption also rises, although not at the same rate. This is because the more people earn, the larger the proportion of their earnings they are prepared to save.

The exact amount people spend on consumption and how much they save depend on several factors. Anticipation of rises or falls in price can bring forward or delay consumption, for example. Changes in the availability and cost of credit will also have an effect. In addition, the marginal propensity to consume—the proportion of extra income spent rather than saved—is likely to be much greater among the poor, who will have more unsatisfied needs than the wealthy.

SEE ALSO:

• Volume 3, page 28: Government and the individual

• Volume 3, page 43: Government and business

• Volume 3, page 105: Organizations and boards

Consumer price index (CPI)

The consumer price index, or CPI, measures the average price of goods and services bought by a typical household. Economists study price indexes such as the CPI so that they can measure the price level—or the level of inflation—in an economy. The CPI may also be referred to as the retail price index or the cost-of-living index.

To measure the CPI, economists look at a selection—often called a basket—of goods and services. This basket of goods usually amounts to approximately 400 items that a typical family needs to buy regularly. The basket is divided into categories such as food and drink, housing costs, clothes, transportation, medical care, entertainment, and anything else that might be considered necessary to maintain a healthy standard of living.

Economists estimate the price of an average basket and compare it to the price of a similar selection of goods and services purchased the month before or the year before, for example. Any increase in price that has occurred in the intervening period provides quite a good indication of inflation over that period of time. This is why the CPI is sometimes known as the core rate of inflation.

Keeping an eye on rises and falls

In market economies, such as those in Europe and the U.S., prices are determined by supply and demand rather than being set by government regulation. In such countries a major concern of government is preventing the overall price level from suddenly rising or falling. Rapid price changes can distort the economic decisions and strategies of consumers and businesses, and thus might ultimately destabilize a whole economy. It is important, therefore, for economists to be able to measure how price levels are changing—if prices are going up or down too rapidly, the government will take action to reverse the trend (*see* Inflation and deflation, page 49; *see* Fiscal policy, page 40).

Although the CPI is quite a narrow measure compared to some other price indexes, it is probably the best-known and most widely referred to because it has a direct bearing on the lives of ordinary consumers. Most news reports on inflation tend to cover changes in consumer prices, and these prices are of direct relevance to people's standard of living. In addition, some labor contracts include a provision to raise wages in line with CPI increases, and labor unions will often base their annual wage increase negotiations on the information provided by this index. Social security payments are also tied to increases in the CPI. Such increases are known as cost-of-living adjustments (COLAs) because they are intended to preserve the purchasing power of people's incomes at its former level. Pensions, too, tend to be index-linked—that is, they are increased in line with inflation so that their real value is not eroded over time.

SEE ALSO:

• Volume 1, page 86: Inflation and deflation

• Volume 3, page 6: Government and the economy

BELOW: Some of the typical regular household purchases on which the consumer price index (CPI) is based.

Cooperatives

Cooperatives differ from ordinary firms in that their main goal is not necessarily the maximization of profits for their shareholders. There are two main types of cooperative: ones that exist for the benefit of their worker-owners—worker or producer cooperatives—and ones that exist for the benefit of their customers—consumer or retail cooperatives.

Producer or worker cooperatives are limited liability businesses that are owned by some or all of their workers. Often worker cooperatives are set up by workers to prevent layoffs or to create employment. Alternatively, they may be established to provide a good or service that the workers feel will benefit society, for example, organic produce or housing. The worker-owners provide the money or finance to set up the business and have to agree some form of management, appointing managers or voting on important decisions, for example. Profits are normally distributed among the workers since they are also the firm's shareholders.

In producer cooperatives there is no conflict of interest between the workers and the shareholders because they are one and the same. As a result there should be no strikes, and the labor force has a greater than usual incentive to work hard.

In practice it is often very difficult for groups of workers to raise enough money to set up and finance their own business. Producer cooperatives also require a great deal of trust and cooperation between the people involved, while members of such bodies often lack the management experience necessary to make the firm successful. As a result producer cooperatives are quite a rare form of business organization—one of the best-known examples of a successful worker's cooperative is the Boothbay Region Lobstermen's Coop in Maine.

Consumer or retail cooperatives are set up for the benefit of consumers. They are also limited liability businesses, but they are owned by members of the general public who can own shares up to a certain limit. Shares can only be sold back to the cooperative, and shareholders each have one vote regardless of how many shares they own. The shareholders elect a management committee and receive a fixed dividend on their shares. The remainder of the profits after this dividend has been paid is dis-

ABOVE: A thriving café at the Boothbay Region Lobstermen's Cooperative in Maine.

tributed to customers according to how much they spend, for example, in the form of food stamps. Among many examples of this type of firm is The French Broad Food Coop in Asheville, North Carolina, a consumer-owned cooperative that sells organic food and environmentally friendly products.

The organization of consumer cooperatives might seem to provide a good deal for customers. But during the last 20 years such businesses had most of their competitive advantages eroded by more conventional firms that were able to take greater advantage of economies of scale (*see* Economies of scale, page 30). In consequence many customers have now deserted cooperatives in favor of large supermarkets where prices are at least as cheap, if not cheaper.

SEE ALSO:

• Volume 2, page 6: An introduction to business

• Volume 6, page 54: Industrialization, urbanization, and modernization

Corporations

A corporation is a business firm owned by shareholders. These owners are not liable for the debts of the corporation. This means that if the corporation goes bankrupt, shareholders only stand to lose the money they put in in the first place—their personal property cannot be seized.

Corporations are an important form of business organization. Although they are fewer in number than other forms of business organization, such as sole proprietorships and partnerships, they include virtually all large businesses and account for more sales, profits, and employment than the other forms of business. All businesses listed on the New York, U.S., and NASDAQ stock exchanges are examples of corporations.

A corporation is a legal entity in its own right. As such, it can engage in contracts, sue and be sued by others for damages, pay taxes, and be accused and convicted of crimes. Corporations are able to raise large sums of capital to finance expansion or other activities by issuing stock. A share of stock represents partial ownership of a corporation. Corporations may be either privately or publicly held. The stock of a privately held corporation is owned by a few individuals and is not traded on a stock exchange. Most small corporations, and some large ones, are privately held. Fidelity Investments, the largest mutual fund company, and the Los Angeles Lakers basketball team are two of the most famous privately held corporations.

A privately held corporation can "go public" by selling shares of stock to the general public. When a privately held company issues stock to the public for the first time, it is called an initial public offering, or an IPO. Several familiar Internet companies, including Amazon.com and Yahoo.com, have gone public in recent years with highly successful IPOs. After its IPO a corporation can raise additional funds by issuing stock in a secondary offering.

Once the stock of a company has been issued, it can be bought and sold by investors via the stock exchanges (*see* Stocks and shares, page 104). There are currently more than 7,000 publicly traded companies in the United States. When an investor buys a share of stock on a stock exchange, the company that issued the stock does not receive any of the funds. For example, when an investor buys a share of McDonald's stock on the New York Stock

Exchange (NYSE), he or she obtains the share from another investor who had previously purchased it. The investor selling the share receives the revenue from the buyer, not from the McDonald Corporation. Occasionally corporations buy their own stock. This strategy, known as a stock buyback, is used when the management of the company believes that the current stock price understates the true value of the business.

The shareholders of a corporation are its owners, and they select the corporation's management. The shareholders vote for a board of directors who oversee the activities of the business. The board of directors, in turn, selects a chief executive officer (CEO) who manages the business on a daily basis. The CEO meets regularly with the board to review, plan, and discuss business operations.

ABOVE: Throughout most of the 20th century General Motors was the world's largest automobile manufacturer and possibly also its largest corporation, with a turnover greater than that of many nations.

LEFT: The trading floor of the New York Stock Exchange, where the value of shares may rise or fall as new investments are made and existing funds are moved between different corporations.

When a corporation is profitable, the board of directors may choose to distribute the profit to shareholders in the form of a dividend. Corporations that pay dividends typically declare and distribute them on a quarterly basis. However, there are some highly profitable companies that have never paid a dividend; rather they have reinvested all their profits back into the business.

Relative to other forms of business organization, corporations are better able to raise large sums of financial capital for business expansion. One method of raising capital is the issuance of stock as discussed above.

Corporations are also able to borrow funds, often at a very favorable rate of interest. To cover short-term capital needs, a corporation may choose to establish and draw on a line of credit with a bank. The interest rate charged by banks for its most creditworthy corporate buyers is called the prime rate.

Long-term borrowing is achieved by issuing bonds—a promise to pay the purchaser of the bond a specified sum of money at some time in the future. Corporate bonds are the debt of a corporation. Corporate bonds are rated by services such as Moody's. If the company issuing a bond is financially sound, it is highly likely to make the required payments to the bondholder, and the bond is rated as investment quality. If there is a high degree of uncertainty as to whether the issuing company will meet its bond obligations, the bond receives a low rating. Such bonds are called junk bonds.

An advantage of the corporate form of business organization is that the owners—the shareholders—have only limited liability for the obligations of the business. The most that a shareholder can lose is the amount that he or she paid for the stock. Should the corporation be successfully sued, winners of the lawsuit cannot claim the personal property of the shareholders. This is not the case with sole proprietorships and partnerships.

One disadvantage is that the profits of the corporation are subjected to double taxation. Corporate profits are taxed by corporate income tax; then, when the profits are distributed to the shareholders in the form of dividends, they are taxed again as income tax. The profits of sole proprietorships and partnerships are taxed only at the individual level.

SEE ALSO:

• Volume 1, page 102: The stock market

• Volume 2, page 6: An introduction to business

• Volume 3, page 43: Government and business

• Volume 3, page 105: Organizations and boards

Costs

The costs of producing and selling goods and services are the costs of the resources used. Costs can be explicit or implicit, or might be variable (costs that vary with output) or fixed (costs that stay the same regardless of how much is produced).

Explicit costs are the payments made by a firm for the use of items such as materials and labor. They also include rent for the use of buildings and the costs of hiring plant and machinery it does not own.

Implicit costs relate to the use of resources that the firm itself owns. For example, if the firm owns the factory in which it produces its output, it will not have to pay rent. However, by using the building, the firm cannot rent the factory out to another firm. The cost of giving up the opportunity to receive rent from another is the implicit cost of using the buildings for its own purposes. Therefore, to ascertain the real cost of producing its output, a firm must impute a rent to itself. This is based on the rent it would receive from a third party given the size of the building, its structure, its state of repair, and its location. An implicit cost is therefore an opportunity cost (*see* Opportunity cost, page 79).

The long and the short run

The short run is a theoretical period of time when one or more factors of production cannot be changed. It is a time scale when plant and machinery are fixed, and the only way of increasing production is by having more variable inputs such as materials and labor. In practice the short run varies from one industry to another. It could well take a firm in the petrochemical industry five years to build additional plant, but a small firm in the clothing industry could increase its capacity in a matter of a week or two by simply buying a new sewing machine.

The long run is the time scale when all factors of production are variable—that is, when plant and machinery can be bought, technology can be developed to increase productivity, and so on.

Costs can also be categorized in different ways. Some vary directly with output, whereas others—at least in the short run—remain constant. This leads to classifying costs as either variable or fixed.

ABOVE: *Cotton production incurs both fixed and variable costs. Wages paid to workers and the cost or rent of machinery are variable—both will increase as output rises, as more workers are taken on, and more equipment is needed.*

Variable and fixed costs

Variable costs are those that tend to vary directly with output. Obviously the more units of output the firm makes, the higher will be its cost of materials—if you want to make more clothes, you need to buy more fabric, dyes, thread, and so on. The wage bill for employees will also vary with output—the more clothes you make, the more people you will need to make them. Typical variable costs are

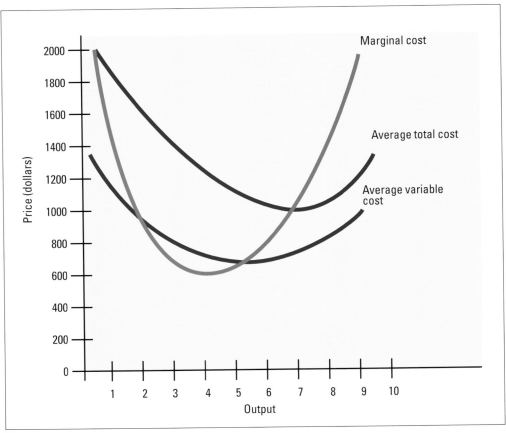

Figure 1 All firms face cost curves similar to the ones shown here.

the cost of raw materials and the cost of labor and power.

Fixed costs are those that do not directly vary in the short run as output increases. They include the administrative costs of running the firm, property taxes, and rent, whether explicit or implicit. They are all costs for which the firm has to pay as a matter of course, even when production is zero. They also include an apportionment of past expenditure to the present. For example, capital depreciation—the wear and tear and loss in value of machinery—is a fixed cost.

Fixed costs are said to be sunk costs since the expenditure is irretrievable. Since these past costs cannot be recovered, they are irrelevant to current decision-making. Advertising is an example of a sunk cost. Sunk costs can be a barrier to another firm entering the market. For example, an existing firm might spend a large amount of money on advertising and establishing its product in a market. This could deter a rival firm from setting up in the same industry with a similar product since the firm will be unable to compete without also spending a lot of money on advertising. If it does not advertise, consumers will continue to buy the established product.

Total, average, and marginal costs

When looking at how decisions are made by firms, economists look at total, average, and marginal costs.

The total cost in the short run comprises a firm's total fixed cost and total variable costs.

The average cost in the short run is the total cost divided by the number of units produced. Average costs can be further divided into average fixed costs—the total fixed costs divided by the number of units produced—and average variable cost—the total variable cost divided by the number of units produced.

Marginal cost is defined as the addition to total cost that is incurred in the short run by increasing output by just one unit. It is one of the most important costs in determining the level of output.

Every firm has cost curves that look like those shown in Figure 1. In the short run it may be expected that the average total and average variable cost would fall per unit of output. However, for every firm as output rises incremental costs initially fall but eventually rise. This is because of diminishing returns (see Diminishing returns, page 27). Marginal costs behave in a similar manner—initially falling quite rapidly as output increases, then rising.

SEE ALSO:

• Volume 2, page 28: How a business works

• Volume 2, page 48: Finance and accounting

• Volume 2, page 80: How firms behave in the real world

• Volume 2, page 100: Market failure and externalities

The demand curve

Demand is a relationship between the price of a good or service and the quantity of that good or service people are willing and able to buy during a period of time. The demand curve is a common graph economists use to show the relationship between the two.

Price is the key determinant of demand. For example, suppose that Jenny has just received her allowance of $10 and decides to meet her friends for lunch. They go to King's Burgers and see that a cheeseburger is $4. Jenny is very hungry and buys two burgers. The fact that she is hungry means that she is willing to buy two burgers; she also has the money to be able to afford them. If the burgers were $3—and if she were very hungry indeed—she could have bought three burgers. If, on the other hand, the burgers had been $6, she would have been able to buy only one no matter how hungry she was. The quantity of a particular good that people—or consumers—would buy at different prices can be represented by what is known as a demand curve. Figure 1 shows the demand curve for cheeseburgers with price (P) on the vertical axis and quantity (Q) on the horizontal axis.

In almost all cases the demand curve shows that the quantity demanded falls as price increases, and the quantity demanded increases as price decreases, giving a curve that slopes downward from left to right. As the price of cheeseburgers goes up, Jenny can afford to buy fewer burgers, so her quantity demanded falls. In order to represent this simple relationship between price and quantity, all other factors, such as the price of other goods and the income of the consumer—in this case Jenny's allowance—are taken as constant in a demand curve (*see* Models and modeling, page 69).

The fact that Figure 1 shows a downward sloping curve reflects the theory of decreasing marginal utility (*see* Marginal analysis, page 62). Initially, Jenny is very hungry and will pay a high price for one or two cheeseburgers. However, once she has eaten three burgers, she is unlikely to want to buy many more no matter how low the price falls.

The price of the good or service itself is not the only factor that determines demand. Another important factor is the income of the consumer—in this case, Jenny's allowance. Other variables include the price of any substi-

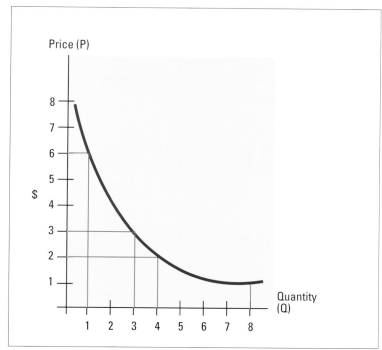

Figure 1 Demand curve for cheeseburgers.

tute or complementary products, advertising, fashion, the cost and availability of credit, and the size of the population.

Price and demand

When the price of a good rises relative to others, it affects demand in two ways, one direct and one indirect. The direct effect on demand is referred to as the substitution effect. Consumers are likely to switch some or all of their expenditure to cheaper versions of the good in order to maximize their satisfaction. In this example, if Jenny went into King's Burgers and saw that the price of a cheeseburger had gone up to $6, she might decide to go across the street to Donald's Burgers, where she knows she can buy a similar cheeseburger for $4. If she does this, she can still afford to buy two burgers, so she is happier than if she had stayed at King's and bought just one.

The indirect result of a price rise on demand is known as the income effect. If the price of a good rises, it reduces the spending power of consumers, whose money no longer goes as far as it did. This may change the way they allocate their resources. At the burger stand, with cheeseburgers priced $4, Jenny could buy two and have $2 left over for a soda. If the price increased to $5, Jenny could still buy two burgers, but would have no money to spend on anything else. In this case she might decide to buy a different combination of goods, such as a single burger, a soda, and an apple pie.

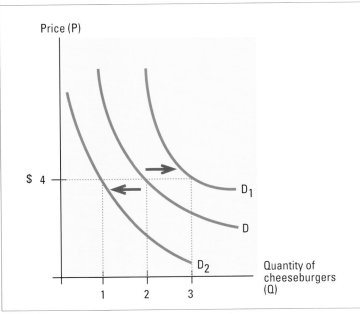

Figure 2 *Effect on change in income on demand.*

Income and demand.

A rise in consumer income—for example, if Jenny's parents increased her allowance—will almost always lead to a rise in demand. Figure 2 shows how a rise in Jenny's allowance to $15 would result in a shift in her demand curve to D1. Similarly, a fall in income—a cut in her allowance to $5—will usually lead to a fall in demand, as in the shift in her demand curve to D2 (*see* Goods and services, page 43).

The increase in total demand is almost always smaller than the increase in income, since people will usually save a proportion of the increase. (In this sense "save" means "refrain from spending" rather than place in a savings account.) Even with an allowance of $15, Jenny may decide to stick to her original purchase of two burgers and a soda, keeping the extra $5 to spend later in the week.

LEFT: The most important determinant of demand is price. If prices are too high, the quantity demanded of a good or service will be insufficient to meet supply, and there will be a surplus, as with these unwanted tomatoes. This excess of supply will eventually reduce the price.

SEE ALSO:

• Volume 2, page 28: How a business works

• Volume 2, page 80: How firms behave in the real world

• Volume 3, page 61: Government and labor

The developing world

A developing country is defined as a poor country that is seeking to develop its commercial and industrial sectors. Chile, Guatemala, Thailand, and India are all developing countries. Others, such as many countries in Africa, are referred to as less developed or underdeveloped countries since they have neither the capital nor the social organization necessary to grow or "develop." Three-quarters of the world's population live in developing and less developed nations.

ABOVE: A street scene in Jaipur, India. India's large, cheap workforce has been an important factor in the development of its manufacturing base, particularly in the computer sector.

The developing and underdeveloped world is sometimes referred to as the Third World. In this context the First World, or the developed world, comprises rich, industrialized, mostly Western, mostly democratic countries such as the U.S., Britain, Japan, and Germany. Most of these countries are based in the northern hemisphere, while most Third World countries are in the southern. The Second World was an expression once used to describe the command or socialist economies of the communist world, countries such as the states of the former Soviet Union, China, Poland, and Bulgaria *(see* Socialism, page 100*)*.

Countries of the developing world have, of course, different histories, populations, cultures, climates, and resources. However, they do have a number of characteristics in common, though to varying degrees:

● Often there are insufficient capital resources such as factories, tools and machines, roads, and schools. The capital that does exist is often in very poor condition.

● People living in developing or underdeveloped countries often have a poor education, with many children unable to attend school. School is either too expensive for families to afford, or children have to work from an early age. Girls are less likely to gain access to education and training than boys. As a result, developing countries are often characterized by having a large, unskilled workforce.

● Labor productivity is also poor. Without the necessary machines or skills workers produce much less.

● Developing countries have a low average income per person, partly as a result of low labor productivity. In many cases low average incomes are accompanied by large differences in income between the rich and the poor.

● People living in the Third World also face lower life expectancies than they would in the First World, and are more likely to suffer poor health and diseases.

● This, in turn, is partly the result of large numbers of people on low incomes being unable to afford a good diet. Many people have poor access to health care, often live in poor, unsanitary, overcrowded housing, and do not have access to clean drinking water.

● Finally, developing countries often have very high rates of population growth (see Population and migration, page 80). This is partly as a result of high child mortality rates—families will tend to have more children if they know that some will die at a young age. Other factors include social attitudes, education, and access to birth control.

Possible ways forward

All these characteristics are related to one another. Low labor productivity is the result of poor capital resources and lack of education. This in turn leads to low incomes, which affects living conditions and health.

However, some developing countries have been able to take advantage of certain of the above characteristics when competing on world markets—e.g. their large populations providing markets for goods and services, and their cheap workforces. India, for instance, has used its cheap labor as a basis for economic growth, developing a large manufacturing base and a highly successful computer industry.

During the 1970s many economists thought the best solution to Third World poverty was lending money so that countries could invest in capital, build up capital stock, expand production of goods and services, and "trade their way out of debt." Institutions such as the International Monetary Fund (IMF), the World Bank, and large banks in the West loaned money to countries such as Mexico, Brazil, India, Zimbabwe, and Malaysia. Many of the loans came with strict conditions. If these institutions were

to lend out vast sums of money, they wanted to be sure they would one day get their money back with interest. A number of economic policy implications came with the loans—a debtor country had to take measures to combat inflation, for example, or had to open up its economy to international trade and investment.

The scale of economic growth that industrialized nations expected from these loans and policies failed to materialize, however. By the 1980s many countries found themselves crushed by debt repayments to the West (see International debt, page 53). Today richer nations are looking at reducing or writing off some of the debt they are owed by Third World countries. The World Bank and the IMF have also reviewed their policies and continue to investigate alternatives such as less technologically complex, smaller-scale, more participative and accountable approaches to development.

ABOVE: Agricultural workers in the Gambia, Africa, face lower life expectancies than they would in the First World.

SEE ALSO:

● Volume 4, page 6: The U.S. government and world economics

Volume 4, page 35: International trade and finance

● Volume 4, page 63: The world economy

● Volume 6, page 106: Today and tomorrow

Diminishing returns

Diminishing returns occur when attempts to increase production—by adding workers or up-to-date technology, for example—fail to generate a continuing increase in output, usually because the production operation has become less efficient.

The law of diminishing returns states that as additional quantities of variable factors such as labor or machinery are added to a production process, the extra output generated by each additional unit of the variable factors will eventually fall. Although the units of these additional variable factors of production are equally efficient, and all other factors remain constant, they are being used less efficiently. The law can be illustrated using a farming example concerning the relationship between the amount of resources used—seed, fertilizer, hours of labor put in to growing the crop, and so on—and the amount of output, i.e., the harvest.

If one farm worker farmed a fixed piece of land, the output would be limited by the amount of labor that individual could do. With each additional worker employed on the farm, output per unit of labor would initially increase. This is because there are more people to help with planting, irrigation, and harvesting, and workers able to take advantage of specialization (see Specialization and the division

LEFT: *Because an apple tree can only produce a certain quantity of apples, increasing the number of workers engaged in picking the crop would eventually lead to diminishing returns in respect of the number of apples each worker could pick.*

SEE ALSO:

• Volume 2, page 28: How a business works

• Volume 6, page 54: Industrialization, urbanization, and modernization

of labor, page 103). Eventually, however, a point would be reached at which the returns from employing an additional hand would start to decrease. Each worker would have less to do, would add less to output. Eventually overall output might even be reduced, as additional workers start to get in the way of those already employed.

In a factory of a fixed size, likewise, a point will be reached where employing additional units of labor will result in diminishing returns per worker. Or the addition of extra units of machinery will increase output initially, but will eventually result in reduced overall output.

The law of diminishing returns naturally affects costs. In the short run, as more of a factor of production is introduced, the marginal cost, and the average cost per unit of output, initially decrease but then start to rise. This is shown in Figure 1 where the cost curves are U-shaped: they fall initially and then start to go up.

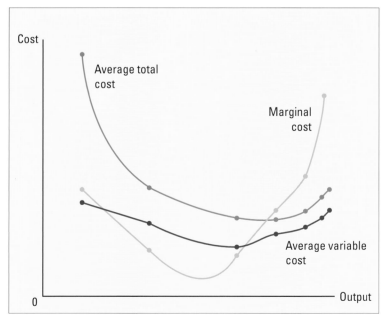

Figure 1 The effect of the law of diminishing returns on costs.

Economic efficiency

Efficiency can be defined as a measure of how well an allocation system satisfies peoples' wants and needs. Economists use several different measures of efficiency: allocative, technical, productive, and Pareto efficiency.

In any economy resources are limited, but people's wants are not. An economy therefore needs some system of deciding how to allocate its resources. The effectiveness of that system is its allocative efficiency. The market mechanism and central planning by a goverment are two possible means through which economic resources might be allocated—goods and services to consumers, for example, or productive resources to producers.

Consider an economy with two individuals, Alice and Bill. The economy produces a set level of output, which is allocated between the two. The allocation is described as efficient if it is not possible to allocate the output differently in such a way that either Alice or Bill is better off, and the other is no worse off.

Whether or not an allocative improvement is possible will depend on the marginal utility derived by Alice and Bill from the various different goods that constitute total output. For example, we can assume that total output consists of two goods, computer games and books. Alice prefers computer games, and Bill prefers books. Transferring a computer game from Bill to Alice in exchange for a book will be a more efficient allocation because both Alice's and Bill's total utility, or satisfaction, will increase (*see* Marginal analysis, page 62).

Technical efficiency

A production method is described as being technically efficient if, in order to produce a given level of output, it is not possible to use fewer resources. In other words, the method makes the best use possible of its materials. A relationship called the production function defines the maximum output that can be achieved for a given level of resources. Each point on the production function is a separate technically efficient combination of the given resources. A technically efficient company, for example, will be producing on its Production Possibility Frontier (*see* Production, page 86). A technically efficient economy extends this efficiency to the economy as a whole.

ABOVE: Traditional small-scale agriculture achieves static efficiency, getting the maximum possible yield from a set area with fixed resources and tools.

Productive efficiency

Productive efficiency is a measure of how resources are divided among sectors of an economy that produces several different goods. Such an economy achieves productive efficiency if, for a given output of all the goods in the economy, it is producing the maximum possible quantity of the last good with the resources available. In other words, the production of no one good is less efficient than the production of the others. Unlike technical efficiency, productive efficiency does not necessarily ensure the maximum possible output of all goods given the total resources available.

Pareto efficiency

The concept of Pareto efficiency—as defined by Italian economist Vilfredo Pareto (1848–1923) in 1909—encompasses all the preceding measures of efficiency. It specifies that an out-

come is Pareto-efficient if, for given consumer tastes, resources, and technology, it is not possible to move to another allocation of resources that would make some people better off but nobody worse off. This implies that resources are being utilized in a technically efficient—and therefore productively efficient—manner, so that total output cannot be increased, and that the current output is being allocated in an efficient manner. In economic theory Pareto efficiency occurs by default in a perfectly competitive market because of the conditions assumed (*see* Competition and perfect competition, page 14).

Static vs. dynamic efficiency

Allocative, technical, productive, and Pareto efficiency all assume a fixed amount of resources and technology in an economy. They are therefore short-term or "static" measures of efficiency. In the long run, however, resources and technology are not fixed.

In order to achieve dynamic efficiency, an economy must expand its production as much as possible. This is achieved by generating additional resources through growth and the availability of finance, and by investing in

research in order to advance production techniques (*see* Growth and development, page 46).

The more that potential output increases, the more dynamically efficient the economy will be. The closer that actual output comes to potential output at any point in time, the more statically efficient it is.

Equity vs. efficiency

Pareto efficiency means that making someone better off should not make anyone worse off. In reality, welfare economics is concerned with ensuring that poorer members of society are supported, usually at the expense of those who can best afford it (*see* Taxation, taxes, and subsidies, page 107). Because this redistribution of wealth leaves some people worse off, it does not improve overall efficiency. It does, however, bring an improvement in equity as the gap between rich and poor becomes narrower.

An efficient outcome is therefore not necessarily equitable, and an equitable outcome is not necessarily efficient. In an ideal world the optimum solution would be both equitable and efficient. If this is not possible, an economy must decide how much efficiency can be traded off against equity.

ABOVE: The use of fertilizers and investment in plant for harvesting means that modern agriculture is dynamically efficient, that is, it is trying to increase its potential output.

SEE ALSO:

• Volume 2, page 62: Competition, expansion, and growth

• Volume 2, page 100: Market failure and externalities

• Volume 3, page 6: Government and the economy

• Volume 3, page 28: Government and the individual

• Volume 3, page 43: Government and business

Economies of scale

Economies of scale mean that as the size of a firm increases, its per unit costs decline.

In the short run, as a company grows, its unit costs initially fall. At some point, however, they begin to rise as output per unit of input decreases as a result of diminishing marginal returns (*see* Diminishing returns, page 27). The same may not be true in the long run, however. The long run is an abstract period of time long enough for other factors to be varied: a firm's plant and buildings can be added to or completely renewed, for example, to allow for an increase in the scale of operations.

When a firm first begins to expand, it enjoys economies of scale. The result is that in the long run an increase in output will lead to a reduction in the average total unit cost. So, if a firm is producing cans of soda, the first few cans will be very expensive to produce—because of costs such as the price of buildings and plant, for example, which do not vary with output—but as output increases, each can will cost less to produce.

One cause of economies of scale is the fact that machines are not divisible. Say a machine can produce 100,000 cans of soda a year. If a company with one machine needs to raise production to 120,000 cans, it has to buy a whole new machine, not one-fifth of a machine. The capital outlay needed to buy a machine is the same if 20,000 or 100,000 cans are produced. Therefore the fixed cost for every can falls the more the machine is used because depreciation charges will be spread over more units.

Other economies of scale might come from economies of increased dimensions. The set up and operating costs of machines do not increase proportionately with size. It does not cost twice as much to buy and operate a machine that has double the capacity of a smaller version, for example. Larger firms also have the benefit of negotiating discounts on bulk purchases and can often borrow money more cheaply than small ones. As a firm becomes larger, it also enjoys administrative economies and managerial efficiencies. Management will be able to adopt sophisticated techniques such as work studies and operational research to benefit the firm.

Larger size does not automatically improve efficiency, however. As a firm expands, it is

ABOVE: Once a company has built a facility such as a warehouse, the more stock it contains, the cheaper that warehouse becomes to use. This, in turn, reduces the unit cost of storing each item.

possible that the long-run average costs begin to rise. When increasing size leads to higher per unit costs, the firm is experiencing diseconomies of scale. The most common cause of such diseconomies is failure of management. The problems of coordinating and controlling an expanding firm may eventually result in disorganization. A manager is needed to supervise other managers; meetings are held more often; paperwork increases. The amount of time and labor not directly involved in producing output grows—this can reduce efficiency and so have an impact on costs.

SEE ALSO:

• Volume 2, page 28: How a business works

• Volume 2, page 80: How firms behave in the real world

• Volume 6, page 54: Industrialization, urbanization, and modernization

Returns to scale

The long-run average cost curve for a firm is normally U-shaped, like its short-run counterpart. Figure 1 shows a firm's long-run average cost curve. Economies of scale change into diseconomies of scale at point X. However, research has shown that for many industries the long-run average cost curve is actually L-shaped, as in Figure 2.

In this case the point at which the long-run cost curve reaches its lowest point is known as the minimum efficient scale. After this point, although the economies of scale are exhausted, diseconomies are no longer encountered. Instead, constant returns to scale begin.

Returns to scale is the term used to describe the relationship between a firm's output and the quantities of inputs used to produce that output in the long run, as for example in the relationship between the quantity of cans of soda produced and the inputs of sugar, water, flavorings, aluminum for the cans, labor, and machines that it takes to produce that quantity. When the long-run average cost curve is declining, the firm is enjoying economies of scale. When it rises, diseconomies of scale are encountered. With L-shaped curves, the minimum efficient scale has been reached—instead of being unable to cope with ever-increasing growth, the firm's management is able to remain efficient. This might be achieved by a management structure where many tasks are delegated, and where vigorous controls and monitoring allow for a smooth administration.

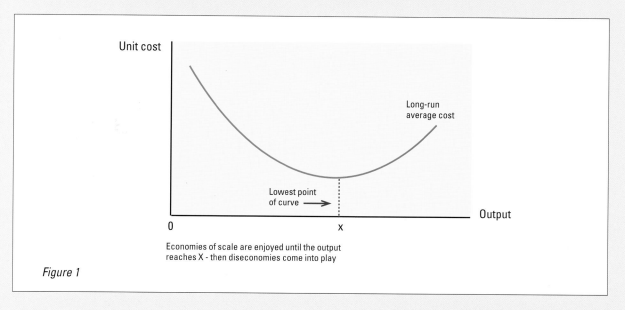

Economies of scale are enjoyed until the output reaches X - then diseconomies come into play

Figure 1

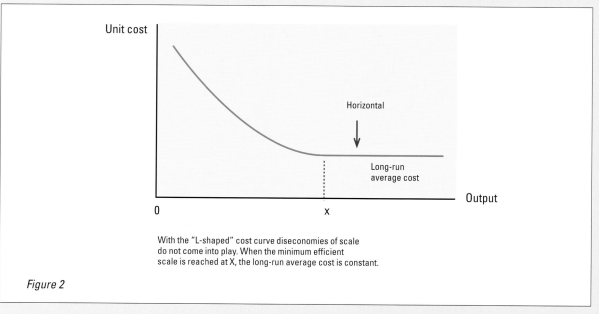

With the "L-shaped" cost curve diseconomies of scale do not come into play. When the minimum efficient scale is reached at X, the long-run average cost is constant.

Figure 2

Elasticity

Elasticity is a measure of the responsiveness of one variable—the dependent variable—to changes in another variable—the independent variable. Elasticity is often used to measure how changes in price (the independent variable) will affect the quantity demanded or supplied (dependent variables) of a good or a service.

Price elasticity of demand (PED) is the responsiveness of quantity demanded to changes in price. Price elasticity of supply is the responsiveness of quantity supplied to changes in price.

Determinants of PED

Many different factors determine the PED for a product. Undoubtedly the most important is the availability of substitutes for a particular product. Where substitutes exist, we tend to find that elasticity of demand for that product is higher than when no substitutes exist. For example, if the price of butter goes up, quantity demanded will fall significantly as more people switch to margarine, which is an acceptable substitute, as in Figure 1. This shows a relatively elastic demand curve. However, demand for products such as salt, for which there are no close substitutes, tends to be relatively inelastic—quantity demanded will not change much with a rise or a fall in price, as in Figure 2. An inelastic demand curve has a steep gradient.

As we have examined elsewhere (*see* The demand curve, page 23), the quantity demanded for a product varies with its price. However, elasticity is also affected by frequency of purchase. Products that are relatively cheap and frequently purchased tend to have a lower elasticity of demand than products that are relatively expensive and which

LEFT: The price of bread is fairly price inelastic—it is a staple food with no close subsitutes. Different brands of bread, by contrast, are fairly price elastic: one brand can be easily substituted for another.

are purchased infrequently. This explains why the elasticity of demand for newspapers is less than the elasticity of demand for automobiles.

Calculating elasticities

We know that changes in price cause changes in quantity demanded, and so PED can be calculated as follows:

$$PED = \frac{\text{percentage change in quantity of good X demanded}}{\text{percentage change in price of good X}}$$

In general, if elasticity is greater than one in absolute value, the relationship between

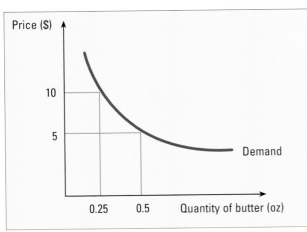

Figure 1 Relatively elastic demand.

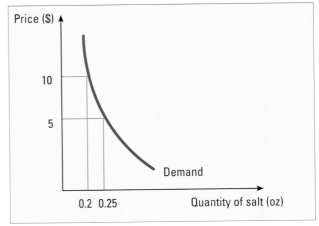

Figure 2 Relatively inelastic demand.

two variables is said to be elastic; and if it is less than one, the relationship is said to be inelastic. One point to note is that although PED is usually negative, by convention we ignore the negative sign.

Another point is that for any two variables, the value of elasticity will vary for different values of the variables. For example, we find that in general, price elasticity of demand is inelastic at relatively low prices and elastic at relatively high prices. To see why, consider the demand curve for good X. Consider a price reduction from $20 to $18 and a price reduction from $4 to $2. In both cases price falls by $2. In the first case the percentage change in price is -10%, and the percentage change in quantity demanded is 50%. So:

$$\text{PED} = {}^{-10}\!/\!{}_{50} \quad \text{or} \quad -0.20.$$

In the second case the percentage change in price is -50%, and the percentage change in quantity demanded is 10%, giving a total value for PED of -5! Since the negative sign is ignored, the values for PED above would usually be written as 0.20 and 5 respectively.

PED and total expenditure

For any product an important relationship exists between price elasticity of demand and total spending on the product. In general, if PED for a product is greater than one and therefore elastic, a price reduction will lead to an increase in total spending on it, and a price increase will lead to a reduction in total spending on it. Exactly the opposite happens when PED is inelastic and therefore less than 1. In this case a fall in price will lead to a reduction in total spending on the product, and a rise in price will lead to a rise in total spending on the product.

Elasticity of supply

Elasticity of supply is the responsiveness of quantity supplied to changes in price. It is measured in the same way as PED, although of course we substitute "percentage change in quantity supplied" for "percentage change in quantity demanded." The elasticity of supply is always positive since the supply curve has a positive slope. One of the main factors determining elasticity of supply is time. An increase in the amount supplied to market depends on the ability of current suppliers to increase their output or for new firms to enter the market. These changes take time—many years in some cases, such as coal or oil production. As a result, elasticity of supply tends to be greater in the long term than in the short term.

Other measures

Other measures of elasticity are income elasticity of demand and cross-elasticity of demand. Income elasticity of demand measures the responsiveness of changes in demand to changes in income. Since incomes generally tend to rise over time, income elasticity of demand has some important implications for the long-term plans and strategies of firms. Cross-elasticity of demand measures the responsiveness of changes in demand for one product to changes in the price of another product. A positive cross-elasticity of demand implies that products are substitutes because an increase in price for one product is associated with an increase in demand for the other. On the other hand a negative cross-elasticity of demand implies that goods are complements—that is, they are jointly consumed—because an increase in the price of one good causes a reduction in demand for the other.

SEE ALSO:

• Volume 2, page 28: How a business works

• Volume 3, page 79: Taxes

Equality and equity

In economics equality and equity are terms used to describe the distribution of income in society, but they are not the same thing. An equal or even division of a nation's economic output among its population might not be fair or just. An equitable division, on the other hand, is fair and just.

If we imagine that the economic output of a nation is like a pie, both equality and equity refer to ways in which that pie may be divided. In a market economy, for example, the division depends on the ownership of resources. Those who own the most highly valued resources will tend to receive a larger slice of the pie. In a socialist or command economy, on the other hand, the government or state owns most resources and divides the pie according to its assessment of people's need.

Economic theories explain various ways in which a society manages its resources—that is, its land, labor, and capital. Those theories have different goals, however, and there are many ways of judging whether an economy is doing a good job or a bad job. When making this evaluation, economists often compare equity and efficiency. A capitalist government tends to put a greater emphasis on efficiency, while a socialist government will typically be more concerned with equity.

Efficiency means that society is getting the most it can from its resources. An efficient economy produces what people want at the lowest possible cost (*see* Eccomomic efficiency, page 28). Whether or not an economy is efficient determines the size of the economic pie to be divided among the population.

Socialist economies work on the assumption that everyone should get the same size piece of the pie. Capitalist economies typically size each piece according to an individual's contribution, so that those who work harder become richer. Most capitalist governments, however, also acknowledge the desirability of achieving a greater or lesser degree of equality.

In the United States, for example, high-income earners are taxed at a higher rate than low-income earners. This is because they can better afford to pay for government programs, including housing, food, and medical assistance for the most needy members of society. In this way the government redistributes income from rich to poor, creating a more

ABOVE: Slum housing standing beside a thriving business district is a stark illustration of the inequality that some economic systems inevitably produce.

equal distribution of the economic pie. If taxing the rich at a higher rate reduces their willingness to work, however, then society sacrifices efficiency for the sake of greater equity. The two ideals are sometimes in conflict. This does not mean that society should not help the poor and disadvantaged, but it does suggest that economic policies need to take account of the trade-off between the two.

> ## SEE ALSO:
>
> • Volume 3, page 28: Government and the individual
>
> • Volume 6, page 106: Today and tomorrow

Exchange rates

Exchange rates set the price of a currency in terms of how much it is worth in other currencies. Because they can rise and fall, exchange rates are particularly important in international trade; they also affect how much money vacationers have when they are abroad.

International trade is often more complicated than domestic trade because exporters prefer to be paid in their own currency. If, for example, a U.S. company exports sneakers to Japan, it will expect to be paid in dollars, but a Japanese exporter of video recorders to the United States may well expect to be paid in yen. Currencies are exchanged in a foreign exchange market. The price of each currency in the market is determined in the same way as the price of any other commodity, through demand and supply (*see* Price and price theory, page 82).

The demand for, and supply of, a country's currency depends partly on that country's level of trade. The demand for dollars will be influenced by the demand for U.S. products in other countries. Japan has to buy dollars to pay for U.S. sneakers, thus increasing the demand for dollars. Similarly, the supply of dollars will be influenced by the demand for Japanese goods in the United States as importers supply dollars to pay for yen and other currencies.

If currency demand and supply are allowed to work without government intervention, exchange rates are said to be floating cleanly. Governments may also set an exchange rate, however, in which base rates are said to be fixed. A government may have to buy its own currency to boost demand or sell it to boost supply so as to maintain it at this fixed rate.

The exchange rate will also depend on how speculators and investors view a particular country's economic prospects. Speculators buy or sell such large amounts of a currency that they can swamp the effect of trade-based transactions: in other words, rises or falls in the exchange rate no longer reflect real trading activity in an economy. In the late 1990s speculators were sometimes able to destablize weaker currencies almost at will in order to profit from rising or falling rates.

For many people their most direct contact with the exchange rate comes if they take a vacation abroad. The exchange rate sets how much of another currency tourists receive in return for their dollars.

RIGHT: The value of a particular currency relative to another currency reflects numerous factors. At the most basic level, however, foreign exchange markets treat money like any other commodity, setting its price according to how much of it there is and how many people want to buy it.

SEE ALSO:

• Volume 1, page 71: Money markets and interest rates

• Volume 2, page 80: How firms behave in the real world

• Volume 4, page 35: International trade and finance

• Volume 4, page 6: The world economy

Externalities, environmental

An externality is the effect that one consumer's or producer's decision has on other individuals, other than through the effect that decision has on market price. For example, if somebody decides to smoke a cigarette in a crowded restaurant, the price that person pays is the cost of the cigarette plus whatever ill effects the cigarette has on his or her health. But what about the costs borne by the other people in the restaurant—in terms of their health and suffering the smell of smoke?

In economic terms an externality is that part of costs not borne by the individual consumer or producer whose activities have given rise to those costs. The value of an externality is represented by the costs or benefits to society as a whole, minus the private costs or benefits. So in the case of the cigarette smoker the value of this externality is the health costs and discomfort suffered by the people in the restaurant minus the costs borne by the smoker him or herself.

Externalities can be both negative and positive. In a negative case, for example, a company may decide to increase production of chemicals. This might result in increased waste being dumped into the river that runs next to the company, which in turn would affect local people's decision to eat fish caught from the river. On the other hand, a town council that decides to keep the town's streets clean will benefit people living there whether or not they have paid their taxes.

Cost-benefit analysis

Externalities exist because transactions that take place in the free market do not always produce a socially optimal outcome. In other words, the people involved in the transaction put their needs first, even if they clash with those of society as a whole. This failure to be socially optimum is measured in terms of marginal social cost, which is determined by cost-benefit analysis. It is carried out in two stages, first by identifying the parties who stand to gain or lose—from the pollution, say—and second by quantifying the extent by which they gain or lose. The sum total of these gains and losses is the net additional social benefit or cost.

Calculating net additional social benefit or cost is a more complicated exercise than might first appear. Many individuals are involved, they are often interdependent, and occasionally it is not clear exactly who they are. To return to the chemical company: the right to pollute benefits the company in the form of higher profits, since disposal into the river costs it nothing. The company's employees benefit from secure employment. The government benefits from higher tax receipts. Local business benefits from higher sales to residents working for the company.

On the costs side local fishers suffer because stocks are reduced by water pollution. Local consumers cannot buy fish caught in their local rivers. Local people suffer generally through not being able to enjoy a clean environment, or they might suffer health problems after swimming in the river. Meanwhile, however, fishers in other areas may benefit as demand for their catch increases.

ABOVE: Pollution often occurs because it is cheaper for companies to pollute their surroundings than to treat waste or dispose of it more cleanly. Eventually, however, the costs of pollution are passed to society as a whole.

Private and social costs and benefits

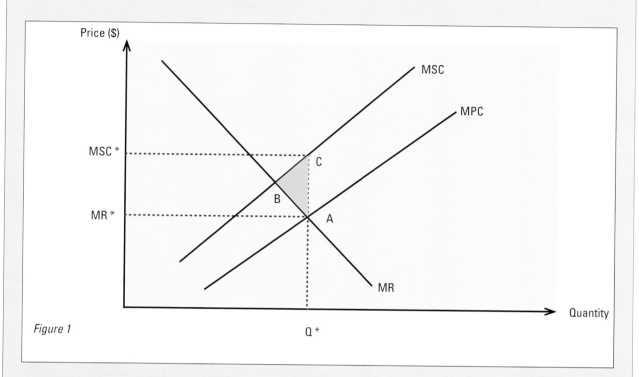

Figure 1

Externalities arise in cases where there is a gap between the private costs and benefits faced by the individual producer or consumer making a decision, and the social costs and benefits faced by others as a result of that decision. In the case of a chemical firm that pollutes a local river, for example, the private cost is the cost of producing the chemicals. The social cost, however, includes the loss of benefit to local people from, among other things, the reduced consumption of fish and the increased dirtiness of the river.

Assuming the firm wishes to maximize its profits, it will continue to produce—and therefore pollute the river—until its marginal private cost (MPC) equals its marginal revenue (MR) (*see* Profits and profit maximization, page 88). The company will produce at point A—quantity Q* of chemicals. Assuming also that individuals consume until their own marginal benefit equals marginal cost—the purchase price—marginal revenue is equivalent to marginal social benefit (MR*). The marginal social cost (MSC*) at this point, however, is greater than the marginal revenue generated. The social outcome is therefore not efficient. Equating marginal social cost (MSC) to marginal social benefit, on the other hand, would have produced an optimal outcome at point B, with the firm producing less chemicals at a higer price. The total additional "social cost" of the suboptimal result (A) is shown by the triangle ABC.

In many cases it is difficult to quantify in monetary terms the value of a social benefit or cost incurred. It is therefore also difficult to compare directly the worth of such variables as job security or the ability to swim in a local river.

Intervention

Assuming that the social cost or benefit of an activity can be identified, the next stage is to intervene in order to "force" a socially desirable outcome. The problem here is the difference between private and social costs and benefits. The solution, therefore, is to make the two as close as possible. This can be achieved by, for instance, imposing tax charges on polluters to increase their cost base or offering subsidies to environmentally responsible producers to reduce additional social costs (*see* Externalities and government policy, page 38).

Green economics

The desire to incorporate environmental responsibility into economic policy has led to "green economics," as for example, in the use of taxation or subsidies to force a socially efficient outcome. In purely economic terms, however, such a strategy is merely an attempt to correct the failure of the free market to take into account costs and benefits other than those faced directly by participants within the market.

SEE ALSO:

• Volume 2, page 100: Market failure and externalities

• Volume 3, page 43: Government and business

• Volume 4, page 63: The world economy

Externalities and government policy

Externalities occur when economic activities generate effects that are not taken into account by the market mechanism. Negative externalities arise when the welfare of an individual is negatively affected by the actions of another agent, and no payment is given to compensate. The reverse is true for positive externalities.

Externalities tend to occur when goods have no markets, and no market prices exist as a result. For example, there is no market for the environment—a firm can dump its waste at sea or pollute the air through its chimneys without having to pay anyone. Environmental problems are negative externalities in which the costs to society of pollution are not considered by economic agents (the firms themselves) when deciding what activities to undertake (*see* Externalities, environmental, page 36).

Externalities are external costs or benefits that the market mechanism fails to reflect. For example, the price you pay for leaded gasoline reflects the cost of its production but not the health costs to society of the pollution that results from its use. Hence the presence of externalities results in a socially inefficient outcome (*see* Economic efficiency, page 28).

Government intervention can, however, "internalize" these external costs or benefits by assigning property rights—social arrangements that govern the ownership and use of economic resources. Many economists believe that externalities arise because of the lack of well-defined property rights, and that this prevents the existence of markets. If property rights are assigned to a resource, then a market and a market price will emerge. For example, the government might decide to sell pollution permits to firms located along a river. These permits represent user rights on the environment and allow the firms to discharge a certain amount of pollutants into the river. The permit price constitutes the payment for using the environment in this way and should guarantee a more efficient use of the environment.

Another remedy—known as the Pigovian solution—requires the establishment of taxes

ABOVE: Oil spills represent a negative externality to oil production and transport.

on negative externalities, or subsidies for positive externalities, on the activities that generate them. An example might be a tax on leaded gasoline, making it more expensive for motorists to buy. Similarly, a subsidy could be paid to firms producing unleaded gasoline, ultimately making it cheaper for motorists.

External costs and benefits are thus internalized by making the economic agents pay a tax to pollute. Subsidies might be paid to encourage firms with less polluting production methods or those making environmentally sound products.

SEE ALSO:

• Volume 2, page 100: Market failure and externalities

• Volume 3, page 43: Government and businesss

Federalism

Federalism is a form of political organization in which power is divided or shared between one central government and several regional or state governments. The way in which power is devolved can vary considerably between different governments and over time.

The United States is run federally. The central or federal government in Washington D.C. is responsible for providing public goods such as national defense, regulating market failures and externalities, setting the government's spending and taxes, and controlling the money supply, along with many social programs (*see* Public sector, page 89; Externalities and government policy, page 38; Regulation and antitrust laws, page 93). State governments, on the other hand, are largely responsible for policies on education and poverty, and for managing the relevant budgets and enforcing the laws in these areas. Other countries that have a federal system of government include Brazil, Canada, Germany, and Switzerland. The various systems that call themselves federal, however, differ in many ways.

In the United States much of the credit for the establishment of the principle of federal government—which is enshrined in the Constitution of 1787—goes to chief justice John Marshall (1755-1835). To begin with, however, federal powers were restricted to areas such as making treaties and printing money. All other powers belonged to the member states. Over the years, however, many state powers and responsibilities were centralized to the federal level. This trend began during the Great Depression when many state governments did not have the finances or resources to cope with the vast numbers of unemployed and needy people. President Franklin D. Roosevelt and Congress passed legislation that included job programs, help for families with children, and financial assistance to people who could not work. Control over many of these programs and services was concentrated in the federal government. This trend was continued in later social programs such as food stamps and Medicare and with the creation of the Environmental Protection Agency in 1970, all of which were federal government responsibilities.

In recent years there has been increasing public demand to transfer power away from Washington D.C. to state and local governments. Scaling back federal government has been a major concern for Congress since the late 1980s and throughout the 1990s. Today Washington has to provide funds for state and local governments to enforce most new federal policies or mandates. This increase in the authority of states has had particular effect on public policy issues such as poverty, education, and the environment.

Still, most of the key policy decisions that affect and shape people's economic lives in the United States are made at the central level. Monetary policy, for example, involves controlling the money supply and setting credit conditions such as interest rates. The Federal Reserve, or Fed—the central bank of America and the U.S. government's banker—is largely responsible for setting policy in this area (*see* Money: its supply and demand, page 72). Similarly, fiscal policy can affect important macroeconomic goals such as price levels and employment. This involves setting government spending and taxation, and is determined by laws that are passed by Congress and signed by the president (*see* Fiscal policy, page 40). Any major change in the direction of fiscal policy is normally the result of a decision by the U.S. president.

ABOVE: The United States has a federal system of government. While power has been increasingly centralized throughout most of the 20th century, the 1990s saw many policy issues moving back to state authority.

SEE ALSO:

• Volume 3, page 6: Government and the economy

• Volume 3, page 28: Government and the individual

• Volume 6, page 86: The West in the 20th century

Fiscal policy

Fiscal policy is a government's approach to changing its expenditure or taxation policy in order to achieve broad economic objectives such as reducing unemployment, cutting inflation, or boosting economic growth.

Fiscal policy is the basic instrument by which government varies its income and expenditure to realize its macroeconomic objectives. Government expenditure includes purchases of goods and services, including highways and public education, and transfer payments, such as Social Security and welfare. Government income comprises tax revenue from individuals in the form of personal income taxes, from businesses as a tax on profits, and on transactions in the form of sales and excise taxes (*see* Taxation, taxes, and subsidies, page 107).

Among the typical primary macroeconomic objectives of fiscal policy are full employment, normally defined as an unemployment rate of or below approximately 5 percent; price stability, normally defined as an inflation rate of 2 percent or less; and economic growth—for example, an annual increase in real per capita national output of 2 percent or more.

In the United States fiscal policy is conducted by the President and Congress. In contrast, monetary policy—changes in the money supply that affect the cost of credit—is set by the central bank, the Federal Reserve.

There are two main types of fiscal policy. Demand-side fiscal policy seeks to influence the aggregate demand, the total demand in the economy for the nation's output. Expansionary fiscal policy, which includes increases in government expenditure or cuts in taxes, increases aggregate demand and boosts employment, but may be associated with a rise in inflation. Contractionary fiscal policy, such as decreases in government expenditure or hikes in taxes, reduces aggregate demand and cuts inflation. Supply-side fiscal policy focuses on increasing the aggregate supply, or total output in the economy, through greater incentives to work, save, and invest. Such incentives might include investment tax credits for businesses and favorable tax breaks for personal savings.

The effectiveness of demand-side fiscal policy is a source of much debate among economists. Actively stabilizing the economy near full employment is in the Keynesian tradition

ABOVE: Governments may seek to control inflation through contractionary fiscal policy—raising taxes and cutting welfare payments, for example. Such policies are liable to be unpopular with many people.

SEE ALSO:

• Volume 3, page 6: Government and the economy

• Volume 3, page 28: Government and the individual

• Volume 3, page 79: Taxes

(*see* Keynesianism, page 54). Monetarists, meanwhile, believe that fiscal policy is ineffective in changing aggregate demand (*see* Monetarism, page 71). Neoclassical economists, on the other hand, argue that the impact on output of any fiscal policy-induced change in aggregate demand will be neutralized by changes in aggregate supply. They also believe that stabilizers built into the tax and transfer system, such as welfare payments, moderate the business cycle (*see* Laissez-faire, page 59; The business cycle, page 7). For example, recessions with rising unemployment are softened by greater government expenditure on transfer payments, an automatic expansionary fiscal policy. Conversely, economic expansions require fewer transfer payments, an automatic contractionary fiscal policy.

Free trade and protectionism

Protectionism is the restriction of imports into a country through government regulations. Free trade is the opposite of protectionism—i.e., when there are no such restrictions.

While classical and free market economists argue that free trade will result in all trading parties being better off in the long term (*see* Laissez-faire and classical economics, page 59), many people argue the case for protecting domestic markets from cheap foreign imports. For example, the United States protected its automobile industry during the 1970s, principally from imports of cheaper Japanese automobiles.

The most common method of protection is a tariff—a tax on imports or exports. Every country imposes tariffs on at least some imports so that the importer has to pay a proportion of the initial price to the home government. This raises the domestic price of the good to consumers, thus making it less attractive to them. Some countries also impose tariffs on certain exports—Brazil, for example, taxes coffee exports—which raise money for the government. Export tariffs are forbidden by the U.S. Constitution.

The case of bananas

In the figure shown here, for example, with no international trade—i.e., if all are bananas produced and sold within the United States—the price of bananas is Pd, where quantity supplied equals the quantity demanded in the domestic market. The world price for bananas is Pw. With free trade imports would be represented by Q2 minus Q1—the difference between the quantity supplied domestically and the quantity demanded at the world price. Domestic production of bananas falls as a result of trade, but domestic consumers are better off because they can buy more bananas at a lower price. If the U.S. puts a tariff on banana imports (Pw+T), imports are reduced to Q4 minus Q3. Domestic producers are better off with a tariff since they can sell more bananas at a higher price. Domestic consumers, on the other hand, are worse off, having to pay higher prices for fewer bananas, but are still better off than they would have been if there were no trade at all.

Another form of protectionism is quotas, where only a specified amount of a good is

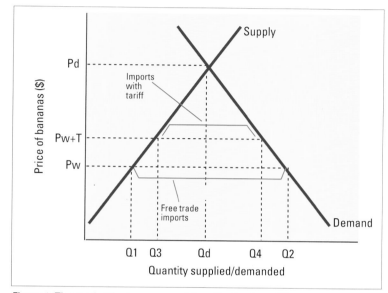

Figure 1 The market for bananas and the effects of a tariff.

allowed into the country during a given period—e.g., no more than 10,000 cars a year can be imported. This restricts the supply of the good, so increasing the price. Nontariff barriers include rules and regulations—such as strict safety regulations—that make it more difficult to import.

In spite of the theoretical advantages of free trade, as justified by the law of comparative advantage (*see* Comparative advantage, page 12), and despite the liberalization of trade that has continued since World War II, many people remain convinced that restrictions on trade can still be beneficial to a particular country.

The arguments for protectionism are varied. Between World War I and World War II a popular argument was that protection of domestic industries was necessary to maintain employment and domestic production during periods of recession. However, many economists now believe that this merely pushed the problem onto other countries, for U.S. tariffs in turn led many countries to retaliate by imposing similar restrictions on imports. The result was that world trade seized up. Many tariffs and restrictions on imports today are "tit-for-tat"—for example, the European Union (EU) banned

RIGHT: Trade between nations is a cornerstone of the world economy. However, the traffic of goods and products is seldom unrestricted by legislation and may sometimes be banned altogether.

imports of beef from the United States in 1999 because of the alleged steroid content in the meat. The U.S. then retaliated by imposing restrictions on certain EU products being shipped into the country.

Protecting inefficiency

Those in favor of some forms of protectionism may also argue that domestic firms cannot compete against cheap foreign labor. In recent years textiles and clothing industries in the West have used this argument when challenged by cheap imports of clothes from Asia, for example, where wages are a fraction of those in Europe and the United States. Meanwhile, those in favor of free trade contend that countries should produce goods they are relatively more efficient at making. There might be some short-term hardship as particular industries are run down, and before resources can be transferred to new industries, but in the long run all countries benefit.

A further argument in favor of protectionism is that it should be introduced to protect infant industries from world competition, at least until they are firmly established. The problem here is that the infant industry may never grow up as a direct result of this protection. Those opposed to protectionism take the view

that free trade forces firms to become efficient, or else they go bankrupt.

A similar argument used by those in favor of protection is that certain imports should be restricted to protect traditional craft industries or small-scale family farming. Advocates of free trade, on the other hand, believe that subsidy is a much more efficient method of helping a threatened business than the imposition of a tariff on its rivals.

Finally, it might be argued that protection is necessary for those industries and raw materials that are considered crucial to a nation's independence and safety. They might include defense and transport equipment, and steel production. If a country is dependent on other nations for its arms and defense equipment, for example, it is vulnerable to embargoes should there be a war. Supporters of free trade might argue that the building up of a strategic stockpile would be more efficient in this case.

Despite all the arguments for free trade, many successful modern economies, such as Japan and Germany, have pursued protectionist policies. Unemployment rates are still high in many parts of the world, and many of the hardest hit countries see protectionism as an important way to protect domestic jobs.

SEE ALSO:

• Volume 3, page 79: Taxes

• Volume 4, page 6: The U.S. government and world economics

• Volume 4, page 35: International trade and finance

• Volume 6, page 38: The Age of Reason and early industrialization

Goods and services

Goods and services, or economic commodities, are the basic units of economic activity. An economic commodity is anything that is both useful and scarce, and thus has a price. Goods are tangible items and might include anything from housing, food, and clothing to vacuum cleaners, TV sets, books, and jewelry. Services tend to be more abstract—they might include doctors' services, telephone calls, going to the movies or theater, video rental, and vacations.

Goods and services are sometimes also classified as necessities and luxuries. Consumption of necessities is seen as essential in order to maintain a minimum standard of living. Consumption of luxuries, on the other hand, contributes to a higher standard of living than the minimum.

The defining economic characteristics of a commodity—scarcity, usefulness, durability, and so on—determine the type of analysis to which it is subjected. For example, free goods are things that are useful but not scarce, such as the air that we breathe. A public good, such as national defense, is characterized by nonrivalry and nonexcludability—it benefits everyone whether or not they directly pay for it—and so has to be provided by the government (*see* Public sector, page 89).

Goods can also be classified according to their durability and end-use. A durable good is any good that yields utility or satisfaction over time rather than being used up at the moment of consumption. Under this definition durable goods include not only relatively expensive and technologically complex goods such as refrigerators and video recorders, but also

ABOVE: In economic terms a theater trip is classed as a serice rather than a good and as a luxury rather than a necessity—theater-going is not essential to maintaining a minimum standard of living.

43

the value of output produced domestically, the

Economic theory

Growth and development

There are various measures of the health of any economy. One of the most important is its rate of economic growth—increases in output per head of the population. Development, on the other hand, is a more complex measure and refers to a sustained improvement in standards of living. Improvements in growth and development are most often achieved by increasing the quantity and quality of land, labor, capital, and entrepreneurship—and by technological progress.

The main sources of increases in output are growth in the quantity and quality of the factors of production and technological progress. The factors of production are physical capital—the factories, equipment, and machinery that constitute the human-made aids to production; labor or human resources; and land, which comprises not only land but also natural resources, such as forests, minerals, and water. Technological progress refers to innovations and inventions that help in the production of goods and services.

Technological progress is often built into new capital equipment as in the case, for example, of more powerful computers and more energy-efficient machinery. This increases the average quality of physical capital stock. Improvements in the quality of labor result from increases in the work force's average levels of education and health. One particular quality of labor important for economic growth is entrepreneurship—the ability to recognize and exploit profitable opportunities.

The natural resources available for production can be increased by exploration or by improving methods of mining or fishing, for example. The quality, as well as the quantity, of natural resources, however, can also be diminished by pollution and improper management. Overfishing reduces fish stocks to a level where they cannot regenerate their original numbers; deforestation results in soil erosion. Economic growth at the expense of environmental deterioration may not be sustainable.

The growth of a nation's population is equal to the difference between the births and deaths in the population, plus immigration into the country minus emigration from it. The

LEFT: Agriculture is an activity in which the growth that can be achieved by advances in technology needs to be balanced by concerns about disturbing local ecosystems or causing soil erosion.

Gross domestic product and gross national product

Gross domestic product (GDP) is the value of all final goods and services produced within the boundaries of a country over a period of time, normally a year. Gross national product (GNP) measures the value of the final goods and services produced by the organizations and citizens of an economy over a period of time, including those based abroad.

GNP is defined as GDP plus "net property income from abroad." Some citizens and organizations in the United States own firms and land in other countries; others have loaned money to foreign countries. These assets earn profits, rent, dividends, and interest that are brought back to the United States—hence they form part of U.S. income. In the U.S. net property income from abroad is this income earned abroad minus what America pays to foreigners who own domestic assets.

So, for example, in the case of a multinational company like General Motors, the profits of a subsidiary based in Europe are not counted as part of U.S. GDP since it is based outside America. However, these profits would be counted as part of U.S. GNP since they are income earned abroad by an American corporation. On the other hand, an American-based branch of a European company would have its profits included in U.S. GDP but not GNP.

There are three different ways of measuring GDP. One is by adding up the market value—that is, the value at market price—of all final goods and services produced domestically. A second way of measuring GDP is to consider the total expenditure that takes place when output is sold. This comprises the total of household expenditure (consumption), plus business expenditure (investment on capital goods, wages paid to labor, etc.), and government expenditure and net exports (exports minus imports). The third way of measuring GDP is by taking it as equal to the total income of everyone in the economy. This comprises all payments to factors of production—land, labor, and capital—in the form of rent, wages, interest, and profits. All three of these measures—the value of output produced domestically, the

value of expenditure to purchase that output, and the value of income received by factors of production—must be equivalent *(see* National income accounting, page 76*)*.

Economic health check

GDP is used by countries to measure the health of the economy. It is calculated by economists and statisticians from data and statistics that are compiled and released quarterly. A decline in the value of the real GDP for two or more quarters is defined as a recession *(see* Recession, page 91*)*. A slowing down of the rate of increase in the GDP is cause for concern in most economies unless they are concerned with controlling inflation.

In the early 1990s the U.S Department of Commerce joined the rest of the world in focusing on GDP rather than GNP as a gauge of how the U.S. economy was doing. GDP has now become the standard measure for the health of the U.S. economy.

SEE ALSO:

• Volume 3, page 6: Government and the economy

• Volume 3, page 79: Taxes

• Volume 4, page 63: The world economy

LEFT: *The value of goods produced by U.S. corporations based in Hong Kong is recorded as part of American Gross National Product, but not Gross Domestic Product.*

Growth and development

There are various measures of the health of any economy. One of the most important is its rate of economic growth—increases in output per head of the population. Development, on the other hand, is a more complex measure and refers to a sustained improvement in standards of living. Improvements in growth and development are most often achieved by increasing the quantity and quality of land, labor, capital, and entrepreneurship—and by technological progress.

The main sources of increases in output are growth in the quantity and quality of the factors of production and technological progress. The factors of production are physical capital—the factories, equipment, and machinery that constitute the human-made aids to production; labor or human resources; and land, which comprises not only land but also natural resources, such as forests, minerals, and water. Technological progress refers to innovations and inventions that help in the production of goods and services.

Technological progress is often built into new capital equipment as in the case, for example, of more powerful computers and more energy-efficient machinery. This increases the average quality of physical capital stock. Improvements in the quality of labor result from increases in the work force's average levels of education and health. One particular quality of labor important for economic growth is entrepreneurship—the ability to recognize and exploit profitable opportunities.

The natural resources available for production can be increased by exploration or by improving methods of mining or fishing, for example. The quality, as well as the quantity, of natural resources, however, can also be diminished by pollution and improper management. Overfishing reduces fish stocks to a level where they cannot regenerate their original numbers; deforestation results in soil erosion. Economic growth at the expense of environmental deterioration may not be sustainable.

The growth of a nation's population is equal to the difference between the births and deaths in the population, plus immigration into the country minus emigration from it. The

LEFT: Agriculture is an activity in which the growth that can be achieved by advances in technology needs to be balanced by concerns about disturbing local ecosystems or causing soil erosion.

growth of a nation's employed labor force depends on increases in the number of people who are of labor-force age and the overall health of the economy, since this determines the employment rate.

Economic growth occurs when there are increases in the average product of labor, that is, the average amount of goods or services produced by each person in the labor force rises. Economic growth also occurs when the percentage of the population in employment increases. A rise in the average product of labor may be due to an improvement in the quality of labor through education or better health; it might also come from an increase in physical capital, so that there are more machines in proportion to workers. Technological progress can also increase the output per unit of labor, as advances in knowledge allow greater output to be produced from given resources.

Growth rates also depend on a country's ability to develop and adapt new technologies (*see* Technology, page 109). Important considerations include the degree of openness of the economy to foreign trade and investment, and the economic-political-legal environment, which can encourage or discourage such stimulants to growth as entrepreneurship, competition, and efficient use of resources.

Growth is a necessary, but not a sufficient, condition for economic development. That is, the rising per capita output and income that define economic growth do not always result in characteristics of development such as a reduction of poverty or widespread improvements in the health and education of the population. Economic growth may produce a very concentrated distribution of income and wealth—there are a very small number of very wealthy people, but the majority of the world's population is still very poor. Moreover, economic development often involves structural change. Historically, this transformation has been from primarily agrarian to urban-industrial economies with modern services, improved infrastructure, and increased international commerce.

There is no one universally accepted measure of economic development. The United Nations Development Program, however, has devised a Human Development Index (HDI) that indicates a nation's relative progress in terms of life expectancy at birth, adult literacy, school enrollment rates, and per capita GDP, the value of each person's output expressed in comparable dollars. The HDI is intended to capture some of the more important dimensions of improving the human condition.

SEE ALSO:

• Volume 2, page 100: Market failure and externalities

• Volume 3, page 6: Government and the economy

• Volume 3, page 28: Government and the individual

• Volume 4, page 63: The world economy

Income distribution

Income distribution shows the ways in which a society's income is divided.

In a market economy the supply of and demand for factors of production, such as labor and capital, determine workers' wages and the return owners of capital receive on their investments. In this way the market determines income distribution.

Free markets usually result in income inequality, which is a highly contentious issue for both the public and governments (see Equality and equity, page 34). Many people believe that income distribution should not be determined by market forces alone but that governments should ensure a more equitable distribution between the population. This is the philosophy of many communist or socialist governments. Other people believe that such intervention takes away the incentive to work hard and innovate.

The table below shows the percentage of money income going to families in the United States in 1993 in terms of quintiles, which split the population into fifths or blocks of 20 percent. The lowest quintile comprises the poorest 20 percent of families, the second fifth is the next poorest, and so on up to the top fifth, which represents the richest 20 percent of families in the country. In 1993 the richest fifth received 46.2 percent of the total income, while the poorest received only 4.2 percent of total income. The table also shows cumulative shares of income. For example, the bottom 60 percent had 30.2 percent of income—this is the combined sum of incomes that the bottom, second, and third fifth received.

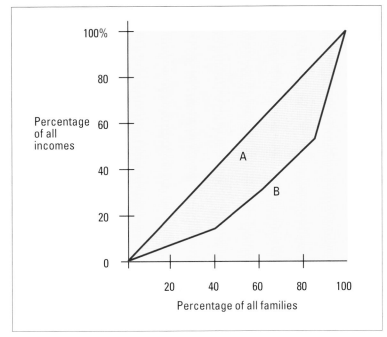

Figure 1 The Lorenz curve.

Income distribution is often plotted graphically by what is called a Lorenz curve. The Lorenz curve in Figure 1 is plotted based on the data contained in the table. The percentage of all families in the economy is plotted along the horizontal axis and the cumulative percentage of all incomes received by those families on the vertical axis.

Since the bottom 20 percent of the population received only 4.2 percent of income in 1993, we plot a point accordingly. For the bottom 40 percent of population, we plot a point at 14.3 percent of income, and so on. At 100 percent of the population the cumulative income must also be 100 percent. Connecting all these points gives the Lorenz curve (B). If income distribution were equal among all members of a population, the curve would be a 45-degree line equidistant from both axes. This line (A) is called the line of income equality. Here 10 percent of the population earns 10 percent of income, 20 percent of the population earns 20 percent of income, and so on. The closer a Lorenz curve is to the line of income equality, the more equal is income distribution; the further it is away, the less equal.

Income distribution in the U.S. 1993

Quintile	Percent of income	Cumulative percent of income
Bottom Fifth	4.2	4.2
Second Fifth	10.1	14.3
Third Fifth	15.9	30.2
Fourth Fifth	23.6	53.8
Top Fifth	46.2	100.0

SEE ALSO:

• Volume 3, page 6: Government and the economy

• Volume 3, page 28: Government and the individual

• Volume 3, page 79: Taxes

Inflation and deflation

Inflation is a sustained rise in the average price level. When inflation is present, a dollar is said to have less purchasing power than it did a year ago—your dollar can buy less today compared to what it could buy last year. With deflation the opposite is true—it is a sustained fall in the average level of prices.

Inflation or deflation is often measured using the Consumer Price Index (CPI) (*see* Consumer price index, page 17).

Since the 1970s a major objective of economic policies has been to curb inflation. Governments have tended to assume that economic goals, such as economic growth and low unemployment, will succeed only if inflation is brought under control.

The purchasing power of money is what money can buy. Suppose that an economy has only one good, bread, which costs $1 per loaf. With $2 you can buy two loaves of bread. The following year the price of bread goes up to $2. Now your $2 can only buy one loaf of bread. Purchasing power goes down as prices rise.

If, however, your income rises by the same percentage as inflation, your purchasing power will remain the same. It doesn't matter to you that bread costs twice as much if you earn twice as many dollars as you did before. If your income remains the same, on the other hand, or increases at a slower rate than prices rise, then inflation is clearly a problem.

Inflation may also hurt savings. If inflation is higher than interest rates, people's savings will gain very little or might even lose value (*see* Interest rates, page 52). This reduces any incentive people might have to save.

Inflation also has international consequences. High inflation means that a country's exports become relatively expensive in foreign markets, while high domestic prices will attract cheaper imports. This will result in a deficit on the current account of the balance of payments since imports are greater than exports.

An extreme form of inflation is hyperinflation, when prices rise by as much as a thousand percent or more in a year. In such situations, as for example in Russia in the 1990s, prices become virtually meaningless, and the price system breaks down altogether. Many price transactions in Russia were carried out in U.S. dollars because people did not trust the Russian currency, the ruble, to keep its value. Similarly

in former Yugoslavia, war caused hyperinflation, one consequence of which was that people going into cafés tried to make sure they paid on entry because the price would have risen before they left!

Different economists account for inflation in various ways. Keynesian theorists, for example, contend that there are two main types of inflation—cost-push inflation and demand-pull inflation.

Cost-push inflation is a sustained rise in general price levels caused by rising production costs. Such rises in costs cause firms to raise their own prices in order to avoid losses. Some economists argue that the high inflation rates suffered

ABOVE: During the 1920s Germany suffered acute hyperinflation. When it reached its peak, a wheelbarrowful of marks would be needed to purchase a simple staple such as a loaf of bread.

LEFT: During the crisis that followed the Arab-Israeli Yom Kippur War in 1973, U.S. oil prices were for a time increasing so rapidly that gas stations could not quote accurately the cost of a gallon.

by the U.S. during the 1970s were primarily due to rising oil prices (see Oligopoly and oligopolistic competition, page 78). Since oil is vital for the production of many goods, higher oil prices lead to effects on prices throughout the economy.

Some economists believe that the major cause of cost-push inflation is pressure from labor unions for higher wages above the level of increases in labor productivity. On the other hand, firms with some monopoly power might push prices up above any rise in costs that they face in order to increase their profit margins (see Monopoly, page 74).

Demand-pull inflation occurs when demand is greater than the capacity of the economy to produce goods and services to meet that demand. As demand increases, supply remains the same, so prices rise. This might occur when an economy has reached full productive capacity—it may have full employment or little surplus capital and cannot expand supply to meet demand.

Monetarists believe that high inflation is caused when the money supply is allowed to grow rapidly. Such growth may occur when a government wants to spend more than it derives from taxation or borrowing—in this case it might simply issue more money. With money supply increasing faster than demand,

spending increases, and prices go up (see Monetarism, page 71).

Experts disagree about the causes of inflation and hence the best way to tackle it. If inflation is caused by excessive increases in the money supply, then it can be reduced by reducing the rate of growth of the money supply. Keynesian economists believe that the money supply is difficult to control, and that inflation is better dealt with by manipulating aggregate demand through increasing government expenditure in the public sector or reducing taxes (see Fiscal policy, page 40).

Deflation

Deflation—a fall in price levels—goes hand-in-hand with unemployment and a drop in national output. It is often caused by government policies such as tax increases or using interest rates to influence the demand for money and attempts to control the supply of money.

Some economists think that the global economy is overproducing—the supply of goods and services is too great to be met by demand. They believe that this will lead to worldwide deflation. Consumers would benefit from falling prices, but firms would find it difficult to make profits, and a recessionary spiral of falling prices and rising interest rates might be difficult to control.

SEE ALSO:

• Volume 1, page 24: Banks and banking

• Volume 1, page 58: Saving and borrowing

• Volume 1, page 86: Inflation and deflation

• Volume 3, page 6: Government and the economy

Intellectual property

Intellectual property is different from real property, such as land or houses, because it is an intangible idea and the product of an individual's mind. Intellectual property is the creative work of inventors, artists, authors, musicians, and entrepreneurs and as such includes inventions, paintings, books, music, and computer programs.

Intellectual property adds value to a book or a compact disc, for example, which may be far above the cost of printing that book or recording and issuing a piece of music. The creative effort of authors, musicians, or inventors needs to be protected so that others cannot copy ideas and profit from them. This is most commonly done through patents, copyrights, and trademarks.

Patents are legal documents issued by the government that grant exclusive rights to the inventor of a product or service. They protect a new product's initial research and development costs. If other individuals or firms wish to make or use the original invention, they are required to pay a license fee or royalty to the inventor.

Copyrights protect authors', artists' and musicians' performing and recording rights. Copyright protection prevents others from copying a piece of writing or music, for example, and enables these individuals to earn royalties for themselves and their heirs. There are international economic agreements stating rules to clamp down on the theft of copyright, including unauthorized recording of live performances and commercial copying of films.

Trademarks and branding help manufacturers protect their reputation in terms of the quality of their products. For example, it is illegal for a jeans manufacturer to produce jeans of a similar design to Levi jeans and then label them as if they were a genuine Levi product. Trademarks have some key benefits—they prevent other companies from copying one another, they differentiate goods for consumers, and they legally enforce this difference or license it.

New ideas can also be protected through licensing agreements. Licensing means that a person or company has to pay a sum of money, usually a percentage of the price of the product, called a royalty, to use a particular trademark, logo, or distinctive product packaging. The licensed product industry grew phenomenally in the 1990s, when companies started producing all kinds of merchandising that were spinoffs from, for example, characters in TV programs or films. In these situations the marketing and advertising for the product are already in place through the high profile of the film or TV program. When Disney makes a new film, for example, it grants a license to producers of toys, books, and tapes that are based on characters in the film. The license is usually granted on a short-term basis, and Disney receives a royalty in return.

SEE ALSO:

• Volume 3, page 43: Government and business

• Volume 2, page 62: Competition, expansion, and growth

ABOVE: Musicians who are on a royalty may earn money from their compositions whenever they are played on the radio or covered by another artist.

Interest rates

Interest is a sum of money received in exchange for making a loan. The interest rate is the amount of interest paid expressed as a proportion of the size of the loan. Interest rates are expressed in terms of percentage per year. They represent the cost of borrowing money.

The interest rate is determined by the supply of and demand for money (*see* Money, supply, and demand, page 72). It is vital for everyone because it ultimately sets how much people or businesses have to pay to get a loan from the bank or a mortgage for a house, or how much interest a savings account will yield.

In the United States the money supply is controlled by the central bank, the Federal Reserve, or Fed for short, which fixes the quantity of money supplied in the economy. This money supply, represented by a vertical line at Q^{MS} in Figure 1, is independent of the current interest rate and income. Money demand, on the other hand, is dependent on the interest rate and income: the quantity of money demanded goes up as incomes rise, or as the cost of borrowing—the interest rate—falls. Money demand can be represented by a line sloping downward from left to right, reflecting the fact that the interest rate is the opportunity cost of holding cash instead of other interest-bearing assets (*see* Opportunity cost, page 79).

Equilibrium is achieved when the money supply equals money demand. If the interest rate is above or below this equilibrium rate,

ABOVE: Few people have cash to pay for everything they want to buy, so they need to take loans on which they will usually pay a set rate of interest.

SEE ALSO:

• Volume 1, page 6: What is money?

• Volume 1, page 58: Saving and borrowing

• Volume 1, page 71: Money markets and interest rates

• Volume 2, page 48: Finance and accounting

• Volume 3, page 6: Government and the economy

people will adjust their holding of interest-bearing assets such as bonds. Suppose, for example, that the interest rate is i_0 on Figure 1. The quantity of money demanded exceeds the quantity supplied. People try to increase their money holdings by reducing their holdings of interest-bearing assets. As a result, there will be an excess supply of bonds, which, in turn, will force bond issuers to offer higher interest rates in order to attract buyers. The interest rate continues to rise until the money market reaches equilibrium. Similarly, at any interest rate above the equilibrium level, an excess supply of money will push the rate down toward the equilibrium level.

Economists distinguish between the nominal interest rate and the real interest rate. Suppose that you deposit $100 dollars at your bank, and the bank pays you a nominal interest rate of 10 percent every year on your deposit. During the year prices rise by 5 percent, so that each dollar buys 5 percent less (*see* Inflation and deflation, page 49). At the end of the year your deposit has gone up to $110. However, the true increase in your purchasing power has only gone up by 5 percent—to $105. The real interest rate that tells you that increase is the difference between the nominal interest rate and the rate of inflation.

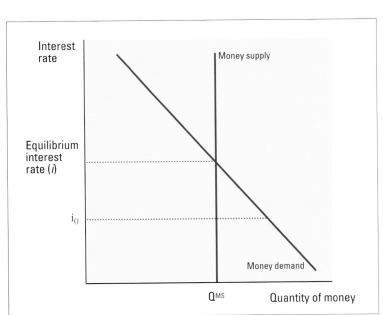

Figure 1 Equilibrium in the money market.

International debt

An international debt is money owed by a government to a government or bank in another country, or to an international financial institution such as the World Bank or the International Monetary Fund (IMF).

Many countries of the developing world—such as Brazil, Indonesia, and Tanzania—owe a great deal of money to banks in the developed world and to the governments of nations such as the United States, Britain, and Japan (*see* The developing world, page 25).

Under the conventional economic theory of development the best way for a nation to increase its output of goods and services is through investment and by increasing its capital stock (*see* Capital, page 8). During the 1970s many developing countries borrowed money, mainly from banks and institutions in developed countries, in order to finance investment. This was done in much the same way as a business might borrow money from a bank to finance expansion. However, in the 1980s many debtor countries in the developing world found that they could no longer afford the repayments on their loans. For example, at the end of 1989 Brazil owed its foreign creditors $111.3 billion, while Mexico owed $95.6 billion. In both cases these debts amounted to many times the annual sales of goods and services by these countries to the rest of the world.

There are several reasons why so many countries in the developing world found themselves in this position. Much of the money they had borrowed was wasted on poor investments or projects—many of which had been promoted by the lenders. These projects did not go on to create the output necessary to cover the debt repayments.

In addition, the cost of borrowing soared in the 1980s as the value of the U.S. dollar went up. Since most loans had been made in dollars, developing countries found they had to export more and more goods and services in order to receive the same number of dollars in return. Meanwhile, interest rates increased worldwide, further increasing loan repayments.

Finally, some of the money that was loaned to developing countries for capital investment was used by military regimes on national defense. Other loans were appropriated by corrupt government officials.

ABOVE: One of the great anomalies of the world economy is that many countries suffer grinding poverty despite having a wealth of valuable natural resources.

Today many developing countries face interest repayments that are greater than all the finance they currently receive through investments, new loans, or aid from overseas. Recently, however, campaigns such as Jubilee 2000 have made many Western governments give serious consideration for the first time to the possibility of writing off the debts of the world's poorest nations.

> **SEE ALSO:**
>
> • Volume 4, page 6: The U.S. government and world economics
>
> • Volume 4, page 63: The world economy

Keynesianism

Keynesian economists believe that governments should intervene directly in the economy to ensure that aggregate demand is sufficient to ensure full employment without losing control of inflation.

Keynesianism arose as a concept following the publication of *The General Theory of Employment, Interest, and Money* by John Maynard Keynes in 1936. This work was written against the background of the Great Depression (*see* Recession and depression, page 91). During this period unemployment soared and remained at exceptionally high levels virtually throughout the 1930s, at times in excess of 20 percent in the United Kingdom and the United States.

Prior to this, classical theory had been the dominant viewpoint among economists, with its claims that markets were always in equilib-rium (*see* Laissez-faire and classical economics, page 59). As the Depression continued, however, this became increasingly difficult to defend as a theory, and the concept of market failure, as put forward by Keynes, gradually gained much wider acceptance.

Key premises of the General Theory

Keynes's General Theory was founded on several new ideas and fresh interpretations of existing data. Among the most important of them were sticky prices, total output, the demand for money, demand management, and animal spirits.

LEFT: After 1945 Western governments—inspired in part by the ideas of Keynes—resolved to increase state-funded social welfare. Here, an English mother collects dried baby milk from a subsidized food sales counter.

Sticky prices

Keynes observed that markets could—and did—fail. Markets might not be in equilibrium as a result of prices, particularly wages, being inflexible or sticky—that is, they resisted the downward movement needed for the market to clear. This meant that involuntary unemployment occurred (*see* Unemployment, page 113), and that consumption fell below the economy's potential output. Since consumer prices also remained inflexible—due primarily to underlying labor costs—the economy as a whole was in disequilibrium, with aggregate supply exceeding aggregate demand.

Determination of total output

Keynes believed that the level of output of the economy was determined by aggregate demand, not aggregate supply. Supply-side factors such as relatively high production costs, scarcity of resources, and poor technology could be restraints on potential output. However, this potential output was not always attained because of the existence of market failure. This contrasted with classical theory, which claimed that prices adjusted to ensure that demand always equaled supply.

The demand for money

Keynes claimed that the demand for money was driven by three motives: carrying money in order to meet specific planned expenditure; holding money in case of unforeseen events; holding cash as an alternative to other investment assets because it carries less risk.

Demand management

Because of the above observations and theories, Keynes advocated that governments should intervene directly in the economy in order to ensure that aggregate demand was sufficient to ensure full employment. This was to be achieved by the use of active fiscal policy—the manipulation of taxation and government spending (*see* Fiscal policy, page 40). During periods of under-employment government expenditure should be in excess of tax revenue, so boosting aggregate demand. Conversely, in periods of inflation tax revenue should exceed expenditure in order to prevent overheating of the economy. This was known as fiscal stabilization, or Keynesian demand management.

Animal spirits

In a period of unemployment Keynes claimed that recovery would be assisted by a phenomenon he referred to as "animal spirits." He maintained that given the foreknowledge that cycles exist (*see* The business cycle, page 7), at some point in any recession the belief would spread that the low point had been reached, and that therefore the upturn was around the corner. This would boost confidence, which would in turn stimulate new investment and greater consumption. Once sufficient numbers of consumers and investors had regained confidence in the economy, their actions would then bring about the very recovery for which they had been hoping by increasing aggregate demand.

Crowding out

Classical economic theory maintains that Keynesian demand management cannot be effective because of the existence of a phenomenon known as "crowding out."

Any fiscal boost causes an increase in people's disposable income. IS in Figure 1 represents all combinations of income levels and interest rates at which aggregate supply equals aggregate demand. An increase in incomes will cause an outward shift in the IS curve from IS to IS* since aggregate demand is

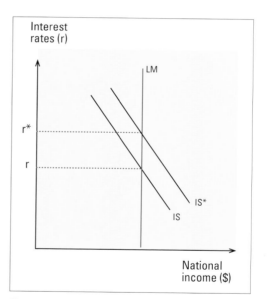

Figure 1 Crowding out.

higher for any given interest rate. Since the demand for money is derived—at least in part—from the demand for goods, an increase in disposable income also causes an increase in the demand for money.

The LM curve in Figure 1 represents all combinations of income levels and interest rates at which the money market is in equilibrium, with money supply equaling money demand. In the short run classical economists believe that the supply of money is fixed. Consequently the LM curve is perfectly inelastic and therefore vertical. Any increase in the demand for money will increase interest rates from r to r*.

Aggregate demand, or consumption, initially increases. However, it is pushed back down as interest rates go up and investment falls. It is through this sequence of events that any increase in national income is ultimately "crowded out."

The Keynesian model

Keynes disputed the classical belief that the money supply was fixed. He claimed that savings and investment were not determined by interest rates. He believed that savings were determined by levels of personal income, and that investment was determined by profits. Consequently, a fiscal boost that increased aggregate demand would also increase the supply of money through its impact on savings and investment.

Because movements in the money supply are not related to the level of interest rates, the LM curve in this case is perfectly elastic and therefore appears horizontal on the graph.

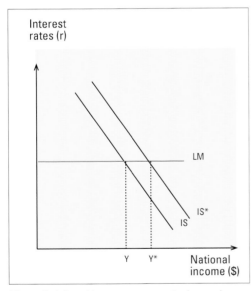

Figure 2 A fiscal boost to aggregate demand.

The outward shift in the IS curve from IS to IS* produces no change in interest rates. Investment remains unchanged, and so national income increases by the extent of the fiscal boost, from Y to Y*.

The scenarios outlined above are the two most extreme possibilities. In reality the true degree of crowding out that occurs in an economy probably lies somewhere between the two.

The vogue for using demand management as a tool of economic policy was at its height

ABOVE: J.M. Keynes believed active demand management by governments could boost economic activity during a recession and could calm boom periods, so reducing the destabilizing effects of the business cycle.

between the mid-1930s and the 1970s. The immense expenditure on rearmament in the buildup to and throughout World War II (1939-1945) provided a much-needed boost to economies still struggling to escape the grip of the Depression. This was crucial in establishing demand management as a realistic method of attaining full employment.

The decline of Keynesianism

For a long period after the end of World War II in 1945 stabilization policy was actively pursued. However, over time booms and recessions became more pronounced, requiring more extreme corrective action. Some economists began to argue that the recessions and booms that followed were even greater as a result of stabilization policy. Others saw the great shocks to the international economy—such as the Vietnam War and the oil crisis of the 1970s (*see* Oligopoly and oligopolistic competition, page 78)—as the true culprits. All over the world economies lurched painfully from very high inflation to very high unemployment.

The purpose of the fiscal stabilization was to maintain aggregate demand at a level sufficient to ensure full employment without losing control of inflation. But variations became so severe that many Western economies could no longer obtain full employment while at the same time experiencing high inflation rates. Keynesianism was seen by many to be failing and has become increasingly unpopular since the late 1970s.

SEE ALSO:

• Volume 3, page 6: Government and the economy

• Volume 3, page 28: Government and the individual

• Volume 3, page 79: Taxes

• Volume 6, page 86: The West in the 20th century

Labor

Labor is defined as the human input into the production process. It is one of the key factors of production used to produce goods, services, land, and capital. Labor is not simply an economic factor, however. The relation of workers to their employers, their working conditions, and the wages they receive for their labor are also politically and socially important.

Economists associate various terms with labor. Demand for labor is the number of workers of a given skill level that firms want to hire at different wage rates in a time period, such as a week. The wage rate is the price of labor. A firm's demand for labor is similar to a student's demand for pizza—the lower the price, the greater the quantity demanded (*see* The demand curve, page 23). Other things being equal, a firm will want to hire more workers the lower the wage it must pay. If wages increase, the firm will employ fewer workers. There is an inverse relationship between the wage and the amount of labor a firm will employ.

The supply of labor shows how much labor workers will offer to firms at different wage rates in a time period. As with the supply of any other commodity, there is a direct relationship between the wage workers receive—the price of labor—and the amount of labor they will supply to the market (*see* The supply curve, page 105). The higher the wage, the greater the quantity of labor workers will offer. This is because the opportunity cost of not working increases as the wage increases. Watching television or playing soccer become increasingly expensive leisure activities when the wage rate rises (*see* Opportunity cost, page 79).

Labor markets

A labor market is the network through which the buyers and sellers of a given type of labor interact. It is through this market interaction that the number of labor units employed and the wage paid to workers are determined. A labor market might be a local market, as in the case when a town has one large employer to whom all workers go when they want jobs. Alternatively, there might be numerous employers seeking a particular type of labor—computer operators, for example. In this case the competition among the employers will tend to drive up the wage and increase the number of workers finding jobs. In a competitive labor

ABOVE: The nature of labor for many people changed with the emergence of new industries such as electronics, but the labor market remains governed by supply and demand.

market, where no individual employer or worker is powerful enough to influence the wage rate, the market or equilibrium wage rate is determined by the interaction between the market demand for labor by firms and the market supply of labor by workers (see box, page 58).

Human capital refers to the skills and education embodied in the workforce. Increases in human capital result from investment in education and training.

SEE ALSO:

• Volume 3, page 61: Government and labor

• Volume 4, page 6: The U.S. government and world economics

The equilibrium wage rate

The equilibrium wage rate is the rate at which the demand for and supply of labor are equal. This table shows an equilibrium wage rate for computer operators of $10.00 per hour. At a wage greater than $10.00 workers offer more labor than firms want to hire, and there is a labor surplus. At a wage of $12.00, for example, there would be a surplus of 300 hours of labor that would be unemployed each week. Such a surplus creates pressure for the wage to fall back to the equilibrium wage of $10.00. At a wage less than $10.00 firms attempt to hire more computer operator hours than workers want to offer. This creates a shortage of labor and forces the wage to rise to the level of $10.00, where the shortage is eliminated.

Hourly Rate	Number of hours of labor by computer operators demanded by firms each week	Number of hours of labor supplied by computer operators each week	Condition of wage labor market at specific wage rate each week
$8.00	1,000	700	Shortage of 300 hours of labor
$9.00	900	750	Shortage of 150 hours of labor
$10.00	800	800	Equilibrium
$11.00	700	850	Surplus of 150 hours of labor
$12.00	600	900	Surplus of 300 hours of labor

This table can also be plotted on a graph showing labor supply and labor demand at various wage rates. The mobility of labor among different labor markets influences the equilibrium wage rates in each of those individual markets. Workers tend to move to labor markets where the wage rates and working conditions are better than they are in the market in which the worker is currently employed. The influx of extra workers into a labor market, however, puts downward pressure on the wage rate in that market. Likewise, the exodus of workers from a market tends to create an increase in the wage in that market. Overall, labor mobility increases the total output in an economy because workers move to jobs where their productivity, and thus their wages, are relatively high.

In the real world there are numerous complexities to the labor market. Often workers cannot move freely between jobs in different locations because of family commitments, links to their community, problems buying and selling property, and so on. Neither are wages decided simply via the demand for and supply of labor—such factors as union pressure and minimum wage legislation, if it exists, also have the effect of pushing wages above equilibrium level.

The total income earned by workers is an important variable in an economy. In the United States workers' wages and salaries account for about two-thirds of all income generated each year. U.S. workers spend approximately 80 percent of their personal income on goods and services; the rest is devoted to taxes (about 15 percent) and savings (around 5 percent).

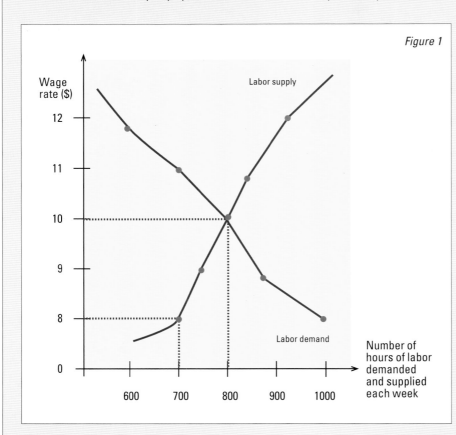

Figure 1

Laissez-faire and classical economics

Laissez-faire ("let them do it" or "let it happen") is a French 19th-century term referring to the belief that the duty of government is to protect property rights, maintain a stable currency, and provide public goods while leaving the production of all other goods and services to free markets. Classical economics has its roots in this belief in laissez-faire, arguing that free markets are highly efficient, whereas government intervention leads to economic inefficiency.

Classical or laissez-faire economics might be seen as the opposite of socialist or planned economics. A laissez-faire society attempts to deal with the basic economic problems, such as unemployment, inflation, and maintaining economic growth, by allowing the free play of market forces. A socialist or planned economy, on the other hand, allocates resources through a planning mechanism and attempts to deal with economic problems through direct intervention (see Socialism and command economies, page 100).

Capitalist governments try to run their countries according to free market or laissez-faire beliefs. This kind of system has some basic traits: people have the right to own houses and land and to gain income, for example, rents, from their land and houses. Enterprising people are free to start factories, run services, and to sell products. In a command economy most of these transactions would be controlled by the government.

Whether a government leans toward a classical or free market economics, or whether it follows a more Keynesian or socialist approach, will have implications for government economic policy. For example, classical economists believe that there is no long-term tradeoff between unemployment and inflation. Rather, unemployment will force workers to accept cuts in their wages and so expand the demand for labor. Or take inflation: in common with monetarists most classical economists believe that inflation can be dealt with by reducing the growth of the money supply (see Monetarism, page 71).

A Keynesian economist, on the other hand, sees unemployment as a situation where the government needs to intervene to stimulate demand in the economy, while moves to reduce inflation by reducing the growth in the money supply are to be avoided because they will lead to high unemployment (see Keynesianism, page 54).

However, in the late 1970s and early 1980s many Western economies faced both high unemployment and high inflation rates after decades of following Keynesian policies. The less interventionist, free market approaches of classical and laissez-faire economics began to gain popularity, particularly in the United States the United Kingdom. The classical approach remains one of the most influential of economic theories in the world today.

ABOVE: In the 1980s Margaret Thatcher and Ronald Reagan led a sustained revival of free market policies.

SEE ALSO:

• Volume 3, page 6: Government and the economy

• Volume 6, page 38: The Age of Reason and early industrialization

Land and natural resources

In economic terms land is defined as including not just land itself but all natural resources, such as minerals, fossil fuels, timber, and water. Like labor and capital, land is an important factor of production, meaning it is used in the production of economic goods and services.

Among land, labor, and capital, land is unique as a factor of production because it is largely fixed in quantity. Labor and capital may be created over a period of time, but the quantity of land stays roughly the same. The quality and productivity of land, however, may be increased by using capital or labor (*see* Capital, page 8; Labor, page 57).

All natural resources—agricultural, mineral, energy, and marine—are considered to be part of the resource known as land. Some of these resources, such as farm crops, forests, and stocks of fish, are renewable. This means that they can be created or renewed by agriculture or natural reproductive processes. If a crop is harvested, new seeds can be planted to produce a new crop; if a forest is felled, new trees will grow in its place. Water is often thought of as a renewable resource because the water cycle ensures that rain replenishes the rivers, lakes, and oceans. Ultimately, however, the total quantity of water on earth is limited, and thus to some extent it is nonrenewable.

Resources such as iron ore, sand and gravel, limestone, coal, petroleum, and natural gas are normally considered nonrenewable. While it is possible to recycle metals, glass, and other products made from minerals, the total quantity of natural ore on the planet is limited. Energy resources, such as coal, oil, and gas, are consumed as they are used and are more obviously nonrenewable. Although they are naturally occurring substances, they are created over such long periods of time that the supply is effectively finite. When natural resources become scarce, their value generally rises.

The price or economic value of land itself—real estate—is largely dependent on its location and potential uses. Since the supply of land is relatively fixed, the more potential uses for land in a given location, the more valuable the land and the higher the price. Land in downtown New York City, for example, is extremely valuable because of the many uses to which it can be put. Land in the middle of the Sahara Desert is not so valuable because it has few uses. The discovery of petroleum reserves

ABOVE: Oil is one of the most valuable forms of land—not only because of its uses, but also as it is a nonrenewable resource that will ultimately run out.

under the Alaskan tundra created valuable land from wilderness; on the other hand, the exhaustion of gold and silver mines in many parts of the western United States has created ghost towns on land that was once among the most valuable in the country. Land values and prices can be enhanced by access to transportation as well as by the discovery of deposits of mineral and energy resources. The availability of water can also make land more valuable for farming or recreation, and the depletion of water supplies normally reduces land values.

Markets for land and natural resources operate according to the laws of supply and demand, just as do the markets for other economic resources. Government, however, also has some ability to control the use of land by the application of zoning ordinances and conservation practices. Local, state, and federal regulations may also have a significant impact on the possible uses of land and thus on the value of the land itself.

SEE ALSO:

• Volume 2, page 100: Market failure and externalities

• Volume 3, page 43: Government and business

• Volume 4, page 63: The world economy

Macroeconomics

Macroeconomic theory deals with the working of the economy as a whole. It involves economists looking at aggregate demand and aggregate supply—demand for and supply of goods and services throughout the whole economy. Alternatively, it might involve economists studying total economic output, income, expenditure, and price levels in the economy.

Macroeconomics contrasts with microeconomics, which is concerned with the analysis of single parts of the economy such as individual households, single firms, and isolated markets (*see* Microeconomics, page 67).

Typically, macroeconomists aim to explain the level of output, inflation and employment in a country. The study of macroeconomics is important because it gives an indication of how well an economy is doing. Is the country producing more or less goods and services than last year or 10 years ago? Are people receiving more or less real income? Are prices going up too quickly? Are there more or fewer people unemployed this year than last? A government can judge how successful or unsuccessful its policies are when it looks at these indicators.

Several performance indexes—ways of measuring the health of the economy—are used for this purpose. Gross Domestic Product (GDP) is the main index measuring national income and output. The consumer price index (CPI) and the unemployment rate index are respectively the most common measure of the level of prices and of the proportion of workers that are unemployed.

Famous theories

In order to simplify the real world economy, a variety of different macroeconomic theories are used by economists. Two of the most famous examples are classical economic theory (*see* Laissez-faire and classical economics, page 59) and Keynesian economic theory (*see* Keynesianism, page 54).

The basis of classical economics is the theory that changes in price will result in equilibrium in the markets for factors of production, as well as in the markets for goods and services. As a result, in the classical framework workers are fully employed, and capital stock is fully utilized. The classical view is used mainly to describe the macroeconomic equilibrium point toward which the economy slowly moves in the long term.

ABOVE: Macroeconomists strive to prevent hyperinflation, one of the great enemies of stability.

The main tenet of Keynesianism, on the other hand, is that in a modern economy, prices and wages are not fully flexible. Partly as a result of this unemployment, economic depression, and inflation can arise, and the state may have to intervene to help solve those problems. The Keynesian view is mainly used to explain fluctuations in the level of output and employment of a country.

SEE ALSO:

• Volume 3, page 6: Government and the economy

• Volume 6, page 86: The West in the 20th century

Marginal analysis

Marginal analysis is the examination of the effect of adding one extra unit to, or of taking one unit away from, a particular economic variable in the production process. Although it is a largely theoretical approach, it is also an important practical tool for businesses assessing economic benefits versus their costs.

Marginal analysis compares two main factors, marginal cost and marginal benefit. Marginal cost is the extra cost in relation to total cost that a firm incurs in the short run when it increases its output by just one unit; marginal benefit is the increased benefit in relation to total benefit that a firm gains by increasing its output by one unit. Marginal revenue is the addition to a firm's total revenue earned by selling one extra unit of its output. The marginal efficiency of capital is the rate of return, or profits, expected on making an additional investment of one dollar.

When marginal analysis is applied to consumers, it is based on the concept of utility (*see* Utility, page 115). Utility is the satisfaction that an individual derives from buying a good or service. It is measured in utils. The law of diminishing marginal utility states that the more an individual consumes of a particular product in a set period of time, the further the satisfaction gained from consuming each additional unit will fall. So, for example, a hungry person derives great satisfaction from eating an ice cream. However, each subsequent ice cream eaten at the same meal provides less satisfaction.

Since consuming more of a particular product gives less satisfaction, consumers will pay less for each additional product or service they buy. Figure 1 shows that plotting marginal utility against consumption produces a downward sloping curve. This explains why demand curves also slope downward for most products.

Early economists considered that utility could be measured in the same way that temperature could be measured in Fahrenheit or Celsius, by using exact measures of each unit of consumption, or utils. It proved impossible to make accurate measurements using this approach. Instead, economists adopted an approach where satisfaction was measured on a relative scale. They asked people to order their preferences for products according to the levels of satisfaction they derived from them.

Measures of utility between two products can be shown visually. If you ask consumers to

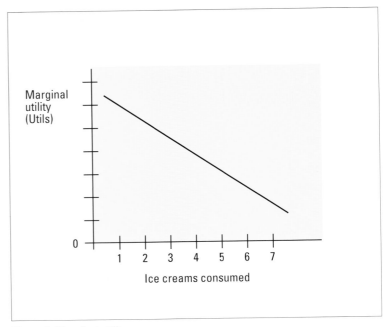

Figure 1 *Marginal utility.*

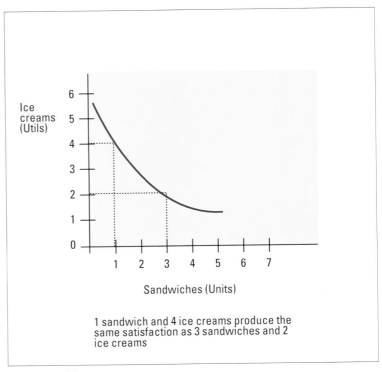

1 sandwich and 4 ice creams produce the same satisfaction as 3 sandwiches and 2 ice creams

Figure 2 *Indifference curve.*

state all the combinations of two products that give them the same level of satisfaction and plot the results on a graph, you get a downward sloping curve. This indifference curve (Figure 2) plots the combination of products to which a consumer is "indifferent." Whether a consumer has more sandwiches and fewer ice creams, he or she derives the same overall level of satisfaction.

Indifference curves slope downward because rational consumers naturally prefer more of both products. Consequently, they will not give up more of one product unless they receive more of the other. From this assumption it is possible to analyze the effect of a change in the relative prices of the products on the quantities demanded.

The laws of supply and demand mean that prices tend to move toward the point where supply equals demand (*see* Price discrimination, page 84). When the actual price in the market is below the price that a consumer would be prepared to pay, the consumer receives additional satisfaction. This extra utility received by the consumer is known as consumer surplus.

The downward slope of the demand curve can also be explained by the income and substitution effect (*see* The demand curve, page 23). When the price of an item falls, usually more of it is demanded. When a consumer has an income of $10 and ice creams cost $1, they can buy 10 ice creams. If the price of ice creams then falls to 50 cents, the consumer has an "extra" $5 to either spend on ice creams or something else. This is known as the income effect. The substitution effect, on the other hand, results from the relative attractiveness of cheaper ice creams compared to a good whose price has not changed. Consumers are encouraged to substitute ice creams for other items in their budget that are now relatively more expensive.

The price of a product is determined by its relative scarcity rather than its actual usefulness. Water, for example, is far more useful than a diamond—water has a far greater total utility. Because water is available in abundance, however, its marginal utility and therefore its price are low. In contrast, diamonds have a low total utility, but because they are rare, their marginal utility and price are high.

SEE ALSO:

• Volume 2, page 28: How a business works

• Volume 2, page 100: Market failure and externalities

• Volume 3, page 93: Pensions and insurance

• Volume 6, page 54: Industrialization, urbanization, and modernization

Market failure and anticompetitive practices

Market failure describes a situation in which there are imperfections in the economy that prevent efficiency in the production, consumption, and allocation of goods, services, and resources.

The importance of markets and the market mechanism has grown in many Western economies in the last decades. Some economists and politicians argue that a perfect free market will automatically achieve the greatest efficiency. Even where markets have been given free rein, however, they are never perfect, and there are instances where markets fail.

Imperfect competition

The conditions for perfect competition are extremely demanding. For example, there must be many buyers and sellers in all markets so that there is no concentration of market power. Buyers and sellers should also have perfect knowledge, there should be no barriers to entry to or exit from the market for producers, and so on. Factor markets—that is, markets in land, labor, and capital—must also be perfectly competitive (*see* Competition and perfect competition, page 14).

In reality these conditions are seldom met, and power is often very concentrated in market economies. For years, for example, AT&T was the only long-distance telephone carrier, and Kodak controlled the film market. In recent years Microsoft has controlled the market for Windows, a PC operating system. Coca-Cola and Pepsi have dominated the soft drink market, making similar but not identical products.

Markets where competition is limited may be divided into three groups. A firm has monopoly power if it is the sole provider of a product and that product has no close substitutes. The result of this monopoly power is a

ABOVE: Markets fail because they cannot take account of externalities such as pollution. Few drivers consider the health costs to others resulting from the smog they create when they drive into a city.

> **SEE ALSO:**
>
> • Volume 2, page 100: Market failure and externalites
>
> • Volume 3, page 43: Government and business
>
> • Volume 3, page 105: Organizations and boards

higher price and a smaller output than would be the case had the industry been composed of a large number of small, highly competitive firms. In factor markets monopoly suppliers exist in forms such as trade unions. There can also be monopoly buyers such as governments (*see* Monopoly, page 74).

Most goods markets are oligopolistic, meaning they are dominated by only a few firms selling similar products. The market for automobiles in the United States is an oligopoly, for example, as is the world market for crude oil, which is controlled by a dozen oil-producing countries (*see* Oligopoly and oligopolistic competition, page 78). Since there are only a few firms in an oligopoly, the actions of any one firm can influence the profits of the other firms. Oligopoly is characterized by interdependence in the firms' decision-making, which is shaped by the potentially contradictory impulses of self-interest on one side and cooperating with other supplies to maintain the oligopoly on the other.

In some cases firms get together and agree on quantities and prices to charge in order to maximize their joint profits. Such an agreement among firms in a market is called collusion, and a group of firms acting collectively as if they were a monopoly is called a cartel. The U.S. antitrust laws find most collusion and cartels illegal and prohibit competing firms from even discussing fixing prices.

In addition, firms may act singly or with others to deter other firms from entering the market. Such actions are called restrictive practices and include exclusive dealing, tie-ins, and exclusive territories.

Externalities

According to market theory, prices and profits should accurately reflect costs and benefits to producers and consumers, so allowing the market mechanism to allocate resources efficiently. In reality, however, prices and profits can be very misleading, creating another example of market failure.

Assume that Firm A and Firm B are non-polluters that use water from a nearby river. They operate in competitive markets and currently produce the amounts of their products that are desired by society. Suppose Firm A now decides to quit cleaning up its wastes and instead dumps them in the river. This reduction in its costs means that Firm A can charge a lower price and sell more of its good. The costs of Firm B, located downriver, will increase because it must now clean up the pollution caused by Firm A. As a result, Firm B will increase its price and sell less output. In this case the presence of an externality—pollution—in a market causes an inefficient allocation of scarce resources between the two firms. Some countries, including the United States, use fines or other restrictions to transfer the cost of cleaning up the pollution back to Firm A (*see* Externalites, environmental, page 36).

Missing markets

There are some goods and services that the market fails to provide or underprovides for a variety of reasons. Public goods, such as defense and policing, need to be provided by the government as a result of market failure (*see* Public sector, page 89). Mixed goods, such as health and education, bear some characteristics of public goods and will also be underprovided by the market mechanism.

For example, a college student's demand for higher education indicates the price the student would be willing to pay for such education. That price would reflect the value the student feels the education has for him or her. The student's demand for higher education does not, however, include additional benefits that education has for society in general, such as increased production, better citizenship, and so on. Because a competitive market for higher education would be based only on the student's demand for education, the amount of education provided would be less than society would desire. Publicly supported universities in the United States receive tax dollars to make up the difference between the actual cost of providing educational services and the tuition paid by students. This encourages the universities to provide more education (*see* Externalities and government policy, page 38).

BELOW: *Education is an example of a market that fails because a student's demand for education reflects only its value to him or her as an individual and ignores its value to society as a whole.*

Mercantilism

Mercantilism is an economic theory that once had many proponents and was practiced by several nations during the 17th and early 18th centuries. The central tenet of a mercantilist's belief was that the wealth, and therefore the power, of any nation depended on the amount of precious metal it possessed.

Since power and wealth were thought to depend on the possession of precious metals such as gold and silver, building up stores of these metals became the main aim of economic policy. Mercantilism seemed a commonsense view of how states became successful: the richer the nation, the greater its capacity to finance wars and other ventures to increase its strength. Later economists largely discounted this theory, arguing that commerce and manufacturing were much better indicators of a country's wealth.

Mercantilist theory stated that if a country did not possess its own gold and silver, then it should endeavor to acquire them by trade. This could happen only if its balance of trade was "favorable," meaning that the nation exported more than it imported. The nations that received these exports would pay for them in gold and silver, thus depleting their own stores while increasing those of the exporting nation. Mercantilism was thus a highly competitive system: a nation could increase its wealth only at the expense of other nations.

Mercantilism made a direct link between the strength of a nation and its trading activity, so governments aimed to create an environment that was favorable to merchants. Many nations passed sumptuary laws that outlawed luxury foods, drinks, and even clothing that had to be imported from abroad. The theory also encouraged the establishment of overseas colonies, which were to provide raw materials for the home country and a marketplace for the goods manufactured from these materials. To ensure that the balance of trade remained favorable to the mother country, all manufacturing was banned in the colonies, and trade was strictly controlled.

According to mercantilist theory, the larger a nation's population, the bigger its workforce, the higher its potential exports, and the greater its wealth. Every available person should therefore be set to work, even young children, in order to increase output. A large population also

provided a large domestic market for goods and a plentiful supply of soldiers, who were important in an age of warfare. Mercantilists also believed in thrift—saving and minimizing the desire for imported luxury goods—thereby encouraging the accumulation of capital within the state (*see* Capital, page 8).

During its heyday in the 17th century the main proponents of this theory were Thomas Mun in England, Jean-Baptiste Colbert in France, and Antonio Serra in Italy. None of them used the word mercantilism, however—the term was first applied to their principles by Adam Smith in *The Wealth of Nations* (1776).

Because of its emphasis on accumulating profit, mercantilism provided a favorable climate for the growth of capitalism. But Smith and other economists believed in free trade with no government regulation and did not regard stores of gold and silver as accurate measures of a nation's wealth. They also argued that trade should not enrich one nation at the expense of another but should benefit all the participants.

ABOVE: According to mercantilists, gold and silver were the foundations of economic prosperity.

SEE ALSO:

• Volume 6, page 22: The emergence of Europe

• Volume 6, page 38: The Age of Reason and early industrialization

Microeconomics

Microeconomics is the term used to describe the behavior of individual economic units, in particular consumers and firms. This contrasts with macroeconomics which is the study of the economy as a whole and large aggregates such as unemployment and the price level.

Within microeconomics the economic analysis of individual behavior is mainly concerned with consumer demand theory and the theory of time preference—i.e. the amount by which people prefer immediate consumption over deferred consumption. The economic analysis of firms in microeconomics is mainly concerned with production decisions and price theory. When analyzing firms, economists often focus on the type of market within which the firm operates, and the degree of competition in that market.

To explain the behavior of individuals and firms, economists identify equilibrium situations that treat each market in relative isolation. An equilibrium exists when there is a state of balance that can only be changed by an external event. For example, individuals are in equilibrium when, given their income, they cannot achieve a greater level of satisfaction by consuming a different range of goods and services than those they already purchase. Microeconomics has several dimensions, including price theory, general equilibrium theory, game theory and social choice theory.

Price theory

The major assumption of price theory is that consumers and firms buy or sell such a small amount compared to consumption and production in the market as a whole that individually they are powerless to influence the price of any product. Instead, the equilibrium price of each product is determined by the collective actions of consumers—as demanders of the product—and firms—as suppliers of the product.

General equilibrium thoery

As the term suggests, general equilibrium theory, looks at the conditions necessary for all markets in the economy to be in simultaneous equilibrium. It attempts to explain what price will exist for each good and what quantities will be traded. General equilibrium theory enables three important questions to be answered: Does a general equilibrium exist? Is there only one general equilibrium? Is general equilibrium restored if something disturbs the equilibrium?

ABOVE: Microeconomics looks to explain the behavior of individuals and firms—how consumer demand changes with income and price, how firms decide what to produce, what price to charge, and so on.

Game theory

Conventional microeconomic theory is concerned with decisions made when complete information exists; game theory is concerned with identifying choice when incomplete information exists. Cooperative game theory looks at situations where individual decision-makers coordinate their strategies so as to achieve a superior outcome. Noncooperative game theory is concerned with how the actions of one decision-maker affect the actions of other decision-makers.

Social choice theory

Microeconomic theory is concerned with decisions about the production of nonmarket goods—goods and services that will not be provided through the market, such as national defense. It is also concerned with group decision-making such as choice of government. Both of these issues have an important bearing on the allocation of resources in an economy.

SEE ALSO:

• Volume 2, page 28: How a business works

• Volume 2, page 62: Competition, expansion, and growth

• Volume 6, page 86: The West in the 20th century

Mixed economies

A mixed economy is a mixture of a planned economy and a free market economy. It is an economy in which some goods and services are produced by the free-market sector, while others are produced by the state.

In practice purely free markets and purely planned systems do not exist. An economy is said to be a planned economy or a command economy if most of its resources are allocated by the planning process (*see* Socialism and command economies, page 100). If, on the other hand, most resources are allocated via the market mechanism, the economy is said to be a capitalist or free market economy (*see* Capitalist or free market economies, page 9). In a mixed economy the balance between planning and the market mechanism is more equal.

The private sector in a mixed economy acts very much as it would in a capitalist economy. Producers, consumers, capitalists, landowners, and workers all aim to maximize their own utility and are motivated by pure self-interest. A significant percentage of the factors of production—land, labor, entrepreneurship, and capital—is privately owned, and competition exists between private producers of goods and services. The public sector, however, also owns some of the factors of production and is motivated more by consideration of the social welfare of the community as a whole. Resources in the public sector are allocated through the planning mechanism rather than through competition, supply and demand, and people's ability to pay.

In a mixed economy one role of government is to regulate the economic activities of the private sector to guard against anticompetitive practices or externalities, for example. Another function of government is to provide public goods, such as law and order, and mixed goods—which have some of the characteristics of public goods—such as education (*see* Public sector, page 89).

There is a great deal of controversy about what proportion of a mixed economy should be run through the planning process, and how much of it should be left to free market forces. In Sweden, for example, around 60 percent of gross domestic product (GDP) goes on public expenditure, compared to around 33 percent in the United States. Some of the questions that governments have to address include how

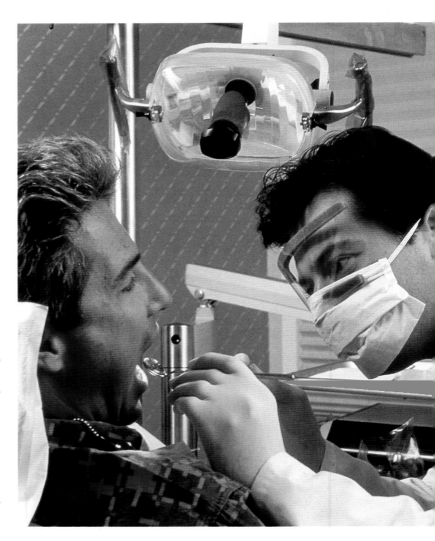

ABOVE: *In a mixed economy dentistry is a typical example of the goods or services that may be provided by the state as part of a national healthcare program.*

much they should take responsibility for ensuring a minimum standard of living for their citizens through unemployment benefits or free medical care, for example. Can the government provide goods and services efficiently, and offer the quality and choice that people demand? Should governments try to iron out the worst inequalities in society? Or will high government spending, and high taxes, reduce peoples' incentives to work and lower economic growth rates?

SEE ALSO:

• Volume 3, page 6: Government and the economy

• Volume 3, page 28: Government and the individual

Models and modeling

Economic research depends on the ability to create models. Models are not accurate representations of the world. Rather, they are attempts to simplify it—a model as complex as the real world would be too difficult to understand. With simplifications models help clarify how a particular factor alters an outcome. This is done by performing comparative statics—changing one factor to see how it alters another while holding all other factors fixed.

Mathematical models

Mathematical models come in two forms: normative models and positive models. Normative models deal with how the world should work; positive models attempt to explain how the world actually does work. Many mathematical models are based on assumptions about the setup of the economy. Given these assumptions, the model seeks to locate an equilibrium, that is, a point where no internal force can produce change.

Different models are based on a wide range of assumptions, some of which may be mutually contradictory for the sake of argument and to help establish a truth. However, there are several common assumptions that appear in mathematical models time and time again.

Rationality

Economic models that rely on individual preference maximization assume that preference orderings are rational. This is an assumption composed of two parts. The first part, which is known as completeness, requires that the individual be able to order all the available choices according to a preference ranking. For example, an individual must be able to make one of the following statements: either "I like zucchini more than or as much as broccoli" or "I like broccoli more than or as much as zucchini."

Second, if the individual prefers zucchini to broccoli and broccoli to asparagus, she or he must also prefer zucchini to asparagus. This assumption is known as transitivity.

Ceteris paribus

This assumption allows all outside factors to remain constant, while the variables that are being studied change around them. This allows comparative statics to be performed in economic models. *Ceteris paribus* is a Latin term meaning "other things being equal."

ABOVE: Models are simplified representations of the world. They attempt to explain, for example, how a reduction in price will lead to an increase in quantity demanded of most goods and services.

Perfect competition

This assumption is commonly used in price theory, general equilibrium, and in some macroeconomic models. Perfect competition requires that firms be small and numerous; further, that all firms produce the same good. In models where these preconditions are satisfied, an individual firm cannot alter the price level, and it is therefore known as a price-taker *(see* Competition and perfect competition, page 14).

Cobweb theory

Given the relevant assumptions, economists then seek to locate the point of equilibrium within the model. There are many ways of measuring it, but one of the most important is known as the cobweb theorem, which was devised in the 1930s by U.S. economist Mordecai Ezekial. It was originally based on a study of farmers—Ezekial showed that their speed of response as producers to changes in price was limited by the time frame in which they were accustomed to working. Because of the long

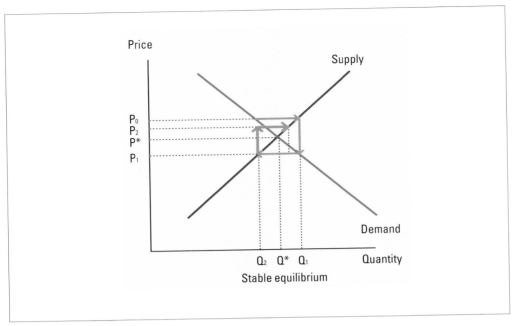

Figure 1 *The cobweb model.*

period between seed time and harvest, for example, farmers tend to charge the price for their produce that they would have received the last time they sold it.

Cobweb theory helps explain how an equilibrium may be arrived at in a supply-demand model. Suppose that the price is higher than its equilibrium level, where quantity supplied equals quantity demanded. At the high price, P_0, producers supply more output than equilibrium requires, Q_1. Once quantity Q_1 is produced, selling the good requires a reduction of the price to P_1, which is lower than the equilibrium level. Given prices are at P_1, suppliers choose to restrict production to a lower-than-equilibrium quantity, that is, to point Q_2. This process continues until prices and quantity converge at the point where the supply and demand curves intersect (at price-quantity combination P^* and Q^*). At this point neither the price nor the quantity produced needs to change. Since, at this point, no internal force can produce change, it is said to be an equilibrium. In particular, **it is** a stable equilibrium—in other words, any attempt to move the price or quantity or both away from this equilibrium point will be countered by a natural movement back toward the convergence.

In economics equilibrium is described as the situation in which the forces that determine the behavior of some variable are in perfect balance and thus exert no pressure on that variable to change. It is a situation in which the actions of all economic agents are mutually consistent. For example, equilibrium price may be affected by the process that drives suppliers to increase prices when there is more demand than supply and to undercut each other when there is more supply than demand—the equilibrium mechanism thus regulates the forces of demand and supply.

Econometric models

Econometric models are constructed in an attempt to explain how the world actually works. Economists hypothesize factors that may influence a particular variable and test them against data from the real world. Very often, econometric models serve as semi-practical tests of previously formulated mathematical hypotheses.

In such models the variable that is being studied is known as the dependent variable. The factors on which the dependent variable depends are known as the independent variables. So, for example, demand might be the dependent variable, with price the indepedent variable. The data collected in order to test the effects created by the independent variables may form a time series, be cross-sectional, or part of a panel. A time series is made up of information taken from a single place at several different points in time; cross-sectional data are gathered from several locations at a single point in time; panels show combinations of time series and cross-sectional data. By seeking to locate the Best Linear Unbiased Estimate (BLUE) of a line fitting the data, the model implicitly locates the effects of the independent variables on the dependent variable.

SEE ALSO:

• Volume 2, page 6: An introduction to business

• Volume 2, page 28: How a business works

• Volume 6, page 54: Industrialization, urbanization, and modernization

Monetarism

Monetarism is a theory about how changes in the money supply affect other macroeconomic variables, particularly national income or a country's level of output. Monetarists believe that changes in the money supply are the main cause of changes in the average price level.

Monetarism and monetarist policies, which attempt to maintain stable prices through control of the money supply, became particularly important in the early 1980s after what many saw as the failure of Keynesian policies (*see* Keynesianism, page 54). After years in which many economies experienced both high inflation and high unemployment, governments were looking for an alternative. Monetarism, as expounded by U.S. economist Milton Friedman, seemed to point the way forward, and the theory was enthusiastically adopted by President Ronald Reagan.

The amount of money in the economy influences supply and demand, inflation, banking, and credit (*see* Money: its supply and demand, page 72). However, monetarists argue that in the long run changes in the money supply affect only prices and leave the overall level of output unchanged.

The demand for money

Monetarist thinking is based on the quantity theory of money. This focuses on changes in the money supply and is written as:

$MV = PY$

Where M = the money supply.
V= velocity of circulation—the speed with which money in the economy circulates, or the number of times each $1 is spent.
P = the average price of final output.
Y = the volume of real final output.

Monetarists argue that V and Y are determined by factors other than the price level or the money supply. For example, Y, the amount of all goods and services a nation can produce, is determined by the skills of the population and the application of new technology. Monetarists believe that changes in M cause changes in P, but they deny that changes in P cause changes in M.

According to Friedman, the demand for money is a stable function of national income. This is important because if the demand for money is stable in relation to income, velocity of circulation must be constant.

So how do changes in the money supply affect output in the economy, or gross domestic product (GDP)? Monetarists argue that an

ABOVE: *Milton Friedman, largely responsible for the popularity of monetarism with some Western governments during the 1980s, advocated strict control of the money supply as a means to keep inflation low.*

SEE ALSO:

• Volume 1, page 24: Banks and banking

• Volume 3, page 6: Government and the economy

• Volume 6, page 86: The West in the 20th century

increase in the money supply will leave people holding excess money balances at the existing level of GDP. Consequently, spending will increase as people release their excess funds. As demand increases, output and prices will rise until people need all their money to finance their transactions. In other words, GDP will rise until the supply of and demand for money regain equilibrium.

However, an increase in GDP can consist entirely of an increase in real output (Y) with prices (P) unchanged, an increase in P with Y unchanged, or a combination of both. Monetarists claim that in the short run GDP will consist of an increase in both, but in the long run the level of output is determined by institutional factors such as capital stock, labor mobility, and technological progress. Such factors are not influenced by changes in the money supply. While it is possible that such changes will bring about changes in short-run output, in the long run output will regain equilibrium. Hence, an increase in the money supply above the rate of growth of output will, in the long run, simply lead to higher prices.

Money: its supply and demand

Money is usually defined as anything that is generally accepted by individuals in payment for goods, services, or for settling financial debts.

ABOVE: Availability of credit is an important part of the transactionary demand for money. A lower interest rate makes borrowing cheaper and hence increases money demand.

Major features of money include easy recognition, uniformity in quality, easy divisibility, and a constant value within a geographic area. In modern economies there are three generally accepted functions of money:
(i) Money is a medium of exchange—it is used to pay for goods and services;
(ii) Money is a store of value—money will keep its value until it can be spent later on;
(iii) Money is a unit of account or a measure of value—it puts a value on goods and services.

However, as the famous Nobel Prize economist John Hicks often repeated, "monetary theory is in history," meaning that the nature of money varies dramatically between societies and over time. What really fulfills the three functions above is a matter of a lively debate.

Monetary authorities such as the Federal Reserve in the United States are extremely concerned with what money is since it can affect key government policy goals. The Fed, in fact, continuously provides official measurements

NAME	COMPONENTS	SIZE (US$bn.)
Currency	Coins and notes in circulation	435
M1	Currency + demand deposits, travelers' checks, other checkable deposits	1,139
M2	M1 + money market mutual fund (MMMF) shares, money market deposit accounts (MMDSs), saving deposits, small time deposits (notice accounts)	3,693
M3	M2 + Repurchase agreements (RPs), Eurodollars, large denomination time deposits, institutional holdings of money market mutual funds	4,453
L	M3 + Savings bonds, banker's acceptances, commercial paper, short-term treasury securities	5,459

Table 1: Money definitions in the U.S. (*Source: Federal Reserve Bulletin, Jan. 1997*`).

based on its definitions of money. Table 1 shows the definitions of money currently used in the United States and their measurements for 1997.

Once money has been defined, then economists can investigate its supply and demand. The interaction between the supply of money and the demand for money provides the link through which the monetary authority, in this case the Fed, can affect policy targets such as output, employment, and prices.

Money demand

Economists in the United States are particularly concerned with what determines the demand for money—i.e., why people hold money. This is because if it is known what determines the willingness to hold money, economists can form some idea of how people will respond if and when the quantity of money—the money supply—changes. Traditionally, the analysis of the demand for money has been segmented into three parts: transactions demand, precautionary demand, and speculative demand.

Transactions demand for money is related to the amount of money people need for current transactions—i.e., for purchasing goods and services. It is therefore related to people's income levels. Precautionary demand causes people to hold money in case of emergencies. Speculative demand for money is the demand for money that people hold in order to speculate on purchases of assets such as shares of stock and bonds.

Together these make up the total demand for money. The amount of money that people hold in order to carry out these three activities is influenced by their income levels and the interest rate.

In Figure 1 Md represents the total money demanded at income Yo, while Md_1 represents the total money demanded at income Y_1. A rise in income from Yo to Y_1 increases the total demand for money from $600 to $800 billion. A fall in the interest rate from 8 percent to 7 percent is an increase in the quantity of money demanded from $600 to $700 billion and is a movement along the existing Md curve.

However, the actual amount of money held by individuals at any time must be equal to the amount of money supplied. Equilibrium in the money market requires that the demand for money is equal to the supply of money.

Money market equilibrium

Figure 2 shows equilibrium in the money market. The Fed is responsible for determining the supply of money and sets it at a level that is inde-

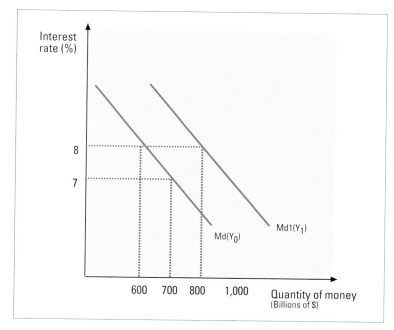

Figure 1 *The demand for money.*

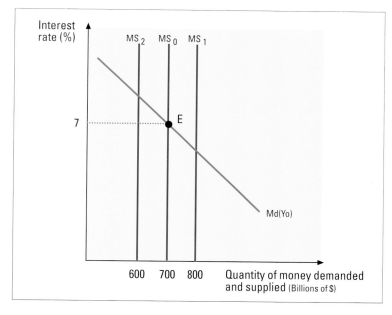

Figure 2 *Money market equilibrium.*

pendent of the level of income and the rate of interest. As a result, money supply MS_0 remains the same—$700 billion—at all interest rates and thus can be represented by a vertical straight line. With money supply set at MS_0, the final equilibrium is at point E with the interest rate at 7 percent. However, for policy purposes the Fed may increase or decrease the money supply. If the money supply is increased to MS_1, the interest rate falls. Since the cost of borrowing is less, overall investment in the economy rises, and aggregate demand increases. For a reduction in the money supply to MS_2 the reverse is true.

SEE ALSO:

• Volume 1, page 6: What is money?

• Volume 1, page 24: Banks and banking

• Volume 3, page 6: Government and the economy

• Volume 4, page 63: The world economy

Monopoly

A monopoly is a situation where there is only one seller of a good or service in a market. This seller has complete control over the market price and totally dominates the production and distribution of a particular product or service for which there is no close substitute.

In order for a monopoly firm to remain the only supplier in the market, there must be barriers to entry that prevent other firms from entering the market and competing. There are several main barriers to entry.

Single ownership of a key resource is an important barrier. A monopoly may grow up as a result of having sole access to a natural deposit of minerals, for example. The great diamond company, De Beers, is a classic case in point.

Patent and copyright laws can also form a barrier. Patent and copyright laws give one person or firm the exclusive right to sell some goods or services to the public. A copyright or patent may protect an invention, a particular design, or a piece of music or writing.

It might also be that the setup costs in an industry make it prohibitively expensive for new firms to enter. In the automobile industry, for example, the initial cost of developing a new brand of car and setting up a mass production plant makes an effective barrier to entry for most firms.

Natural monopoly is another barrier to entry. A natural monopoly arises when economies of scale lead to just one firm producing in the market (*see* Economies of scale, page 30). Economies of scale in this case mean that the largest firm can set a price below that which any smaller firm would need to stay in business. For many years in the U.S. it was widely agreed that the railroads were natural monopolies, along with electric utilities and telecommunications. With natural monopolies there might be a case for government ownership, or at least for some kind of government regulation.

Finally, marketing barriers may exist in the form of advertising. A monopolist may develop a very strong brand image for its product so that consumers will continue to buy it even if cheaper or better products appear on the market.

If a monopoly is protected from potential competitors by high barriers to entry, it can charge a high price and earn excessive profits. In this case a monopoly can be harmful to the

ABOVE: In the United States the Federal Trade Commission judges whether or not a firm is abusing monopoly power.

economy, and some kind of government or legal regulation may be required. In the U.S. some industries are regulated, and antitrust laws are in place to restrict abusive practices of a monopoly. For example, in the 1990s the Microsoft software company was found by the Federal Trade Commission to be monopolizing the internet and software industries (*see* Regulation and antitrust laws, page 93).

However, the mere fact of monopoly does not prove that any economic harm is done. If barriers to entry are low, lack of actual competitors may not be a great concern. The threat of potential entry by competitors may be enough to make a monopoly firm behave as if it were a competitive firm. Today most economists think that market contestability—that is, the question of whether or not barriers to entry are low enough—is more important in judging the social cost of monopoly.

Recent studies have also found that innovation, research and development, are critical for long-term economic growth. By allowing investors to reap profits from new ideas or inventions, the patent and copyright system effectively sets up monopolies and gives an incentive to individuals and firms to engage in research.

SEE ALSO:

• Volume 2, page 80: How firms behave in the real world

• Volume 2, page 100: Market failure and externalities

• Volume 3, page 43: Government and business

• Volume 6, page 22: The emergence of Europe

Multinational corporations

A multinational or transnational corporation or business is a firm that owns and operates factories or production units in foreign countries.

Most multinational enterprises—firms like Esso, Ford, Nestlé, Pepsi, IBM, and Mitsubishi—were originally founded and are owned by the residents of developed countries, particularly the United States. Such firms normally enter the international market when they start trading abroad, selling their products overseas. As international sales increase, the owners or managers of the business might decide that it would be advantageous to locate subsidiaries in foreign countries.

With continuing progress and development in transportation and communication technologies multinationals are set to grow in size and number. Today, the combined output of the world's 200 largest multinational corporations is already equivalent to one-third of the total world output. The output of General Motors alone exceeds the output of many countries, including Denmark, Norway, and Poland.

Multinationals may derive many advantages from owning operating units in several countries. Producing and selling in a major market abroad will reduce a company's transportation costs, while at the same time enabling the firm to maintain direct contact with its customers. Producing and operating in a particular country may also enable the multinational to overcome any resistance to buying products made outside that country.

Firms also go abroad in order to avoid import restrictions or to gain access to raw materials and natural resources that are not available in the home country. In some cases multinationals set up in countries where wages are lower and health and safety regulations and other employment legislation are more lax than at home.

Other factors also influence a firm's decision to start up in a particular country. In the early 1990s, for example, many overseas firms, especially from the United States and Japan, started subsidiaries in the United Kingdom. These companies were attracted by the lack of restrictions on working hours, subsidies to firms that went into areas of high unemployment, and by the native language. The last

ABOVE: Since the collapse of communism, Western multinationals have made significant and highly profitable inroads into the former Soviet Union.

consideration influenced even multinationals from Japan, where English is the most widely spoken second language.

Multinationals can benefit their host countries by providing new jobs, new technologies, and new approaches. The production and management techniques of the Japanese companies based in the United Kingdom have been copied by a number of British firms. Multinationals also contribute to the exports of the host country, while consumers benefit if the multinational firm increases competition in the area, since there will be a greater choice of products, higher quality, and lower prices.

However, not all effects are beneficial. Multinationals may force local producers out of the market, reducing competition and consumer choice. Some multinational corporations have been accused of exploiting local populations, with low wages and poor health and safety records.

In addition, many multinationals have the potential to shift production around the world. This gives them great bargaining power in wage negotiations and even in discussions with governments. Large multinationals may threaten to close down plants in order to win concessions.

SEE ALSO:

• Volume 2, page 80: How firms behave in the real world

• Volume 4, page 6: The U.S. government and world economics

• Volume 4, page 63: The world economy

• Volume 6, page 106: Today and tomorrow

National income and national income accounting

National income is the value of income, output, and expenditure of an economy over a period of time, usually a year. National income accounting measures and summarizes national income.

Gross domestic product (GDP) is a measure of national income and therefore a measure of overall economic performance. It is defined as the market value of all final goods and services produced within a country in a given period of time. Defining and measuring GDP are major goals of national income accounting. In the United States the Department of Commerce issues the "National Income and Product Accounts" to provide a measure of the position and movement of the U.S. economy.

There are three different but equivalent ways to measure GDP:

The first, and perhaps the most straightforward method, is to add up the market value of all final goods and services produced domestically—for example, computers, apples, haircuts, and so on. Estimates are used for valuing some services not sold in the market such as government services. It is also necessary to distinguish between intermediate goods—raw materials such as steel, for example—and final goods such as automobiles. Intermediate goods are not included in GDP. One way to avoid double-counting—adding the intermediate goods to the final goods—is to add up the value added at each stage of production. This will equal the value of the output less the cost of intermediate inputs.

Another way of calculating GDP is to consider the total expenditure that takes place when output is sold. Since every transaction has two sides—a buyer and a seller—total expenditure must be equal to the total value of output. Expenditure is divided into four categories: consumption (C), investment (I), government purchases (G), and net exports, which are exports (X) minus imports (M). So GDP = C+I+G+X-M.

Finally, GDP is equal to the total income of everyone in the economy since all expenditure must first have been received as income. In other words, the value of the goods and services produced by an economy over a period of time must equal what is spent and what is earned in that economy.

SEE ALSO:

• Volume 3, page 6: Government and the economy

• Volume 6, page 86: The West in the 20th century

BELOW: Measures of national income attempt to include the value of, expenditure on, and income from all final goods and services in the economy—even the more obscure services, such as those provided by this Elvis impersonator.

Nonprice competition

Imperfectly competitive markets—which, in practice, include most markets—allow firms to compete in ways other than through the price of the product they are selling. Nonprice competition might include promotion and advertising, product placement, and branding.

Under perfect competition firms producing the same goods and services compete with each other on the basis of the price of those goods and services alone (*see* Competition and perfect competition, page 14; Price discrimination, page 84). In practice, however, very few markets, if any, are perfectly competitive, and price is only part of the story.

Most firms, when they introduce a new good or service to the market, will form a marketing strategy. The first part of this strategy involves the firm developing a product that its customers will want to buy. Suppose that a firm wishes to market a new kind of sunglasses. Market research might be necessary to identify a gap in the market—a radical kind of lens, for example, or a fashionable new design.

The marketing department will then have to set a price. It may be above or below the price of other sunglasses on the market. If the firm is aiming to sell large quantities of standard, mass-produced sunglasses, it will set a low price, $10 a pair, say. Alternatively, the firm might be looking to sell designer or very high-quality sunglasses, in which case the price will be a lot higher, perhaps $200 per pair.

Once product and price have been determined, the firm must use advertising and promotion to inform potential customers about the new sunglasses and to try to influence them to buy their product rather than that of their competitors. They also need to make sure they have a good distribution system, so that the sunglasses are in the right place at the right time to meet the hoped for demand.

Branding is a very important part of nonprice competition, and many markets are dominated by branded goods—famous examples include Coca Cola soft drinks and Levi's jeans. Branded goods are goods produced by a particular firm that appear to have various unique characteristics that distinguish them from other similar goods. Some products actually are unique—a Les Paul electric guitar, for example, or a Rolls Royce automobile. Others, such as many brands of cereal, toothpaste, or detergent, are very similar but are merely packaged and advertised differently. A branded good that has been heavily promoted through advertising will often sell more than an exactly equivalent unbranded product, even if the unbranded product carries a much lower price.

ABOVE: Advertising is one of the most powerful weapons of nonprice competition.

SEE ALSO:

• Volume 2, page 62: Competition, expansion, and growth

• Volume 2, page 80: How firms behave in the real world

• Volume 3, page 43: Government and business

Oligopoly and oligopolistic competition

An oligopoly is said to exist in a market where there are a small number of interdependent firms competing with each other. Most markets in the western economies are oligopolistic to a greater or lesser degree.

Oligopolistic firms have a high degree of control over both the output and the price of products. As a result, the prices established are higher than they would be in a competitive market.

An oligopolistic market is created when supply is controlled by a relatively small number of large firms, as for example when three or four firms control 80 percent of the total market output. These firms are interdependent—the actions and strategies of one will affect significantly the others in the same industry. With perfect competition there are many small producers, all of which are independent. An action by one firm will not affect the others (*see* Competition and perfect competition, page 14). With oligopolistic competition, if one large firm decides to increase its sales, this increase will normally be at the expense of the sales of other firms in the market.

Some economists believe that an oligopolistic market is characterized by barriers to entry. If there were no such barriers, smaller firms would enter the market, attracted by the abnormal profits being earned. This would reduce the market share of the large producers and bring down prices.

Firms operating in an oligopolistic market may adopt a wide range of strategies. However, one feature they have in common is that they tend to spend a lot on marketing, advertising, and branding products (*see* Nonprice competition, page 77). This is because they need to maintain market share against rival producers' products without resorting to cutting prices. A cut in prices is liable to trigger a price war, which would reduce profits.

Firms in oligopolistic markets often use ingenious marketing devices to maintain customer loyalty—money-off coupons, loyalty cards, air miles, free gifts, and other promotions.

ABOVE: *A 1982 meeting of the Organization of Petrol-Exporting Countries (OPEC) in Vienna, Austria. The world oil market is a classic example of an oligopoly in which a few producers control the market.*

Advertising is also used to tell consumers about new, revamped, or repackaged products. For example, the launch of the new blue Pepsi logo in 1996 was supported by a lavish advertising campaign. Advertising may also be used to counteract the launch of a rival's new or improved product.

Strong branding is another of the ways in which firms compete in oligopolistic markets. Companies tend to spend a lot of money on a distinctive product design, packaging, and corporate logos.

In an oligopoly price competition may also be avoided by collusion and cooperation. Firms might agree among themselves to restrict competition, set prices, or cut supply in order to push up prices and increase profits. In most developed countries such practices are illegal (*see* Market failure and anticompetitive practices, page 64; Regulation and antitrust laws, page 93).

Opportunity cost

Opportunity cost is the highest valued alternative that must be forgone or given up when a choice is made.

When a consumer chooses to do one thing or buy one good, the benefits he or she might get from other activities or goods are forgone. The opportunity cost of playing a game of tennis, for example, is whatever else the player could be doing instead—watching TV, working, playing computer games, or taking a walk, for example. Opportunity costs are an important measure of the choices made by individuals, businesses, or other organizations.

Consumers, firms, and governments all constantly have to make choices similar to an individual's decision of whether to play tennis rather than watch TV or take a walk. Consumers, for instance, want to buy or be given more goods and services, while governments might like to to increase the amount of money they spend on education and law and order. Resources in an economy are scarce, however. There are not enough raw materials, or factories, or workers, or time to produce everything that people want or to allow people to do everything they want to do.

Whenever an individual makes a choice—to buy a car, for example—then other options have to be given up. The opportunity cost of buying a car might be the holiday that has to be forgone in order to afford it. A government could make a decision to spend more money on and allocate more resources to national defense: the opportunity cost of this decision is the forgone benefit of spending that money or allocating those resources to other areas of government activity, to education or welfare benefits, for example.

Opportunity costs and resources

Opportunity cost can also be used as a measure of the cost to a firm of using scarce resources—land, labor, or capital—to produce a particular product or service in terms of the various alternatives to which those resources could have been put. For example, if a company or economy choose to devote more resources to producing televisions, the opportunity cost is that fewer resources are then available to produce personal computers.

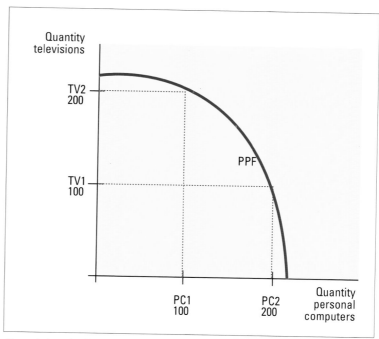

Figure 1 A production possibility frontier shows the opportunity cost of producing televisions in terms of computers, and vice versa.

Figure 1 plots the number of televisions and personal computers that could be produced using the resources available in a particular economy. It shows that if firms decide to increase the production of televisions from TV1 to TV2, the output of personal computers then has to be decreased from PC2 to PC1. In this case the opportunity cost of producing an extra 100 TVs is 100 PCs.

Production possibility frontier

The curve on Figure 1 joining all the possible combinations of the manufacture of televisions and personal computers is known as the production possibility frontier (PPF) (see Production, page 86). The slope of the PPF is the marginal rate of transformation—the ratio between the marginal cost of producing televisions and the marginal cost of producing personal computers. The PPF assumes a direct reallocation of resources: in practice, however, it is not always possible to switch resources from one particular good or service to another.

SEE ALSO:

• Volume 2, page 28: How a business works

• Volume 6, page 54: Industrialization, urbanization, and modernization

Population and migration

The population of a community, region, or nation is the number of people living there. The population of a nation, and its makeup, are important not only as the source of labor or the workforce in that country. Rapid population growth can also be an obstacle to economic growth (see Growth and development, page 46).

Migration is the shift of people from one region or nation to settle in another. Often migration comes about as a result of economic factors such as unemployment (*see* Unemployment, page 113) and where businesses choose to locate.

People will often be forced to leave a rural community in which there is not enough land to farm in order to find work in a city. Such economic migrants may also be forced to leave a country in which capital, land, and natural resources are insufficient to provide them with jobs.

It might be argued that a large population means a greater market for goods and services, and is also a greater pool of labor, a key productive resource. This in turn can lead to greater specialization, more division of labor, and therefore a greater economic output. However, the makeup of the population is key. If a country is poor and experiences a rapidly expanding population, then the ratio of dependents to workers will also grow. This in turn will result in an increasing proportion of capital being devoted to supporting that population—through expenditure on schools, hospitals, roads, and the like—and less capital actually producing goods and services (*see* Capital, page 8). Those resources actually creating wealth—such as workers, factories, and machines—will find it increasingly hard to support the rest of the population—children, the elderly, the sick, and the unemployed.

Thomas Malthus was the first to talk about the negative possibilities behind an ever-expanding population. Since then many other economists have cited rapid population increase as a major obstacle to economic growth and development. The last quarter of the 20th century saw the population of the world growing at a rate of 2 percent every year, with the number of people in the world doubling every 37 years. There are about 6 billion people in the world today. With present population growth rates many people believe that there will come a time when the earth can no longer support so many human inhabitants. Many of the earth's natural resources are finite (*see* Land and natural resources, page 60)—eventually supplies of oil, coal, and other minerals will run out. Even some renewable resources are being exploited at a far greater rate than they can renew—fishing stocks and hardwood forests, for example.

Others argue, however, that developments in technology will overcome many of the problems of depleted natural resources. They claim that alternative energy sources such as solar and wind power will be fully developed, together with innovations in recycling paper, glass, and other materials. Whether such technological advances will prove remedy enough remains to be seen.

SEE ALSO:

• Volume 2, page 28: How a business works

• Volume 4, page 63: The world economy

• Volume 6, page 38: The Age of Reason and early industrialization

BELOW: A large population means larger markets for goods and services, but is also a drain on limited natural resources.

Poverty

A person is said to be in poverty if he or she is living on less than the level of income that would meet basic human needs or provide a particular standard of living in a country.

Unequal wealth means that some people are relatively well off, while others are relatively poor—some people have more assets (money, possessions, property, and so on.) than others and thus have unequal income. The concept of poverty is closely related to that of wealth—like wealth, poverty is to some extent a relative concept (*see* Wealth, page 116). Poverty must be understood in relation to the general standard of living in a particular time and place.

Living standards and the cost of living vary from country to country, and even within countries. Therefore the poor in a country where living standards are high might not be poor in a country where living standards are low. Someone with a fairly low standard of living in the U.S., for example, would probably be looked on as being quite wealthy in a country such as Angola or Bangladesh.

However, there is also a dimension of poverty that is absolute, since human beings have basic subsistence needs that are not socially constructed, but are given by our biology. Anyone who lacks access to the minimum amount of food and drink necessary to avoid malnutrition, or who lacks protection from the elements in the form of housing or clothing is said to be in absolute poverty.

Measuring poverty

The poverty level, or poverty line, in the United States is an amount of money meant to reflect the cost of food. It is a somewhat arbitrary concept, created by the Department of Agriculture in 1901, which takes the sum of the prices of the food commodities judged necessary to sustain a family and then multiplies this sum by three. In 1998 a family of four was said to be in poverty in the U.S. if their income fell below $16,036 each year. However, the poverty line does not take into account the differences in the cost of living between urban and rural areas, which can be substantial, with housing costs, transportation, and food generally a lot higher in cities.

Poverty in the United States

In the United States statisticians measure the number of people classified as living in poverty and the percentage of the population that this represents. During the 1960s and early

LEFT: Critics of free market or capitalist systems point out that while many benefit from this method of resource allocation, other people lose out. The homeless lack access to even the most basic necessities for living—food, shelter, and clothing.

1970s both the number and the percentage of poor people declined, but rose sharply during the late 1970s until the early 1980s. Poverty then declined again until 1990, when the United States hit another recession. The late 1990s, with fairly good economic growth rates, saw another decline in poverty levels. The health of an economy is very important in determining whether poverty rates are rising or falling. If output in the economy is falling, many of those people who are living on or just above the poverty line will find their incomes falling and thus standards of living starting to fall below it. Often this is because a lot of people become unemployed during a recession—the main cause of poverty is whether or not a person has a job (*see* The business cycle, page 7; Recession and depression, page 91).

Many social critics have pointed out that although capitalism is a system that generates enormous wealth, it also generates staggering levels of both relative poverty and the elements of absolute poverty: homelessness, malnutrition, and starvation. According to the Institute for Food and Development Policy, 60 million people starve to death every year worldwide, of whom 15 million are children.

SEE ALSO:

• Volume 3, page 28: Government and the individual

• Volume 3, page 61: Government and labor

• Volume 4, page 63 The world economy

Price and price theory

The price of a commodity is the rate at which it can be exchanged for something else—usually money or other goods or services. Price is determined by demand and supply. The market-clearing or equilibrium price is the price at which quantity demanded equals quantity supplied.

To illustrate price theory in operation, take the price of tennis rackets. Suppose there are many firms producing tennis rackets. If one firm wants to sell more—that is, supply more rackets to the market—it needs to persuade more people to buy them. The simplest way to do this is to reduce the price. It might be that tennis suddenly becomes very popular during a particular period—at the beginning of the summer, for example, when people want to get fit. As a result, more people want to buy rackets, and many will be prepared to pay higher prices for those rackets that are available at the time they want them. In general, if supply increases or demand decreases, prices will fall. Similarly, if supply decreases or demand increases, prices will go up.

This can be shown using a supply and demand diagram, such as that shown in Figure 1 (right).

Excess demand and supply

At $25 people would want to buy 400,000 tennis rackets. Unfortunately, only 200,000 rackets would be supplied at this price, and many customers would be disappointed. In this situation there is said to be an excess quantity demanded. At $35, on the other hand, 400,000 tennis rackets would be supplied to the market. However, only 200,000 people would want to buy a racket at this price, and many would therefore be left unsold. In this case there is said to be an excess quantity supplied.

Only at a price of $30 will quantity demanded equal quantity supplied, that is at point E. This is said to be the equilibrium or market-clearing price. This is the price at which the forces of demand and supply are balanced, and there is no tendency to change either way. If there is an excess quantity supplied, suppliers will cut production and reduce prices. If there is an excess quantity demanded, producers will take advantage of the situation by increasing production and increasing their prices. This trend will continue until quantity supplied equals quantity demanded.

The tendency to move toward the equilibrium price occurs as the result of the

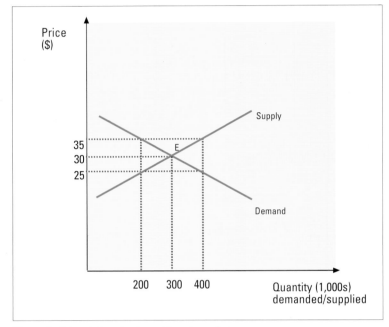

Figure 1 *Price determination of tennis rackets.*

logical process of competition, rather than through any direct intervention. This is the "invisible hand" written about by Adam Smith in his definitive and groundbreaking book *An Inquiry into the nature and causes of the Wealth of Nations*, which was first published in 1776.

In the short run price equilibrium might be impossible to achieve, just as it may be physically impossible for suppliers to respond immediately to market forces. It may be that they are already producing at full capacity and will have to invest in new plant, machinery, tools etc. or hire more labor if they are to increase supplies. Even if manufacturers have stockpiled the good in question, it may still have to be physically brought to the marketplace or distributed to retailers, both of which can be time-consuming and potentially costly measures.

Interaction between markets

Although for the sake of convenience economists may consider markets in isolation—as with the above example—in practice price

LEFT: The price of a good will tend to be high when demand for it is high or its availability is low. When demand is low or supply is abundant or excessive, the price will fall.

changes in one market tend to affect demand and supply in several other markets. For example, if goods or services are considered to be complementary—that is, the use of one is linked to that of one or more others—then a fall in the price of one good or service could lead to a rise in the demand for both. So, for example, if the price of compact disc players goes down, this could lead to a rise in demand for both CD players and CDs.

On the other hand, if certain goods are seen by consumers as being to some extent substitutes for each other—as mailing a letter may be regarded as a straightforward alternative to making a telephone call—then a rise in the price of one is likely to lead to a rise in demand for the other. If telephone calls become very expensive, more people are likely to write letters.

A third possible link between markets is through derived demand. In this case the demand for a particular factor of production (*see* Land and natural resources, page 60; Labor, page 57; Capital, page 8) depends indirectly on the level of demand for the product to which it contributes. For example, the demand for looms, weavers, and wool derives—wholly or in part—from the market for woven cloth. A fall in the price of cloth, and hence a rise in the quantity of it demanded, will lead eventually to a rise in demand for the factors used in its production. So this fall in cloth prices will eventually lead to a rise in demand for looms and weavers. In this way more cloth can be manufactured and supplied to the market to cater for the rise in demand for cloth.

SEE ALSO:

• Volume 2, page 28: How a business works

• Volume 2, page 62: Competition, expansion, and growth

• Volume 2, page 80: How firms behave in the real world

Price discrimination

Price discrimination occurs when a supplier sells the same good or service at different prices to different people. Children or senior citizens will be charged less for movie theater tickets, for example, or people might be charged more to travel on the subway early in the morning when it is busy than during the day.

For price discrimination to succeed, a special set of market conditions must apply. Most importantly, the price elasticity of demand for the good in question must vary between the markets (*see* Elasticity, page 32). In some markets people will respond differently to a change in the price of a product. For example, when it comes to travel by air, a business traveler is often on a much tighter schedule but has fewer restrictions on the price he or she can afford than a tourist, who has more options for when they can fly. The business traveler's demand for airline services is less price elastic than a tourist's: it will remain virtually constant even if the price rises. As a result, the airline can increase the price of tickets to the business traveler and lower the price for tourists, thus increasing its revenue. If demand is price inelastic, an increase in price will increase revenue; if demand is price elastic, a decrease in price will increase revenue.

Further examples of price discrimination are movie theaters where children and senior citizens will be charged less than other people. Senior citizens' demand for movies has a higher price elasticity because they have more free time than workers. Similarly, large warehouse stores such as Price Club and Sam's will sell larger quantities of a product at a lower price. Customers shopping at these stores have a higher price elasticity of demand for certain products than people who do not want to buy such large quantities.

For price discrimination to work, the two or more markets, in addition to having different price elasticities, must be sufficiently separate to make arbitrage—the practice of buying in one market and selling at a profit in another—impossible. For example, you cannot buy a children's ticket at a movie theater and then sell it to an adult for a profit. The supplier must also have some monopoly power to prevent consumers from switching to cheaper suppliers (*see* Monopoly, page 74).

International discrimination

Price discrimination also takes place across national boundaries. A monopolist, for example, might "dump" goods abroad at a much lower price than at home. Different levels of taxation may create price discrimination between neighboring states. If the gap gets too wide, goods are likely to be smuggled across the border for sale on the black market.

SEE ALSO:

• Volume 2, page 28: How a business works

• Volume 2, page 80: How firms behave in the real world

LEFT: Airline tickets are subject to such price discrimination that it is possible that virtually everyone in the same check-in line paid a different price for the same journey.

Privatization

Privatization is the transfer of state-owned enterprises to private control and ownership. It is the opposite of nationalization, which involves the acquisition of private enterprises by the government or public sector.

A state-owned enterprise (*see* Socialism and command economies, page 100) is not subject to the same economic forces as a private enterprise. Being within the public sector, such an enterprise is funded—or at least subsidized—out of central tax revenue. As a result, it is protected against bankruptcy and is not faced with the same pressures of competition as a private enterprise.

Although not totally efficient (*see* Economic efficiency, page 28), state ownership is often desirable, especially in the case of industries that provide fundamental products such as water, electricity, or rail services that private enterprise would not produce because of the high setup costs involved. The cost of the necessary infrastructure—laying tracks, signals, power stations, waterpipes, and so on—make it difficult for private enterprise to enter the market. As a result, many state-owned enterprises are natural monopolies (*see* Monopoly, page 74). While they are in the public sector, they can be directly influenced by government to ensure that they do not exploit their privileged position in the market. State- or government-owned industries also provide public goods such as national defense or law and order (*see* Public sector, page 89). There are, however, many economists who believe that as many as possible of these state-owned industries should be put into private hands.

Efficiency

Those in favor of privatization argue that exposing state-owned industries to competition and market forces drives them to become more efficient. Without the pressures of competition managers and workers allow costs to rise. Inefficiency, previously subsidized by state funding, will now reduce profits and the funds available for further investment. Firms will have to become more efficient in order to survive.

Cost and consumer choice

Cost reductions can be passed on in the form of lower prices for consumers. The pressure of competition is also an incentive to provide bet-

ter service and greater consumer choice. Private firms are also more likely to be innovative and sensitive to consumer demands.

Regulation

Although the government no longer makes decisions on behalf of privatized industries, they can still be controlled by efficient regulation. Regulation often takes the form of a limit on profitability. This restricts the prices such industries can charge and ensures a more socially acceptable outcome.

Privatization can be desirable if resulting increases in efficiency produce a better social outcome. In the U.S., for example, parts of the prison service are now privatized, while in the United Kingdom many previously state-owned industries were privatized in the last 20 years of the 20th century. In these cases infrastructure such as prison buildings or electricity lines were already established. The right to use this infrastructure was sold off to smaller private firms that compete with each other for contracts to run a prison or to provide electricity to customers.

ABOVE: Many U.S. prisons—which were historically state-run—have recently been privatized. Supporters of this change in ownership argue that the move will achieve at least as good a service at significantly lower cost.

SEE ALSO:

• Volume 3, page 43: Government and business

• Volume 6, page 106: Today and tomorrow

Production

Popcorn, baseball bats, cars, education, movies, and nuclear weapons are just some of the goods and services produced in the world economy. In the production process firms combine existing products with factors of production—typically machinery (capital), natural resources (land), and employees (labor)—to make the final product.

The resources or factors of production available to a firm—typically capital and labor—are limited. Management must therefore make decisions about production to ensure the most efficient use of those resources.

The production function

A company makes two products—popcorn and donuts. Management have three options:

1. To make only popcorn
2. To make only donuts
3. To make both popcorn and donuts.

Option 1 maximizes output of popcorn; option 2 maximizes output of donuts. The level of output of popcorn and donuts under option 3 depends on what proportion of total resources is allocated to the production of each.

The production function for popcorn and donuts—also known as the production possibilities frontier (PPF)—is the set of possible combinations of each for the limited resources that are available.

Efficient production and productivity

In Figure 1 any point inside the PPF—A, for example—is inefficient because it is possible, given the available resources, to produce more of one good and no less of the other. Any point on the PPF, on the other hand—B, for example—maximizes output for given resources. This is optimal productivity, and a firm that achieves this is producing efficiently.

In order to maximize profit, management either minimizes costs for a given output or maximizes output for given costs.

Diminishing marginal returns

If all resources are allocated to popcorn, no donuts are produced. As resources are switched from the production of popcorn to the production of donuts, output of popcorn falls, and output of donuts rises. The amount of donuts produced rises quickly at first, but more slowly as each unit of resource is switched to it.

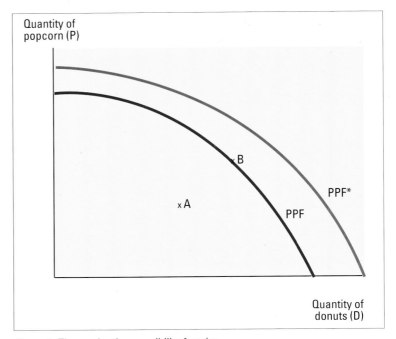

Figure 1 The production possibility frontier.

This is known as diminishing marginal returns (*see* Diminishing returns, page 27).

Suppose the firm's capital resources comprise six machines—three to make popcorn, three to make donuts. In terms of labor the firm has six machine operators and two supervisors. Initially, all operators and supervisors are producing popcorn.

One operator is switched to a donut machine, with one supervisor to assist him. Output of donuts rises steeply to the capacity of the first machine. Then another operator is switched to a second donut machine. Output of donuts rises again, but the supervisor now has two operators to assist, so problems take twice as long to solve. The increase in donuts is therefore less than for the first switch. For each operator switched, the additional output of donuts is less because of increased demands on the supervisor's time. Operators get in each other's way after switching three operators, since there is more than one operator to a machine.

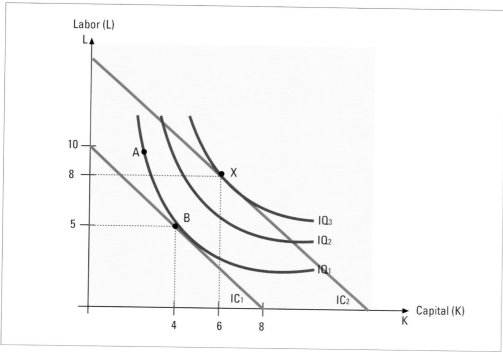

Figure 2 Isocost and isoquant curves.

While the output of donuts is rising, the opposite is happening to popcorn. The first operator switched to producing donuts was effectively the last one originally allocated to popcorn, and therefore the least productive. Therefore, output of popcorn falls slowly at first, but faster as each succeeding operator is taken away.

Shape of the production function

The curved shape of the production function is determined by diminishing marginal returns. If increases or decreases in output of popcorn and donuts were constant with each switch, the function would be a straight line. The stronger the effect of diminishing marginal returns, the more pronounced the curvature of the production function.

Short and long run

The above is a short-run scenario, in which all key factors—resources and production techniques—are fixed. The PPF cannot move.

In the long run this is not the case. Companies can generate additional resources by growth or other financing activity. Technological advances will also improve the productivity of these resources. Additional resources or improved productivity will expand the PPF to PPF*. In the short term management will produce on the PPF. Longer term they will attempt to shift the PPF outward.

Isocosts and isoquants

Cost is defined as a function of the available resources—in this case capital (K) and labor (L). The "isocost" curve (IC_1) represents different combinations of capital and labor that generate the same total cost. So in Figure 2 ten workers and no machines would cost the firm the same as eight machines and no workers, or four machines and five workers.

Each combination of resources, however, produces a different total output. The "isoquant" curve (IQ_1) represents the combinations of capital and labor required to produce a given level of output. For example, point A on IQ_1 produces the same total output as point B, but A requires more labor and fewer machines to do so.

The managers of the company know the maximum resources available—six machines and eight workers, for example—and therefore they know their maximum isocost is IC_2 in Figure 2. If they aim to reach the highest possible output given these resources, they will produce on isoquant IQ_3. They could produce along a number of points on IQ_2, but this will give a lower output than is possible with the resources available. The efficient combination of resources is that at the point of tangency IC_2 and IQ_3, point X. This will maximize output for a given cost. It will also ensure that the company is producing on its PPF, since it also maximizes output for given resources.

SEE ALSO:

• Volume 2, page 28: How a business works

• Volume 6, page 54: Industrialization, urbanization, and modernization

• Volume 6, page 72: Experiments in planned economies

Profit and profit maximization

Profit is the difference between a firm's total revenue and its total costs. When total costs exceed total revenue, profits are negative, and the firm makes a loss. A firm will maximize profits at the price and quantity where marginal revenue equals marginal cost.

Economic theory measures profits in slightly different ways from accountants working with the financial records of individuals or businesses. Accountants are interested only in explicit costs, such as payments for raw materials and labor. Economists, on the other hand, are concerned with both explicit and implicit costs (*see* Costs, page 21). The explicit cost of a company using its own premises, for example, is the rent or mortgage it pays on the property; the implicit cost, however, is the opportunity cost of the potential rent forgone by not leasing the property to a third party (*see* Opportunity cost, page 79).

Economists categorize profits as being either normal or abnormal. A normal profit is just sufficient to ensure that the firm remains in business. In market theory normal profit is an integral part of the cost of providing the goods and services being produced. If the level of profit in a particular market is low compared to another market with equal risk, a firm may transfer its resources to that other market.

Abnormal profits—also known as excess or economic profits—are greater than those needed to keep the firm in business. In the short run profits may be above normal because of a temporary imbalance in the market. If, for example, supply is insufficient to meet demand, a firm will be able to increase its prices and output, and enjoy abnormal profits. However, the profitability of the market will encourage new firms to enter, and eventually profits will decrease as supply increases and prices decline. If a firm enjoys a monopoly, it could also receive excess profits in the long run. A monopoly is only sustainable if new firms are prevented from entering the market by barriers (*see* Monopoly, page 74).

Businesses face cost curves similar to those shown in Figure 1. A firm maximizes its profit when it produces output so that the marginal cost (MC) of the last unit produced is equal to the marginal revenue (MR) of the last unit sold. Profit is the difference between the average total cost (ATC) and the average revenue (AR)

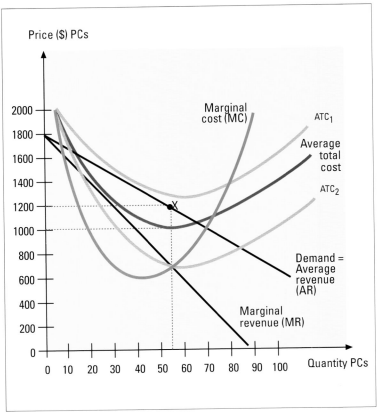

Figure 1 Profit maximization for a firm.

of that last unit. Figure 1 shows the AR, MR, MC, ATC_1, and ATC_2 curves for a computer firm. The optimal output is always output 0X, where MR equals MC and the firm produces 55 computers at $1,200 each. At any output less than 0X, MR is greater than MC, and expanding output to 0X would generate additional marginal profit. At any output greater than 0X, MC is greater than MR, and reducing output to 0X would increase profit. The level of ATC relative to AR at output level 0X determines the actual level of profit. If ATC is equal to or higher than AR at output level 0X (ATC_1), the firm will suffer a loss or earn only normal profit. If ATC is lower than ATC at output 0X (ATC_2), the firm will profit until other firms enter and reduce its AR curve or increase its costs and raise the ATC curve until it is earning normal profits again.

SEE ALSO:

• Volume 2, page 28: How a business works

• Volume 2, page 80: How firms behave in the real world

Public sector

The public sector is the part of the economy that is owned and controlled by government. In in the United States the term relates to activities at the federal, state and local levels, primarily taxation and government expenditure.

Government expenditure is used for a variety of reasons, such as the provision of certain social benefits (*see* Taxation, taxes, and subsidies, page 107). It is also used to fund the provision of what are known as "public goods," goods and services such as national defense, education, police, and fire protection.

A pure public good is a good from which everyone benefits equally and cannot be prevented from doing so. This feature is called nonrivalry. For example, the existence of the armed forces provides security for all individuals irrespective of whether they pay the taxes that fund the army or not. In addition, the fact that one person benefits from this security in no way prevents anyone else from benefiting from it to an equal extent. This feature of a good or service is called nonexcludability.

Reasons for public goods

A public good has to be provided by the government when the market system fails to provide it. There are numerous reasons why this might happen (*see* Market failure and anticompetitive practices, page 64).

The free-rider problem is a consequence of the nature of a public good, which means that there is no incentive for individuals to be honest about how much they would pay for it. A person might argue, for example, that given that their benefit from police protection is in no way reduced by anyone else's, why should he or she offer to pay for it? He or she can let others pay, sit back, and still benefit. This feature of public goods is the prime reason why they are generally best provided by government.

Another reason why public goods are left to the public sector is setup costs. The cost of setting up a business to provide a good such as law and order would include police stations, squad cars, communications networks, courts, prisons, and so on. These costs would be too high for a private enterprise to meet. Likewise, even if private enterprises could fund the initial setup costs, they would not recover their investment because there is no market on

which to sell a public good. Because of the free-rider problem, it is impossible to identify which individuals benefit from the good and how much they benefit, who would be prepared to pay for it, and so forth. It is therefore impossible to set a selling price. Private enterprise will not participate in the provision of such a good. Private enterprise has different motives from the public sector. Private enterprise aims to maximize profit. In the case of public goods such as national defense or law and order this is hardly an appropriate goal.

Mixed goods

Pure public goods account for only a small part of total expenditure in the public sector. Another important area of government expenditure is mixed goods—goods that would be underprovided by the market as a result of externalities or because costs occur today, but

ABOVE: Law and order is one of the public goods that have to be provided by the public sector.

ABOVE: *Education is a mixed good. If provision is left entirely in the private sector, firms will underprovide education since they will not take account of the long-term value of education to society as a whole.*

a whole—that are not taken into account in the provision of education and in its demand. Other similar examples include roads and health services, where some government intervention is also necessary.

Public choice theory

Given that the private provision of public goods is not a realistic option, and that some government intervention is necessary in the provision of mixed goods, the government has to decide which goods to provide and how much of them. Although it is substantial, the public treasury is not unlimited. Increasing revenue by raising taxation is also usually a politically unpopular decision. A cost-benefit analysis is therefore required to determine what level of provision, and of which goods, will maximize the social benefit obtained from a given level of resources.

The main problem associated with such an exercise is identifying the "value" of the benefit of providing a good. Consider the example of national parks and their role in the conservation of wildlife and plant species. The benefit derived from the recent reintroduction of wolves to Yellowstone National Park, for example, is that it helps conserve a species that might otherwise die out. There is an ethical aspect to such conservation, as well as certain educational benefits and the pleasure people will derive from being able to see the creatures in the wild. On the other hand, might not the reintroduction of wolves make Yellowstone a more dangerous place for people to visit? If so, is there a justification for only putting resources into conserving those species that do not present any danger to human beings? Is it desirable or even possible to "value" one species above another? Such questions have to be addressed if finite resources are to be allocated efficiently.

benefits may only be received far into the future. An example of a mixed good is education. The future prosperity of the United States or any other country depends on having a well-educated workforce. In addition, people who cannot read or write, or who cannot understand numbers, are unlikely to find a job and are therefore going to be a drain on society, rather than an asset. If all schools were private, however, some parents might not be able to afford to, or might not want to, send their children to school. In this case there are significant positive externalities—the benefits to society as

Recession and depression

A recession occurs when an economy has experienced falling levels of output—negative growth in real GDP—for at least two consecutive quarters of a year (i.e., for 6 months or more), but has not reached its low point or trough. A depression is a very severe, deep, or prolonged recession—in this case output falls a great deal and remains in the trough a long time, sometimes years.

The Great Depression of the 1930s is a classic example of a severe depression. Between 1929 and 1933 output in the United States fell by about 30 percent, and in 1933 about 25 percent of those seeking work in the U.S. were unemployed. These results were mirrored worldwide, as firms, unable to sell their products, closed their factories and offices on a scale not seen before or since.

Different economic theories have looked at the causes of recession and depression in terms of the business cycle. The business cycle refers to the regular recurring fluctuations in economic activity that follow a pattern of recession or depression followed by a period of recovery and expansion of output, and then back to recession again (*see* The business cycle, page 7*)*.

The classical view

Classical economists (*see* Laissez-faire and classical economics, page 59*)* knew very little about why economic activity fluctuated, and the causes of the business cycle were viewed as obscure and diverse. However these economists believed that expansions and recessions were self-correcting features of the economy. They took the view that the economy would settle in equilibrium at full employment. The mechanism that would ensure this was changes in wage rates. For example, during a recession supply of labor would exceed demand, and as a consequence, wage rates would fall. As wages fell, workers would be priced back into jobs and would use the incomes they earned to purchase the increased output they produced. The opposite occurs during periods of growth and expansion.

A major problem with this mechanism is that it cannot be relied on to restore full employment if wages are inflexible. Because of this, recessions can persist for a considerable period, as happened in the 1930s. This self-correcting mechanism is also based on an important assumption that changes in aggregate supply (total supply of goods and services) cause changes in aggregate demand (total demand for goods and services).

ABOVE: *As the economy worsened during the early 30s, many Americans had trouble accepting the country's situation. Protests and demonstrations were organized, and blame began to be leveled at President Hoover and his government.*

Keynesian theories

The Keynesian view, on the other hand, is that firms produce greater output in response to increased demand. In other words, changes in aggregate demand cause changes in aggregate supply. Keynesians therefore argue that the business cycle results from changes in aggregate demand. In particular, random, temporary fluctuations in private sector investment and consumption spending are viewed as the main causes of fluctuations in economic activity. To Keynesian economists the solution is simple. When the level of economic activity is depressed, governments should cut taxes and borrow (and then spend) the savings of people and organizations. The result of this should be that people's incomes rise, employment goes up as a result of increased government spending, and aggregate demand rises. This, in turn, leads to increased consumer spending that encourages increased production from firms. When the economy is booming, the government should do the opposite. In this way, according to the Keynesian view, one function of the government is to smooth fluctuations in economic activity by contra-cyclical policies.

Real business cycle theory

A third view of the business cycle is termed real business cycle theory. Real business cycle theorists, like classical economists, argue that changes in aggregate supply (rather than demand) cause fluctuations in economic activity. However, unlike classical economists, they argue that there is no reason why changes in aggregate supply should be temporary and instead suggest that they represent permanent adjustments in the economy. For example, the information-technology revolution has had a profound impact on techniques and costs of production. These changes are not reversible, and so there is no reason to believe that the effect of such changes is temporary.

Real business cycle theorists therefore argue that upswings in the cycle are caused by improvements in supply-side conditions that encourage entrepreneurs to invest. Downswings are caused by a deterioration in supply-side conditions, such as a sudden rise in the price of oil, which would tend to discourage investment by entrepreneurs. One important implication of real business cycle theory is that government intervention in the economy to smooth the business cycle is unnecessary—not because the economy is self-correcting, but because there is nothing governments can do!

Economic loss and the business cycle

Apart from the human cost of unemployment, economists are concerned with the business cycle because it implies an economic loss to society as a whole. Economic losses arise in two ways. First, output falls during recessions and depressions, and this output is lost forever. It has also been suggested—though not all economists accept this view—that when output fluctuates in the economy, uncertainty increases, and this discourages investment by entrepreneurs. The implication is that if fluctuations associated with the business cycle could be smoothed, investment would be greater, and this in turn would encourage greater economic growth.

ABOVE: Many unemployed people relied on handouts for food. There were long, hungry lines, like this one in New York City in 1932, in every town and city across the United States.

Economic policy and the Great Depression

The start of the Depression has been historically linked to the Wall Street Crash of October 1929, when there was a massive drop in share prices. However, modern economic research has shown that the Federal Reserve had begun tightening monetary policy (see Monetarism, page 71) in early 1929 and then continued to tighten its monetary grip after the stock market crashed. While the monetary causes of the Depression were not obvious for many years, the loss of value in the stock market was.

It is now widely agreed in economic circles that not only did the U.S. Federal Reserve help start the Depression, it also prolonged it. The Fed continued to tighten its monetary policy, and this caused or contributed to the massive bank failures across the United States. In the early 1930s the Fed again tightened monetary conditions just as the United States was beginning to come out of the recession under the New Deal Policies of President Roosevelt. The U.S. economy suffered another recession from which it did not recover until pulled out by the military expenditure before World War II. Monetary economists, while not agreeing with the Keynesian analysis of the Great Depression, do agree that economic analysis failed to keep the Great Depression from happening and failed to even shorten it.

SEE ALSO:

• Volume 3, page 6: Government and the economy

• Volume 4, page 6: The U.S. government and world economics

• Volume 4, page 63: The world economy

• Volume 6, page 86: The West in the 20th century

Regulation and antitrust laws

An important economic role of government is the regulation of business activities that are not in the public interest. Regulations might be required to prevent employment discrimination, environmental pollution, or unsafe products. Governments may also need to make laws— antitrust laws—to prevent anticompetitive business practices, such as price-fixing.

Many types of business activity are subject to government regulation. For example, there are laws that prohibit the use of child labor, protect worker safety, prohibit employment discrimination on the basis of ethnicity, age, or gender, and impose a minimum wage. Other government regulations are designed to protect consumers by, for example, ensuring product safety and prohibiting the sale of alcoholic beverages to minors. Before physicians may prescribe a new medicine, the drug company that developed it must prove its effectiveness. Furthermore, governments require that practitioners in many fields— including medicine, law, and schoolteaching—obtain licenses. Drug testing and professional licensing are regulatory methods of consumer protection.

Government regulations require that businesses provide accurate information to consumers. For example, firms that process foods are required to provide nutritional information on food packages, and banks are required to provide interest rate information to potential borrowers.

Governments may also impose regulations because of externalities, such as pollution from automobiles and factories (*see* Externalities, environmental, page 36; Externalities and government policy, page 38).

Antitrust laws are federal laws that restrict anticompetitive business practices. These laws prohibit firms in an industry from making agreements—to fix prices, or restrict supplies, for example—and prohibit mergers that restrict competition, increase prices, or limit choice (*see* Market failure and anticompetitive practices, page 64; Oligopoly and oligopolistic competition, page 78). In industries where a single monopoly can provide the product at the lowest cost—for example, public utilities—governments may grant an exclusive franchise to one firm, but regulate the price that the firm may charge for its good or service (*see* Public sector, page 89; Monopoly, page 74).

ABOVE: The sale of medicines is closely monitored by government to maintain safety standards and ensure that drugs are not made available to the public until it is as certain as it can be that they are safe to use.

When businesses are required to comply with government regulations, production costs increase and this may result in higher prices. Society also bears the administrative costs needed to enforce regulations. Those regulations for which the benefits exceed the costs are in society's interest. However, in practice it is difficult to measure benefits such as the prevention of unsafe or discriminatory practices and compare them with costs.

SEE ALSO:

• Volume 2, page 100: Market failure and externalities

• Volume 3, page 43: Government and business

Rent and economic rent

Most people see rent as payment received by a land or property owner in return for allowing others to grow a crop on their land, for example, or live in their house. Economic rent, however, is something quite different—it is the amount of earnings a resource, such as land, labor, or capital, receives above what that resource would receive in its next best use.

The term "rent" has several different meanings in the field of economics. In one context rent represents the income received by those people who own land, a resource category that includes soil, timber, water, minerals, and other natural resources.

Economic rent, by contrast, is the amount of rent a particular resource or factor of production such as land or capital receives, or the amount of money a worker receives, that is above the earnings of that factor if it were doing or being used for something else (see Resources, economic, page 95).

For example, a piece of land might be rented by its owner either to a business for $30,000 a year to build a factory or to a farmer for $20,000 a year to graze cattle. In this case the owner rents the land to the business for the factory. The rent is $30,000, but the economic rent is $10,000—the $30,000 minus the $20,000 of the next best use of the land.

A football player earns $300,000 a year. The next best job he can get might be working behind a bar earning $25,000 a year. In this case the economic rent he receives is very high—$275,000.

Since nearly all resources have alternative uses, the concept of economic rent is an important determinant in the allocation of a society's resources. In terms of capital equipment a truck could be used to transport fresh fruit, for example, while its next best use might be to carry crates of chickens. In terms of natural resources timber could be used to make furniture; its next best use might be as domestic fuel.

Rent seeking

Economic rent seeking refers to efforts by individuals to develop new products or to find new ways to produce existing products at lower costs. People who do these things will increase their own economic rent and so gain an economic advantage over others. Society benefits because the result is a wider variety of products and lower prices.

Political rent seeking consists of activities undertaken by individuals, firms, or groups to influence public policy in a way that will benefit them. If successful in their efforts, these people will find income directly or indirectly redistributed to them and away from others. Because such activities tend to use valuable resources without producing more output or income overall, economists consider political rent seeking to be inefficient.

Special interest groups—such as tobacco manufacturers, whale fishermen, and the oil industry—and the lobbying organizations that represent them devote large amounts of time and money to making sure that the government passes legislation that will benefit them even though such legislation may harm others in society. The emphasis in such cases is on a transfer of income from one group to another, rather than on the creation of additional income for all of society.

SEE ALSO:

• Volume 3, page 43: Government and business

• Volume 6, page 38: The Age of Reason and early industrialization

LEFT: Top athletes are likely to earn a high economic rent. The difference between the income Michael Jordan receives as a basketball player and the income he could earn in another profession is probably quite large.

Resources, economic

Economic resources comprise four categories—labor, land, capital, and entrepreneurship. Economic resources are also called factors of production.

The most basic economic problem facing every society is the scarcity of its factors of production (*see* Scarcity, page 99). There are not enough of these economic resources—material for making things and the people and machines to do the job—available to produce all of the goods and services that members of a society would like to have. Resources are limited; human wants, on the other hand, are not. As a result, individuals and societies must make choices about how best to use their resources, whether it is by personal preference or by government policy.

Each country has a unique distribution of land, labor, capital, and entrepreneurship. The types of goods and services an economy can produce, therefore, will vary from nation to nation. International trade allows nations to specialize in producing those goods and services for which they have suitable resources, at the same time buying others they need from abroad. Those nations with vast holdings of resources are likely to produce more output and create more income than countries with small quantities of resources.

The quality of a nation's labor resource has several dimensions. The size of the country's population is important in setting the overall size of the work force. Economists also judge labor by considering other factors, such as the education, nutrition, and gender and age distribution of the work force. Economists refer to society's level of education and training, the amount of knowledge the workforce has been taught, as its human capital.

Land consists of a country's whole stock of natural resources, including not just land itself, but also resources such as water, mineral deposits, timber, oil, and clean air. Some resources, such as certain kinds of trees, are easily renewable. Others, such as fish stocks, may take time to renew. Supplies of oil and coal, on the other hand, are nonrenewable and cannot be replaced.

The tools, factories, and machines a country uses to help it produce output more efficiently are called the capital resources of that country. Capital resources are goods that are used to produce other goods and services, but are not used up in the production process. So, for example, a sewing machine is used to make jeans, but is still available to make more jeans even after making several hundred pairs.

Money is sometimes referred to as capital, as in the term capitalism, but in economic terms capital is taken to be a productive resource.

Entrepreneurship is sometimes included as part of labor. It refers not to a thing but to ability and attitude, and describes the willingness of some people to take risks in developing a new product, or a new production process, starting up a new business and so on. Entrepreneurship might take the form of a large corporation testing a new model of automobile or a couple opening a local store. Such activities are important because they advance economic activity and knowledge. Each new generation of entrepreneurs learns from the successes and failures of previous entrepreneurs, but all entrepreneurs run a greater or lesser risk of failure.

ABOVE: Farming brings together all categories of economic resources: land, the farmer's labor to grow the crop, capital equipment to plant and harvest the crop, and entrepreneurship from the farmer starting up in business.

SEE ALSO:

• Volume 2, page 28: How a business works

• Volume 2, page 100: Market failure and externalities

Revenue

Firms earn revenue by selling goods and services to customers. Total revenue is the total receipts of a firm from the sale of its output of goods and services. It is the unit price of a good or service multiplied by the quantity sold at that price (P x Q).

Because revenue is determined by price, it is also intimately linked to demand. A firm has to be able to know what the demand is for its goods and services if it is to calculate what price to charge for them and the quantity to produce. Since demand is the relationship between price and quantity, the firm will be able to calculate what its revenue will be at a range of possible prices if it knows the demand for its product (*see* The demand curve, page 23).

Economists analyze revenue in various ways. Average revenue is the revenue received per item sold. It is the average price of the product or service, taking no account of factors such as variations of unit price. Average price can be calculated by dividing the total revenue by the total number of items sold. Marginal revenue is the revenue gained from the sale of one additional unit of output (*see* Marginal analysis, page 62).

A firm's average revenue curve is the same as the demand curve facing the firm. In Figure 1, for example, the quantity of second-hand cars demanded at a price of $18,000 is two. Average revenue at this point is the total revenue—$36,000—divided by the number of cars sold. The firm's average revenue when it sells two cars is therefore $18,000.

Figure 1 shows the average revenue curve and the marginal revenue curve faced by the second-hand car firm. As the price declines, the per unit revenue also goes down—hence the average revenue, or demand, curve slopes down. The marginal revenue curve also slopes down, but it is steeper than the average revenue curve. This is because each additional unit of output, or car, sold brings in less additional revenue than did the previous unit.

Elastic and inelastic demand curves

A firm's revenue is partly dependent on how responsive the demand for its product is to any change in price. This, in turn, depends on the elasticity of the demand curve being faced by the firm's product. If demand is price-inelastic, then the firm can increase prices without there

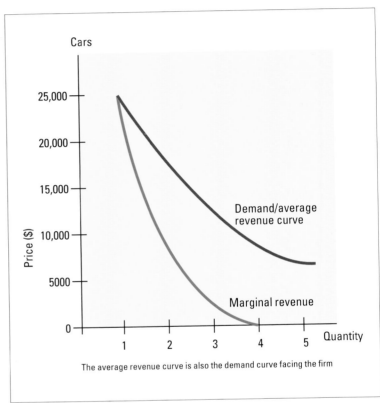

Figure 1 *Revenue for a second-hand car dealer.*

being a significant fall in demand. A rise in price will thus inevitably bring an increase in the firm's revenue. Gasoline, for example, is fairly price inelastic—even if the price rises, people cannot reduce their consumption to any great degree. Some people will start using public transport, walk, or cycle, but trucks still need gas for business, and many people still need their cars to get to work. A rise in the price of gasoline will increase an oil firm's revenue.

If demand is price-elastic, the reverse is true—the firm cannot raise its prices without there being a resulting significant fall in demand and a corresponding reduction in revenue. If the price of comic books rises, for example, many readers might decide that they are too expensive and stop buying them (*see* Elasticity, page 32).

SEE ALSO:

• Volume 2, page 28: How a business works

• Volume 2, page 62: Competition, expansion, and growth

Savings and investment

National income accounting classifies two types of savings: private and public. Private saving is the income households have remaining after they pay for taxes and consumption. Public saving is the tax revenue governments have remaining after they pay for their spending. The sum of private and public saving is called national saving.

Most people use the terms savings and investment to mean the same thing. However, in economics investment is taken to mean an increase in the capital stock—an increase in tools, machines, factories, and so on—or any other expenditure designed to increase output in the future (*see* Capital, page 8).

Suppose Jennifer earns more than she spends and deposits her unspent income in a bank or uses it to buy stock or bonds from a corporation. Since her income is higher than her consumption, the leftover income is considered saving. She might think of herself as "investing" her extra income, but in the language of economics she is in fact saving rather than investing.

Investment, on the other hand, is the purchase of new physical capital, such as machines, buildings, or houses. When Jim borrows from the bank to build a house, he adds to the nation's investment. Similarly, if the corporation that sold Jennifer's stock uses the proceeds to fund a new project, they add to the nation's investment.

It is easy to understand saving and investment in terms of supply of and demand for loanable funds. Saving is the supply of loans; investment is the demand for loans. Matching one person's savings with another person's investment takes place through a large variety of formal financial institutions such as banks, credit unions, insurance companies, pension funds, and the stock and bond markets. These institutions help channel savings to individuals or firms that need money to buy physical capital. Physical capital may be houses and cars in the case of a consumer or machinery and factories in the case of a firm. Individuals can lend their savings to investors by buying corporate bonds and stocks. Or they can deposit their savings in a bank that makes loans to other individuals or firms.

Savings and investment depend on the price of loanable funds—i.e., interest rates.

Interest rates, in turn, depend on liquidity and risk. We can look at these factors from the point of view of an individual, firm, or a nation's assets and liabilities. Assets and liabilities together determine wealth.

Assets represent property or rights to property, while liabilities are debts owed to others. Assets might include cash, bank deposits, corporate bonds, government bonds, stocks, houses, and the like, which are all different in terms of liquidity (*see* Figure 1). Liquidity is defined as the ease and speed with which an asset can be traded for other goods.

ABOVE: Most people who use their savings to buy shares of stock see this as a form of investment. In economic terms, however, it is seen as private saving.

Liquid			Illiquid
Cash	Bank deposit	Stocks and bonds	Real estate (houses)

Figure 1

Very liquid assets, such as cash and checking account deposits, can be readily used for any transaction. This is not possible with less liquid assets such as a house.

Assets will have different rates of return—interest rates—in accordance with their liquidity and their level of risk (*see* Interest rates, page 52). Given their advantages, liquid assets generally pay a low interest rate. Risky assets, on the other hand, pay a higher rate of return in order to convince savers to hold them. So, for example, stocks have a higher average interest rate than bonds because they have greater risk. Similarly, because corporations are more likely to default than the federal government, corporate bonds have a slightly higher interest rate than government bonds. Long-term bond interest rates are usually higher than short-term interest rates because the saver's money is tied up and illiquid for longer.

In general, savings depend positively on the level of interest rates. That is, the greater the return on their money, the more that people are likely to save. Liquidity and risk, however, are also important factors that have to be taken into consideration. Savers have to weigh the benefits of receiving a high interest rate against the costs of not being able to access their savings at short notice. They must counterbalance the benefits of a high interest rate with the costs in terms of the risk of losing their savings.

Investment, on the other hand, depends negatively on interest rates. Firms and businesses are more likely to invest if the price of borrowing to finance investment is low.

Savers supply their surplus income in the hope that they will be paid back with interest. In this way they provide for their future buying power. Investors demand loanable funds because the benefits of the added investment today provide them with additional capital for the future. This benefit more than offsets the interest costs they must pay savers—otherwise they would not do it. Financial markets, then, have the unique role of linking the present to the future.

Savings and investment are key ingredients for economic growth. When a nation saves a large portion of its gross domestic product, more resources are available for investment in capital, and higher capital raises a country's productivity and standards of living.

LEFT: *Excavation machinery in Spain. The funds necessary for firms to invest in capital equipment such as this are provided by savers who put their unspent income in a bank account or buy bonds or shares.*

SEE ALSO:

• Volume 1, page 58: Saving and borrowing

• Volume 2, page 48: Finance and accounting

• Volume 3, page 93: Pensions and insurance

• Volume 6, page 38: The Age of Reason and early industrialization

Scarcity

Scarcity is the most fundamental concept in economics. All the different topics that make up the field relate either directly or indirectly to the problem of scarcity, which is caused by the fact that there are not enough economic resources to satisfy all human wants or desires.

Scarcity exists because individuals and societies have more wants than they have resources—labor, entrepreneurship, land, and capital—available to satisfy those wants. As a result of scarcity these productive resources, or factors of production, face many competing uses. A field might be plowed to grow crops, for example, or used to build a housing development or a parking lot. Choices have to be made, and some wants are left unmet. Scarcity is the essential reason why some goods or services cost more than others. If everyone had enough of everything, no single commodity would be more or less valuable than any other.

All economic factors are subject to scarcity. The labor or human resources needed to produce goods and services for consumers—the workers to manufacture cars and clothes or to provide services, as do teachers and medical doctors—may be limited by population size, by the numbers of people that there are of working age, or by inadequate education and training. Entrepreneurship, another limited factor often included as part of labor, is limited by the same factors and might also be subject to political discouragement.

The second category of limited resource is land, which includes land itself along with natural resources such as minerals, petroleum, and water. Different countries face very different availability of land and resources. Some nations have large oil reserves, for example, or abundant arable land, while others are not so lucky. The final limited factor is capital goods—the factories, equipment, and tools used to produce the goods and services that consumers want (*see* Resources, economic, page 95).

Scarcity exists for individuals, businesses, communities, and nations. Because of scarcity it is necessary for these different groups to make choices and to try to choose the alternative that will produce the greatest benefit. When an individual or business makes a choice, the next best alternative is given up. This next best alternative is the called the opportunity cost (*see* Opportunity cost, page 79). People have to make many decisions relating to scarcity every day. For example, a student who has an economics test tomorrow

ABOVE: Manhattan has some of the most expensive real estate in the world because, while demand for property on the island is high, the land to build it on is relatively scarce.

may decide to watch a popular television show tonight instead of studying. Time is scarce, so the opportunity cost of this decision is not being prepared for the economics test. A business person may decide to install a new piece of equipment that will replace workers. A city council may decide to use a vacant lot for a community park instead of a new manufacturing plant. A nation may decide to spend more public money on interstate highways and education and less on national defense.

Whether the decision is big or small, individual or international, it is necessary because of scarcity—the unlimited wants of consumers versus the finite availability of resources.

SEE ALSO:

- Volume 2, page 100: Market failure and externaliteis

- Volume 4, page 6: The world economy

Socialism and command economies

Socialism is an economic and political theory that broadly advocates collective or government ownership and control of all resources and factors of production in a society. Socialist theory also advocates that goods and services should be allocated by the government, rather than by market forces.

Socialism has its roots in Marxist theory. Within this theory socialism is a transitional stage in society's development from capitalism to communism. It is the stage at which the distribution of goods and services remains unequal, and payment is made according to work done rather than need. Communism is the final stage in which people work "according to ability," and resources are allocated "according to need."

A command or planned economy is an economy that is run on communist or socialist principles—it is an economy in which resources are allocated by the government through a system of planning.

Although Marx was quite vague about what would eventually replace capitalism, he did state clearly the view that capitalism was bound to decay and that it would eventually turn into socialism, which would then in due course become a superior entity, communism. Communism would resolve the class struggle, leading to a classless society and finally to the complete abolition of the state or government.

Command economies

In a command or planned economy all economic decisions are made by the government. Such economies tend to be run by governments which, in theory, want greater economic equality

ABOVE: Communism in the Soviet Union was bolstered by the state's powerful armed forces and substantial munitions industry. They enabled the nation to repel the German invasion in 1941 during World War II, which Russians call "The Great Patriotic War."

Marxist theory

ABOVE: For many years communism was seen as the salvation of the USSR, which had turned to this previously untested system of government after hundreds of years under the autocratic and often capricious tsars.

Marxist economics, the work of Karl Marx, radical economist and political philosopher, has had a profound impact on both economic theory and practice. His critique of capitalism (*see* Capitalist and market economies, page 9) created a distinct school of economics and influenced economic policy not only in the communist nations, but in most countries worldwide. Marx saw the economy as comprising two interdependent parts—the means of production, which provides the technical ability to produce, and the relations of production, which provide the structure within which this production can occur. According to Marx, the relations of production are based on class, and history is a history of class struggle.

The main relationship in capitalism is between capitalists—who own the means of production—and workers—who own nothing but their own labor. The importance of this can be seen if we look at the labor theory of value. Commodities have a use value and an exchange value. Use value is based on individual preferences. But what links different commodities so that they can be compared in value and exchanged? For Marx this link was that all commodities are the product of labor. Therefore their exchange value is the value of the labor taken to produce them. Within capitalism this labor is itself sold to capitalists who benefit from workers' ability to create exchange values.

Capitalists use money to purchase the means of production—tools, equipment, land, raw materials, and labor. When these factors are combined, the end products have a higher value, and capitalists make a profit. According to Marx, this is possible because labor, and only labor, produces more value than it costs to buy. A worker might work for 12 hours in a day, but would earn his or her salary in just six or seven hours. The exchange value created by the production process—the value above the exchange value of labor used in that production process—is called surplus value or profit. Capitalists alone benefit from this surplus value through control of the means of production. However, it is the workers that produce the surplus value. Marx saw this as exploitation of labor.

This exploitation leads to competition between workers and capitalists as capitalists try to increase the rate of exploitation, and hence their profits, and workers try to resist. But capitalists must also compete among themselves for a share of the profits. This makes capitalists look for new technologies and techniques to gain an advantage over other capitalists and to increase the rate of exploitation.

Marx went on from his analysis of current and former methods of economic organization to make predictions about the future of capitalism. He believed that capitalism had contradictions and would suffer from crises that would eventually lead to its destruction. It had created a working class that would demand and go on to create a new mode of production through revolution.

between consumers. Through planning, goods and services can be produced to satisfy the needs of all the citizens in the country, not just for those who have the money to pay for them.

Although we usually talk of command economies in relation to the former communist states, especially the Soviet Union, even the U.S. during World War II had elements of a command economy. Still today around 25 percent of U.S. goods and services are produced by the government. On the hand, even in the most strictly planned economies of China and North Korea some goods and services are provided through the free market.

In a command economy the workers own the means of production—this is through the government that they theoretically control. The government, through various planning agencies, plans the economy on a yearly and sometimes a five-yearly basis. The plan is based on the previous year's figures, which are generated by the government statisticians.

In order to plan production in a command economy, the government assesses its assets—workers, land, raw materials, and capital equipment—and decides what commodities to produce using these assets. It then passes this information on to the firms that are to carry out the production process and allocates the necessary resources to the firms.

The government also allocates the goods and services produced. It estimates the people's needs and supplies products accordingly. The state can also prioritize state goods in the production process—for example, weapons and defense equipment or the production of public goods, such as free health care.

In a command economy labor is controlled through trade unions. Workers are motivated with traditional incentives such as productivity bonuses. This is the traditional or Soviet model of the command economy. Other communist or socialist countries later tried to decentralize planning, allowing workers self-management and using moral incentives.

Full employment

Essentially, socialists believe a government can make rational decisions about the direction of economic life that will result in a fairer allocation of resources than Adam Smith's "invisible hand" (*see* Capitalist economies, page 9). Most command economies provide full employment and a greater equity of incomes than in free market economies. The planning system in the Soviet Union also provided for the rapid industrialization. However, these systems tend not to produce the choice of goods, nor the quality of products that people want. The undemocratic nature of the systems and their bureaucratization led to inefficiencies, waste, and environmental destruction. In the 1980s communist governments in Eastern Europe began moving away from command economic structures. By the early 1990s communist governments had been forced out of power in Eastern Europe, and the Soviet Union had collapsed (*see* Transitional economies, page 112).

ABOVE: In the crisis that followed the 1917 October Revolution and the foundation of the communist Soviet Union many previously rich people were forced to sell their possessions in the streets.

SEE ALSO:

• Volume 3, page 28: Government and the individual

• Volume 3, page 61: Government and labor

• Volume 4, page 6: The U.S. government and world economics

• Volume 4, page 63: The world economy

• Volume 6, page 72: Experiments in planned economics

Specialization and the division of labor

The division of labor is a form of specialization in which each individual worker performs only a few of the tasks in an entire production process. Specialization might also involve machines being set to do specific tasks, or land being devoted to the production of a single product.

With the division of labor workers become more proficient in the limited number of tasks they perform. Workers can also perform these tasks more quickly since they are not constantly switching between different activities. This leads to greater wealth for an entire nation. Adam Smith, writing in *The Wealth of Nations*, observed the advantage of the division of labor in the manufacture of pins. He concluded that if each person performed all the tasks in manufacturing pins, one worker could produce only a few pins each day. However, if all the different jobs were divided, with workers specializing and using machines, 10 people could produce around 48,000 pins in a day. The results of specialization are therefore increased efficiency, productivity, and consequently a higher standard of living.

There are other forms of specialization in addition to the division of labor. Machines such as robots and computers are made to do specific tasks. Geographic regions often develop particular industries because of their particular natural resources and climate. An area with large forests may develop an important timber industry, for example, while the climate in France and California allows vineyards to produce grapes for fine wines.

As living standards rise and societies become more complex, specialization increases. Compare farms in the United States only a few generations ago with those of today. Historically, a farm was almost a self-sufficient economic entity that raised hogs, cattle, and chickens and grew vegetables, corn, and fruit. Today's modern farm specializes. It may be a dairy farm, a small grain farm, or a beef cattle farm. To a large extent this increased specialization in agriculture explains why modern farms are so productive.

Specialization creates networks of interdependence. People specialize in the production of a particular good or service, so they are dependent on others for what they are unable to produce themselves. This necessitates trade. Trade occurs when both parties to the trade expect to benefit. Trade takes place between individuals, between communities, between regions, and between nations (*see* Trade and international trade, page 110). Nations also specialize in some goods and services, exporting those products in which they have a comparative advantage (*see* Comparative advantage, page 12). For example, the United States is known for the export of agricultural products throughout the world. Just as individuals benefit from trade because of the division of labor, nations also enjoy greater wealth because of specialization and international trade.

ABOVE: *It is often quicker and cheaper for a worker to specialize in part of the production process.*

SEE ALSO:

• Volume 2, page 28: How a business works

• Volume 2, page 80: How firms behave in the real world

• Volume 6, page 38: The Age of Reason and early industrialization

Stocks and shares

The stock of a corporation is the value of its assets in terms of the capital and funds it has available for investment at a particular point in time. A share is a fraction of the stock of a corporation.

Most firms pay their day-to-day running costs from revenue gained by selling their product. But firms may also need money to finance further investment—perhaps to develop a new product or or to buy new plant or to fund research and development. To raise this money, they may draw from existing (retained) profits, borrow from a bank or other financial institution, or sell shares in the company.

In the case of a share issue the firm hopes that these shares will attract investors. Investors in turn hope that once they have put their money in, the firm will become more profitable, and their investment will start to benefit them financially. If the firm then becomes more profitable, investors will be paid a share of the firm's profits (a dividend) that is in proportion to the number of shares they own (their holding). Thus, for example, if an individual buys 250 shares in a company with a total share issue of 100,000 shares, and the total dividend in a given year is $10,000, the shareholder might receive a dividend of $25. This dividend will be paid to the shareholder at the end of the firm's financial year. The shareholder still holds the shares, which may make further profits the following year.

In practice many stocks and shares are not sold directly by firm to investor but are traded on a stock market. If all 100,000 shares in the imaginary firm above have been sold, and the company is very profitable, the shares may become highly sought after by other investors who want a slice of the action. Such demand would result in an increase in the value of the shares above their face value—a $1 share might change hands on the stock market for many times that amount. Thus, in addition to the profits that may be made through dividends, shareholders may also benefit from increases in the market value of their shares.

Investors may gamble by buying shares in a firm that is currently having a hard time in the hope that its performance will improve, thus rendering them a profit. When firms with a good long-term track record have a poor period, new money may pour in from people who believe that things can only get better.

Another characteristic of a stock market is that thinking something sometimes makes it so—in other words, if lots of people start to buy shares in a particular firm, others may get the idea that the newcomers know something they do not and buy shares in the same firm themselves. This drives the price of the firm's shares up. If many investors suddenly decide to sell, this may have the opposite effect on other investors and on the share price.

ABOVE: Stocks and shares not directly traded from a firm to an investor are traded on a stock market, such as the Mercantile Exchange in Chicago, Illinois.

SEE ALSO:

• Volume 1, page 102: The stock market

• Volume 2, page 48: Government and business

• Volume 6, page 38: The Age of Reason and early industrialization

The supply curve

Supply of a good or service quantity offered for sale at each price over some period of time, such as a day or a week. The main factor determining quantity supplied of a product is its price. In general, as the price of a product rises, quantity supplied rises—that is, suppliers will produce more of any good or service as prices for it rise.

Consider a firm that sells its entire output at the same price per unit. In this case the profit per unit sold is simply the difference between the price of the product and its average cost of production. For example, if a firm sells its product for $10 per unit, and on average each unit costs $8 to produce, the firm earns $2 per unit sold. If it sells 10,000 units per week, the total weekly profit of the firm is therefore $2 x 10,000 = $20,000.

Now imagine that for some reason the price of the product rises to $11. If the firm continues to produce 10,000 units of output per week, its weekly profits rise to $30,000. This is a significant increase, and it is likely that the firm's owners or managers will wish to earn even more. To do this they will need to increase the amount they produce each week. This seems easy enough; but if the firm is interested in earning higher profits, why do they not simply increase output from 10,000 units per week to 15,000 units per week? To answer this question, we need to understand how average costs behave as output changes.

Output and costs

When firms increase the amount they produce, they incur additional costs. For example, they have to purchase more raw materials. However, costs are unlikely to rise proportionately with output. Indeed, the law of diminishing returns (*see* Diminishing returns, page 27) tells us that in the short run, as firms employ additional factors of production, average product falls. If average product falls as output increases, average cost must rise. Look at Table 1 (*see* page 106), which shows the relationship between average product and average cost for company A.

In constructing Table 1 we have assumed that the firm is able to buy or hire additional inputs at a constant price.

Deriving a supply curve

How much company A will supply per week depends on the price at which its product sells. If we assume that costs include the minimum level of profit the company requires, we can say that at a profit per unit of $3, compa-

BELOW: The amount of packaged food this firm produces each week will depend on the price it receives for its product. If prices rise, the firm will supply more food to the market.

ny A will supply somewhere between 20,000 units and 30,000 units. At a profit of $4 the firm will supply somewhere between 30,000 units and 36,000 units. As price rises, the firm supplies more output to the market—but so do all the other firms that produce this product. However, there is another reason why more is supplied as price rises. Firms differ in levels of efficiency. Less efficient firms have higher costs of production. Table 2 shows hypothetical data for company B, which produces the same product as company A.

Output	Quantity of inputs	Average products	Total cost of inputs ($)	Average cost of production ($)
2,000	10	200	5,000	2.50
3,000	20	150	10,000	3.33
3,600	30	120	15,000	4.10

Table 1 Company A.

Output	Quantity of inputs	Average products	Total cost of inputs ($)	Average cost of production ($)
2,000	15	133	7,500	3.75
3,000	25	120	125,000	4.17
3,600	35	103	175,000	4.86

Table 2 Company B.

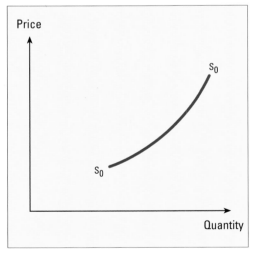

Figure 1 Market supply curve.

At a profit of $2.50 per unit company B would not supply anything. At a profit of $4 company B will supply somewhere between 2,000 units per week and 3,000 units per week. If these were the only firms in the market, we could say that at a profit per unit of $2.50 market supply would be made up entirely of what company A supplies. However, at a profit of $4 market supply would consist of the combined

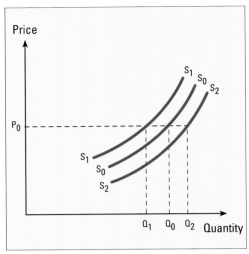

Figure 2 Effect of rising or falling costs.

outputs of companies A and B. The lesson is clear. As the price of a product rises, firms with higher costs are able to earn a profit and will therefore undertake production. Our arguments therefore enable us to construct a typical market supply curve such as the one illustrated in Figure 1.

The effect of changes in costs

Any supply curve, such as that shown in Figure 1, is drawn on the assumption that a given set of costs exists. What would happen if costs were to rise at all levels of output for all firms, for example, because input costs increase? The answer is simple. At any given price firms will be unable to supply the same quantity as previously and will therefore reduce supply. This is shown in Figure 2 by a shift of the supply curve from S_0 to S_1. The opposite will happen if costs fall at all levels of output. In this case the supply curve will shift from S_0 to S_2.

Time and supply

We have argued that quantity supplied responds to changes in price, but we have not considered the length of time taken for supply to respond to price changes.

Economists argue that the momentary period is so short that supply cannot respond—in other words, supply is completely inelastic in the momentary period. In the short run, however, supply can be increased as more variable factors of production—those that can obtained quite easily—are acquired. So, for example, a firm producing processed food can buy in more fruit, vegetables, meat, and so on. Finally, in the long run firms can acquire additional amounts of all factors of production; supply is most elastic in the long run. The firm could buy another factory, for example, or take on more labor.

SEE ALSO:

• Volume 2, page 28: How a business works

• Volume 3, page 61: Government and labor

• Volume 6, page 38: The Age of Reason and early industrialization

Taxation, taxes, and subsidies

A tax is a charge imposed by government on individuals and organizations. It is generally based on income, profit, or the value of goods and services.

There are two main reasons for taxes: to raise revenue, and to correct a market failure. The opposite of a tax is a subsidy, which is an amount paid by government to producers.

Tax revenue serves two main purposes—to fund government expenditure on public goods and services, and to redistribute wealth.

Because of the nature of pure public goods and mixed goods—the high setup costs involved, the free-rider problem, and the positive externalities (*see* Public sector, page 89)— it is unrealistic to expect them to be provided by private enterprise. As a result, government funds or subsidizes goods such as police protection, national defense, education, and healthcare out of central tax revenue.

Wealth is not distributed equally throughout an economy (*see* Income distribution, page 48; Equality and equity, page 34). While some individuals struggle to provide for themselves, others can afford a comfortable lifestyle with money to spare. Income redistribution is not done directly, but by using tax revenue. Taxes are imposed on those earning income or making profits in order to fund social welfare payments such as unemployment benefits.

Correcting market failure

In the market socially inefficient outcomes can result when there is a difference between private and social costs. That is, the difference between the costs borne by an individual producer involved in an activity such as burning waste material from the production process, and the costs incurred by society as a whole as a result of that activity in terms of air pollution, for example, which causes suffering to individuals and damage to the environment.

Governments may attempt to correct this imbalance by imposing a tax on producers—a charge for burning waste products, for example. Such a tax increases the producers' cost base, and consequently private costs become closer to social costs. This forces the market toward a more socially efficient equilibrium (*see* Externalities, environmental, page 36; Externalities and government policy, page 38).

ABOVE: *One reliable way of raising revenue is to impose taxes on luxury products that people have to—or feel they have to—buy.*

Direct and indirect taxes

Taxes can be direct or indirect, progressive, regressive, or proportional.

A direct tax is a tax that individuals or businesses become liable to pay automatically when earnings are made. Examples of direct taxes include income tax and business tax. An indirect tax is a tax paid on goods and services. Indirect taxes will be incurred when an individual chooses to spend his or her income on a product that bears such a tax. It can therefore be avoided, unlike a direct tax. The prime examples of indirect business taxes are excise taxes and sales taxes. Assume a hotel room in New York costs $100 per night. The government imposes an excise tax at 10 percent. The hotel must now charge $110, of which $10 is paid to the government and the original $100 is paid to the hotel.

A progressive tax is a tax under which the wealthy pay a greater proportion of their income than the less wealthy. For example, an income tax system that increases the proportion of tax you pay as your level of income increases—as the U.S. tax system does—would be considered progressive. Progressive tax narrows the gap between rich and poor by taking more from the former than from the latter. It can therefore be used to redistribute wealth.

However, increasing tax rates can be a disincentive to work. If a large proportion of your additional income goes to the government, you may decide that it is not worthwhile earning additional income.

A regressive tax, on the other hand, is one under which the less wealthy pay proportionately more. For example, the Community Charge—or "Poll Tax"—that was introduced in the United Kingdom in the late 1980s charged a flat rate per head of population regardless of income. The main objection to this form of taxation is that if you earn $20,000 per annum and are charged an $800 tax, you are paying proportionately more than if you earn $40,000 and are charged the same tax. Such a tax has a disproportionate effect on the poor. Indirect taxes are also regressive in that they are based on product values, not on income. A rich person paying $11 for a product instead of $10 can better afford the difference than a less wealthy person.

As its name implies, proportional tax is a tax levied at all income levels but at a constant percentage of that income. Hence it is intermediate between a progressive tax and a regressive tax. Proportional taxes result in a tax liability that is a constant proportion of the individual's income—thus someone who earns $100,000 a year will pay ten times more proportional tax than someone who earns $10,000 a year.

Tax and elasticity

Because an indirect tax can be avoided by choosing not to spend, or by spending on untaxed products, it is more efficient for the government to tax goods for which demand is inelastic—i.e., for which there are no real alternatives (see Elasticity, page 32). Since an indirect tax increases the selling price of a product, if demand for that product is elastic, any tax imposed on it will reduce sales. Revenue raised will be low as a result, thus defeating the purpose of the exercise. However, if demand for the products is inelastic—as with cigarettes and alcohol, for example—then sales will fall only slightly as a result of a price increase, and the revenue raised will be higher.

The optimal tax rate is that which maximizes revenue, given that demand for the product will fall as the rate of taxation imposed on it gets higher. Beyond a certain level the decrease in sales volume as a result of this tax will outweigh the increased revenue per unit, and total revenue will fall. Figure 1 (below) shows the effect graphically—this is known as the "Laffer curve."

SEE ALSO:
• Volume 2, page 48: Finance and accounting
• Volume 3, page 6: Government and the economy
• Volume 3, page 28: Government and the individual
• Volume 3, page 79: Taxes
• Volume 3, page 105: Organizations and boards

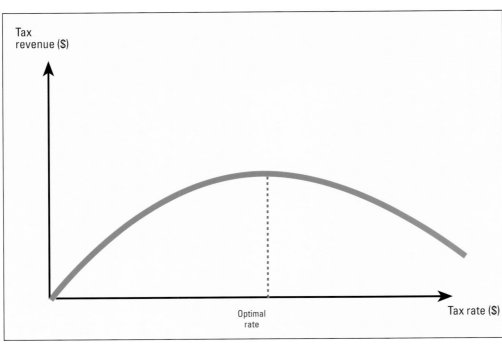

Figure 1 The Laffer curve.

Technology

Technology is the set of methods by which different resources are combined to produce goods and services. Technological innovations allow a firm to increase the productivity of its existing resources of land, labor, and capital.

Technology aids efficiency—for example, an accountant will be more productive if she has a calculator rather than if she has to work out all her figures using a pen and paper. Similarly, a piece of land is more productive if the farmer has access to a combine harvester than it is if he has to harvest his crop by hand. In both cases the output that can be produced by each unit of input has been increased by the application of technology.

Technology is an important element of economics because it is one of the key ways in which a nation can expand its output of goods and services. The acquisition or development of technology and technological improvement are vital for economic growth (*see* Growth and development, page 46).

Suppose that a farmer has a fixed plot of land which she farms on her own. She grows only one crop, cotton, which she plants by hand and irrigates by fetching water in a bucket from a well. She harvests the cotton by hand and digs the land using a spade before she plants the next crop the following year. Working 10 hours a day and using these methods, she can plant cotton on around half her plot of land and harvests five sacks of cotton each year.

Now suppose the farmer decides she wants to produce more from her land. She continues to work for 10 hours a day, but devotes only eight hours to digging, planting, and irrigating her crop, putting aside two hours each day for laying irrigation pipes on her fields, developing a pump for the well, and drawing up designs for an animal-drawn plow. That year she only harvests four sacks of cotton. However, the following year she can dig the land more quickly and efficiently using her plow and can irrigate her crop more effectively pumping water from the well along the irrigation pipes. With the development and application of this technology the farmer harvests eight sacks of cotton the following year.

In this case simply buying another spade or another bucket to transport water would have made no difference to the farmer's output. However, by improving the quality of her cap-ital resources by acquiring or developing technology, the farmer has increased her own productivity and the productivity of her plot of land.

What is true for individuals is also true for nations. When a country wishes to expand its production of goods and services, it needs to do more than simply combine increasing quantities of land and natural resources with further capital and labor. It must also ensure that it improves the productivity of each of those resources. For any given increase in the workforce and stocks of capital equipment, technological progress will accelerate economic growth.

RIGHT: *The development of the wheel was, of course, one of the greatest technological developments in human history. But even this great discovery has been improved by thousands of years of technological refinement.*

SEE ALSO:

• Volume 2, page 62: Competition, expansion, and growth

• Volume 6, page 38: The Age of Reason and early industrialization

• Volume 6, page 54: Industrialization, urbanization, and modernization

Trade & international trade

From the beginning of history people have traded with each other, neighbor with neighbor, tribe with tribe, then town with town and region with region.

In its earliest days trade broadly took the form of barter—the exchange of one good or service for another. In this simple form, however, barter is extremely limited. If it is to operate at all, there needs to be what economists call a double coincidence of wants—the person trading meat for cloth needs to find someone with cloth who wishes to exchange it for meat. Barter also gives rise to the problem of how to put a value on goods and services. These problems were perhaps not so great in prehistoric society, but became much more acute as economies developed, and the number of tradeable products and services grew. The solution was the development of money. Money (*see* Money, its supply and demand, page 72) provided both a means of exchange and a means of valuing items, allowing trade to grow and flourish.

From localized dealing trade quickly spread across the world as people sought to improve their standards of living. They bought products they were unable or unwilling to manufacture, selling the goods they produced in return. The first commodity exported from the Northern American colonies was animal fur. Later exports included tobacco, sugar, and cotton to England. Early imports to America—commodities bought from overseas—included wine and salt, which were imported directly from southern Europe and the Canary Islands. Slaves were one of America's largest early imports.

Over the years there have been different theories as to the most beneficial way a nation might engage in international trade. During the 17th century, for example, many people believed a country should attempt to export more than it imported, using the surplus payments to bolster its wealth with the purchase of gold and silver (*see* Mercantalism, page 66). There was also a great deal of protection of markets, with certain imports banned or taxed heavily. Later, economists argued that international markets should be allowed free reign, with countries specializing in those products they were comparatively more efficient at producing (*see* Comparative Advantage, page 12).

ABOVE: A U.S. trading post in mineral-rich Alaska. Animal fur was the earliest of America's exports abroad.

Economies that engage in international trade with few or no restrictions are known as open economies (*see* Free trade and protectionism, page 41). The degree of openness between countries can be estimated by their exports measured as a percentage of gross domestic product (GDP). The United States, for example, is the world's largest exporter, with more than $600 billion worth of exports in 1996. This was almost $100 billion more than the second largest export nation, Germany. However, exports from the United States comprised only 12 percent of GDP in 1996, ranking it far behind many European countries. Meanwhile, the Netherlands' exports made up 56 percent of its GDP, yet amounted to less than $200 billion in value. The United States the world's largest economy. Its sheer size and the huge amounts of imports, over $800 billion in 1996, obscure the fact that trade is extremely important even if, as a percentage of GDP, it appears not to be.

RIGHT: Countries in the developing world rely heavily on the export of raw materials. The problem with raw materials is that their value rises and falls more quickly than that of manufactured goods.

International trade has grown rapidly since the end of World War II in 1945 and has become increasingly important to the world economy. This can be partly explained by increases in wealth in both the developed and the developing worlds, and partly by huge technological improvements that have made the transportation of goods safer, more efficient, cheaper, and quicker than ever before. However, an even more important factor has been the collective determination of many countries to reduce tariffs and other barriers to trade. Immediately after World War II several international organizations were established to improve the world order—these included the International Monetary Fund (IMF), the World Bank, and the General Agreement on Tariffs and Trade (GATT), which aimed to remove restraints on trade such as tariffs and quotas and to create a truly global market.

Changing patterns of trade can mean that the world price of some goods and services changes at a different rate from that of others. This will have a different impact on different countries depending on the types of products they produce for export and what they import from abroad.

One country's loss is another's gain

For example, developing countries such as Sri Lanka, Chile, Brazil, and Malaysia are traditionally reliant on exports of raw materials or primary products such as copper, tin, coffee, sugar, rubber, and timber. The prices of these raw materials might rise more slowly (or fall more quickly) than the prices of manufactured products. These fluctuations will affect the country's terms of trade—that is, the ratio of export prices to import prices. So, for example, if the world market price for coffee is falling rapidly, the terms of trade will move against exporters of coffee, such as Brazil. However, such a fall in price will result in the terms of trade moving in favor of countries producing and exporting manufactured goods, such as the United States. They will still receive a good price for their exports of automobiles, computers, and so on, but can import coffee at a cheaper price.

Transitional economies

Transitional economies is a term applied to those economies of the former Soviet Union and Eastern Europe that are in the process of transforming themselves from command or planned systems to a more market-oriented approach.

In 1986 Mikhail Gorbachev became the leader of the Soviet Union and began reforms of the communist system that were to lead, ultimately, to its collapse. Gorbachev introduced new policies based on the ideas of *glasnost* (the Russian meaning "openness") and *perestroika* ("reconstruction"). As the Soviet Union changed, so too did its satellite states in Eastern Europe. One by one the rulers of Bulgaria, Czechoslovakia, East Germany, Hungary, Poland, and Romania began to implement policies that moved the countries away from planned economies toward more market-based systems or mixed economies (*see* Mixed economies, page 68).

During this long and often painful process all the former communist countries received financial support from the International Monetary Fund (IMF) and were given advice on transforming their economies by neoclassical economists at the IMF.

Shock therapy

Governments in the former communist nations had to adopt certain measures as part of the "shock therapy" prescribed by the IMF, including:

● The liberalization of prices—prices were no longer to be set by the government, but were instead to be determined through the market mechanism alone.

● The elimination of the subsidies formerly provided by the government to publicly owned corporations. Hard budget constraints were now placed on these firms so that they would not run up bad debts.

● Private enterprises were now allowed to form and operate freely, while some government firms were privatized.

● Economies had to become more geared to producing goods for export and had to be more open to foreign investment.

● Governments adopted monetary policies that were aimed at creating a stable macroeconomic environment.

These policies were followed, to a greater or lesser degree and at varying speeds, by all the former communist countries in Europe.

ABOVE: Hungary was one of the first former communist states to reap the potential benefits of a free market economy. Other Eastern European countries have not been as successful.

The effects were dramatic. The government or public sector in each of the countries was unable to function as relations between highly interconnected firms broke down, while the private sector was also slow to emerge. As a result, output fell rapidly, unemployment, previously unknown, climbed, savings lost their value, and pensioners found their pensions had became worthless.

In some countries—notably the Czech Republic and Hungary—the drop in output slowed after a number of years, and then growth resumed. These countries had the confidence and support of the West and had been able to contain opposition to the reforms. In other countries, however, powerful interests forced the government to maintain subsidies and support for large, public-owned corporations, while criminals took control of private firms, creating gangster terrorism. Many years after the beginning of the transition, only a few of the former command economies can be said to have successfully completed their attempted transformation to market-oriented or mixed economies.

SEE ALSO:

● Volume 4, page 63: The world economy

● Volume 6, page72: Experiments in planned economies

Unemployment

Unemployment is the excess of the supply of labor over its demand—the excess of those seeking employment as compared to the number of jobs available.

In an efficient market an excess of quantity supplied causes the price of the good—in this case labor—to fall until the quantity demanded rises and the quantity supplied falls enough for the market to clear. Many economists believe that unemployment indicates that the market has failed.

They say that market failure occurs because the price of labor—the wage rate—is maintained artificially high (at W in Figure 1), preventing it from falling to its equilibrium level where quantity supplied equals quantity demanded. Unemployment (u/e) is the difference between quantity of labor supplied at W (Ls) and quantity demanded (Ld). Wages are artificially high as a result of factors such as trade union pressure or rules, or minimum wage laws. While these factors guarantee higher pay levels for those employed, they also restrict the level of employment itself.

Costs of unemployment

Unemployment has both public and private direct and indirect costs. Direct private costs are lost income. Direct public costs are the decreases in tax revenue as earnings fall and increases in welfare payments such as unemployment benefits.

Indirect public costs derive from the social impact of unemployment. As unemployment rises and incomes fall, there are externalities such as increased crime and diminished health among the unemployed. Society pays in the form of increased policing and health-care costs. If there is a large number of unemployed, it will also have an effect on aggregate demand as people's incomes fall. This can cause further increases in unemployment.

The workforce is comprised of those of working age who are fit and able to work. However, not every member of the workforce is willing to work. Some economists argue that the very existence of social security benefits can be a disincentive to work if people believe that the additional income they can earn from working does not justify the effort involved. Such individuals are classified as "voluntarily

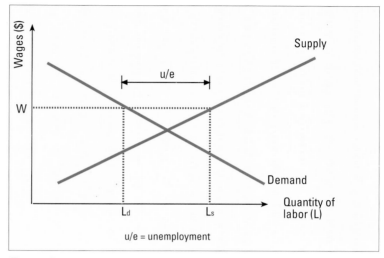

Figure 1 The labor market.

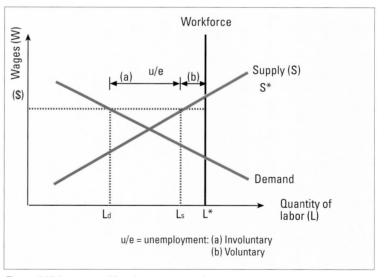

Figure 2 Voluntary and involuntary unemployment.

unemployed"—they are not working because they do not wish to. This contrasts with the "involuntarily unemployed," who are willing to work at the available wage but cannot do so because there are no jobs available. Figure 2 shows both cases. The supply of labor with social security benefits is now represented by the S curve. The supply of labor without social security benefits is shown by curve S*, and the quantity of labor supplied in the short term is noted as L*. Involuntary unemployment is the difference between Ld and Ls as before (a). The difference between Ls and L* (b) shows voluntary unemployment.

Types of unemployment

Involuntary unemployment is driven by a number of factors, each of which leads to a different type of unemployment.

Classical unemployment is the result of a market failure, such as wage inflexibility. Many factors influence the labor demand and supply curves. However, classical economists believe that if the labor market is allowed to clear, with wages adjusting until equilibrium is reached, then there will be no unemployment.

Frictional unemployment, on the other hand, occurs because most people switch jobs at some point in their working lives. Often these switches take time. Any time spent looking for a new job after leaving the old one is known as frictional unemployment.

Structural unemployment occurs because over time the types of industry that dominate economies change. During the 1950s and '60s, for example, mining and manufacturing were major employers, but these industries are now in decline in the Western world, while in other industries there have been moves toward more automated production, which requires less labor. As demand for labor falls, large numbers of workers find themselves unemployed. Many, particularly the old who can have difficulty retraining for new jobs, or who may be discriminated against because of their age, remain out of work for long periods.

Another type of unemployment is demand-deficient unemployment. This occurs when the gap between demand for and supply of labor expands—that is, if supply increases or demand falls. The supply of labor depends on factors such as the aging of the population and the desire to work, which tend to be relatively stable in the short run. Labor demand, however, is likely to vary. Economies go through periods where growth is very low (*see* The business cycle, page 7), and demand for labor falls in line with the demand for the end product. If at the same time the supply of labor remains steady, then unemployment rises.

The Phillips curve

Unemployment levels and inflation rates are interrelated. In general, high inflation rates tend to coincide with low unemployment since they both occur in periods of high growth. Similarly, high unemployment rates tend to coincide with

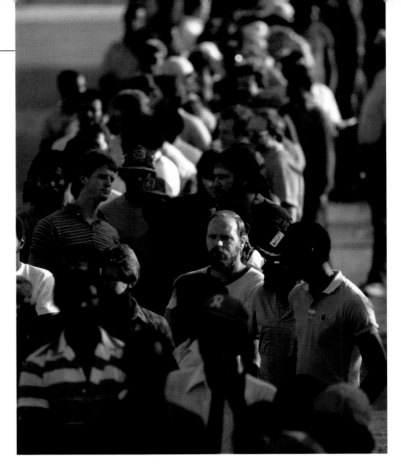

ABOVE: The number of people who are jobless is a reliable indicator of the overall state of the national economy.

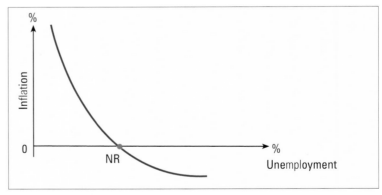

Figure 3 The Phillips curve.

low inflation. In 1958 Professor A.W. Phillips of the demonstrated a strong statistical relationship between unemployment and inflation based on historical data from the United Kingdom. Similar relationships have since been identified for other economies, including the United States. The Phillips curve—see Figure 3, above—suggests unemployment can be traded off against inflation. That is, low inflation can be achieved but at the price of high unemployment, and vice versa. The level of unemployment associated with zero inflation is known as the natural rate (NR) for an economy and includes an allowance for frictional employment.

SEE ALSO:

• Volume 3, page 6: Government and the economy

• Volume 3, page 28: Government and the individual

• Volume 3, page 62: Government and labor

• Volume 4, page 6: The U.S. government and world economics

Utility

Utility or satisfaction is the benefit that is gained from the consumption of a good or service.

Individual preferences are crucial in building economic models. Preferences reveal that Bob would rather buy an apple than an orange, but they do not tell us how much more he prefers one fruit to the other—that is, they do not reveal intensity. The measurement of preference is called utility; the unit of analysis is a util.

A utility function is a mapping from a level of goods to a number of utils. Figure 1 shows the utility function for one good. In this case it is assumed that as the level of the good consumed increases, the pleasure or benefit the consumer receives also rises.

Figure 2 illustrates utility when the consumer has preferences for two goods, apples and oranges. The individual can achieve a particular level of utility by choosing different combinations of apples and oranges. The curve indicating a particular level of utility is known as an indifference curve. So, for example, five baskets of apples and one basket of oranges will give the consumer the same level of satisfaction as three baskets of apples and two baskets of oranges (point A on IC_0). Since the individual prefers a higher level of any good to a lower level, an increase in utility is depicted by a rightward shift of the indifference curve such as IC_1. IC_1 shows a higher level of satisfaction, where, for example, the individual consumes four baskets of apples and three baskets of oranges (point B on IC_1).

The individual's goal is to maximize utility in order to achieve the most pleasure possible. However, the individual consumer is constrained. For instance, if your income is limited, you cannot consume an infinite amount of every good. Instead, you will consume the feasible combination of goods and services that is preferred to all other feasible combinations. We can show the set of feasible combinations of apples and oranges for the example by drawing in our consumer's budget line for the $24 she has to spend on apples costing $4 per basket and oranges costing $6 per basket. Given her income and these prices, our consumer buys the highest level of utility, IC_0, at point A. If her income were to increase enough, shifting the budget line out parallel until it became tangential to IC_1, she could buy

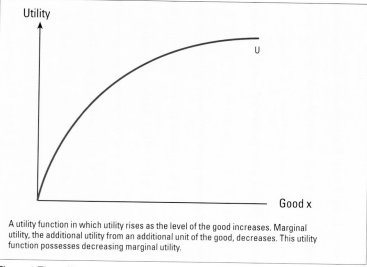

A utility function in which utility rises as the level of the good increases. Marginal utility, the additional utility from an additional unit of the good, decreases. This utility function possesses decreasing marginal utility.

Figure 1 The utility function of a single good.

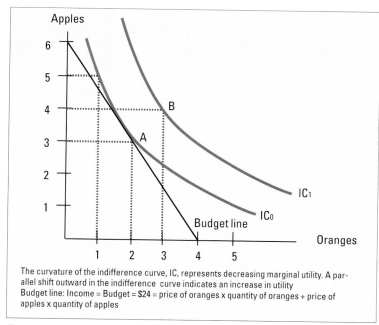

The curvature of the indifference curve, IC, represents decreasing marginal utility. A parallel shift outward in the indifference curve indicates an increase in utility
Budget line: Income = Budget = $24 = price of oranges x quantity of oranges + price of apples x quantity of apples

Figure 2 The utility function of two goods.

the higher level of utility. If the prices of apples or oranges fall enough to push out the budget line so that she could buy some combination on IC_1, she could buy that level of happiness. Even though we cannotmeasure utility, consumers' responses to changes in budget or price show that they behave in a utility-maximizing manner.

SEE ALSO:

• Volume 3, page 93: Pensions and insurance

• Volume 6, page 54: Industrialization, urbanization, and modernization

Wealth

A person's wealth is defined as the stock of assets (land, labor, capital, and entrepreneurial ability) they own at a particular point in time. A wealthy person owns assets of substantial value. These assets may include such things as money, bonds, and other financial instruments, works of art, or other commodities of value, property, and labor skills.

The concept of wealth is closely related to that of poverty (*see* Poverty, page 81). Wealth is a relative concept—it can only be understood in relation to the general standard of living in a particular time and place. Where poverty can be seen in terms of a person having an income below the general standard of living, wealth might be seen in terms of a person having assets generating income in excess of that general standard of living.

Living standards, and the cost of living, vary from country to country, and even within countries. For example, $10,000 would hardly qualify as a substantial income in the United States, Europe, or any other industrialized nation, but in a country like Bangladesh, where the per capita gross domestic product was around $286 in 1999, it is a fortune. Similarly, in urban areas the cost of living tends to be far higher than in rural areas, largely due to the higher costs of housing, food, and transportation.

Wealth, therefore, cannot be solely understood in terms of the numerical amounts of currency it generates, but rather in terms of the number and range of commodities which that currency can command in the market. Many argue that wealth should also be considered in terms of how it relates to poverty and the distribution of income in society (*see* Income distribution, page 48).

There is a strong belief in most industrialized societies that the rich earn their wealth through hard work, taking risks, and through saving and thrift. However, it should also be noted that a substantial portion of the Fortune 400—a list of the richest 400 people in the U.S., published annually—actually inherited most of the assets they own. Karl Marx argued that the first capitalists initially "earned" their fortunes through stealing land and thus dispossessing many peasants, forcing them to become factory workers (*see* Socialism and planned economies, page 100). Others, however, see wealth—the fact of there being the potential to gain a substantial stock of assets—as an essential motivating force in a freely competitive economy. The potential to become wealthy will lead to innovation,

ABOVE: *A shopper in New York City shows all the trappings of a wealthy lifestyle.*

choice, and the efficient production of goods and services (*see* Competition and perfect competition, page 14). It might also be argued that in most economies wealth drives demand, which in turn drives economic growth.

Whatever the causes, it is true that the poorest two-thirds of the world's population consumes less than one-fifth of all wealth. A middle income group accounts for one-fifth of the population and consumes one-fifth of the world's output. A further one-fifth—living in the richest countries, like the U.S., Canada, Japan, and Western Europe—consume the remaining two-thirds of the world's output.

SEE ALSO:

• Volume 3, page 28: Government and the individual

• Volume 6, page 22: The emergence of Europe

Glossary

accounts records of earnings, expenditure, assets, and liabilities kept by individuals, firms, and governments.

balance of payments a record of a country's international trade, borrowing, and lending.

balance of trade an indicator of a country's financial condition produced by subtracting the value of imports from the value of exports.

balance sheet a list of assets and liabilities that shows the financial condition of a firm, individual, or other economic unit.

barter a system of trading in which goods are exchanged for other goods rather than for money

black market an illegal part of the economy that is not subject to regulation or taxation and that often deals in high-priced, illegal or scarce commodities.

bond a legal obligation to pay a specified amount of money on a specified future date.

boom and bust a phrase that describes a period of wild swings in economic activity between growth and contraction.

business cycle the periodic but irregular fluctuation in economic activity, usually measured by GDP, which rises and falls for reasons economists do not fully understand.

capital the physical assets owned by a household, firm, or government, such as equipment, real estate, and machinery. Capital is also used to mean financial capital, or money used to finance a business venture.

capitalism an economic system based on private ownership and enterprise and the free market. Capitalism has been the dominant economic system in the western world since around the 16th century.

central bank a public organization, sometimes subject to government influence but often independent, established to oversee and regulate a country's monetary and financial institutions.

commodity a primary product such as coffee, cotton, copper, or rubber. In economics, "commodity" is also used to describe a good or service created by the process of production.

communism a political doctrine based on the ideas of the philosopher Karl Marx that seeks to establish social equality through central regulation of the economic activity and communal ownership. *See also* planned economies.

comparative advantage the advantage gained by a producer—an individual, firm, or government—if they can produce a good at a lower opportunity cost than any other producer.

consumer good an economic good or commodity that is bought for use by a household rather than by industry, for example.

consumer price index (CPI) an economic indicator based on the price of a range of goods and services to calculate an average for expenditure of a U.S. family.

cost benefit analysis the appraisal of a project or policy, for example, by comparing all the social and financial costs with the social and financial benefits arising from that project or policy.

curve a line plotted between points on a graph; an economic curve can be a straight line.

deflation a general downward movement of prices.

demand the desire for a particular good or service backed by the ability to pay for it.

depression a deep trough in the

business cycle, usually marked by high prices and high unemployment.

developing country a poor country that is undergoing a process of economic modernization, typically including an increase of GDP through the development of an industrial and commercial base.

economies of scale factors which cause the average cost of producing a good to fall as output increases.

entrepreneurship the ability to perceive opportunities in the market and assemble factors of production to exploit those opportunities.

externality a cost or benefit falling on a third party as the result of an economic activity which is not accounted for by those carrying out that activity.

factors of production the productive resources of an economy, usually defined as land, labor, entrepreneurship, and capital.

fiscal policy the attempts a government makes to maintain economic balance by altering its spending on goods or services or its revenue-raising through taxation.

foreign exchange rate the rate at which one country's money is exchanged for another. The rate is often used as a measure of the relative strengths and weaknesses of different economies.

free trade international trade that is not subject to barriers such as tariffs or quotas.

gross domestic product (GDP) the total value of the final output within the borders of a particular economy.

gross national product (GNP) GDP plus the income accruing to domestic residents from investments abroad, less the income earned in the domestic market by foreigners abroad.

inflation an upward movement in the general level of prices.

interest the amount earned by savers or investors on their deposit or investment or paid by borrowers on their loan. The amount of interest is determined by the interest rate.

Keynesianism an economic doctrine based on the theories of J. M. Keynes that advocates government intervention through fiscal policy to stabilize fluctuations in the economy.

labor the workforce who provide muscle or brainpower for economic activity.

laissez-faire a French term for "let it do," originally used in classic economics to describe an economy with no government intervention.

land land and all natural resources such as oil, timber, and fish.

liquidity a measure of how easily an asset can be converted into cash.

macroeconomics the name given to the study of the economy as a whole rather than with the detailed choices of individuals or firms. *See also* microeconomics.

the market an arrangement which facilitates the buying and selling of a good, service, or factor of production. In a free market the prices which result from this are regulated by the laws of supply and demand rather than by external constraints.

mercantilism an economic policy popular in Europe from the 16th to the 18th centuries that stressed the importance of exports to earn reserves of gold and silver and used high tariffs to prevent imports.

microeconomics the study of individual households and firms, the choices they make in individual markets, and the effects of taxes and government regulation. *See also* macroeconomics.

monetarism an economic doctrine that regards the quantity of money in an economy as the main determinant of aggregate demand. As such, attempts by government to increase output by stimulating demand will only result in inflation.

monetary policy the attempt to regulate inflation and economic activity by varying the money supply and interest rates. Monetary policy is often the responsibility of a central bank.

money supply the amount of liquid assets in an economy that can easily be exchanged for goods and services, usually including notes, coins, and bank deposits that can be transferred by writing checks.

monopoly a market in which there is only one supplier of a good or service for which there is no close substitute.

neocolonialism a relationship between a country and a former colony in which the business interests of the first continue to dominate the economy of the latter.

opportunity cost the best alternative that must be given up when an economic choice is made.

planned economy an economy in which production and distribution are determined by a central authority, such as a ruler or a government.

private sector that part of an economy in which activity is decided and the means of production owned by individuals or firms rather than government. *See also* public sector.

productivity the ratio between the input of resources such as capital and labor and the resulting output of goods and services.

protectionism an economic doctrine that attempts to protect domestic producers by placing tariffs on imported goods.

public sector that part of an economy owned by a government or other public bodies such as state administrations.

recession a severe contraction of economic activity marked by two successive quarters of falling GDP.

specialization the decision by an individual, firm, or government to produce only one or a few goods or services.

sustainable development a form of economic growth that seeks to use renewable rather than finite resources and to minimize the permanent damage done to the environment by economic activity.

supply the quantity of a good or service available for sale at a particular price.

taxes and tariffs compulsory charges placed on economic activity by governments. Taxes might be placed on wealth or income, on business profits, as a sales tax on transactions, or as license fees on activities such as driving. Tariffs are taxes placed on imports into a country.

trusts anticompetitive alliances formed among businesses to force prices up and bring costs down. Trusts were outlawed in the United States by the Sherman Antitrust Act of 1890.

unemployment the condition of adult workers who do not have jobs and are looking for employment.

wealth the total assets of a household, firm, or country less its total liabilities.

welfare state a system of welfare provision by a government to keep its citizens healthy and free from poverty. Welfare provisions typically include free health care, insurance against sickness or unemployment, old age pensions, disability benefits, subsidized housing, and free education.

The World's Economies, 1996

	Population (millions)	GDP $m		Population (millions)	GDP $m		Population (millions)	GDP $m
Afghanistan	20.9	12.8	Germany	81.9	2,364.6	Nigeria	115.0	27.6
Albania	3.4	2.7	Ghana	17.8	6.2	North Korea	22.5	21.5
Algeria	28.8	43.7	Greece	10.5	120.0	Norway	4.3	151.2
Angola	11.2	3.0	Guadeloupe	0.4	3.7	Oman	2.3	15.3
Argentina	35.2	295.1	Guatemala	10.9	16.0	Pakistan	140.0	63.6
Armenia	3.6	2.4	Guinea	7.5	3.8	Panama	2.7	8.2
Australia	18.1	367.8	Guinea-Bissau	1.1	0.3	Papua New Guinea	4.5	5.0
Austria	8.1	226.5	Haiti	7.3	2.3	Paraguay	5.0	9.2
Azerbaijan	7.6	3.6	Honduras	5.8	4.0	Peru	23.9	58.7
Bahamas	0.3	3.5	Hong Kong	6.2	153.3	Philippines	69.3	83.3
Bahrain	0.6	5.7	Hungary	10.0	44.3	Poland	38.6	124.7
Bangladesh	120.1	31.2	Iceland	0.3	7.2	Portugal	9.8	100.9
Barbados	0.3	2.0	India	944.6	357.8	Puerto Rico	3.7	30.3
Belarus	10.3	22.5	Indonesia	200.5	213.4	Qatar	0.6	7.5
Belgium	10.2	268.6	Iran	70.0	132.9	Réunion	0.7	2.9
Benin	5.6	2.0	Iraq	20.6	21.9	Romania	22.7	36.2
Bermuda	0.1	2.1	Ireland	3.6	62.0	Russia	148.1	356.0
Bhutan	1.8	0.3	Israel	5.7	90.3	Rwanda	5.4	1.3
Bolivia	7.6	6.3	Italy	57.2	1,140.5	Saudi Arabia	18.8	125.3
Bosnia	3.6	3.3	Jamaica	2.5	4.1	Senegal	8.5	4.9
Botswana	1.5	4.8	Japan	125.4	5,149.2	Serbia, Montenegro	10.3	15.7
Brazil	161.1	709.6	Jordan	5.6	7.1	Sierra Leone	4.3	0.9
Brunei	0.3	4.6	Kazakhstan	16.8	22.2	Singapore	3.4	93.0
Bulgaria	8.5	9.9	Kenya	27.8	8.7	Slovakia	5.3	18.2
Burkina Faso	10.8	2.4	Kirgizstan	4.5	2.5	Slovenia	1.9	18.4
Burundi	3.2	1.1	Kuwait	1.7	31.0	Somalia	9.8	3.6
Cambodia	10.3	3.1	Laos	5.0	1.9	South Africa	42.4	132.5
Cameroon	13.6	8.4	Latvia	2.5	5.7	South Korea	45.3	483.1
Canada	29.7	569.9	Lebanon	3.1	12.1	Spain	39.7	563.2
Central African			Lesotho	2.1	1.3	Sri Lanka	18.1	13.5
Republic	3.3	1.0	Liberia	2.2	2.3	Sudan	27.3	10.7
Chad	6.5	1.0	Libya	5.6	23.1	Suriname	0.4	1.3
Chile	14.4	70.1	Lithuania	3.7	8.5	Swaziland	0.9	1.1
China	1,232.1	906.1	Luxembourg	0.4	18.9	Sweden	8.8	227.3
Colombia	36.4	80.2	Macau	0.4	7.4	Switzerland	7.2	313.7
Congo	46.8	5.7	Macedonia FYR	2.2	2.0	Syria	14.6	16.8
Congo-Brazzaville	2.7	1.8	Madagascar	15.4	3.4	Taiwan	21.5	275.0
Costa Rica	3.5	9.1	Malawi	9.8	1.8	Tajikistan	5.9	2.0
Cote d'Ivoire	14.0	9.4	Malaysia	20.6	89.8	Tanzania	30.8	5.2
Croatia	4.5	18.1	Mali	11.1	2.4	Thailand	58.7	177.5
Cuba	11.0	18.0	Malta	0.4	3.3	Togo	4.2	1.3
Cyprus	0.8	8.9	Martinique	0.4	3.9	Trinidad and Tobago	1.3	5.0
Czech Republic	10.3	48.9	Mauritania	2.3	1.1	Tunisia	9.2	17.6
Denmark	5.2	168.9	Mauritius	1.1	4.2	Turkey	61.8	177.5
Dominican Republic	8.0	12.8	Mexico	92.7	341.7	Turkmenistan	4.2	4.3
Ecuador	11.7	17.5	Moldova	4.4	2.5	Uganda	20.3	5.8
Egypt	63.3	64.3	Mongolia	2.5	0.9	Ukraine	51.6	60.9
El Salvador	5.8	9.9	Morocco	27.0	34.9	United Arab Emirates	2.3	44.6
Eritrea	3.3	0.8	Mozambique	17.8	1.5	United Kingdom	58.1	1,152.1
Estonia	1.5	4.5	Myanmar	45.9	63.4	United States	269.4	7,433.5
Ethiopia	58.2	6.0	Namibia	1.6	3.6	Uruguay	3.2	18.5
Fiji	0.8	2.0	Nepal	22.0	4.7	Uzbekistan	23.2	23.5
Finland	5.1	119.1	Netherlands	15.6	402.6	Venezuela	22.3	67.3
France	58.3	1,533.6	Netherlands Antilles	0.2	1.9	Vietnam	75.2	21.9
Gabon	1.1	4.4	New Zealand	3.6	57.1	West Bank & Gaza	0.8	3.9
Gambia, The	1.1	0.4	Nicaragua	4.2	1.7	Yemen	15.7	6.0
Georgia	5.4	4.6	Niger	9.5	1.9	Zambia	8.3	3.4
						Zimbabwe	11.4	6.8

Further reading

Allen, L. *Encyclopedia of Money*. Santa Barbara, CA: ABC-Clio, 1999.

Ammer C., and Ammer, D. S. *Dictionary of Business and Economics*. New York: MacMillan Publishing Company, 1986.

Atrill, P. *Accounting and Finance for Non-Specialists*. Engelwood Cliffs, NJ: Prentice Hall, 1997.

Baker, J.C. *International Finance: Management, Markets, and Institutions*. Engelwood Cliffs, NJ: Prentice Hall, 1997.

Baites, B. *Europe and the Third World: From Colonisation to Decolonisation, 1500-1998*. New York: St. Martins Press, 1999.

Bannock, G., Davis, E., and Baxter, R.E. *The Economist Books Dictionary of Economics*. London: Profile Books, 1998.

Barilleaux, R.J. *American Government in Action: Principles, Process, Politics*. Englewood Cliffs, NJ: Prentice Hall, 1995.

Barr, N. *The Economics of the Welfare State*. Stanford, CA: Stanford University Press, 1999.

Barro, R.J. *Macroeconomics*. New York: John Wiley & Sons Inc, 1993.

Baumol, W.J., and Blinder, A.S. *Economics: Principles and Policy*. Forth Worth, TX: Dryden Press, 1998.

Begg, D., Fischer, S., and Dornbusch, R. *Economics*. London: McGraw-Hill, 1997.

Black, J.A. *Dictionary of Economics*. New York: Oxford University Press, 1997.

Blau, F.D., Ferber, M.A., and Winkler, A.E. *The Economics of Women, Men, and Work*. Engelwood Cliffs, NJ: Prentice Hall PTR, 1997.

Boyes, W. and Melvin, M. *Fundamentals of Economics*. Boston, MA: Houghton Mifflin Company, 1999.

Bradley, R.L., Jr. *Oil, Gas, and Government: The U.S. Experience*. Lanham, MD: Rowman and Littlefield, 1996.

Brewer, T.L., and Boyd, G. (ed.). *Globalizing America: the USA in World Integration*. Northampton, MA: Edward Elgar Publishing, 2000.

Brownlee, W.E. *Federal Taxation in America: A Short History*. New York: Cambridge University Press, 1996.

Buchholz, T.G. *From Here to Economy: A Short Cut to Economic Literacy*. New York: Plume, 1996.

Burkett, L., and Temple, T. *Money Matters for Teens Workbook: Age 15-18*. Moody Press, 1998.

Cameron, E. *Early Modern Europe: an Oxford History*. Oxford: Oxford University Press, 1999.

Chown, J.F. *A History of Money: from AD 800*. New York: Routledge, 1996.

Coleman, D.A. *Ecopolitics: Building a Green Society* by Daniel A. Coleman Piscataway, NJ: Rutgers University Press, 1994.

Cornes, R. *The Theory of Externalities, Public Goods, and Club Goods*. New York: Cambridge University Press, 1996.

Dalton, J. *How the Stock Market Works*. New York: Prentice Hall Press, 1993.

Daly, H.E. *Beyond Growth: the Economics of Sustainable Development*. Boston, MA: Beacon Press, 1997.

Dent, H.S., Jr. *The Roaring 2000s: Building the Wealth and Lifestyle you Desire in the Greatest Boom in History*. New York: Simon and Schuster, 1998.

Dicken, P. *Global Shift: Transforming the World Economy*. New York: The Guilford Press, 1998.

Economic Report of the President Transmitted to the Congress. Washington, D.C.: Government Publications Office, 1999.

Elliott, J. H. *The Old World and the New, 1492-1650*. Cambridge: Cambridge University Press, 1992.

Epping, R.C. *A Beginner's Guide to the World Economy*. New York: Vintage Books, 1995.

Ferrell, O.C., and Hirt, G. *Business: A Changing World*. Boston: McGraw Hill College Division, 1999.

Frankel, J.A. *Financial Markets and Monetary Policy*. Cambridge, MA: MIT Press, 1995.

Friedman, D.D. *Hidden Order: The Economics of Everyday Life*. New York: HarperCollins, 1997.

Friedman, M., and Friedman, R. *Free to Choose*. New York: Penguin, 1980.

Glink, I.R. *100 Questions You Should Ask About Your Personal Finances*. New York: Times Books, 1999.

Green, E. *Banking: an Illustrated History*. Oxford: Diane Publishing Co., 1999.

Greer, D.F. *Business, Government, and Society*. Engelwood Cliffs, NJ: Prentice Hall, 1993.

Griffin, R.W., and Ebert, R.J. *Business*. Engelwood Cliffs, NJ: Prentice Hall, 1998.

Hawken, P., et al. *Natural Capitalism: Creating the Next Industrial Revolution*. Boston, MA: Little Brown and Co., 1999.

Hegar, K.W., Pride, W.M., Hughes, R.J., and Kapoor, J. *Business*. Boston: Houghton Mifflin College, 1999.

Heilbroner, R. *The Worldly Philosophers*. New York: Penguin Books, 1991.

Heilbroner, R., and Thurow, L.C. *Economics Explained: Everything You Need to Know About How the Economy Works and Where It's Going*. Touchstone Books, 1998.

Hill, S.D. (ed.). *Consumer Sourcebook*. Detroit, MI: The Gale Group, 1999.

Hirsch, C., Summers, L., and Woods, S.D. *Taxation : Paying for Government*. Austin, TX: Steck-Vaughn Company, 1993.

Houthakker, H.S. *The Economics of Financial Markets*. New York: Oxford University Press, 1996.

Kaufman, H. *Interest Rates, the Markets, and the New Financial World*. New York: Times Books, 1986.

Keynes, J.M. *The General Theory of Employment, Interest, and Money*. New York: Harcourt, Brace, 1936.

Killingsworth, M.R. *Labor Supply*. New York: Cambridge University Press, 1983.

Kosters, M.H. (ed.). *The Effects of Minimum Wage on Employment*. Washington, D.C.: AEI Press, 1996.

Krugman, P.R., and Obstfeld, M. *International Economics: Theory and Policy*. Reading, MA: Addison-Wesley Publishing, 2000.

Landsburg, S.E. *The Armchair Economist: Economics and Everyday Life*. New York: Free Press (Simon and Schuster), 1995.

Lipsey, R.G., Ragan, C.T.S., and Courant, P.N. *Economics*. Reading, MA: Addison Wesley, 1997.

Levine, N. (ed.). *The U.S. and the EU: Economic Relations in a World of Transition*. Lanham, MD: University Press of America, 1996.

MacGregor Burns, J. (ed.). *Government by the People*. Engelwood Cliffs, NJ: Prentice Hall, 1997.

Magnusson, L. *Mercantilism*. New York: Routledge, 1995.

Mayer, T., Duesenberry, J.S., and Aliber, R.Z. *Money, Banking and the Economy*. New York: W.W. Norton and Company, 1996.

Mescon, M.H., Courtland, L.B., and Thill, J.V. *Business Today*. Engelwood Cliffs, NJ: Prentice Hall, 1998.

Morris, K.M, and Siegel, A.M. *The Wall Street Journal Guide to Understanding Personal Finance.* New York: Lightbulb Press Inc, 1997

Naylor, W. Patrick. *10 Steps to Financial Success: a Beginner's Guide to Saving and Investing.* New York: John Wiley & Sons, 1997.

Nelson, B.F., and Stubb, C.G. (ed.) *The European Union : Readings on the Theory and Practice of European Integration.* Boulder, CO: Lynne Rienner Publishers, 1998.

Nicholson, W. *Microeconomic Theory: Basic Principles and Extensions.* Forth Worth, TX: Dryden Press, 1998.

Nordlinger, E.A. *Isolationism Reconfigured: American Foreign Policy for a New Century.* Princeton, NJ: Princeton University Press, 1996.

Painter, D.S. *The Cold War.* New York: Routledge, 1999.

Parkin, M. *Economics.* Reading, MA: Addison-Wesley, 1990.

Parrillo, D.F. *The NASDAQ Handbook.* New York: Probus Publishing, 1992.

Porter, M.E. *On Competition.* Cambridge, MA: Harvard Business School Press, 1998.

Pounds, N.J.G. *An Economic History of Medieval Europe.* Reading, MA: Addison-Wesley, 1994.

Pugh, P., and Garrett, C. *Keynes for Beginners.* Cambridege, U.K.: Icon Books, 1993.

Rima, I.H. *Labor Markets in a Global Economy: An Introduction.* Armonk, NY: M.E. Sharpe, 1996.

Rius *Introducing Marx.* Cambridge, U.K.: Icon Books, 1999.

Rosenberg. J.M. *Dictionary of International Trade.* New York: John Wiley & Sons, 1993.

Rye, D.E. *1,001 Ways to Save, Grow, and Invest Your Money.* Franklin Lakes, NJ: Career Press Inc, 1999.

Rymes, T.K. *The Rise and Fall of Monetarism: The Re-emergence of a Keynesian Monetary Theory and Policy.* Northampton, MA: Edward Elgar Publishing, 1999.

Sachs, J.A., and Larrain, F.B. *Macroeconomics in the Global Economy.* Englewood Cliffs, NJ: Prentice Hall, 1993.

Shapiro, C., and Varian, H.R. *Information Rules: A Strategic Guide to the Network Economy.* Cambridge, MA: Harvard Business School, 1998.

Smith, A. *An Inquiry into the Nature and Causes of the Wealth of Nations,* Edwin Cannan (ed.). Chicago: University of Chicago Press, 1976.

Spulber, N. *The American Economy: the Struggle for Supremacy in the 21st Century.* New York: Cambridge University Press, 1995.

Stubbs, R., and Underhill, G. *Political Economy and the Changing Global Order.* New York: St. Martins Press, 1994.

Teece, D.J. *Economic Performance and the Theory of the Firm.* Northampton, MA: Edward Elgar Publishing, 1998.

Thurow, L.C. *The Future of Capitalism: How Today's Economic Forces Shape Tomorrow's World.* New York: Penguin, USA, 1997.

Tracy, J.A. *Accounting for Dummies.* Foster City, CA: IDG Books Worldwide, 1997.

Tufte, E. R. *Political Control of the Economy.* Princeton, NJ: Princeton University Press, 1978.

Varian, H.R. *Microeconomic Analysis.* New York: W.W. Norton and Company, 1992.

Veblen, T. *The Theory of the Leisure Class (Great Minds Series).* Amherst, NY: Prometheus Books, 1998.

Wallis, J., and Dollery, B. *Market Failure, Government Failure, Leadership and Public Policy.* New York: St. Martin's Press, 1999.

Weaver, C.L. *The Crisis in Social Security: Economic and Political Origins.* Durham, NC: Duke University Press, 1992.

Werner, W., and Smith, S.T. *Wall Street.* New York: Columbia University Press, 1991.

Weygandt, J.J., and Kieso, D.E. (ed.). *Accounting Principles.* New York: John Wiley & Sons Inc, 1996.

Williams, J. (ed.). *Money. A History.* London: British Museum Press, 1997.

Websites

Consumer Product Safety Commission: http://www.cpsc.gov/

Equal Employment Opportunity Commission: http://www.eeoc.gov/

Environmental Protection Agency: http://www.epa.gov/

Federal Reserve System: http://www.federalreserve.gov/

Federal Trade Commission: http://www.ftc.gov/

Food and Drug Administration: http://www.fda.gov/

The Inland Revenue Service: http://www.irs.gov/

Occupational Health and Safety Administration: http://www.osha.gov/

Social Security Administration: http://www.ssa.gov/

The U.S. Chamber of Commerce: http://www.uschamber.com

The U.S. Labor Department: http://www.dol.gov/

The U.S. Treasury Department: http://www.treas.gov/

Picture Credits

Index

126

Fluvanna County High School
1918 Thomas Jefferson Parkway
Palmyra, VA 22963

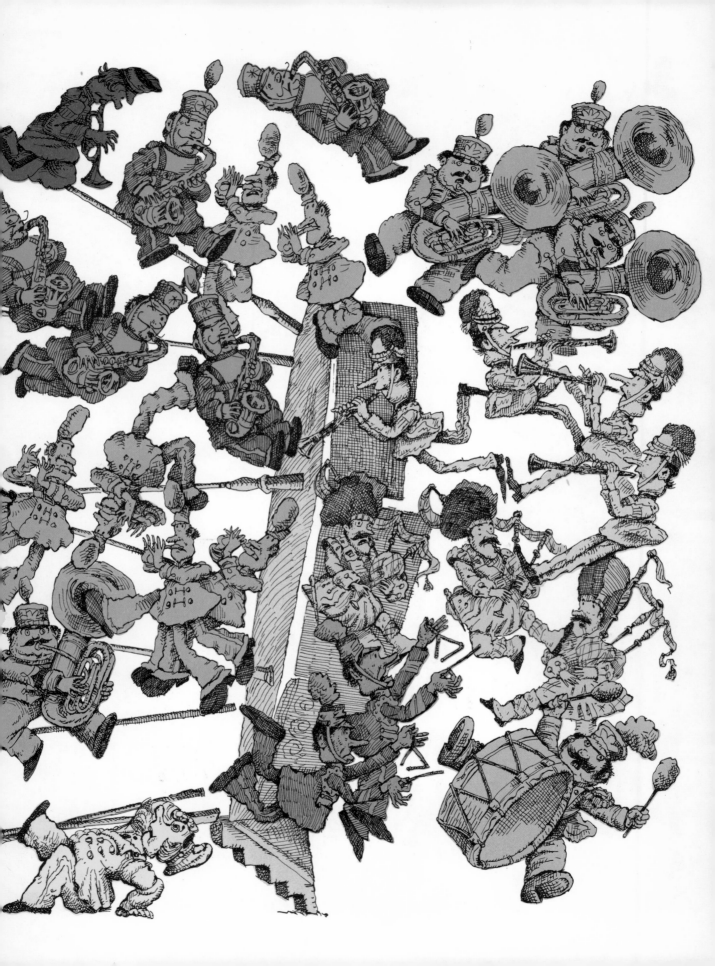

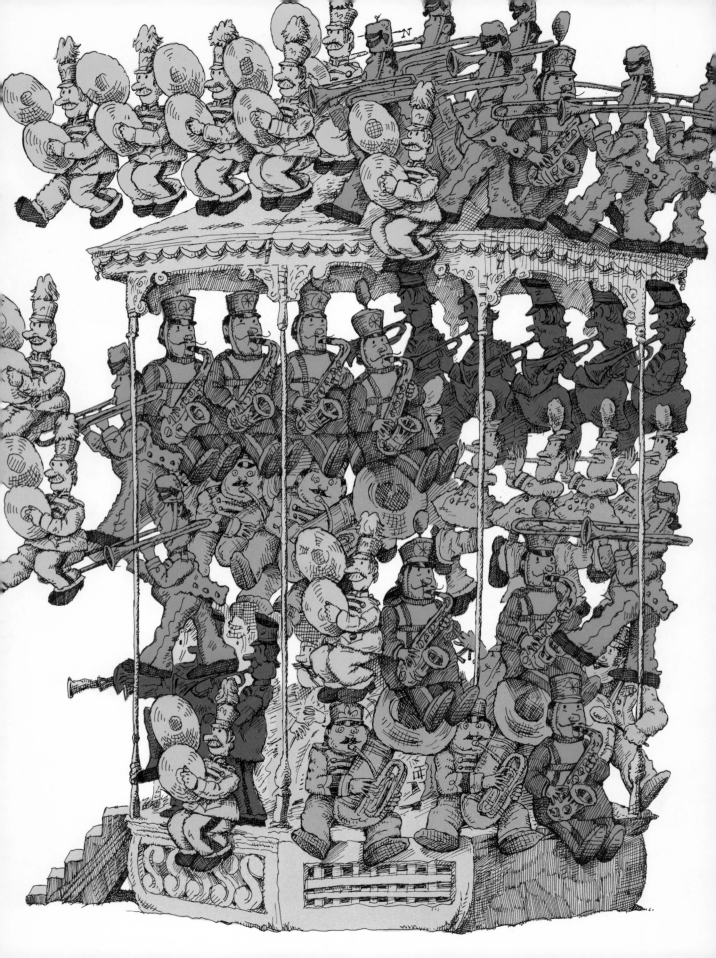

10
TEN

crashing cymbals

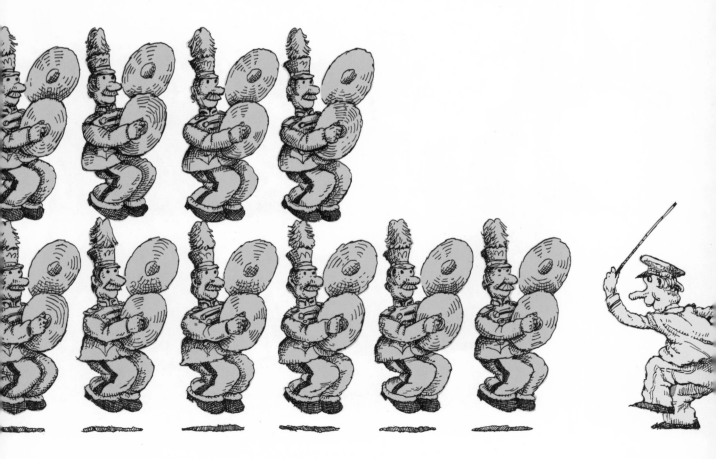

9

NINE

tootling trombones

8

EIGHT

syncopated saxophones

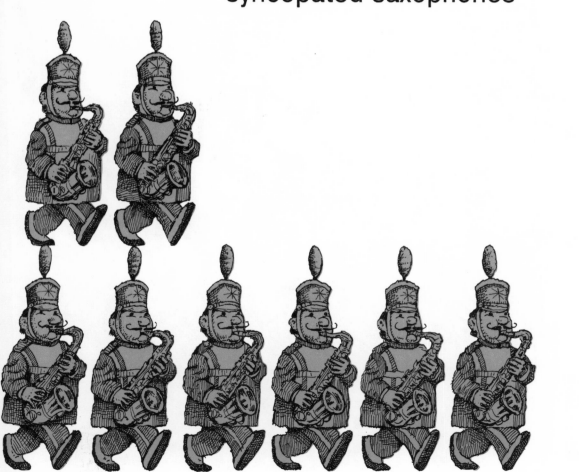

7
SEVEN
triumphant trumpets

6
SIX

persnickety piccolos

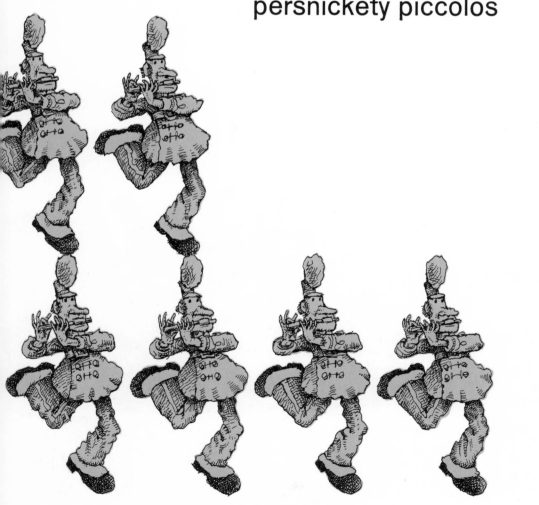

5

FIVE

tumbling tubas

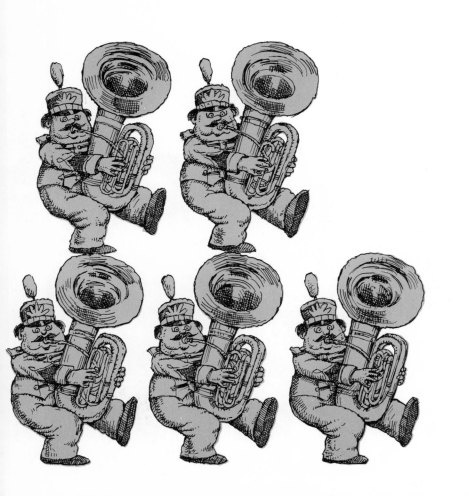

4

FOUR

crooning clarinets

3
THREE

bellowing bagpipes

2
TWO

tinkling triangles

84249

dancing drum

J
K

dancing drum

a counting book for children
(and parents) who are tired of
puppies and chickens and horses...

by Gail Kredenser and Stanley Mack
pictures by Stanley Mack

S. G. Phillips ⚡ New York

Text copyright © 1971 by Gail Kredenser and Stanley Mack
Illustrations copyright © 1971 by Stanley Mack
Library of Congress Catalog Card Number 79-146845. ISBN 0-87599-178-5
Manufactured in the United States of America. All rights reserved

*For
Kenneth
and
Peter*

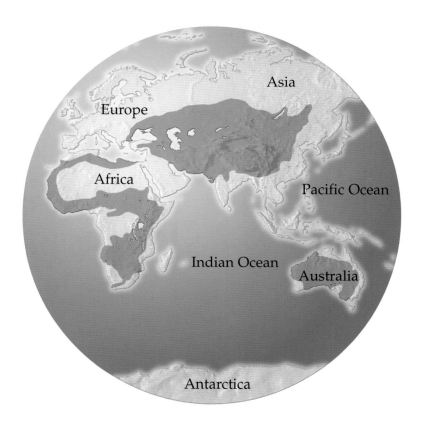

Europe
Asia
Africa
Pacific Ocean
Indian Ocean
Australia
Antarctica

In Asia there are grasslands on high plateaux between huge mountain ranges where it is too cold and dry for many trees to grow.

America's Great Plains are grasslands. They are next to the Rocky Mountains in what is called "rain shadow land", land that is dry because the mountains shelter it from rain.

What on Earth?

New word!
"Savannah" is a Native American word for "grassy plain". A savannah is a grassland with scattered trees.

What's in a name?

Grasslands grow on every continent except Antarctica at the South Pole. In Africa and South America, grasslands are called "savannah". In North America they are called "prairies". The Russian word for grasslands is "steppes" and in South America tall swaying grasslands are called "pampas".

9

Are Grasslands Hot or Cold?

Hot tropical grasslands are hot all year round. Temperate grasslands bake in hot summers but are bitterly cold in the winter. High in the central Asian steppes, summers are short and fiercely hot but winters are long and freezing. Grasses here are short and ground-hugging to survive the blasts of icy wind.

Elephants

The African elephant is now only found in the grasslands of east and central Africa. The elephant is considered an endangered species.

wet or dry?

Grasslands grow in areas that are too dry for forests to grow but have more rainfall than deserts. Some hot tropical grasslands have about three very wet months a year. But others have up to eight months of rainfall, enough for some trees and grasses to grow.

wild?

Yes. Fierce thunderstorms, hailstones, high winds and tornadoes can rage across the grasslands. Tornadoes often occur in the North American prairies. Lightning sometimes sets fire to dry grasslands.

What on Earth?

Big muscles!

An elephant's trunk has 40,000 muscles which give it great strength and movement.

An elephant uses its trunk like an arm. The tip of its trunk is sensitive enough to pick up a pin.

How Does Grass Grow?

Grass root systems can spread outwards and **downwards**! Waxy stems grow up from the roots and sprout leaves. As the plant grows it makes a spikelet. Seeds form in the spikes. Some grasses sprout fresh leaves from **scattered** seeds. Others grow from buds just under the surface of the soil.

A grass seed spikelet is like a feathery arrow-head. When the seeds are blown off by the wind each seed has a sharp tail to help it hold on to the soil where it lands. This is how grass spreads.

Can grass get eaten to death?

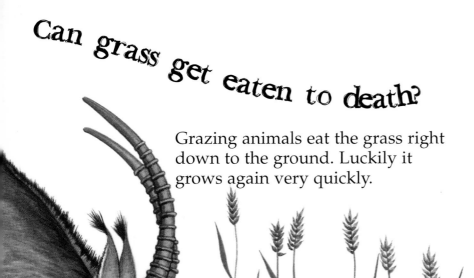

Grazing animals eat the grass right down to the ground. Luckily it grows again very quickly.

chomp chomp!

Tufts of grass

12

What on Earth?

Disaster?

Fierce fires turn grasslands into miles of ash. But after a fire, grass plants make new shoots. Fire can actually **renew** the grassland!

sizzle!

sizzle!

sizzle!

An African buffalo herd in the Okavango Delta, Botswana, Africa.

What's Underground?

O nly a third of the grass plant grows above ground. The rest of it forms a tangle of roots and runners in the soil. Tiny hairs on the grass roots take in the minerals and water it needs from the soil. Grassland soils vary. Some grasses grow in dry, shallow soil. Other grasses grow in deep, rich, dark soil. A teeming mass of wildlife share the grassland soil.

Prairie dog family

Grass

Roots

Prairie dog

What on Earth?

Too small to see?

Protozoa

Algae

Bacteria

Fungus

Virus

Tiny bacteria and protozoa, which are too small to see, help to break down dead matter. Algae and fungus help to feed the soil.

These insects eat smaller insects that can cause plant disease. They also clear up dead plant matter.

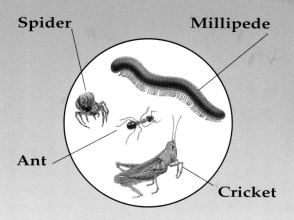

Spider

Millipede

Ant

Cricket

The burrowing owl often lays its eggs in other creatures' empty nests.

This is a North American prairie dog. It is a member of the rat family. Like rats, its teeth keep growing because it wears them down with constant chewing. Prairie dogs live in packs and build huge networks of underground burrows called towns.

The rattlesnake lives in a burrow.

Burrowing owl

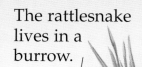

Coyote

Rattlesnake

A black-footed ferret kills a prairie dog and then takes over its home

Slug

Worm

15

What plants Grow in Grasslands?

Grasslands are full of wildflowers. There are also shrubs and sometimes trees. These plants have to survive in difficult conditions. Flowers in temperate grasslands must cope with freezing weather. They grow low to the ground to stay safe from strong winds. Their leaves are tightly curled to keep in warmth.

Spring on the Texas prairie (*left*). Wildflowers bloom everywhere. This temperate grassland brims with bee–loving flowers like clover. Some flowers like broom snakeweed and rayless goldenrod are very poisonous.

Where is the Serengeti?

The Serengeti grasslands are in Tanzania in Africa. Thorny shrubs grow here; so do acacia trees. The broad, leafy branches of the acacia tree spread into a thick canopy overhead.

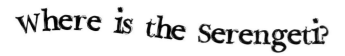

These are acacia trees growing in the Serengeti grasslands, Africa.

What on Earth?

What's so special about the baobab tree?

In drier parts of the grasslands sits the great baobab tree. Its huge hollow trunk holds water. Every part of the tree can be used by humans.

What Animals Live There?

Great herds of large animals have roamed grasslands for millions of years. They have strong hooves for galloping across hard ground. Their teeth and stomachs help them chew and digest stiff grasses. They eat grassland plants. Bison and cattle have **four** stomachs!

spiky seeds?

Some grasses have smooth seeds which are eaten and scattered along with an animal's droppings. Other plants have spiky seeds which spread when they land on an animal's fur.

Which animal is a nibbler?

Zebras

Giraffe

Zebras and giraffes drink from a water hole. Giraffes are browsers. They nibble leaves from trees and tall shrubs.

Why do leopards have spots?

A leopard's spots help to hide, or camouflage, it among the grasses.

What are predators?

A leopard is a predator, a creature that hunts other animals for food. Leopards and other big cats are attracted by huge herds of herbivores that graze the grassland. Predators stalk weak, old or very young animals or those that have strayed from the herd.

What on Earth?

Ants beware!

The giant anteater has no teeth. But its sticky tongue is two feet long and can slurp up to **30,000 ants** each day!

Do Birds Live in Grasslands?

Greater rhea

Grasslands are perfect habitats for lots of bird species from huge Australian emus to tiny Hungarian larks. Smaller birds eat grass seeds, berries, insects and grubs. Larger, pecking birds such as emus, ostriches and rheas chew leaves and roots as well as seeds and berries. They also eat small lizards, birds, and snakes. Birds are good for the grassland. They spread seeds, which are shed in their droppings, and also eat insects and pests.

The greater rhea lives on the South American pampas.

Speedy rhea!

Like ostriches, the rhea cannot fly but it runs at 40 miles (64 kilometers) per hour!

What do vultures eat?

Not all birds are seed and insect eaters. These huge vultures are scavengers that feed on carrion (meat from dead animals). Vultures often pick at the bones left behind by predators like cheetahs and lions.

Big rhea!

The greater rhea is a huge bird. It can grow to the amazing height of 5 feet (1.5 meters) — that is taller than most cars!

Vultures

21

What Insects Live in Grasslands?

Grasslands buzz with thousands of insect species. They drink the sweet nectar from flowers. As they feed, pollen lands on them and they carry it from one flower to another. This fertilizes the flowers and makes them produce seeds and berries. But insects aren't all good. In temperate zones, insects and worms can eat more grass than any other creatures!

Termite mound (Inside)

skyscrapers?

This huge earth mound is a termite city. These mounds can be 20 feet (6 meters) tall! Inside millions of termites live and work in a maze of rooms, tunnels and holes. The Queen termite lays about 20,000 eggs each day which are cared for by worker termites.

What do butterflies drink?

Regal fritillary butterfly

This very rare butterfly lives on the North American prairies, meadows and marshes. It drinks the nectar of flowers like red clover, milkweed and mountain mint.

What on Earth?

Invasion!

A locust swarm looks like a vast swirling black cloud. There can be more than **fifty billion locusts** in a swarm!!!!

chomp chOmp!

What are locusts?

Locusts are a kind of large, leaf-eating grasshopper. When there is no rain for a very long time they swarm together in tall columns which can be as high as 1 mile (1.6 kilometers)! Then they swoop down and eat every plant in sight.

Locusts

23

Why Are Grasslands Important?

There are at least 7,500 different grass plants. Grasses like wheat, oats, corn, barley and rice have been a vital source of food for thousands of years. Exotic grassland flowers grow in our parks and gardens and are used in some medicines too. Farming has reduced natural grasslands and some plants have been lost forever.

What can you make with grass?

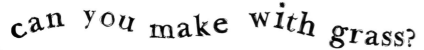

Building bricks can be made by mixing grasses with earth and dung. It can also be used as roof thatch.

Dustbowl!

Cereals like wheat, oats and corn are grown on North American prairies. These crops do not have deep natural roots like grass which holds the soil in place. In the 1930s, a drought turned the loose soil into a huge dustbowl. Huge clouds of dust blew for hundreds of miles. It affected over 97 million acres of land across five states. Crops failed and thousands of farmers were ruined.

What on Earth?

Hot Earth

Grassland roots hold lots of moisture. They also provide much of the world's oxygen and absorb gases that can create a harmful rise in temperature, or global warming, if they reach up into the atmosphere.

Are Grasslands Under Threat?

Nearly three quarters of the world's food is grown in grassland areas, yet only two percent of original grasslands remain. Many of its plants and creatures are now under threat. When a natural grassland area is cleared for other use, species that are good for the environment are lost too.

How would you survive in grasslands?

We grow wheat, maize and barley on grassland, to make anything from cornflakes to bread. But be careful – some grasslands are home to tigers, leopards, lions and rattlesnakes and they would love to have you for lunch!

Grassland dangers

Lion If a lion attacks you make a lot of noise and try to scare it away.

Rattlesnake If you are bitten by a rattlesnake - keep the wound below where your heart is in your chest. Call emergency services on your two-way radio.

Malaria This disease kills over a million people a year and is transmitted by mosquitoes. Sleep under a mosquito net and wear some repellent.

What to take checklist

Carry a long **knife** to hack your way through tall grasses. Don't get lost – be sure to take a **compass.** The biggest grassland in Russia stretches over 2,500 miles. Take a good pair of **boots** for walking and a **box of matches** to light a fire at night to keep warm. Take an **alarm** to scare off attacking animals and be certain to take a **two-way radio** to call for help. Remember to take **traps** to catch your dinner and enough fresh **water** for the journey.

Grassland Facts

A blue flower called a gentian grows in temperate grasslands across the world. Its roots have been used to cure stomachaches!

In one flying group of locusts there can be as many as 80 million locust adults.

Giraffe

The horned lark from the North American grasslands nests on the ground. It sings as it flies because there are no trees to perch on.

There are 100 types of grasshopper on the American prairies! Some only eat flowers and clear the soil for grass to grow. But farmers think they are pests.

The outer part of a seed is called a coat.

Some termites make their own food! They grow vegetable molds and then eat them.

Female elephants are pregnant for almost two years.

The giant anteater has spit like glue. It drowns ants in slime.

The Queen termite is up to 100 times bigger than the workers.

Glossary

bacteria tiny living animals

burrow a hole or tunnel dug by a small animal

camouflage patterns and colors that help a plant or creature to hide in its habitat

continent large land mass (like Australia)

dry temperate a climate that has cold winters and hot summers

fungus spongy vegetable growth, like a mushroom

global warming a rise in Earth's temperature

habitat the natural environment of a plant or animal

herbivores plant-eating mammals

hot tropical a climate that is always hot through its dry season and wet season

migrate to move on from one place to another

pampas the South American name for tall, swaying grasslands

plateaux areas of high flat ground

protozoa tiny living animals

species a group of plants or creatures with similar features and habits

Ostrich

What Do You Know About The Grasslands?

1. What are tall swaying grasses called?

2. How fast can the greater rhea bird run?

3. Why is the baobab tree so useful?

4. What is the Russian word for grasslands?

5. Whose home does the black-footed ferret steal?

6. Which creature builds a mound with air vents?

7. How many stomachs do bison and cattle need to digest grass?

8. How can animal droppings be useful?

9. Do fires kill off grasslands?

10. What do vultures feed on?

Can you guess how much a rhinoceros weighs?

Go to page 32 for the answers!

31

Index

Pictures are shown in **bold**.

Answers

1. Pampas (See page 9)
2. They can run over 40 miles (64 kilometers) per hour (See page 20)
3. Its hollow trunk holds water (See page 17)
4. Steppes (See page 9)
5. The black-footed ferret steals the prairie dog's home (See page 15)
6. The termite builds a home with air vents (See page 22)
7. Bison and cattle have four stomachs to digest grass (see page 18)
8. Seeds are shed in their droppings (See page 18)
9. No, the grasslands quickly recover (See page 13)
10. Carrion, meat from dead animals (See page 21)

An adult rhinoceros weighs about 5 tons. That's as much as three and a half cars.

1. The People and Their Lands

> Not Afghans, Turks or sons of Tartary,
> But of one garden, and one trunk, are we;
> Shun the criterion of scent and hue—
> We all the nurslings of one springtime be.
>
> *Mohammed Iqbal*

In 1947 the subcontinent of South Asia was host to violence as had not befallen the land since the great Indian uprising ninety years before. Neighbor fell upon neighbor, trainloads of families perished in massacre, villages were burned and their inhabitants slaughtered. Within six months, more than half a million people perished brutally by the hand of man. Amidst the carnage Pakistan was born.

The years since then have witnessed the 100,000,000 people of Pakistan struggle for survival against continuing, but less devastating odds. Floods and droughts have destroyed their crops, neighboring countries have encouraged their disunity, and their own leaders have sometimes failed them.

Yet Pakistan has survived and her people have achieved the purpose for which they joined in 1947: an independent homeland for South Asia's Muslims.

The motivation for Pakistan was Islam, a religion founded more than thirteen centuries ago in Arabia. In undivided India in 1947, about 25 per cent of its 437,000,000 inhabitants were Muslims, believers in Islam. Most of the rest were Hindus. It was for Muslims that the leaders of the Pakistan movement claimed to speak during the drive for independ-

1

ence. Led by a brilliant lawyer named Mohammed Ali Jinnah, they sought a nation of their own in order to avoid living as a religious minority, a nation in which they might develop an Islamic society.

Perhaps under different circumstances the Muslims and Hindus of India could have continued to live together as citizens of one secularly ruled nation. In the previous centuries people in the South Asian subcontinent with varied patterns of living had often dwelt amicably side by side. But the tensions created by the struggle for power during the move toward independence from Great Britain prior to 1947 emphasized differences almost to the point of civil war.

Religion lay at the root of these differences and surface manifestations of it appeared throughout the society. In villages Hindus and Muslims lived next to each other, but not together. Intermarriage was rare. Religious practices were not only different, they were often conflicting. With only a little stimulation, submerged fears that one group would attack the other rose to the surface and erupted.

Among educated Muslims, the "need" for self-determination was felt even more strongly than among the villagers. Social intercourse between educated Muslims and Hindus was the exception, not the rule. In government and industry, Muslims could not advance as rapidly as Hindus. Because of their religion and traditions, these Muslims could not accept the permanent status of "minority."

With the reluctant acquiescence of British and Hindu leaders, Mohammed Ali Jinnah and his followers pieced together Pakistan out of those areas in the subcontinent that were predominantly Muslim. In the west, these included the provinces of Sind and the Northwest Frontier, the western part of the Punjab, the vast Baluchistan Agency, and, finally, the small princely states of Amb, Bahawalpur, Chitral, Dir, Kharan, Khaipur, Kalat, Las Bela, Makran and Swat. In addition,

certain Pathan tribes along the Afghanistan border gave their allegiance to the new government. In 1955, all of these were merged into the single province of West Pakistan, although certain tribal groups retained a special relationship with the central government. The area, some 311,000 square miles, is the size of Texas and Louisiana combined; its population in 1964 is more than 44,000,000, over four times that of Texas.

In the east, the areas comprising Pakistan include the eastern half of Bengal Province, a portion of Assam around the city of Sylhet, and the tribal territories of the Chittagong Hill Tracts. More densely populated than West Pakistan, the area of 54,000 square miles—about the size of Wisconsin—contains 53,000,000 in 1964, five and a half times that of Texas. Together, East and West Pakistan form the sixth most populous country in the world.

Pakistan has been called a "double" country. East and West Pakistan are separated by 1,000 miles of India and are as different from each other as Florida and Nevada. Western Pakistan, with its deserts, mountains and the vital Indus River, sits on India's western shoulder, snuggling into the side of Afghanistan and a portion of Iran in the west, touching Communist China along the northern Himalayas, and stretching south to the Arabian Sea. The average rainfall is less than 20 inches, but this statistic is deceiving. West Pakistanis may experience long and harsh dry spells, which suddenly end with torrential rains. Most of their agriculture depends upon irrigation, and along the Indus River the United States, in cooperation with other Western countries, is helping Pakistan to build a giant irrigation and flood control system.

East Pakistan, with its jungles and an alluvial plain which includes nearly 80 per cent of the province, borders India, Burma, and the Bay of Bengal. Here the climate is just the opposite from West Pakistan. Rainfall ranges from 50 inches

3

a year in the western areas to more than 200 inches in Sylhet district. But as in West Pakistan, rainfall is uneven—as much as 70 per cent of the rain falls in the monsoon months between June and September, creating violent floods on the deltaic plains along the Brahmaputra and Ganges rivers.

Neither province differs significantly from the lands on the other side of its borders. Only rarely do rivers or mountains form natural boundaries between Pakistan and its neighbors.

The name, Pakistan, was suggested by a student, Rahmat Ali, in 1931. The first syllable, *pak,* is the Persian word for "pure." *Stan* means "land." In addition, "P" stands for the former province of (P)unjab, "A" for the (A)fghan area of the northwestern frontier dominated by Pathan tribes, "K" for (K)ashmir, the mountainous land of Muslims ruled by India, "S" for the former (S)ind province and "TAN" for Baluchis(TAN). Bengalis, however, are quick to point out that this description omits more than one-half of the country's population.

Most Pakistanis are farmers and live where water is most accessible. In West Pakistan, all but a scattered few live in the area irrigated by the Indus River and its tributaries which flow 1,000 miles, from the Himalayas in the north to the Arabian Sea in the south. East Pakistan is both blessed and cursed by the abundant waters of the Brahmaputra and Ganges rivers which also rise in the Himalayas and flow together in the center of the province to empty into the Bay of Bengal. Like the Indus, they give and they take away—a source of life, but in rampant flood, also a source of death for the millions who live along their banks.

Fewer than 15,000,000 Pakistanis—about 15 per cent—live in urban areas larger than 5,000 population. In East Pakistan, fewer than 6 per cent live in cities. Yet these relatively few produce the political leaders, government officials, scientists, teachers, doctors and other trained personnel who steer the

society. The city dwellers most enjoy the benefits of progress —education, public health and material prosperity.

Like villagers everywhere else in the world, rural Pakistanis are as warm and hospitable to know as they are parochial and conservative in their ways. The changes that have taken place in Asia over the past centuries have largely passed them by, leaving them illiterate and poor, ill-clothed, ill-housed and in ill health. Fewer than 15 per cent can read or write. Their average annual income is estimated at less than $70 a year. Malnutrition is common. Few villagers receive as much as 2,000 calories a day.

A villager's family, which includes numerous relatives beyond his wife and children, is vitally important to him and plays a far greater role in life than families in more urban societies. Indeed, the world of the rural Pakistani is his family and his tribe or village. He is affected chiefly by events that take place within a day's journey from his home. The laws that rule him are mainly the traditions of his immediate society, not those that come to him from the city. To the exasperation of the westernized and educated "man with a plan," who indeed is now very active in Pakistan, change seems to creep into the lives of most rural Pakistanis with the speed of a somnambulant camel.

Encouraging change, yet controlling it, is one of the aims of Pakistan's leaders. Like their counterparts in other relatively new countries, they seek to develop their society rapidly, yet peacefully. "Development" is a popular word. Since 1947, many have worked diligently and successfully towards Pakistan's advancement through programs to improve agriculture, raise the quality of education and welfare services, improve nutrition and health, promote investment in industry and strengthen government administration. Advancement, however, has not been uniform; some areas have progressed

5

faster than others, a reflection usually of how willing the people are to change their ways of doing things.

Pakistan is a land of great variety. Just as there are sandy deserts and steaming jungles, wide plains and soaring mountains, so, too, are the people varied in speech, looks and behavior. It is remarkable that they could be joined together in one nation. Linguists have counted thirty-two different languages. Anthropologists have found five major religions and many sects and cults. There are Sindis and Baluchis, Pathans and Punjabis, Brahuis and Chitralis, Bengalis and Kashmiris. Most are Muslim, but others are Christian, Hindu, Buddhist and Zoroastrian. Not all of them give the nation of Pakistan their first loyalty. Although unity is the aim of their leaders, diversity is a fountainhead of strength as well as a source of many problems. To know something of each major group of people in Pakistan, whether it is distinguished by language, religion, or origin, is to know something about the country's dynamics.

The Bengalis

Most Pakistanis are Bengalis, inhabitants of East Pakistan. They are acutely aware that they constitute slightly more than half the population of the country. Long before there was any thought of Pakistan in the subcontinent, Bengalis had established a national awareness. Their ethnic sensitivity creates the foremost internal political problem in Pakistan.

Twenty-four out of every twenty-five Bengalis dwell in villages and rural homesteads, tied to the land by tradition, following ancient patterns of living. In arable areas their population density exceeds 1,500 people per square mile. For East Pakistan as a whole, the density is 922 per square mile, higher than the density of Japan. To exacerbate an already serious problem, many villagers are migrating to East Pakistan's few

6

cities, swelling the ranks of the unemployed and bloating the slums.

Bengalis are often called a "riverine" people because of the extensive river system in East Pakistan. The climate is so wet during the summer monsoons that urban Bengalis are seldom without umbrellas. Soaked by rains and swollen rivers, the land can grow abundant crops of rice, tea and jute, the fiber from which burlap is made. Homes are built of bamboo and often are so isolated by water that the boat is to a Bengali what a donkey is to a Punjabi. Boiled rice is the food staple; fish and meat are luxuries.

To their advantage, most East Pakistanis speak the same language—Bengali, an Indo-Iranian tongue of which the intellectuals are exceedingly proud. For centuries it was the language of India's most gifted poets and, despite its distinct dialects, it is a potent political symbol. Its written form derives from a fifth century script. Sharing with Urdu the designation as an official language of the country, Bengali is also spoken by some 25,000,000 people outside East Pakistan across the border in India.

Not all Bengalis are Muslims. There are also 10,000,000 caste Hindus and "untouchables," termed "Scheduled Castes." Many are landowners, proprietors of textile mills, bankers and merchants. Most "untouchables" share the extreme poverty of Muslim Bengalis. Violent antagonism between the communities—called communalism—which is based primarily on religious sensitivities, sometimes causes great concern in Pakistan and India.

One ethnic variation among East Pakistanis is the quarter of a million tribesmen who live in the Chittagong Hill Tracts along the Burmese border. Here among the forested hills live twelve different tribal groups completely unrelated racially or linguistically to the average Bengali. Primarily Buddhist, but including some Muslims, Hindus and Christians, they

7

follow a sedentary life as cultivators, usually of tea. Hunting is popular, but for food, not for the sport of shooting the famous Bengal tigers which still inhabit the forests. They speak variations of the Tibeto-Burman languages and have more Mongoloid features than their fellow Bengalis.

When compared as a group to West Pakistanis, Bengalis are more literate, and have a greater degree of political sophistication. Without broad traditions of a landed Muslim aristocracy, they have experience in democratic processes, although not in administration. But they are also among the poorest Pakistanis. Famine and epidemic, often the result of floods and cyclones, are frequent visitors in East Pakistan. In the crowded homesteads, villages, and towns, malaria saps the strength of the workers who, when healthy, have trouble enough providing for their usually large—and always expanding—families. While the jute grown by the farmers earns most of Pakistan's foreign exchange, they receive little for it. Their overall advancement has been slow, although there have been gains in some areas. For instance, near Comilla, home of East Pakistan's Academy for Rural Development, experiments in creating rural cooperatives and introducing modern farming techniques have been quite successful. So, too, has the work of the Water and Power Development Authority in creating projects for controlling floods, providing irrigation and generating power.

The major Bengali city in East Pakistan is Dacca, its capital and seat of the Pakistan National Assembly. It is an old and crowded city of more than half a million people located 150 miles east of Calcutta. In centuries past, Dacca was the capital of several Bengali empires. In the recent past, Dacca was only one of many small towns in this densely populated land, living on the income from jute, fruit, and rice shipped by river barge to its wharves. Nearly all industry was in Calcutta, which remained in India after 1947. Today, Dacca is

an administrative and intellectual hub with dozens of new government offices and a fast-developing university. Nearby, new jute mills provide employment. To the south, Chittagong and Chalna are thriving commercial ports. In other parts of the province Rajshahi, Bogra, Rangpur, Sylhet, Mymensingh and Comilla are developing centers of trade, education and industry. All will soon be linked by commercial helicopter service.

The Punjabis

The Punjab—"land of five rivers"—is the home of Pakistan's second largest group, the largest in West Pakistan. Not only are Punjabis more numerous—26,000,000 against a combined total of 16,000,000 in all other West Pakistani groups—but from the Punjab come most of West Pakistan's intellectual and political leaders. To the dismay of other West Pakistanis, particularly the Pathans, the Punjabis have usually controlled the provincial government from their capital of Lahore.

Before partition, the Punjab was a large province in northwestern India. While most people spoke a dialect of Punjabi, an Indo-Iranian language akin to Urdu, they were far from being united. Many were Muslims, especially in the west, while others were Sikhs, Hindus and Christians, each having distinctive traditions and beliefs. Nearly all were farmers who tilled the soil made fertile by the Ravi, Sutlej, Jhelum, Chenab and Beas rivers that flow out of the mountains to meet the Indus.

From India's earliest days, the Punjab was one of the subcontinent's richest sources of food. In the late nineteenth century, the British created there the largest irrigation system the world had ever known.

At the time of partition, the Punjab suffered great stress. West Pakistan's boundary had been drawn through the heart of the province, bisecting irrigation systems, rivers and even

villages. While most Punjabi Muslims lived west of the boundary, many also lived in non-Muslim areas to the east. At the same time, many Hindus and Sikhs lived in western Muslim areas where they were the best farmers and most skillful workers. In a frenzy of fear and anger during 1947, more than 4,500,000 Sikhs and Hindus in the west fled to the east, while approximately 6,500,000 Muslims in the east fled westward. Frequently, as their paths crossed, they fell at each others' throats. In the great cross-migration, the largest in modern times, some 11,000,000 people left their homes to settle on strange lands and to clog city slums.

The resettling of new farmers, mostly unskilled, and the accommodation of refugees in the Punjabi cities of Lahore, Sialkot and Multan were among the monumental tasks facing the new nation. The problems were complicated by continuing antagonisms with India.

Yet Pakistan's Punjabi leaders found an incidental blessing in the tragedy of migration. When people move their homes, they become more susceptible to adopting new ways of living and working. With the aid of technicians from Europe and America, Punjabis have undertaken land reform and village development programs that hold out hope for a better life.

A Punjabi's life is simple, filled with the everyday problems of raising a family, plowing the soil and reaping a harvest of cotton, grain or sugar cane. With his oxen, camel, donkey, or horse, his few sheep and goats, and perhaps a milk cow or buffalo, he earns a living that allows him few luxuries. His thatched-roofed, mud-brick home provides shelter for his animals as well as his wife, children and, if he is getting on in age, his children's children. He lives in a village of several hundred people, all of them of the same religion—usually Islam—and many of them related. To get to town, he must walk, ride on an animal or in a cart, the most common being the two-wheeled *tonga*. He must travel for many hours along

a rutted dirt road. He may be lucky enough to live near a railroad or a main highway, in which case he can, if he can afford it, ride a train or bus.

The greatest of all Punjabi cities is Lahore, a center of commerce, learning and government in northern Pakistan. With its university, newspapers, railroad terminal and romantic history, it is a more significant city to the people of West Pakistan than is Islamabad, Pakistan's new capital-under-construction 150 miles to the northwest. Lahore is an ancient capital on the Ravi River which, since partition, has become modernized with new bazaars, apartment buildings and housing developments.

The Pathans

West of the Punjabis live the Pathans, a tribally-oriented people who are second to none in their spirit of independence. They are sometimes called Paktuns, or Pashtuns, after their Indo-Iranian language, Pashto, which, however, stems from a different branch than Urdu, Bengali, and Sindi. They are the rigidly-Islamic warriors who so intrigued Rudyard Kipling. Blessed for centuries with good, if erratic, leaders, Pathans have made and unmade rulers in Afghanistan and India and, by their very aggressiveness, have become involved in international affairs. The Russians, Germans, and British have competed for Pathan allegiance in days gone by. The governments of Pakistan and Afghanistan seek their loyalty today.

The land of the Pathans is the Suleiman Mountains, a spur of the great Himalayas. Its barren peaks and fertile valleys form a major physical barrier between central Asia and the subcontinent. Across its passes—among them, the Khyber, Tochi and Gomas—invaders have repeatedly fought to gain entrance onto the lush plains of India. Control of the passes and the proud Pathans who inhabit them has been the object

11

of all of India's rulers. Such control remains of vital concern today.

Pathans inhabit both sides of Pakistan's northwestern border with Afghanistan. They number some 11,000,000, half of whom live in Pakistan east of what is called the Durand Line, a boundary drawn on a map by an English colonel and officially accepted by the Afghan king, in 1893. Pakistani Pathans live in two different areas. One, primarily on the plains, is controlled by the West Pakistan government. The other is mostly in the highlands along the Durand Line and is called the Tribal Area, responsibility for which resides in the central government. In most Tribal Area matters, the government defers to the wishes of the tribes. Most Pathans not living in Pakistan live in Afghanistan and include among their leaders the ruling family of King Zahir Shah.

As tribesmen, Pathans extend their loyalty beyond their immediate families to groups of related *kheyls,* family systems that comprise a tribe. Often, members of a tribe are distinguishable from those of another tribe by their dress, dialect, occupation or the area in which they live. Their tribal leader, called *khan* or *malik,* performs a role similar to that of a local governor, but the realm of his responsibility is tribal rather than geographical. Although not elected by secret ballot, the leader derives his authority from the support of his tribal followers. While some leaders acquire their position through family or tribal influence, nearly all of them base their strength on the voluntary support of their people.

The major tribal groups among Pathans are the Khattak, Yusufzai, Mohmand, Mahsud, Shinwari, Afridi, Wazir, Orakzai, Bangash and Ghilzai. The Ghilzai Pathans live primarily in Afghanistan, but, when the borders are open, thousands of them, called *powindahs,* or nomads, cross into Pakistan to graze their animals and seek work.

Pathan tribal society has its own laws, which do not always conform to the formal laws of the Pakistan government. Called *pashtunwali*, they cover both moral and criminal matters. One of the most compelling is *badal*, the law of revenge which leads to innumerable blood feuds among Pathans. *Melmastia*, protection, requires that Pathans provide asylum to anyone seeking haven from an enemy, whoever he might be. By the same token, Pathans have made hospitality to strangers almost a fetish.

According to pashtunwali, a Pathan is a man of courage whose warrior-like acts are greatly admired. In Pathan society the *jirga* interprets pashtunwali. Jirga is an assembly of elders which not only conciliates disputes, but also acts as the political representative body of the tribe.

The power of pashtunwali and the jirga over a particular Pathan is largely based upon how tribally-oriented he is. Among the more isolated Pathans in the Tribal Area, tribal laws and loyalty are strong; they accept the laws of the Pakistan government only incidentally. But to its credit, the government has in the past been remarkably sensitive to Pathan feelings and has permitted these Pathans considerable latitude in self-government. The High Court of West Pakistan is prohibited by the constitution from interfering in tribal affairs and the central government's representatives act more as ambassadors than rulers.

Among the lowland Pathans, those living in the province of West Pakistan who have entered to some degree into the mainstream of national life, tribal ties and traditions are proportionately weaker and the influence of government is stronger. Among all Pathans, however, the rifle is an important symbol of manhood and independence.

Regardless of their country of residence, many Pathans are intensely loyal to their tribe and Pathan way of life. This attitude has led some Pathans, and particularly the ruling

13

family of Afghanistan, to promote the growth of Pathan nationalism. The movement seeks to create an independent Pathan country, to be called Pashtunistan, which would include all of Pakistan's northwestern frontier and much of the former province of Baluchistan. The Pashtunistan movement, which has often exacerbated relations between Pakistan and Afghanistan, has not been successful. One reason is that the divisions between the tribes, their own lack of unity, are more overpowering than the existence of a national consciousness. Many Pathans have pledged their loyalty to Pakistan and have been a source of strength to the new country. They have given Pakistan some of its most dynamic personalities, among them Abdul Ghaffar Khan; his brother, the late Dr. Khan Sahib; and Abdul Qayyum Khan.

The failure of the drive for Pashtunistan and the extensive, though sometimes tenuous, loyalty of Pathans to Pakistan is one of the greatest achievements of Pakistan's successive governments. Beginning with Mohammed Ali Jinnah, who immediately after partition removed "foreign" troops from the tribal areas, each government leader has generally respected the distinctiveness of the Pathans. This respect has been supplemented by considerable government subsidy. With few exceptions, Pathans have been allowed to rule themselves, even to manning thir own frontier militia and to developing their economy and social programs at their own speed and with their own talent. The result is that no other group has advanced in education, health, and general prosperity so rapidly as the Pathans.

Nowhere is their advancement more apparent than in the city of Peshawar. A trading center on the land frontier between Pakistan and Afghanistan, this Pathan city has been prized for centuries as the citadel of the Khyber Pass. It is a growing city of 200,000, with new industry and a flourishing university. The Kabul River, flowing through the Peshawar

14

Valley, provides by its new Warsak Dam an increasingly important source of electric power for factories and water for expanding irrigation systems. Other major Pathan cities are Dera Ismail Khan, Kohat and Bannu.

The Sindis

The Sindis may well be the oldest group in Pakistan. In the heart of their land lies the dusty ruins of Mohenjo Daro, inhabited over 4,000 years ago, although the ties between these ancient people and the Sindis of today are obscure. At any rate there are few Pakistanis so primitive in their ways or so backward in their economic development.

The southern sandy shore of West Pakistan is hundreds of miles wide. On this infertile dry plain known as the Sind Desert, after the Indus River that flows through it, more than 5,000,000 villagers live a bleak and monotonous life. Here where temperatures reach 130° in the shade in summertime and raging sandstorms obliterate the brightest of days, life's most vital problem is control of the water supply, which usually derives from the irrigation systems of the great Indus River or a few wells. Beyond the irrigated reaches, the Sind becomes pure desert, one of the hottest and cruelest in the world.

Once the Sind was a thriving little empire, at least, the portions of it along the Indus River. When an Arab adventurer named Mohammed bin Qasim arrived there in 710 A.D., he found busy towns trading cotton and dyes with the rest of the world. Bin Qasim was among the first to bring Islam to the subcontinent. Later, a dynasty arose under the Talpur Mirs, who ruled the towns until the British conquered the area in 1843, in the course of a war with Afghanistan. Today, crumbling remnants of tombs and monuments attest to the prosperity of the rulers, if not of their subjects.

15

Sindis, who speak a distinctive Indo-Iranian language, are farmers who till lands generally belonging to city-dwelling landlords. Little of the land reform movements in the past decade have reached them. For those who have been "liberated" from landlords, the dry earth still provides only scanty crops of cotton, wheat or sugar cane.

Sindis are a hospitable, but shy people. They usually wear black clothes but brighten their garb with red turbans or sashes. They also paint elaborate and colorful designs on their furniture.

While a few Hindus live in the Sind—before partition they held considerable power there—most Sindis today are Muslims of various sects. They include in their religion a strong belief in folk spirits. Far from major currents in Pakistani life, they know little of Pakistan and even less of the efforts being made by their leaders to help them. A few have established a reputation as brigands.

The cities of Sind, such as Hyderabad, Sukkur and Larkana, live off the land around them as trading centers. And being within the irrigation system of the Indus, their inhabitants are able to grow beautiful gardens which, unfortunately for visitors, they usually surround with high mud walls.

Karachi, the largest city of Pakistan, was once primarily a Sindi city. Formerly a small port on the Arabian Sea involved mainly with exporting Sindi cotton and importing foreign goods for other Sindi cities, Karachi has become the major commercial center of the country, tied to the north by rail. Its population before partition was fewer than half a million. When Mohammed Ali Jinnah selected it as Pakistan's new capital, refugees poured into its quiet streets and government clerks crowded into its few office buildings. Today, it has approximately 2,000,000 people and, while no longer the official capital, it boasts of luxury hotels, elaborate embassies, busy wharves, fishing fleets and many new industries.

16

The Baluchis

To the west, toward Afghanistan and Iran, live the Baluchis, a tribal people who toil a land even less hospitable than that of their Sindi neighbors. No major river flows through Baluchistan, only seasonal creeks. Speaking a language all their own, but with the same Indo-Iranian roots as Pashto, they are divided into tribes that live not only in Pakistan but also in southern Afghanistan and Iran; the Baluchis in Pakistan number some 300,000. A proud people, they have in the recent past shown a belligerent concern for their independence. Amid the barren lowlands or pine-scrub hills, these tribesmen have for unchanging generations herded their flocks of goats and sheep, scratched patches of wheat, tended fruit trees and fought off foreign intruders. In Pakistan, they form one of the least advanced groups in terms of economic development.

Living alongside the Baluchis are some 250,000 Brahuis who speak a language affiliated with the ancient tongues of southern India, not the more recent Indo-Iranian languages of the Baluchis or Pathans. In the past these people led a nomadic life as herdsmen. They are slowly becoming integrated into the more sedentary society of the Baluchis.

Quetta is the center of trade and commerce in Baluchistan. Situated 5,490 feet above sea level, it is a cool haven for those living on the hot desert below. It was to Quetta in the heat of the summer that the British often brought—and many Pakistanis now bring—their families from Karachi. In the surrounding hills, Pakistani and foreign prospectors search for minerals that will hopefully bring prosperity to the area. On the cooler slopes above, farmers cultivate one of the world's major sources of juniper, whose berry provides the oil that gives flavor to gin. Baluchi fruits are superb.

Other Pakistanis

Another distinctive and important group in Pakistan are Christians of mixed English-Indian ancestry. They are often better educated than most Pakistanis because of the influence of foreign missionaries and British administrators. At the time of partition, they were a source of skilled manpower for Pakistan and they remain influential in many industries and in government service. One of their most prominent leaders is the Chief Justice of the Supreme Court of Pakistan, A. R. Cornelius.

One important segment of Pakistan's population is composed of descendants of Persians who fled many years ago from persecution in their homeland because of their minority religion—Zoroastrianism. Called Parsees (after their place of origin, Persia), they number fewer than 15,000. In Karachi, where most of them live, they participate actively in the commerce and industry of the country.

Although not ethnically nor religiously different, another distinctive group within Pakistan's population are the refugees or *muhajireen* who migrated from other parts of the subcontinent after the summer of 1947. While many traveled from West to East Bengal or East to West Punjab, and therefore had much in common with their Bengali or Punjabi brothers, others came from greater distances and brought with them cultural variety. Some of Pakistan's intellectual and political leaders, even some of the very founders of the nation, came from Bombay, Calcutta and New Delhi, possessing academic degrees from the world's greatest universities. Most spoke English well, but nearly all spoke Urdu, an Indo-Iranian language similar to Hindustani, but written from right to left in the Persian script. While the educated muhajireen were few among the total number—an estimated 6,000,000 to 9,000,000—they acquired a place of importance

18

in the early political, economic and social life of the country. Their lack of identification with any of the political areas which comprised Pakistan after 1947 permitted them to assume roles of mediators in the rivalries that emerged as Pakistan began its new life.

Essentially, then, the development of Pakistan is the process of welding together these individuals—from family, tribe, ethnic, and religious group—into a single force working toward collective betterment. While religion was the magnet which brought them together, Pakistanis have found that the differences among them run deep and unity has been difficult to achieve.

In 1947, many Europeans and Americans who were sympathetic to the Indian independence movement proclaimed loudly that the partitioning of the vast subcontinent with its great variety of people would never work. The skeptics failed to understand the depth of religious feeling among South Asian Muslims. Pakistan's leaders went doggedly forward to create a South Asian nation which Muslims could call their own.

2. The Forces of Religion

No single element in the lives of Pakistanis plays a more pervasive role than religion. It affects the way they work, their adjustment to hardship, the course of their government. Religion helps determine what they eat, whom they marry, what they learn in school and how they develop their society. For millions, religion is the very reason they are Pakistanis at all, rather than Indians.

Religion was responsible for the creation of Pakistan and contributed greatly to its success in remaining independent and united. Economics played a part as did the personal ambitions of some politicians. But religion lay at the heart of the Pakistan movement in the years before 1947, creating the drive and longing necessary to tear apart the popular dreams of a united Indian subcontinent.

The influence of religion might have been less had circumstances been different in the years between 1900 and 1947. Mahatma Gandhi and other Indian leaders, many of them Muslims, who sought independence from the British, were emphatic that Muslims and Hindus could live under one government. However, among the millions of farmers and urban workers religion was not a sometime thing. It closely affected their lives and proved grist for the mills of politicians. During the subcontinent's struggle for independence, the harmony that often existed between religious groups withered away. Differences loomed so large that they overpowered brotherly love, which both religions preached.

20

Religion was effective in creating Pakistan in two ways—one negative, the other positive. On the one hand, Muslims came to fear domination by Hindus. "Islam in Danger!" became a widening cry. On the other hand, many educated Muslims sought Pakistan in order to develop their community into what they believed a true Islamic society should be. "Pakistan an Islamic State!" also gained appeal.

The apprehension of subcontinent Muslims was based on both theological and socio-economic grounds. Among villagers religion was an emotional subject. Religious laws were to be strictly followed or at least followed as defined by the religious leaders of the villages. Threats or rumor of threats to Islam could touch sparks of anger among Muslims. Among Hindus, Muslims were always suspected of plotting to violate their Hindu mores. Each came to mistrust the other.

Among India's more educated, urban groups, religion's role was expressed more in terms of social and economic behavior than in the Muslim mosque or Hindu temple. Muslim families befriended other Muslim families. Social clubs catered to either group, seldom both. Economically, Muslims found it difficult to advance in certain kinds of business—the textile industry, banking, finance, and above all, government service. As independence drew near, Hindus felt confident of their future role as leaders of the majority. Muslims were apprehensive.

Religion thus produced the high-pitched enthusiasm which carried Pakistan into existence and kept it going when the world believed it would soon collapse. It was a bulwark to sustain a burdened people, many bereft of their homes and facing extreme poverty in the wake of floods and droughts. For all their diverse languages and cultures, Pakistan's Muslims shared a common creed that cemented them in common action.

21

Islam

Along with Judaism and Christianity, Islam is one of the great monotheistic religions of the world, having more than 400,000,000 adherents. Distinct from Judaism and Christianity, it nevertheless has many common beliefs which Muslims ascribe to the same single God and the same prophets, with the addition of Mohammed. Indeed, Muslims group themselves with Jews and Christians as "People of the Book," those whose beliefs are said to follow the revealed word of God and are recorded in testaments. The Muslim "bible" is the Koran.

Islam was formally established in 622 A.D. when an Arab merchant named Mohammed ibn Abdullah, after several years of declaring that he had received divine revelations, fled from his home city of Mecca to temporary haven in Medina. These messages were later compiled in the Koran. This book provides the basis of Islam, a word meaning "submission" (to the will of God). Followers of Mohammed also recorded his way of life, his deeds and ideas, which are called the *sunnah,* or Traditions. The sunnah is expounded in a vast collection of short narratives called the *hadith,* which supplement the Koran in providing guidance to Muslims.

To the many-sected Christians, and Jews and pagans of Arabia in Mohammed's day, his simple messages, coupled with political events, had considerable appeal. Mohammed's following grew and within a few years, thousands had affirmed their belief in the new religion. Supported by militant tribesmen seeking new lands, Muslim Arabs quickly extended their influence beyond the Arabian peninsula. They soon ruled from central Asia to Spain. Today, they live in many lands from the Philippines to West Africa. Pakistan is second to Indonesia as the largest Muslim nation—85,000,000, or 88 per cent of the population.

The actual tenets of Islam are few, although interpretation

22

is endless. Muslims believe that there is only one indivisible God who is immutable and omnipotent, vengeful yet compassionate. Mohammed was an ordinary mortal through whom God (Allah) presented to erring man the scriptures through which he could gain immortality in Paradise. Orthodox Muslims believe that while God had previously revealed "the way," the scriptures as revealed through Mohammed are the truest of all—and the last. Indeed, to be a Muslim a person need only say—and believe—the *shahadah,* the profession of faith:

"There is no God but God, Mohammed is the Apostle (or Messenger) of God."

Islam proclaims the doctrine of the Last Judgment, Grace, the existence of Angels and the Devil, and the truths of prophets, the most important of whom, next to Mohammed, are Adam, Noah, Abraham, Moses and Jesus. Muslims accept the Virgin Birth and the Immaculate Conception of Jesus, but not the concept of Christ's divinity.

Islam encourages its believers to have a sense of membership in a vast community of Muslims, all equal in the eyes of God. In the mosque everyone prays together; in the courts, all receive equal justice. No man has more religious authority than another. Each is free to develop his own character. Many orthodox Muslims go farther and believe that the community of Muslims is divinely inspired and that all actions within it are determined by the laws of Islam—called *shari'a.* All aspects of community life are as much a part of religion as praying in a mosque. The community is a religious community seven days a week and the Koran provides instructions for proper living. Some are personal laws, others apply to the community as a whole. Through Mohammed, God provided directions for business, for relations between man and wife, for government and for worship. To suggest that a court of

23

law can be non-religious in theory is to suggest that a mosque is a secular institution.

Upon this sense of brotherhood and Islamic interpretation, Muslims in pre-partition India were able to develop and justify the existence of "a second nation" within the country. Among the leaders of Pakistan, many educated in secular British universities and trained in English law, the problem of reconciling classical Muslim philosophy with twentieth-century liberalism in government has been one of major proportions. As of 1964, the influence of modern secularism has been greater in Pakistan's government than Islamic orthodoxy.

To most Pakistani Muslims, however, religious practices and the demonstration of faith are of more concern than theological doctrine. These practices are described in the Koran and, with some minor variations, are consistent throughout the Muslim world.

The most common—and important—duties of a Muslim are those called "the five pillars of the faith." The first requires recitation of the shahadah, followed by prayer, fasting, almsgiving and a *hadj* (pilgrimage) to Mecca, the holiest of cities for orthdox Muslims.

A devout Muslim prays five times daily, always facing Mecca, with each prayer performed in a prescribed way from various standing, bowing, kneeling and prostrate positions. It is a simple, quiet, unaccompanied ceremony, the only sound often being the muffled chant of the *imam* who leads the prayers. Following prayers on Friday, the holy day of the week, a religious leader will usually preach a sermon. Most prayers are verses from the Koran, spoken in Arabic which many Pakistanis do not understand. It is preferable for Muslims to pray in congregation to emphasize the community nature of the religion.

Muslims fast during the month of Ramazan (or Ramadan), the ninth month in the Muslim calendar which, being based

24

on lunar months of less than thirty days, comes at varying seasons of the year. The fasting period is from sunrise to sunset during which neither food nor drink may enter the faster's mouth. During hot days, when Ramazan occurs in the summer, tempers tend to grow short among the fasters. In some countries, especially Tunisia and Turkey, political leaders have supported moderation in the fast because of the decreased efficiency of the population. But in Pakistan, nearly all Muslims observe the fast.

The Koran requires each Muslim to show charity. *Zakat*— giving away part of one's possessions each year—has in the past been a religious substitute in Muslim countries for the income tax, and in Pakistan some leaders still advocate it as a basis for the country's fiscal system. When he gives zakat, the remainder of a man's possessions become *pak* or purified.

Not everyone is expected to make the hadj to Mecca, but the person who does acquires Grace as well as prestige. He is entitled to prefix his name with "hadji." It is not unusual for a Pakistani to dye his hair and beard red following a hadj.

There are other practices in Islam which play or have played in recent years, an important role in a Pakistani Muslim's life. Among these is *jihad,* meaning "exertion," which has been understood at times to mean holy war against nonbelievers. Many Muslims called for jihad against India to free the state of Kashmir from Indian control. The most frequent use today of jihad is to demonstrate a continuing effort to propagate the faith.

The dietary practices of Muslims are a combination of tradition and Koranic law. Pork is shunned and the Koran several times mentions the evils of drinking alcohol.

The Koran prohibits *riba,* or usury, the taking of interest on money loans. This injunction has been a problem to Muslim society in the modern business world, and in pre-partition

25

India, most of the moneylending was handled by Hindus and, in urban areas, foreigners. Although Muslims have been moneylenders, particularly the Pathans, most have been so away from their home districts. When Pakistan came into existence, few Muslims were trained in banking. While Pakistan's constitution calls for the elimination of riba, few Pakistanis know just how this can be done.

What the Jews and Christians consider God's commandment to Moses regarding monotheism and idolatry applies equally for Muslims. Many orthodox Muslims believe that representation of humans in any way, such as in statues or paintings, violates this injunction. They are especially sensitive when paintings or films depict Mohammed.

Throughout their history, Muslim artists have generally confined their skills to design and they adorn buildings and religious paraphernalia with elaborate Arabic and Persian script. Artists who paint the human figure—and many do in Pakistan as a result of Persian and Moghul influence—must go against orthodox tradition.

Islam has developed rules in regard to women which reflect the traditional view of their responsibilities within the family. While theoretically equal to men, they play a subordinate role which limits their opportunities to participate in modern society outside the home.

Initially, Islam was a boon to women. Before Mohammed, polygamy was uncontrolled, wives had no inheritance rights nor protection from divorce. Islam limited a husband to four wives provided he could treat them equally, gave daughters half the inheritance rights of sons, and required husbands to divorce their wives in front of a witness. In Pakistan today, polygamy is diminishing, women have increasing inheritance rights and wives have more protection in divorce, but the changes in recent years have benefited relatively few.

26

The practice of *purdah*, the seclusion of women, is widespread in Pakistan. To a great extent, it is a cultural manifestation, not religious, although the Koran prescribes modesty. Veiling of women is commonplace and it is a usual sight to see women walking the streets draped from head to toe in a white or black tent-like *burqa*, looking much like a large inverted badminton shuttlecock. Many of these women will go through life without ever showing their faces to anyone outside their family. Village women do not veil themselves so much as city women and poorer women veil themselves less than the wealthy.

While Muslims of all societies accept certain basic dogma of Islam and share a common belief, the degree to which any Muslim observes the letter of orthodox theology depends upon many circumstances and to this extent, there is little difference between Muslims and non-Muslims throughout the world. "Unorthodox" practices abound in Pakistan, particularly among illiterate Muslims who have lived intimately among Hindus, as in Sind and East Pakistan. To those who believe them, these adulterations are as much "religion" as the written word of the Koran. Some of the unorthodoxies among Pakistani Muslims also derive from the Hinduism of their converted forebears.

A folk belief prevalent in Pakistan—and not uncommon elsewhere—is the existence of an "evil eye" which, when focused on an individual, can bring harm. This "eye" may be any place, but it is often associated with strangers, especially if they are carrying cameras. To ward off the effects of the "evil eye," charms of all sorts are available. It is common to see donkeys, camels and even automobiles and trucks decorated with blue pendants to protect the owner's means of transportation. Infants wear amulets, frequently containing words from the Koran, around their necks to assure safe passage through childhood.

27

Muslim Leadership

Islam is essentially an equalitarian religion in which all members of the faith are equal in rights, privileges and authority. It has no organized church and no formal hierarchy of priests. Because each Muslim is responsible individually to God, Islam does not provide for either saints or earthly representatives. Yet the worship of Muslim saints flourishes in Pakistan.

Certain individuals in Muslim society do exert varying degrees of religious leadership. They acquire this through study and knowledge of Islam or through experience in religious matters. In some countries, such as Afghanistan, they are appointed by the government. In villages, some men ordain themselves as religious leaders and obtain acknowledgement from villagers through their piety. Frequently, a man (rarely a woman) acquires religious authority by inheritance, following his father's footsteps.

The most common religious leader in Pakistan is the *mullah*. He may have a small following, as in a village, or a large following in a city. Generally, he is associated with a particular mosque in which he preaches and otherwise ministers to his flock, assisting in births, weddings, funerals and other celebrations in which a religious connotation is desired. Mullahs usually need another job in order to live.

A Pakistani who is quite learned in religion acquires the title of *maulana* or *maulvi*. Scholars and judges of Islamic law, they form a *ulema* to consider religious questions. The ulema, with its collective learning and experience, has come to speak for the community on religious—and sometimes secular—affairs. A conservative group, it has acted as a brake on Pakistan's social and political reformers.

Two functional titles common in Pakistan are *imam* and *muezzin*. The imam, as used here, is the individual who pre-

28

sides over prayers in the mosque. He may be anyone of the congregation, but more often he is the local mullah or, if the ceremony is important, a visiting maulana or maulvi. He is usually paid by his congregation or by income from property owned by the mosque which has been given to it by a benefactor. The muezzin is another paid employee of the mosque who calls the faithful to prayer five times a day from one of the minarets of the mosque. A *khatib,* another functionary, is a man who reads—or more accurately, chants—from the Koran in the mosque.

Another group of religious figures in Pakistan are the *pirs,* unorthodox Muslims who acquire a close personal following among villagers and tribesmen. On his death, a pir is often revered as a saint and his tomb becomes an attraction to pilgrims. A pir need not have formal religious training, but he displays great devotion and knowledge of mystical experiences which he shares with his followers. Most pirs perform nothing other than religious duties, for which their followers reward them. Bengalis tend to ascribe superhuman powers to most of their historical warriors, called *ghazi,* and use the terms pir and ghazi interchangeably.

A particularly effective and personal mullah can be venerated as a pir upon his death. A lower-grade pir with less religious endowment is sometimes called a *fakir.* Other terms for pirs are *ghau* and *wali.*

In recent times, it is not uncommon for a pir or fakir with a large following to engage in politics. One such was the late Fakir of Ipi, a Pathan who was active in starting the Pashtunistan movement. Another was the Pir of Manki Sherif who encouraged Pathans to support Pakistan in 1947. Pirship may be inherited as well as earned, a practice common in the former Sind province where, among many pirs, the Pir Pigaro of the Hurs is the most famous. To many, he is a living saint.

Other Muslims may acquire respect and influence by being descended from Mohammed. They prefix their names with *sayyid*.

Muslim Sects

As in other religions, Islam has schisms. Some are small in the total picture; others are important and vitally affect life in Pakistan. Most divisions began in politics.

Mohammed had been dead only a few years before quarrels erupted over who was to succeed him as leader of the faithful. Some said that the caliph, or successor, should be selected by Mohammed's tribe, the Qureysh, and then approved by the entire community. This group predominated and have come to be known as Sunnites, those who follow the sunnah, the traditions of the Prophet.

Others felt that leadership was hereditary and that only Ali, Mohammed's cousin and son-in-law, was the true caliph. Those who supported this position were called "partisans of Ali" or Shi'at Ali, later simply called Shi'ites.

Three-fourths of the world's Muslims today are Sunnites. In Pakistan, they comprise more than 90 per cent of the Muslim community and are usually considered the "orthodox" Muslims, although within the community there are all kinds of religious opinion ranging from conservative to liberal. Shi'ites, themselves divided, comprise most of the rest, but not all.

The existence of a large religious minority Muslim group has not made unification of Pakistan any simpler. Shi'ites, although observing many of the same tenets and practices as Sunnites, reject the orthodox sunnah, have different traditions and ceremonies and feel themselves a distinct group. They have more than once felt the ire of Sunnites because of their differences.

Shi'ites, who are a large majority of Iran's population, be-

lieve that Ali was the true successor to Mohammed. Most Pakistani Shi'ites also believe Ali was the first of twelve succeeding Imams, spiritual leaders considered to have divine authority. The twelfth Imam disappeared as a young man and the faithful believe he will return as a *mahdi,* or messiah. Most Shi'ites are also called "Twelvers" to distinguish them from others who do not recognize all twelve Imams.

Shi'ism is a more passionate expression of Islam than is orthodox Sunnism. Some scholars say this results from the quantity of martyrs within the history of the sect, which in the past has suffered the discrimination of any religious minority. Foremost among their martyrs was Hussein, Ali's son, who was killed in 680 at Karbala (in present-day Iraq) by the troops of the Sunni caliph, Yazid.

Another Muslim minority is also Shi'ite, but its followers disagree over the identity of the seventh Imam. Called "Seveners," they are also known as Ismailis. They have recognized a succession of Imams down through history, and today the Imam is known to the world as the Aga Khan. The Ismailis of Pakistan—as in other countries—are well organized and relatively more educated and prosperous. They are adept at caring for their own people, seeing that schools are available for Ismaili children and that welfare institutions minister to the community's poor.

While a minority religion, Shi'ism has given Pakistan many of its leaders, although they have not been identified very strongly with religion. Among them are Pakistan's founder, Mohammed Ali Jinnah, former President Iskander Mirza and a former Prime Minister, the late Ismail I. Chundrigar.

The Ahmadiyas are a third Muslim minority and the subject of considerable controversy. They number about 200,000, but weigh more in terms of influence. Founded in 1901 by Mirza Ghulam Ahmad (1835–1908), a wealthy Muslim from the village of Qadian in the Punjab, Ahmadiyism is an at-

tempt to "purify" existing beliefs and practices. Ahmad claimed to have had revelations and declared himself a prophet, although some of his followers did not accept his prophethood, which they felt was contrary to the teachings of Islam.

Ahmadiyas have revived a missionary spirit among Muslims and their proselytizing has spread into Africa and Asia where they preach orthodox Islam with a touch of mysticism, ascetism and modern liberalism. In Pakistan they, like the Ismailis, have become a close-knit community with their own schools and welfare institutions. Better educated than most groups, they have acquired positions of importance in the government, a circumstance that fed the fires of riot in Pakistan's early days. One of their prominent leaders is Mohammed Zafrulla Khan, a former foreign minister, ambassador, and, in 1964, a justice of the International Court of Justice.

Through all Muslim groups in Pakistan, regardless of sect, there runs a thread of mysticism that lends a warm, and often poetic element to what is otherwise a fairly unemotional religion. Called *sufism,* it is an inspirational approach to knowledge of God and is widespread in Iraq and Iran. Those influenced by sufism feel that the individual is able to reach a personal communion with God through meditation, physical exertion in a frantic sort of way (for example, in what Westerners call "whirling dervishes"), pious asceticism, recitation of poetry, or chanting of music.

Religious fraternities have grown up in the Muslim world that have usually developed from the leadership of a particularly saintly sufi. Each order has its own litany and ceremony designed to assist the communicant to reach a mystical state. In Pakistan, the four major fraternities are called Chishtiya, Suhrawardia, Qadiriya and Naaqshbandiya. Some scholars estimate that more than half of Pakistan's Muslims, especially in East Pakistan, are influenced to some degree by

sufism. Most of Pakistan's pirs are sufi, while many outstanding poets and musicians have attributed their inspiration to sufism.

Over the centuries, Sunni scholars have tried to codify the laws of the Koran and sunnah. Four major schools of law exist today, each named after its founder: The Hanafite, Hanbalite, Shafi'ite and Malekite. They are all agreed that the four principle sources of law are the Koran, the sunnah, the consensus of the community (*ijma*) and analytical deduction of the intent of the principle sources. They differ only in the degree of emphasis given to each course. In Pakistan, the Hanafite school predominates. Founded in the eighth century by Abu Hanafah, it places major emphasis on deduction of intent rather than on the literal instructions of the primary sources. Consequently, the development of shari'a law in the subcontinent has been accompanied by considerable debate over what is and is not proper Muslim behavior.

In the first ten years of Pakistan's existence, lives were lost and blood was spilled in the streets of Lahore and Karachi in the dramatic search for an "Islamic constitution." To conservative Sunnites, their shari'a was the only law and those who did not accept it were heretics. In the resulting short-lived constitution of 1956, Pakistan was declared an "Islamic Republic" based on the Koran and orthodox sunnah.

In promulgating a new constitution in 1962, President Ayub dropped the "Islamic" designation of the republic and tried to avoid making decisions in regard to shari'a. The constitution did not mention the sunnah at all, instead calling the "way" of Islam the "Islamiat." But the religious forces were too great and in the first amendment to the constitution, passed by the parliament—and approved by the President— in December, 1963, Pakistan once again became an "Islamic Republic."

According to the 1962 constitution, Pakistan is a "demo-

33

cratic state based on Islamic principles of social justice." These are generalized as follows: All citizens are equal before the law and may freely express their opinions, associate peacefully, move about the country, acquire property, follow any vocation and practice any religion. They may not engage in slavery or forced labor.

Certain other features of the constitution reflect shari'a. The head of the state must be a Muslim and religious instruction should be compulsory for Muslim children. Riba, usury, should be eliminated and the use of alcoholic beverages discouraged. Above all, no law should be passed that is "repugnant to Islam."

To guide Pakistan's government on Islamic affairs, the constitution establishes an Advisory Council on Islamic Theology consisting of leading theologians and lawyers appointed by the President. It is this council which is intended to suggest how Muslims may live in accordance with Islamic concepts and to decide which laws passed by the National Assembly violate Muslim principles.

The constitution also recognizes the Islamic Research Institute, an organization established by prominent Islamic scholars to study problems of constructing a Muslim society.

The formalities of the constitution in regard to Islam primarily concern the lawyers, students of religion and mullahs. They have little effect upon the lives of Pakistan's ordinary Muslim citizens, who follow the rules of custom and tradition as developed within a Muslim society.

Ceremonies

Muslim ceremonies are important in Pakistan. They occui in accordance with the twelve-month Muslim calendar which is based on the cycles of the moon. While Pakistan's official calendar is Gregorian, as in the West, villagers and religious celebrants live by the Muslim calendar.

34

In their frequency, Muslim ceremonies demonstrate the proximity of religion in everyday life of Pakistanis. In the intensity with which they are observed, they demonstrate the depth of religion in the ordinary person. Among them all, Pakistanis enjoy the ceremonies as the only recesses in what is normally a colorless, monotonous life.

For most, the observance of Ramazan, the holy month of fasting, is the major "ceremony" of the year, although many city Muslims observe the fast more through token abstinence. Two weeks before Ramazan, villagers celebrate the Shab-i-Barat, during which God is supposed to fix the destinies of all for the coming year.

The most joyous holiday is Id-ul-Fitr, the end of Ramazan. On this day, new clothing appears on even the poorest backs, friends exchange gifts and food is served in amounts far in excess of what the host can afford. It is a day when friends embrace and dance in the streets. At noon, nearly everyone goes to the mosque for a ceremonial prayer.

Perhaps the most important ceremony in the religious sense is the observance of Id-ul-Zuah, also called Bakr-al-Id, which celebrates Abraham's willingness to sacrifice his son, Isaac. Those who can afford it sacrifice an animal, usually a goat or a calf, by cutting its throat. One-third of the animal goes to charity; the rest is prepared for the year's major banquet. Id-ul-Zuah takes place on the tenth day of Zulhijjah, the twelfth month.

Id-i-Milad celebrates the birth of the Prophet Mohammed and occurs on the twelfth day of Rabi al-Awwal, the third month. The day is marked with special prayers and a feast.

The first day of the year, the first of Muharrum, is celebrated by all Muslims, usually with a feast and a vacation. For Shi'ites, it marks the beginning of ten days of mourning over the martyrdom of Hussein and his brother, Hassan. The Sunni caliph, Yazid, is hanged in effigy. The ceremony ends

35

with a procession of mourners who dance with increasing frenzy, often drawing blood from their bodies with swords brandished in symbolic gestures. Feeling between Sunnites and Shi'ites is frequently tense and rioting is not uncommon. In 1963, more than 100 people were killed in Muharrum riots.

Hinduism

There are an estimated 10,500,000 Hindus in Pakistan, most of whom are called caste Hindus, although many are "untouchables," designated as Scheduled Castes. About 95 per cent of them live in East Pakistan. The rest live mainly in Sind and Kalat, where one Hindu group numbers 18,000. To the extent that Hinduism allows generalizations, East Pakistani Hindus follow the same religion as Indian Hindus, particularly those living in West Bengal.

To Hindus, the Sanskrit equivalent of the word "religion" is *dharma,* meaning "duty" or "law." Simultaneously, it is a theology, a philosophy, a way of life. It exerts far more influence over the daily lives of ordinary Hindus than Islam over most Muslims or Christianity over most Christians.

Unlike Islam or Christianity, Hinduism has no single source of theology. It has no fixed creed or dogma. In fact, scholars say that Hinduism is composed of as many religions as there are people professing Hinduism. It has no founder, as in Islam or Christianity, and its beginnings are lost in time.

Hinduism developed after central Asian tribes, today called Aryans, settled in the subcontinent over 2,000 years before Christ. They left written records, called the *Vedas,* which show how ancient Aryan cults incorporated indigenous beliefs. As time passed, other literature, much of it mythological and symbolic, added to the content of the religion. The *Upanishads,* a collection of philosophical treatises, were written toward the end of the Vedic period (ca. 1400 B.C.). The years to about 800 B.C. form the "Epic Age" during which

Hinduism's great epic poems, the *Ramayana* (The Book of Rama) and the *Mahabharata* (Great India), with its beloved poem, the "Bhagavad-Gita" (Song of God), were produced. A combination of history and legend, like most of the early Greek and Biblical literature, they tell of an ancient kingdom —called Bharata—whose heroes and villains are today part of the family of Hindu gods. Rama, the hero of the *Ramayana* and ruler of Bharata, and Krishna of the *Bhagavad-Gita,* are considered by most Hindus to be *avatars,* incarnations, of Vishnu, one of the Hindu trinity. While there are no beliefs which are essential to Hinduism, most Hindus venerate this literature and take guidance from it. Many pious Hindus pray for the return of the golden age of *Ram Raj,* the Rule of Rama. Pakistani Muslims often derisively called modern India "Bharat."

At a philosophical level, many Hindus recognize God as the only reality. The visible universe is all *maya,* an illusion, a projection of the mind. As there is spirituality, then, in everything, it follows that man has a dual nature; an outer, visible self and a divine soul or inner self, called *atman.* To many Hindus, man's highest aim is *moksha,* the mystical union with God when man becomes aware of true reality, sheds his outer self and is free from mundane existence. Buddhists call this union *nirvana.*

The individual Hindu is free to decide for himself what kind of God he worships and with whom he seeks moksha. Many educated Hindus see God as one Supreme Reality, an impersonal spirit, called *Brahman.* Others view Him as a personal God. Others recognize no god at all. To most Hindus, the villagers, there are many personal gods, each with different realms of responsibility.

The principal gods are the triple manifestation of Brahman, which appears primarily as Brahma, the Creator; Vishnu, the Preserver and Shiva, the Destroyer. Shiva, one of the most re-

vered gods, is also worshipped as the god of asceticism, fertility and death. The lives of the many gods and their multiple personalities are the subjects for most Hindu folk ballads and contribute richly to the color and imagination of Hindu art forms.

Idols abound in Hindu temples and homes, and worshippers make obeisance and sacrifice before them. To the modern intellectual, idols are the symbolic conception of the images of God. Many village Hindus take the idols for the deities themselves. In contrast to Muslim worship which is congregational, Hindus generally worship individually or in family units, a practice which reflects the individual rather than the community emphasis of the religion.

Shaktas and Vaishnavas are prominent Hindu sects in East Pakistan. The former worship Shiva and the goddess, Shakti, who is also personified as Kali and Durga. The latter worship Krishna, the incarnation of Vishnu, and his consort, Radha. Kali is represented as an angry dancer symbolizing the destructive forces of nature and the destroyer of evil. Durga is presented as a multi-armed goddess slaying a buffalo demon with one hand and bestowing blessing, hope, plenty and protection with the others. Among Vaishnavas, the longing of Radha for union with Krishna and the drama of their love-making symbolizes the relation which every believer should have with the Supreme Deity, Vishnu. Around this love affair Bengali poets and singers have created a large body of literature, much of it erotic. Students of Islamic theology also believe that the Hindu tradition of mystical Vaishnavism influenced the development of sufism in Bengal.

There are several ways to achieve moksha, but the most common are those outlined in the philosophy of *yoga*. Union with God may be achieved through knowledge (*jnana yoga*), love and devotion (*bhakti yoga*), physical discipline of one's body (*hatha yoga*), action or deeds (*karma yoga*) and the best,

a combination of the others in their advanced stages propelled by concentrated will (*raja yoga*). The various forms of yoga are major values and ideals of human conduct which guide Hindus.

The stages along the paths to moksha are the repeated lives a person lives in the process of birth and re-birth. Man, according to the theory of reincarnation commonly accepted by Hindus, is reborn to a higher and better existence if he lives his life properly; if he lives improperly, he is re-born into a lower existence. The right-living man will eventually achieve moksha and freedom from this miserable life. What is proper living? Yoga provides the answer to many people. For millions, it means especially *karma,* acting righteously and fulfilling one's dharma as prescribed by the caste system.

One of the most common elements in the Hindu way of life is the division of society into many castes. The more modernized Hindu philosophers see caste as a purely social manifestation growing out of a past in which occupational distinctions developed into higher and lower social orders. For the millions of uneducated Hindus, the rationale of the caste system is the joint doctrine of karma and reincarnation.

The roots of the caste system lie deep in history, dating from the Aryan invasions of the subcontinent. Originally disdainful of the natives, the Aryans did not intermarry nor mix socially with them. Although intermingling occurred eventually, distinctions continued, supported by the divisions of labor. Society was divided into four major groups: the *Brahmins,* or priests and teachers; the *Kshatriyas,* or rulers and warriors; the *Vaisyas,* or tradesmen; and *Sudras,* the farmers and laborers. These divisions—called *varna,* meaning "color" in Sanskrit—became, in time, infinitely sub-divided, hereditary and, within Hinduism, endowed with religious sanctity. They became the castes into which Hindus are born today.

Many village Hindus believe that an infant at birth is

entering his caste either as a reward or penalty for his actions in previous life. He must live, marry and die within his caste and perform the duties ascribed by tradition to members of that caste. Each caste has rules about acceptance of food and water from lower castes, conventions of speech and deportment toward other castes and, above all, shunning the "untouchables." Some Hindus are believed to have led such unrighteous lives that they are at the bottom of the caste hierarchy. Mahatma Gandhi called these "untouchables," so numerous in East Pakistan, *harijan,* "Children of God." It was the existence of so many lower and non-caste Hindus in Bengal centuries ago and the prolonged period of Muslim rule there that permitted Islam, which offered equal opportunity to all the faithful, to gain so many converts in Bengal.

The many areas of variance between Hinduism and Islam helped in the development of Muslim society in the subcontinent and created many of the fears and antagonisms that led to the making of Pakistan. The caste system is the most obvious tradition distinguishing Hinduism from Islam. While Hinduism places an individual in a better or worse relationship to others at birth, Islam decrees equality. While one permits the worshipping of idols, the other abhors it. While Hinduism is what each worshipper generally wishes it to be, Islam is dogmatic in what a Muslim must be. Hinduism is intellectually and religiously tolerant; Islam allows little room for compromise. Most Hindus do not accept a single, revealed source of religion; Muslims are "People of the Book."

On a personal level, many Hindus revere all kinds of life and do not eat meat of any kind; Muslims have fewer restrictions. Hindus accompany their devotions with music and ritual; Muslims worship in comparative quiet. Each of the differences, while not prohibiting close and amicable relationships between Hindus and Muslims, is nevertheless a potential point of intellectual or physical friction.

Ceremonies

The celebrations of Hinduism are colorful, religiously oriented and often excited. The major *puja,* or festival, in East Pakistan is in the autumn and commemorates Durga's slaying of the buffalo demon and her joyous visit to her father's house. One of Durga's daughters is Lakshmi, the goddess of wealth and prosperity. Shortly after the homage to Durga, Hindus celebrate Lakshmi Puja.

A third festival comes twenty days after Durga Puja and is dedicated to Kali. It is a festival of lights when every house is illuminated and men carry torches to the water in remembrance of the dead.

In January, Hindus, especially students, celebrate Saraswati Puja in honor of the goddess of learning. Her image appears in almost all Hindu schools in East Pakistan.

Another festival celebrates the coming of spring and is dedicated to Vishnu, Krishna (sometimes called Narayan) and Radha. Steeped in fertility rites, the festival is called Holi (or Dol Yatra) and is a time of gaiety, when celebrants throw colored water and powder over everyone in sight.

In summer, Bengali Hindus pay homage through fairs and festivals to the Car of Jagannath, the Lord of the World. Its most famous centers are Dhamrai, a village near Dacca, and Comilla.

The Hindus of East Pakistan are represented in political life by the Pakistan National Congress, a surviving remnant of the All-India National Congress of pre-partition days and which now is the leading political party of India. The Scheduled Castes Federation represents the non-caste Hindus. East Pakistani Hindus have special government-supported schools and cultural organizations, foremost of which is the Varendra Research Society and the Rama Krishna Mission, founded by followers of a nineteenth century saint. Among prominent

41

Hindu leaders are Mrs. Neli Sengupta, Dhirendranath Dutta, and Shrischandra Chatterji.

The 1962 constitution of Pakistan states as a "principle of policy" that "steps should be taken to bring on terms of equality with other persons, the members of under-privileged castes, races, tribes and groups. . . ." Hindu leaders express hope that President Ayub will be able to carry out this policy because in 1964 the vast majority of Hindus in Pakistan are among the poorest and least socially advanced of all Pakistanis.

Buddhism

There are approximately 400,000 Buddhists in Pakistan, nearly all of whom live in the vicinity of Chittagong. Many are tribesmen who have intermixed the Buddhist religion with varying degrees of animist cults and folk superstitions.

Buddhism was once the dominant religion of the subcontinent, but its influence waned after the fourth century A.D. It is the major religion in many Asian countries, including Burma and Ceylon.

Buddhism grew out of a protest in the fifth century B.C. by a reformer named Gautama Siddhartha (ca. 563–483 B.C.) who objected to the rigid controls of the Brahmin Hindu priests. Buddha, "The Enlightened One" as his later followers called him, did not criticize the religion itself so much as the way it was practiced.

In his boyhood, Gautama was distressed by the suffering of mankind. He left his princely home, his young wife and baby son to find a solution for overcoming these sufferings. After meditating nine years, he discovered that through renunciation of all desires one could achieve nirvana while still in this life. Transmigration, the travel of the soul from stage to stage (not necessarily through re-birth), can bring a person to the point of identification with the Cosmos. Buddha did not

42

preach any god or gospel, but spoke against artificial ceremonies, rituals and idol worship for one's progress.

Popular Buddhism in Bengal has come to include a galaxy
of gods. The Buddhist shrine is the center of village life. The
most devout Buddhists become monks in the many mona-
steries around Chittagong.

Buddhist festivals generally commemorate different episodes
in Buddha's life. The most important is Baisakhi Purnima, in
late spring, which celebrates the Buddha's birth and his at-
tainment of nirvana. The festival coincides with a great Buddhist fair, held near Chittagong, when Buddhists from all
parts of Pakistan assemble to pay homage to Buddha.

Christianity

Nearly a million Pakistanis are Christians who live in both
provinces, but chiefly in the Punjab. They are about evenly
divided between Roman Catholics and Protestants.

Christianity first came to South Asia with the Apostle St.
Thomas, who is said to have preached in southern India.
Roman Catholicism was permanently established in Goa in
the sixteenth century when the Portuguese founded colonies
there. Other Portuguese missionaries settled in Chittagong,
Dacca, and Karachi. The leading Roman Catholic today is
Valerian Cardinal Gracias, a native of Karachi who lives in
India. Most other Roman Catholic clergy are foreigners.

The first Protestant sects arrived with the British in the
seventeenth century. In Bengal the Baptist Mission, active
since 1801, the Oxford Missions and others have worked successfully among low caste Hindus and among tribal peoples
in Mymensingh and Sylhet districts. In West Pakistan, the
Seventh Day Adventists and Presbyterians are strong. The
Punjab has been particularly important to the American
Presbyterian Mission, established in 1834. Forman Christian
College in Lahore is one of the subcontinent's outstanding

educational institutions, while the Seventh Day Adventist Hospital in Karachi provides one of the few centers in Pakistan for modern American medicine.

Foreign Christian missionaries, whom Pakistanis associate with the Western non-communist world, have been allowed to teach in their own schools and to practice medicine, but periodic waves of Muslim emotion have sometimes curtailed their activities. In May, 1962, more than 200 Muslim students of Forman Christian College demonstrated against alleged interference by college authorities in their religious activities, accusing them of having an anti-Muslim bias. Such demonstrations occur every few years.

Religion and Government

In their constitution, Pakistanis have included a declaration of religious freedom. The constitution states:

"No law should (a) prevent the members of a religious community or denomination from professing, practicing or propagating, or from providing instruction in, their religion, or from conducting institutions for the purpose of or in connection with their religion; (b) require any person to receive religious instruction, or to attend a religious ceremony or religious worship, relating to a religion other than his own; (c) impose on any person a tax the proceeds of which are to be applied for the purpose of a religion other than his own; (d) discriminate between religious institutions in the granting of exemptions or concessions in relation to any tax; or (e) authorize the expenditure of public moneys for the benefit of a particular religious community or denomination except moneys raised for that purpose."

The constitution attacks "untouchability" in any form. It further states that "the legitimate rights and interests of the minorities should be safeguarded, and the members of minor-

ities should be given due opportunity to enter the service of Pakistan."

Religious prejudice does exist in Pakistan, as it does in every country. Discrimination can also be found, particularly against Hindus, perhaps the most economically depressed group in the country. The tensions of partition in 1947 are still alive, whetted periodically by the undulating relations between Pakistan and India, especially over Kashmir. Both India and Pakistan accuse each other of permitting communal riots. In May, 1962, Muslim refugees from West Bengal reported more than 1,000 deaths in Malda. In early 1964, riots occurred in Kashmir over the theft of a religious relic from a Muslim mosque. In East Pakistan, infuriated Muslims attacked and killed many Hindus. In retaliation, Hindus in India began killing Muslims.

Yet the official policies of both India and Pakistan are clearly opposed to religious discrimination. How these policies affect the daily lives of Muslims, Hindus, Buddhists and Christians, however, depends upon the people themselves.

Except among the few educated people, religion in Pakistan is a mixture of folk superstition and formal principles. In the manner of many societies of poor, illiterate villagers, religion is a means of adjustment to nature, which, in their ignorance, they see as largely uncontrollable. Hinduism, Islam, Christianity, and Buddhism in Pakistan reflect the circumstances of a man's life. A poverty-stricken Hindu or Buddhist must find hope for release from his misery—hence, he is prone to believe in reincarnation. In the next life, things will not be so miserable. To a poor Muslim or Christian, release is found in the hope of immortality, in Heaven. While a Muslim may blame fate (*Kizmet*) for a crop-destroying flood, a Hindu will blame the anger of a particular god. Both resist the notion that man himself can change fate or a god's revenge. To the educated government worker, seeking to mobi-

45

lize village initiative in development schemes such as flood control dams, the folk beliefs of both Hindus and Muslims mitigate against him. Man-made change violates the sanctity of nature and threatens the very religion by which the villager explains nature.

The development of Pakistan in achieving political stability and economic well-being depends largely on how its leaders utilize the ethical and moral teachings of religion as a guide to public policy, yet overcome the inertia which religion places so firmly in the path of the country's progress.

3. *The Distant Beginning*

The people of Pakistan came to identify themselves as Pakistanis only shortly before, and in some cases, only after partition in 1947. Yet many can trace their ancestry back hundreds of years while scholars are able to surmise that their cultural and ethnic origins pre-date 2000 B.C. Politically new, Pakistan is culturally very old.

The immediate ancestors of those South Asians who were to become involved in the creation of Pakistan were, with exceptions, settled in their pre-partition homes, adherents of Islam, Hinduism or Sikhism, and speaking their present-day languages by 1858, the year the British government formally established its rule over India. Where these ancestors came from, how they got there and how they acquired their religions and languages is a story not yet completely written. But the bits that can be pieced together indicate that no story could be more colorful, fascinating, or vital to understanding Pakistan.

Only in recent decades have scholars tried systematically to understand the origins of South Asians. With outstanding exceptions, these historians have been Europeans and Americans. South Asian scholars themselves have generally devoted their intellectual energy toward other subjects, particularly politics and philosophy.

To a large extent, the dearth of knowledge of South Asia's past is the fault of that very element which distinguishes the people of the subcontinent—religion. For hundreds of years religion has dominated scholarship in India. The intellectual's

emphasis was upon the development of the spirit, the philosophy of existence. Hindu-oriented history, whose earliest records, the *Vedas,* appeared 3,000 years ago, tells much about the origins of ideas and philosophies; it tells little of the day-to-day development of society. Muslim-oriented history, while more concerned with man's cultural growth and the chronological reign of kings and conquerors, nevertheless begins only in the tenth century. To the ancient Muslim scholar, the years before Islam were periods of darkness and evil and thus unworthy of scholarly attention. Early Muslim schools, *madrassahs* and *maktabs,* were institutions for the study of Islam.

Ancient Civilizations

Modern Pakistani historians like to date the origins of the people from Mohenjo Daro, a city which some 4,000 years ago flourished on the banks of the Indus River as it flowed through the Sind desert. Here, today, amid sun-baked ruins, is evidence of a civilization emerging from the Bronze Age and similar in development to those in ancient Mesopotamia and Egypt. Vessels of copper and bronze, kiln-baked pottery and elaborately-built public baths testify to the existence of an early urban society. In Harappa in the Punjab, similar ruins add to the belief that the subcontinent may some day yield up secrets of an antiquity equal to that of any other part of the world.

At the time of Mohenjo Daro (or shortly thereafter—scholars disagree) the northern lands of the subcontinent were inhabited by a short, dark-skinned people living in villages and a few towns and dependent primarily upon agriculture and trade. These people would be to South Asia what the Indians were to the North American continent centuries later.

Some time around 2000 B.C., in known-history's first great migration, a tribal people emerged out of central Asia, crossed the Hindu Kush and poured onto the plains of present-day

48

Iran, Afghanistan and Pakistan. Whether or not these tribesmen were the first "invaders" of the south is not really important to the story of Pakistan—they were certainly the first significant ones. They are known as Aryans, after a Sanskrit word meaning a tiller of the soil. They brought with them a new language, a different social system and a body of religious beliefs which they forced upon the inhabitants they found on the fertile lands along the Indus. They laid the foundations upon which modern man developed in the subcontinent.

The Aryan invasions are important to the understanding of Pakistan. Although they took place 4,000 years ago, the effects are apparent today. Through their language, the Aryans tied together the peoples of Europe and Asia. The classical Hindu language of Sanskrit was an Aryan tongue. The chief languages of Europe, as with Urdu, Persian, Pashto and Bengali, all belong to the Aryan-based linguistic family called Indo-European. The Hindu religion developed from Aryan beliefs.

To Aryan descendants, these origins are significant. Afghanistan's national airline is called Aryana Airlines. The word "Iran" itself means "land of Aryans." Pakistani political leaders occasionally propose the idea of an "Aryan Federation" composed of Pakistan, Iran and Afghanistan, similar in political structure to new Malaysia in Southeast Asia or the Mahgreb plan among Arab-speaking nations in North Africa.

From the Vedas and other accounts of life handed down by the Aryans, scholars see only glimpses of the origins of modern-day society.

The Vedic family was patriarchal—in contrast to the society of Mohenjo Daro, which apparently gave dominance to the maternal side of the family. The family, while doubtlessly nomadic in the beginning, became settled and earned its livelihood from cultivating the soil and herding animals. Groups of families, living in villages, developed a sense of community

49

organization. Representatives of the various families met to-gether to solve their common problems and determine courses of action primarily, it appears, in defense of their villages. These ancient "committees" or assemblies have become basic to subcontinent villages. They are known as *panchayats,* "as-semblies of five," a word as well as an idea used today through-out South Asia. The village assembly was the predecessor of Pakistan's Union Councils.

By 500 B.C. the Aryans had expanded their civilization throughout most of the subcontinent, reaching into what is now Bengal in the east, Mysore in the south, always pushing the "darker" people before them. The subcontinent became a kaleidoscope of small kingdoms which rose, merged, fell and rose again in such confusion that historians have yet to un-ravel their identity or chronology. The religion of Hinduism spread across the land and the priestly Brahmins acquired great power over the people, demanding respect for the Sacred Law and the chief Vedic gods.

Religious tyranny often breeds reform and about 540 B.C. South Asia's first great reformer, Gautama Siddhartha, began protesting the restrictive practices of the Brahmins. Through his efforts he laid the foundations for Buddhism.

During the Buddha's lifetime another great change was tak-ing place. By 550 B.C. the tribes of Aryan descendants living on the Iranian plateau had formed the first great Aryan em-pire, called the Achaemenid. Their capital was Persepolis, near what is now the Iranian city of Shiraz. In 538, King Cyrus pushed an army across the Hindu Kush. A short time later, Darius, his successor, reached the Indus River. The bas-relief sculpture in Persepolis records the tribute brought from the subcontinent to help support Darius' wars against the Greeks. Henceforth, control of the wealthy and strategic lands watered by the Indus would be the aim of many rulers

west of the Suleiman Mountains, from Alexander the Great to Napoleon, Hitler, and Stalin.

The story is told, by a Greek historian who was there, that when Alexander the Great invaded the Punjab in 325 B.C., he was met by a native general who asked the Macedonian's cooperation in defeating a mighty empire farther east—in Magada. Alexander and his tired, rebellious army refused and headed home by boat down the Indus, leaving behind a few Greek soldiers. The general, named Chandragupta Maurya, incited the Punjabis to overthrow the Greeks and with new strength went on to conquer Magada himself. He established an empire that lasted more than a century. The Mauryan dynasty produced Asoka, the first great king of the subcontinent.

Asoka ruled from 275 to 232 B.C. In his youth, he was a ruthless warrior who led his Mauryan troops to great military victories in central India. In his middle years, however, he was introduced to the gentle philosophies of Buddhism and a great change came over him. Compassion and piety replaced the carnage and depredation which had characterized his earlier life. Throughout his empire he erected pillars of stone on which were written edicts commanding love and peace.

"Work I must," Asoka vowed, "for the welfare of all the people."

He transformed his army officers and ambassadors into missionaries who, in turn, spread the ideas of Buddha among South Asians. In the northwestern Greek-dominated areas, Buddhist *stupas* (temples) appeared in great profusion and statues of the Buddha within bore a strong resemblance to those of Greece's classical age.

Apparently South Asia was not yet ready for the kind of life advocated by Asoka. After he died attacks came from all

sides. Provinces broke away. By 185 B.C. the "Kingdom of Love" was dead.

The people of the northwest—what is now West Pakistan—knew little peace after Asoka's death. First, Greeks from Bactria, north of the Hindu Kush, conquered the local rulers of Sind and Punjab. They in turn were driven out by the Sakas, who fell to the Parthians and they, ultimately, to the Kushans, all from central Asia. None contributed much to the culture.

While many of the conquerors left South Asia with their booty, many more of their soldiers remained to be absorbed into the great assimilative population of the subcontinent. Scholars today discuss what influence they had on society. Greek methods of sculpture and coinage certainly caught hold, and perhaps even Greek science. It is possible that the Greeks absorbed new philosophies from the Vedic Hindus. Near Peshawar, in the ancient province of Gandhara, a Greco-Buddhist architectural style was set that lasted for centuries. But whatever these invaders gave to South Asia, it did not prevail. Hinduism and its peripheral influences rose to supremacy under the subcontinent's second great indigenous rulers—the Guptas.

Like the Mauryan Empire before it, the Gupta Empire began in bloodshed and oppression under its first two leaders, but reached great heights of law and order under its third, Chandragupta II. He administered his vast kingdom through appointed provincial governors. He encouraged the development of literature and art. Sanskrit became the language of learning. Hinduism was in ascendancy and the caste system became an integral part of Hinduism. To many Indians today, the period from 320 to 500 A.D. was "The Golden Age of Civilization."

After Chandragupta's death the governors began fighting among themselves. From central Asia, new invaders, particularly the White Huns, crossed the passes of the Suleiman

Mountains and bore down onto the plains of the Punjab. In Kashmir, a separate kingdom arose which helped establish that land as a politically-distinct part of the subcontinent. In Bengal, a Buddhist dynasty called the Pala inaugurated a period of prosperity that for several centuries produced a culture honored by Bengalis today. South of the Punjab, a group of warriors declared themselves Rajputs—"Sons of Kings"—and claimed tribal membership in the Hindu Kshatriya, or warrior, caste.

Islam Arrives

Islam first came to the subcontinent through its port towns not long after the Prophet Mohammed conquered the Arabian peninsula in the seventh century. Arab sailors and traders brought the new religion as they plied the ancient sea lanes of the Persian Gulf and Indian Ocean. In 710, Mohammed bin Qasim conquered Sind. Then came new warriors, bent as much on looting the riches of the Punjab and Kashmir, like the invaders before them, as in carrying out jihad to convert the idol-worshippers.

Four different groups of Muslims implanted Islam into the soil of the subcontinent. First came the Turks from central Asia; second were the Pathans from Afghanistan and the Suleiman Mountains; third were the Moghuls—part Turk, part Mongol—also from central Asia. With each conqueror came Muslim missionaries from all parts of the Middle East. Among Buddhists and low caste Hindus they made thousands of converts.

Some of the conquerors gave new directions to the growth of Islam. Mahmud of Ghazni, once a Turkish slave, led the first true invasion of the northwest in 1000 A.D. His soldiers destroyed thousands of Buddhist and Hindu temples. At Ghazni, in what is now Afghanistan, he built a university which supported great scholars such as the historian al Biruni

53

and Khwaja Abdullah Ansari, a poet quoted today in the teahouses of Pakistan. After Mahmud came Mohammed of Ghor who by 1200 established the Muslims' capital in Delhi. With few interruptions, Muslims ruled the subcontinent from Delhi until the British replaced them some 658 years later.

A century or so later, Timur, descendant of Genghis Khan, marched across the Punjab. His sack of Delhi in 1398 was so complete that one witness wrote, in moving poetic phrase, that after Timur's departure: "Not a bird moved a wing in the city for two whole months."

Timur, sometimes called Tamerlane (Timur-i-lang, or Timur the Lame) did not enter South Asia easily. By the fourteenth century, the Pathans had gained control of the Suleiman Mountains. Descended from Aryans, although their own genealogies often claim descent from the children of Israel, the Pathans—who were then (and sometimes still are) called Afghans—had developed in rugged isolation from other groups. From such strongholds as Bannu and Kohat they fought Timur and all other central Asian invaders, as well as the Turkish sultans of Delhi, with considerable ferocity.

It was not difficult for these aggressive tribesmen to move into Delhi amid the wreckage left by Timur of the Turkish Sultanate. One Pathan chief, Bahlol Lodi, brought to the throne the tribal concept of rule by one chief, but with the accord of other tribal chiefs. The entire Pathan population pledged allegiance to him and many tribes moved out of the highlands of the Suleiman Mountains and onto the northwestern plains of what is now West Pakistan.

Pathan rule extended Islam even farther into the Hindu-controlled lands of the subcontinent, but like its predecessors, the Pathan dynasty weakened from internal strains. It became an easy victim of Babur, "the Tiger," history's next invader from central Asia and the founder of the Moghul Empire.

The 200 years of Turkish-Pathan rule established in the

subcontinent forever the existence of two major cultural streams—Hindu and Muslim. Other streams appeared during the time, Sikhism for one, and others disappeared, such as Buddhism. But Islam came to stay. It was not conducive to assimilation, as Greek culture, nor to retreat. Dogmatic and non-mystical, it left little room for compromise on such principles as the existence of one God, the authority of Mohammed's revelations and the sinfulness of image-worship. The warriors and missionaries who brought Islam sought converts, not compatibility. They were contemptuous of the caste restrictions of Hinduism.

Islam even brought its own languages. Turks, Persians and Arabs composed most of the armies that invaded from the west. The "foreign" rulers in Delhi surrounded themselves with Persian scholars, while religious teachers taught Arabic, the language of the Koran. Local South Asian languages, derived from Sanskrit, were the bases onto which these "foreign" languages built. The eventual result in much of the northern areas was Urdu, written in Arabic-Persian script, heavily laden with Persian, Turkish and Arabic words, but intelligible to speakers of Hindi, the language of Hindus living in the same area.

Thus Islam, nurtured by its believers, guarded by its leaders and sometimes enthusiastically propagated by its missionaries, avoided absorption. It was eventually able to grow and Muslims to multiply within Hindu culture, particularly, of course, where Muslim kings held power. Foreign soldiers married Hindu girls, who then adopted the religion of their husbands. For low caste Hindus, Islam offered salvation without the caste indignities prescribed by the Hindu Brahmins. The tribal and extended family system of the society made possible the conversion of many more. If one leader adopted the new religion, many of his relatives followed. One encouragement to conversion was a tax, called *jizya*, which many Muslim rul-

55

ers throughout the world levied on non-Muslims. To avoid the tax, many Hindus became Muslim. While most rulers followed the Turkish practice of utilizing native talent in government, Hindus also found that by becoming Muslim they could sometimes rise much higher in the government.

One early attempt to bring Hinduism and Islam together was made in the latter part of the fifteenth century by a Punjabi mystic named Nanak. He founded Sikhism as a composite of what he considered the best of each religion, such as monotheism from Islam, karma and reincarnation from Hinduism. Although Sikhism endured, it never spread beyond the Punjab.

By the time Babur defeated the Pathan Sultan of Delhi, Ibrahim Lodi, at Panipat in 1526, Islam had taken firm root in the subcontinent's soil. It had also begun to reflect some of the color of its environment, despite its resistance to compromise. Babur, himself a pious Muslim who considerately left behind a well-written diary, noted the Muslims' peculiar "Hindustani way." Here Muslims developed practices that contrasted with the Islam which had arrived from Arabia and these differences remain today to distinguish the Islam of Pakistan from that of Saudi Arabia.

For instance, although Islam by doctrine is emphatically opposed to the Hindu caste system, many convert Hindus continue to observe caste identification. In Pakistan today, many Muslims will not consider marriage with any of darker color nor associate with those of certain occupations. Among some Muslim groups, as Babur found, marriage rites are first performed in Hindu style, then in Muslim style. And some Muslims in India still do not eat meat.

More important than these outward manifestations were the ideological interpretations that developed in South Asian Islam from the earliest days. Mysticism and contemplation, dominant in Hinduism, influenced Indian Muslims; the wide-

56

spread reverence for saints and pirs grew from local non-Islamic customs.

The Moghul Empire

The cultural development of Islam and the emergence of Indian Muslims as a large, separate group were greatly accelerated during the reign of Babur and his Moghul successors. For many Pakistani intellectuals, certain periods during the 330 years of Moghul rule rank as the most glorious in the history of the Muslim peoples in the subcontinent.

Many Indians and Western historians, and some (but not all) Pakistanis, look upon the reign of Akbar from 1556 to 1605 as the greatest of the Moghul period. Coming to power at the age of 15, Akbar was an unusually sensitive ruler, as concerned with the problems of the spirit as with the mechanics of building and governing an empire. Like Asoka long before him, he was distressed at the growing religious antagonisms. His solution was to expound a new religion called "The Divine Faith," of which he was the sole interpreter. He abolished the taxes on non-Muslims and brought many Hindus into the higher ranks of government. Many Pakistanis consider Akbar's concessions to Hinduism as little less than heresy.

Under Akbar, many administrative practices introduced by earlier rulers were refined. The system was based upon authoritarian power in the hands of a few who ruled the apathetic masses. Moghul rulers wished first to maintain order. Consequently, the army and police were vital arms of government, carefully treated, protected and well-trained. The rulers sought wealth from within the existing agricultural system and adopted the land-taxing system of previous Hindu rulers. They employed Hindus to administer the treasury. Islamic law predominated and Muslim courts dispensed Moghul justice, frequently violating Hindu caste require-

ments. Akbar introduced a professional civil service which was a precedent for that introduced by the British and which, in turn, stood Pakistan and India in good stead after 1947. Akbar also concerned himself with social reform. He opposed child marriage and the Hindu practice of *suttee,* the sacrificing of living wives with their dead husbands. He encouraged his Persian and Turkish followers to marry local Indians at all levels and to seek some popular support. Akbar's rule, nevertheless, was autocratic. The masses had no part in the business of governing.

Tolerant and judicious rulers such as Asoka and Akbar appear only rarely in any country's history. None of Akbar's successors matched his genius, although some made contributions to the development of Islam in the subcontinent.

Corresponding with the era of King James I in England, Selim, called Jahengir, or "Conqueror of the World," followed Akbar in 1605 and ruled until 1627. He had both Hindu and Muslim wives, the most powerful of whom was Nur Jahan, a Persian who encouraged the culture of her homeland in the court. It was to Jahengir's court that England sent its first diplomatic mission and established formal trade ties. Moghul days were then numbered.

Europeans arrived like the Arabs, by sea. Portugal was the first to gain a foothold with the arrival of Vasco da Gama, who sailed around the Cape of Good Hope and anchored off India's west coast in 1498. Not long afterwards, the Duke of Albuquerque defeated Arab sea power and for the rest of the sixteenth century the Portuguese monopolized South Asian trade.

Portuguese motives varied, like those of most invaders. They desired trade and found lucrative commercial resources at Goa. Many Portuguese possessed a fervent missionary spirit and wherever a trading post appeared Christianity followed, generally to stay. Finally, the Portuguese dreamed of empire,

and it was not long before they and the Dutch, French and British were fighting over who would control South Asia. The British won.

Britain's interest in South Asia began formally in 1599 when a group of businessmen in London formed the East India Company to "trade with the orient." The next year, Queen Elizabeth gave them a charter which permitted them a monopoly on British trade in the east. The charter gave the company the right to acquire territory, coin money, defend its property with arms, administer justice within its property, collect income from the land—in other words, to behave like a sovereign power if it could get away with it.

Jahengir unwittingly let the East India Company assume control and for the next 347 years no South Asian leader was able to prevent Britain's domination of the subcontinent. In 1614, the East India Company established its first trading center in Surat, near what is now Bombay; other posts appeared near Madras in 1616 and in Bengal in 1633. In 1650 the British built a major fort—Fort William—on the Hooghly River near present-day Calcutta.

At first the advent of the new foreigners had little effect upon the "Muslim stream" in the subcontinent. Other influences pertained, Persian and Indian. Under both Jahengir and his son, Shah Jahan, the intellectual traditions of their ancestors flourished. Persian scholars and artists flocked to their courts. New institutions of learning appeared in Delhi and also in provincial capitals such as Jullundur, Hyderabad and especially Lahore, where, like their predecessors, the rulers frequently established their court. Persian remained the language of literature and learning, its influence seeping deeply into the Urdu language of the common Muslim people. Even Hindu poets began writing in Persian and Urdu. Both rulers had a passion for extravagant monuments and their architects built some of South Asia's most notable structures,

59

among them the Taj Mahal in Agra, and the royal palace and the lovely Shalimar Gardens in Lahore.

These intellectual attainments diminished after Shah Jahan was imprisoned by his son, Aurangzeb, who made himself king in 1658. Aurangzeb was rigidly orthodox and attempted to practice literally the various political and economic instructions of the Koran and sunnah. He re-established taxation of non-Muslims, pressed for conversion of Hindus, and supported expansion of Muslim ownership of Hindu lands. In Lahore, he built the giant Badshahi Mosque.

The great Moghul Empire, which incorporated territory from Kabul to Chittagong and Kashmir to Mysore, had reached its zenith, and now, under Aurangzeb (who died in 1707), it began to disintegrate. Throughout their reign, the Moghuls kept up a continual rivalry with the Persians, the former wishing to keep the northwestern door shut, the latter, like so many others, to keep it open. The Pathans sat in the middle.

Akbar was able to control these independent-minded frontiersmen by first subduing the Yusufzai tribes and then paying the Afridi and Orakzai tribes to keep the Khyber Pass under their control. On Aurangzeb's orders, the Moghul governor of Kabul bribed various other tribes in an effort to stimulate internal Pathan strife, preventing them from joining forces. This policy destroyed whatever chance there may have been for the development of a united spirit among the Pathans of the Suleiman Mountains. The British continued the same policy of fostering disunity.

One Pathan group, however, grew strong despite Moghul efforts. This group, the Ghilzai, invaded Persia and captured Isfahan. The great Persian leader, Nadir Shah, drove them back, captured Kabul and in 1739 reached and plundered the Moghul capital itself.

The fragmentation of the subcontinent begun in Aurang-zeb's time continued even faster with the sacking of Delhi. In Bengal, the Muslim governor, the Nawab of Dacca, be-came virtual monarch and acquired a great fortune selling land to the East India Company. Hyderabad in central India gained independence under a Muslim ruler, the Nizam, as did the southern province of Mysore under its Muslim sultans, Haider Ali and Tipu Sultan. In Sind, the Talpur Mirs estab-lished virtual independence.

By the beginning of the eighteenth century, the French were vying with the British for trade rights on the subconti-nent. Their first foothold was near Madras in 1670 and in following decades they established themselves in Pondicherry and Bengal, not far from the British near Calcutta. British-French rivalry, reflecting their struggle for supremacy in Europe, reached its peak in 1756. The Nawab of Dacca, Siraj-u-Dowla, with French backing, captured Fort William in Calcutta. The subsequent imprisonment of the British led to stories in England of the "Black Hole" of Calcutta in which many British soldiers, packed together in a tiny cell, were supposed to have perished.

Public reaction to the news in England was immediate and intense. Robert Clive, an obscure clerk in the East India Company who rose in the military service through sheer in-genuity, led troops against the French up and down the east-ern coast. In the Battle of Plassey in 1757, he defeated the Nawab of Dacca, recaptured Calcutta and inaugurated a new period of British control over Bengal and, gradually, the entire subcontinent. The French lost forever their oppor-tunity for dominance.

The long and colorful story of British imperialism in South Asia more properly belongs in a history of India than of Paki-stan. As the British gradually overthrew centers of Muslim

61

power, they replaced it with either their own or Hindu strength except in a few, significant places. For the 190 years after the Battle of Plassey, the development of Muslim culture and political thought was confined to certain areas and was important only at certain times. Although these developments, such as in the Punjab and Bengal, were part of the whole subcontinent's move toward independence from the British, they were more specifically important to the development of Pakistan.

The Punjab

The Punjab's capital, Lahore, had long been a symbol to conquerors arriving from the west. Having fought through the Pathan tribesmen, invading armies usually established their major encampments in the Punjab, where they could gather and feed their forces before forging eastward. By the same token, rulers in Delhi used Lahore as their major forward post for protecting the empire from Pathans and other unfriendly visitors from beyond the Suleiman Mountains.

As a meeting ground for invaders and defenders as well as a land of relative prosperity, the Punjab spawned a large variety of ideas and political experiments. It was here, for instance, that Sikhism was born and developed into a militant faith.

In 1845 the British, with the aid of such minor chieftains as Gulab Singh, the ruler of Jammu, defeated the Sikh army and stationed a garrison in Lahore. In 1846 they sold Jammu and Kashmir to Gulab Singh as a reward for his help. Three years later, the Sikhs rose again, but were again and finally defeated at the Battle of Chillianwalla, and the Punjab was annexed in the name of the East India Company. Until 1947, Sikh princes owned considerable amounts of land and numerous small Punjabi states remained in Sikh hands.

Islam in Bengal

Developments in Bengal were also of particular importance in the creation of Pakistan. It was here that the first real Muslim movements toward a common national purpose began.

Bengal's geography contributed to its distinctive development. Mountains and rivers limited the area's accessibility to the sea and through two major gateways in the north—the valleys of the Brahmaputra and Ganges rivers. Mass migrations, which affected so much of the subcontinent, generally missed Bengal where transportation was so hampered. But the Aryans reached Bengal to intermix with earlier inhabitants—called Pundras—and contribute to the language and religion. Buddhism flourished under Asoka. Toward the end of the Gupta era, the great Pala Buddhist kingdom arose in Bengal to unite the people for the first time. While Buddhism in the rest of South Asia (except Ceylon) declined before the rejuvenation of Hinduism and the introduction of Islam, it remained strong in Bengal until the twelfth century and the rise of the Hindu Sena dynasty (1100 to 1204).

The first Muslim visitors to Bengal were probably Arabs, traders seeking the tea, rice and spices of the east. The first documented invasion by a Muslim was that of the Turkish general, Bakhtiyar Khalji, in 1204. He replaced Hindu power in the name of the Sultan of Delhi and brought with him teachers and missionaries to spread the gospel of Islam.

A century later, a Bengali warrior named Shamsuddin Ilyas Shah affirmed his independence from Delhi and set up a small empire of his own in Bengal. The Bengali Sultanate permanently established Islam in Bengal and laid the foundation for the changes that would occur there in 1947. Among the people, these newcomers were not unwelcome. Bengalis were largely Hindus, but members of the lowest castes. Buddhism had degenerated under tyrannical Hindu rulers. As in

the Sind and the Punjab a few centuries earlier, conditions provided an opportunity for Islam. Thousands were converted to the new religion.

With the encouragement, patronage and subsidy—in land and cash—of the Bengal sultans, Muslim pirs and sufis came to Bengal from Arabia, Persia, and other parts of South Asia. It was said at the time that there was not a single town or village in Bengal without a Muslim priest. Madrassahs, mosques, and *khanqahs* (missionary centers) arose in numbers, usually and cleverly on the site of a revered Buddhist or Hindu shrine.

New races with new languages arrived to affect the composition of Bengal society. Some, like the Chinese, were fleeing tribal uprisings north of Assam. Many refugees fled to Bengal, accounting for traces of Turk, Persian and Punjabi in the origins of Bengalis. Imported Abyssinian slaves once occupied the Bengal throne.

In 1538 the Moghul emperor, Sher Shah, reconquered Bengal, putting an end to the independent sultanate. During this time, many Pathans migrated to Bengal and gained control of the government, despite the objections of Akbar. Bengalis themselves developed a resentment against these "foreign," albeit Muslim, intruders that continued to modern times.

In the two centuries following the demise of the Bengal Sultanate the province had little unity. Rebellion and piracy flourished and members of the Muslim aristocracy gave loyalty to no one. Finally Robert Clive's victory in 1757 brought Bengal under the control of the British.

Changes then occurred in the province. Hindus replaced Muslims in government and the subsidies to Muslim educational institutions decreased, although a school in Calcutta continued to educate "sons of Muslim gentlemen for reasonable and lucrative offices in the government and to produce competent officers for courts of justice." A new English gov-

ernor of Bengal, cooperating with Hindu merchants loyal to the East India Company, literally denuded the province of its economic wealth.

Under Warren Hastings and Lord Cornwallis, fresh from his military campaigns in America, new land programs came into being. Hindu money-lenders became the new landowners. British capital supported Calcutta's Hindu entrepreneurs who transformed the economy of Bengal, to the disadvantage of the old Muslim gentry. Commerce in such cash crops as indigo and the importation of British textiles destroyed the ancient agricultural and weaving economy that had supported millions of Bengalis.

Culturally, Bengal rose to importance as Hindus found new opportunities for self-expression. Western scholars followed the East India Company to Calcutta, where they translated Hindu and Muslim works into English. Charles Wilkins invented type for the Bengali language. The Asiatic Society of Bengal, founded in 1748, began serious study of Sanskrit. In 1800, Lord Wellesley founded Fort William College, where demands for the first time were made for textbooks in Hindi and Urdu. Spreading out from Bengal, English replaced Persian as the official and cultural language of the subcontinent. Throughout the nineteenth century, Bengali literature, with increasing emphasis on English and Hindu scholarship and ideas, was important in nearly all of India.

British expansion in all the subcontinent followed much the same pattern of Bengal and the Punjab. Muslim strength diminished, local rulers fought among themselves and the British stepped in. In rapid succession, they conquered Sind, lower Burma, the kingdoms of Oudh and Nagpur, and they stationed garrisons in many other states. Resistance grew accordingly and, by 1857, the stage was set for the first major rebellion against British control.

The causes, actions and results of the uprising of 1857—the British call it a "mutiny," Pakistanis and Indians call it a "war of independence"—are many and varied. It began among a few Muslim princes still loyal to the Moghul emperor, among mullahs seeking revival of Muslim life at the expense of growing Christian influence, among former Hindu rulers and among the East India Company's Muslim and Hindu soldiers who had been subverted. Later, the villagers joined, their fears aroused by Muslim and Hindu agitators.

Disorganized and without foreign help, the rebels were no match for the British with their superior generalship and arms. The British found allies among the Sikhs, always ready to fight against Muslim ascendancy, and those Muslim and Hindu rulers who from the start had confidence in a British victory. The rebels captured Delhi, but they soon lost it. In less than a year, the uprising collapsed, the last Moghul emperor, Bahadur Shah, was exiled to Burma and the British government replaced the East India Company as ruler of South Asia.

Henceforth, British, Hindus, and Muslims would each seek a separate destiny.

4. Toward Nationhood

Centuries ago Emperor Asoka, the tolerant Mauryan, tried to unite Hindus and Buddhists to form an empire based on justice and peace. His succesors failed him. Later, Emperor Akbar, the pious Moghul, tried to unite Hindus and Muslims to form an empire based on justice and peace. His successors failed him also. In 1858, the British assumed the role of peacemaker.

The story of British failure to unite Indians is the story of Pakistan's success. It begins with the uprising of 1857, two significant results of which affected Muslims. First, the British government formally replaced the East India Company and the Moghul emperor as ruler of the subcontinent. Under the India Act of 1858, the British Cabinet, through a Secretary of State for India, became responsible for appointing the Viceroy of British India whose power, in turn, extended through all the provinces and all government services. Many princely states—Muslim, Hindu and Sikh—maintained nominal sovereignty except in foreign affairs and certain other matters only so long as they cooperated with the British.

Secondly, the British, who blamed the Muslims for the uprising, turned increasingly against them. Following the pattern begun in Bengal after the Battle of Plassey in 1757, the British gave preference to Hindus in government, education and business. In succeeding decades, Muslim influence waned, even in the army as the British, while relying heavily on Pathan and Muslim Punjabi soldiery, stopped forming all-

Muslim units. English systems of law continued to replace Muslim law and Hindus held most of the financial and administrative posts not held by foreigners.

Sir William Hunter, who wrote of Indian Muslims after the uprising, reported that there was only one Muslim among the 240 Indian lawyers admitted to the Calcutta bar between 1852 and 1868 and there was not a single Muslim High Court Judge. Of 1,338 civil service appointments in Bengal, Muslims received only 92.

The Muslim community, already bitter, withdrew further from the mainstream of intellectual, economic and political activity.

In taking on the rule of India, the British assumed a gigantic task. Millions of people who worshipped different gods in countless different ways and who spoke hundreds of different languages and dialects were sorted into scores of different provinces and states, the latter often ruled by despotic princes little concerned with the well-being of their subjects. Poverty, hunger, corruption, and cruelty were common. The British sought to bring order to the chaos and re-fashion the complex political structure. Like the Moghuls before them, they wished only to rule a peaceful society, develop the economy to support the British trade system and administer the law.

History records the work of many conscientious British individuals and many progressive actions in India. In the Punjab, John Lawrence created a province with a strong economic base. New penal codes brought a new era to Indian law. Schools brought education to the upper class children so they could fill the administrative needs of government. The English language brought modernization in scholarship.

But the British were authoritarian in the tradition of Indian rulers and colonizers everywhere. With few exceptions,

top jobs in government were closed to Indians. In local councils, British governors appointed the membership. Indians were barred from British clubs and felt the effects of racial discrimination.

In 1885, a few Europeans and Indians in Bombay organized the Indian National Congress. Their objective: social reform under "the blessings of British rule." Before long, this objective was lost and a new one took its place: parliamentary government. Indian nationalism found its first real vehicle to drive to independence. But it was a Hindu-driven machine.

Nature, always heavy-handed in India, spurred the Indian National Congress into action. In 1895 a severe famine, accompanied by plague, ravaged the villages around Bombay. More than 1,000,000 people died and the conciliatory attitude of the Bombay reformers turned to anger. Two Englishmen were murdered. The Congress began to speak more militantly.

The British compounded the work of nature and at the same time gave Muslims an opportunity to experience the heady brew of Muslim nationalism. In 1905, they partitioned Bengal.

The purpose of partition was reasonable and without malice. The province, its capital in Calcutta, covered more than what is today just East and West Bengal. It included Bihar and Orissa and had a population of 80,000,000, far too many to administer efficiently. The British established a new province of East Bengal and Assam under a lieutenant-governor, whose capital was Dacca, the ancient Muslim capital of the Bengal Sultanate.

Many Muslims were overjoyed. Nearly all Bengali Muslims lived in the eastern sector, yet since 1757 they had been governed by English and Hindus from Calcutta, in the western part. To these Muslims, partition held out hope for social and economic emancipation.

The Muslim Re-awakening

The partition of Bengal was a climax in the development of Islam in the subcontinent. It ended a long period of aimless intellectual wandering and gave new direction in the search for self-determination.

Nurtured by Turkish, Pathan, and Moghul patronage, Muslim scholarship in previous centuries had been more vibrant than anywhere else in the Islamic world. Its content was largely theological, but in Muslim life everywhere politics is never far away from the Koran. Reform movements easily developed into political action.

The lines of Muslim thought that extend today into the idea and substance of Pakistan took identifiable form in the reform movements of the eighteenth century. They began with a scholar named Shah Wali-ullah who brought a measure of harmony between Shi'ites and Sunnites. He was followed by a more aggressive reformer named Sayyid Ahmad Shahid, whose movement led to a jihad against the Sikhs. Sikh-Muslim antagonism was never allowed to abate.

Long before the Hindu nationalists began their drive against the British, Muslims sought to expel the foreigners who had usurped their own tenuous authority in province after province. The center of trouble was in Bengal and Patna where Muslim leaders such as Sayyid Ahmad Shahid declared India to be *dar-ul-harb,* or "place of war" (against Islam). Muslims, they said, could never live in a country ruled by non-Muslims. Until their homeland was *dar-ul-Islam,* they would resist. The British called them "Hindustani fanatics," but their influence was great. Eventually, they helped rouse Muslim villagers to support the uprising of 1857.

The effectiveness of these Muslim leaders and thinkers diminished after 1858. They became even more bitter against

Europeans and sought to shield Islam from all modern influences.

One man stood out in his sharp dissent. His name was Sayyid Ahmed Khan. Born in 1817, he was the son of a greatly-respected religious recluse descended, as the name "sayyid" denotes, from the Prophet Mohammed. He grew up, however, in the home of his more secular-minded grandfather, a mathematician in the East India Company who dabbled in local politics. Thus, Sayyid Ahmed Khan became a writer of religious tracts on the one hand, and a sub-judge under the British on the other. During the uprising he not only remained loyal to the British, but helped save British lives in Bijna.

In a book addressed to the British entitled *The Causes of the Indian Mutiny,* Sayyid Ahmed Khan stated that the way to avoid future mutinies was for the British to permit Indians —Hindu and Muslim—to participate in law-making. He also pleaded with Muslims to join in the modernization of India and said that so long as Muslims stood apart they would be relegated to inferior positions. Although he sought Hindu-Muslim cooperation, he felt that there was a fundamental difference between the two groups.

Despite the enmity of his more orthodox contemporaries, Sayyid Ahmed Khan, with British help, opened schools and welcomed both Muslims and Hindus, emphasizing the secular curriculum of the Europeans. In 1873, with the backing of the Nizam of Hyderabad and the Amir of Afghanistan, he founded the Mohammedan Anglo-Oriental College, which later became Aligarh University. The British rewarded him with knighthood.

Slowly, students of Aligarh and other Muslim intellectuals began to identify themselves with the "progressive" movement of Sir Sayyid. Among them were Sir Sayyid's successors as chancellors of Aligarh, Mohsin ul-Mulk (1837–1907) and

71

Viqar ul-Mulk (1841–1917), as well as the theologian, Maulvi Chiragh Ali. Nasir Ahmed (1936–1912), a civil servant, wrote extensively on social reform among Muslims, while Altaf Hussein Hali (1837–1914), a poet, was influential in awakening a group consciousness among Muslim villagers and city masses. He became known as India's first Muslim "national poet." Wrote Hali:

> Why do you idly stand, my countrymen?
> Arise and lend a hand, my countrymen.
> If you are men, help others in some way,
> Or simply eat and drink and pass away.

Others not directly connected with Aligarh sought to move Muslims forward. In Bengal, Nawab Abdul Latif (1828–1893) organized the Mohammedan Literary and Scientific Society in 1863 in an attempt to counteract the conservative influences there. An English-educated judge, Sayyid Amir Ali (1849–1938) was more critical of Europeans in India and more of a revivalist in religion, but nevertheless spoke out for modernization of the Muslim intellectual. Unfortunately, he wrote mostly in English so his influence among Muslims was limited.

The Punjab, too, saw renewed intellectual activity among Muslims in the birth of Ahmadiyism. Ahmadiyism was founded by Mirza Ghulam Ahmad (1839–1908) in 1901, and the movement's followers were active missionaries and zealous teachers. They, more than any other single Muslim group, attacked illiteracy and poverty among villagers.

Muslim traditionalists were not idle. Their main center of influence was in the town of Deoband near Dehli. The Deoband movement rejected government support for education and tried to isolate itself from the general stream of secular progress. Its social and political ideal was the life led by Muslims under the seventh century caliphs. The ideas of this school were best voiced by Hussein Rizvi Akbar (1846–1921),

72

a renowned poet from Allahabad who satirically attacked Aligarh's educational policies.

Another conservative trend developed in the Pan-Islamic movement, which sought to bind Indian Muslims more closely to the political and intellectual activities of Muslims in the Middle East. For centuries the question of unity had involved Sunni Muslims of the subcontinent through the recognition or non-recognition of the various caliphs, the leaders of the faithful. The caliphate had shifted frequently—from Arabia to Damascus to Baghdad to Cairo and, eventually, to Constantinople with the rise of the Ottoman Empire. Some subcontinent Muslim emperors recognized the reigning caliph, requiring that his name be mentioned in the calls to prayer and other religions ceremonies. Others, such as Akbar, ignored the western caliphate and claimed it for themselves.

Pan-Islam became important after the fall of the last Moghul emperor because orthodox Muslims had no person to turn to for religious leadership—or, symbolically, to mention in Friday prayers—other than the Ottoman Sultan. They received encouragement from Jamal al-din al-Afghani, a Muslim nationalist in the Arab world who visited India—in exile —from 1878 to 1882. Pleading for Pan-Islamic unity and the revival of glories that were once Islam's, al-Afghani denounced Sir Sayyid Ahmed Khan's pro-European movement as well as his "progressive" attitudes toward religion. Sir Sayyid's insistence that the truth of Islam was its "conformity to Nature," he said, was "the root of corruption, the source of untouchable evils."

A particularly effective conservative spokesman was Maulana Shibli, and although he graduated from Aligarh, he encouraged support of the Ottoman caliphate. He was later decorated by the Ottoman Sultan, Abdul Hamid II.

In 1893, Shibli and a group of Muslim divines organized a movement called the Nadva-tul-Ulema which joined the Deo-

band school in attacking Aligarh. Among its followers was Maulana Abul Kalam Azad who called Aligarh "a slave factory." Azad later became the foremost Muslim opponent of Pakistan. He was India's first Minister of Education. It was the plan of Shibli and others to have the Nadva assume the political leadership of Muslims.

By the end of the nineteenth century, both conservative and liberal schools of Muslim thought in India had contributed to some religious and intellectual re-awakening of Muslims in the subcontinent. Indeed, one European scholar, W. S. Blunt, wrote that "India is the most important land where the Mohammedan faith is found." He added: "It may safely be affirmed that the course of events in India will determine more than anything else the destiny of Mohammedanism in the immediate future of this and the next generation."

With the partitioning of Bengal in 1905 it was apparent to many Muslim leaders that the time had come to have a political instrument of their own. In 1906 they met in Dacca to discuss the subject. Out of the meeting came the All-India Muslim League, "to promote the feeling of loyalty to the British, to protect and advance the political rights of Muslims and to prevent the rise of hostility among Muslims toward other communities." Mohsin ul-Mulk and Viqar ul-Mulk of Aligarh were made secretaries. The Aga Khan, leader of the world's Ismaili Muslims, was elected permanent president.

These leaders went a step further. They called for British acceptance of the principle of "separate electorates." Such acceptance would mean recognizing the existence in India of two separate communities. It would also mean a negation of European parliamentary democracy based on majority rule.

India's Muslims feared Western democracy. Sir Sayyid Ahmed Khan had pinpointed this fear by writing: "Now suppose that all the English . . . were to leave India . . . then who would be the rulers of India? Is it possible that

74

under these circumstances, two nations—the Mohammedan and Hindu—could sit on the same throne and remain equal in power? Most certainly not. It is necessary that one of them should conquer the other and thrust it down. To hope that both could remain equal is to desire the impossible and the inconceivable."

The only solution, these Muslims felt, was to allocate a certain number of seats in each legislative body to each religious group. Each would have its own voters, candidates and representatives.

In 1909, Viceroy Minto and Lord Morley, Secretary of State for India, formulated an India Councils Act which for the first time permitted elections above the local level. It also recognized the principle of separate electorates. Known as the Minto-Morley Reforms, the move started a roulette of religious politics that caused alternate moments of anguish and elation until it ended in the creation of Pakistan. Indians claim that the British granted separate electorates in order to divide the people and weaken opposition to their rule.

Elation was the mood among Muslims in the first decade of the twentieth century. Bengal was partitioned. The All-India Muslim League and the award of separate electorates assured Muslims of increasing influence. It was a brief moment, however. In 1911, the British revoked the partition.

Jinnah: Ambassador of Unity

What started as a love affair between the British and Muslims, each seeking from the other assistance against the Indian Hindu nationalists, turned suddenly to a bitter quarrel. Muslims began supporting the Indian National Congress against the British. Events abroad fed their antagonism. Maulana Shibli called the Italian-Turkish War of 1911 another Christian Crusade against Muslims. As World War I began, more and more Indian Muslims, led by Abul Kalam Azad and other

religious conservatives, supported the Ottoman Empire against the British. News of the British defeat at Gallipoli, where many Indian Muslims served in the British-Indian army, set off rounds of celebration in India. The British, in what seemed almost a spite measure, built a railway line through the principal mosque in the city of Cawnpore.

One prominent Muslim, one of the few Muslim Leaguers who also belonged to the Indian National Congress, felt that Congress and the League should work together toward Indian self-government, each suppressing its religious bias. His name was Mohammed Ali Jinnah. He was later known as the "Ambassador of Hindu-Muslim unity," and the person most responsible for the creation of Pakistan after "unity" proved impossible. He became Pakistan's first governor-general.

Jinnah was born in Karachi on Christmas Day in 1876, the year Disraeli gained for Queen Victoria the title of "Kaisar-i-Hind"—Empress of India. He was the son of a prosperous hides merchant, a member of the Khoja sect of Ismaili Muslims and descended from Hindu converts. An excellent student, he was sent at the age of sixteen to study law in England. The traditions of English society, so contrasting to the ways of the crowded port town of his native Karachi, impressed him. He adopted English fashions, even to the detail of a monocle. When he returned to India in 1896 to begin practicing law in Bombay, he was more English than Indian, stiffly proper and unable to speak any language well except English.

Jinnah's bearing and idiosyncrasies left him open to criticism throughout his life—he was called arrogant, uncompromising, cold, aloof, egotistical. At times he displayed all of these characteristics and he made many enemies. But his integrity was seldom questioned, by Muslims, Hindus, or foreigners. If his tongue was sharp, it was without personal

malice. And if he lacked warmth, he worked indefatigably to better the lot of his people.

Jinnah was a lonely man. His parents bound him in marriage before he was fifteen, but his wife died soon after. His close friends were few, as were his pleasures. When he later re-married, it was to a Parsee twenty years his junior. The marriage did not last.

Jinnah's genius in dialectics, his unbending resolve to move Muslims forward along constitutional lines, won for him at a very early stage in his career a high reputation among British and Indian officials, despite his unapproachable demeanor. When the British government enlarged the Legislative Council in the India Councils Act of 1909, Jinnah, at the age of thirty-three, was elected to it by the Muslims of Bombay. In this forum he boldly pleaded the cause of Hindu-Muslim unity and Indian self-government. His concern was not so much religion as constitutionalism. He became a member of the Home Rule League of Mrs. Annie Besant, a group of upper and middle class Indians who, for the first time, joined together to advance the principle of Indian self-government, but within the British empire. In 1913, he joined the Muslim League and, as a member of both League and Congress, sought to bring the two into working harmony.

World War I found Indians in an angry mood. Agitation against the British was sometimes extreme. In Bengal, Muslims responded to the Ottoman caliph's call for jihad against Turkey's Christian enemies. Such leaders as Maulana Mohammed Ali and his brother, Shaukat, and Abul Kalam Azad went to jail amidst rioting. In the Punjab, Sikhs, angered at the killing of fellow Sikhs in Calcutta who were demonstrating against the British, plotted rebellion under the banner of the Ghadr (Mutiny) Party.

Into this scene stepped another London-educated lawyer, Mohandas K. Gandhi, known to the world as Mahatma (Great

Soul) or as Gandhiji to Indians (but as "Mr. Gandhi" to Jinnah). For the next thirty years, Gandhi led the Indian independence movement. He was also the most effective spokesman against the recognition of a "two nation" character of Indian society. To Gandhi, Indians were Indians first, Hindus or Muslims second. To many Muslims, including Jinnah, Gandhi represented Hindu nationalism.

Only a society as heterogeneous as India's could produce such contrasting leaders as Gandhi and Jinnah. Gandhi, while born of prosperous parents, identified himself with the poor and struggling masses, whom he brought into the independence drive. Jinnah had to force himself to leave the cloisters of the intellectual world, and even then could not speak the language of the people. Gandhi was a humanist, a man whose heart was with the suffering. He was emotional, driven by what he called an "inner light." His very presence among them brought Hindu masses to *darshan,* a sense of ecstasy caused by being near a deified person. Jinnah called him a "Hindu revivalist" and said that to stir the masses by way of emotions was wicked. Throughout their many years of rivalry, neither the austere Jinnah nor the humble Gandhi really understood what the other was talking about. They never learned to communicate.

The peak of Hindu-Muslim cooperation came in 1916 when, in Lucknow, Jinnah talked the Congress leaders into supporting the League's stand on separate electorates. This demand, he said, "is not a matter of policy, but a matter of necessity to the Muslims, who require to be roused from the coma and torpor into which they have fallen so long." In the Lucknow Pact, the Congress agreed that Muslims could occupy one-third of the seats in the Central Legislative Council.

The British, concerned with the war in Europe, sought to assuage Indian antagonism through reforms. These were promulgated later in the Government of India Act of 1919—

called the Montagu-Chelmsford Reforms—which, in effect, gave India its first constitution. The Act decentralized some of the governor-general's authority, giving more power to provincial governments. It also permitted elected councils to control wider areas of government, especially in education, health, and agriculture. The nationalists claimed the reforms did not go far enough.

Riots and bloodshed swept India as the cycle of "Indian demonstration-British repression-Indian demonstration" began. For example, several thousand people crowded into a city park in Amritsar one day in 1919 to listen to speeches in violation of British orders. The British general in charge ordered his troops to fire. In minutes, more than 300 people were killed and 1,200 wounded. Throughout India, nationalism became more violent.

In response, the British passed the Rowlatt Acts, giving the courts the right to hold secret trials or no trials at all. Jinnah and many others, their sense of law and British justice violated, resigned in protest from the Legislative Council.

Jinnah had more to protest than British injustice; the Indian nationalists began to repel him. Increasingly, the leadership of the nationalist movement seemed to be dominated by Hindus employing religion in their cause. In 1920, he followed Annie Besant in resigning from the Home Rule League because, as she said, it was "so intertwined with religion." Gandhi, only shortly before, had introduced *satyagraha*—mass, non-violent resistance. The word was Sanskrit, the principle was that of *ahimsa,* an ancient Hindu rule of non-violence. The result was bloodshed as riots against the British broke out in Delhi, Bombay and the Punjab. Jinnah was appalled at the use of unconstitutional methods and at the Hindu-Muslim antipathy they produced. He resigned from the Indian National Congress and retired from politics.

In 1921 Muslims joined the general clamor of protest with

an issue of their own—"Islam in Danger!" With the Ottoman Turks defeated in war, the European powers faced the problem of the caliphate. Thousands of Indian Muslims in Sind, the Punjab and the Northwest Frontier marched toward Turkey to flee the "infidel" rule of India and to "save" the caliph. Abul Kalam Azad went to jail again, the marchers returned home, but Muslims throughout India were inflamed. Gandhi, seeking Muslim cooperation against the British, led the formation of the Khilafat (caliphate) movement and called for non-cooperation, including *hartal,* economic boycott. As respect for authority declined across the country, violence increased. When Gandhi called off the movement in 1924, Muslims were resentful and frustrated. Hindus were bitter and an era of communal violence between Hindus and Muslims began which buried the spirit of Jinnah's Lucknow Pact. Henceforth, Muslims would become more anti-Hindu than anti-British, more pro-Muslim than pro-Indian.

Fear increased between members of each religious community, both in rural and urban areas, and they found petty excuses for violence, particularly in neighborhoods where neither could claim a large majority. An insult here, a spoken word there, produced a riot; a Hindu band marching past a Muslim mosque, a Muslim slaughter of a Hindu sacred cow, caused explosions of fury.

In 1928, Indian nationalists proposed a new constitution for India which rejected the principle of separate electorates. The British equivocated and called for conferences in London. The moribund Muslim League was powerless. Jinnah was out of it all, practicing law in England.

Iqbal and Pakistan

Only one voice lent real dynamism to the Muslim cause. It came from a poet-philosopher named Mohammed Iqbal. Since Shah Wali-ullah more than 100 years before, few Mus-

lim thinkers contributed to the development of Muslim culture in the subcontinent as much as this one man.

Iqbal was born in Sialkot in the Punjab in 1873 to a family from Kashmir. His father, a craftsman, was also a sufi. From these beginnings, Iqbal wended his way through the complex of Muslim thought, adopting first one and then another idea, contributing to each with his melodious Persian and Urdu poetry. His following was enormous among intellectuals and as his ideas changed, so did those of his followers.

After a period of study and research in Europe, during which he, like Jinnah, was influenced by British liberalism, Iqbal returned to Lahore to teach and to write. Rejecting sufism, which he condemned as self-abomination, he emphasized the development of the human personality. His orthodox Muslim critics were pacified by his glorification of Muslim life under the first four caliphs, his opposition to the British and his support for Pan-Islamic movements.

Above all, Iqbal became a champion of Muslim rights in India and found a following among the Aligarh modernists because of his support of the Muslim League and the principle of separate electorates.

Iqbal was elected President of the Muslim League in 1930. In his inaugural address at Allahabad, he voiced what he considered the only logical next step in the progress of Muslim-Indian-British relations:

"I would like to see the Punjab, Northwest Frontier Province, Sind and Baluchistan amalgamated into a single state. Self-government within the British Empire or without the British Empire, the formation of a consolidated Northwestern Indian Muslim state appears to me to be the final destiny of Muslims, at least of North West India. . . ."

Muslims throughout India were shocked—no one of importance had ever suggested Muslim political *and* geographic self-government. A few months later, a Cambridge University

81

student named Rahmat Ali coined the word "Pakistan" for Iqbal's state.

As Muslim League president, Iqbal traveled to London for the 1930 Round Table Conferences, there to join Jinnah and the Aga Khan in discussions of Indian constitutional reform. By this time, Gandhi was India's most dominant figure and in London he claimed to speak for all Indians, Hindu and Muslim. His claims were rejected. In 1932, the British Prime Minister announced the "Communal Award," separate electorates which would be part and parcel of any future constitutional reform in India. Congress accused the British of "dividing and ruling." Gandhi commenced a fast.

The Communal Award became an integral part of the Government of India Act of 1935, which established the constitution of India as inherited by Pakistan. The Act gave increased autonomy to the eleven Indian provinces in legislative matters. It widened the elective support of government and called for nationwide elections in 1936.

Jinnah was dubious of carrying the idea of separate electorates into a state of Pakistan. He was not certain that it was legal in British constitutional law. However, few Muslim leaders had given serious thought to Iqbal's idea and therefore it was not difficult for Jinnah to accept an invitation to return to India and lead the Muslims as he had once done. The appeal came to him in London in 1933, carried by Liaquat Ali Khan, a Muslim politician from the United Provinces and a graduate of Aligarh. Liaquat, twenty years younger than Jinnah, proved to be a good counter-balance to Jinnah's imperfections. While Jinnah dreaded contact with the uneducated masses, Liaquat courted them, held them spellbound with his oratory and eventually molded their collective thinking after his own. Jinnah finally returned to India, holding stubbornly to the idea that Hindus and Muslims could work together.

Tirelessly, and with Liaquat at his side, Jinnah sought first to unite the Muslims. "The Hindus and Muslims must organize separately," he said, "and once they are organized, they will understand each other better." He became president of the Muslim League Election Board.

His failure was colossal. In the 1936 elections, the National Congress, led by Jawaharlal Nehru, won an overwhelming victory. While Muslims comprised 30 per cent of the electorate, the Muslim League had the support of less than 5 per cent of the Muslim vote. The remainder of Muslim votes went to the various Muslim parties and individuals in the provinces who had rejected the League. In Bengal, Fazlul Haq who, with Hussein S. Suhrawardy, founded the Krishak Praja Party, proved to be the most able Muslim politician. In the Punjab, Fazl-i-Hussein led to victory his Unionist Party, a coalition of Muslims, Hindus and Sikhs. In the Northwest Frontier Province, Dr. Khan Sahib's Muslim Nationalists allied themselves with Congress to prevent outside Muslim influence. Only in the central Indian provinces, where Hindu majorities were great, did the Muslim League gain any significant votes.

In Bengal and the Punjab, Muslim leaders, although not members of the Muslim League, formed coalition governments with non-Muslims. The Muslim League expected also to join coalition governments in other provinces, but instead was rebuffed by the National Congress, which demanded that Muslims resign from the League if they wished to participate in governments. Indignantly, Jinnah, Liaquat Ali Khan, and other League leaders stormed across India demanding recognition for the League. Their list of grievances grew and with it more support. Bengal's Fazlul Haq and the Punjabi Prime Minister, Sikander Hayat Khan, backed the League.

The League had one major weakness. It was composed of the urban elite and had little contact with the masses. Its

Aligarh graduates represented businessmen, landlords, and professional people who were modernists in religion, but conservative in economics and naive in politics. If anyone had contact with the Muslim masses it was the Deoband conservatives such as Maulana Abu Ala Maududi and his Jama'at-i-Islami (Community of Islam) and Abul Kalam Azad. More sympathetic to the Congress, they rejected the League for its "Aligarh" leadership, and its equivocal stand against the British.

Iqbal saw the problem. He wrote: "I believe that a political organization which gives no promise of improving the lot of the average Muslim cannot attract our masses." Again he wrote: "The League will have to finally decide whether it will remain a body representing the upper classes of Indian Muslims or the Muslim masses, who have so far, with good reason, taken no interest in it."

Nor was Jinnah convinced that Iqbal's two-nation theory meant Pakistan. Iqbal believed that Jinnah would inevitably have a change of heart. The poet stressed his case repeatedly and in 1937 he wrote to Jinnah: "Don't you think the time for such a demand has already arrived?" Iqbal died the next year and still Jinnah resisted Pakistan.

In 1939, war broke out in Europe and the British, without consulting the National Congress, declared India a belligerent and suspended constitutional reform. The Congress ministries in seven of India's eleven provinces resigned in protest. Jinnah called it a "Day of Deliverance" from Hindu rule. With Congress members such as Nehru and Gandhi alternately in and out of jail, the Muslim League grew stronger and Jinnah's authority over party members greater.

The path toward Muslim nationhood was cleared of dialectical and political debris in 1940 at the Muslim League's annual conference in Lahore. Jinnah had finally accepted the

inevitability of Pakistan and the honor fell to Fazlul Haq of Bengal to introduce the "Pakistan Resolution":

"No constitutional plan would be workable in this country or acceptable to Muslims unless . . . the areas in which Muslims are numerically in the majority as in the northwest and eastern zones . . . shall be autonomous and sovereign."

A few months later, Jinnah stated: "No power on earth can prevent Pakistan."

He threw himself fiercely into the political maelstrom. He began wearing the *shalwar* and *shamian,* the native dress of educated Muslims. He was sixty-four years old before he felt the effects of popularity; it rejuvenated his spirit and, in return, he rejuvenated the Muslim League. Muslims, high and —finally—low, called him "Quaid-i-Azam," or Great Leader. He organized an All-Indian Muslim Students Federation to attract young people in the Pakistan movement. Fazlul Haq, H. S. Suhrawardy and Liaquat Ali Khan rallied the Muslim masses. League members appeared more frequently in the ministries of the Punjab, Bengal, the Northwest Frontier, Sind and Assam.

Opposition to the League was intense. Nehru called the idea of Pakistan "absurd." Later, Gandhi met with Jinnah and proposed that the League and the Congress unite and achieve independence, *after* which the people of the various areas could vote for the kind of future they wanted. Jinnah replied that he doubted Gandhi's authority to make such a promise and the talks collapsed.

Some Muslim leaders opposed Pakistan and the League. Religious conservatives such as Maulana Maududi believed that nationalism was incompatible with Islam. In the Northwest Frontier Province, Khan Abdul Ghaffar Khan, the "Frontier Gandhi," allied his followers with the Indian National Congress. His Khuda-i-Khidmatgars (Servants of God), called "Red Shirts" because of their clothing, believed that Pathans

85

would be able to retain their separate identity more effectively under a Congress government in Delhi than a Muslim government in Pakistan. In Kashmir, Sheikh Mohammed Abdullah, the most popular Muslim leader in this Hindu-ruled state, felt confident that an independent India led by his close friend, Jawaharlal Nehru, would respect the semi-autonomous status which he hoped Kashmir would have. He linked his Jammu and Kashmir National Conference Party with the Congress and against the League.

At the end of World War II Britain faced with little heart the continued rule of India. It was apparent to all that India must soon be freed. In India, Muslims, Hindus, and Sikhs were tense with anticipation, each fearful of their position under a future government. Riots shook Calcutta and the Royal Indian Navy mutinied. Britain's new Labor government called for elections in India in the winter of 1945.

The Muslim League Succeeds

With more vigor than his frail body could stand, Jinnah, accompanied by his lieutenants, began touring northern India, speaking to all the Muslims he could reach. Although he spoke in English, his eloquence, coupled with dramatic gestures with his monocle and an admonishing forefinger, swept his listeners with him. Thousands upon thousands of Muslims thrust their devotion upon a man whose words they could scarcely comprehend.

"Vote for a Muslim Leaguer even if it be a lamp-post," he urged. Many took him literally.

This time, the League had a colossal success. It won all 30 Muslim seats in the Central Legislative Assembly. In provincial parliaments, it won 427 out of 507 Muslim seats. It failed to capture Khan Abdul Ghaffar Khan's Northwest Frontier and in the Punjab where, although it gained 78 out

of 175 seats, the Unionist Party joined with Congress and the Sikhs to form the government. Nehru's National Congress won the non-Muslim constituencies.

The elections over, the British sent a Cabinet Mission under Sir Stafford Cripps to India to promote "the early realization of self-government." It suggested that an interim government be set up to oversee elections in the provincial legislatures for a constituent assembly which would write India's new constitution. When the Muslim League demanded that Muslim members of the interim government must belong to the Muslim League, Congress refused to join. The British dropped plans for the interim government and called for elections anyway.

Jinnah protested. "Goodbye to constitutional methods," he said.

Muslims felt let down at the failure of the interim government plan. To maintain their confidence and press their claims, the League prepared for demonstrations.

In July, 1946, elections were held in the provincial legislatures. The League won all but 3 of the 79 Muslim seats. However, the future of Pakistan obviously lay in the good intentions of the 292 National Congress members, few of whom had ever accepted the premise of a "divided India" with provinces grouped according to the predominant religion. These intentions were made clear in a remark by Congress President Nehru:

"The big probability is that there will be no grouping (of provinces)."

The angry League took to the streets and sanctioned plans for a Direct Action Day on August 16. Both Britain and the National Congress poured fuel on the fire. On August 8, the Viceroy invited Congress to form an interim government without the League. Muslims were furious. On August 9, the Na-

tional Congress also called for demonstrations. They came at a time when famine was spreading across the land, laborers were striking in the cities, and lawlessness was rampant.

In Calcutta, a tinder box of violence, Muslims on August 16, 1946 marched toward government headquarters on Direct Action Day. Hindus tried to bar their way. Houses were set on fire, shops were looted, hospitals were jammed. After three days, the Great Calcutta Killing cost the lives of more than 5,000 people, mostly Hindus, and more than 20,000 were injured.

Sir Francis Tuker, the British officer then commanding the army in the Eastern Command, reported how events in Calcutta led to violence in Bihar as Hindus sought revenge. There, the death toll exceeded 8,000. Tuker describes a typical day's "unrest":

"On the evening of the 6th of November, 1946, at a sideshow run by Muslims, there was a motor-cycling display called 'The Wall of Death.' There was a fair crowd watching when a Muslim performer threw a jest at a Jatni (a person of a racial group called the Jats) woman spectator. . . . A sudden shout went up that a Muslim had insulted a Hindu woman. At once on this alarm a number of small bands of Jats rushed out and, in concerted fashion, set to work to massacre the Muslim stallholders at the *mela* (fair), scattered all about the fair grounds quietly plying their trade. Practically every Muslim man, woman and child was murdered with appalling cruelty. Either here or later even pregnant women were ripped up, their unborn babies torn out and the infants' brains bashed out on walls and on the ground. There was rape, and women and children were seized by the legs by burly fiends and torn apart. These hellions looted and burnt the show, casting the dead and dying into the flames. Most were killed with spears but some of the killings were by strangulation.

88

. . . The murderers' women stood about, laughing with glee at the burning booths, egging on their menfolk." *

While much of the violence in these days was spontaneous, some was carefully plotted. Each community had its organized, militant battalions. Among Muslims, the League had formed a National Guard with units in Bengal, United Provinces and the Punjab. Extremist Muslims formed the Khaksars, chiefly in the Punjab. Hindus had the R.S.S.S., a militant arm of the extremists with training camps in Bihar and Bengal, and the Congress-run Seva Dal. According to their religion, Sikh men carry swords; they also have traditions of military action and many served in the army. Each Sikh village could thus boast of a body of trained warriors prepared to act in a crisis.

On February 20, 1947, Prime Minister Attlee announced that the British would leave India in June, 1948, and, to direct the operation he sent Lord Louis Mountbatten to India as Viceroy.

The announcement of Britain's impending departure heightened the anxiety, particularly in the Punjab. Up to 1947, most of the blood had flowed in the cities and villages in Bengal, Bihar, and United Provinces. Now it was the Punjab's turn.

In one of its proposals for the future India, the British Cabinet Mission placed the Punjab in one unit, Bengal in another. Whoever controlled the unit controlled the province. Jinnah had accepted this grouping. So had the Congress. Not so the Sikhs of the Punjab or the Hindus of Bengal and Assam. They would be minorities under the Muslims and were as fearful of this possibility as the Muslims were of being a minority in India.

The Sikhs of the Punjab had always opposed the idea of

* Sir Francis Tuker, *While Memory Serves* (London: Cassell & Co., 1950) p. 198.

Pakistan. Most of them lived in the eastern part, but many lived around Lahore. Should the Punjab be declared part of Pakistan, Sikhs would be ruled by their traditional enemy, the Muslims.

Some Sikh leaders preferred to solve the problem by constitutional methods. Others adopted the tradition of the ancient Sikh warriors. Led by war-trained ex-soldiers of the Indian National Army, which fought with the Japanese against the British during World War II, many Sikhs joined private communal armies.

Trouble began in earnest after March, 1947, following the resignation, under Muslim League pressure, of the Unionist Party-Congress Party-Sikh coalition government in the Punjab. Communal riots swept the streets of Lahore, Rawalpindi and Amritsar. British authority at the local level collapsed as marauding bands of Sikhs and Muslims attacked each others' villages mercilessly.

Master Tara Singh, a revered Sikh leader, cried: "There can be no settlement if Muslims want to rule the Punjab."

Said another, Gyani Kartar Singh, president of the Akali Dal: "Our battle-axes shall decide if the Muslims shall rule."

Violence lent urgency to all three parties—British, Congress, and the Muslim League. Nehru demanded that in any partition arrangement the Punjab and Bengal be cut in two. Jinnah accepted, saying: "Better a moth-eaten Pakistan than no Pakistan at all." Lord Mountbatten returned to London and on June 4, 1947, announced suddenly that independence would be given to India *and* Pakistan on August 15. The following month, the British Parliament passed the India Independence Act creating the two new nations.

The very urgency that led to independence—and partition —months before either side expected it, produced chaos as tens of thousands fled from their homes, killing and being killed. Out of the chaos came Pakistan.

90

5. The Faltering Start

Two words, shouted rhythmically, marked the spirit of the new country after August 15, 1947. *"Pakistan Zindebad!"* *"Pakistan Zindebad!"* (Long live Pakistan.) Near Karachi, a defective tie derailed a train. Dozens of workers shouting "Pakistan Zindebad!" lifted it back onto the tracks within thirty minutes. People who had known little happiness found hope in the cry, "Pakistan Zindebad!" With not much else but spirit and a resolute leader, they set about creating a country.

Mohammed Ali Jinnah had been flown to Karachi a week before independence day, landing amidst a vast sea of people who had come to pay him homage. He was tired and sick, but he smiled as his car moved slowly along the hot Sind desert road to Government House.

"You are free," he told them, and they shouted, "Quaid-i-Azam Zindebad!"

To the discomfort of Sind government officials, Jinnah selected his home town of Karachi as the capital. Lahore was too close to India, and Dacca . . . well, that was in East Bengal. So thousands of strangers, mostly government clerks, descended on the quiet Arabian Sea port from New Delhi and Bombay with authority to take over desks, chairs, telephones and even houses. When Jinnah found the bookshelves of the Sind Governor's mansion empty, he insisted that the governor return the books. He ordered some "borrowed" croquet mallets and wickets sent back from Lahore.

Commissions under Sir Cyril Radcliffe set out to define the borders of the two countries. In Bengal, precedence helped. The partition in 1905, revoked in 1911, set a pattern for the 1947 borders, with West Bengal to include the city of Calcutta. A few sub-districts in Assam around the city of Sylhet became part of Pakistan. Yet many small areas were left undefined to create later controversy with India.

The Punjab was not so easy. Radcliffe's Boundary Commission could make no mark on the map without antagonizing someone. District by district, *tehsil* by *tehsil,* the line was drawn harshly through villages, farmlands and irrigation systems. Both leaders, Nehru and Jinnah, stood valiantly by their agreement to accept the Radcliffe decisions, even as their countrymen howled in protest.

The violence of pre-partition days was only a prologue to the anguish that followed August, 1947. For months before, families had been packing their few belongings and heading toward lands of their faith, where, presumably, they would be safe. Now, with the Punjab partitioned, the roads were clogged with frightened people seeking haven some place beyond. Trains leaving New Delhi for Lahore were jammed with Muslims; many did not get there. Near Amritsar, Sikhs slaughtered entire trainloads of men, women and children. In Lahore and West Punjab villages, Muslims killed great numbers of Sikhs and Hindus.

Within a few months, between 100,000 and 200,000 people died violently. The exact number may never be known. When the thousands who died from starvation and disease are added to these, the estimates exceed 500,000. The number who left their homes to settle in another land was close to 12,000,000. No other population movement in history involved so many people in so short a time. Bitterness was deep.

In cities across Pakistan and India, from Peshawar to Chittagong, hordes of poor and hungry *muhajireen* (refugees)

sought shelter, food and jobs. Karachi, before the war a modest port town of 25,000, suddenly became a swollen and squalid metropolis of nearly 1,000,000. The lucky ones lived in cane-built lean-to's propped against the sides of buildings and in shantytowns. The less fortunate passed their days and nights in the gutters or on the sidewalks. In all the towns of the new country, starvation, exposure, disease and despair marked the cost of partition. In Indian cities, Hindu and Sikh refugees created squalor and unrest no less fearful than in Pakistan.

Colossal Problems

Partition involved more than dividing peoples. Filing cabinets, naval vessels, railway cars, airplanes, bank accounts, and surgical instruments had to be shared. A commission established general rules for dividing the subcontinent's assets, with India getting the larger share. Division of the "spoils" plagued relations between the two countries in succeeding years and remains an aggravating friction.

As if the violent emotions generated by partition were not enough, the realities of economics seemed even more calamitous. Pakistan's two wings had no industry of significance, they had poor transportation, little electric power, and few administrators and technicians. What little economic strength existed was largely sapped by collisions with India and the demands of the refugees.

In 1947, Pakistan's economy depended upon four crops—cotton, wheat, rice, and jute. The population movements in the wheat- and cotton-producing Punjab caused a sharp drop in production and the vital irrigation systems were broken in two. Cotton, the major export product of West Pakistan, lost its Indian market and great mounds of cotton bales rotted on the wharves of Karachi. In East Pakistan, heaps of jute bales sat in Dacca unable to be moved by rail or shipped to the jute mills of Calcutta. A jute war between the two countries, each

93

side raising its demands and duties against the other, led to a complete economic break between East and West Bengal.

Partition left Pakistan without any industrial wealth to fall back on as its agricultural base deteriorated. What few small factories existed in the Punjab were Hindu- and Sikh-operated and they began to deteriorate when the Hindus left. There was a banking system but no one to operate it and investment capital, except for some funds from Hyderabad State in India, was scarce. Even the traditions of Muslim society worked against industrial progress. Muslims had habitually invested in land and trade, not industry or banking. One group of Muslims, the Ismailis from Bombay, were trained in banking. After partition, many of them migrated to Karachi where they played a vital role in financing the new government.

The formidable task of setting up a government fell to fewer than 100 top Muslim, British-trained administrators, not one of whom was a Bengali. At their side stood three other groups, two Muslim and one non-Muslim. The first was the military, whose dedicated, non-political cadre of leaders, all British-trained and experienced in administration, assured a degree of stability. A second was the judiciary which contained some of India's outstanding legal minds. Islam's emphasis on law had led many Indian Muslims into the legal profession where they attained considerable stature. Pakistan's courts were to be a bulwark in the stormy years ahead.

Another group who gave initial help was the Christian Anglo-Indians. For generations, these people, a part of each culture, yet belonging to neither, had performed a unique role in society. Both English and Indians had confidence enough in them to entrust them with vital responsibilities. While political bombshells burst around them, they kept the trains running, the telephone and telegraph lines open and the police force under control.

94

But helpful as these dedicated and loyal groups were, Jinnah realized they were inadequate to fill Pakistan's needs. His solution to the manpower problem was in keeping with his realism. He hired the British and, fortunately, there were many former "colonialists" who were willing and able to assist. Throughout the government in its early days, the British held posts requiring special skills and experience.

The government of Pakistan on August 15, 1947, was based on the Government of India Act of 1935 and the India Independence Act of 1947. This "constitution" provided for a parliamentary government along British lines with a Crown-appointed governor and a legislature from which a cabinet was to be selected to carry out executive functions. It divided the responsibilities of government between the central parliament—called the National Assembly—and the parliaments of the various provinces. The central cabinet theoretically had authority over the defense and security of the country—the armed forces, communications, railroads—and finance and foreign affairs. The provincial cabinets controlled health, education, agriculture, local government and law enforcement. The largest administrative units of the provinces were called divisions, headed by an appointed divisional commissioner. Divisions were administered through districts, each with a magistrate or commissioner, whose main functions were to collect taxes and maintain law and order in the tradition of Moghul and British government in the subcontinent. There was no machinery for involving the villagers in government.

Jinnah accepted the Crown appointment of governor-general of Pakistan, while in India Lord Louis Mountbatten assumed this post. Presumably it was a figure-head job, as it was in India, but Jinnah established a precedent. He was boss.

Pakistan's new legislature was composed, with a few exceptions, of Muslim Leaguers elected in 1946 to the Indian Constituent Assembly. Jinnah was also president of the As-

sembly, whose cabinet comprised members of the Muslim League and one Hindu. Liaquat Ali Khan, Jinnah's long-time aide, was prime minister, minister of defense and minister of foreign affairs. (In India, Jawaharlal Nehru became prime minister.) The finance minister was Ghulam Mohammed, a strong-willed Punjabi educated at Aligarh University and one of the few Muslims to rise to the top of the Indian Civil Service. From Bengal, Jinnah selected Fazlur Rahman, a lawyer, and J. N. Mandal, a Hindu "untouchable" who had been president of the Bengal Scheduled Castes Federation.

New Pakistan appeared in the family of nations as an independent state, geographically divided, but constitutionally united. Mohammed Ali Jinnah was its head and his loyal cabinet represented the various parts. In fact, however, Pakistan in late 1947 was a very unstable mixture of provinces and powerful leaders who, amidst the emotions of religion and the harsh realities of politics, joined together under a strong leader to meet an emergency. Each had interests of its own which spread the disease of dissension that threatened Pakistan soon after its birth.

East Bengal had the largest number of special interests. A thousand miles from the capital of Karachi and separated from the western provinces by an enemy as yet unresigned to Pakistan independence, East Bengal felt neglected from the start. Indeed, Bengal's chief minister in early 1947, Hussein S. Suhrawardy, demanded Bengal's complete independence and, on being rebuffed by Jinnah, decided not to live in Pakistan. While he was a member of the Pakistan National Assembly (elected by the East Bengal legislature), he joined Mahatma Gandhi in West Bengal and spent many months attempting to settle communal problems in India. He did not reside permanently in Pakistan until after Jinnah's death.

Suhrawardy's views were indicative of the chauvinistic views of many Bengalis, but in 1947 millions of them were enthusi-

96

astic about the new "Islamic" state. Besides their religious feelings, many also remembered the elation of partition forty-two years earlier.

East Bengalis entered the nationhood of Pakistan with pride; their beloved leader, Fazlul Haq, had presented the "Pakistan Resolution" to the Muslim League in 1940. They outnumbered West Pakistanis 47,000,000 to 33,000,000. Their agricultural cash crops, jute and tea, earned 70 per cent of Pakistan's foreign exchange. Compared with the West Pakistanis, East Bengalis knew they were better educated, more experienced politically and more united. Independence, as with partition years before, was their hope of solving their poverty and their dependence upon the Hindus of Calcutta. Out of 2,237 large landholders, only 356 were Muslims.

Yet their country's new capital was Karachi, in the province of Sind. In the nation's new parliament, legislators spoke English and Urdu, not Bengali. The power of the Muslim League belonged to Indian refugees, not to East Bengalis. Muslim League spokesmen from Bengal, Fazlur Rahman and Khwaja Nazimuddin, were political conservatives, members of a landlord dynasty who represented urban wealth, not rural poverty. Bengalis felt that their new Pakistan government was neglecting them, particularly when Punjabi troops arrived in Dacca "to keep order" and Punjabi administrators took over government offices (although there were no trained Bengalis to handle these chores).

Each West Pakistan province contained special interests and severe problems, too. The Punjab, largest by far of the western provinces and also the wealthiest, swarmed with powerful leaders, nearly all landlords, each seeking to control provincial governments and, ultimately, the central government. The problems of the Punjab were immense. For a while, refugees descended on Lahore at the rate of 51,000 a day. Dozens of factories stood idle. Agricultural land lay fallow. The head-

waters of West Punjab's great canal system were in the hands of the enemy, India, which intermittently cut off the flow of precious water. The future of the people depended upon prompt attention to the province's agriculture, industry and restless population. Extremist groups such as the Majlis-i-Ahrars and the communists sought to foment revolution.

The Northwest Frontier Province always played a special role in South Asian affairs and its leaders demanded special attention after partition. Pathan nationalism was strong and Pathan loyalty to Pakistan was tenuous. Abdul Ghaffar Khan, loved and respected by many tribesmen, had persuaded his followers to support the Indian National Congress, and his brother, Dr. Khan Sahib, had been chief minister in a Frontier Congress ministry.

The growing appeal of the Pakistan movement had finally found adherents in the Frontier, among them the influential Pir of Manki Sharif and Abdul Quayyum Khan. In July, 1947, Pathans in the "administered" area of the NWFP voted to join Pakistan and in August the Muslim League leaders joined the National Assembly in Karachi. The cooperation of some Pathans was not wholehearted; Jinnah soon ordered Abdul Ghaffar Khan imprisoned and Dr. Khan deposed as chief minister and placed under house detention.

Jinnah knew his people. Immediately after partition, he withdrew Pakistani army units from the Frontier and left the responsibility for law and order in the hands of the Pathans themselves. Eventually such Pathan leaders as Abdul Quayyum Khan and Sardar Rab Nishtar were able to develop among Pathans a sense of identity with Pakistan strong enough to resist Afghan and Indian attempts to stir up demands for Pashtunistan.

Sind Province created no special problems equal to those of Bengal, Punjab or the Frontier. Most Sind politicians—all wealthy landlords—were generally loyal to the Muslim

League, but prone to misconduct and corruption. The first prime minister of Sind was M. A. Khuro, one of the province's largest landlords who, when Jinnah dismissed him in 1948, was charged with sixty-two specific allegations of maladministration. Sind's problems were acutely social and economic, although for a period the existence of the capital in Karachi caused friction between the provincial leaders and government.

Jinnah had proclaimed that Pakistan could succeed only through "unity, faith and discipline," and these were the goals he constantly sought during the one year left to him to lead his people. As the summer heat descended on Karachi in 1948, Jinnah moved his little court to the spruce- and juniper-covered hills above Quetta in a village called Ziarat. Here in the cool heights he lived his last days, issuing orders, fretting over government papers and worrying about the bitter battle between India and Pakistan over Kashmir. On September 11, an airplane flew him back to Karachi on a stretcher. That night, he died.

The invincible leader, then, was gone. For the first time in many years, South Asian Muslims had no single individual to direct their course. Jinnah had held the country together through the sheer force of his will. Admonishing politicians, lecturing civil servants and commanding obedience, he literally ordered Pakistanis to unite. Quaid-i-Azam spoke and his people obeyed.

Jinnah's personality made the position of governor-general important, although its powers were limited by the British constitutional tradition. To fill this post, the Muslim League selected a Bengali landlord, Khwaja Nazimuddin. Liaquat Ali Khan continued as prime minister and upon him fell the mantle of leadership. He had the advantages not only of being Jinnah's chief lieutenant, but he was also a refugee and not identified with any particular province.

99

Nevertheless, Jinnah's death released a torrent of suppressed ambitions. They fell into two general fields. One involved the controversy over the role of religion in the new country, as expressed specifically in the writing of a new constitution. The other was the struggle by urban politicians for power within the various provinces and among the provinces for control of the central government. Neither issue involved or was meant to include the millions of Pakistani villagers.

Religious Debates

The responsibility for writing a constitution lay with the National Assembly, which had also been designated a Constituent Assembly. In the latter role, the members met on the average of ten days a year during the first six years of Pakistan's existence. They could not produce a constitution. They did stir up considerable argument, however, some of which led to bloodshed.

The arguments over Pakistan's future laws were, in a real sense, a continuation of the reform movements and dialogues over Islam in the subcontinent begun in the eighteenth century. They involved many of the descendants of the early reformers, such as Maulvi Tamizzudin Khan, who was President of the Constituent Assembly. They included movements which had their birth over a century ago. For the first time, the followers of Sayyid Ahmed Khan's Aligarh "progressive" movement met in open debate with the classical and fundamentalist followers of the Deoband school of theology to try and produce a practical constitution for a twentieth century state. Very little of the discourse concerned the people of Pakistan.

The extreme—and loudest—position was led by Maulana Maududi, president of the Jama'at i Islami, who, after partition (which he had opposed) brought his followers to Pakistan in hopes of creating there a true Islamic community. Among the refugees in Lahore, to whom he and his adherents

100

ministered devotedly in both material aid and spiritual sustenance, he gained many supporters. Students and workers also came under his influence as their frustrations found an outlet in Maududi's religious fundamentalism.

Some of Maududi's demands were that the state should be declared an "agent of God," the basic law should be the shari'a, and only Muslims could hold major offices. Maududi did not consider Ahmadiyas true Muslims. The economic system and social structure would be that revealed by the Koran and sunnah. Maududi called for an Islamic revolution to re-create the life of Arabia 1,325 years ago.

A less reactionary position was held by the ulema of respected Muslim divines, the Jama'at-i-Ulema-i-Islam, led originally by Maulana Shabbir Ahmed Usmani (who died in 1949). Maulana Usmani was a member of the Muslim League and a partisan of an "Islamic" state. He once wrote: "The mullah does not want to rule, he only wants the rulers to be somewhat like the mullah."

To the academicians and politicians went the task of presenting the various degrees of secularism. They included conservative landlords, students of British liberalism and Muslims still enamored by the ruthless, but effective leadership of Kemal Ataturk who brought secular government to Turkey after World War I. They were joined by members of religious minorities—Hindus, Christians, Parsees, as well as Shi'ites and Ahmadiyas—who were apprehensive of their positions in a state based solely on Islamic law as interpreted by Maulana Maududi and Maulana Usmani.

Their fears were heightened by religious riots, aimed mainly at the Ahmadiyas. Serious agitation against this minority Muslim sect began in 1952 as debate of the Islamic constitution reached an emotional pitch. The Ahmadiyas represented to many Sunnites the epitome of heresy. Even more galling was that Mohammed Zafrulla Khan, the foreign minister, was an

101

Ahmadiya. Accusing him of packing the foreign ministry with Ahmadiyas, Maulana Maududi and other Muslim groups, especially the Ahrars in the Punjab, called for his resignation and demonstrated in the streets. In Lahore and Karachi, sporadic protests fanned into violence. After the army quelled the riots, a military court sentenced Maududi to death, but the sentence was later commuted. The Ahrars were banned.

Provincialism

Provincialism plagued Pakistan from the start and provided Liaquat Ali Khan with his greatest test of leadership after Jinnah's death. That he passed the test could be attributed to his strong personality and favorable economic conditions brought on by good harvests and the Korean war. He was also aided by public fear of India. While many Pakistani politicians placed their own personal and provincial interests ahead of Pakistan's national interest, they were first of all more anti-Indian than anything else. If the alternative to unity was re-association with India, they would be patriotic Pakistanis.

On October 16, 1951, Liaquat Ali Khan was assassinated while making a speech in Rawalpindi. The seeds of disruption burst into full bloom as the Punjabis and Bengalis fought for power. In the next seven years, Pakistan had six prime ministers and one revolution.

To fill the vacancy left by Liaquat's death, the Muslim League selected the Bengali Governor-General, Khwaja Nazimuddin, as prime minister. The Punjabis were able to have the finance minister, Ghulam Mohammed, made governor-general. He, like Jinnah, applied a firm hand in the position. Unlike Jinnah, he was identified in Bengal with the Punjabi partisans who controlled the civil service and the army. He was blamed by Bengalis for Pakistan's refusal in 1949 to devalue its currency in the face of devaluation by India and

102

Great Britain. At the time, devaluation helped India's jute industry at the expense of East Bengal's.

Nazimuddin was not a forceful person, yet he was surrounded by forceful politicians. Indeed, many members of his own cabinet, although members of the League, formed their own personal followings in the National Assembly. The League became increasingly splintered and, finally, powerless.

The Muslim League had come to life in the sheltered salons of India's more prosperous, educated Muslims. For a few years, Jinnah and Liaquat had drawn support from the Muslim masses, but on their deaths the League forgot them. It returned to the salons from which it came, offering no philosophy, ideal or program to the people of Pakistan.

Nazimuddin was a loyal Muslim Leaguer who, though he was from Bengal, was not a Bengali nationalist. He spoke Urdu himself, and even called upon Bengalis to accept Urdu as *the* only national language. Protests spread through the province and Nazimuddin and the Muslim League lost support. Inability to control the anti-Ahmadiya riots in Lahore and Karachi, continued defeats in the negotiations with India and the United Nations over Kashmir, and serious economic reverses combined to bring about Nazimuddin's downfall. In 1953, the governor-general summarily dismissed him, thereby violating—for the first time, but not the last time—the principles of parliamentary democracy.

The new prime minister was also a Bengali, from Bogra, Mohammed Ali, whose main qualifications for the position were his successful ambassadorship in Washington, D. C. and his lack of involvement in politics. He, too, failed to provide leadership or strength equal to that of Ghulam Mohammed and before long, the specter of Bengal nationalism rose to defeat him. The very fact that he was *not* a politician turned out to be a weakness.

103

In March, 1954, Bengal held its first elections. Into the fray came the old pre-partition parties—Suhrawardy's Awami League and Fazlul Haq's Krishak Sramik Party, as well as other small groups, including the communists. As a United Front, they overpowered the impotent Muslim League, which gained only 10 out of the 309 seats. Fazlul Haq became provincial chief minister in the midst of labor riots. He exacerbated the situation by calling for an "independent" Bengal. The central government in Karachi, still controlled by the Muslim League, charged Fazlul Haq with treason and ousted him. A new governor was sent to control the rebellious province. His name was Iskander Mirza, an army major-general and longtime civil servant who within days had his army arrest more than 1,000 people.

The collapse of the Muslim League in Bengal and subsequent demonstrations throughout the country, as well as the National Assembly attempt to curb his powers, led Ghulam Mohammed on October 24, 1954 to declare a national state of emergency. He dissolved the National Assembly—many of whose members represented the defunct League in Bengal—only to have the courts declare his move illegal. On other grounds, he declared a new state of emergency and again the courts contradicted him. Rather than call back the old unrepresentative assembly, Ghulam Mohammed, under prodding from the Supreme Court, called for a new parliament. In the summer of 1955, the provincial legislatures elected eighty members to Pakistan's Second National (and Constituent) Assembly. The Muslim League won twenty-six seats.

In the face of Bengal's repudiation of the Muslim League, Mohammed Ali resigned as prime minister. In October, 1955, due as much to illness as politics, Ghulam Mohammed also resigned as governor-general. He died a year later.

The new Assembly politicians called upon General Iskander Mirza to be governor-general. He was a bureaucrat, autocratic

and impatient. He had no hesitation in announcing publicly that what Pakistan needed was a "controlled democracy."

His prime minister was a Punjabi civil servant named Chaudhri Mohammed Ali. One of his first acts was to carry out a plan that Punjabis had been hatching for some time—the unification of West Pakistan. Called the One Unit scheme, the integration of West Pakistan's four provinces and ten small principalities into one unit, with its capital at Lahore, would be economically advantageous and put West Pakistanis on an equal footing with East Pakistanis. Through the Muslim League in West Pakistan, Punjabis expected to control the new province. While their Muslim League-dominated legislatures approved the plan, many Pathans, Sindis and other non-Punjabi groups took a dim view of this development. Bengalis were particularly incensed.

Under Chaudhri Mohammed Ali, Pakistan also acquired its first constitution, which came into effect on March 23, 1956. By late 1955, the ingredients of Pakistan's new constitutional cake were ready for mixing. They had been studied, discussed, fought over and written into numerous documents and proposals, generating considerable political heat. Unfortunately, the cake fell in the baking. It lacked the leavening of reality and opportunity.

The 1956 constitution, which was meant to continue the old parliamentary system, was basically a "foreign" document, imported by British-trained Muslim lawyers who were steeped in British-Indian parliamentary history. It took the British 700 years to develop the basis of British common law and political responsibility. Pakistanis, over 80 per cent illiterate and independent for only nine years, were expected to provide this basis almost overnight. With good leadership, such as Prime Minister Nehru gave to Indians, the system might have worked. But such leadership in Pakistan was lacking

and it had no opportunity to prove itself. Elections were never held under the 1956 constitution.

Many hopes rode on the new government of President Iskander Mirza and his new prime minister, Hussein Suhrawardy. Both were honest men. Mirza supplied administrative talent; Suhrawardy was a genuine and practical Bengali politician, capable of understanding the country's needs. Together, they sought joint electorates for Muslims and Hindus, reversing the very principle of Pakistan's formation. They kept Pakistan's pro-Western alliances strong, even in the face of the tempestuous Suez crisis. But eventually, General Mirza's desire to "control" democracy and his suspicion and contempt of political institutions collided with Suhrawardy's political activity and the two men parted company.

Beginning of Collapse

At the end of its first decade of life, Pakistan was a cauldron of political furor. The Punjabi politicians had begun to fight among themselves as well as with Pathans and Sindis. New parties appeared, old ones re-appeared. Few of them involved the villagers and small tradesmen who played little part in the first ten years of Pakistan's political life. Except in East Pakistan, where such leaders as Fazlul Haq genuinely sought the participation of villagers, politics and self-government was an urban activity limited to the educated few, especially the landlords, industrialists, and lawyers. Stripped of the personalities of their leaders, the political parties were ideologically similar—and empty.

President Mirza joined the political fray and engineered the appointment of the Pathan leader, Dr. Khan Sahib, as chief minister of the new single province of West Pakistan. Many prominent Punjabi politicians, members of the Muslim Leaguers, protested bitterly, especially when Dr. Khan Sahib

formed the new Republican Party in 1956 with President Mirza's backing. Each side found support from feuding landlord families across the province. The National Awami Party, led by a Sindi, G. M. Syed, and some Pathan followers of Abdul Ghaffar Khan, held the balance of power in the National Assembly between the League and the Republicans. Its major platform: dismantling the One Unit scheme.

In East Pakistan, disunity was no less intense. The United Front of Suhrawardy and Fazlul Haq collapsed, Suhrawardy's Awami Party rivaled Haq's Krishak Sramik Party, each seeking aid from the seventy-two Hindu and other minority members of the provincial assembly.

Across the country, moral standards seemed to deteriorate. Wealthy families and wholesale merchants hoarded food and smuggled gold. Food riots broke out in East Pakistan and a new movement began there with successionist claims. Smuggling between East Pakistan and West Bengal in India reached such proportions that the army inaugurated a campaign, called "Operation Close Door" to stop it. Labor strikes closed vital industries and Pakistan's foreign exchange reserves plummeted. The continued failure of Pakistan's diplomats to obtain concessions from India over Kashmir kept tempers high and the refugees still slept on the streets, ill and idle. Government officials resigned by the dozens as politicians hampered their work. Others resorted to corruption. In the villages, even the politically-disinterested farmer began to show his resentment. No one knew this better than the army recruiting officers, the few men in government service who had continual contact with Pakistan's rural masses. In the army, normally non-political officers became restless as they saw graft and greed subvert Jinnah's ideals for a Muslim nation.

In 1958, plans were laid for new elections under the 1956 constitution. Intrigue, especially in West Pakistan's legislature

in Lahore, rose to new heights. Dr. Khan Sahib was assassinated. Students in high schools and colleges were organized to electioneer for whichever candidate paid them the most. Landlords' agents toured their villages compelling voters to support their landlord. In East Pakistan's parliament, rivalry reached a violent climax when a fight broke out September 23, 1958. The deputy speaker was injured so badly when struck by a flying piece of furniture that he later died. President Mirza was unable to "control" his rampaging "democracy."

Once before, during the riots of 1955, the governor-general (Ghulam Mohammed) had asked the army's commander, General Mohammed Ayub Khan, to take over the country. General Ayub had refused. The army was solidly built upon British traditions of disassociation from politics; administer, yes, but govern, no. Its leaders had generally stayed out of politics and had done their work efficiently and effectively, gaining a good reputation for the army by quelling various riots in which it had been ordered to act. That it now took action on its own pointed to the low state into which Pakistan's leadership had fallen.

Early in October, 1958, General Ayub confronted President Mirza with the fact that the army was planning a coup d'état. On October 7, at General Ayub's insistence, President Mirza illegally suspended the constitution, abolished the legislatures and ordered political parties disbanded. He declared martial law throughout the country and appointed General Ayub as Chief of the Martial Law Administration.

General Ayub was prepared for the assignment. His troops had been placed quietly and strategically throughout the cities. There was no resistance and Pakistan's government fell peacefully without bloodshed.

At first, President Mirza and General Ayub, colleagues for years, attempted to work as a team. Only a few days passed,

108

however, before it was obvious to Ayub that Mirza was a liability. His reputation was tarnished, and he appeared to be more of a competitor than a partner. On October 27, Mirza reluctantly flew off to London and General Ayub declared himself "Head of State." Pakistan had become a military dictatorship.

6. Experimental Democracy

In October, 1958, many who cared for Asian affairs shrugged their shoulders. Another "underdeveloped country" had fallen to its army in a coup d'état. As had gone Egypt, Burma, Iraq and Syria, so went Pakistan.

"My authority is revolution," General Mohammed Ayub Khan openly admitted. "I have no sanction in law or constitution."

Promptly he began to act. He appointed "experts" to his cabinet—three army generals and eight civilians, four from each province. As minister of rehabilitation, he named General Azam Khan, whose army troops had quelled the Punjab riots of 1953. Mohammed Shoaib, a financier, took over the empty treasury. A lawyer and son of a respected judge, Manzur Qadir, became foreign minister. Zulfikar Ali Bhutto, a young and brilliant economist and lawyer, became minister of commerce. Behind closed doors, a powerful team of army officers, each in control of vital units of the armed forces, sat in continual conference.

As with many modern-day dictators, General Ayub ordered a literal cleanup of the country and soon Pakistanis were comparing the number of flies in Karachi with fly statistics from Communist China. But General Ayub wanted more than flies. Before the Martial Law Regime was ended on June 8, 1962, more than 1,660 government servants had been dismissed or forcibly retired for misconduct, corruption and inefficiency. Hundreds of businessmen and politicians had gone

110

to jail for blackmarketeering, hoarding and smuggling. More than two tons of smuggled gold had been uncovered and millions of rupees in unpaid taxes collected. New price controls and police action against hoarders stabilized the food markets. Ayub appointed commissions to study economics, education, health, land reform, and the entire political system. Within a few months these commissions had submitted their recommendations.

The efficiency of dictatorship brought startling results. Ayub was a man of quick decisions. On the advice of his land reform commissioner, Akhtar Hussain, he decreed new changes in land tenure and ownership which stripped power from some of the biggest landowners. He commanded General Azam Khan to settle Karachi's refugees without delay. A new Muslim Family Laws Ordinance, decreed in 1961, tore at the fabric of classical Islam, to the dismay of the mullahs. A Commission on National Education recommended sweeping changes in the educational system.

Many Pakistanis, those who had lost faith in their dream for a Muslim country, found new hope in the pronouncements and actions of Ayub's military government. It was as though Jinnah had returned and the enthusiasm of 1947 was felt anew. Former government servants who had resigned out of discouragement came back to join the move forward. Students who had been studying abroad rushed home.

Like many dictators, General Ayub vowed that his revolution was temporary.

"Let me announce in unequivocal terms," he said, "that our ultimate aim is to restore democracy." Throughout the world and particularly in India, many were skeptical.

Mohammed Ayub Khan was born on May 14, 1907, in Rihana village in the mountainous Hazara district between the former Northwest Frontier Province and the Punjab. Many Muslim military officers have been reared in this area

111

and, because of their family ties, have sometimes been called Pathans. However, few of them are considered Pathans by those tribesmen living to the west and few can speak good Pashto. For instance, General Ayub does not speak fluent Pashto.

Following modern tradition, Ayub as a young man attended Aligarh University and then entered the Royal Military College at Sandhurst, England. He served with a British regiment for a year, then joined the Fourteenth Punjab Regiment which saw action against the Japanese in Burma during World War II. By 1947, he was one of only thirty-two pre-war Muslim army officers; the rest were wartime recruits. Thus after partition, he rose rapidly in the service. He became a brigadier and led a brigade in the tribal area of Waziristan. Later, he commanded troops in East Pakistan and in 1951 became the first Pakistani Commander-in-Chief of the army, with instructions to re-organize and modernize the military.

A hearty, personable individual, over six feet tall, with a clipped mustache and a precise command of English, General Ayub was the model of British-Indian soldiery. He was an expert horseman. He loved to hunt, fish, and play tennis. His major interests were military history and international affairs. Local politics bored him, as did pompous politicians.

General Ayub was a seemingly reluctant dictator. His influence in the army had been strong for many years, ever since some army officers were implicated in a 1951 conspiracy to overthrow the government. On several occasions, he could have put the army into power—during the Punjab riots in 1953, after Nazimuddin's dismissal the same year, and after the dissolution of the first Constituent Assembly in 1955. At that time Governor-General Ghulam Mohammed literally begged him to take over. Ayub may have been tempted to step in earlier, but his training opposed it. Although an impatient person, he was a disciplined soldier. Besides, he had

112

not completed the modernization of the army. In 1954, he joined the government's cabinet only to quit in disgust in 1956 over the game of politics.

The key to democratic government, said Ayub, lies in the effectiveness of institutions that represent and include the masses of people. Such institutions did exist in Pakistan and had been there for years, but they were stagnant from neglect.

Foremost among these were the panchayats, the village councils whose origins were centuries old. While empire after empire rose and fell, the villagers paid their taxes and, in relative isolation, governed themselves through these institutions. The members of the panchayats were the elders, the venerated religious leaders, the landlord or, later, his agent.

In Pakistan, the panchayats had little opportunity to perform constructive political work. They were not integrated into the framework of government. There was no regular election system. Ignored in West Pakistan, they were controlled by the landlords and the mullahs. They had no resources to undertake constructive action.

East Pakistan was more fortunate than West Pakistan. In the late nineteenth century, British administrators in Bengal established some 4,000 village councils called Union Boards, many based on the panchayats. The boards were primarily local security units which kept law and order and tried minor disputes. Sometimes they concerned themselves with the water supply, sanitation, or other social and political problems. Like the panchayats, however, they were isolated from the general structure of government; they were separate little political arenas often under the thumb of the landlord.

There were also municipal committees and councils throughout the larger towns of East and West Pakistan. These, too, had shown signs of positive action in meeting urban problems but more often than not they were torn with

political rivalries and again isolated from the government structure.

More recently, new village councils came into being through the Village AID (Agriculture and Industrial Development) program. Started in 1953 with the help of American technicians, the councils were more concerned with economics than politics, but they did give villagers an opportunity to work together. Nevertheless, the councils, grown to more than 19,000, also lacked contact with the political structure.

In a democracy, said Ayub, "every man, woman and child must participate to the fullest possible extent." In looking at these village and urban institutions and seeing that under previous parliamentary governments they had had little relationship with the political system, he concluded that they would not work. He said:

"Without going to the hard core of our nation at a really intimate level, every system of democracy in our country is bound to become a farce, as it did in the past. The large majority of our people live in villages. They are mostly uneducated and illiterate and, therefore, unable to exercise their right of vote except at a community or village level. Their personal contacts, and the immediacy and urgency of individual community interests make it practical and possible for them to judge people and elect only those in whom they have full confidence, based on personal knowledge of the candidate's background, temperament, behavior towards other people, and past performances in general. This also applies to the urban areas. . . ."

The institution for making democracy "intimate" was a new system (for Pakistan) called "Basic Democracies." General Ayub had formulated a plan for creating grass roots political institutions before he came to power. A year after his take-over, he promulgated the Basic Democracies order.

114

Basic Democracies

The "primary constituency" in the Basic Democracies is a group of neighbors numbering about 1,000. All persons in the group, men and women over twenty-one years of age, who are not government employees, may vote for a representative, who must be over twenty-five. This elected individual is called a Basic Democrat.

Basic Democrats are grouped together, like platoons, into councils. The smallest, with ten Basic Democrats and five others appointed by the government, is the Union Council or, in the cities, the Town Committee. There are 4,000 Councils in West Pakistan and 4,200 in East Pakistan, each representing about 10,000 people. After the 1965 elections, the government plans to dispense with appointed members.

The elected chairmen of the councils are members of the next higher group. In West Pakistan this is the Tehsil Council, named after the administrative district established long ago for tax purposes. In East Pakistan, the council is called Thana Council for the same reason. At least half the members of these councils must be Basic Democrats; the rest are appointed.

The next higher body is the District Council, composed of Basic Democrats from the Tehsil and Thana councils and other appointed members, with the latter outnumbering the former. Chairmen of these are members of Divisional councils. Theoretically, there is a Provincial Council, but this step has not yet been taken. Provincial matters are in the hands of Provincial Assemblies, whose members need not be Basic Democrats.

Each council in the chain has judicial, police, and developmental responsibilities. Each has limited taxing and spending authority. It is expected to respond to village needs in health, education, and economic development, initiating "self-

115

help" projects wherever possible. Its members work with government specialists assigned to its area. Each council chairman is president of a "conciliation court" which attempts to settle village disputes. These frequently involve marriage and divorce or controversies over water and grazing rights. Throughout, however, the government bureaucrats have complete authority over all council actions.

One of the greatest problems in Pakistan's governmental systems has been the ignorance of both the governed and the governing about the activities and needs of each. Through the Union Councils, villagers are expected to learn how and why government officials levy taxes, maintain law and order, operate schools and direct thousands of the experts trained to help with village problems. The villager learns that the government is not omnipotent and is unable to meet all his desires, or even his needs. The bureaucrat, on the other hand, is expected to become familiar with the primary needs and the limitations and strengths of the villagers.

The councils are above all expected to be educational, providing training grounds for future leaders. The government has established training centers so that Basic Democrats may learn how to conduct meetings, maintain correspondence and records, draw up and keep budgets, find new sources of revenue, utilize the skills of government servants, seek advice and obtain financial aid.

General Ayub ordered the first elections in the Basic Democracies program in December, 1959. Touring West Pakistan in a private train called "Pak Jumhuriat Special"—and East Pakistan by airplane—he spoke before thousands of villagers and townsmen, explaining the program and answering hundreds of questions. Student volunteers, radio, films, and pamphlets helped to "sell" the idea.

Government figures report that 67 per cent of the men and 42 per cent of the women of Pakistan voted. They elected

116

83,245 Basic Democrats, of whom 50,000 were village leaders, 30,000 were shopkeepers and tradesmen, and the remainder were businessmen, journalists, retired civil servants and lawyers. About 10,000 were illiterate. Many Village AID leaders were elected.

The elections were relatively honest, although there were cases of purchased votes. Indeed, one of the problems inherent in the system is that a candidate need secure less than 1,000 votes to be elected.

Other weaknesses appeared. Illiterate villagers did not suddenly acquire a sense of social responsibility overnight. They elected many landlords, mullahs and pirs, the old panchayat leaders who were able to perpetuate their power through the traditional social system. Urban groups, who number only about 15 per cent of the population, yet contain nearly 100 per cent of the educated, professional leaders, lost considerable representation. Non-Muslims elected only 7.5 per cent of the Basic Democrats whereas they comprise 12 per cent of the population.

The concept of the Basic Democracies reflects a soldier's attempt to organize the entire society along military lines. It is an experiment in limited, but expanding, self-government, which requires the test of time before it is proven. It could prove no less effective, however, than the program Pakistan tried half-heartedly during its first ten years.

It was to the 83,000 Basic Democrats that General Ayub turned in early 1960 to confirm his command of the revolution. In an election in which the Basic Democrats were given a choice of General Ayub or no one, 95.6 per cent voted for General Ayub. On February 14, 1960, he took the oath of office as president. A few days later, he appointed a commission of five East and five West Pakistanis to draw up a new constitution.

The Constitution of 1962

President Ayub's call for a new constitution relighted all the old fires of controversy over the meaning of Pakistan. This time, however, the fires were carefully tended by the Pakistan army which, under the Martial Law Regime, effectively controlled the country. Political parties attempted to re-emerge only to be suppressed. Many politicians went to jail.

President Ayub laid down four conditions for his democracy. It should:

1) Be simple to understand, easy to work and cheap to run;
2) Put to the voter only such questions as the voter can understand without external prompting;
3) Ensure the effective participation of all citizens to their full intellectual capacity;
4) Produce reasonably strong and stable governments.

The constitutional commission reported in a little over a year. It said that Pakistan had no deep traditions in parliamentary government. British colonial government in pre-partition India was certainly not "parliamentary" so far as South Asians were concerned. The commission claimed that the failure of parliamentary government after 1947 was not the fault of the system, but an absence of proper elections, undue interference from heads of state, irresponsible political parties and poor leadership. The commission recommended a stronger presidential role, but an equally powerful legislature. President Ayub disagreed and challenged the suitability of the parliamentary system. Behind the scenes, with General Azam Khan and Manzur Qadir, he prepared another version which became the new constitution on March 1, 1962.

In a stroke, the President made Pakistan a republic governed by a single president (no vice-president), a single na-

Women stroll in the spacious gardens of the Tomb of Jehangir in
Lahore

Tribesmen of the Frontier

A modern office building in Karachi

The Mahabat Khan Mosque at Peshawar

Thelma Johnson

Village children examine dead locusts at the scene of locust spraying operations in the desert area

A staff technician explains X-ray apparatus to students at the TB Control Demonstration and Training Centre

Unations

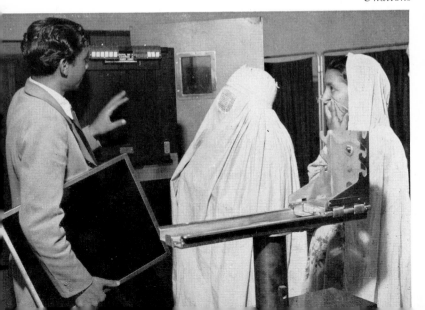

Girl students from Dacca University

Basic Democracies—polling scene in Karachi

The ancient Persian Wheel is still in use in parts of West Pakistan

Right: A Sindi farmer of the Ghulam Mohammad Barrage area of West Pakistan

Below: Jhoomer—a colorful dance of West Pakistan

Havoc caused by devastating floods in East Pakistan

tional assembly (legislature) and two provincial assemblies, with the position of president dominant. The president and all legislators are elected by an electoral college (the Basic Democrats), not directly by the people.

Unlike the constitution of 1956, President Ayub's constitution did not designate Pakistan as "Islamic." However, on December 25, 1963, in response to pressure by religious interests, the National Assembly amended the constitution and Pakistan became an "Islamic Republic" again. The amendment also restored the bases of all laws as being the Koran and the sunnah.

According to the new constitution, the president, who must be a Muslim, is the sole executive authority of government. He appoints his own ministers, who need not be members of the National Assembly, but if they are, they must then resign. He obtains legislative advice through appointed parliamentary secretaries from the Assembly who serve with each minister at the president's pleasure. He appoints the attorney-general, the judges of the courts, and the governors of the two provinces. He has complete responsibility for the Tribal Areas, which include the states of Amb, Chitral, Dir and Swat as well as the areas bordering Afghanistan and the Chittagong Hill Tracts. The president can control finances and lay down financial policy. He can veto laws passed by the National Assembly and dissolve the Assembly, provided he calls new elections, in which case he himself must seek re-election. Except for President Ayub, who may serve eight years, a president's term is limited to five years, unless a joint session of all three assemblies permits him to continue. When the National Assembly is not in session, the president may declare ordinances, good for six months. If he declares a state of emergency, his ordinances are good indefinitely.

The few restrictions on the president would be difficult to enforce. The Assembly may impeach him if it can obtain a

75 per cent majority. Those who initiate impeachment proceedings must resign if they fail to get a simple majority. The Assembly may override a veto with a two-thirds majority, but if it does, the president may then ask for a referendum among the Basic Democrats to confirm his veto.

The National Assembly, with each province equally represented, consists of 156 members, 150 of whom are elected by the Electoral College plus 3 additional members from each province who must be women. Their terms run for five years, although present members are allowed eight years if they are re-elected in 1965. No one may be a member who works for the government, who is a foreigner, who has been bankrupt or convicted of an offense within five years. The last provision thus eliminates all the politicians indicted under the Martial Law Regime. If a member is absent for thirty consecutive days, he loses his seat.

The National Assembly meets in Dacca under its elected Speaker, who acts for the president when he is out of the country or incapacitated. The Assembly may pass bills on national, but not provincial affairs, and pass on the president's budget, which it then may not alter in succeeding years unless it is to vote an increase. When election time comes, the Assembly, in joint session with the provincial assemblies, selects the presidential candidates, numbering no more than three.

The two provincial assemblies are organized along the lines of the National Assembly. Their relationship to the provincial governors is similar to that of the National Assembly's to the president. The West Pakistan Assembly meets in Lahore, the East Pakistan Assembly in Dacca. Each has 155 members, at least five of whom must be women. The governor, appointed by the president, has a council of ministers in the same manner as the president. The ministers and governors must be

120

from the provinces they are administering and must resign from the assemblies if they have been elected members.

On paper, the constitution transferred several responsibilities to the provincial governments which had previously been the concern of the central government. Agriculture, water and power development, health, social welfare, and industrial growth were among these and East Pakistan achieved equality with West Pakistan in the authority it presumably could assert in these fields. The transfer of powers, however, has been difficult to achieve in fact. Not only have the provincial governments, especially East Pakistan, not been prepared for assuming greater responsibilities, but the central ministries have been reluctant to give up power they have wielded so long.

Under the new constitution, the judiciary consists of a Supreme Court for the entire nation and High Courts and subsidiaries in the provinces. The president appoints all judges. The High Courts do not have authority in Tribal Areas, where tribesmen administer their own justice through traditional assemblies (among the Pathans called *loy jirgas*). The courts may overrule a president's decree, as they did in 1963 when they defied President Ayub by ordering government ministers to resign from the assemblies to which they had been elected.

The constitution originally contained no "bill of rights" guaranteeing certain basic freedoms and protection to the citizens. But in the amendment passed in December, 1963, such a "bill" was approved. It was limited, however, in that it did not apply to those living in Tribal Areas nor to activities covered in some thirty-one previous laws. Among these, were freedom of speech and the press, which are only as free as the president wishes, depending upon what he considers a danger to the safety of the country.

Other issues dealt with in the constitution include:

—The elimination of riba (usury);

—The capital of Pakistan is to be the new city of Islamabad, with Dacca a "second" capital;

—The national languages are Bengali and Urdu with English acceptable in governmental affairs;

—A two-thirds majority of the National Assembly may amend the constitution with presidential approval.

The role of the Basic Democracies is left vague. The constitution provides no formal link between the Union Councils and higher groups with the centers of power in government. The amount of responsibility they have depends upon the president and his administration. Their influence on the course of government is informal except when the Basic Democrats are asked to vote for members of the assemblies, for a president or in a referendum.

Pakistan held its first national elections under the new constitution in April and May of 1962. The voters were Basic Democrats grouped into 300 constituencies for provincial elections and 150 constituencies for the central election. The candidates did not have to be Basic Democrats themselves, but they did have to be approved by an Election Commissioner. Again, the small number of voters per candidate made the cost of influencing them lower than in previous years and there was some illegal persuasion involved. But on the whole, the elections appear to have been relatively free and honest.

The results showed that despite the new constitution the people themselves, as represented by the Basic Democrats and the winning candidates, had not discarded their traditions. To the National Assembly the Basic Democrats sent many old-line, but unindicted politicians, mullahs, pirs, and powerful landlords. Many new faces did appear in the provincial assemblies, however, including village farmers and shopkeepers, urban laborers and tradesmen. Many did not support

President Ayub's constitution or policies, especially in the National Assembly.

Pakistani critics felt that the new experiment produced "government for the people by the bureaucratic elite" and was no different from what had gone before. They asked how a system could be democratic when the top representatives in government were not elected directly by the people.

When the National Assembly met for the first time on June 8, 1962, President Ayub withdrew martial law and Pakistan began the trial run of democratic government, Ayub-style. From the day General Ayub assumed power in October, 1958, to the day he relinquished it to his own constitution, the elapsed time was forty-four months.

Interested Groups

With the rebirth of constitutional government, Pakistan set off on a new course. The old problems remained: ethnic rivalry, Islamic government, provincial autonomy, economic and social distress, Kashmir, India, Pashtunistan and political leadership. Various groups had a vital stake in each issue, but the framework in which they sought to meet these problems was different.

The Military and Civil Service

The most powerful group in the society has been the trained professionals in the executive branch of government, all of whom are responsible to Mohammed Ayub Khan, President, Field Marshal, Supreme Commander of the Armed Forces and Minister of Defense. At the top are the "superior services," a small group of select, well-trained administrators. Under them is a mass of regular government employees. Beside them stand the military forces. Of these, the most effective are the officers and enlisted men of Pakistan's army, numbering an estimated 170,000. Pakistan's military establishment is the most stable

123

institution in the country. The Army's enlisted personnel are primarily Punjabi farm boys and young Pathans whose fathers probably also served at one time in the service. Few are Bengali.

The officers of these troops are trained in the British military system. The traditions of their military units derive from years of experience under British commanders. Among these traditions is participation in civil administration, particularly in the areas of West Pakistan where the British in pre-partition India used army commanders as local governors. Nearly every major town was flanked by a military encampment called a cantonment and these, today, form a broad network of military power throughout West Pakistan. Most of them, however, are concentrated along the borders of Afghanistan and Kashmir.

In recent years, American influence in the armed forces has increased, particularly in the air force. American-made F104's and F86F jet fighters give the air force a fighter strength unequaled in South Asia. Hundreds of Pakistani pilots have received training in the United States and have proved equal in ability to pilots anywhere in the world.

The Pakistan navy is the country's weakest defense unit. After partition, Pakistan received a few minor warships, the largest being a cruiser. Numbering no more than 10,000, the navy officers and enlisted men are British-trained. Many of them are Bengalis, who have a tradition of the sea.

The morale of the defense personnel is generally high, kept that way through discipline, fair treatment, a fairly high standard of living, and, especially in West Pakistan, public respect. The forces have received as much as 80 per cent of the government's budget, although in recent years, this has fallen to about 60 per cent. Among West Pakistanis, the army has a good reputation and soldiers are treated as national heroes. In East Pakistan, the army often represents control over free-

dom. To many East Pakistanis, the army is a "foreign" force because it is composed chiefly of Punjabis and Pathans. Most military governors in East Pakistan have been from the West.

Another major force in the executive branch is the bureaucracy—the elite "superior services" and thousands of lower functionaries. The structure was laid down by the Moghuls, solidified by the British and continued faithfully by the Pakistanis. A conservative group on the whole, they tend to see their responsibilities as primarily regulatory—keeping the peace, administering justice and collecting taxes, in the manner of their predecessors. Planning for development and sharing responsibility with technical specialists are unfamiliar to them. At the top of the bureaucracy sit the well-educated members of the Civil Service of Pakistan, the Pakistan Foreign Service, Police Service of Pakistan and Accounts and Revenue Service. These services attract the best university graduates, usually members of families already in the services. Many have foreign education and are of outstanding quality. Yet they are a class unto themselves. President Ayub has expressed a desire to abolish the system.

Below this group are the masses of government servants, whose salaries are relatively low, as is their morale. Promotions are limited and based upon time served, not merit. There is little mobility from one level to another. Many second-level bureaucrats often live, work, and die in the same job.

From the highest official to the lowest *patwari* (village clerk), the machinery of government is almost automatic. Lower officials make as few decisions as possible, depending always upon orders from the top. While the system discourages initiative, it does usually assure that once an order is formulated by the president or his ministers action eventually takes place at the bottom.

125

One of President Ayub's proudest achievements is the reforms he has inaugurated in the field of public administration. In 1960, he established the Pakistan Administrative Staff College in Lahore to improve the quality of senior administrators with more than fourteen years service. National Institutes of Public Administration in Karachi, Lahore, and Dacca seek to upgrade lower level officials, as does the Secretariat Training Institute. The Civil Service Academy trains young university graduates for government service. The Academies for Rural Development in Peshawar and Comilla train administrative supervisory personnel for village aid and other nation building departments. An Institute of Development Economics trains officials in the business of planning.

While not a political action group, members of the executive branch of government have wide vested interests. When the constitutional organs of government weaken, as they have done in the past, both military and civilian groups can apply effective controls over the direction Pakistan moves.

The Bengalis

The largest group with a special interest in President Ayub's "experimental democracy" are the Bengalis, whose strong identification with East Pakistan sometimes overshadows their loyalty to the country as a whole. The 1962 National Assembly had barely convened in Dacca before Bengalis rose to complain about their role in the republic.

President Ayub, quite aware of the problems of East Pakistan, gave increased attention to Bengalis during the Martial Law Regime from 1958 to 1962. His cabinet included Bengalis as ministers of transportation and industry. New irrigation and flood control schemes were started in the province and the budget for water and power development increased 700 per cent. In 1962, East Pakistan gained control over its own railroads and the constitution not only increased pro-

vincial authority but placed the seat of the National Assembly in Dacca. Ayub appointed a Bengali, Abdul Munim Khan, as governor.

Soon after the National Assembly met, President Ayub reluctantly permitted the revival of political parties. In Bengal, Munim Khan and A. T. M. Mustafa led forth the old Muslim League, still claiming the mantle of Mohammed Ali Jinnah and now supporting President Ayub. The League was able to corral about 100 of the 156 members of the East Pakistan Assembly. Like previous Muslim Leaguers, they faced the problem of supporting the central government and at the same time, satisfying their own Bengali demands.

Former Bengali prime minister, Khwaja Nazimuddin, could not go along. He had opposed the One Unit scheme making West Pakistan a single province and he was a strong advocate of the parliamentary system which gives weight to numbers through legislative power. With other old League members, he started a party called the Councillors Muslim League and began seeking support across the country.

Other Bengalis were more vehement in opposition. Among them were Maulana Abdul Hamid Khan Bashani, the firebrand head of the National Awami (Peoples) Party. Another was H. S. Suhrawardy, the former prime minister who, from a jail cell where President Ayub had put him, resurrected his old Awami League. He did not have long to lead his party, however. Soon after his release from imprisonment, he left Pakistan for foreign countries. He died in 1963.

By 1964, all the old Bengali parties had been revived with most of the same leaders working behind the scenes, except for Fazlul Haq and Suhrawardy, both of whom were gone. Young and new politicians began preaching the cause of Bengal in opposition to the government. They opposed the Basic Democracies, the 1962 constitution and, among some, Pakistan's alliance with the United States. They were particularly

127

opposed to strong central government at the expense of provincial autonomy, despite the increased federalization in the 1962 constitution. Said one Bengali leader:

"We have been turned into a colony of West Pakistan."

Some observers foresee the eventual break-up of Pakistan as Bengalis seek increased independence from West Pakistan. That Bengali Muslims have not openly sought independence can, in part, be credited to (or blamed on) India. While Kashmir does not greatly concern Bengalis, India and its threat of Hindu domination certainly does. Shortly after partition, there was talk of rejoining West Bengal, but this interest lagged as Bengali Muslims achieved a greater sense of their own unity and strength. Now, most Bengali Muslim leaders fear India more than they dislike disparity with West Pakistan. The extreme alternative is independence, which few Bengalis openly espouse. But increased autonomy appears to be the future Bengali goal.

The Pathans

Pathans are equal to Bengalis in their awareness of ethnic identity. They look to the government to protect their way of life and to prove that it is better to be a Pathan Pakistani than a Pashtunistani. The dissolution of the Northwest Frontier Province in 1955 made those Pathans not living in Tribal Areas subject to the laws of West Pakistan provincial government in which Punjabis predominated. Many Pathans have been angry ever since.

Like the Bengalis, the Pathans entered the political arena with enthusiasm after 1962. President Ayub sought their support and found some among the followers of Khan Pir Mohammed Khan, the Pir of Manki Sharif and Khan Habibullah Khan, whom Ayub brought into his cabinet as minister for Home and Kashmir Affairs. Joining the Muslim League, these

men expressed confidence that the Ayub government would continue to support Pathan interests.

Opposition to President Ayub has been strong, however, among Pathans. Yusuf Khattak from Peshawar, a member of a tribe noted for its literary as well as military talent, joined the Councillors Muslim League. Khan Abdul Wali Khan, son of the frequently-jailed and widely-respected Abdul Ghaffar Khan, joined the National Awami Party. With their Bengali counterparts, Pathan oppositionists seek dissolution of the One Unit Scheme in West Pakistan and decentralization of government.

The Punjabis

The educated and wealthy leaders from the Punjab seek to maintain their dominant influence in provincial affairs. Although the 1962 constitution limits the number of Punjabi representatives in the West Pakistan legislature to less than one-half, Punjabis generally control the government. The One Unit Scheme thus places Punjabis on a level almost equal to that of the Bengalis, who far outnumber them in the population. New spokesmen have appeared among the Punjabis, but behind the scenes such politicians as Firoz Khan Noon, Mian Mumtaz Daultana and Mushtaq Gurmani still bargain for Punjabi strength.

Other regional groups play only a small part in Pakistan's over-all political life. Baluchi nationalism occasionally disturbs the government, as it did in April, 1963, when police arrested Atahullah Khan Mengal, a member of the National Assembly, tribal chieftain and champion of Baluchi autonomy.

As governor of West Pakistan, President Ayub appointed Malik Amir Mohammed Khan, the Nawab of Kalabagh, an area between the Punjab and the former Northwest Frontier Province. It is his difficult task to maintain the precarious bal-

ance between the Punjabis and the Pathans, Baluchis, and Sindis.

Religious Groups

The constitution of 1962, by being vague on Islamic institutions, literally invited a public furor from religious leaders. They do, after all, represent a deep sense of Muslim consciousness throughout the society. No ruling group can safely ignore them for long.

The loudest and most effective of the religious leaders has been the Jama'at-i-Islami's Maulana Maududi, a learned and eloquent theologian. Although frequently arrested and his activities proscribed, Maududi remained in touch with the mullahs and pirs during Martial Law. Subsequently, in the new assemblies and on soapboxes throughout cities and villages, he and his followers have continued to reject Anglo-Saxon law and European influences, such as social mingling of the sexes and women's franchise. Maulana Maududi has considerable appeal among West Pakistani villagers.

Another religious group has re-appeared under the leadership of Maulana Athar Ali. Called Nizam-i-Islami, the party is composed of Muslim scholars and mullahs who seek a more moderate interpretation of Islam than does Maulana Maududi. Former Prime Minister Chaudhri Mohammed Ali, has become one of the party's new leaders.

In the National Assembly, considerable influence on legislation is exerted by the Islamic Democratic Front, headed by Maulana Abdul Bari. Its members, nearly all mullahs, were successful in making Pakistan's constitution more Islamic in the writing of the first amendment.

Lesser, but more extreme religious groups include the Khaksars and the often-banned Ahrars. Their particular strength lies in their ability to inflame passions over Kashmir. In various assemblies certain politicians wearing the mantle of reli-

130

gious leadership stand ready to espouse religious causes. One Sindi pir, a member of the National Assembly, claims 900,000 followers. The Pir Pigaro of Sind claims to control 18 out of 33 Sindi members of the West Pakistan Assembly.

So long as President Ayub remains in power, it is likely that the strongest official influence in religious affairs will be asserted by the Advisory Council of Islamic Theology. Its members include a lawyer, Justice S. A. M. Akram as chairman, a former Columbia University professor and vice chancellor of Karachi University, I. H. Qureshi, and Maulana Abul Hashim, the director of the Islamic Academy in Dacca. All are repeated targets for conservative religious leaders who claim they are deserting the true path of Islam. Opponents call the Academy "a laboratory of the government to create a new Islam not preached by the Holy Prophet."

Nearly all politicians include religion in their political appeals, just as they did before the revolution. Khwaja Nazimuddin calls for "Islamic socialism" with zakat made compulsory in industry. Khurshid Khalid, head of the militant Khaksars, cries for jihad against India. Thus religious dissension and extremism, some observers feel, are more of a threat to Pakistan's survival than ethnocentrism. Certainly, since to many Muslims the formation of an Islamic state was the whole purpose in creating Pakistan, the subject of religion will be part of the dynamics of the country for many years.

Urban Groups

Two urban groups are important to Pakistan's great experiment. Both are relatively small in number, but large in power. The largest is the labor force: underpaid, restive workers who live in crowded slums. They are only partially organized and disciplined. Like their counterparts in other countries they can influence the course of government, if only because of their common frustrations and accessibility

to the centers of power. Their frustrations are easily exploited by communists and other disruptive elements, especially in the jute and textile mills of East Pakistan. Agitators can, with little effort, stir up a street demonstration or a riot.

The second group is the intellectuals. They do not, as a rule, identify themselves with the bureaucracy, any ethnic group, or religious movement. Many are refugees from India. They are lawyers, newspaper editors, professors and students, a few industrialists and professional men. Articulate and influential, they are often critical of government, whatever kind it is. Lawyers are particularly disturbed by President Ayub's constitution, which diverged from the British system under which they were trained.

Political Parties

In most European and American countries, political parties represent the competing ideologies of various groups within the society. This is not so in Pakistan. For the most part, parties are composed of politicians who have banded together to advance themselves rather than ideologies. Those who vote do so to support the leader, not "the cause." President Ayub's opinion of them has been unequivocal. He said: "Political parties have been our bane in the past."

In 1962 President Ayub permitted political parties to reappear. In one respect, he was responding to public pressure. In another, he became aware that he himself needed a vehicle through which to mobilize mass support for his programs.

In 1964, the major party in Pakistan was the refurbished Muslim League, which called itself Conventionist to distinguish itself from Muslim League splinter groups. Its aim was to support President Ayub, who, in May, 1963, joined the party and later became its president. Its leaders seek to enroll Pakistanis from all walks of life and they have succeeded in gaining more than 2,000,000 members. The League controls

all the legislative assemblies, but not by large majorities, especially in the National Assembly.

Opposition parties are, so far, more irritating than disruptive. Continually splitting and re-forming, they are not often strongly identified with any program except, perhaps, the National Awami Party of Maulana Bashani which stands for neutralism in foreign affairs. In addition to the multiple provincial and Islamic parties, various groupings appear periodically in the assemblies. In the National Assembly, the most important is the Pakistan People's Group, a coalition under the leadership of Yusuf Khattak which seeks a return to the 1956 constitution. The Communist Party and the Islamic fundamentalist Jama'at-i-Islami are banned.

The instruments of political influence have always been limited in number. They now are limited in strength with the absence of direct elections and the weakened position of the legislature. The press, radio and the speakers' platforms are of value in urban areas. They are particularly limited for opponents of the government, which operates all broadcasting facilities and asserts considerable control over the press.

There are some 80 daily newspapers, most of them privately-owned and printed in Urdu and Bengali. A few are in English. Their total circulation is less than 400,000, although each paper may be read aloud several times to non-readers. Perhaps as many as 3,000,000 people thus know roughly what goes on in the country through the press. Within defined limits, the newspapers may print opinions of the editors. These opinions are frequently critical of the government regardless of the party or person in power. They have been quite critical of President Ayub, who has appealed to the press to revise its attitude and "adopt a more objective approach toward national issues." To support his appeal, he has forced newspapers to print only government-approved versions of assembly proceedings, which are usually critical,

to print all government releases fully and to open their financial records to government inspection. Editors charge that the law muzzles criticism. They also cite the case of the Urdu newspaper, *Kohistan,* banned for a month in 1963.

President Ayub has recognized that radio broadcasting is important in a country whose people are over 80 per cent illiterate. Radio reaches perhaps 15 per cent of the area of Pakistan and no more than 5,000,000 people, nearly all urban dwellers. But the government is building new transmitters and distributing radio receivers through the Union Councils and Town Committees and hopes that by the end of 1964 the system will cover 100 per cent of East Pakistan and 25 per cent of West Pakistan. The government owns and operates the only broadcasting facilities, Radio Pakistan.

Public speaking is an effective means of political influence. Passions are easily inflamed and it is not unusual for a quiet political meeting to turn into a riot.

President Ayub has tolerated little extended criticism. As he said in 1963, "mutual suspicion, recriminations and hostility" in Pakistan were even a greater threat to its survival and safety than a hostile and well-armed India. Stability of government, he feels, is essential if his plan to reach the villagers and workers through his Basic Democracies is to succeed.

He obviously feels that the major burden of leadership rests on his shoulders and will continue so in the foreseeable future. He has selected a few followers upon whose advice he increasingly relies. These include Zufikar Ali Bhutto in foreign affairs, Mohammed Shoiab in finance and economics, and West Pakistan's Governor Mohammed Khan in political affairs. But he does not, he says, see anyone around to succeed him who can appeal to both East and West Pakistanis. Indeed, absence of a strong Bengali leader to support him is one of President Ayub's major political deficiencies.

134

Those who shrugged their shoulders in 1958 when Pakistan fell to a military dictator are watching Ayub's great experiment with interest. Pakistan's problems are similar to those of many underdeveloped nations, although none can claim the handicap of being split so far in two.

What the world thinks, however, will not particularly disturb Pakistanis. Their search is for their own unity, the need is for their own discipline. They can only hope that their struggling economy does not drag them down before the great experiment has a chance to succeed.

7.   Planning a Livelihood

Pakistan's people work hard and earn little. Few are trained for industry or modern agriculture and their methods are old-fashioned. The realities of life, most of which have to do with the business of keeping alive, take precedence over their interests in politics, debates over religion, speeches on constitutional law and alarms over Kashmir.

In more industrialized countries, millions of people work at many different tasks. Each task is related to the work of others. Together they support their entire society. In Pakistan, millions of people work at a few tasks and little of the work of one man is related to that of another. One of the characteristics of an "underdeveloped country" is the unorganized nature of its economy. Each man or working unit labors pretty much alone. Farmers and their families are nearly self-sufficient except when floods or droughts wipe out their crops.

At times, being unorganized is an advantage. After partition, Pakistan's economy, according to economists from developed countries, was chaotic. There was not enough food. There were few markets for cash crops, and transportation was disrupted. There was little industry or money. Yet Pakistanis survived, partially because of their disorganization. While economic malnutrition struck one part of the country's body, it was isolated from the rest. Each little unit worked on, relatively unaffected by the disorder around it.

But at all times, hunger and poverty are curses and Pakistan's unorganized agricultural economy has given her people

very little other than life itself. Economists guess—statistics are never reliable for an underdeveloped economy—that the average income of a Pakistani in 1949 was $50 a year. In 1964, the most generous economists estimate that the average Pakistani earns no more than $70 a year. While production has increased, so too, has the population, which grows at the rate of about 2,500,000 people annually.

From the start, Pakistan's leaders have sought to improve the economy by "organizing" agriculture, creating industries and strengthening the many related fields to support them. "Development" has become the key word in the vocabulary of government and economists have prepared numerous plans.

The first Six Year Plan died before its birth for want of money and trained guidance. A First Five Year Plan was to begin in 1955, but did not get started until two years later. Under this plan, some $2,800,000,000 was expended with priority given to projects for power, irrigation and industry. Some attention was paid to agriculture, particularly through the Village AID (Agricultural and Industrial Development) program, established in 1953. While many worthwhile projects were born which added to Pakistan's development, the plan did not meet its objectives. There was not enough money; it had given agriculture too little emphasis and Pakistan's population grew too fast. Economics got lost in the maelstrom of politics. President Ayub said later:

"The real and pressing problems of the country were ignored in this hide-and-seek for power."

In 1960, Pakistanis adopted a Second Five Year plan which called for spending $4,600,000,000. It was based on $3,000,000,000 in foreign aid. This time, agricultural improvement was emphasized; more than 35 per cent of the planned expenditure was for farming and water development. In the Third Five Year Plan, starting in 1965, these fields will receive nearly 50 per cent of the development funds.

137

As leaders of newly-independent countries in Asia have discovered, sometimes to their surprise, the most important "economic unit" in their society is the villager and his family, not the industrialist. Upon the farmer rests the real sustenance of the nation; upon him also lies the burden of improvement and organization.

Agriculture

Nearly 83,000,000 Pakistanis, 85 per cent of the total population, live in approximately 100,000 villages and depend upon agriculture for their livelihood, although not all farm the land directly. They produce, depending upon the weather, about 60 per cent of the national income. The sale of farm products abroad earns 71 per cent of Pakistan's foreign exchange. Except for tea, none of these sales are in food products: jute and cotton are the major cash crops.

Farmers are able to cultivate only 17 per cent of the soil in West Pakistan; 75 per cent is cultivated in East Pakistan. These amounts can be increased as much as 40 per cent with better drainage and irrigation, which Pakistanis are trying to do. Crop yields are among the lowest in the world. With double-cropping and better farming practices, Pakistanis can eventually become self-sufficient in food. Advances have been made. Since 1958, the index of agricultural production has increased from 102 to 114. Even so, in 1964, Pakistanis cannot grow enough food to feed themselves. They must import food from other countries.

One reason why the Pakistani farmer fails to grow enough is that he has little incentive to do so, once he is assured that his family is fed. The traditional land tenure systems, those customs and laws that determine who owns, controls and uses the land and its products, discourage efforts to improve. While these systems vary with the area, they all contain similar im-

pediments to initiative. The farmer rarely owns the land he cultivates.

"Land reform" is a simple phrase to define a solution to a complicated problem. Pakistanis have attempted it for years, without making much headway, although there has been recent progress.

The most significant advances have been made in East Pakistan, where, before 1947, the great landlords were often Hindus. After partition, the East Pakistan government limited holdings to 33 acres per family or 3.3 acres per family member and gave ownership rights to villagers. Landlords were compensated in forty-year bonds. General Ayub announced sweeping reforms in West Pakistan in 1959. In theory, the government purchased land from large landlords, giving them in return twenty-five-year bonds, and resold the land to the farmers on an installment plan. At the same time, the government put ceilings on land holdings: 500 acres of irrigated or 1,000 acres of unirrigated land. In practice, many large landholders have deeded land to relatives but have maintained control, thereby circumventing the ceiling.

Lack of incentive is only one reason why Pakistani farmers are poor. If they have a surplus, the buyers in the marketplace pay little for it even though a few miles away there may be a food shortage. There is little marketing information. But surpluses are rare and the most ambitious cultivator needs more than he has. In West Pakistan, water is scarce; in East Pakistan, it regularly floods his crops. The fields, which the villager surrounds with thick embankments, *bunds*, are usually too small to farm efficiently. The soil is frequently debilitated. In West Pakistan, where irrigation is so widespread in the Punjab, salinity and waterlogging have reached such proportions that some experts predict the once-fertile Indus valley will be a desert within fifty years. Because of salinity, West Pakistan loses an acre of cultivated

139

land—enough to feed one person—every five minutes (and in the same time, gains ten more mouths to feed). The government has committed large sums to combat this problem, but admits that much more must be done. The U. S. Government has obligated some $5,000,000 to assist in demonstrating that salinity and waterlogging can be controlled.

Seeds are poor and lack variety. Pests sweep through the crops. It does little good if a farmer understands fertilization, because there are few fertilizers available and these are expensive. The best fertilizer is animal manure, but, because of fuel shortage, women pack it into dung cakes to be dried on the household wall and burned in the fireplace.

In many parts of Pakistan, undernourishment and diseases such as malaria, tuberculosis, and dysentery frequently limit the efficiency of the farming family. Even if a farmer is enterprising, he cannot easily borrow money to buy a better plow or better seeds. The banking system is just beginning to reach into rural areas. The local moneylender, from whom he borrows cash to meet wedding or funeral expenses, charges up to 100 per cent interest.

Above all, the Pakistani farmer lacks knowledge. He is generally illiterate. He plows and sows as his father did, turning the soil with pointed sticks and sowing seed by hand. Farming methods are traditional and sometimes complicated by religious custom. For example, one Baluchi farmer, when he found that his fields would grow two crops a year instead of one when using "foreign" seed, refused the seed because it came from a non-Muslim land.

Pakistan has what is known as a subsistence economy. Farmers who grow food do so primarily to feed themselves and their families, and pay their taxes or their landlord. They do not generally grow surpluses to sell to the cities except when they need to buy a few manufactured items in the local bazaar. The cities cannot depend upon the villages for food—from

140

1947 to 1960, when food imports increased, food was rationed in West Pakistan's cities. Changing the rural economy to produce surpluses is one of President Ayub's goals.

In West Pakistan, farmers raise wheat, barley, gram, corn, fruit, vegetables and livestock as consumable products. Wheat is the staple and is grown in thousands of tiny patches, the seed hand-sown, the harvest hand-cut and the grain hand-winnowed. Although mechanization is negligible, Pakistan ranks thirteenth among the nations in wheat production. Other consumer crops include sugar cane and oil seeds such as mustard and rape.

In East Pakistan, rice is the major food crop, utilizing 70 per cent of the cultivable acreage, but it is highly vulnerable to destruction by floods. In 1963, the loss to weather was so great that rice production declined nearly 10 per cent, drastically cutting Pakistan's rate of economic growth, from 5 per cent to 1 per cent—far below the natural population increase. While Pakistan is the world's third largest rice producer, in most years East Pakistan must import rice. Other consumable products include oil seeds, sugar cane, and tea, half of which is exported.

Pakistan grows two major cash crops which provide most of its foreign exchange. By far the most important is jute, a tall, fibrous plant much like hemp, grown in the inundated, silty lowlands of East Pakistan. The plants are sown in February and cut in July and August, in water three or four feet deep. The stalks are placed in a pool of water called a *khal* where, for two weeks, they decompose. At the end of this period, a worker beats the stalks until the fibers are loosened and can be stripped off and hung out to dry. House to house buyers, called *farias,* who sail small country boats, pick up the dried jute, take it to market and sell it to middlemen, called *beparis.* These in turn sell the jute to a baler or his agent and the bales are sent by boat to jute mills or docks for

141

shipping raw jute to mills abroad. Before partition, these mills were in Calcutta. New ones in Pakistan now handle much of the raw jute, turning out burlap and rope for sale abroad, chiefly to the United States and England. With so many individuals between the farmer and the buyer, the man who did the original work gets little, especially when he doesn't even own the land.

Pakistan's second cash crop is cotton, grown mostly in West Pakistan on 12 per cent of the cultivated area, almost all of it irrigated. In pre-partition days, high-grade, long-staple cotton was the pride of Sikh and Hindu farmers, all of whom fled to India in 1947. Subsequently, the quality of Pakistani cotton has fallen and the world markets, already switching to artificial fibers, demand less from Pakistan. Nevertheless, efforts are being made to improve the cotton industry. New gins, high payment for quality grades and better growing practices, including mechanization, are increasing the benefits of cotton farming. New textile mills have made Pakistan self-sufficient in cotton cloth, and cotton products now help raise export earnings.

Few items in their lives are more important to villagers than their animals. Frequently, a farmer's wealth is judged by how many bullocks or horses, camels, or sheep he owns. It is a lucky young bridegroom whose bride brings with her a farm animal in her dowry.

Unfortunately for the economy, farm animals perform many functions and are not particularly good at any of them. Cows, water buffalo and she-camels not only must give milk, but must pull loads. For this they need plentiful food, but food is often scarce. To use a steel plow, which would better turn the soil, a farmer needs a strong animal.

Sheep and goats range unfenced throughout West Pakistan, uprooting precious grass and destroying saplings that

142

could prevent erosion. Their hides and skins are exportable products.

For animals, crops, and humans alike, water in Pakistan is the key to survival. The rivers that flow from the Himalayas through Afghanistan, Kashmir, and India, and the monsoons that bring rain in the summer, are more important to the people of the land than any other single element. Unhappily, nothing is more unreliable. In West Pakistan a late winter can delay the melting of snows and cause drought. Heavy spring rains or an early snow-melt can flood the lands, carrying off precious topsoil, crops and sometimes the villages themselves. In East Pakistan monsoon rains when accompanied by cyclones inundate entire villages.

The most productive soil in West Pakistan is in the irrigated land of the Punjab and it was here that partition so affected farming.

The source of water for many irrigation canals was in India and the Indian Government frequently impeded the flow of water into Pakistan. Rights to Indus water became a heated subject between the two countries. As early as 1951, foreign experts sought to aid India and Pakistan in reaching riparian agreements. Not until 1960 did they sign a treaty agreeing to the joint development of the Indus River system, in cooperation with the International Bank and a consortium of countries including Australia, Canada, West Germany, New Zealand, the United Kingdom and the United States. By the treaty, India agreed not to interfere with Pakistan's western rivers, while Pakistan agreed to build canals which in ten years would replace water it required from the eastern rivers flowing from East Punjab. The total cost of the Indus Development Project is expected to exceed $1,800,000,000 with the donor countries supplying more than half of the cost. Pakistanis predict that the project will ensure the water sup-

143

ply of more than 50,000,000 people living in an area covering some 30,000,000 acres.

Responsibility for developing Pakistan's water resources lies with the provincial governments' Water and Power Development Authorities (WAPDA), established in 1958. They develop irrigation, fight waterlogging and soil salinity problems, and produce hydro-electric power. In West Pakistan, the WAPDA is responsible for the Indus Development Project and has become one of the most effective government agencies. In East Pakistan, WAPDA's program follows the lines charted by the 1956 United Nations mission under the former United States Secretary of the Interior, Julius Krug. It has endeavored to build embankments to protect villages from sudden flood and sought to increase power from new dams.

Along with water control, village development is another program to improve the rural economy. It began in 1953 with Village AID and continues today through the Basic Democracies.

Village AID was based on the American agricultural extension system in which county agents, called "village workers" in Pakistan, brought farming and home improvement advice to farmers and their wives, demonstrated new techniques, introduced new seed, supplied better implements, and encouraged farmers to construct roads, dams, ditches, and better houses. The image of the dedicated village worker pedaling his bicycle along a dirt path from village to village became a symbol of rural progress. By 1960, nearly 5,000 workers had received training in Village AID Institutes, five in each province. Their supervisors had been trained at the two Academies for Village Development in Peshawar and Comilla. They had established 176 development areas of 100,000 people each, organized 19,625 village development councils, planned 150,000 demonstration plots, dug 1,000 miles of canals, built 3,000 miles of dirt roads, and intro-

duced new farming practices in hundreds of villages. In 1961, to the dismay of the village workers, the government suddenly canceled the program and incorporated it into the Basic Democracies.

One difficulty in the Village AID program lay in the attempt to adopt—and Americans to promote—a system foreign to the people. The principal weakness of the American county agent system in Pakistan was that it sent into a village a person not from that village whose task was to "change" the villagers. Pakistani villagers are suspicious of "foreigners," even if that foreigner is from the next village, much less the city, which is where most village workers came from. Another weakness was that the village worker appeared to the local government administrator as a competitor and disrupter of the peace. Few village workers found the administrator cooperative.

Lack of village enthusiasm for change reflected also the individualistic nature of the Pakistani farmer. Cooperative action between village leaders, except in emergencies, is unusual in Pakistan. While one of every three farms in West Pakistan is operated by more than one household working cooperatively, the number of family leaders involved is few. There is little joint ownership in Muslim societies and Pakistan's is no exception. There are about 28,000 cooperative societies in West Pakistan involving some 1,400,000 members, but these are primarily government-backed banking institutions.

One direction of rural improvement will probably be along the lines set by Dr. Akhtar Hameed Khan, the imaginative head of the Academy for Village Development in Comilla. Using some eighty square miles as a development laboratory, Dr. Hameed Khan went into the villages and asked the villagers to select a representative to come to Comilla for training. When the representative returned, his fellow villagers

145

listened to him and accepted many of the new ideas he acquired at the Academy.

His next step was to introduce cooperative action and before long cooperative societies grew up to provide supervised credit, cooperative purchasing and marketing, and cooperative use of machinery. By 1963, there were 120 village cooperatives in Comilla district and a central association providing a variety of services to the farmers. The experiment was considered so successful that similar programs have grown up in seven districts in West Pakistan and six sub-districts in East Pakistan. President Ayub has ordered this program extended to all thirty districts in East Pakistan. What Dr. Hameed Khan had proved was that the Union Councils in the villages could produce if given the means, that throughout the countryside there was plenty of leadership talent, and, finally, that cooperatives could work in a Muslim society.

To provide administrative and technical guidance to the rural program, the Pakistan government has given increasing emphasis to secondary and advanced agricultural education. Under the Second Five Year Plan, Pakistan has opened two new agricultural universities at Mymensingh in East Pakistan and Lyallpur in West Pakistan, both of which had previously been undergraduate schools. Other agricultural schools are at Peshawar, Tandojam, and Dacca.

Industry

Pakistanis see industrialization as a partial solution to their economic problems. Industry will give employment to urban workers, whose numbers increase drastically each year as population pressures force villagers to seek work in the cities. Industry will reduce the country's dependence upon manufactured imports, make greater use of natural and human resources, diversify investment and, above all, give Pakistanis a sense of self-sufficiency.

146

The growth of Pakistan's industry has been more spectacular than the progress made in agriculture, although it has affected relatively few people. Manufacturing accounted for less than 7 per cent of the country's national income in 1950; in 1963, it accounted for 14.4 per cent. In 1947, Pakistan had an almost invisible industrial establishment. West Pakistan inherited from India only nine of the subcontinent's 400 textile factories. All the jute factories of Bengal became Indian property and many trained factory workers and owners migrated to India. The new Muslim migrants to Pakistan were unskilled. But by 1964, East Pakistan had over a dozen jute mills; new textile factories in West Pakistan produced over 750,000,000 yards of cloth, against 100,000,000 in 1952. New fertilizer and cement factories, petro-chemical plants, paper and sugar mills, and hundreds of small industries had altered the complexion of urban economic life. The index of manufacturing rose from 38 in 1950 to 205 in 1963.

What industry that did exist in Pakistan would have collapsed altogether if a few wealthy industrialists had not been willing to risk new investment. Even these individuals might have avoided the risks had India been cooperative. In denying its factories to Pakistani raw materials and, in 1950, de-valuing its currency, India effectively forced Pakistanis to rush into industrialization. Said one industrialist a few years later: "India easily could have killed us with kindness."

Consequently, new industries began appearing on the outskirts of Karachi, Lahore, and Dacca. The Adamjee family built new jute mills in Narayanganj and the Ispahanis, besides establishing a bank, started an airline to link the two wings. Europeans and Americans came to provide technical assistance.

Quite early it was apparent that government would have to give private enterprise a helping hand. Credit was lacking, as was planning. So in 1952, the government created the

147

Pakistan Industrial Development Corporation (PIDC) which began investing government funds in industries. Small consumer goods factories appeared in every city to make matches, light bulbs, cigarettes, and the many small items so expensive to import, yet so in demand by the people. By mid-1962, when it was divided into provincial units, the PIDC had established fifty-five industrial projects in cooperation with private investors.

One of Pakistan's first needs was electric power. Created by coal and oil generators, the total installed capacity was barely 100,000 kilowatts, among the lowest in the world. Pakistani and foreign engineers planned new dams, among them the Canadian-assisted Warsak project on the Kabul River and the United States-assisted Karnafuli dam in East Pakistan. When natural gas was discovered in the Sind desert, a pipeline was laid to bring new power to Karachi. By 1964, Pakistan's power capacity had increased to nearly 1,000,000 kilowatts; still Pakistan was one of the lowest-powered countries.

In its Second Five Year Plan, Pakistan hopes by 1965 to have 1,300,000 kilowatts, one-third of which will be hydroelectric, the remainder deriving from natural gas, coal, and diesel fuel. Plans are afoot to build an atomic reactor in East Pakistan, which is particularly short of power resources. Little oil has been found in the country and Pakistan must import much of her fuel, especially oil and coal. A new refinery in Karachi will have an annual capacity of 1,500,000 tons of crude.

A second problem in industrialization was—and is—mineral resources. Russian, American, and other foreign prospectors have scoured Pakistan's barren hills in search of raw materials. In 1963, United Nations experts decided that an iron ore deposit near Kalabagh, a coal-mining area in the northwestern corner of the former Punjab province, could produce 150,000,000 tons of low-grade ore. Pakistanis feel

148

this is adequate to support a steel mill, to be built in Karachi. Another steel mill is under construction in Chittagong, under Japanese guidance. Although some chrome ore has been found, exploration for other minerals has not been so productive.

While industrialization is usually thought of as urban, villagers and residents of small towns have also helped create new wealth. More than 1,000,000 Pakistanis are involved in small industries scattered throughout the country, which produce carpets, cigarettes, wood and bamboo products. In a few villages in the former Northwest Frontier Province, Pathans make guns. Nearly all products, especially the guns, are for local use.

Pakistanis are understandably proud of their industrial growth. Not only did their industrial output increase nearly 200 per cent from 1950 to 1963, but they almost reached their 1965 goal two years ahead of schedule. One reason for this is that the government was successful in encouraging private investment in industry, both domestic and foreign. By giving individuals and foreign companies preferential treatment, President Ayub departed from the practice of his predecessors. Shipping, trucking and all small-scale industry are privately-owned and government investment is only minimal in business, mining and large and medium-scale industry.

Government investment is aimed primarily at resource development and the major public services, including railroads, airlines, telegraph and telephone systems, radio and television (in 1964). Some industries, such as the Karnafuli Paper Mill, were started by government and sold to private owners. To promote investment in East Pakistan, the government has given new industries there eight tax-free years, against only two tax-free years in Karachi.

The result of Pakistan's policy has been a private investment boom, which by 1963 had attained 92 per cent of the

149

1965 target set for the "private sector" in the Second Five Year Plan. Outstanding successes were in textiles and chemicals. The government has declared that it will not nationalize industries and has guaranteed the repatriation of foreign capital and unrestricted remittance of profits. The United States and West Germany have been primary sources of foreign private capital while Japan has shown increasing interest.

Manpower for Development

Whether in agriculture or industry, progress depends upon the development of people, not machines. President Ayub and his advisors have recognized that this development centers on education, not as an academic exercise but as a public investment in economic progress.

The mass of Pakistan's manpower is unskilled, particularly in industrial pursuits. Workers have little familiarity with mechanical or electrical devices and only among certain groups, such as the Pathan tribesmen and urban dwellers, is it easy for them to learn mechanical skills. Nearly all unskilled laborers are illiterate so that training is especially difficult. Yet, the cities are clogged with unskilled migrants from villages and from India who seek employment.

At the other end of the manpower scale are the managers and executives who must mobilize and direct the country's development. While Pakistan has been more fortunate than many other new countries in Asia in having inherited—and subsequently trained—a large body of high-level manpower, there are still too few trained leaders. Both the absence of opportunity and the system of education have prevented the society from producing enough men with managerial talent or technical knowledge. The educational system has been designed largely to produce civil servants, not industrial or agricultural managers.

150

Between the unskilled worker and the industrial manager lies an even greater vacuum in manpower: the skilled worker and the technical supervisor. To have such manpower, a nation needs a large group of workers seeking training and an educational system equipped to give them the skills. Pakistan has neither. Those few individuals who go to school beyond the elementary grades—less than 1 per cent of the population —are children of urban families who view manual labor with aversion. The educational system reflects their desire to enter government service in a "white collar" capacity and provides little opportunity for technical training.

Aware of these deficiencies, the Commission on National Education, which reported to the President in 1959, stated that "only through vigorous action in training the people needed for this technological and agricultural progress can we escape from the situation in which our vast manpower, instead of being a source of national wealth, is a constant drag on our economy."

Domestic Trade

One of the most private of all economic activities in Pakistan, and one of the least organized, is domestic trading—the buying, storing, selling, and transportation of goods. The government, in its Second Five Year Plan, allotted one-fifth of its investment toward improving commerce and trade, especially transportation.

To most Pakistanis, "domestic trade" means the local village or town bazaars which they visit weekly. There are, of course, millions of villagers who depend but slightly upon the products available in distant markets.

Only in recent decades has the use of money become widespread among villagers. In the past, buying and selling was by barter, the village farmer trading a skin or other farm product for the equivalent in value of a manufactured item.

151

Considerable bargaining accompanied the transaction. While the use of money has become common in Pakistan, the absence of a fixed price and the technique of bargaining are still common in trading.

In West Pakistan, villagers and townsmen alike do most of their trading in small shops, although many villagers, particularly in Baluchistan and northwestern frontier areas, also depends on nomadic tribesmen who bring manufactured goods from the major trading centers. In East Pakistan, few villages have shops. Instead villagers attend weekly *hats* (bazaars) in nearby larger villages and sometimes wait for the periodic *melas* (fairs) to do their shopping. They also await itinerant vendors who travel by boat from village to village.

Trading in towns and cities is a combination of European and village systems. Each major town has a European section in which stores, both specialty and general, provide goods for across-the-counter sale. The prices are standard and little bargaining occurs. But most urban trading takes place in older town bazaars with stalls and shops specializing in various goods and commodities. Sellers of one kind of item ordinarily group their shops together so that a person wanting to buy shoes, for instance, goes to the shoe bazaar; if pots or pans are desired, the buyer finds the metal bazaar. Goods seldom have fixed prices and bargaining is necessary as buyer and seller reach agreement on values. While barter is common in smaller towns, money is used in cities.

The problems of marketing are serious impediments to economic progress. There are few standards of quality, so that each item bought or sold must find its own relative value. Weights and measures are not standardized. Each region and sometimes each merchant uses distinctive definitions of quantity. Local vendors frequently use bits of metal to determine weights. The usual measures are the *maund* (officially 82 2/7 pounds) which is divided into 40 *seers* and the

seer into 80 *tolas*. In East Pakistan, a maund may weigh anything from 30 to 60 seers. In some areas, a maund can be simply *pukka,* high grade, or *kutcha,* low grade. Pakistan's economists hope eventually to introduce the metric system.

The monetary system also varies from place to place, although in recent years considerable standardization has been achieved, particularly in cities. In 1947, the basic unit of currency was the *rupee,* equal to about 20 U. S. cents. This was divided into *annas* and *pies.* In 1961, President Ayub inaugurated the metric system for money, with the rupee divided into 100 *paisas.*

Improvement of the trading system depends greatly on the state of storage facilities and transportation. Economists estimate that up to 10 per cent of the country's desperately needed grain crops are spoiled or lost in storage after harvesting. With foreign help, the government is introducing modern storage silos in the Punjab and East Pakistan.

Transportation in West Pakistan follows routes established by the British for defense, not internal trade. These routes usually run toward the border of Afghanistan and seldom provide a north-south connection for most towns and villages except along the border. Thus, while a village in one valley could have a food surplus, villagers only a few miles away across a hill could be facing starvation. While some major new roads are tying larger towns together, the absence of feeder roads to villages keep millions of people isolated. Here the Basic Democracies are achieving admirable results by encouraging villagers to build their own access roads to the major trunks.

Local transportation in West Pakistan consists mostly of oxcarts and other animal-drawn vehicles which travel on dirt paths to reach nearby markets. In East Pakistan, boats do the chores of oxcarts. As new roads have connected larger towns, the use of buses and trucks has increased. Trucking holds out

great hope for improving trade and represents the ultimate in private enterprise. Competition is keen. The industry has provided jobs for many, particularly Afridi tribesmen of the Pathan area who find in truck driving an outlet for their carefree spirits.

Railroads are one of Pakistan's most potentially valuable assets, but they are sadly neglected for want of money. Partition left Pakistan with about 8,000 miles of track, almost all built for military defense rather than economic support, and with badly deteriorated rolling stock. Subsequently, Pakistan has improved the Karachi-Lahore-Peshawar system, which services the cotton export industry, and has built new railroad shops in Karachi and the Punjab. East Pakistan has only 1,700 miles of railroad and this is particularly hard to improve. Both systems use diesel power.

Until recently, the central government managed the railroads, but in 1962, their administration was transferred to the provincial governments, which have concentrated their efforts on rehabilitating the existing system rather than expanding it.

There is some trading between the two provinces, but not nearly so much as Pakistanis would like. West Pakistan buys tea, paper products, tobacco, and a little jute from East Pakistan, which in turn buys cotton products and small consumer items from West Pakistan. The trade advantage lies with West Pakistan.

Inter-province trade relies on ocean shipping. In 1947, Pakistan owned three ancient and rusted cargo ships. In 1963, there were forty-three, all privately-owned, and for the first time there was adequate cargo space to handle traffic between Karachi and Chittagong and Chalna.

Passenger and mail transportation between the two wings and within the provinces has been revolutionized with airline development. Because of ill feeling between Pakistan and In-

dia, air travel is the most effective method of linking the two provinces.

In its early days, Pakistan had two privately-owned airlines flying Dakota and Convair airplanes. The government established Pakistan International Airlines in 1955 and today it is perhaps one of the most efficiently run businesses in the country. Jet airplanes whisk politicians and businessmen back and forth between the wings of Pakistan like commuters. Smaller airplanes reach out to nearly all major towns. East Pakistan has started one of the world's first transportation systems based on helicopters. A government-subsidized shuttle service between twenty-two towns costing the same as first class riverboat fares will eventually serve more than 200,000 passengers a year.

Government-controlled Pakistan International Airlines also services major cities of the world, providing regular jet flights to London, Frankfurt, Geneva, Rome, Beirut, Teheran, and New York. The government negotiated an agreement in 1963 with Communist China to begin flights to Canton, Shanghai, and Peking, much to the disappointment of Pakistan's anticommunist allies. The first flights began in April, 1964.

Foreign Trade

While agriculture and domestic trade form the major part of the work Pakistanis do, foreign trade is vital to the general economy. It is through trade with other countries that Pakistanis earn most of the foreign exchange with which to buy manufactured goods, fuel and capital equipment, as well as hardware for their armed forces. What foreign exchange Pakistan does not earn by trading, it obtains through grants and loans from industrial countries.

As in most new Asian countries, Pakistan exports raw materials chiefly. These are limited to two main products: jute and cotton. The sale of jute and jute products accounts for

155

about 59 per cent of the value of all exports and provides the world with nearly half of its raw jute and jute products. Raw cotton and cotton products earn about 10 per cent of the foreign exchange. The market for these exports is threatened by synthetics, so Pakistanis hope that they can increase their exports of tea, fish, hides and skins, wool, cottage industry products, paper and other minor products which make up the balance of the export trade.

For many years, Pakistan's best customers were, in order of importance: the United Kingdom, the United States, Japan and West Germany. India, in 1959–1960, purchased only 5 per cent of Pakistan's exportable products. In that year, however, the two countries worked out the Trade Agreement and Special Payments Arrangement and in 1960–1961 India was suddenly Pakistan's best customer, buying 58 per cent of her exports, in rupee value. Great Britain was next with 16.6 per cent, followed by the United States, 9.2 per cent and Japan, 6.8 per cent.

With the United Kingdom and other West European countries moving toward closer economic relations, Pakistan has worried about the security of its export markets. This apprehension, combined with a shift in foreign policy, brought about development of new markets. In 1963, Pakistan signed barter agreements with the Soviet Union for railway ties and cement in exchange for jute; with Communist China, cement in exchange for jute; with Poland, cement in exchange for jute; with Czechoslovakia, automobiles and other manufactured items in exchange for chrome ore; and with Hungary, electrical equipment in exchange for jute. With all this trading, the total value of the barter agreements is a mere $5,000,000.

With such a limited economy, Pakistanis need to import a substantial amount from other countries. The range of desired consumer goods increases every day as more people learn,

by radio, newspapers and word-of-mouth, what other people in the world have. But consumer goods must compete with fuel and machinery for Pakistan's limited foreign exchange. The government generally controls foreign exchange and from year to year varies the amount allowed for various kinds of purchases. In 1958–1959, 24 per cent of imports by value was for consumer goods; in 1960–1961, the amount was 42 per cent. Purchases of raw materials for industry and fuel and spare parts for machinery and vehicles accounted for the rest.

Pakistan has purchased more goods from the United States than any other country. In 1960–1961, the U. S. supplied 24 per cent of her imports. Other countries who sell to Pakistan include the United Kingdom, 18 per cent; West Germany, 8.5 per cent; Japan, 8 per cent and India 4 per cent

To the dismay of the East Pakistanis, whose jute crops are the major export item, most of the imports purchased with foreign exchange have gone to help West Pakistanis. However, since 1962 the government has funneled an increasing amount of export earnings to East Pakistan and in the Third Five Year Plan Bengalis will receive more of the available development funds than West Pakistanis.

The chronic deficit between import costs and export earnings has been one of Pakistan's most serious problems—as it is with nearly all developing countries. Up to 1956, when jute was selling well and harvests were bountiful, imports and exports were generally in balance. Since then, there have been ever-increasing deficits as food production fell, jute competition increased and imports rose drastically. While exports between 1956 and 1961 rose only 25 per cent, imports doubled. In 1962, exports reached the equivalent of $397,000,000; import costs were $738,000,000. The continued deficit makes it even harder for Pakistan to borrow money or in other ways meet its development costs.

In its foreign trade policies, Pakistan is guided by several external factors. Because it borrows heavily from agencies controlled by the United States government, which also furnishes grants-in-aid, Pakistan is forced to make large—and relatively expensive—purchases in the U. S. Pakistan's association with the British Commonwealth and its membership in the sterling area permits relatively free exchange of money, an encouragement to trading with other sterling bloc countries. Pakistan is also a member of the General Agreement on Tariff and Trade (GATT), whose members give each other preferential tariff and trade treatment.

Government Participation

Muslim and British traditions in the subcontinent, the lack of natural resources and money, and the concentration of talent in the bureaucracy have all led to an increasing government role in Pakistan's economic development. The amount of government activity has varied with the years. After partition, the government tried to take responsibility for nearly every economic problem. Both the First and Second Five Year plans reflected an awareness that the government could not control and operate everything. Many responsibilities in industry were returned to private enterprise and control of public industries was decentralized. The provincial Pakistan Industrial Development Corporations, the Pakistan Industrial Development Bank, Pakistan International Airlines, and Karachi Electric Supply Corporation were made semi-public. But in agriculture and development of water and power resources, government activity has, if anything, increased.

Another area in which government has had to play a major role has been banking. Prior to partition, the banking structure in Pakistan's part of the subcontinent was in the hands of Hindus, Sikhs, and foreigners. The Koranic injunction against riba and the dearth of opportunities for Indian Mus-

lims to enter the banking business left the field to others. In mid-1947, there were 631 registered bank offices in the Pakistan area. A year later, after partition and the departure of non-Muslims, there were 195. By 1963, the number had grown to 861.

The government formed the State Bank of Pakistan in 1948 and it has become the most important money-lending institution in the country. Like the U. S. Federal Reserve Bank, it issues money and acts as a "banker's bank." It was instrumental in founding the privately-owned National Bank of Pakistan (1949), the House and Building Finance Corporation (1952), the Pakistan Industrial Credit and Investment Corporation (1957), the Agricultural Development Bank (1961) and the Industrial Development Bank of Pakistan (1961). It also regulates the sixteen foreign and domestic private banks which actually do most of the banking business. Government postal savings banks try to serve Pakistanis on the lower economic levels and government-operated agricultural credit cooperatives attempt to aid farmers.

Sitting atop all these government activities and directing them with a firm hand is the powerful National Economic Council, whose chairman is President Ayub. Composed of leading government officials such as Mohammed Shoiab and economic planner Said Hassan, it is the final arbiter of economic affairs and frequently, the only source of decisions for development matters. The Council leans heavily on the Central Planning Commission which, since 1955, has been advised by economists from Harvard University. Powerful and influential, the Commission helps formulate development policies and oversees the implementation of development plans.

Upon the National Economic Council and the Planning Commission rests the responsibility for carrying out the Second Five Year Plan. They also have now drawn up the outlines of the Third Five Year Plan which will cover the years

159

1965 to 1970. Latest estimates place the cost for the Third Plan at more than $10,000,000,000, twice as much as the Second Plan. Significantly, the Third Plan envisages an acceleration of 150 per cent in the development program of East Pakistan with the long-term objective of removing the economic disparities between East and West Pakistan by 1985. Its goals include raising the national income by 30 per cent (against 24 per cent in the Second Plan), increasing power and agricultural production and reducing dependency on foreign aid from 50 per cent to 40 per cent.

Foreign Aid

Pakistan began receiving help from other countries soon after independence. First, its wealthier Commonwealth colleagues (Australia, Canada, Great Britain, New Zealand) organized the Colombo Plan to assist less fortunate members. The first major project was the development of the Thal region in the Punjab for resettling refugees. Then the United Nations and the United States sent technicians and funds to attack basic economic, social, and welfare problems. With its entry into the Baghdad Pact, later called the Central Treaty Organization (CENTO) and the Southeast Asia Treaty Organization (SEATO), and its foreign policy commitment against international communism in 1954, Pakistan's benefits from U. S. foreign aid increased perceptibly. For instance, in 1956 Pakistan received $154,000,000 in foreign economic aid. In 1958 it received $145,000,000, and in 1962, after the revolution, it received $323,000,000.

United States aid has varied in kind and amount depending upon the foreign policy changes of both countries. U. S. economic aid in grants and loans was $404,000,000 in 1962. Only one country, India, received more from the U. S. in that year. Since 1947, Pakistan has received more than $1,500,000,000 in economic assistance from the U. S.

United States aid has helped nearly all economic projects, but most of the funds have gone for food and major development programs in transportation, power, and irrigation. Investment surveys, dollar and local currency loans, investment guarantees, and support for development banks have aided private enterprise. A large amount of aid has been in surplus food. One of the most recent projects supported by low-interest loans has been the construction of the Wah Cantt industrial center near Rawalpindi. Originally an ordnance factory, the two square miles of buildings will eventually turn out products as diverse as safety pins and bulldozers. In 1963, U. S. aid was aimed at the saltwater intrusion problem, increasing rice production, improving rural health, streamlining the bureaucracy, supporting an all-out education program, and promoting private industry. Pakistan is one of four "pilot" countries selected by the U. S. government for special emphasis on private enterprise activity (along with Thailand, Colombia, and Nigeria). Special efforts are being made to encourage American companies to invest in Pakistan's industries.

Pakistanis welcome foreign aid, aware that without it they cannot possibly improve their low standard of living. But, like patients receiving a vaccination for their health, Pakistanis do not like the treatment. They are sensitive and deeply resent the necessity of having to be injected with foreign aid. The very pride which led subcontinent Muslims to seek a country of their own forces them to accept with reluctance a dependence upon other people for their welfare.

This pride also encourages Pakistanis to work harder than they perhaps would work otherwise to reduce their dependency and in this effort they are somewhat successful. For instance, in 1963 exports of cotton textiles were the highest in Pakistan's history, up some 10 per cent over the previous year. Pakistanis expect that exports will increase steadily so that

161

their dependence on foreign aid will drop from 49 per cent to 41 per cent before the Second Five Year Plan is completed.

Yet increasing exports do not, in the short run, answer the needs of most Pakistanis, the villagers. In 1962–1963, manufacturing increased, as did exports, but floods and drought brought such calamity to the farmers that Pakistan's overall national income declined 1 per cent. Until the 83,000,000 villagers of Pakistan are able to produce more and obtain real compensation, Pakistan's development programs will be only superficial. It is in the development of its human resources that Pakistan must find the key to its prosperity.

8. *Traditions Under Attack*

As Pakistanis seek prosperity they face a constant conflict with their age-old customs. Progress requires change and for a people whose traditions are ancient and revered change does not come easily. Most Pakistanis live by rigid code, bred of a need to survive in a hostile world. Religion has confirmed these codes, making modification of them even more difficult.

The most powerful institution guiding a Pakistani's life is his family. Be he villager or city dweller, educated government official or simple farmer, Muslim, Hindu, Parsee, or Christian, Punjabi or Bengali, a Pakistani is a family man. His membership in a particular family or tribe forms the guidelines of his life.

The family is the basic economic unit in which a man works, earns and retires. It provides his security, not only as a fighting unit for tribesmen, but for protection against physical disability, unemployment and old age. In industrial societies, these functions have been usurped by the state—and insurance companies. Not so in Pakistan.

Family systems vary in South Asia, but anthropologists agree that they have one thing in common: a family consists of more than the husband, wife, and their children. It extends outward to include fathers and mothers, a married brother and his children, perhaps a widowed sister, all living in the same household. Among tribesmen, the "family" may include all parents, brothers and sisters, cousins, uncles and aunts. In the Punjab and Sind area, the lineage of a family is called a *biraderi*. Among Pathans it is called a *kheyl*, which incor-

porates a particularly large number of relatives. Bengalis call their lineage *athaya-shajan*. The degree to which a Pakistani recognizes a relative as part of his biraderi or kheyl depends on how "modernized" he has become.

Among most families, especially of the Muslim faith, the father is the family head. The members of the biraderi trace their relationship patrilineally to a common male ancestor. Among non-tribal families, the eldest son becomes head of the family when the father dies. Among Pathans, this is not always so. While ancestry extends back through the father, family leadership falls to the son who, in the eyes of the kheyl, is the most competent.

Toward each member of his extended family, a Pakistani child has certain prescribed obligations. The father commands great respect and the relationship between father and child is formal, and often restrained. A Pakistani's warmest attachments are to his mother and, next, to his sister and his maternal grandmother. For aunts and uncles, the family code sets forth strict rules of behavior. The child who best follows this code becomes a favorite, defended by all.

A family performs as a team. Each male fulfills certain tasks in the trade or occupation of the family. Women attend to the household and child-rearing needs. Married daughters have the obligation to settle quarrels between family members while sons are expected to defend their sisters' honor. The removal of a family member, as when a boy goes off to school, threatens the functioning of the family team.

While the family unit's strength gives protection and security to its members, it also inhibits development of new institutions which new nations demand. It may impede the development of the individual by limiting his education or mobility. It breeds nepotism in government.

Family or tribal loyalty can and does conflict with a man's loyalty to the larger "family" of his nation. Some farming

families resist education and mechanization which would disrupt the traditional unit. "Teach my boy to read and write," says a farmer, "show him the world beyond our village, and he will leave home. Without my son, I cannot plow, sow, or reap. And who will care for me in my old age?"

To insure protection and security, families must be strong and large, with many sons. Because disease takes so many children, a husband and wife will try to have a lot of children and they look with suspicion on attempts to persuade them to limit the size of their family.

Generally, then, a Pakistani's first loyalty is to his family. He will guard it against defamation and maintain its honor. If a member commits a crime that reflects on the family's prestige, the offender is severely punished and threatened with the ultimate penalty—expulsion. Yet, a family will defend its members, even if they are wrong, if by doing so the family's reputation remains unaffected.

It is because of the family's importance that marriage is such a highmark in Pakistani life. Planning marriages and selecting mates are of concern to the entire family. Early in a child's life, parents begin searching for a partner. They look first within the lineage, seeking a second or third cousin from a more important family unit. Usually this is in another village. The job of husband- and wife-finding is the mother's, although the father must bargain over the dowry a girl takes with her.

Muslim marriages are contractual affairs, not religious. The family of each partner works out precisely the responsibilities of each child. The daughter's family must make sure that if there is a divorce the daughter will receive as much "alimony" as possible. When the contract is settled, the families sign it, the boy and girl then agree to it and the marriage is consummated accompanied by joyous festivities which sometimes stretch over an entire month. While child marriages still ex-

ist in many villages, it is becoming more common for parents to wait until the boy is at least 16 and the girl 15.

President Ayub's government has tried to eliminate many of the traditions of Pakistani marriages. For instance, the Muslim Family Laws Ordinance of 1961 decreed every marriage must be registered with the Union Council and that divorce had to be a two-way proposition. Under orthodox Muslim law, a husband may divorce his wife merely by saying to her three times in front of a witness, "I divorce you"— the woman is thus divorced. Now, the woman must either consent or her husband must obtain permission from the Union Council. Religious leaders are quite upset by this intrusion of the government into personal Muslim law.

While the Pakistani family forms the core of the society and is the basic economic unit, few families are completely self-sufficient or independent. Over the centuries, society has developed occupational groups and social classes within each village or group of villages, each of which depends upon the other for security. Among Hindus, this stratification is solidified into the caste system, which has religious sanctity. For Muslims, distinctions exist without religious basis.

Thus, in a village there will be a barber, carpenter, weaver, baker, cobbler, mullah, *hakim* (folk doctor) and others whose families have acquired specialization through the years. Each is like an occupational caste. Children marry within their caste and wherever they go tend to follow the occupation and customs of the caste. This system applies equally in the cities among manual laborers, shopkeepers and government servants, modified, of course, by the degree of "modernization" that has taken place.

Social distinctions stem not only from a family's occupation, but from ancestors. One such distinction is called *ashraf*, or high-born, as against *ajlaf*, or low-born. Much of Pakistan's aristocracy is ashraf, descendants of Arab and Afghan con-

querors and Moghuls who once ruled South Asia. They are proud of their ancestry and maintain a class awareness, usually marrying other members of the class. Millions of Pakistanis—indeed, most of them—are descendants of converted Hindus. These the ashraf classify as ajlaf, a distinction without great significance to most Pakistanis.

Another division in the social structure is the *zamindars,* the landowners, or, in East Pakistan, *talukdar.* Many zamindars are also ashraf and thus are in the highest echelons of society. But a zamindar may also be a small landowner, far from wealthy. By owning land or being a member of a family which owns land he acquires membership in this group. He seldom marries outside it.

Millions of Pakistanis classify themselves as *kammis.* They are the craftsmen who generally do the non-farming jobs of the community, although they may also do field work. Kammis are divided into various occupational groups. Between kammis themselves and between kammis and zamindars contractual relationships exist which insure that everyone is fed and cared for. While each has a higher or lower relationship to the other, no one is indispensable. The lower seek favors and give gifts to the higher who, in turn, protect the lower. Changing any part of the system—even to removing the landlord—threatens the entire community.

Village life in Pakistan revolves around the family and caste relationships. The leading family is usually that of the wealthiest zamindar who himself is the *choudhury,* or chieftain. In East Pakistan, he is called the *morol.* It is he who must act as representative of the village to the government, be public spokesman, settle disputes (unless the dispute is such that he must call in the village elders, the panchayat) and maintain a guest house for visitors. He usually gets elected to the Union Council, although in some cases, the mullah or the peripatetic barber may gain enough stature to get elected.

167

At village level, the choudhury acquires his position by inheritance, but with the acquiescence of the other villagers. They may, if they are unhappy enough, change their allegiance to another zamindar, in which case, rivalries develop and biraderis compete for first place.

Among Pathans, the chieftain is called malik or khan. While his authority is considerable, he must first gain acceptance by the minor tribal leaders. When he speaks, it is only after the leading members have met together in jirga to discuss matters.

A West Pakistani desert or plains village is composed of dried clay houses with flat roofs covered with mud some twelve inches thick, laid upon timbers. Some have thatched roofs. Usually, each group of family houses is surrounded by a mud wall. Narrow lanes wind among the houses and act as sewers as well as paths. In many areas, especially in tribal territory, the entire village is surrounded by a wall. Many villages have a central "courtyard" which may have a store or two. It is common for the mosque to be off to one corner of the village. The courtyard may have the only well in the village. Some villagers keep their animals in their own houses; others keep them in a common stable in the village, but in nearly all cases animals at night remain very close to their owners. In higher terrain, West Pakistanis depend more upon wood, stone, and thatch in construction of their houses.

East Pakistan villages are quite different from those in the West. A Punjabi or Sindi village may have as many as 1,500 people, but a Bengali village will have fewer than 1,000. While a West Pakistan village will include many families living close together geographically, an East Pakistan village will have only a few families, each living apart in a subdivision called a *para*. There are not enough large areas of dry land on which to build an extensive village. Each family builds a row of bamboo huts around a central courtyard,

which usually has a pond. The sloping roofs of the houses are thatched with dry grass and their eaves droop in response to the heavy rains. More a group of separate homesteads than a village in the ordinary sense, the collection of paras in a banana or coconut grove has no store or other commercial enterprise, although it may have a small mosque.

More than 95 per cent of the people in East Pakistan live in such family villages, many of which are so close together that densities sometimes exceed 2,000 people per square mile. In the Lohanjang *thana* in Dacca district, more than 3,000 persons inhabit a square mile.

Villages in both provinces are usually connected in such a way as to form groups. Intermarriage between youths of the same caste in nearby villages and trade and craft relationships bind many villages together. Villagers share festivals and celebrations and there is much visiting back and forth. One village will become prominent and perhaps have a school and even a store available to other villagers. For most rural Pakistanis, this cluster of villages is their world and it is upon this cluster that President Ayub has built his Basic Democracies program. While villagers learn of events in the cities from radios, itinerant vendors, and other visitors, they really know only individuals and events within their cluster.

One characteristic of village life is its routine. Any variation from the routine is welcomed and villagers eagerly look forward to celebrations, religious festivals, visits from outsiders (who, properly, always give advance warning of their visit) and market days.

Zekiye Eglar, a Muslim scholar who did graduate work at Columbia University in New York, lived among Punjabi villagers for five years. She describes a sample of village life—a typical winter day.*

* Zekiye Eglar, *A Punjabi Village in Pakistan* (New York: Columbia University Press, 1960) p. 59 ff.

"By the time the sun is quite high, the woman at home has finished her morning chores. She rose before sunrise and in the dim light of a small lamp started to grind the grain. The sound of the grinding mill reaches the children in their beds, but they sleep on. Then she begins to churn the milk; in spring and summer she would churn outside. . . . The children wake up, but still remain for some time in bed, while the mother lets the chickens out from under the large basket with which they were covered at night. Then she kneads the dough and lights the fire. The children come outside and warm themselves near the hearth. They do not change their clothes for they sleep in the same clothes they wear during the day. They eat bread with butter and pickles, drink buttermilk and go to the mosque.

"Not every woman cooks on winter mornings. Some give the children bread or rice from the previous evening with buttermilk. In some houses people eat both breakfast and lunch, but other women prefer to prepare an early lunch.

"Children hardly wash their hands and faces in the mornings, for they are cold and the mother doesn't insist too much. She will wash them in the afternoon when it gets warm, and will change their clothes. The woman herself changes into fresh clothes in the afternoon, after she has finished her work, has washed, and has combed her hair; she finds little time in the morning to attend to her toilette.

"Men do not wash themselves at home. They go either to the well or to the bath attached to the mosque. A man wraps himself in an old sheet and sits in the sun while his wife washes and dries his clothes.

"After the children leave, the woman washes the dishes from the previous evening and from the morning, and feeds the chickens. She rolls up the bedding and puts it away, and carries the cots out into the courtyard for they are used during

170

the day. A neighbor may stop in for a few minutes, but morning is a busy time.

"The smoke rising over the walls of the baker's house is a sign that the oven is being heated. The baker's wife heats the oven twice before noon on winter mornings—for the people who eat an early lunch and for those who eat after noon. The baker's wife, as she works, squats by the side of an earthenware oven sunk in the ground. A small roof protects her from too much sunshine. Other women squat around her with their earthenware platters of dough which they shape into flat round breads and pass to the baker's wife to stick to the sides of the heated oven. For every eight loaves baked, she lays aside a piece of dough for one loaf as payment for her work. But even though she is paid every time bread is baked, at harvest time the *zamindars* who are her customers send her some grain. While they wait for their bread to be baked, women's tongues are as busy as their hands. This is the social club for women, where they exchange all the news and gossip of the village; how many outfits a certain woman brought from her visit to her parents' home; how, to spite her daughter-in-law, a farmer's mother was trying to persuade her son to take a second wife; and how the weavers threatened to leave the village unless the daughter of a weaver who had eloped with the son of a poor *zamindar* was returned to her parents. . . .

"As the sun rises higher and if the well is working, some women go there with their laundry, which they have soaked in boiling water and washing soda, and, placing a washboard under the running water, they beat the clothes with a wooden club, rub them with soap, and rinse them out. They spread the clothes to dry on the grass in the fields next to the well. . . . While the clothes are drying, a woman squats and washes herself in a small enclosure through which a thick jet of water from the well runs on its way to the fields. . . .

171

"While the little children are playing by the well, the older boys are in the mosque, where they go for an hour every day to learn to read the Quran from the village *imam,* and the girls study in the *imam's* house under the tutoring of his wife. This is the extent of the children's formal education. . . . Instead, they help their fathers in their work and thus, if the fathers are *kammis,* learn their fathers' trade. All boys learn how to cultivate the land and take care of the cattle. . . .

"The afternoon is the time for leisure and for visiting. A few women neighbors may drop in, and they all sit crowded together on a cot. Someone may read the popular poem, for women love it, too. The barber's wife or his mother may drop in, but she does not stay very long for she is on her way to the *chowdhri's* [choudhury] house where she will wash and comb and braid the *chowdhrani's* hair and will also massage her body, for this is her duty. . . .

"There are always people from the outside who pass through the village. There are vendors who sell children's toys, cheap crockery, and fruit; the men who pewter the copper pots; in summer, the ice cream man; a juggler; a man with a trained monkey and a bear; a group of professionals whose specialty it is to sing a lullaby to a baby; a village bard who travels with an orphaned son; a traveling *fakir* . . . the beggar begs in the name of God. They usually know which are the doors to knock at, and people give them grain or food—never leftovers, for that is a sin. . . .

"In the men's guest house, a small group of men play cards —a cobbler, the driver of a carriage who has come back from the city early in the afternoon, a *zamindar,* and the old servant of the *chowdhri.* A few men are also watching them. They play bridge and trumpet cards, and are intent on playing their best, for they never play for money, but are proud to play well.

"Late in the afternoon some men come in from the fields laden with huge piles of fodder. Others go home to milk the

172

buffaloes. The children are already at home, playing in the courtyard.

"As sunset nears, a few men go to the mosque to take their ablutions. Women who pray take their ablutions at home. Sunset is announced by the chanting of the call to prayer from the veranda of the mosque. Silence falls on the men sitting outside, as each says a prayer in his heart. Women pray on small mats spread in the courtyards or on the verandas of their homes. When the prayer is over, the men go home for their evening meal. . . .

"The evening meal is served right after sunset. The family squat near the hearth, except for the father who sits on a cot and is served there. After the meal, men get together in small groups. If they have work or some intrigue to discuss, they will visit each other's houses; otherwise they leave their houses and go outside to the places they usually frequent—the men's guest house, the place where some wealthy landowner keeps his cattle, or the workshop of the cobbler who always keeps a fresh *huka* [hooka]. Young men and boys join the older men or sit and tell stories or guess at riddles. . . .

"Everything becomes quiet after the night prayer. The only sound heard is the tinkling of the bells of the buffaloes working at the well, the regular flow of the water, and the song of a young man who is working at the well the whole night."

Time for the villager does not move by the clock. The sun is his major timepiece and the seasons determine how daily chores may vary. During fall and late spring, he is planting and sowing. In the winter and early and late summer, he has little to do. Except in times of emergency like a flood, life moves slowly. Phases of the moon set the dates for religious festivals.

City life is largely an extension of village life, modified to meet new conditions. During partition, refugee farmers from India fled to the cities of Pakistan. Since then, many Pakistani

villagers have migrated to the cities, as shown by the fact that, in the past ten years, the rural population has increased 19.8 per cent while the urban population has increased by more than 56 per cent. Millions of urban dwellers are still villagers at heart and are bound by the same traditions. Even the urban aristocracy is attached to the land and government and busiless leaders often have ties to one village or another.

Thus, in the cities, the same occupational caste distinctions pertain. Between occupational and social groups, there is little intermarriage except as modern-educated youth are able to ignore traditions. Like their village relatives, the family is a close-knit unit. Each member depends upon the other for security and livelihood. The arranging of proper marriages is as important to city folks as to villagers. In a country where prosperity is reserved for the very few, family members frequently give each other preference in jobs.

As in the village, a city man's prestige derives as much from the social level of his biraderi or kheyl as from the quality of his work. Money naturally plays a much larger role among urban Pakistanis and wealth brings honor of sorts. But wealth, combined with a good family ancestry and caste, means ever so much more.

In the cities and towns life becomes frustrating for Pakistanis. Their traditions were set in the village or tribe and have little relation to the pace and demands of modern city life. One example of frustration is the conflict between living according to time—as measured by the clock and as measured by traditional means. Promptness for appointments is a foreign manifestation and producing work according to a deadline or plan acquires an adjustment often beyond many Pakistanis. To the military-trained leaders of Pakistan, whose lives have been strictly regimented, the casual tempo around them demands great patience.

174

City life in Pakistan is superficially like life in any city. The calendar is Gregorian for most purposes. Work for the men begins at a specified time in the morning, stops for lunch, begins again an hour or so later, stops for tea, resumes and finally ends about 5 P.M., at which time every one goes home. Shops and the bazaars stay open much later. For a woman, life is more flexible, but she must spend at least half of each day in the bazaars. There being few "general" stores, she must go to one place for vegetables, another for meat, another for shoes or cloth. Fortunately, in the cities there are schools for her children, a blessing her village cousin does not always have.

Like the villagers, people in the city use the evenings as a time to socialize, meet with friends, listen to music, tell stories, and exchange gossip. If they can, families walk or ride a bus to the outskirts of town to escape the city heat. On weekends, a picnic and more visiting enlivens the routine. For men, and a few women, movies are a favorite recreation. In fact, the cinema in Pakistan is one of the more successful businesses. One theatre owner reported that he did not consider a movie popular unless the average movie-goer had seen the same film at least five times.

Recreation, especially group sports, plays a large role in the life of Pakistani youth. Most sports require little equipment but considerable output of energy. One popular game is called *kabadi* or *hadudu* in which two sides of any number of players oppose each other on a large field. Team members alternate as raiders, trying to cross the center line to touch a member of the opposing team without getting caught, all the while repeating in one breath the syllables "ka-ba-di-ka-ba-di." Another game is *hinga dari* or *laban dari*. Here teams attempt to steal salt from the center and place it in squares about the field. Inter-village matches bring forth enthusiasm similar to that found at American football games. In the Punjab and

175

among the Pathans sports on horseback are popular, ranging from polo to tent-peg sticking. So, too, is hunting.

On a national scale, although mostly in the cities, Pakistanis have produced athletes in nearly all sports. Their cricket teams play regularly against those of their Commonwealth partners. In the British Empire and Commonwealth Games in 1962, Pakistan's wrestlers won seven gold medals (in eight weights). For many years, the brothers Kashim, Azam, and Rowshan Khan have been world champions in squash rackets. Soccer is a popular school sport as is field hockey, in which a Pakistan team captured a gold medal in the 1960 Olympic Games. In basketball, track, tennis, and swimming, Pakistan is trying to develop Olympic competitors, although these sports, while popular, are relatively new to the country.

One distinguishing feature of Pakistani life, village or city, is the role of women. It is prescribed by tradition, religion and the men. Just as there are detailed obligations between individuals within a family or biraderi, so, too, is there a carefully defined occupational and social role for women to play, whether they like it or not. Basically, this role is similar to being a contractual servant to the man, satisfying his sexual desires, bearing and raising his children, preparing his food, finding a good mate for his children, keeping him informed of family affairs, comforting him in his old age, and supporting him in all his pursuits. In return, he provides her with children to raise, food to cook and a family to organize. He protects her, gives her the alimony previously agreed upon if he divorces her, and sometimes defers to her commands in the running of the household. If she is strong-willed, he may even permit her to advise him in business affairs. Each depends upon the other, but each has a separate place in society.

In this traditional role, Pakistani women are usually secluded from affairs outside their family. They generally may not meet male strangers who visit their husband's home. When

they walk beyond the confines of their house, they must be unobtrusive. In the towns, where there are many strangers, "unobtrusive" means veiled from head to toe. The practice of purdah, or seclusion, remains prominent in Pakistan, more so than in almost any other Muslim country except, perhaps, Afghanistan or Saudi Arabia.

Tradition has kept women isolated from those few streams of progress running through Pakistan. Education has largely passed them by. Most schools are for men and co-education is permitted only at the most primary level. While 80 per cent of the men are illiterate, over 90 per cent of the women are.

In a few corners of Pakistani society, women are escaping from the "separate but unequal" role. Some have cast off the veil, literally and figuratively, to become some of Pakistan's most adept and prominent leaders. They have achieved eminence in nearly all professions. Many of them are from families who migrated from India and who left behind not only their lands, but also their bondage.

The All-Pakistan Women's Association (APWA) is typical of the women's attempt to break with the past. Headed by Begum Liaquat Ali Khan, wife of Pakistan's first prime minister, who was assassinated in 1951, APWA is as formidable a force for Pakistan's progress as any other single organization in the country. From its ranks of young, dedicated women have come village workers, welfare aides, nurses, and social action leaders who have swept away years of lethargy among women and stubbornness among men and brought change into Pakistani homes.

In addition to Begum Liaquat Ali Khan, who has also been Pakistan's Ambassador to the Netherlands, other leading women have been Fatima Jinnah, the sister of Pakistan's founder, and Begum Mujibunnissa Akram, at the age of thirty-seven a member of the National Assembly and delegate

177

to the United Nations. Begum Sarwari Irfannullah participated in the World Congress of Women held in Moscow in June, 1963, while Begum Ruqqaya Anwar is an outstanding East Pakistan member of the National Assembly. Begum Mahmooda Selim Khan is a West Pakistan minister. Begum Jehanera Shah Nawaz from Lahore is a leader in the opposition and a prominent feminist. Together, these leaders have been able to break the centuries-old injunction against equal inheritance rights for women, much to the anger of religious leaders who continue to hold by the Muslim law which allots to daughters only half the amount of inheritance as sons.

Whether Pakistanis live in a village or town, they place the same high values on various aspects of life. Although some are common to all Asians, others are characteristic of Pakistanis.

Foremost among their values is a firm belief in the essential equality of all Muslims. Like most people, they breach the code of equality in practice, but Pakistanis are firm in their acknowledgement of the right of any man to sit at another man's table or pray by his side in his mosque (although women must pray separately).

Pakistanis also place value on loyalty—to the precepts of Islam, to their families and to their villages. The codes of behavior are well defined and the person who observes these codes attains stature. The young man who shows respect for age, the young girl who acts modestly, the zamindar who sacrifices an animal on Id al-Bakr, the son who returns to his village to visit his family, the person who does not eat pork and who fasts during Ramazan—each gains in the eyes of his community.

Hospitality, too, is a basic value, to the Punjabi or Sindi villager as much as to the Pathan whose codes are the most strict. To strangers and friends alike, Pakistanis accept an obligation to open their doors to those who seek shelter or

178

friendship, and as poor as he might be, a man must share what he has with a guest in his house.

Among townsmen, and an increasing number of villagers, formal education has great value. It is a means of rising in the social scale despite one's birth. For a farmer who is enlightened enough to permit his son to leave home temporarily, it is an opportunity for the son to do better than his father and to improve the life of the village family. For the patriotic—and there are many so motivated—education is an assurance that their country will progress. Some place such a high value on formal education that the university degree becomes the end of all endeavor rather than a step toward greater achievement.

Materially, villagers and many urban Pakistanis place great value on land. Here is tangible security. Muslims in South Asia have been farmers and rulers, not tradesmen or industrialists. Ownership of land evokes feelings of dignity and safety. This attitude has kept many urban Pakistanis so emotionally close to the soil they are reluctant to invest earnings or their future in factories or commerce. By the same token, Pakistanis also place value on jewelry which, over the years, has proved the safest means of hoarding wealth. Governments may come and go, economies may rise and fall, but gold earrings conserve their value in the marketplace and please the womenfolk as well.

In the life of nearly every Pakistani "The Government" asserts some influence, directly or indirectly. Although there are many who do not even know there is such a nation as Pakistan, few are oblivious to some kind of superstructure riding herd on their lives. What they think about it affects the government and the activity of people as citizens.

Pakistanis have two conflicting attitudes toward government. Both grew out of past experience. On the one hand,

the government is expected to solve most of the country's problems; on the other, it is the cause of most problems.

During most of India's history before 1947 the attitude of government leaders, whether Hindu, Moghul or British, was paternalistic, while the attitude of the people was one of passive submission. The state satisfied all needs; it built schools, roads and hospitals; maintained law and order and dispensed justice. In return, it expected from the people obedience, co-operation and the performance of assigned tasks. Initiative was seldom expected or encouraged and the relationship between government and the people was impersonal. This attitude still is deep-seated among government officials and the ordinary citizen today. But it has been modified by increasing mutual disrespect.

As the various nationalist movements gained strength after 1857, particularly after Mahatma Gandhi's movement of non-cooperation at the end of World War I, government became singularly unpopular among South Asians. Political awakening brought increasing criticism. Every action of government, good or bad, met with a storm of protest. "Government" came to be viewed as evil and its laws oppressive; non-cooperation was a badge of patriotism.

Pakistan came into being with combined attitudes of apathy toward personal or community initiative and resentment toward authority in public life. Both attitudes plague the advancement of Pakistani society. Many government servants see people as subjects and the people see government as a ruler, the cause of all problems and the source of all solutions.

As surely as the monsoons sweep into Pakistan every year, so change is creeping into its society and affecting patterns of living, attitudes and values, welcome or not. It is this progress and control of the changing social system that is a major challenge to Pakistan's leaders. If they must threaten the protective link in the family's chain of security, then they must

180

provide—or convince the people to provide for themselves—a substitute.

A son leaving his village to seek his way in the city appears to threaten his family's security, yet such a move gives greater opportunity for a young man to build a better life. A daughter seeking education violates the traditions of village life yet broadens her horizon. An unarranged marriage between a couple of different occupational castes defies the practices of centuries, yet gives both boy and girl opportunity to find greater happiness and a more meaningful life. A young girl joining APWA against the wishes of her father contravenes the code of family loyalty and female modesty, yet brings another soldier into Pakistan's army of welfare workers.

Few villagers in Pakistan and even fewer city dwellers have escaped acquaintance with abrupt change in the past decade, particularly since the advent of President Ayub. For many years to come, zamindars and kammis, ashrafs and ajlafs, Muslims and Hindus, villagers and urbanites, will follow the traditional ways of living in the subcontinent. But more and more they will all shed certain habits and values as they get caught up, willingly or not, in the twentieth century.

9. The Absent Necessities

Although sought by many, formal education and good health are luxuries available to relatively few Pakistanis. For the majority of the people—the villagers—development of the mind and care of the body depend upon family convention. In its Second Five Year Plan, Pakistan has embarked upon an ambitious course to adapt these conventions to modern technology. Already, the benefits of science and education have been extended to many thousands who could not previously perform effectively in their changing society.

Education

Pakistan's leaders have come to realize that investment in education is an integral part of the country's investment in economic development; that without trained manpower there can be little growth in industry or agriculture. Unfortunately, the initial costs of such an investment are enormous because Pakistan has so far to go. Literacy is a good indication. Only some 15 per cent of the people can read or write—less than 20 per cent of the population aged five years or over. What literacy gains Pakistan makes in expanding primary education are practically nullified by the rapidly expanding population.

Centuries of poverty prevented the establishing of educational institutions in South Asian villages. But two other factors contributed as well. One was the traditional Islamic approach to learning and the other was the narrow scope of education supported by Muslim and British rulers.

Formal education among Muslims generally, whether in

182

South Asia or the Middle East, has largely meant learning about religion, although there are exceptions. Various Muslim courts throughout history—in Baghdad, Ghazni, Khorosan, and Delhi—encouraged scholarship in a broad range of subjects. For the masses, however, the educational process was in the hands of mullahs, whose primary purpose was the teaching of Islam—and Arabic. And as the world progressed about them, the mullahs made little use of modern knowledge. In Bengal, Muslim missionaries established madrassahs which taught only religious subjects until a group of "reformed madrassahs" introduced arithmetic, history and geography in 1915. In the area that is now West Pakistan, these schools were called maktabs and, at a more advanced level, *dar-ul-ulums*.

Religious schools were once the chief educational institutions for Muslims and they still play an important role in education in Pakistan, as do religious schools for Hindus in East Pakistan. Subjects offered remain predominantly theological. The government has begun an intensive program to organize classes for mullahs and imams in hopes of raising the level of their teaching. Among Hindus, the government supports some 100 special schools known as *tols,* supervision of which it leaves to Hindu leaders.

The Moghul rulers of India encouraged some Muslims and a few Hindus from important families to seek broader education in order to serve in the top ranks of the government. The British who followed them continued the same policy.

Beginning in 1835, the British promoted a limited system of public education, which Christian missionaries supplemented with private schools. The objects were to propagate Christianity and to train young Indians for government service. The architect of the system was T. B. Macaulay, who wrote at the time that the British system of education was designed to produce "a class of persons, Indian in blood and

183

color, but English in taste, in opinions, in morals and in intellect." Classes were offered in philosophy, English literature, grammar, European economics, English history, and some science. With this broad base, graduates could then serve in administrative posts demanding general knowledge. Little or no effort was made to provide technical training or mass education.

For many years, British-styled education appealed primarily to Hindus, especially after the uprising of 1857 when they received preference in government service. While Hindus advanced academically, Muslims continued to rely on their madrassahs and maktabs. It was to overcome this Muslim disadvantage that Sayyid Ahmed Khan established the Mohammedan Anglo-Oriental College at Aligarh in 1875. In 1920, it became Aligarh University and was the primary institution for training subcontinent Muslims for government. Its graduates formed the core of Pakistan's early leadership. Few of the newly-independent countries of the world today have a more qualified group of educated leaders than Pakistan did at the time of its independence.

Yet the very system which produced well-educated leaders provided only minimal training for those who were needed to build the country, the engineers, doctors, scientists, businessmen and technicians.

In Pakistan's inherited educational system, a student progresses in four stages to reach the university level. The first five years are called "primary," the next three "middle," the next two "high school," and the final two "intermediate." The curriculum in all stages, beginning with the first grade, contains subjects of a predominantly theoretical nature and a student need only memorize facts from books and from copious notes carefully written verbatim as the teacher speaks. While the object of the student may not be to enter university or government service, the plan of studies is designed with

these goals in mind for everyone. Those who do not succeed are not prepared for anything else.

In the early days of Pakistan, the government's approach to education was primarily to expand what it had inherited. More schools and teachers seemed to be the answer. By 1955, Pakistan had doubled the number of primary school teachers to 75,000. It was not long before Pakistanis realized that increased facilities and teachers did not provide the quality of education which the society needed. The First Five Year Plan made a small beginning at giving teachers better training, but it alloted only one-fifth of its development funds to education. The government's biggest step was to appoint a Commission on National Education, headed by S. H. Sharif, with freedom to look into all the corners of Pakistan's educational system.

In 1959, the Commission made its report. It minced no words in pointing out the weaknesses of the old system and, indeed, its report was praised in many parts of the world. Of more importance, President Ayub supported its recommendations, appointed an autonomous Planning and Development Division in the Ministry of Education and instructed Mr. Sharif to hurry. In the Second Five Year Plan, investment in education was doubled. Against the resistance of many teachers, who had not been consulted or been involved in the educational planning and who opposed many of the new plans, the government made slow headway. In some areas, such as home economics education and agricultural training in East Pakistan, advancement has been remarkable. On a country-wide basis, however, the system strongly reflects that which Pakistan inherited.

No more than 40 per cent of Pakistan's children enter primary school. Of these, nearly 75 per cent drop out before they have reached the fifth grade, the stage at which a child is considered literate. Only about 5,000,000 children, 4,000,000

of whom are boys, enter the 50,000 primary schools each year. Nearly all live in the towns and cities.

Children do not go to school for several reasons. First, there are not enough schools, especially in West Pakistan, or enough teachers. But even when schools are available, some village parents do not see the sense of formal education. Children are an important part of the working unit and farmers often feel that their children are more useful in the fields than in school.

Ever so slowly, attitudes toward education are changing. Zekiye Eglar states: *

"Formerly, many well-to-do *zamindars* sent their sons to school, but if the boy did not show much eagerness to study the parents did not insist because the land was always there. Today, both sons and daughters are being educated. The demand for educated girls has become widespread, and in the villages people have already learned to inquire whether a marriageable girl has completed primary or high school. . . . The *kammis* are equally eager to educate their children. Most of them send their children to the village school opened by the government, but not all of them as yet send their daughters to the same school with their sons. Instead, they still prefer to have their daughters study the Quran, which is taught by the wife of the *imam*. However, among the young men who have had some education, there is a strong desire to marry an educated girl who has studied in a regular school."

The Commission hoped to see the number of primary schools expanded by 22,000 by 1965 and educational reforms made which would decrease the drop-out rate and increase enrollments. After two years, the Implementation Commission was far from its goal, although advancement in East Pakistan was encouraging.

* Eglar, *op. cit.,* page 191.

186

Students from the secondary stages of education form the bulk of the educated community. They have attended one of 6,000 public and private schools. Most teachers have only a secondary education themselves, but since their only requirement in the present system is to read lectures, the pedagogical demands on them are not great. The goal of the students is to pass a year-end written examination in which success can be achieved through memorization. Throughout the year, all intellectual effort is aimed toward this single examination. The student receives no credit for work done during the year.

The Commission on National Education wrote:

"Our own secondary system is so far removed from our actual and immediate needs, as to make it hopelessly inadequate." The Commission recommended that the curriculum be diversified, that it "include such additional subjects and training as will form a preparation for specific vocations and careers."

Teacher resistance to the Commission recommendations has been particularly strong in secondary education, especially in changing the examination system, broadening the curriculum and up-grading the teachers. An effort has been made to establish an "educational extension" program in major cities to give in-service training to teachers and supervisors. In addition, new "demonstration" secondary schools have been built, with American assistance, to show how a different system of education can be effective. The experiments are too new to have made an impact on the system.

In higher education, Pakistan has had to overcome great handicaps, not all deriving from the educational system. For instance, in 1950, Pakistan had only three universities, one each in Sind, the Punjab and East Bengal. Dacca University was originally affiliated with the University of Calcutta, India's major teaching institution. It and the University of the Punjab in Lahore were considered outstanding. They trained top

187

level civil servants. However, most of the university professors were Hindus who migrated to India in 1947. Both schools deteriorated drastically. Only in recent years have they begun to improve their standards with young, foreign-trained Pakistani teachers. Today, Pakistan has six universities: University of Sind, University of Punjab, Peshawar University, Dacca University, University of Karachi, and Rajshahi University. Their total enrollment in 1960 was about 7,400. Affiliated with them, or sending students to them, were some 209 non-professional two-year colleges, many privately-owned, with an enrollment of 110,000.

As in secondary schools, university students obtain a degree, their passport to government service, by passing a year-end examination. Teachers lecture only on those subjects contained in the examination and students generally concern themselves only with preparing for the final test. The Commission on National Education claims that teachers "have substituted cramming for education" and says that the "emphasis has been on the successful retention of some facts about a subject for a brief period rather than on the more arduous but rewarding aim of mastering a subject, understanding its basic principles, and learning how to apply this understanding to real situations."

Those Pakistanis who pass the examination—and retain what they have previously memorized—are well-educated in a narrow sense. With additional study abroad, many have become singularly well prepared to assume positions of leadership in government and in education. But many students entering universities are not equipped for it and they fail, only to repeat the process the next year, and perhaps the next. For instance, in 1957, more than half the students of Punjab University did not pass examinations for the various degrees. Nearly all returned the following year. Even the failed student has more education than most Pakistanis and

is proud of what little he has. It is not unusual for applicants for white collar positions to include in their applications, "B.A.-Failed."

The Pakistan government in its Second Five Year Plan accepted most recommendations of the National Commission, but it sees an advantage in a continued, although restricted, university course preparing students for government service. It seeks to raise academic standards, improve selection of students and the quality of teachers.

While there is a recognized place for generalized university education in Pakistan, the Commission has also noted the urgent need for more professional and technical manpower. While 75 per cent of the employed persons in Pakistan are in agriculture, for instance, only some 200 students take degrees in agriculture each year compared to 800 graduates in law.

A start has been made in meeting this problem. In 1963, there were sixteen polytechnic schools open, against three in 1958. Since 1960, the government has developed agricultural universities at Lyallpur in West Pakistan and Mymensingh in East Pakistan. Two engineering schools in the universities of Dacca and Lahore have been made into four year degree schools and two new technical universities are being built. New home economics colleges in Lahore, Dacca, and Peshawar joined the one previously existing college in Karachi.

Perhaps the greatest impediment to developing technical education is the attitude of students—and their parents and teachers—towards manual labor. The Commission on National Education wrote:

"One of our greatest weaknesses as a people is our unwillingness to use our hands and a misconception of the true nature of manual work. So long as this remains a feature of

189

our educated class, progress in developing our country will be slow."

For students, graduates and teachers alike, education has meant freedom from manual labor. Regardless of when the student leaves school, he expects to find office work. Even those who study for vocations such as agriculture and engineering often feel excused from working with their hands. Few agricultural students intend to farm the land themselves. They look forward to clerical and administrative positions in government.

The aim of President Ayub's government is, as the Commission on National Education recommended, "to reverse the national aversion to the use of the hands" and "develop in our people a sense of dignity of manual work and a pride in technical achievement. We must develop our manpower skills at all levels if national progress, self-sufficiency and welfare are to be achieved."

A second handicap in training manpower is the absence of discipline among student bodies. This attitude goes back to pre-partition days when students led much of the criticism of authority, in that case, the British government. Students were, after all, an elite, organized group within an illiterate, unorganized society. Contempt for authority was widespread and when Pakistan became independent it continued rather than abated. Political opportunists have taken full advantage of the students' mercurial interest in politics and used them for non-academic purposes. Students who are often unsuited for higher education, with much free time on their hands and lacking guidance from the faculty, have acted with a predictable degree of irresponsibility. They have rioted when they felt that their examinations were too difficult; they have intimidated voters, marched on and stoned government offices and have frequently forced the government to close their schools.

190

At the heart of the problems lies the fact that education is for the few; most Pakistanis receive no formal education at all. Mostly these are villagers, not many of whom are averse to manual labor. But teaching them is expensive, requiring more than mere construction of schoolhouses or training of teachers. When village parents can neither read nor write, and follow patterns of living that resist change, their children soon lose whatever gains they made in a schoolroom. Pakistan's educators have begun an adult education program, but they have only rippled the surface of a deep sea of illiteracy and ignorance. In no field are the effects of this ignorance and poor communications between those with modern knowledge and those without it so apparent as in the field of health.

Health

Perhaps the saddest part of life for Pakistani parents is the sickness of their children and their inability to do anything about it. Throughout the villages, particularly in crowded East Pakistan, malnutrition is commonplace, disease is widespread, doctors are few, and death is a frequent visitor. The average life span of a Pakistani villager is under thirty years and over half of all deaths are among children under ten. Life expectancy in Pakistan is less than in India, Indonesia, and many other Asian countries.

Health statistics are difficult to gather. Most people die without benefit of an attending physician. The man responsible for reporting deaths and who usually makes the diagnoses is a poorly-paid *chawkidar,* or watchman, who often attributes death to "fever." Villagers are under no obligation to give him information. But from what little is known, few people in the world suffer more from ill health than Pakistanis.

Much ill-health stems from a poor diet, which leaves the body susceptible to disease. Few villagers eat more than 2,000

191

calories a day (against a needed 2,400 to 3,000 calories). Their meals are ill-balanced, with very little protein. The villager who eats meat once a month is fortunate. A recent study among 1,500 villagers near Dacca revealed that 76 per cent were malnourished.

Another related cause of ill health is ignorance of sanitation. Water polluted by both animals and humans washes the clothes and dishes and also quenches the thirst. The idea that flies and other insects carry disease is foreign to most villagers, including those responsible for selling and preparing food.

More than 24,000,000 Pakistanis suffer from malaria every year, nearly a quarter of the population. Of these, 500,000 die and another 6,000,000 become susceptible to other diseases due to the debilitating effects of malaria. No other disease causes such mortality. And unfortunately, mosquitoes in Pakistan are becoming resistant to DDT.

Tuberculosis, too, is prevalent, especially in crowded city slums and villages. Rapid industrialization and overpopulation, coupled with poverty and undernourishment, help tuberculosis spread. Villagers frequently contract the disease from cattle, which often share sleeping quarters with the families. Public health officials estimate that more than 1,000,000 Pakistanis have tuberculosis and more than 150,000 die from it each year.

Cholera is one of the major epidemic diseases of East Pakistan. It sweeps the province twice a year, causing up to 30,000 deaths annually.

Smallpox is also endemic, as is typhoid. Dysenteries affect nearly all village children. A study of children in a village near Dacca in 1958 revealed that every single child had intestinal worms. Throughout West Pakistan, millions face blindness from trachoma.

It is common for villagers to attribute their illness to the will of God and to accept their fate. There is little they can

do about it anyway, except to try what folk remedies they know, such as washing sores in the warm blood of a freshly-sacrificed animal. Usually a sick villager will first seek help from the local mullah, who will probaly give him an amulet or some holy water. If a doctor is near, he then may seek medical help. It is not unusual for a disease to be far advanced by the time a doctor is called in.

There are two kinds of doctors in Pakistan, both recognized by the government: those trained in modern medicine, who number about 10,000, and those trained in traditional medicine, who far outnumber modern doctors. In Muslim society, the traditional system is called *unani,* which was introduced during the Muslim conquests and is derived from Greek science. A practitioner is called a *hakim,* although many apply this name to any doctor. In East Pakistan, particularly among Hindus, the predominant system is *ayurvedic* and the practitioner is called *vaid* or *kaviraj.* This system follows medical texts compiled twelve to fifteen centuries ago. Its pharmacy influenced the development of medicine in Europe. Both the hakim and vaid practice healing techniques long since abandoned in most developed countries. However, the Unani Research Center in Karachi seeks to discover the benefits that may exist in the many herbs and remedies employed by these doctors. The manufacture of ayurvedic medicines is an important local industry in East Pakistan. Government officials do not consider these medical men effective and hope to replace them with scientifically-trained doctors. Meanwhile, the government is trying to persuade them to incorporate more modern techniques into their practice.

With fewer than ten modern doctors per 100,000 persons, Pakistan's medical corps is less developed than in most Asian countries, including India and Burma. This is not surprising since Pakistan had to begin from scratch to build a public health service. Before partition, the medical and technical

staff in the various provinces now constituting Pakistan were mostly non-Muslims, nearly all of whom migrated to India. For instance, in the Northwest Frontier Province in 1951 there were only 53 medical officers to man 121 government medical positions. West Punjab lost 75 per cent of its nurses to India.

Partition left Pakistan with only one fully-operating medical school, the King Edward Medical College in Lahore. By 1963, there were six medical schools in West Pakistan, one exclusively for women and three in East Pakistan. They graduate about 600 doctors each year. Nearly all of these, like their colleagues before them, seek private practice in the cities, shunning the rural villages where facilities and compensation are meager.

Nursing has developed especially slowly. There are about 2,600 in the country. There is considerable social pressure against women entering any profession, including nursing. Many nurses are Christian and Parsee, but the number of Muslim girls in nursing is increasing. A college of nursing was established in Karachi in 1956 and some twenty training centers now prepare young women as auxiliary nurses.

Partition also left Pakistan with few hospitals. By 1963, the number of beds per 100,000 people was about 30, less than India (35) or Burma (37). In the Second Five Year Plan, the government hopes to add another 8,000 beds. Development of health facilities is almost entirely in the hands of the government, especially the provincial governments, although foreign missionaries still make an important contribution.

A Medical Reforms Commission has noted that the problems of ill health and malnutrition can only be solved when the general economic and social conditions improve substantially and when education is more widespread. But it has recommended to President Ayub, who has forcefully backed it, an intensive program of improvement with most of the

194

emphasis on preventive, rather than curative, medicine. The Second Five Year Plan assigns close to 60 per cent of its health development funds to raising general health standards, recognizing that the cost of trying to cure all present ills is prohibitive.

Special emphasis has been laid on malaria eradication and many areas of Pakistan have been sprayed with DDT. World Health Organization experts have guided the program and training courses have started at the Malaria Institute of Pakistan in Dacca. A new country-wide B.C.G. vaccination campaign continued to attack tuberculosis in 1963 with thirty-two mobile teams touring both provinces, bringing to more than 16,000,000 the number of people vaccinated.

Two new programs begun by President Ayub's administration are the first hope in years for real progress in preventive medicine. The first is the establishing of 300 rural health centers. By 1963, 10 demonstration and training centers were opened and construction started on 48 more. Each health center serves 30 to 40 villages and is staffed by one male and one female doctor with an auxiliary staff consisting of a woman "health visitor" and several technicians. Every health center has 3 sub-centers with a health technician and a midwife who attend to 10 villages. Three days a week, the male doctor serves at the Primary Health Center and on the other three days he visits the sub-centers. Similarly, the woman doctor visits sub-centers while the male doctor is in the Primary Center, because in Pakistan women usually demand women doctors. These centers provide for medical treatment, maternal and child welfare, sanitation, family planning, control of communicable diseases, and health education. Patients needing confinement are referred to tehsil or thana and subdivisional hospitals. The government plans to assign medical interns to these centers before granting them their medical certificates.

A second new program is in family planning. In few other areas in the world is population growth more "explosive." The percentage increase is 2.4 per cent annually; in West Pakistan, it is 2.7 per cent. Rapid population growth (spurred by health programs that cut the death-rate) limits the opportunity for children to develop properly, curtails investment resources in favor of current consumption, raises the net cost of supporting the population and creates serious obstacles to social and economic development. As parents see their children die from unknown causes—one of every four dies before the age of ten—and as the economic and social system depends upon working children to support their parents in old age, couples, particularly husbands, tend to look favorably on frequent childbirth. But above all, ignorance of planning, the lack of knowledge that they can do anything about recurring births, prevents couples from limiting the size of their families to a number they can support.

Through the Basic Democracies, the rural health centers and some 1,920 (in 1963) family planning centers, the Pakistan government is undertaking an ambitious program to slow the rate of population growth. Advised by demographers and health experts from the Population Council in the United States, Pakistan has trained 605 doctors, 446 health visitors and nurses, and 4,800 village workers and *ansars* (helpers) in family planning techniques. It has also carried out research on the acceptability and effectiveness of different methods of birth limitation.

Foreign advisory help has figured prominently in Pakistan's efforts to meet health problems. The Colombo Plan nations, the United States and the United Nations agencies—World Health Organization (WHO) and United Nations Children's Emergency Fund (UNICEF)—have been active in medical education, preventive medicine and research.

196

Social Welfare

As in all developing countries which have such a large proportion of poor people, there are millions unable to find for themselves even the basic requirements of life. Rapid urbanization caused by refugees from India and migrants from the villages have swelled Pakistan's towns with individuals sick in both body and heart, without housing, food, or work. Cyclones and floods have uprooted thousands more. While government agencies have begun an attack on specific social problems such as education and health, most government energy has gone toward building an economy which hopefully in the long run will create a society strong enough to care for its poor. Meanwhile, these millions of urban poor must rely on a few public and private social welfare agencies.

Few societies have had to face such a serious refugee problem as Pakistan. After 1947, nearly nine million Muslims from India flooded into East and West Pakistan without the means to survive. They clogged city streets with makeshift huts devoid of sanitation facilities. Many died of virulent disease which swept through their miserable refugee colonies.

Pakistan's Commonwealth partners first came to its aid in resettling agricultural refugees in the Punjab. In the sandy wastes of the Thal desert, irrigation projects opened new lands and newcomers began building a new life, each receiving land based on the amount of land he farmed in India. Villages sprouted from the once barren soil and new market towns with such names as Qaidabad (after Mohammed Ali Jinnah) and Liaquatabad (after Liaquat Ali Khan) began to flourish. Other settlement projects began wherever new irrigation works were built, especially after the 1958 revolution, when Ayub Khan ordered immediate attention to the refugee problem.

Many Pakistanis, particularly the women, helped by foreign

197

friends, made heroic efforts after 1947 to meet the refugee problem in Karachi. While their efforts were of an emergency and shortrange nature, they won praise for preventing a miserable situation from becoming worse. After 1958 they found substantial help from the Pakistan government. Under the energetic command of General Azam Khan, General Ayub's Rehabilitation Minister, an entire new community was built in Korangi, on the outskirts of Karachi. Today some 30,000 houses and their inhabitants now form a new city with mosques, schools, markets, playgrounds and hospitals. Elected Town Committees organize the people within the Basic Democracies program and urban development projects run by the government help the refugees adjust to their new life. By 1965, the government expects all the Karachi refugees to be settled.

With General Azam Khan transferred to East Pakistan, new resettlement schemes and town planning began in that province. By 1962, three of seven schemes were completed and 11,500 families resettled. Slowly, but at an increasing pace, the refugees are finding homes. Concurrently, the government is supporting both public and private house construction generally, although private builders have tended to concentrate on homes for the wealthy.

Traditionally, care of the helpless in Pakistani society is the responsibility of the family. It is the family which cares for its members who become lame, blind, or mentally ill. In old age, parents find security through their children. As the family system weakens, inevitable in today's changing society, its economic role decreases. As the families move from village to city, so too does the family's welfare function deteriorate. In such circumstances, society must provide an alternative welfare service, and in Pakistan the society is ill-equipped. Except among a few factory workers' organizations, Pakistan has no formal social security system.

198

Under the First Five Year Plan, the government began a program based on the local community, utilizing as far as possible the services of private agencies. It established schools of social work in Dacca and Lahore and formed, in 1956, the National Council of Social Welfare. In the Second Five Year Plan, more use was made of the Basic Democracies with trained advisers attached to local councils. Furthermore, a social welfare unit was made a permanent part of the powerful Planning Commission, assuring that in most future development programs social welfare will not be ignored. By 1965, the government hopes to have 1,100 social workers and 900 other professional workers for instruction of the physically handicapped and in adult education programs. Two new schools of social work were established in Karachi and Rajshahi. All social welfare activity is now under provincial directorates of social welfare, which are advised by social welfare councils.

Most welfare activity, however, stems from the work of private, voluntary agencies, both religious and secular. Traditionally, care of the poor has been a religious, as well as family, responsibility and Islam has within its instructions the firm obligation of charity. Religious taxes such as zakat supported some welfare work and the meat and skins of animals sacrificed in religious ceremonies helped a few of the poor.

At the time of partition, the only major voluntary agency equipped for social service was the Red Cross, which immediately established a Pakistani branch. Since then, the Pakistan Red Cross has been the chief private organization for meeting welfare emergencies. It is the only private agency yet able to coordinate world-wide efforts to help Pakistanis in time of need.

However, the largest and most effective general social service organization is the APWA, organized shortly after partition to distribute food and clothing, and to nurse the sick.

With branches in each province and every city, it has mobilized women to serve their country by running schools, helping in adult education projects and organizing maternal and child welfare centers. APWA has demanded of political groups to include women and has encouraged the government to appoint women to units of the Basic Democracies. Above all, APWA has kept pressure on the government to give increasing attention and money to social welfare.

Through local organizations, some religious, including Christian missions, foreign help has also brought support for social service programs. Red Cross groups in many European and American countries have responded to appeals for aid. Western church groups such as the Church World Service and the National Catholic Welfare Council in the United States maintain liaison with Pakistani organizations. The U. S. government's foreign aid program assists in training social service workers as well as providing surplus food for free distribution.

WHO and UNICEF participate in social service activities, working through both governmental and private groups such as the Pakistan National Tuberculosis Association, Tuberculosis Patients Welfare Association, Pakistan Leprosy Relief Association and the Association for Mental Health. The Population Council helps family planning associations, the key groups which are attempting to slow the rate of the country's population expansion.

10. In Search of an Identity

In the fading twilight of a Pakistani day, clusters of village men gather around hookas, squatting on the ground or sitting on *charpois* (rope beds) to talk. They tell stories, recite poems, sing. The women sit nearby, sometimes joining in song. Some are hand-spinning coarse wool. Children play, perhaps the popular game of striking a small stick with another to see how far they can hit it. Together, they form a tableau common in thousands of villages across the countryside, a tableau that is part of Pakistan's personality and its pastoral people.

The stories are often accounts of the day's events or, if one has returned from a visit, his adventures. Or the stories may be about a man who lived long ago—a pir, a ghazi, or a great zamindar. Told again and again, never written, these tales become history as the villager understands it. A man with a poetic or musical ear may turn the story into a poem or song and it becomes a part of Pakistan's great wealth of folk culture.

Whether Sindi, Pathan, Punjabi, or Bengali, songs and poems tell of the land and the mysteries of religion. As farmers who are deeply attached to the soil, Pakistanis live in constant awareness of the elements. Few folk songs ignore the environment of their authors who often use pastoral subjects as romantic allegory.

A Bengali villager sings:

> The month of Aghran brings the new crop
> Some reap the harvest,
> While others are engaged in the harvest festival.
> One who has reaped well is happy,
> One who has none awaits others' mercy.

> The month is almost over,
> But the maiden's desire remains unfulfilled.
> Shortly comes the month of Paush
> With all its youthful vigor.

In each region of the country, the variations in climate and land are reflected in the literature of the people. Thus the Bengali writes and sings of rivers and boats. He usually has a song for every occasion, even for plying his boat upstream (in which case he sings a type of song called a *sari*) or downstream (when he sings a *bhatiali*).

> Take back thine oar, O boatman,
> I can no longer ply it.
> All my life I have struggled
> To bear my boat upstream,
> But backward it has gone;
> And now in my old age
> I find my efforts gone for nought.

A Sindi shepherd weaves his tale on the loom of a hot and dry desert which is rarely watered by an irrigation canal.

> The jackals are howling across the dark stream,
> My love is a peacock, in beauty supreme.
> The forest of myrtles spreads up to the brink
> The love of my girl is like heavenly drink.

Religion is always near the consciousness of the villager. During religious festivals, a chant called a *qawwali* expresses the universally deep devotions of Pakistanis.

> How rich and mighty is God!
> He has set up the panorama of the world,
> Which He will break up any time He likes without
>   paying heed to anyone.
> In this market-place of the world
> Many are engaged in selling and buying.
> (They seldom feel that)
> God and the Prophet are its owners.
> Adore the deepest truth.

202

But perhaps the most common folk songs and poems are concerned with romance. Whether sung or written by men, they are usually about a woman's lost or departed love. In West Pakistan, the forlorn young woman often dreams of her lover as a warrior, as in this Baluchi folk song:

> When he walks, it seems he is going to conquer the enemy fort;
> When he turns to look at his foes, they tremble with fear.
> He is pledged to see me;
> I am certain he will turn up,
> Walking sportively with his silvery gun,
> Because Baluchi blood flows in his veins.

A Punjabi maiden inevitably visualizes her man on horseback and sings a song called a *dholak,* after a drum which accompanies it:

> I have green trees
> In my courtyard.
> Turn round thy horse, O swain,
> Come let us sit in the shade.
>
> I have a pair of cows
> In my courtyard.
> Turn round thy horse, O swain,
> Come, have a cup of milk.
>
> I have a mango tree
> In my courtyard.
> Turn round thy horse, O swain,
> Have a few mangoes.

While the villager seems relatively contented with the various styles of expression he has developed, the urban poet, musician, dancer, painter or architect in Pakistan is restless and often frustrated. He wants to be recognized by the rest of the world, particularly Europe and the United States. He is sometimes guilty of gross imitation, rejecting his cultural traditions as unworthy of the modern world or the new Pakistan. But he is beginning to search his own heritage for artistic inspira-

tion. He is experiencing the forms of feeling universal to man and he seeks a greater opportunity for self-expression. Slowly, he is discovering the personality of Pakistan.

Literature

The oldest literary stream in Pakistan flows in Bengal, where the continuity of recorded history and language extend back more than 1,000 years. Under the Buddhist Pala dynasty, a colloquial language developed that was the beginning of Bengali. Songs in this ancient Indo-Aryan tongue were recorded by Buddhist monks. Suppressed by the Hindu Senas (1100–1200 A.D.), who established Sanskrit as the language of literature, Bengali began to flourish again when Muslim Turks conquered Bengal in the 13th century. The sultans of Bengal (1351–1575) patronized art and literature. While they imported Persian poets, local bards such as Shah Mohammed Saghir (1389–1410) composed in Bengali and sent down to modern times epic songs of romance and mysticism. *Puthi* poetry, ballads of mythical adventure similar to the *Arabian Nights*, became a popular literary form. Under the Moghul governors, Persian culture was deeply implanted in Bengal. New words appeared in the Bengali language, Shi'ism, with its traditions of tragedy and suffering, and sufism became part of an expanding Bengali Muslim literature which existed side by side with Hindu mythological poetry and song.

During British rule, Hindus dominated the literary scene in Bengal. In Calcutta, modern Bengali literature developed through non-Muslim scholars: Michael Dutt, Bankimchandra Chatterjee and, finally, Rabindranath Tagore (1860–1941), perhaps the greatest of all Bengali literary figures. With lyrical charm, Tagore expressed a mystical philosophy of life. An artist, novelist, dramatist and poet, he was awarded the Nobel prize for literature in 1913.

Muslim poets were lost and outmoded, engrossed in their

puthis and religious tracts. The first sparks of a Muslim renaissance were struck by Nawab Abdul Latif who organized the Mohammedan Literary and Scientific Society in 1863. But Muslim Bengali literature did not burst forth until shortly before World War I when a young poet named Nazrul Islam rebelled against Tagore's mysticism, and declared his own war against social injustice and colonialism.

> How much longer will the weak suffer thus?
> Those whose bones have gone to run the iron train,
> Babu Sahibs throw them out as coolies in disdain.
> Have you paid wages? Oh, stop you band of crooks!
> You paid in *pies,* but pray confess how many millions you took.

A soldier by training, who had a scholar's passion for language and music, Nazrul Islam (b. 1899) composed lyric poetry that was recited in nearly every Bengal village. He introduced into Bengali poetry the Persian *ghazal,* a sweet lyric easily put to music. He also set to music hundreds of poems. He predicted with joyous optimism the end of British rule and sang of a new order for his people. Sadly, Nazrul Islam could not know that his predictions came true. In 1942, he suffered a mental breakdown, from which he has not recovered.

While Bengalis created their own literature, influenced in part by Persian and Arabic words, styles and ideas, and partly by the Hinduism around them, Muslims of northern India fed another literary stream. More so than in Bengal, these Muslim poets and composers wrote and sang in Turki and Persian rather than in the native languages of India. Each Turkish and Moghul court included artists from foreign lands who imposed upon the indigenous cultures the languages and ideas of their home countries. The mingling of foreign languages with local Indian tongues produced Urdu and by the fourteenth century some poets were experimenting in the new language.

205

In the princely state of Hyderabad, the first "school" of Muslim poets and scholars flourished, attracting intellectuals from the Middle East. Here lived and wrote such revered poets as Vali of Deccan (1668–1744), and Sultan Quli Shah who more than any other gave Urdu a respectability in scholarship. Later, Delhi became the center of Muslim Urdu literature while Lucknow and Lahore each had schools of its own. Mir Taqi Mir (1720–1808) composed romantic ghazals which also reflected the crusading reformation among Muslims. Asadullah Khan Ghalib (1797–1869) and the last Moghul emperor himself, Bahadur Shah Zafar (1775–1862), set high standards of Urdu poetry as they lamented the fate of Muslims.

Muslim poets were probably the most important influence in reviving the spirit of Muslims toward the end of the nineteenth century, a spirit that grew into a nationalist movement. Pakistanis call them "poets of freedom." Their lyrics, satires and patriotism awakened Muslims throughout the subcontinent to their special heritage, language, religion and culture. Among the leaders were Mohammed Hussein Azad (1823–1910), Altaf Hussein Hali (1837–1914), Hussein Rizvi Akbar (1846–1921), Maulana Shibli (1857–1914) and Zafar Ali Khan (1870–1950), the latter a brilliant orator and editor who founded the outspoken newspaper, *Zamindar,* in Lahore. But the greatest in more recent times was the man who first suggested a nation of Pakistan: Mohammed Iqbal (1873–1938), the poet-philosopher.

> India, I gaze at you, and weep and wail,
> For never was there such a tragic tale.
> The pickers have not left a flower in sight,
> The while the gardeners all amongst them fight.
> The heavens have many thunder-bolts in store;
> O nightingales, be watchful evermore.

Iqbal wrote a clear and virile prose on politics, philosophy, economics, sociology and religion. He is remembered notably, however, for his beautiful ghazals in Urdu and Persian. Iqbal was a visionary, prone to mysticism, but he was also a man who demanded action.

Iqbal was a philosophical poet, but departing from themes of his predecessors whose thoughts were chiefly of despair, he advanced a philosophy of hope. Real life finds expression, he said, "when the swimmer dives into the boundless ocean of life, fighting the huge waves and surmounting them." The basis of much of Iqbal's poetry was *khudi,* the ideal of the "self." He wrote:

"Loyalty to God virtually amounts to man's loyalty to his own ideal nature." But "self," he added, is nothing without love and without perception and awareness, there can be no love.

> The hand of knowledge grasps an empty sheath,
> If in the breast a heart illumined beats, then
>   warmth of words will breathe the fire of life,
> But if no light there be, words are forever dead.*

Increasingly, literary scholars of Europe and America are discovering Iqbal's works, finding therein new thoughts and writing techniques which only a handful had previously appreciated. Through the work of the Iqbal Academy, this philosopher-politician is becoming better known as a prose writer and poet.

Many others, of course, have made major contributions to Pakistan's literary heritage. In Sind, where song springs from nearly every breast, there are few villagers who cannot quote lines from Shah Abdul Latif (1699–1752) of Bhit or who have not made a pilgrimage to the tomb of this revered saint. A patriot and poet, this ancient mystic adapted classical forms

* Edward McCarthy, "Iqbal as a Poet and Philosopher," *Pakistan Anthology* (Karachi: Pakistan Publications, June, 1961), p. 82.

of music and verse to the spirit of Sind, where the earthen jar (*ghaghan*) is often used as a drum and the desert gives man an endless range for his imagination. Farther north near Multan, another sufi saint, Khwaja Farid, wrote mystical poetry in the last century, which Multanis sing today. In the Punjab, Waris Shah, another nineteenth century poet, wrote in the vernacular, developing the *hir*, a romantic story told in rhyme.

One of the most venerated of all regional poets, however, is a Pathan, Kushhal Khan Khattak (1613–1691), whom Pathans still quote endlessly. Khattak was a warrior and his ghazals extolled the virtues of honor, battle and Pathan greatness, at the same time condemning those who swayed from the Pathan codes. He wrote:

> I, only I, care for my nation's honor.
> The Yusufzais are at ease tilling their fields;
> Afridis, Mohmands, Shinwaris, what are they about?
> See! The Moghul host lies in Ningrahar,
> And the true Pathans, every one from Kandahar to Attock,
> Should stand openly or in secret to the cause of honor.

From the seventeenth century until today, the Khattak tribe has produced outstanding Pushtu poetry.

Poets remain the most popular writers in Pakistan. Among Bengalis, the name of Jasimuddin stands about the highest. He is noted for his historical epics, love songs, and poems about nature. Sometimes called the "folk poet of Bengal," he is also a dramatist and folk singer. Here is one of his more romantic poems:

> O my boatman of the wide river!
> In the evening, rowing your boat,
> To whom are you going?
>
> O my boatman of the wide river!
> Rowing downstream into the mysterious shadows,
> My heart is roaming, weeping.
> My beloved beckons from the shadowy clouds.

208

> O my boatman of the wide river!
> Beyond the bend on the further bank
> Is my wife's field.
> The gentle wind from her banana grove
> Lifts my hair.
> Give her this message.
> A poor wretch dies of weeping
> From the grief she causes him.

Also writing in classical Bengali style is Ghulam Mustafa who, in addition to using a rural setting for his works, writes of Islamic history and religion and is strongly nationalistic. Begum Sufia Kamal and Farrukh Ahmed are two more Bengalis, both lyric poets who write of romance, although the latter is also noted for his nursery rhymes.

The so-called poet laureate of Pakistan is Hafiz Jullundri, equally praised for his epics and lyrics which he writes in Urdu. Yet he has also developed several new forms of poetry and has successfully put to verse the history of Islam. He is also the author of Pakistan's national anthem:

> Blessed be the sacred land
>   Happy be the bounteous realm
> Symbol of high resolve
>   Land of Pakistan
> Blessed be thou citadel of faith.

> The Order of this sacred land
>   Is the might of the brotherhood of the people
> May the nation, the country and the State
>   Shine in glory everlasting
> Blessed be the goal of our ambition.

> This flag of the Crescent and Star
>   Leads the way to progress and perfection
> Interpreter of our past, glory of our present,
>   Inspiration of our future,
> Symbol of Almighty's protection.

209

Faiz Ahmed Faiz is as famous as Hafiz. After independence, Faiz skillfully used the ghazal to protest vehemently the social inequities, economic disparities and political discords in Pakistan, and was once imprisoned by the government. More recently, he has turned to blank verse and has originated new forms in modern Urdu poetry to write of love and lust as well as social reform. His personal following is large and devoted.

Sometimes called the "poet of youth" and "poet of revolution," Josh Malihabadi is, like Faiz Ahmed Faiz, a critical Urdu poet whose reputation was earned before partition when he urged the people to rise against the British.

Other well-known Urdu poets include Sufi Ghulam Mustafa Tabassum, who excels in romantic ghazals and nursery rhymes, and Jafar Tahir, the originator of a new style of canto in Urdu which makes use of majestic words and phrases. One of the founders and chief exponents of blank verse in Urdu, N. M. Rashed, writes forcefully on social and political subjects. He is responsible for many innovations in metre and rhyme. Among the favorite young poets today are Salimur Rahman, Abbas Athar, and Majid Amjad.

Prose in subcontinent Muslim literature is a relatively recent form except for religious and political essays. Prior to British rule, some Muslims had written prose epics, tales of fantasy and history. But the novel and short story became popular only in the twentieth century, beginning most notably with Prem Chand, who used social conscience themes with considerable literary quality.

In Bengal, Shaukat Osman is well known for his social and political satires. Allauddin Azad writes popular Bengali fiction and Syed Waliullah's short stories about family life in East Pakistan are widely published. Bengali essayists include Dr. Shahidullah and Dr. Sajjad Hussain.

For several years after independence no significant novel appeared in Urdu. Finally, in the fifties, three outstanding

210

works were published. *Ag Ka Dariya,* by Q. A. Haider, is an attempt to tell the history of mankind, whose characters spiral back and forth through time. Miss Haider's humanistic approach was first seen as pessimistic and subversive by many critics and for some time she was the target of controversy. A second good novel, *Alipur Ka Eli,* by Mumtaz Mufti, is somewhat reminiscent of Sartre's *Nausea.* But Mufti has developed a simpler and more straightforward manner of narration. The third is *Udas Naslen,* by Abdullah Husain, considered by some the best novel written in Urdu. Through his central character the author describes life in the period from 1910 until after independence.

The major literary output in Urdu in past twenty years is the short story. Dozens of writers have turned to this form. Chief among them are Ahmad Abbas, Manto, Mumtaz Mufti, Ahmad Qazmi and Ghulam Abbas. Younger writers, such as Intizar Husain, have re-discovered their heritage of romances and prose epics. With unblushing realism, these authors are contributing a new dimension in Pakistani literature. Hopefully, efforts will be made to translate the better works into other languages.

Few writers are able to live on their work; they must depend for their livelihood on other professions. Some are journalists, others are teachers and a few work for the provincial and central governments. Various government-subsidized societies promote literary activity and lend assistance to writers. Among them are the Pakistan Writers' Guild, the Iqbal Academy, the Society for the Advancement of Literature in West Pakistan and academies for Urdu, Pashto, Punjabi, Sindi and Bengali. The Urdu Academy, the most authoritative body on the lexicography and usage of that language, is preparing a dictionary which, with its 200,000 entries, will be the longest and most complete dictionary of the Urdu language ever attempted. A few philanthropists extend patronage on an indi-

vidual basis and to societies. In 1960, for instance, the Adamjee family established an annual prize of 20,000 rupees for the best literary work of the year.

Most literary efforts appear in the 1,400 or so periodicals and newspapers, rather than in book form. However, the combined circulation of all the journals published in Lahore, Karachi, and Dacca does not exceed 400,000. Only 10 of the 80 or so dailies exceed 10,000. But readership—or even more important, the "listenership" of a publication—is far greater than its sales figures might indicate. It is not at all unusual for those who are literate to read newspapers to those who cannot read. In this way, probably about 3,000,000 people are reached by the printed word.

More than 900 publications are printed in Urdu, the language of some 70 daily newspapers. Prominent among them are: *Jang* (War), a pre-partition paper from Delhi; *Nawa-e-Waqt,* a paper with considerable cultural interests, especially in the works of Mohammed Iqbal; and *Imroz,* once a far left-wing paper since converted to the cause of the Ayub government. *Kohistan* is another outstanding daily printed in Rawalpindi, Lahore, and Multan. Briefly closed by the government in 1963, it has a well-developed news service, good reporters and an enterprising owner who has introduced new techniques in printing.

Bengali, spoken by most Pakistanis, is the language of a dozen dailies and some 150 other periodicals, although most of these have a greater circulation than publications in West Pakistan. The outstanding Bengali newspaper is *Azad,* which supports the government. It is an important medium for Bengali literature. *Ittifaq* and *Sangbad* are strongly regional-istic and frequently critical of any government in Karachi or Rawalpindi.

English, the language of officialdom and the universities, is also the language of about 10 daily newspapers and over 200

212

other periodicals. Some have a long history and hold an important place in the intellectual life of Pakistan. *Dawn,* founded in New Delhi by Mohammed Ali Jinnah, is published in Karachi by the wealthy Haroon family. Edited by the choleric Altaf Hussein, it takes extreme views on most issues, but nevertheless provides a good outlet for writers in English. From Rawalpindi and Lahore, the *Pakistan Times* provides probably the most unslanted news and gives more space to serious literary efforts as well as to discerning coverage of cultural events. Other English newspapers are *The Pakistan Observer* in Dacca, and *The Morning News,* published both from Karachi and Dacca. *Evening Times,* Karachi, is an important tabloid.

Periodicals are in a more nascent stage than newspapers. With poor financial backing and small circulations, they number in the hundreds. Some are religious, others are political, but most are literary and are good media for poets and short-story writers. One of the best is probably *Lail o Nahar* (Day & Night), edited by Ghulum Hustafa Sufi Tabussum. Other serious literary magazines are *Nuqoosh, Naya-Daur, Sat-Rang, Mah-e-Nau,* highly sophisticated critical journals which set the taste in Urdu literature in both India and Pakistan. English language outlets for literary works include *Vision,* published by Yunus Said, a Karachi writer, *Scintilla,* a quarterly on arts, crafts and literature, and the government's *Pakistan Quarterly,* which for the most part is devoted to the publicizing of Pakistan's cultural heritage in the arts, architecture, literature and philosophy. *Mah-e-Nau* (The New Moon), a monthly Urdu journal published by the government from Karachi is, unlike most official publications, a genuine literary force and has attracted the most influential writers in Pakistan for over sixteen years.

Radio, too, provides writers with new opportunities, especially in drama. There are few theatres in Pakistan and only

213

limited interest in live drama, but this interest is increasing as a result of radio plays.

Performing Arts

Musical programs, the most popular output on radio, support many musicians who would otherwise have to turn to other occupations. It is principally through radio that Pakistani musicians are able to experiment with new forms of music and seek in music an expression of the Pakistani personality.

Music, like poetry, is an old and vital part of the culture of South Asia. Indeed, the two are not far apart for a poem is, more often than not, to be sung rather than recited. And across the land, whether in the fields and meadows of the Punjab or along the banks of Bengal's rivers, a listener is seldom out of earshot of a song being sung or a tune being played by a shepherd, a farmer, or a boatman.

Unlike European music, Pakistani music is based on a single line of notes, a complicated melody without chords or harmony. The instruments accompanying a singer or a lead instrumentalist play in unison. Rhythmical and infinitely variable, it is easily adapted to the emotions and ideas of the performer who is not bound by rules of harmony. Little of the music is written, so that players and singers display considerable improvisation, spontaneity, and freshness.

The most ancient South Asian music was devotional, sung and played by Hindus in their temples. The early Muslims rejected this music because the religion of Islam discouraged the formal playing of music. Such "orthodoxy" fell into unhappy days with the coming of the Moghuls, whose respect for the Persians, the least "orthodox" of Muslims, was high. Under the Moghul emperors, musicians from Arabia and Persia brought new musical techniques. In the Moghul courts, during the sixteenth and seventeenth centuries, classical mu-

sic reached heights similar to that of the contemporary European composers, Beethoven, Bach, and Brahms.

The earliest great master among Muslims in South Asia was Amir Khusro, a scholar and poet who established the present classical styles of Pakistani music. He invented musical instruments, notably the *sitar,* a stringed guitar with a long finger-board that is one of the most sophisticated instruments of today's music. It is usually played as a solo instrument. Khusro and his successors reconciled Hindu and Muslim styles so that now the music of Pakistan and India are essentially the same, although there are regional variations.

Among the various classical styles is the *dhurpad,* a vigorous, manly type of music that became popular in the time of Akbar and is used for heroic tales and praises to God. The *qawwali,* which originated in Persia, is a monotonous, hypnotic mode used by mystics in their devotional music. *Tappa* is quick tempo music which developed out of folk songs centuries ago. *Thumri,* light and frivolous, is sung by women, who move seductively with the music.

Pakistani music, classical or folk, is music to be sung or danced to, and most songs are romantic. Although there are religious songs (which inevitably elicit strong criticism from mullahs when they are sung on Radio Pakistan) and a few patriotic songs, nearly all subjects revolve around a girl's longing for a boy, who is usually some place else than beside his loved one. The basic instruments used to play the music include the stringed *sarangi,* the harmonium (a table-top accordion), and the *tabla* (drums), with additional stringed and reed instruments and flutes. Generally, there are few instruments playing at one time as each is essentially a solo instrument. There are no orchestras as such to play Pakistani music.

While the government of Pakistan has not encouraged the progress of classical music (out of fear of antagonizing the

mullahs), popular music has nevertheless developed remarkably. The countryside abounds wth strolling groups of minstrels who travel from village to village and city to city, playing at weddings and festivals. Few villages are without a singer or instrumentalist who, when the mullah is not around, entertains the people and accompanies their evenings songs. With the advent of radio, singers such as Roshan Ara Begum, and instrumentalists such as Ustad Alauddin Khan, have achieved wide popularity. As in all cultures, modern interpretations and rhythms greatly influence the music of the people. It is not unusual today to hear attempts at combining the harmonic system of European music with the single note style of South Asia.

Dancing, like music, had its origins in the religion of the Hindus and received from Muslims new interpretations and styles so that today there is little difference between Hindu and Muslim dancing. What is different are the regional variations; in East Pakistan, dances are usually subtle, delicate and symbolic, although the *jari-gan* is a dance (and song) about warriors which is popular during the festival of Muharrum. Among Pathans and Baluchis, dancing is more virile and martial. In the Punjab and the Sind, romance is the usual theme. Dancers, like the music accompanying them, perform in unison. When a dancer performs alone, he (or she) has freedom to make innumerable interpretations as the dance develops.

Two classical dances of West Pakistan are the *bharata natyam*, a Hindu-based temple dance secularized by the Moghuls and now shared by all, and the martial *Khattak*, of Pathan origin. In the latter, dancers perform with swords or sticks. Folk dances in West Pakistan include the festive *bhangra* of the Punjabis and the *jhoomer*, a swaying, swinging, seductive dance popular among Sindis and Baluchis.

Dancing professionally is not so respectable in the eyes of Pakistanis as the performers would wish and few women make a career of classical dancing. Consequently, a tradition has emerged whereby male dancers take female parts, a practice common among Sindis and Pathans. One notable exception is Mrs. Ghanshyam who, with her husband as a partner, is a well-known classical dancer. Other popular dancers are Afroza Bulbul and Rafi. The Institute of Culture in Karachi and the Bulbul Academy in Dacca, commemorating the great performer, Bulbul Choudhury, and the Ghanshyam Rhythmic Art Center train future dancers and bring folk dancing before a wide public.

Dancing and music are important in entertainment. An example of this is the experience of an Indian film producer who spent large sums of money making a movie without music. When the film failed to draw audiences, the producer recalled it, inserted irrelevant dances between various dramatic sequences and released it again. The film was an instant success.

Drama has never mattered much in Pakistan's culture, although millions of Pakistanis are avid movie-goers. India is one of the world's leading film-producing countries and movie-going is the single most popular commercial entertainment for urban dwellers, who pay about 20 cents for admission. Pakistan has begun a modest film industry whose rate of growth depends on whether or not the government permits the import of Indian films. There are a dozen studios producing about 50 films a year. The most popular stars are Shamim Ara, Sabiha, Nayyer Sultana and the comedian Nazar. Western films, especially musicals, spectaculars and cowboy pictures, whose action may be followed whether the sound tracks are dubbed or not, attract large audiences.

In Bengal, the *jatra,* a dramatic performance based on provincial myths and legends, is popular among villagers and is

217

acted out by amateurs. Bengali playwrights such as Hussein Ali, and Urdu playwrights such as Imtiaz Ali Taj and Asghar Butt, have found that their satires and farces are popular in both provinces. Amateur theatrical groups such as the Shilpi Chakra in Dacca, the Karachi Art Theatre Society and the Avant Garde Arts Theatre, have not found many angels nor do they draw enough paying customers; consequently, they have not been too successful. The Parsee community theatre group in Karachi, however, has fared better.

Painting and Architecture

Painting as an art form has developed slowly in Muslim South Asia. For centuries after Mohammed the Prophet reproduction of the human form was considered blasphemous and a violation of the Islamic injunction against idol worship. Consequently, design and ornamental calligraphy grew into a great art in many Muslim countries. Iranians, however, did not accept the orthodox injunction and Persian miniature painting, including representation of the human form, came with the Moghuls to India, there to intermix with Hindu styles and colors. The conventions of Asian painting, such as strong symbolism, the absence of shadows and deliberate disregard of perspective, were combined with the Persian use of flowers in profusion, hunting scenes, and romantic motifs.

Today, the most noted artist in the Moghul tradition is M. A. Rahman Chughtai, whose works are only slightly influenced by European styles. His simple line drawings and Persian-style miniatures are displayed and sold throughout the world.

While some new Pakistani painters have followed Chughtai's style, others have sought expression through the entire range of Western art patterns from representational to abstract. Zainul Abedin, a Bengali who founded the Dacca Art Group, is the foremost representative of Westernized painting.

218

In recent years, his themes more and more center on village life. He has begun to experiment with abstract forms.

Other artists, such as folk-painter Allah Buksh, muralist Fyzee Rahamin, abstractionists Zubeida Agha and Shakir Ali have received acclaim in Pakistan and abroad. Behind them is a growing number of young and spirited artists groping for styles and idioms that will better express what they consider the "new" Pakistan. Many are influenced by Japanese painting. Among them are Sadequain, Gulgee, Hamidur Rahman, Khalid Iqbal, Aminul Islam, Ajmal Hussain, and Atiya Hasan, all of whose works are beginning to appear in the United States.

Painting has received more public support than literature, music or drama, although few artists are able to earn a living from the products of their brushes. In Lahore, the Mayo School of Art and the Punjab University Art Department have a pre-partition history, while in Dacca the Art Institute has attempted to replace the important position once held in art education by Calcutta. Arts councils in major cities receive government subsidy and provide young artists with opportunities for exhibition. A National Exhibition of Paintings each year gives recognition and awards as an encouragement to artists.

As in so many other art forms, traditional architecture is a synthesis of imported Muslim influences and native Hindu styles. And, as with other artists, architects are still searching for a distinctive Pakistani personality, one that does not reject the past yet expresses their modernizing society.

Hindu and Buddhist architecture which Muslims found when they invaded the subcontinent was lavish with sculpture in which various forms were piled together seemingly without plan. The low domes of Buddhist stupas, Bengali convex roofs whose eaves kept rain off the sides of the building, and dark

219

and mysterious interiors, reflected an adjustment to environment and fitted the contemplative and mystical religion.

Muslim conquerors brought with them styles of geometrically simple buildings with open and light interiors. Mosque builders sent slender minarets reaching skyward and giant, single domes arching above each place of worship. Gradually, these forms changed; domes became lower and broader, minarets became fatter and buildings developed a complexity more akin to the native Indian manner. The great Moghul builders—Akbar, Shah Jahan, Jahengir—employed Hindu as well as Persian designers and left in their ornate monuments such as the Taj Mahal in Agra and the Moghul palace in Lahore a new architectural synthesis.

In perhaps no other visual art field have Pakistanis ignored their cultural heritage as in architecture. In their efforts to become "modern," home builders, government planners, factory owners and their architects have demanded "Western" design. The result is too often imitative of the West's worst, and additionally look alien on Pakistani soil.

Some builders, however, are recognizing their rich heritage and here and there are attempting to reconcile their desire to be "modern" with their Asian traditions. In the residential area of Gulberg in Lahore, some of the new homes reflect these attempts. The houses display riotous color and decoratian, some are original in design and indicate that a true Pakistani architecture may be developing. In East Pakistan, architects are experimenting with bamboo as a structural element.

Handicrafts

Aesthetic sensibilities of a people, reflected in their music and art, are also found in their folk handicrafts. Like their stories and songs, the motifs and patterns derive from centuries of aritstic traditions beginning perhaps as long ago as

the Indus valley civilization in pre-Aryan days. While the ancient styles have continued to the present, much of what is included in the contemporary minor arts and handicrafts displays the impact of Muslim society, introduced by invaders and settlers. The floral and geometric surface decorations on objects of everyday use can be traced to Muslim influence, as can Muslim predominance in certain handicraft trades such as shoemaking.

In the area that is now Pakistan, certain indigenous handicrafts have achieved particular excellent. Glazed pottery in Sind and the Pathan areas feature colors of turquoise, green and brown and are covered with floral patterns from ancient designs. The potters of Multan and Bahawalpur are adept in making an extremely light and elegant "paper" pottery. The Ceramic Institute in Lahore helps adjust old practices and styles to modern marketing demands.

Fashioning jewelry and utensils from gold and silver is a long-established art in the Punjab, Pathan areas, and East Pakistan. The continual demand for jewelry as a means of "banking" wealth encourages the industry, which still follows the ornate and filigree styles of the Moghuls.

In weaving, each district has its own distinctive patterns. The Muslims of East Pakistan have lost much of their quality with the introduction of machine-made goods, but they remain unusual. Heavily decorated woven flax cloth is a specialty of Sindi weavers. Embroidery is universal, but in the Punjab, Sind, and Baluchistan nearly every piece of material displays extensive needlework with a profusion of sequins.

Muslims, less prohibited by their religion than Hindus from working with leather, have become skilled shoemakers. They have created artistic and practical styles of footwear. Pathans excel in making *chapals,* marketed in Europe and the United States as "chaplees," while in the Punjab richly ornamented shoes with upturned toes are the pride of every bridegroom.

Afridi Pathans are also noted for the craftsmanship of their homemade rifles which they turn out in village workshops, copying Western models. The industry is as old as the rifle itself and attempts by the Pakistan government to assert some control over the industry have not been very successful.

In Bengal, village crafts center around bamboo and cane work, palm leaf matting, rope and quilt weaving, and the potter's products. Except for pottery, most craftwork is done by women. Dacca and Rangpur are famous for their ivory and horn carvings. Bangles made from conch shells are popular.

Partition and the subsequent migration of Muslims brought new artisans to Pakistan. Wood and ivory carvers and carpet weavers from Kashmir, potters from Bidar, brass and coppersmiths from Delhi, and silk embroiderers from Benares have added to the talent available for an expanded handicraft industry. The government gives some support in its economic planning for development of small industries based upon these skills.

In all the various fields of artistic and intellectual expression, the government has taken some interest, but not a great deal. In literature, it has created its own publishing facilities, most of which are devoted to propaganda for government purposes, although they do provide new outlets for nonpolitical writers. Radio Pakistan and the government information bureaus employ many artists. The government is building a National Arts Center in Karachi and subsidizes local arts councils. A cultural center in the Sindi town of Shah Abdul Latifabad is a model for other centers scheduled for construction. New museums and libraries are proposed in the Second Five Year Plan. But essentially, development of the arts and the search for a Pakistani personality depend upon what each artist can find for himself. Increasingly, those artists and writers who are creating something new are finding inspiration in their own centuries-old culture.

11. Kashmir

The symbol of all that separates Pakistanis from Indians and Muslims from Hindus in the subcontinent is Kashmir. A subject that stirs the deepest emotions, Kashmir is a barrier between two peoples who can ill afford to be at odds. For Pakistanis, Kashmir is a land whose Muslim inhabitants, 75 per cent of the population of 4,400,000, have not yet been permitted to decide whether they wish to join Pakistan or India as a result of partition. For Indians, Kashmir is a beloved part of their country; they hold it and intend to keep it.

Few problems on the international scene are so tangled in prejudice. Both governments involved disseminate considerable propaganda explaining their respective positions. In the United Nations, spokesmen ramble tediously through the intricate by-ways of history, law and logic, myth, passion, and illogic. The future of the people and land of Kashmir remains no clearer in 1964 than in 1947.

As the Punjabi plains roll northeastward along the Indus, Jhelum, and Chenab rivers, they rise toward the Himalayas which separate south from central Asia. A few miles beyond Lahore and Rawalpindi in Pakistan and Amritsar in India, the mountains begin, first as foothils, then as towering ranges, deeply carved with gorges. To the west toward Afghanistan these hills and ranges become Pakistan's northwestern frontier, the home of the Pathans. To the east, the higher ranges become Chinese-occupied Tibet. Between them lies Kashmir, part of whose northern boundary is Communist China.

Kashmir—technically the "State of Jammu and Kashmir"—

comprises several distinct geographical and cultural areas, each with a separate history. The most important, economically and politically, is Kashmir proper, a small province of about 2,000 square miles noted for its beautiful "Vale" and the tourist-loved city of Srinagar. South of Kashmir is the province of Jammu, which borders India, and its small, but distinct territories of Poonch and Mirpur which border Pakistan. Other areas include the isolated northern district of Gilgit with the unique principalities of Hunza and Nagar, and the mountainous lands of Baltistan and Ladakh along the borders of Tibet and China. Together, they form a state some 85,000 square miles in size. It is an area of alpine beauty and lush, fertile valleys. Its rushing streams feed the plains below in India and Pakistan. Only a few passes provide land routes to the outside world. Yet despite its scenic grandeur, and except in isolated centers, Kashmir is an unhappy and poverty-stricken land.

Centuries ago Aryan tribesmen settled in the valleys of Kashmir and developed their culture in semi-isolation from others who swept down onto the subcontinent. To the plainsmen, the greatest Hindu gods lived in the mountains of Kashmir and the aloof Kashmiris believed themselves to be closest to these gods. Here lived the purest of the Brahmins, the highest caste Hindus. Consequently, here also lived the poorest of the lowest castes, kept in virtual social slavery by the Brahmin priests.

Buddhism, offering hope to even the lowest, met with success in Kashmir. But by the third century A.D., Hinduism had re-established itself. By the thirteenth century, a Buddhist prince in Ladakh captured Kashmir and, under the influence of a Muslim missionary named Bulbul Shah, he embraced Islam. Eventually most Kashmiris became Muslim and Kashmir became a center of Muslim learning. Seldom united, however, the people were constantly being conquered by out-

siders. In the nineteenth century, they finally succumbed to the great Sikh general, Ranjit Singh.

In the Sikh emperor's court in Lahore, a Hindu chieftain from Jammu rose to eminence. His name was Gulab Singh of the Dogra caste of Rajputs. In return for his services, he received rulership of Jammu. In the British-Sikh wars, however, he backed the British who, in 1846, sold him the rest of Kashmir for the equivalent of $1,500,000. Thus began the rule of the Dogra Rajputs of Jammu and Kashmir. Not one of their twenty-eight prime ministers before 1947 was a Muslim.

The Dogras reigned over the largest, but one of the poorest, of the princely states of India and placed upon the people a tyranny unmatched in the subcontinent. The Brahmins enforced the harshest Hindu caste and dietary restrictions. Slaughtering a cow meant ten years imprisonment. Slavery was openly practiced until the 1920's. Taxes were harsh.

Over the decades of Dogra rule, Kashmir's ties with the rest of India were tenuous. In the winter, the people were snowbound. Down the rivers and few roads in summer came a few exports of wool, animal products, and carpets. Tourists sought the coolness and beauty of Kashmir's "Vale," and the British government stationed an unwelcome representative in the capital of Srinagar to watch the strategic northern border and to "guide" the Maharaja.

There was little homogeneity or unity among the population. While three-fourths of the people were Muslim, the area contained more than a dozen distinct language groups. Kashmir province was perhaps the most united. Here, nearly 90 per cent of the 2,000,000 inhabitants were Muslims and nearly all spoke Kashmiri, or *Kashiru,* an Indo-European tongue laced with Persian and Turkish words and phrases. Jammu province had nearly 2,000,000 people, most of whom spoke Dogri, akin to Punjabi. On a province-wide basis, about 61

225

per cent were Muslims, the rest Hindus, although in Poonch and Mirpur, Muslims (who spoke Punjabi) accounted for more than 90 per cent. In the northern district of Gilgit and the little principalities, the 300,000 or so inhabitants were almost 100 per cent Muslim, but they spoke several different languages. Ladakh and Baltistan were about 80 per cent Muslim and in the sub-district of Leh, near the Tibetan-Chinese border, the majority, about 40,000, were Buddhist.

Only in Kashmir province itself was there a sense of being "Kashmiri." Most people identified themselves with their religion, district, village, or language. Thus, a man considered himself, for instance, to be a Punjabi-speaking Muslim from Poonch or a Dogri-speaking Hindu from Jammu rather than a "Kashmiri."

In 1932, a Muslim schoolteacher in Srinagar founded the Muslim Conference which he hoped would help lead Muslims to a better life in Kashmir. His name was Sheikh Mohammed Abdullah and he became known as the "Lion of Kashmir." As the independence movement in undivided India grew in the 1930's, he believed that Kashmir would probably be able to retain its semi-autonomous position within a future secular India, especially if India was led by his close friend, Jawaharlal Nehru. He rejected the communal position of the Muslim League and in 1938 formed the Jammu and Kashmir National Conference, which he associated with Nehru's Indian National Congress. Henceforth, he fought for independence, but not for Pakistan. His place at the head of the Muslim Conference was taken by Choudhury Ghulam Abbas, a communally-minded Muslim from Jammu who supported Mohammed Ali Jinnah and the Muslim League.

With independence approaching, the British, Congress, and the League agreed that, among the British-governed provinces, contiguous Hindu-majority areas should form the territories of India and contiguous Muslim-majority areas should form

the territories of Pakistan, with the Punjab and Bengal being partitioned. All three parties agreed on the principle of self-determination in British India. The rulers of the princely states were given the opportunity to decide their own futures, although the Congress insisted that their only choices were to accede to either India or Pakistan.

Thus it was that Hindu- and Sikh-ruled states with Hindu and Sikh populations joined India. Most Muslim states acceded to Pakistan. Some created confusion. For instance, the Muslim Nizam of Hyderabad, whose subjects were mainly Hindu, wanted independence for his state even though it was surrounded by India. Indian troops entered the state in what India called "police action," and Hyderabad became Indian.

The Muslim Nawab of Junagadh decided to accede to Pakistan even though his state did not touch Pakistan and his 800,000 subjects were Hindus. Jinnah accepted his accession, giving, in effect, tacit recognition to the principle that the ruler need not consult his people. The Indian army reversed the Nawab's decision and Junagadh became Indian over Pakistan's vociferous objections. India held a plebiscite and, in so doing, reaffirmed its support of the principle of self-determination. Pakistan has yet to relinquish its claim to Junagadh and it has become enmeshed in the Kashmir dispute.

The Maharaja of Kashmir wished to delay making a decision and asked both India and Pakistan to sign a "Standstill Agreement." Pakistan accepted, but India refused, claiming that to do so would be to recognize the Maharaja's right to declare Kashmir independent. Pakistanis assumed that the Maharaja would defer to the wishes of his Muslim subjects and accede to Pakistan. Indians hoped he would not. Gandhi sped to Srinagar to assert his immense influence. Sheikh Abdullah's National Conference, while opposed to the Maharaja (Sheikh Abdullah was in jail at the time), wanted Kashmir to join India. The Maharaja equivocated.

Indecision in India in 1947 was tantamount to provoking violence. Insecurity bred tension and fear which led to riots and massacre. In the Punjab, frightened Hindu and Sikh families fled to Jammu and from there they raided Muslim refugees pouring into West Punjab. Punjabi Muslims, in turn, raided Jammu and violence swept the land of the Dogra Rajputs.

In the summer of 1947, the Muslims of Poonch, inspired by a lawyer named Sardar Mohammed Ibrahim, revolted against the Maharaja's army. The rebellion spread. The Muslims were not only farmers and tradesmen; some were well-trained soldiers who had fought in World War II. Their revolt was so successful that leaders of the Muslim Conference met in Rawalpindi on October 1, 1947, and formed the Azad (Free) Kashmir government. This was later reconstituted on October 24 to include non-Muslims.

Communal violence in the Punjab and the Muslim revolt in Poonch stirred the emotions of the Pathans in the hills a few miles west. Fellow Muslims, they felt, were under attack. Besides, British authority had collapsed. So in October, 1947, thousands (estimates range from 2,000 to 30,000) of Pathans—Mahsuds, Waziris, and Mohmands—swept up the valleys from Abbottabad into the Vale of Kashmir. They overpowered the meager forces of the Maharaja and threatened to capture Srinagar. They probably would have entered the captured city had they not stopped to loot the town of Baramula.

The revolt of the Poonch Muslims caused little concern among Kashmir's Muslim leaders. But the incursion of the Pathans created consternation. Here was an invasion of "foreigners." Sheikh Abdullah, released from jail in September, was outraged when the Pathans turned toward Srinagar, threatening his beloved Kashmir. So, too, was the indecisive Maharaja who pleaded for Indian troops to save him.

On October 26, the Dogra ruler officially and precipitously acceded his country to India and fled to Jammu. India's governor-general, Lord Louis Mountbatten, provisionally accepted the Maharaja's accession, pending, he said, "a reference to the people" of Kashmir. Prime Minister Nehru confirmed the decision to hold a plebiscite once the "invaders" had left Kashmir soil. In Srinagar, the Jammu and Kashmir National Conference set up an interim government, as part of the accession agreement. The Indian government began to air-lift troops to the Kashmir capital.

The fighting for Kashmir now approached full-scale war as Indian troops fought the forces of Azad Kashmir and Pathan tribesmen. Jinnah wanted to send Pakistani army troops, but his British commander-in-chief, Sir Douglas Gracey, counseled against the move. Jinnah had not accepted the Maharaja's accession to India and called it a violation of the Standstill Agreement. He called for a cease-fire, withdrawal of both Indian troops and Pathan tribesmen, and then a plebiscite administered either by both governments or by an international body. To this, Nehru disagreed, maintaining that the accession was proper, Pakistan was interfering and supporting the Azad Kashmir forces and that Indian troops would not withdraw until Kashmir was cleared of all invaders.

India took its complaint to the United Nations on January 1, 1948, and asked the Security Council to charge Pakistan with "an act of aggression against India." Pakistan's foreign minister, Zafrulla Khan, countered with charges of genocide and placed the question of Junagadh before the U. N. The Security Council's answer was that both sides should stop fighting, Pathan tribesmen should withdraw, India should reduce the number of Indian troops and Sheikh Abdullah's government should admit Azad Kashmir officials preparatory to holding a plebiscite. Both India and Pakistan rejected this

suggestion, but agreed that a U. N. Commission for India and Pakistan (UNCIP) could try to "exercise its good offices."

Although each country had agreed to a plebiscite, they disagreed on the conditions under which it would be held. Arguments over details became increasingly complex and bitter. And in Kashmir the fighting continued, with the Indian army steadily pushing the Azad Kashmir forces back. Muslim refugees fled into Azad Kashmir and Pakistan. In May, 1948, the Pakistan government committed its own army forces, took over operational control of the Azad Kashmir army and sought to protect Muslim gains in Poonch. That warfare did not become more widespread can be attributed to the calmer heads of the respective armies, each commanded by an English general and each composed of Hindu and Muslim officers whose respect and affection for each other outweighed their communal passions.

The U. N. Commission arrived in July, 1948, and on August 13 it adopted its first resolution on the subject, approved by both Pakistan and India. The resolution provided for a cease-fire, reliance upon U. N. military observers, withdrawal of all Pakistani troops, citizens and tribesmen, eventual withdrawal of most Indian troops, and joint determination of the prerequisites for a plebiscite. Details of the plebiscite implementation were spelled out in a subsequent resolution on January 5, 1949. The U. N. Secretary-General appointed U. S. Admiral Chester Nimitz as Plebiscite Administrator.

On January 1, 1949, after fourteen months of battle, formal fighting stopped in Kashmir as the UNCIP arranged a cease-fire. By July, the cease-fire line had become stabilized, so stable, in fact, that fifteen years later, it was almost unchanged. It became the boundary between Kashmir and Azad Kashmir.

By 1949, the Azad Kashmir government had lost the town of Poonch to the Indian army. The only lands it controlled—some 5,000 square miles—were a western strip of Jammu with

the town of Mirpur and part of Poonch, and a portion of western Kashmir province, including the city of Muzaffarabad. Sheikh Abdullah's government controlled most of Kashmir and Jammu provinces, including Srinagar and the Vale, plus some of Ladakh along the Tibetan border, in all about 55,000 square miles with a population of about 3,000,000. The Pakistan government assumed control of the mountainous, sparsely settled, northern frontier lands—Gilgit and that part of Ladakh bordering Communist China—which it termed its "Northern Area." In size, it covers approximately 23,000 square miles.

The significance of Kashmir to Pakistan is the same today as it was in 1949. It is partly economic, partly strategic, and largely emotional.

Economically, Pakistanis see Kashmir as vital to West Pakistan's development. While not economically wealthy itself, Kashmir does contain the headwaters of the major rivers which mean life or death to West Pakistan's agriculture. The Indus, Jhelum, and Chenab rivers all enter Pakistan from Kashmir, and Pakistanis fear that a hostile government in Srinagar could assert disastrous control over these streams.

Strategically, Pakistanis see a hostile Kashmir as a northern sword hanging over their heads. Although the Indians have now built roads to connect Kashmir and India, the former routes out of Kashmir are still available to troops wishing to march into Pakistan.

Finally, many Pakistanis see Kashmir in the context of Hindu-Muslim communalism. Pakistan came into existence in order to provide a home for South Asia's Muslim minority, yet nearly 3,000,000 Muslims living across a cease-fire line in Kashmir are not permitted an opportunity to choose Pakistan. To these Pakistanis, Kashmir's Muslims are enslaved brothers, held down forcibly by an occupying Hindu army. Kashmir is

symbolic of India's enmity towards Muslims in general and Pakistan in particular.

The significance of this emotion lies not only in Pakistan's efforts to obtain a plebiscite in Kashmir. It has provided a unifying factor within the strained body politic of Pakistan itself. By throwing out emotional pails of Kashmir water, Pakistani leaders have been able to douse many small fires of disunity among Pakistanis, especially among the Pathans, the embittered refugees and important religious leaders who now and then call for jihad against India. Keeping external issues in an emotional realm is a technique used by many countries to mobilize sentiment in support of unstable governments. This one was particularly effective in West Pakistan during the depressing days of earlier political maneuvering.

Not all Pakistanis view Kashmir with the same intensity. Most East Pakistanis have less concern for Kashmir than West Pakistanis. Farther from the scene, they are also deeply concerned with their own problems. Indeed, many of them have resented the attention Pakistan governments have given to Kashmir to the detriment of economic development and political rights in East Pakistan.

For Indians, Kashmir's significance is also based on strategic and emotional factors. Economics are not very important; in fact, Kashmir is more of an economic liability than an asset. Strategically, Kashmir contains passes through which invaders might march. Already India and China have fought over parts of Kashmir. In the hands of a hostile nation, Kashmir would threaten India's security.

Kashmir holds a special place in the hearts of many Indian Hindus. It is the homeland of the gods, the heart of the revered Himalayas. For Kashmir to belong to Pakistan is, to many Hindus, unthinkable. Its presence as a Muslim area in India, is evidence of the validity of India's secular policies. Pakistanis claim that Prime Minister Nehru, who was a Kash-

miri Brahmin, was so personally and emotionally tied to Kashmir that he would countenance no change in its status.

Like Pakistanis, not all Indians feel equally intense about Kashmir. Indeed, some Indian groups are prepared to see Kashmir go to Pakistan and the issue settled. Others have openly espoused partition of the state along the present lines or granting Kashmir independence. But many fear that should partition be made officially permanent the result would be renewed communal violence.

In the futile negotiations that followed the cease-fire of January 1, 1949, the significance of Kashmir to each party appeared in various guises. The next step after obtaining the cease-fire was demilitarization of Kashmir, with Pakistan to start withdrawing its troops first. This Pakistan began to do, but trouble arose over the disarming of the Azad Kashmir army. India refused even to reduce its forces unless all Muslim forces were disarmed first. Since then, neither side has agreed to the other's proposal for demilitarization. By 1963, four different U. N. teams had attempted to bring about a reconciliation. The Kashmir dispute had appeared dozens of times on the Security Council's agenda, each time producing hours of rhetoric without results. Almost every Pakistani prime minister attempted to negotiate directly with Prime Minister Nehru and in 1963 Pakistani and Indian ministers sat together for many days seeking an understanding, without success.

In Kashmir itself, India strengthened its position, albeit with difficulty. In October, 1950, the Jammu and Kashmir Conference Party, now controlling Kashmir politics, called for elections of a constituent assembly to determine Kashmir's future. Much of the Western world was dismayed and in March, 1951 the United Kingdom and the United States led the Security Council to adopt a resolution condemning such an election as an inadequate substitute for a fair plebiscite.

Pakistan naturally accepted this resolution, while India naturally rejected it. But the elections were held anyway in the autumn of 1952 under the auspices of Sheikh Abdullah's party—and the Indian army. Only two seats out of seventy-five were contested and all were won by the Jammu and Kashmir Conference Party.

Sheikh Abdullah's goals were the development of Kashmir as a state with special relations with India. While India might logically concern itself with Kashmir's foreign affairs, defense and communications, Kashmiris should otherwise be "completely free and autonomous." Although Prime Minister Nehru and Sheikh Abdullah reached an agreement in 1952 for this "special status," Sheikh Abdullah found it difficult to maintain. The Indian army still controlled the country and in India politicians rejected the idea of special treatment for Kashmir. As with other states, they said, Kashmir should be integrated into the Indian Republic on the same basis. Meanwhile, Hindus and Sikhs in Jammu, resentful of Sheikh Abdullah's predominantly Muslim government, also insisted on Kashmir's complete integration. They commenced demonstrating and rioting. In 1953, Sheikh Abdullah made a speech in Srinagar reminding the Indian government that Kashmir's accession was provisional and that the Constituent Assembly had no authority to pronounce on the question of accession. A plebiscite should be held, he said. Six days later, he was dismissed from office and imprisoned.

With the "Lion of Kashmir" in jail, the Assembly, led by the new prime minister, Bakshi Ghulam Mohammed, voted to work toward the complete accession of Kashmir to India.

Pakistanis seethed anger. They found considerable support from the rest of the world, although not from the Soviet Union which, two years earlier, had thrown its support to India. In 1954, Pakistan and the United States signed a Mutual Defense Assistance Agreement which had been in

234

preparation ever since the Soviet Union sided with India. A few months later, Pakistan joined the anti-communist pacts sponsored by the United States. Pakistan and its Kashmiri obsession had entered the Cold War.

Now it was India's turn to seethe. In both countries, the military's share of the national budgets climbed to more than 60 per cent at the expense of needed development programs. Indian and Pakistani armies faced each other on the borders of Kashmir and the Punjab.

An able, but harsh administrator, Bakshi Ghulam Mohammed began building that part of Kashmir under Indian control. With two-thirds of his budget coming from New Delhi—nearly $700,000,000 by 1963—he expanded Kashmir's tourist facilities, bolstered the carpet industry and built schools.

In January, 1957, he promulgated a new constitution which formally acceded the entire state to India, dissolved the Constituent Assembly and called for elections. These were held in March and, to no one's surprise, Bakshi Ghulam Mohammed's National Conference Party won an overwhelming victory. A Plebiscite Front Party, pledged to the popular Sheikh Abdullah, found little chance to gain votes. In November, amidst a great ovation, Kashmir's representatives took their seats in the Indian legislature in New Delhi. So far as the Indian government was concerned, the status of Kashmir was no longer a subject for serious discussion.

The "Lion of Kashmir" thought otherwise. In late 1957, the Kashmir government released the imprisoned leader. Promptly, he began accusing India of violent repression of Kashmir's rights, demanded a plebiscite and called for United Nations troops to occupy Kashmir. After fifteen weeks of freedom, he was back behind bars.

In succeeding years, the question of plebiscite appeared to become more irrelevant as Indian-held Kashmir became increasingly a part of India. While it retained its own citizen-

ship laws and political institutions, and its leader was called "prime minister" instead of "chief minister" as in India's other fourteen states, Kashmir was publicly a problem only to Pakistanis—and many Kashmiris. In 1963, Bakshi Ghulam Mohammed resigned, to be succeeded by his Finance Minister, Khwaja Shams-ud-Din. With Bakshi active behind the scenes, integration went forward as the prime minister tried to get his title changed to "chief minister."

In 1964, events occurred in India and Kashmir which seemed to offer hope for progress. In March, Ghulam Mohammed Sadiq, a politician with close ties with Indian neutralists, became prime minister of Kashmir. And in April, to the surprise of many, Sheikh Abdullah was released from prison with all charges against him dropped. He promptly repeated his familiar call for self-determination in Kashmir and traveled to New Delhi to meet with his old friend, Prime Minister Nehru. He followed this with a visit to Pakistan for talks with President Ayub.

In the preceding years, Pakistan, like India, had been consolidating its control over Azad Kashmir, whose government was now "temporarily" established at Muzaffarabad. Since 1949, this government had been careful to avoid the appearance of being permanent, maintaining throughout that its real capital was Srinagar and its citizens the people of Kashmir Jammu. It recently changed its name to "The Azad Government of Jammu and Kashmir."

The land of Azad Kashmir is the least fertile part of the area. Few streams flow through it and hardly any roads exist to carry in the tools of development to the people. The approximately 1,000,000 Kashmiris of Azad Kashmir, 200,000 of whom are refugees, are among the poorest of the subcontinent. The refugees are also among South Asia's bitterest, for their homes are under Indian rule. Their capital, they feel, is Srinagar, not Muzaffarabad or Islamabad.

236

Since they came together in 1947, the leaders of Azad Kashmir have fought amongst themselves and with the Pakistan government for control. The competing groups within the Muslim Conference Party are the Muslims from the Poonch-Mirpur-Muzaffarabad area, the refugees from Kashmir province led by Mir Waiz Usuf Shah, and the Jammu Muslims under Choudhury Ghulam Abbas. More communally-minded than the others, Abbas pleads for jihad and forceful "liberation" of Kashmir. Once imprisoned by the Pakistan government, he remains a strong figure in the background of the Kashmir Liberation League. In 1952, the rivalries between the groups led to open warfare and the Pakistan government stepped in to assert firm control. This control has remained strong.

The President of Azad Kashmir in 1964 is Khurshid Hasan Khurshid, a journalist, who seeks international recognition for his government. He has built his strength through the support of President Ayub.

Regardless of their political feelings, all Azad Kashmir leaders are agreed in their support for a plebiscite in Kashmir, which they believe would result in accession to Pakistan. They also agree that the cease-fire line is temporary.

While the administration of the Azad Kashmir government is solely Kashmiri, the Pakistan government, through its Ministry for Home and Kashmir Affairs (headed, in 1964, by Khan Habibullah Khan) guides its affairs. It also helps in the development of the area, although not always as much as Azad Kashmiris would like. It has supplied technicians, both military and civil, and alloted a portion of each annual budget to Azad Kashmir. Through the Basic Democracies, it has sent agricultural experts into the valley villages. New roads have tied isolated communities together and new schools and hospitals have been built. A great new dam—the Mangla Dam—is being constructed on the Jhelum River to provide power

and irrigation. From its own imported supplies, the Pakistan government distributes food. And over the Azad Kashmir Radio network, broadcasts through more than 10,000 radio receivers in both Azad and Indian Kashmir encourage a spirit of "free Kashmir."

Between Indian Kashmir and Azad Kashmir runs the cease-fire line, manned by Swedes, Canadians and other United Nations forces who keep the armies of the two parties apart—most of the time. The U. N. personnel wish to leave. The Indians, Pakistanis, and Kashmiris also wish them to leave, but each group has its own conditions for bringing about the departure. Obtaining a meeting of minds on these conditions has plagued them all, but especially the Kashmiris, since 1947.

In the years of battle and debate over Kashmir, the basic arguments of either side in the dispute have changed little:

—Pakistan maintains that the accession of Kashmir has yet to be determined because the action of the Maharaja was illegal and no plebiscite has been held. India replies that the accession of the Maharaja was legal (did not Pakistan accept the accession of the Nawab of Junagadh?) and that the will of the Kashmir people was expressed in the elections of 1957 under the new constitution.

—Pakistan maintains that the partition of the subcontinent on the basis of communal determination in areas contiguous to either state has not been completed and that Kashmir should be dealt with in the spirit of the 1947 partition agreements. India replies that Kashmir was a special problem and to re-open the issue now would lead to communal violence.

—Pakistan maintains that India is committed to holding a plebiscite in Kashmir. India replies that conditions have changed since this commitment and that there is no further question over Kashmir's accession.

—Pakistan maintains that the government of Azad Kashmir is the true government because it grew out of the first

238

rebellion against the Maharaja. India replies that the Azad Kashmir rebellion was not successful and the government is a puppet of Pakistan with no separate identity.

—India maintains that Pakistan committed aggression in Kashmir and continues to support aggression through its support of the Azad Kashmir government. Pakistan replies that its forces entered Kashmir only after Indian troops threatened the security of Pakistan.

—India maintains that Pakistan did not abide by the U. N. Commission resolution to withdraw its troops so demilitarization could be achieved. Pakistan replies that it could not withdraw its troops so long as Indian troops in Kashmir threatened Pakistan.

—India maintains that by Pakistan's joining CENTO and SEATO pacts, the Kashmir problem changed character, became part of the Cold War, and all previous agreements over Kashmir were thereby nullified. Pakistan replies that Kashmir has nothing to do with the Cold War, but is a subcontinent problem.

—India maintains that its position on Kashmir is irrevocable and conclusive: Kashmir is an integral part of India and shall so remain—there can be no negotiation over past issues. Pakistan replies that Kashmir remains an unresolved problem and that Pakistan will accept arbitration.

Essentially, the status of Kashmir is not determined by legalistic arguments or United Nations resolutions, but by the simple fact of possession. India occupies its part of Kashmir and is not about to relinquish it. Conversely, Pakistan possesses the frontier regions of Kashmir and effectively controls Azad Kashmir. It is not about to relinquish what it controls. To prove its position, Pakistan in 1963 reached agreement with Communist China over demarcation of 300 miles of Kashmir's border. India fought with Communist China to maintain possession of parts of Indian-controlled Kashmir.

The meetings between Sheikh Abdullah and the prime ministers of India and Pakistan appeared to be the beginning of constructive action toward solving the Kashmir problem. Many talked of partitioning Kashmir; others suggested that the land be given autonomy, but under the joint guidance of India and Pakistan. The death of Prime Minister Nehru on May 27, 1964 brought a temporary halt to the discussions. Despite the enmity between Pakistan and India, Pakistanis generally agreed that, with time, Nehru would have eventually reached agreement with them.

The status of Kashmir continues to plague the lives of Pakistanis and Indians and will probably do so for years to come, regardless of the formal solutions reached by government leaders. Kashmir stands, in Pakistani eyes, for all the hostility the world has shown to Pakistan. To deny the right of Kashmiris to accede to Pakistan if they wish is to deny the right of Pakistan itself. Desperately, Pakistanis reach out for support in their private "cold war" in the Himalyas.

12. *A Need for Friends*

From the day Mohammad Ali Jinnah led Pakistanis to independence, they have wanted and needed friends, particularly friends who could help them. Such friends were hard to find in 1947, and even today those who claim friendship often appear to Pakistanis to be less than helpful.

Pakistanis keenly felt that the world was against their new country. While a few Muslim nations applauded perfunctorily in 1947, the nations that counted—the United Kingdom, the United States, the Soviet Union—rushed to congratulate the Indians. The first test of friendship was Kashmir, and here Pakistan's failure to achieve any form of success was evidence of the minor role Pakistanis felt the major nations ascribed to them.

Unlike India, Pakistan faced a single, overpowering problem: survival. From without, India seemed to be purposely exacerbating the economic plight of new Pakistan while at the same time threatening Pakistan with its stronger army. Afghanistan appeared to be grabbing at Pakistan's northwestern frontier. The Soviet Union rushed to support the communists, who found fertile fields for subversion. From within the country, tensions between the various provinces, particularly those of West Pakistan and East Pakistan, tore at the unity the Quaid-i-Azam so painfully had created. Survival was a real concern to Pakistanis in 1947.

As the early years passed and enmity with their neighbors increased, Pakistanis placed more importance on the questions of security and independence than anything else. Today, their

extreme sensitivity over these concerns is an outstanding characteristic in Pakistan's foreign affairs.

Pakistanis recognize that they can only advance in peace. Thus they seek friendship with those countries and organizations which work for peace and which at the same time will assist their development. Most Pakistanis bitterly reject colonialism and support the self-determination of all dependent peoples. And many also have a strong sense of identity with Muslims of other countries and wish to associate with them so long as this association does not work against their efforts to achieve military and economic strength.

These feelings help explain Pakistan's enthusiastic support of the United Nations, of which Pakistan has been a member since 1947. Through the United Nations, Pakistan has sought aid—futilely, it seems—for its Kashmir stand. It has, however, gained economic and welfare support from various U. N. agencies. In 1963, Pakistani troops participated in the U. N.-supervised transfer of West Irian from Dutch to Indonesian control.

Survival, development, and Kashmir also help explain Pakistan's acceptance of military and economic assistance from the United States, its alignment with Turkey, Iran and the West in CENTO, and with Thailand, the Philippines and the West in SEATO. They explain Pakistan's apprehension of communism but also the country's developing ties with the Soviet Union and Communist China, whose delegates Pakistan has supported for seating in the United Nations and with whom Pakistan has signed border, trade, and cultural agreements.

India

With few exceptions, those Pakistanis concerned with "foreign" affairs would like to seek friendship among the people they have known best, and for so long—their Indian neighbors. Personal friendships, in fact, have continued across the

borders between Muslims and Hindus and these have helped keep minor problems from becoming major crises. In times of relative peace, travel between Pakistan and India increases ten-fold as Muslims "go home" to visit families and friends. The "hated" Sikhs cross into Pakistan by the hundreds to visit shrines. With so much in common in their backgrounds, especially during British rule, antagonisms are sometimes difficult to maintain. Both know that together their economies would be stronger, as would their armies.

Yet on a national level, these realizations, friendships, and the logic of cooperation are overshadowed by the actions of the respective governments. To Pakistan, India is the bitterest of enemies and the greatest foreign affairs problem. The ruling minority—government, religious, political ,and intellectual leaders—are still afraid of India's Hindu leaders. They feel that these individuals, all of whom opposed Pakistan's creation, have not accepted the permanency of Pakistan. Pakistanis accuse these leaders of being motivated by Hinduism, not the proclaimed secularism, and charge that Indians seek to control Asia through a doctrine of neutralism and armed force.

To justify these charges, Pakistanis point primarily to Kashmir. They also include India's action in "occupying" Junagadh, which Pakistanis still claim—and show as Pakistani territory on their official maps. Another case of "Indian aggression" arose over the Hindu-majority state of Hyderabad whose Muslim Nizam tried to assert his independence after 1947. As in Kashmir and Junagadh, the Indian army marched in to assure Hyderabad's accession to India. In all three cases, Pakistan blames India for thwarting the will of Muslims, asserting the "right of possession" based on military force. When India attacked the Portuguese enclave of Goa in 1961, Pakistanis felt that their charges of Indian imperialism were confirmed. Said President Ayub in 1963:

"Indian leaders somehow feel that every country from Afghanistan down to Indonesia, where there is a semblance of Indian culture, forms a part of Indian heritage, and so it must also form a part of the Indian political empire."

To Pakistanis, the communal nature of Indian society was not eliminated with the partition of the subcontinent. Hindus are still Hindus and more than 40,000,000 Muslims remain as a minority in a caste-ridden society. Daily reports of Hindu suppression and violence against Muslims are constant reminders to Pakistanis that India is anti-Muslim. Indeed, Pakistanis accuse India of "blackmailing" Pakistan by holding the Muslims of India as "hostages" in a "cold war." Indian leaders lend credence to this charge by saying that communal violence will break out if Kashmiris ever vote to join Pakistan.

Indians, of course, deny that any such evidence exists for Pakistan's fears. Quite the contrary, they say that Pakistan is a threat to India, was an aggressor in Kashmir and could well become an aggressor again. They feel that Pakistan's membership in anti-communist military pacts are really attempts to strengthen the Pakistani armed forces for an eventual attack upon India. While Pakistanis point to Indian persecution of Muslims, Indians also feel that Muslims in East Bengal persecute Hindus. Refugees straggle across the borders between the two countries to support both viewpoints.

Despite these fears, Pakistanis and Indians have been able to settle some of their disagreements. As a result of efforts by Eugene Black and the International Bank for Reconstruction, the two countries agreed to the joint development of the rivers of the Punjab. India paid most of Pakistan's claims for cash assets in pre-partition India and both sides settled on payments for evacuee property left behind by refugees. The Indian government gave up small parts of Bengal to Pakistan, although the Indian Supreme Court ruled that the government had no right to do so. And Indian trade crossing East

Pakistan to Assam and Tripura exceeds 200,000,000 rupees a month as the two countries gradually reach a few economic agreements.

While these successes remove much of the fringe frustration on both sides, they do not perceptibly reduce the suspicions and fears which prevent solutions to major problems. They do not prevent both sides from aiming their armies at each other across the Kashmir cease-fire line rather than at other possible aggressors, or deflecting expenditures from military purposes to economic development.

The Chinese communist attack on India, begun in 1959 but intensified in 1962, greatly affected Pakistani-Indian relations. Public reaction in Pakistan to India's involvement could have been predicted: India had invented the entire affair in order to obtain military aid to use against Pakistan. Pakistanis feel that Indian claims to "neutralism" were proven false and that, in order to obtain arms without admitting the error of their past policies, Indian politicians provoked the Chinese. When the United States and the United Kingdom began sending arms to India, Pakistan officially protested that the West was merely arming India against Pakistan, thereby creating an arms race. In reaction, Pakistan intensified its search for friends.

Afghanistan

While India has been Pakistan's major concern, neighboring Afghanistan has also appeared to Pakistanis as a threat to their unity and security. The issue over which they have quarreled is "Pashtunistan." From the day Pakistan became a nation, Afghan leaders, themselves Pathans, have claimed that the Pathans in Pakistan should be given the right to form a country of their own—if they wish.

Control over all the Pathans has long been the aim of the Pathan rulers of Afghanistan. It is understandable. In a tribal

society such as Afghanistan's, in which the ruler is the tribal leader who can subdue all the others, any Pathan tribe not under his control is a threat. In 1893, the British rulers of India, seeking to keep the Pathans divided and the Afghan king weak, instructed Sir Mortimer Durand to draw a line down the map of the northwest frontier. Until 1946, the Afghan government accepted this line. The Pathans on the Afghan side of the Durand line were theoretically the responsibility of Afghanistan. The Pathans on the Indian side were the concern of the British. The Pathans themselves, particularly the strong Mohmand, Afridi, Wazir, and Mahsud tribes who lived along both sides of the Durand line, felt themselves responsible to no one. Well-armed and strategically located in the hills of the borderland, they were able to maintain considerable independence from the sovereigns in Kabul and New Delhi.

At the time of partition, the strongest Pathan leader was Abdul Ghaffar Khan, the "Frontier Gandhi." He opposed the creation of Pakistan and in the referendum held to decide whether Pathans wished to join Pakistan or India he asked his followers to abstain. He wanted a third choice: independence. Only slightly more than 50 per cent of the Pathans voted in the referendum and of these 99 per cent selected Pakistan. To the Afghans and Abdul Ghaffar Khan, the referendum was not a true indication of Pathan wishes. When Pakistan applied for admission to the United Nations in September, 1947, only Afghanistan voted in opposition.

Afghanistan is a landlocked country whose foreign trade depends upon its neighbors—Pakistan, the Soviet Union and Iran, primarily the first two. Long a target for political exploitation by Russia, even before the communist revolution, it has also been a buffer between the rulers of India and other imperialists wishing to march through its rugged terrain. Afghan rulers have often toed a neutralist line, either by

246

necessity or design, hoping to remain independent yet survive economically. And they have dreamed of obtaining an outlet to the sea. In the years after 1947, King Zahir Shah faced the choice of securing the allegiance of the Pathan tribesmen through the Pashtunistan issue (and obtaining an outlet to the sea) or maintaining good relations with Pakistan, which controlled the only alternative trade routes to those through the Soviet Union. The Pathan ancestry of the royal court, dominated by the prime minister, Mohammed Daoud, led the King to worry less about the Soviet Union and more about the Pathans. Any unrest among the Pathans was not only to be supported, but encouraged.

Hostility toward Pakistan among Pathan hill tribes did not diminish in the early years of Pakistan. Although Abdul Ghaffar Khan was jailed for a time, others took his place. Among them was the Fakir of Ipi, a mullah with considerable following. Until his death in 1960, the Fakir of Ipi was the Afghan government's chief hope in the frontier area. He used pamphlets printed in India and funds supplied by Kabul to exhort dissident Pathans to raid Pakistani-controlled lowlands. Propagandists from India traveled across Europe and the United States pleading the cause of an independent Pashtunistan. The Fakir even proclaimed himself President of Pashtunistan, a country that would extend to the Indus River and the Arabian Sea. His appeals reached all of the subcontinent over Indian and Afghan broadcasting facilities; Soviet broadcasts supported his claims.

One of the peaks of tension between Pakistan and Afghanistan came in 1955 when Pakistan announced the unification of West Pakistan. The Afghan government mobilized its armed forces and Pakistan evacuated its citizens from Afghanistan, simultaneously blocking Afghanistan's borders. The Soviet Union denounced Pakistan and rushed to Afghanistan's aid with new purchasing credits and transit fa-

247

cilities. Neither Kabul nor Karachi liked the Soviet intrusion and in 1956 relations eased. But not for long.

In 1960, trouble flared again when the Afghans supported a tribal attack on the small frontier state of Dir. Pakistan aided the opposing tribal chief, the Khan of Khar, who finally emerged victorious. In the melee, Pakistan deposed the old and autocratic Nawab of Dir, bringing the territory under the administration of the Pakistan government.

Tension from this episode spread throughout the Pathan valleys and violence increased to the point that the Pakistan air force began bombing dissident Mohmands. The year 1961 became the bloodiest in the history of the Pathans since 1937 and, in September of that year, Afghanistan and Pakistan broke off all relations.

For twenty months, Pakistan and Afghanistan remained bitter diplomatic enemies, to the advantage of the Soviet Union, which promptly secured additional trade concessions from the Kabul government. Tons of American aid supplies sat on the piers in Karachi while Afghanistan signed trade agreements with Communist China and strengthened its air force with Czechoslovakian airplanes.

Attempts to bring the two countries together failed repeatedly until the Shah of Iran offered to mediate. In May, 1963, the Shah induced Pakistan and Afghanistan to resume diplomatic relations and both began opening their trade offices. Although Afghanistan did not agree to bury its hatchet for a Pashtunistan, King Zahir Shah did take one significant step toward this end. He dismissed Prime Minister Daoud, the most powerful individual in Afghanistan behind the Pashtunistan issue.

A period of peaceful relations between Pakistan and Afghanistan can help each country. They share the Kabul River and could benefit by its development. Annually, thousands of Pathan tribesmen, the powindahs, move across the Afghan-

Pakistan border seeking work and grazing lands. The settling of these tribesmen would be to the advantage of both countries. But above all, the increasing flow of trade would bring greater prosperity and security to Afghans and link them more closely with the non-communist world rather than with the Soviet Union.

Iran and the Muslim World

Afghanistan has two special claims to the affections of Pakistanis and these they also share with the Iranians. All three are primarily Muslim in religion (Iranians are Shi'ites, Afghans are Sunnites) and Aryan in origin. As recently as 1962, President Ayub Khan called on all three countries to form an Aryan Confederation and in both Afghanistan and Iran cultural leaders replied in friendly terms, if not in political action.

More than any other Muslim country Iran holds a special place in the hearts of Pakistanis. It was the first Muslim country to recognize Pakistan. For centuries, the language of Muslim poetry and song in India was Persian, as was the language of government. Artists drew in the fashion of Persian painters and the sufism of Persia's mystics found enthusiasts among India's Muslims.

Iran and Pakistan are back fence neighbors, sharing a common border. This border is remote and undeveloped, but recent efforts through CENTO have led to improved communications and there are plans to link the two countries by rail. A single track leads from Quetta to Zahedan in Iran, but there the line stops.

Unfortunately, the two countries have little else to share. Both have an underdeveloped agricultural base to their economies and neither is able to provide the other with its needs. Although Iran has great quantities of oil, it is neither able nor willing to share this wealth with any other country.

In their search for friends, Pakistanis look longingly toward other Muslims, if not for material support at least for solace and votes in the United Nations. Even the country's constitution states that "the bonds of unity amongst Muslim countries should be preserved and strengthened."

The old dream of Pan-Islamic unity has pretty well disappeared now in Pakistan. Once a goal of some Indian Muslims, particularly after World War I when the fate of the Ottoman caliph was being decided by Kemal Ataturk, it has been mislaid in the secular nationalisms of the Middle East.

Yet the Arabic greeting among Muslims—*"Salaam aleikum"* —can be heard from West Africa to the Philippines. There are indeed deep emotional ties and sympathetic understanding among Muslims wherever they are. And Pakistan is one of the largest of Muslim nations.

After partition, the hopes of many Pakistanis for a rejuvenation of Muslim brotherhood brightened perceptibly. Muslim friendship societies sprouted in Karachi, Lahore, and Dacca. Said the Minister of Education:

"With the Muslim countries we claim a community of outlook based on spiritual and moral affinities. We have the same faith and the same cultural traditions as they have, and, like us, they too are emerging from the sloth of centuries and are becoming increasingly conscious of the important historical role which Islam has to play as a unifying force. It is only natural that our first cultural links should be with them."

Societies such as the Pakistan-Iraq and Pakistan-Iran cultural associations were helpful in establishing contacts between public groups in various countries. The Pakistan-Arab Cultural Association undertook to publish an Arabic-Urdu dictionary and a Council of World Muslim Affairs provided a forum for Islamic subjects. The Jama'at-i-Ulema-i-Islam in Pakistan sought to make Arabic the official language of all Muslim nations, to create an independent Islamic bloc in

the United Nations, to introduce a central inter-Islamic currency and to promote free trade among Muslim nations. The former Grand Mufti of Jerusalem, al-Hajj Amin al-Husayni, brought his anti-British World Muslim Organization to Karachi in 1951 and called for the creation of a commonwealth of Islamic countries.

In its adolescent years, Pakistan sought to befriend every Muslim nation, to support every Muslim cause in the United Nations and to assume leadership among Muslims. It supported the Arabs on the Palestine question and has not yet recognized Israel. It opposed France in Algeria, Italy in Libya, the Dutch in Indonesia (after World War II, Indian Muslim troops deserted the British to help Indonesians in their fight for independence), and the British occupation of Suez.

Not all Muslim countries accepted Pakistan's aggressive brotherly love with open arms. Many Turks were apprehensive over the appearance of budding theocracy in Pakistan, even asking Pakistan to recall one of its envoys on the grounds of encouraging religious reactionaries in Turkey. Many Arabs suspected the Islamic orthodoxy of these "foreign" Muslims who could not even speak Arabic. The rector of the Muslim university in Cairo, Al-Azhar, protested that too many Islamic conferences were being held in Pakistan. Iranians spoke contemptuously of the Pakistani language, Urdu. Pakistan's prime minister, Hussein Suhrawardy, once complained bitterly that the Egyptians were insulting to Pakistan.

Eventually, Pakistan's self-interest dampened some of its fraternal ardor. Economically, Pakistan's Muslim brothers could do little for the new country and Pakistan sought help elsewhere. No Muslim nation came to Pakistan's aid over Kashmir except to vote against India in the United Nations. Even Islamic Afghanistan became a predatory neighbor allied in the Pashtunistan cause with India. In joining what was

then called the Baghdad Pact, Pakistan antagonized most of its Arab friends, but at least allayed the fears of the Turks, with whom Pakistan signed a military pact in 1954. Pakistan has not joined the Arab economic boycott against Israel.

Sentiments of Muslim brotherhood are nevertheless strong in Pakistan and, so long as religion remains as deeply-rooted as it is among the people, the fate of any Muslim nation in the world will affect Pakistanis. Properly directed, these genuine desires for Muslim unity can help Pakistan play a more significant role in aiding Muslim nations to find strength and stability. Should President Ayub's experiment in the Basic Democracies prove successful, other Muslim nations as politically and economically underdeveloped as Pakistan will be among the first to follow Pakistan's lead.

Non-communist Asia

Many Pakistanis have also searched for friends among their fellow Asians. They share with them a feeling of resentment against Europeans who have long ruled, directly and indirectly, the lives of Asians. The resentment is based on political and racial grounds and, throughout Pakistan, emotions are strong against evidences of racial discrimination in Western countries, especially in the United States.

Relations with neighboring Burma have been of particular concern to East Pakistanis; these relations have not always been completely amicable. While Burma is primarily a Buddhist country, a community of Muslims lives in the Arakan region bordering Pakistan. Shortly after independence, these Muslims rebelled, many fleeing—with their arms—to Pakistan, where they fed anti-Burmese sentiments. Minor problems over delineation of the borders aggravated the situation, although later most of these problems were settled. Occasional stresses, including Burma's threat to deport Pakistani (and Indian) traders and businessmen living in Burma, have not

prevented Pakistan and Burma from enjoying friendly diplomatic relations or joining together in various Asian conferences to seek ways of strengthening Asian influence in world affairs.

In Ceylon, Pakistanis see another country menaced by India and thus a potential friend. Indeed, many Buddhist Ceylonese fear the Hindu minority in Ceylon. They have also not forgotten that India's Nehru once referred (apparently in jest) to Ceylon as a potential Indian province. In 1963, President Ayub visited Ceylon and was warmly received.

India has fostered Pakistan's interest in Asian affairs through its rivaling search for friends. While India has attempted to gain a leadership position based on the late Prime Minister Nehru's "neutralism," Pakistan has spoken for those Asians committed to containing the expansion of communism. At numerous Asian conferences prior to 1964 Pakistanis have been the most effective spokesmen in moderating Asian resentment against the West and opposing the virulence of Asian communists.

Pakistan committed itself to opposing communism in 1954 when it joined Australia, France, New Zealand, the Philippines, Thailand, the United Kingdom, and the United States in forming SEATO, the Southeast Asia Collective Defense Treaty Organization. Under this treaty, Pakistan agreed to uphold the U. N. Charter and to develop its capacity to "resist armed attack and to prevent any counter-subversive activities directed from without against [the] territorial integrity and political stability" of the treaty members. Pakistan agreed to join with the members in meeting common dangers to any territory which the members might designate, by unanimous agreement. Cambodia, Laos and the free territory under the jurisdiction of Vietnam were so designated. Pakistan also agreed to cooperate in economic, social, and cultural fields.

While consistent in its commitment to SEATO, Pakistan has continued to seek friends among the non-committed Asians. These drives reflect a growing discontent among Bengalis with anti-communist commitments in Asia and Pakistan's increasing skepticism over the efficacy of these postures, particularly in solving the Kashmir problem. This skepticism was expressed in 1963 when Foreign Minister Zulfikar Ali Bhutto called for another meeting of Asian leaders similar to that held years before in Bandung, at which time the principle of neutralism and the Asian feelings of resentment were predominant.

The Commonwealth

While Asian and other Muslim nations rushed to congratulate Pakistanis on their independence in 1947, Pakistanis themselves found their most effective friends among their old rulers, the British. This effectiveness, however, was limited in Pakistani eyes. Pakistanis felt the British had let them down during the Punjab massacres and, later, in Kashmir. India's Prime Minister Nehru appeared to be Britain's hero. Nevertheless, it was, in fact, the British and their Commonwealth partners who first helped Pakistan along in those crucial early years.

Great Britain's impact on Indian Muslims before 1947 was great. Among the Muslim intelligentsia, government servants, political and educational leaders who formed the majority of the articulate Muslims, Great Britain and its traditions were deeply respected. Almost to a man, these Muslims spoke English, were educated in British institutions, wore British clothing, admired the British court system and rose to prominence within it. Parliamentary government along British lines was a more natural constitutional system to them than any other and association in the Commonwealth after independence was a logical consequence of this respect.

After partition, Mohammed Ali Jinnah appointed British officers to head each military service and British civil servants as provincial governors. Nearly every ministry had a British expert and Britons were called in to help write the constitutions. It was as easy to find British customs and ideas in Pakistan's cities after 1947 as it was to find native Indian or Muslim ones. The British-trained armed forces wore British-styled uniforms. English was the language of Pakistan's universities and the most influential daily newspapers—*Dawn, Pakistan Times,* and the now defunct *Civil and Military Gazette.* The first economic development projects, such as the reclamation of the Thal desert in the Punjab, grew out of the Commonwealth-inspired Colombo Plan.

Pakistan's membership in the Commonwealth is a voluntary association which prescribes no rigid rules of behavior but does encourage each country to work closely with other members. Each member may follow an independent foreign policy. At first, the Queen of England was also Queen of Pakistan, but this relationship disappeared when Pakistan became a republic in 1956. Now, the Queen is merely "Head of the Commonwealth" and there is no formal or legal link between the British sovereign and Pakistanis.

As a Commonwealth member, Pakistan participates in the various conferences and committees of the Commonwealth. Pakistan is a member of the Imperial Economic Committee, the Imperial Shipping Committee, the Executive Council of the Imperial Agricultural Bureau and the Committee on Imperial Defence. Pakistan's monetary base is British sterling, controlled through the Commonwealth, and Pakistan shares in the trade "preferences" which Commonwealth members give to each other. Great Britain's proposed membership in the European Common Market would threaten Pakistan's economic advantages within the Commonwealth and this is one reason for the reluctance of many Britons to support

255

fully the Common Market idea. Above all, Pakistan has joined with Great Britain in two major alliances—CENTO and SEATO.

But in spite of British and Commonwealth ties, Pakistan's relationships with Great Britain are sometimes strained, usually over the Commonwealth's inability to solve the Kashmir dispute to Pakistan's advantage. Great Britain's representative to SEATO, Lord Louis Mountbatten, was denied a welcome in Pakistan in 1962 because of his previous activities as India's governor-general during the initial stages of the Kashmir troubles. When Great Britain invaded Egypt in 1956, there were widespread demands that Pakistan quit the Commonwealth. If the invasion had not been halted, these demands might well have become irresistible. The most recent strains have arisen over British assistance to India during India's controversy with Communist China. In this, Great Britain shares the criticism leveled by Pakistanis at the United States.

The United States

In the early days of independence, when it appeared that Britain was favoring India on the subject of Kashmir, Pakistanis looked longingly to the United States for friendship. They welcomed American Admiral Chester Nimitz as the first plebiscite administrator for Kashmir. Many asked that American technicians be employed to replace the British. The Mir of Hunza sought to make his little principality the forty-ninth state of the United States.

The United States was slow to respond to these entreaties. Even after Prime Minister Liaquat Ali Khan visited the U. S. in 1951, Washington attempted to follow a neutral course in the conflict between India and Pakistan. American public opinion lionized India's Nehru. Books by Louis Fischer, Vincent Sheean and other American visitors to the subcontinent gave a villain's role to Mohammed Ali Jinnah. U. S. foreign

aid flowed into India appropriately heralded by Ambassador Chester Bowles, whose every move and statement demonstrated to Pakistanis that Americans liked India best.

United States policy toward the Soviet Union, enunciated by Secretary of State John Foster Dulles after 1953, brought sudden change in the relations between Pakistan and the U. S. Advocating the creation of bi-lateral military pacts between the U. S. and non-communist countries and multi-lateral regional groupings to deter Soviet expansionism, this policy found many friends, each of whom was rewarded by economic assistance. As Pakistan's search for friends was limping along ineffectually and the struggle for Kashmir was particularly unsuccessful (in 1952, the Soviet Union openly sided with India), Pakistan eagerly grasped Mr. Dulles' outstretched hands. In 1954, the U. S. and Pakistan signed a mutual defense pact and in 1955, Pakistan joined CENTO. Ambassador Bowles returned to the United States. Pakistan had found a friend which, it presumed, would support it against "neutralist" and "imperialist" India. The U. S. had found a friend which, it presumed, was stalwart in its opposition to international communism. Both ignored the facts of life.

The growing affection between Pakistanis and Americans was phenomenal. U. S. government policy denigrated Prime Minister Nehru's attempt to be neutral between the Soviet communists and American anti-communists. To Pakistanis any foe of Nehru's was a friend of Pakistan's. Many Pakistani leaders—Governor-General Ghulam Mohammed (who was primarily responsible for obtaining U. S. support), Prime Minister Mohammed Ali (Bogra), Minister of Defense Iskander Mirza, and General Ayub—genuinely feared Soviet expansionism and stood unhesitatingly on the side of the Western allies. They also saw what could be gained through alliance with the U. S. in terms of economic and military

257

development. They had cast envious eyes on the progress of Turkey after that country's alliance with the United States.

These leaders were not soon disappointed. U. S. military aid arrived through Karachi faster than men could be trained to use it. Supersonic jets—better than India's—and the latest tanks gave the American-advised armed forces a strength undreamed of by the original British commanders. By 1963, the cost of this military hardware and personnel training exceeded $1,000,000,000. Economic aid in the form of cash gifts and loans, surplus food and industrial equipment, and thousands of technicians, landed in Karachi and Dacca to help Pakistanis bolster their languishing economy. Nearly all sectors of Pakistan's economic and social development program found some support from the U. S. Through the Pakistan Industrial Development Corporations, loans helped start hundreds of small and medium-size factories. Agricultural projects, especially those involving irrigation, soil improvement and rural education received backing. The U. S. helped build the giant Karnafuli dam in East Pakistan and poured funds into the Indus River development scheme. Loans helped begin rehabilitation of West Pakistan's railroads and construction of airfields in East Pakistan. And by May, 1963, the U. S. had sent more than 146 Peace Corps volunteers into Pakistan (only 47 to India). Meanwhile, private American philanthropic agencies and universities gave help to programs in birth control, village development, and urban planning. By 1963, the value of economic aid to Pakistan was $1,500,000,000, or approximately $15 per person. India in the same period received $3,900,000,000 in economic aid from the U. S., or about $9 per person. Few countries in the world had gained more— economically and militarily—than Pakistan from American friendship.

Visits of dignitaries also increased along with aid. In 1959, President Eisenhower arrived in Karachi to be met by the

biggest reception Pakistan had ever given a foreigner. More than 700,000 people turned out to meet him. In 1961, then Vice President Johnson visited Karachi and captured the peoples' hearts by stopping to talk at length with a camel-cart driver named Bashir Ahmed. The next year, Bashir Ahmed was guest at the Johnson ranch in Texas and returned to Karachi loaded with gifts, including a pickup truck. Both Pakistanis and Americans were touched by the gesture.

Also in 1961, President Ayub made a triumphal visit to the United States and spoke before a joint session of Congress. Americans found him genial, outspoken and obviously a friend. Early in 1962, his visit was repaid by Mrs. Jacqueline Kennedy, wife of the U. S. President, who spent five days in Pakistan. As a few Americans and Pakistanis had long before discovered, the peoples of the two nations could easily develop warm and lasting friendships.

But still, Kashmir remained in Indian hands and, in 1963, there were no signs that Pakistan's friendship with the U. S. was helping solve the problem Pakistanis felt was their most important. Indeed, if anything, the friendship had made solution of the Kashmir problem more difficult. Pakistan's anti-communist alliances had hardened India's anti-Pakistan positions. The armies of the two countries still faced each other across the Kashmir cease-fire line, with even greater belligerence.

As though it was designed to weaken U. S.-Pakistani friendship, the invasion of Indian territory by Chinese communist forces in 1962 led both countries to re-examine their policies. The U. S. (and Great Britain) offered to aid India which, in turn, refused to withdraw troops from the Pakistani front to fight China. On April 15, 1963, Pakistan's Foreign Minister Bhutto said that if India should receive massive military assistance from the "Western powers" without a solution to the Kashmir dispute, it would mark a turning point for Pakistan

and the "abandonment of our friends and allies." As military aid began to flow into India—and Ambassador Bowles returned to New Delhi to herald the renewed friendship—Bhutto said that Pakistan's foreign policy was being "reshaped." Later, he and U. S. officials met in Washington. Afterwards, the U. S. announced that it had agreed to "recognize" Pakistan's fear of India, although it was apparent that the U. S. policy-makers did not share this fear. The U. S. also made it clear to Pakistan that it would build its anti-China policy around India, regardless of Pakistani policies. Pakistanis, acting as though any enemy of India's was a welcome friend of theirs, as they did when Pakistan first signed a military pact with the United States, intensified their friendly associations with the communist world.

The Soviet Union

Most of Pakistan's leaders have acted firmly against the growth of communism within the country and opposed the spread of communist power outside the country. With the exception of their unequivocal stands on India and Pashtunistan, few other subjects have brought forth more clearly defined attitudes. Yet these leaders have not generally viewed the Soviet Union or Communist China with the same degree of alarm as has the United States.

Pakistan inherited from British India the geo-political headaches of defending the passes between central and western Asia and the subcontinent. As early as 1713, Peter the Great of Russia indicated a desire to rule India. In 1800 Tsar Paul and Napoleon planned a joint invasion and the British strengthened their forces on India's northwest frontier. During World War I, Germany also made threatening gestures and the British rushed a railroad line from Quetta to Zahedan in Iran and fortified the valleys of the frontier. Marx and Lenin both reiterated Peter the Great's belief that control of India was

essential to the control of Asia. In World War II the British built tank traps in the Khyber and Kurram passes to defend the borders against either Germany or the Soviet Union, whichever enemy decided to attack.

After partition, Pakistan found itself responsible for a 310-mile border with Communist China and a 1,448-mile border with Afghanistan, both potential targets for an aggressor. Pakistanis have usually assumed that the aggressor would be Russian, not Chinese.

Despite this history of strategy, Pakistanis' concern over these borders has been subordinate to their fear of India. Few army units face toward either the Soviet Union or China, much to the distress of U. S. military advisors who have been instructed to re-orient Pakistan's army and air force toward the potential aggressor whom Americans believe is the most sinister.

Pakistan's relations with the Soviet Union have only lately become friendly. After partition, the Soviet Union, like most other nations, sought to befriend India. In the context of Prime Minister Nehru's neutralism, Russians found a warm welcome. Thus the Soviet Union gave no support to Pakistan on Kashmir. It openly backed Afghanistan on the Pashtunistan issue. Consequently, Pakistan was able to commit itself to an anti-Soviet military pact—and permit American U-2 reconnaissance planes to take off from Peshawar—without compromising any friendly associations it might have developed with Moscow.

Communist China

While admitting the expansionist tendencies of Communist China in Southeast Asia—hence, Pakistan's membership in SEATO—Pakistanis have shown little concern over China as a threat to Pakistan itself. Pakistan was one of the first countries to recognize Communist China and has always supported

Peking's claims to the Chinese seat in the United Nations. During the Korean war, Pakistan supported the U. N. position, but sent no troops to Korea. Trading between the two countries began in 1950 and each year Pakistan has tried to increase its exports of jute and cotton to China. Apprehension over Great Britain's possible entry into the European Common Market has caused Pakistani salesmen to search for new markets everywhere, particularly in Asia. In 1963, China and Pakistan signed a new trade agreement which, although it called for no change in basic trade patterns of the two countries, alarmed the western world because it coincided with a Chinese-Pakistan border agreement and the heightened fury of Pakistani-India relations.

When Chinese communist troops thrust deep into Indian territory in the fall of 1962 and Indian troops retreated, elation in Pakistan superseded any fear for Pakistan's security. Not only was its greatest enemy under attack, but the part of India which Communist China appeared to covet most was the barren Aksai Chin, or whitestone desert, in the eastern part of Kashmir's Ladakh district. Few Muslims lived in this area and Pakistanis thus were able to exclude it from their own areas of interest in Kashmir.

The brightening of Pakistan-China relations actually began in 1959 when India and China began arguing over the undefined Himalayan borders. It appeared then that Indian refusal to meet China's border demands would result in a worsening of affairs between the two largest Asian nations. In March, 1961, Pakistan approached China requesting negotiations over the borders of Pakistan-occupied Kashmir and China. The area involved was approximately 3,400 square miles running some 300 miles southeastward from Gilgit toward the Karakorum Pass. Only months after the outbreak of full-scale mountain warfare between India and China, Pakistan announced that on March 2, 1963 China and Paki-

stan had agreed on a new border. Pakistan claims to have gained about 800 square miles. Large areas of Kashmir, sovereignty over which had never been determined, were confirmed as being under Chinese control. The agreement also stated that "after the settlement of the Kashmir Dispute between Pakistan and India, the sovereign authority concerned will re-open negotiations with the Government of the People's Republic of China, on the boundary . . . so as to sign a boundary treaty to replace the present Agreement."

Before long, Pakistan took other steps to strengthen its relations with Communist China. In June, 1963, the head of Pakistan International Airlines visited China to work out details of air service from Karachi and Dacca to cities of China. At the same time, Chinese trade officials began arriving in Pakistan for new talks. Then in February, 1964, Chinese Premier Chou En-lai made an eight-day visit to Pakistan. On February 23, he suddenly announced that Communist China supported Pakistan's demand for a plebiscite in Kashmir.

In the serious business of international relations, the old Machiavellian principle of "my enemy's enemy is my friend" frequently guides a nation's policy. For Communist China, now competing with India for Asian leadership, friendship with Pakistan fits the principle. Besides, the existence of such friendship can be a disrupting influence within the United States-backed anti-communist pacts of which Pakistan is a member, and perhaps strengthen China's hand in its struggle with the Soviet Union for communist leadership. To many Pakistanis, the test of friendship is not whether it results in an improved economy or strengthened military establishment, but whether Pakistan gains vis-à-vis India and, more particularly, comes closer to acquiring Kashmir. In the Chinese, Pakistanis find this kind of friendship—and from Asians for whom many Pakistanis have a particular and natural affinity.

Since independence in 1947, Pakistanis have made giant steps forward in the development of their military, economic, and social institutions. And no one in the country is more aware than President Ayub that this advancement can continue only with the aid of the industrialized countries of Europe and America. But many Pakistanis have lived for years with less materially than they have now; what is more real to them than machines and foreign technicians are the intangibles of life—their religion, their self respect, their independence. Pakistanis seek friends who understand these emotions. They hope that with such understanding will come not only Kashmir, but the tangible tools of progress.

13. *Underdeveloped?*

Pakistan is labeled an "underdeveloped" country. In terms of certain economic and social institutions, such a label is accurate when Pakistan is compared to the countries of Europe and North America. It is accurate when it refers to the distance Pakistan has to go in bringing prosperity to its people. But in fact, the label, like all labels, is neither accurate nor fair. Regardless of how far Pakistan must go, the distance it has traveled in seventeen years is remarkable. If labels are necessary, "progressing" and "developing" are more apt. These labels can also be applied to the most industrialized of nations.

Less than thirty-five years ago, the name "Pakistan" did not exist. Since then, nearly 100,000,000 people have drawn upon their ancient heritage, their deep religious faith and have come together to form the sixth most populous country in the world.

The problems to overcome are colossal. Indeed, when Mohammed Iqbal suggested an independent nation for South Asia's Muslims, many of his countrymen, including the very founder of Pakistan, Mohammed Ali Jinnah, thought he was unrealistic. In 1940, when the grand old man of Bengal, Fazlul Haq, asked the Muslim League to endorse the idea, Pakistan was still only a dream. Yet within seven years, the dream came true.

Even in 1947, there were many who doubted that Pakistan could exist for long. It was, they said, an artificial creation born of tense emotions and British manipulation. Half the people lived 1,000 miles away from the other half and the two groups spoke completely different languages. All were desperately poor. Few could read and write. The means of making a living were primitive and scarce. The institutions for

265

self-government were foreign and only briefly used. Perhaps in 1947 it was fair to call Pakistan an "underdeveloped" country; it was hardly a country at all.

No Indian should have been surprised that Pakistan survived, if only because in South Asia religion is such a vital part of a person's life. Westerners could be excused for not understanding the depth of an Asian Hindu's or Muslim's devotion to his faith. More than anything else, religion bound these diverse Pakistanis together when logic seemed to demand their disintegration.

Few people, too, understood in 1947 the size and strength of the appallingly thin and emaciated man named Mohammed Ali Jinnah. The Quaid-i-Azam figuratively towered over his people like a Gulliver and gave them a warm sense of belonging. He commanded his people to be a nation and they obeyed.

The ingredients of revolt and civil war in Pakistan have been there, awaiting the proper catalyst. Poverty, hunger, frustration, jealousy, corruption, and insecurity—all have begged Pakistanis to destroy their country. Other nations with similar problems have turned to internal violence. But in Pakistan, the only revolt was a bloodless coup d'état, carried out almost before breakfast. And from it came a new leader, Mohammed Ayub Khan, who, within five years, had become a new "father image" to millions.

The gains Pakistanis have made in their seventeen years belie the depressing statistics of illiteracy, poor health, and insufficient economic growth. They are chiefly in the field of unostentatious groundwork constructed for future progress. Materially, however, they are such things as the Warsak and Karnafuli dams, the new ports of Khulna and Chalna, the massive Indus River development scheme, the blossoming factories and mills on the outskirts of every city, sprawling housing projects, and irrigation canals that wind through the parched farmland.

266

But more importantly, the gains are in the development of human institutions such as the successful rural cooperative movement in Comilla, the graduates of new technical training schools, scientists from new universities, the active Industrial Development Bank and the provincial Water and Power Development Authorities. They are the graduates of the public service training institutes, men and women who have learned to plan their progress rationally through the various government departments. They are the commercial entrepreneurs who have developed confidence in the future of their country. Such people and institutions have never been there before.

For many Pakistanis, these gains have taken place at the expense of political freedoms, because under the 1962 constitution (and with the backing of the army) President Ayub is eminently powerful. The National Assemblymen are not elected directly by the people, but indirectly by Basic Democrats. And the Basic Democrats voted 95.6 per cent for President Ayub.

But none can ignore the results. In 1963, despite poor crops, Pakistan could boast that consumer prices were stable as was the value of money. Foreign exchange reserves increased, there was tight control over recurring government expenditures and there was no major labor trouble. Politics had not seriously impeded national development. The same conditions prevailed into 1964. Few other countries in Asia, or any place else for that matter, had such a record.

The key to the continuation of Pakistan's progress lies not only with Pakistanis, but with all the people of the South Asian subcontinent. The violence of 1947, when neighbor killed neighbor with abandon, left deep scars of bitterness on Indians and Pakistanis. And the wound of Kashmir is not bound up. Not until that wound is treated and healed and the bitterness dissolved will either people find the progress each seeks. The Pakistani, like his Indian neighbor, waits.

267

Appendix

SOME FACTS ABOUT PAKISTAN
(based on the 1961 census)

Area 365,524 square miles*

Population: 93,831,982*

Density per square mile: 256.4*

Capitals: Islamabad (future capital under construction), Rawalpindi (provisional capital), Dacca (seat of National Assembly)

Flag: Green field (green is the color of Islam) with a white band near the staff (white represents the minorities) with a white star and crescent (symbols of Islam) in the center of the flag.

Religions: Muslim 88.1 per cent, Hindu 10.7 per cent, other (Buddhist, Christian, Zoroastrian, etc.) 1.2 per cent.

Official languages: Bengali, Urdu, English (until 1972).

Literacy: 19.2 per cent (persons over five), East Pakistan 21.5 per cent, West Pakistan 16.3 per cent.

University Graduates: 82,069 (.08 per cent); East Pakistan 28,069, West Pakistan 54,000.

SUBDIVISIONS OF PAKISTAN

Name	Area (sq. mi.)	Population (000's)	Density (sq. mi.)	Major city	Language
East Pakistan	54,141	50,854	922	Dacca	Bengali
West Pakistan	311,383	42,978	138	Lahore	Urdu**

* Excludes Junagadh and other territory claimed by Pakistan, but held by India as well as Azad Kashmir and the Northern Areas of Kashmir held by Pakistan.

** Although Urdu is the official language, West Pakistan is composed of the following distinctive linguistic-cultural areas:

Baluchistan	134,002	1,384	10	Quetta	Baluchi
Northwest Frontier	38,259	7,563	197	Peshawar	Pashtu
Punjab	79,716	25,643	323	Lahore	Punjabi
Sind	57,259	8,488	150	Karachi	Sindi

268

MAJOR CITIES OF PAKISTAN

Name	Population	Province	Comment
Karachi	1,916,000	West Pakistan-Sind	Former Capital
Lahore	1,297,000	West Pakistan-Punjab	Capital of West Pakistan
Dacca	558,000	East Pakistan	Capital of East Pakistan
Hyderabad	434,000	West Pakistan-Sind	Former Capital of Sind
Lyallpur	426,000	West Pakistan-Punjab	Fastest growing city
Chittagong	363,000	East Pakistan	Port of East Pakistan
Multan	358,000	West Pakistan-Punjab	
Rawalpindi	343,000	West Pakistan-Punjab	Present Capital
Peshawar	213,000	West Pakistan-Frontier	Former Capital of N.W.F.P.
Gujranwala	107,000	West Pakistan-Punjab	

HEADS OF STATE

Name	Title	Started Term	End of Term
Mohammed Ali Jinnah	Governor-General	August, 1947	September, 1948
Khwaja Nazimuddin	Governor-General	September, 1948	October, 1951
Ghulam Mohammed	Governor-General	October, 1951	September, 1955
Iskander Mirza	Governor-General	September, 1955	March, 1956
	President	March, 1956	October, 1958
Mohammed Ayub Khan	President	October, 1958	In Office

PRIME MINISTERS

Name	Started Term	End of Term	Political Party
Liaquat Ali Khan	August, 1947	October, 1951	Muslim League
Khwaja Nazimuddin	October, 1951	April, 1953	Muslim League
Mohammed Ali (Bogra)	April, 1953	August, 1955	Muslim League
Chaudhuri Mohammed Ali	August, 1955	September, 1956	Muslim League
Hussein S. Suhrawardy	September, 1956	October, 1957	Awami League
Ismail I. Chundrigar	October, 1957	December, 1957	Muslim League
Firoz Khan Noon	December, 1957	October, 1958	Republican
Mohammed Ayub Khan*	October, 1958	October, 1958	

*Mohammed Ayub Khan seized power in a coup d'etat on October 7, 1958, abolished the office of Prime Minister, proclaimed martial law, and declared himself head of government as Chief Martial Law Administrator. On October 27, 1958, Ayub deposed President Iskander Mirza and proclaimed himself President.

For Further Reading

AHMAD, COLONEL MOHAMMAD. *My Chief*. Lahore: Longmans, Green 1960.

AHMAD, MUSHTAQ. *Government and Politics in Pakistan*. Karachi: Pakistan Publishing House, second, revised edition, 1963.

ALBIRUNI, A. H. *Makers of Pakistan and Modern Muslim India*. Lahore: Mohammed Ashraf, 1950.

ASAD, MUHAMMAD. *The Principles of State and Government in Islam*. Berkeley: University of California Press, 1961.

BINDER, LEONARD. *Religion and Politics in Pakistan*. Berkeley: University of California Press, 1961.

BIRDWOOD, CHRISTOPHER B., LORD. *India and Pakistan; A Continent Decides*. New York: Frederick A. Praeger, 1954.

BOLITHO, HECTOR. *Jinnah; Creator of Pakistan*. New York: The Macmillan Co., 1955.

BROWN, W. N. *India, Pakistan, Ceylon*. Ithaca, New York: Cornell University Press, 1951.

——. *The United States and India and Pakistan*. Cambridge: Harvard University Press. Second edition, 1963.

CALLARD, KEITH. *Pakistan, A Political Study*. New York: The Macmillan Co., 1957.

——. *Pakistan's Foreign Policy; An Interpretation*. New York: Institute of Pacific Relations, 1959.

CAMPBELL, ROBERT D. *Pakistan: Emerging Democracy*. Princeton: D. Van Nostrand Co., 1963.

CHOUDHURY, GOLAM WAHED. *Constitutional Development in Pakistan*. New York: Institute of Pacific Relations, 1959.

——. *Democracy in Pakistan*. Dacca: Green Book Co., 1963.

Crescent and Green; a miscellany of writings on Pakistan. London: Cassell & Company, Ltd., 1955.

270

FOR FURTHER READING

EGLAR, ZEKIYE. *A Punjabi Village in Pakistan.* New York: Columbia University Press, 1960.

HUSAIN, A. F. A. *Human and Social Impact of Technological Change in Pakistan:* A Report on a Survey conducted by the University of Dacca and published with the assistance of UNESCO. New York: Oxford University Press, 1956.

IKRAM, S. M. and PERCIVAL SPEAR. *The Cultural Heritage of Pakistan.* New York: Oxford University Press, 1955.

KIERNAN, V. G. (Translator). *Poems from Iqbal.* London: J. Murray, 1955.

KORBEL, JOSEF. *Danger in Kashmir.* Princeton: Princeton University Press, 1954.

MARSHALL, SIR JOHN HUBERT. *A Guide to Taxila.* Cambridge, England: Cambridge University Press, 1960.

MOON, PENDEREL. *Divide and Quit.* Berkeley: University of California Press, 1962.

MUQEEM KHAN, MAJOR-GENERAL FAZAL. *The Story of the Pakistan Army.* New York: Oxford University Press, 1963.

MURRAY, JOHN, publisher. *A Handbook for Travellers in India and Pakistan, Burma and Ceylon.* London: J. Murray, 1949.

PHILIPS, CYRIL HENRY, ed. *The Evolution of India and Pakistan, 1858 to 1947, selected documents.* New York: Oxford University Press, 1962.

QURESHI, I. H. *The Muslim Community of the Indo-Pakistan Subcontinent.* The Hague: Mouton & Co., 1962.
——. *The Pakistani Way of Life.* New York: Frederick A. Praeger, 1956.

RAWLINSON, H. G. *India; A Short Cultural History.* New York: Frederick A. Praeger, 1963.

SASSANI, ABDUL HASSAN K. *Education in Pakistan.* Washington: U. S. Department of Health, Education and Welfare, 1954.

SAYEED, KHALID B. *Pakistan; The Formative Phase.* New York: Institute of Pacific Relations, 1960.

271

SIDDIQI, ASLAM. *Pakistan Seeks Security.* Lahore: Longmans, Green, 1960.

SPAIN, JAMES W. *People of the Khyber, The Pathans of Pakistan.* New York: Frederick A. Praeger, 1963.

——. *The Way of the Pathans.* London: R. Hale, 1962.

SPATE, OSKAR HERMANN K. *India and Pakistan: A General and Regional Geography.* New York: E. P. Dutton, 1954.

SPEAR, PERCIVAL. *India, Pakistan, and the West.* New York: Oxford University Press, 1958.

STEPHENS, IAN. *Pakistan.* New York: Frederick A. Praeger, 1963.

SYMONDS, RICHARD. *The Making of Pakistan.* London: Faber and Faber, 1950.

TINKER, HUGH. *India and Pakistan, A Political Analysis.* New York: Frederick A. Praeger, 1963.

TOYNBEE, ARNOLD. *Between Oxus and Jumna.* New York: Oxford University Press, 1961.

TUKER, SIR FRANCIS I. S. *While Memory Serves.* London: Cassell & Co. Ltd., 1950.

WHEELER, ROBERT ERIC M. *Five Thousand Years of Pakistan; An Archeological Outline.* London: C. Johnson, 1950.

WILBER, DONALD N. *Pakistan: Its People, Its Society, Its Culture.* New Haven: Human Relations Area Files, 1964.

——. *Pakistan Yesterday and Today.* New York: Holt, Rinehart & Winston, 1964.

WILLIAMS, L. RUSHBROOK. *The State of Pakistan.* London: Faber and Faber, 1962.

Twayne's English Authors Series

Sylvia E. Bowman, *Editor*

INDIANA UNIVERSITY

Charles Churchill

TEAS   197

Charles Churchill

CHARLES CHURCHILL

By RAYMOND J. SMITH

University of Windsor

TWAYNE PUBLISHERS

A DIVISION OF G. K. HALL & CO., BOSTON

Copyright © 1977 by G. K. Hall & Co.

All Rights Reserved

First Printing

Library of Congress Cataloging in Publication Data

Smith, Raymond J.
    Charles Churchill.

    (Twayne's English authors series ; TEAS 197)
    Bibliography: pp. 149-51
    Includes index.
    1. Churchill, Charles, 1731-1764 — Criticism and
interpretation.
PR3346.C8S55   821'.6   76-42988
ISBN 0-8057-6669-3

MANUFACTURED IN THE UNITED STATES OF AMERICA

For my wife, Joyce

Contents

About the Author

Raymond J. Smith is Professor of English at the University of Windsor in Windsor, Ontario, where he teaches courses in Restoration and eighteenth century English literature, modern and contemporary poetry, and Shakespeare. In addition to teaching, he edits *The Ontario Review: a North American Journal of the Arts*. Recipient of B.A., M.A., and Ph.D. degrees from the University of Wisconsin, he has published essays on Jonathan Swift, Henry Fielding, Samuel Taylor Coleridge, James Dickey, and Howard Nemerov. His essays and reviews have appeared in *The Southern Review, The Bucknell Review, Modern Poetry Studies, Literature and Psychology, The Ontario Review*, and other periodicals.

Preface

The twentieth century has witnessed a considerable effort to reestablish the literary reputation of Charles Churchill, whose fame as a verse satirist was unsurpassed during his brief career (1761-1764); and the most notable attempts occurred during the last twenty-five years which saw the publication of Wallace Cable Brown's critical biography (1953), Edward H. Weatherly's edition of Churchill's correspondence with John Wilkes (1954), Douglas Grant's edition of the poetry (1956), and Yvor Winters's provocative critical essays (1961, 1967).[1] These would-be rehabilitators have made some extravagant claims about Churchill. Brown, in a chapter entitled "The Heights of Parnassus," states that the "nature of Churchill's poetry places him in the great English tradition of neo-classic satire, and in that tradition, dominated by Dryden and Pope, Churchill is one of the major figures."[2] Winters claims that the "Dedication" to the *Sermons* is "the greatest English poem of the eighteenth century and one of the great poems in our language."[3]

Unconvinced, the academic establishment has been content, as if following the precedent of Samuel Johnson's *Lives of the English Poets*,[4] to let the works of this political satirist die from neglect. Significantly, while the Louis I. Bredvold anthology of eighteenth century English literature (1939, 1956) includes one of his poems (*The Prophecy of Famine*), the newer Geoffrey Tillotson anthology (1969) contains none.[5] Professor Tillotson has given the space that was once Churchill's to poets like Walter Titley, John Hoadly, and Sneyd Davies. Although Churchill may not be a "major figure" as Brown claims, he deserves more recognition than Tillotson gives him.

An attempt to describe, analyze, and evaluate the writings of Churchill, this study treats each of the major poems, together with his prose contributions to *The North Briton*, in terms of structure,

technique, and characteristic themes. While the poems are discussed individually, for the most part in the order in which they were first published,[6] each one is considered in the broader contexts of Churchill's times and his work as a whole. Chapter 1 discusses the writer and his age, with emphasis on Churchill's role as a political satirist; Chapter 2, his early, miscellaneous satire; Chapters 3 and 4, his political satire from *The North Briton* to *Gotham*; Chapter 5, his later, miscellaneous satire and posthumous verse; Chapter 6, his achievement and significance in terms of his development of the heroic couplet and his role as an eighteenth century political satirist.

Central to Churchill, both man and poet, is his refusal to conform which looks forward to the iconoclasm of the Romantic era rather than reflects the traditionalism of the neo-Classical period. Proud of the independence that success as a writer gave him, Churchill vigorously opposes tyranny in any form — the tyranny of the literary establishment *(The Apology)*, public opinion *(Night)*, superstition *(The Ghost)*, government *(The Conference, Gotham, Independence)*, and privilege *(The Times, The Farewell)*. At his worst, Churchill was reckless and self-indulgent in both his personal life and his writing; at his best he was a witty and daring critic of his country's political establishment.

This study would not have been possible without the scholarship that has gone before it, most notably the work of Professors Brown, Weatherly, and especially Grant, whose notes to Churchill's poems I have relied upon extensively. Particular debts are also owed to the Clarendon Press, Oxford, for permission to quote from *The Poetical Works of Charles Churchill*, edited by Douglas Grant; and to Columbia University Press for permission to quote from Edward H. Weatherly's edition of *The Correspondence of John Wilkes and Charles Churchill*. I would also like to thank the librarians at the University of Windsor, University of Michigan, and Huntington libraries. Finally, this book owes much to my wife, Joyce, whose patience, encouragement, and criticism helped greatly in bringing it into existence.

RAYMOND J. SMITH

Windsor, Ontario

Chronology

1731/2 Charles Churchill born during February in Vine Street, Westminster; oldest living son of the Reverend Mr. Charles Churchill, curate and lecturer of St. John the Evangelist in Westminster and vicar of Rainham in Essex.

1741- Attended Westminster School.
1748

1745 Designated Captain of King's Scholars at Westminster.

1748 Admission to and abrupt withdrawal from St. John's College, Cambridge.

1749(?) Marriage to Martha Scott. Resided at his father's house in Westminster.

1751 Moved to Sunderland, where he prepared for the priesthood.

1754 Ordained deacon and licensed to serve cures of South Cadbury and Sparkford in Somerset.

1756 Ordained priest; appointed curate to his father at Rainham.

1758 Death of father, whom he succeeded as curate and lecturer at St. John the Evangelist.

1760(?) Saved from debtor's prison by Dr. Pierson Lloyd, father of Robert.

1761(?) Separation from his wife.

1761 Publication of *The Rosciad* (March), *The Apology* (May), and *Night* (November).

1762- Edited *The North Briton* with John Wilkes.
1763

1762 Publication of *The Ghost*, I and II (March), III (October).

1763 Resignation from St. John the Evangelist. Elopement with Elizabeth Carr. Publication of *The Prophecy of Famine* (January), *An Epistle to William Hogarth* (June), *The*

Ghost, IV and *The Conference* (November), and *The Author* (December). Publication of first volume of collected poetry.

1764   Publication of *The Duellist* (January), *Gotham, I-II* (February-March), *The Candidate* (May), *The Farewell* (June), *Gotham, III* (August), *The Times* (September), and *Independence* (October). Died in Boulogne of a miliary fever, November 4; buried in Dover.

1765   Posthumous publication of the *Sermons* with the "Dedication" to William Warburton (February) and of *The Journey* (April). Publication of the second volume of collected poems (April).

CHAPTER 1

Life and Times

Astriking portrait of Charles Churchill is provided by his contemporary William Hogarth's engraving "The Bruiser,"[1] a caricature depicting the satirist as a bear wearing tattered clerical bands. The left paw of this "Russian Hercules" grips a club; the right, a tankard of foaming ale. The tattered bands represent Churchill's role as an Anglican priest, which he abandoned soon after he had achieved economic independence with the spectacular success of his poetry. The tankard of ale suggests Churchill's unpriestly lifestyle. The poet was an avowed hedonist, whose gravestone was appropriately inscribed with the following line from his poem *The Candidate:* "Life to the last enjoy'd, *here* Churchill lies."[2]

That Hogarth, in his engraving, armed the satirist with a club seems appropriate when we consider that the portrait was the artist's revenge against Churchill for his poem *An Epistle to William Hogarth*, which was blunt enough to hold up to ridicule the infirmities of the aging Hogarth.[3] A mutual friend, David Garrick, perhaps a bit dramatically, referred to the *Epistle* as the "most bloody performance that has been publish'd in my time."[4] The club, then, can be seen as representing a certain bluntness in Churchill's approach — a bluntness that is underlined by his style, which is vigorous and often careless. To him, in *The Apology*, the polish of an Alexander Pope elicited boredom: "E'en excellence, unvary'd, tedious grows" (369); and he prided himself upon "Th' gen'rous roughness of a nervous line" (355). So far was his verse from unvaried excellence, he announced in *The Ghost*, that his "measure flows / In halting rhime, half verse, half prose" (II, 247-48).

As for the bear in Hogarth's engraving, it suggests such things as physical bulk, vitality, and audacity. Physically, Churchill was a big, unshapely man. With Hogarth's caricature probably in mind, he

13

referred to himself in *Independence* as an unlicked bear: "A *Bear,* whom from the moment he was born, / His Dam despis'd, and left *unlick'd* in scorn" (149-50).[5] As for his size:

> Vast were his Bones, his Muscles twisted strong,
> His Face was short, but broader than 'twas long,
> His Features, tho' by Nature they were large,
> Contentment had contriv'd to overcharge
> And bury meaning, save that we might spy
> Sense low'ring on the penthouse of his eye;
> His Arms were two twin Oaks, his Legs so stout
> That they might bear a Mansion House about. (157-64)

Churchill's energy was in direct proportion to his size. He was so prolific that, in the last year of his brief career, he published a long poem (or section of a poem) almost every month. These ranged in length from *The Conference* (392 lines) to *The Duellist* (1016 lines). Mockingly, he spoke of his astonishing creative energy in terms of a compulsion, writing in *The Journey* near the end of his life: "In Verse I talk by day, I dream by night; / If now and then I curse, my curses chime, / Nor can I pray, unless I pray in rime" (50-52).

"The Bruiser's" audacity is evident when one glances at a list of his satiric victims. It includes, in the realm of letters, no less a personage than Samuel Johnson, who left himself open to ridicule by assisting in the investigation of the Cock Lane Ghost.[6] In the area of politics, Churchill swung his club at such dignitaries as the chief justice, the prime minister, and even, less directly, the king when he felt that they were acting in a way detrimental to English liberty. On the eve of the formal outlawing of his friend the political activist John Wilkes, he published a virtual taunt to the administration, challenging it to do its worst. "Why let her come," he boasts,

> in all her terrors too;
> I dare to suffer all She dares to do.
> . . . .
> This melting mass of flesh She may controul
> With iron ribs, She cannot chain my Soul.
> No — to the last resolv'd her worst to bear,
> I'm still at large, and *Independent* there.
>   (*Independence*, 527-34)

The fierce independence evident in these lines is central to Churchill, both poet and man.

I *From Priest to Poet*

Although knowledge of Churchill's earlier years is limited, the facts that are available do provide a sort of profile that suggests the character which later emerges from his poems and letters. It is a picture of thwarted talent and of a potentially independent, even licentious, youth held in the bondage of economic misfortune. One can assume that Churchill inherited a high degree of literacy, as well as a relatively low social-economic status, as the son of a Westminster cleric who served as curate and lecturer of St. John the Evangelist in Westminster and as vicar of Rainham in Essex. The young Churchill's record as a schoolboy gives some evidence of his intellectual capabilities. At Westminster School, where he had been enrolled in 1741, he won first place in the competition for the highly prized distinction of King's Scholar in his fifth year. He completed his preparatory schooling successfully in 1748 and was admitted on a Westminster scholarship to St. John's College, Cambridge.

Churchill's first rebellion, and an ill-advised one, was his clandestine, "Fleet" marriage[7] to his childhood sweetheart, Martha Scott. The marriage was probably responsible for ending his academic career, even though it may have been contracted some months after his abrupt withdrawal from St. John's College shortly after his admission.[8] It also circumscribed his social and cultural life when, after living with his father for a few years, Churchill and his wife retreated to Sunderland, a small seaport in Northeast England. Here he stoically prepared for the priesthood, about the only career open to a young man of his background. Many years later Churchill expressed rather negative feelings toward the clerical life in a passage that defended his recent resignation from that life. Picturing his career in the church as a form of enslavement, he wrote:

> Bred to the Church, and for the gown decreed,
> 'Ere it was known that I should learn to read;
> . . . .
> Condemn'd (whilst proud, and pamper'd Sons of Lawn,
> Cramm'd to the throat, in lazy plenty yawn)
> In pomp of *rev'rend begg'ry* to appear,
> To pray, and starve on forty pounds a year . . .[9]
> (*The Author*, 341-52)

Whatever may have been his misgivings, Churchill persevered in his studies and, in 1754, was ordained deacon and licensed to serve

the cures of South Cadbury and Sparkford in Somersetshire in Southwest England. Two years later, he was ordained priest and became curate to his father at Rainham. Upon the death of the elder Churchill in 1758, his son succeeded him as curate and lecturer of St. John the Evangelist, a move that brought him back to the vicinity of London. During these early years of his ministry, his three children were born.[10]

Although Churchill was probably writing poetry since his school days, he apparently did so without any real determination until about his twenty-eighth year when his motivation for writing became stronger. He was no doubt influenced by the examples of two of his friends since Westminster days, Robert Lloyd and George Colman. Like Churchill, both men had earlier made a certain commitment to one of the more conventional professions — Lloyd, to teaching; Colman, to law. Recently, Lloyd had abandoned a teaching position at Westminster to become a freelance writer. By 1760, he had gained a degree of success with the publication of his verse essay *The Actor;* and the same year saw the successful production of Colman's one act play *Polly Honeycombe.*

More important, however, was Churchill's growing indebtedness which obliged him to look for other ways to supplement his income from his clerical offices. Since 1756, he had attempted to do this by teaching, first in his own school for boys at Rainham and later at an exclusive girls school in London. But this extra income was not enough. By about 1760, he found himself on the threshold of debtor's prison ("My Credit at last gasp, my State undone, / Trembling to meet the shock I could not shun" [*The Conference,* 109-10]), where he was relieved by Dr. Pierson Lloyd, his friend Robert's father. During these days, Churchill must have decided to seek his fortune in poetry. Later he was to write, in *An Epistle to William Hogarth,* of the time when poverty had compelled him to "trade in rime" (89-90).

Churchill's early attempts at publication met with failure. According to his first editor, William Tooke, a poem called "The Bard" was rejected by the booksellers as poorly written; another, "The Conclave," was thought to be too libelous.[11] Focussing next on the London theatrical world, with which he had become quite familiar since his return to Westminster, Churchill wrote *The Rosciad.* Similar to Lloyd's poem in its general subject, acting, *The Rosciad* was quite topical and, hence, potentially more popular.

When the booksellers refused him the twenty pounds that he had

asked for the poem, Churchill decided to have it published at his own expense. *The Rosciad,* an immediate success, earned him over 750 pounds. He became as famous in the London literary world as another unknown clergyman, Laurence Sterne, had become a year before upon the publication of the first two volumes of *Tristram Shandy.* The Monthly Review, somewhat sardonically, was to suggest that "the present age may, perhaps, be as much distinguished for its merry Parsons, as the reign of Charles II. was for a set of waggish and witty Courtiers."[12]

With the success of *The Rosciad,* Churchill achieved a degree of economic independence. Freedom of another sort had been gained probably earlier that year when he had separated from his wife. Accounts of this incident are many and contradictory. One passed on by Horace Walpole says that Churchill and his wife were "tired of each other" and that "she went housekeeper to an officer and became his mistress."[13] Churchill furthered his cherished independence a few years later when he resigned from St. John the Evangelist, for he was no longer able to reconcile his old role as priest with his new one as libertine poet.

Even before Churchill's resignation from St. John's, he must have been devoting a good deal of his time to those two pursuits of his later years, poetry and pleasure. That he was writing fairly steadily is testified by the fact that he published two more major poems before the end of the year. Within two months, *The Apology* had appeared. Addressed to the "Critical Reviewers," the poem ridiculed the novelist Tobias Smollett and the dramatist Arthur Murphy, one of whom Churchill was convinced had written the article in *The Critical Review* that attributed the unsigned *Rosciad* to several of the poet's more renowned friends, Lloyd, Colman, and Bonnell Thornton. *The Apology* was followed later in the same year by *Night,* in which Churchill developed the theme of nonconformity. In the following March, he published Books I and II of *The Ghost,* which capitalized on the much-publicized Cock Lane Ghost incident.

In the four years of Churchill's brief career as a professional writer, he, in addition to his duties as co-editor of *The North Briton,* published thousands of lines of verse. At the same time, he did not let his writing interfere substantially with his hedonistic pursuits. His avowed aim was "To live as merry as I can" (*The Ghost,* IV, 268); and the merry life, for Churchill, included dining with the Sublime Society of Beefsteaks, one of the famous eating clubs of the

time. Boswell's *London Journal* affords the following glimpse: "We were entertained by the Club. Lord Sandwich was in a chair, a jolly, hearty, lively man. It was a very mixed society: Lord Eglinton, Mr. Beard, Colonel West of the Guards, Mr. Havard the actor, Mr. Churchill the poet, Mr. Wilkes the author of *The North Briton*, and many more. We had nothing to eat but beefsteaks, and had wine and punch in plenty and freedom. We had a number of songs."[14] A less reputable club visited by Churchill and Wilkes was the Hell Fire Club, which met at the rebuilt Medmenham Abbey, where the members dressed as monks were joined by London prostitutes garbed as nuns.[15]

Churchill's correspondence with Wilkes is spiced with references to their various mistresses. In one instance, Churchill ironically speaks of a new affair in terms of physical discipline. "When we meet . . . you will be amazed to see how I am alter'd. Breakfast at nine — two dishes of tea and one thin slice of bread and butter — Dine at three — eat moderately — drink a sober pint — Tumble the bed till four — Tea at six — walk till nine — Eat some cooling fruit and to bed. There is regularity for you —"[16]

The most notorious of Churchill's affairs was his elopement, in the autumn of 1763, with a young Westminster girl, Elizabeth Carr. Naturally, the elopement created quite a stir. Wilkes advised Churchill that the girl's "family are in the greatest distress, and you are universally condemn'd for having made a worthy family unhappy." So great was the Carr family's distress that Churchill's life seems to have been in danger. "I fear not for your person," Wilkes wrote, "tho' I hear many schemes against your life, if you persevere — The father, brother, and a servant, went with pistols charg'd, to Kensington Gardens, in consequence of an anonymous letter, to have assassinated you —"[17] Churchill's reply to Wilkes is characteristically audacious and a sharp statement of his libertine values. "Assassination — a pretty word, fit for boys to use, and men to laugh at — I never yet play'd for so deep a stake, But if call'd on think I dare set my life on a cast, as that rash Young Man her Brother shall find if he puts me to the proof. My Life I hold for purposes of pleasure; those forbid, it is not worth my care."[18] Churchill, apparently, was not put to the proof. As for Miss Carr, she seems to have returned to her family only to leave them again, in a short time, for her lover. It was at this time that Churchill published *The Conference*, which has generally been read as a public apology for the affair.

Churchill's sexual licentiousness had already resulted in venereal disease,[19] which may have helped to weaken his constitution to the point that he was unable to recover from a miliary fever, contracted in France, where he was paying a visit to the fugitive Wilkes. On November 4, 1764, death cut short Churchill's promising career as a poet.

II *Wilkes and Liberty*

Churchill's brief literary career coincides with the early years of the reign of George III, who ascended the British throne in 1760. The idealistic young king wished to weaken the hold of the long-established Whig oligarchy and to institute a government centered upon king and an impartial ministry. To further his aims, he employed his former tutor, the earl of Bute, whom he gradually advanced in his service until he became his chief minister in 1762. Bute was generally unpopular, not only because he was a favorite of the king but because he had been born in Scotland. Although the Act of Union between England and Scotland had been ratified more than a half century earlier, in 1707, there was still a great deal of rivalry and hostility between North and South Britons. The English associated Scots with the Stuart Pretenders and their unsuccessful attempts to recapture the crown in 1715 and 1745. The Rebellion of 1745 was still fresh in the minds of many Englishmen. The English were also disturbed by another, non-military invasion from across the River Tweed — the steady migration of highly capable Scots into England, where they were achieving high positions in almost all walks of life. The best example was Bute himself, who at this time held the highest political position in the land as the king's first minister.

One of the jobs of Bute's ministry was to end the costly Seven Years' War with France and her allies, even if peace demanded a few concessions to the French. To support Bute and the unpopular peace negotiations, which culminated in the Peace of Paris in February 1763, the administration fostered two periodicals, *The Briton* and *The Auditor*. The former was edited by Smollett; the latter by Murphy. The administration was opposed by Arthur Beardmore's *The Monitor* and by *The North Briton*, edited by Wilkes and Churchill. Churchill had already come to blows with Smollett and Murphy over literary matters; but his association with Wilkes in the editing of *The North Briton* turned their aquaintanceship into a much stronger bond. Wilkes, recovering in France from a wound

received in his duel with Samuel Martin, one of the joint secretaries to the treasury, testified to the quality of that friendship when writing to Churchill in the spring of 1764: "My spirits are as usual, and I believe they will never fail, while I have so noble a cause in view, and so noble a poet to immortalize my actions, and to tell posterity, that, superior to the mean, selfish views of others, and their little passions, we were ever constant and warm friends. I have often reflected with pleasure, that I cannot recollect a single clouded day between us."[20] More important to this study than their friendship is the new, political direction that Churchill's satire took as a result of his association with Wilkes. Churchill's first political satire in verse was *The Prophecy of Famine*, which predicts a Scottish takeover of England under Bute. Published in January 1763, it grew from notes for a *North Briton* essay.[21]

The Peace of Paris had been concluded and the harassed Bute had resigned by the spring of 1763, when what was to be the last issue of *The North Briton*, the notorious Number 45, was published. Written by Wilkes, the essay was an insulting attack against the king's speech in April 1763 at the closing of Parliament. The administration, headed now by the "triumvirate" — George Grenville, the earl of Halifax, and the earl of Egremont — felt that it was necessary to silence Wilkes, and, in attempting to do so, it helped transform him into a popular hero as the defender of individual rights against the oppressions of government.[22] Churchill's self-imposed task was to expose the maneuvers of the administration and to evoke popular support for "Wilkes and Liberty."

The administration arrested Wilkes, as well as numerous others, on a general warrant against those responsible for the "seditious and treasonable" *North Briton* 45. During the subsequent examination of Wilkes, Hogarth drew a caricature of the defendant, which he immediately published. Churchill came to the aid of his friend by punishing Hogarth in *An Epistle to William Hogarth* (June 1763), which earned for the satirist the title of "The Bruiser"; but little defense was actually needed by Wilkes, who was able to plead immunity from arrest as a member of Parliament. He then sued for illegal arrest and seizure of his papers Halifax, who had issued the warrant as joint secretary of state, and Robert Wood, undersecretary of state, and eventually won a total of five thousand pounds.[23] Churchill looked upon Wilkes's legal action against Halifax and Wood as a significant measure in the struggle with tyranny.

This attitude, as well as Churchill's great admiration for Wilkes, is

evident in his letter of September 1, 1763, in which he presents arguments for and against his friend's acceptance of a challenge to duel: "Your Country Demands your Life; the Cause of Liberty is in your hands; and that blessing, so much dearer than Life, must remain precarious if not fix'd by you. No one can try the Secretaries of State if you do not, and tho' there is no doubt but there may be arbitrary ministers in future times, yet it is with me a question whether there may ever be another Wilkes."[24]

Not content to remain silent, Wilkes continued his attack against the administration by privately republishing the collected *North Briton* articles. His enemies responded when Parliament reassembled on November 15, for the House of Commons voted that *North Briton* 45 was a "seditious libel," and the House of Lords attacked Wilkes for a rather loosely related offense — printing an obscene poem called *An Essay on Women.*[25] Leading the attack in the upper house, ironically enough, was the notoriously libertine earl of Sandwich, who was seconded by the bishop of Gloucester, William Warburton, to whom the mock footnotes to the poem had been attributed. The peers found *An Essay on Women* "obscene" and "blasphemous," as well as a breach of parliamentary privilege against the bishop. Churchill reacted, as he had with Hogarth, by making Sandwich and Warburton each the subject of a satirical poem. *The Candidate,* published in May 1764, focusses on the hypocritical earl; the "Dedication" to the *Sermons,* published posthumously in February 1765, on the bishop.

During debate in the House of Commons, Samuel Martin deliberately insulted Wilkes, virtually ensuring a challenge to duel. Wilkes obliged; and, in the exchange that followed, Martin seriously wounded him. Churchill set about writing *The Duellist,* published in January 1764, to support the opinion that the duel was an attempt by the administration to assassinate Wilkes. The fact that Martin was known to have intended to make the challenge and to have been practicing marksmanship months before gave this interpretation some credibility.

The administration continued its action against Wilkes in the Court of the King's Bench before the chief justice, the earl of Mansfield. Churchill had earlier, in November 1763, attempted to arouse public opinion against Mansfield in Book IV of *The Ghost* by associating him with the rebellious Stuarts and by accusing him of injustice. Wilkes, nevertheless, was found guilty of reprinting *North Briton* 45 and of publishing *An Essay on Women* on February 21,

1764. Nine months later, he was formally outlawed upon his failure to appear for sentencing.[26] Wilkes, at this time, was nursing his friend Churchill, who had just come down with a miliary fever in Boulogne.

Churchill's sudden death was a blow from which Wilkes did not soon recover. Several months afterward, we find him expressing his sense of loss to Boswell in a letter that pays tribute to Churchill as a great patriot:

You touch . . . a string which sounds most harsh and discordant to my ear, the death of poor Churchill. I endeavour by every way I can devise to divert my mind from the gloomy idea of so irreparable a loss. . . . I will say no more on this head, but in the words of Tully, "We have lost an excellent patriot and a great man, a man whose magnanimity was tempered by politeness. There is, however, one comfort left us, though a melancholy one, which should alleviate our grief at his death; I think that some favourable providence of the gods rescued a patriot like him from the conflagration of his country."[27]

Early, Miscellaneous Satire: Poetry of 1761-1762

IN *Night,* Churchill has the earl of Bute instruct his pupil, the future king George III: "Outward be fair, however foul within; / Sin if thou wilt, but then in secret sin" (313-14). This attribution of hypocrisy to the king and his favorite is only incidental. *Night,* like Churchill's other early, miscellaneous satire, while showing an awareness of political concerns and an antagonism toward the administration based chiefly on current Whiggish prejudices, focusses on an extra political concern of the poet, social nonconformity. Similarly, *The Rosciad,* in the course of boldly meting out praise and blame to the better-known actors and actresses of mid-eighteenth century London, only glances at the "foreign" origin of the Scotsman Bute (205).

While political satire in Churchill's poems of 1761-1762 is incidental, these poems embody in varying degrees of development some themes that inform his later, more serious works. One, exemplified in the lines from *Night* quoted above, is the eighteenth century concern with the discrepancy between appearance and essence. Actors and ghosts are both rather playful realizations of this theme which he later treated more seriously in the exposure of John Wilkes's hypocritical political enemies. Churchill's opposition to tyranny, his chief political theme, is also reflected in his early poems in which the objects of his attacks range from the tyranny of critics to that of public opinion.

These early satires anticipate Churchill's later works in other ways. Most obviously, they are shaped by the neo-Classical tradition of verse satire. The poems tend to be topical, occasional, and public. Formally, *The Rosciad* is notable for its mock-epic characteristics, *The Apology* and *Night* are modelled after the loosely organized verse epistle, and *The Ghost* returns to the mock-epic mode. As for versification, Churchill shows a preference for the heroic couplet of

John Dryden and Alexander Pope, but he chooses for *The Ghost* the octosyllabic couplet of Samuel Butler and Jonathan Swift.[1] The neo-Classical age is also noted for its mastery of irony, which Churchill, who later utilizes it effectively in his ironic eulogies, uses only occasionally in these earlier works.

I   A Mirror for the Players

One of Churchill's chief nonpolitical interests was theater, which he turned to for the subject of his first published poem, *The Rosciad.* As a King's Scholar, he had probably participated in the annual Latin play at Westminster School.[2] His return to Westminster in 1758 as curate of St. John's gave him access to the London theater, which had already gained the devotion of his friends Lloyd and Colman. The actor Thomas Davies, thought to have been forced from the stage by *The Rosciad,*[3] reported that Churchill frequented the Drury Lane Theatre regularly in preparation for his satire against the players: "His observatory was generally the first row of the pit, next to the orchestra. In this place he thought he could best discern the real workings of the passions in the actors, or what they substituted in the place of them."[4]

Churchill's observations were keen, and he recorded them with precision and wit. Published on March 14, 1761, *The Rosciad* gained immediate fame; and it all but panicked the London theatrical world. Writing of the reception of the poem, Davies notes that "the players spread its fame all over the town; they ran about like so many stricken deer; they strove to extract the arrow from the wound by communicating the knowledge of it to their friends."[5] While the severity of Churchill's criticism was thus manifested, we have the testimony of another actor, Henry Woodward, satirized at fairly great length in the poem, as to its validity. Wilkes, who met the actor in Paris several years later, told Churchill that Woodward "talks in the highest terms of your skill in his business, and of the infinite desire he has to amend by the useful hints you are capable of giving him."[6]

As Churchill was to do often later, he chose to present his criticism of the prominent actors and actresses of his day in a fictional framework. Typically, he does not develop his fiction with the sort of imaginative verve that is evident in the best satire of the era, in works like Jonathan Swift's *Gulliver's Travels* and Pope's *The Rape of the Lock;* instead, his fables are rather strictly functional and often somewhat traditional. In *The Rosciad,* he employs the fiction

of succession, in the mock-epic vein, as did Dryden in *MacFlecknoe*. The poem opens with the actors and actresses, as well as the spectators, squabbling about who is to fill the vacant chair of the ancient Roman actor Roscius. After both contemporary writers and critics, as well as the ancients (in the person of Sophocles), are rejected, William Shakespeare and Ben Jonson are chosen as judges. As the contenders for the chair of Roscius file by the judges, Churchill comments sometimes favorably, more often unfavorably, upon each of them. His chief criterion is grace, "the striking elegance of Ease" (744). David Garrick is finally chosen to succeed Roscius, and the poem ends with Shakespeare's short speech in his praise.

The mock-epic nature of *The Rosciad*, signalled by the title, is evident in the presence of such traditional epic devices as the invocation and the extended simile. As Pope did in *The Rape of the Lock*, Churchill satirically aggrandizes a rather petty contention by the use of a military metaphor. Thus the famous actresses of the day are satirically inflated as Churchill describes them as a band of Amazons, while, at the same time, he keeps before the reader's eyes their unheroic stage roles:

> Next to the field a band of females draw
> Their force; for Britain owns no Salique Law:
> Just to their worth, we female rights admit,
> Nor bar their claim to empire or to wit.
> First, giggling, plotting chamber-maids arrive,
> Hoydens and romps, led on by Gen'ral CLIVE.   (681-86)

The fable itself is most essential to the mock-epic nature of Churchill's poem. It allows him to treat with ceremony the petty rivalries between actors, managers, theaters, and even between the sexes by calling down the great Shakespeare and Jonson to rub shoulders with contemporary would-bes and by dignifying the striving after fame with all the pomp attendant upon the succession of a new sovereign.

The appropriateness of Churchill's choice of the mock-epic for his criticism becomes questionable when we recall that many of his portraits, including those of most of the actresses who are mockingly introduced as a band of Amazons, are positive ones. Chief among the positive portraits, of course, is Garrick's; for Churchill did not wish to deflate Roscius and his heir to another Richard Flecknoe and Thomas Shadwell.[7] Yet, when we consider that actors, good or bad,

are only players, the mock-epic becomes appropriate for even Garrick. The aggrandizement of the mock-epic may be seen as underscoring the discrepancy between appearance and essence inherent in the acting profession. This contrast, which is elaborated in Churchill's *The Apology*,[8] is suggested in *The Rosciad* by the following lines:

> Behind a group of figures awe create,
> Set off with all th' impertinence of state;
> By lace and feather consecrate to fame
> Expletive kings, and queens without a name. (311-14)

If awe can be created with lace and feather, an unassuming exterior may prejudice the consideration of merit. For example, physical coarseness may blind the spectators to the extraordinary acting ability of a Hannah Pritchard, or a lack of physical stature may affect the judgment of the real talent of a David Garrick. Churchill would have it that talent eventually triumphs:

> Figure, I own, at first may give offence,
> And harshly strike the eye's too curious sense:
> But when perfections of the mind break forth,
> Humour's chaste sallies, Judgment's solid worth;
> When the pure genuine flame, by Nature taught,
> Springs into Sense, and ev'ry action's Thought;
> Before such merit all objections fly;
> PRITCHARD's genteel, and GARRICK six feet high. (845-52)

The deception of appearances is underscored early in the poem when Churchill comments about personified Order which leads the procession of actors and actresses. Order's "only care" is to save appearances, he explains; "So things seem right, no matter what they are" (299-300).

In addition to the appearance-reality theme, Churchill deals with two other, related dichotomies that were of special interest to the neo-Classical mind: ancients versus moderns and art versus nature. The eighteenth century debate as to whether the writers of Classical antiquity were superior to those who came after them, a debate most memorably expressed in Swift's *The Battle of the Books*, emerges briefly in *The Rosciad* in connection with the selection of judges. Included in this debate was the question of respect for the so-called rules, criteria for composition derived from the practice of the Clas-

sical writers. Like most of the English neo-Classics, Churchill rejected any unquestioning acceptance of the rules; to him such acceptance was a form of servility. In *The Rosciad*, a "servile race" of "cold-blooded critics" declares that only Sophocles is fit to judge the cause. These critics are described as men "Who blind obedience pay to ancient schools, / Bigots to Greece, and slaves to musty rules" (185-86).

Opposed to the traditionalists is Churchill's friend Lloyd, whose position in the controversy is rather moderate:

> He talk'd of ancients, as the man became
> Who priz'd our own, but envied not their fame;
> With noble rev'rence spoke of Greece and Rome,
> And scorn'd to tear the laurel from the tomb.   (195-98)

When Lloyd, much like Neander in Dryden's *Essay of Dramatic Poesy*, recommends Shakespeare and Jonson as co-judges, he not only rejects blind homage to the ancients but his argument also reflects the nationalistic sentiment of many of the English neo-Classical critics: "They'll judge like Britons, who like Britons wrote" (226).

Much the same sentiments are expressed by Churchill in a short verse essay about criticism that was published in the same year as *The Rosciad*.[9] Addressed appropriately enough to Lloyd, the poem focusses upon the ancient-modern dispute, and Churchill again rejects slavish compliance to the rules and defends that favorite of the English neo-Classical critics, Shakespeare. At the same time, he argues for the irrelevance of both time and place to individual genius: "Born at what place or time you will, / Homer would have been Homer still" (75-76). The fact that he says this about Homer and not Shakespeare is revealing; this pose of objectivity cannot hide his basic nationalism.

While the ancient-modern controversy is the context for the choice of judges in *The Rosciad*, the art-nature dichotomy is the basis of Churchill's criticism of the players. He vigorously attacks artificiality in gesture, speech, and expression of emotion; and he scorns the actor Spranger Barry who "conn'd his passions, as he conn'd his part" (920). In the role of Hamlet, Barry registers fear at the ghost's approach with ludicrous artificiality:

> Some dozen lines before the ghost is there,
> Behold him for the solemn scene prepare.

> See how he frames his eyes, poises each limb,
> Puts the whole body into proper trim, —
> From whence we learn, with no great stretch of art,
> Five lines hence comes a ghost, and, Ha! a start.   (907-12)

Criticizing the older, more formal, declamatory style of delivery, Churchill ridicules the Shakespearean actor James Quin, who had won his fame earlier in the century:

> His words bore sterling weight, nervous and strong;
> In manly tides of sense they roll'd along.
> Happy in art, he chiefly had pretence
> To keep up numbers, yet not forfeit sense,
> No actor ever greater heights could reach
> In all the labour'd artifice of speech.
> Speech! Is that all? — And shall an actor found
> An universal fame on partial ground?
> Parrots themselves speak properly by rote,
> And, in six months, my dog shall howl by note.   (945-54)

To the artificiality of Quin, Churchill opposes the more natural manner of Garrick, whom he particularly praises for his ability to experience and to express emotion. In Garrick, "Nature [is] link'd with Art" (1081). Churchill's choice of Shakespeare and Jonson as co-judges now takes on an added significance; for, if we recall the well-worn neo-Classical distinction between Shakespeare as the "natural genius" and Jonson as the "learned genius," we see that Churchill is using the two as representatives of the nature and art so happily united in Garrick.

During the two years following the publication of *The Rosciad,* Churchill gradually added to the poem until, in its eighth edition, it was half again its original length.[10] As a result, the poem as we know it today is, in the words of a recent critic, "structurally a hodgepodge."[11] Those additions pertinent to Churchill's central purpose — a critique of the London stage — are no problem. Among them are some new critical portraits of hitherto excluded actors and actresses and, more significant, a sharp defense of the poet's right to attack the players, many of whom were outraged by his violation of their "prescriptive rights" (499). Defending his freedom of speech in the second edition of the poem, published within a few months after the first, he writes:

> What! shall opinion then, of nature free
> And lib'ral as the vagrant air, agree
> To rust in chains like these, impos'd by Things
> Which, less than nothing, ape the pride of kings?
> No, — though half-poets with half-players join
> To curse the freedom of each honest line;
> Though rage and malice dim their fad'd cheek,
> What the muse freely thinks, she'll freely speak. (501-08)

The theme here, as well as the harsher sytle, anticipates Churchill's later satire in which he recklessly comes to the defense of Wilkes, whose freedom to publish what he wished was being challenged by the political establishment.

As *The Rosciad* grew in length and price, Churchill found it a convenient means of holding up to public ridicule the men who had the misfortune of becoming either his enemies or those of his friends. Thus several of the long additions in the later versions of the poem tend to be careless of Churchill's central purpose.[12] Two of these further the satirist's revenge against Arthur Murphy, first a literary and then a political enemy. When Churchill ridicules Murphy's theatrical ambitions, we obviously have no objection; but such is not the case when he extends his portrait to include Murphy's abortive legal and business careers. More obviously out of place is the lengthy portrait of Thomas Fitzpatrick, the critic who culminated his quarrel with Garrick by leading the "half-price" riots (Garrick tried to abolish the custom of admitting people for half-price after the third act) against the Drury Lane Theatre. Perhaps the characteristic that disturbed Churchill the most about Fitzpatrick was his effeminacy, and this revulsion comes as no surprise in a man who has devoted an entire poem (*The Times*) to chastize what he felt to be the widespread homosexuality of his era. At any rate, this quality in Fitzpatrick, not his critical ability, is the focus of Churchill's attack — a focus that recalls Pope's attack against Lord Hervey as "Sporus" in *An Epistle to Dr. Arbuthnot*.

Any discussion of *The Rosciad*, finally, should not ignore its topicality, a quality that characterizes in varying degrees all of Churchill's verse. *The Rosciad* is studded with allusions to players, dramatists, theater managers — contemporaries of Churchill who, if known at all, are known only to the specialist today. If Wilkes complained about the obscurity in his friend's recent poems after being away from London for eight months, what might be our complaint

after two centuries?[13] Identification of each of the proper names in
The Rosciad, however, is not essential to our enjoyment of the poem.
In this regard, we would do well to recall Pope's comment on the
topical allusions in *The Dunciad:* "I would not have the reader too
much troubled or anxious if he cannot decypher them [the names] in
the poem; since when he shall have found them out, he will
probably know no more of the Persons than before."[14]

II   *A Reply to the Critics*

The first edition of *The Rosciad* was unsigned. Churchill may
have understood that the name of an unknown author affixed to the
poem would likely have prejudiced it for the critics. Unsigned, the
poem, if it had any merit at all, could be praised as the work of an
established and currently popular writer who had chosen to remain
anonymous because of his love of mystification, his fear of reprisal,
or both. Because of such anonymity, *The Critical Review* cannot be
blamed for failing to attribute *The Rosciad* to the unknown Churchill;
but the reviewer was a bit overly confident about his ability to distinguish style and to affirm that it was the work, "jointly or
separately," of Churchill's more renowned friends Lloyd, Colman,
and Thornton. "It is *natural* . . . for them [young authors] to
imagine," boasted the reviewer, "that they may conceal themselves
by appearing in different shapes, and that they are not to be found
out by their stile; but little do these *Connoisseurs* in writing conceive, how easily they are discovered by a veteran in the service."[15]
This critical overconfidence gave Churchill the impetus for *The
Apology,* which was published two months after *The Rosciad,* in
May 1761.

Addressed to the "Critical Reviewers," *The Apology* focusses
upon critics in the first of its three major parts before going on to actors and, finally, the satirist himself. The Critical Reviewers emerge
in Churchill's satire as jealous, established authors and tyrannical
critics; Churchill scorns both the anonymity and presumption of
these "vet'ren critics" who "publish ev'ry name — except their
own" (125). The general attack against critics leads to specific as-
saults against Smollett and Murphy, one or the other of whom
Churchill suspected had written the review of *The Rosciad.*[16] The
second part of the poem, while defending Churchill's choice of actors as a topic for satire ("All Common Exhibitions open lye / For
Praise or Censure to the Common Eye" [188-89]), continues *The
Rosciad's* attack against them; but it does so in general terms

without mention of specific names. The actual apology, or defense, comes in the third part of the poem in which Churchill defends both the style of his verse and, curiously enough, his right as a clergyman to deal in poetry in the first place.

Probably the most significant aspect of Churchill's attack against the Critical Reviewers is that it presents a picture of the individual writer as pitted against the literary establishment that is represented by one of the influential critical magazines of the time. Employing a political metaphor, he depicts himself as a "novice in the rhiming trade" who is invading with "lawless pen the realms of verse" (35-36). The metaphor continues with members of the literary establishment appearing as usurpers who possess absolute power and do not tolerate dissent. Rhetorically, Churchill asks:

> How could these self-elected monarchs raise
> So large an empire on so small a base?
> In what retreat, inglorious and unknown,
> Did Genius sleep when Dullness seiz'd the throne?
> Whence, absolute now grown, and free from awe,
> She to the subject world dispenses law.
> . . . .
> Who shall dispute what the Reviewers say?
> Their word's sufficient; and to ask a reason,
> In such a state as their's, is downright treason.   (83-96)

Churchill's satire of the Critical Reviewers shifts from a direct general attack to an ironic, specific approach, when he turns to the editor of *The Critical Review*, Smollett. The attack begins in the mock-panegyric vein which Churchill was to use with increasing effectiveness in later poems:

> Oft hath my tongue been wanton at thy name,
> And hail'd the honours of thy matchless fame.
> For me let hoary FIELDING bite the ground
> So nobler PICKLE stand superbly bound.
> From LIVY's temples tear th' historic crown
> Which with more justice blooms upon thine own.
> Compar'd with thee, be all life-writers dumb,
> But he who wrote the Life of TOMMY THUMB.   (148-55)

Churchill is alluding here to the rivalry between Smollett and his fellow-novelist Henry Fielding which resulted in the defeat of the

former's heroes (thinly disguised as "Peeragrin Puckle" and "Rodorick Random") by "a younger brother of General Thomas Jones" in a battle of the books written by Fielding a few years before his death.[17]

The ironic praise of Smollett, in itself a form of doubleness, becomes additionally complicated by another kind of ambiguity — the double meaning of particular words: "wanton," "fame," "hoary," "nobler," and "bound." "Wanton," meaning "excessive," usually has a negative connotation. The second line of the excerpt quoted, however, suggests a positive one — but only if "hail" and "fame" are given their usual positive connotations. In the second couplet, "hoary" is opposed to "nobler," and both words refer at once to appearance and essence. The hoary man is gray and/or venerable; the noble man is imposing in appearance and/or moral character. The amoral connotation of "noble" is reinforced by the surface meaning of "superbly bound," which refers to the material binding, or appearance, of Smollett's novel. On another level, the phrase alludes to the triumph of General Thomas Jones's brother in Fielding's mock battle. Thus, in the lines, "For me let hoary FIELDING bite the ground / So nobler PICKLE stand superbly bound," Churchill with a characteristic lack of delicacy *seems* to be praising Smollett at the expense of the deceased Fielding; but the diction employed suggests that the *real* meaning may not be on the surface, and it prepares the reader for the sudden reversal in the last couplet which suggests that Smollett's novels are second only to Fielding's farce *The Tragedy of Tragedies; or, the Life and Death of Tom Thumb the Great.*

A different kind of doubleness occurs in the second part of *The Apology,* where Churchill defends his satire of the players by attacking them for their unfounded arrogance. While Churchill only suggested the theatrical world's confusion of appearance and reality in *The Rosciad,*[18] he develops that topic more fully and in a skillful and interesting manner in *The Apology.* He begins his attack with a picture of the lowly strolling players, at this time still risking punishment as "Rogues and Vagabonds."[19] The noble roles often played by these people sharply contrast with their essential poverty:

> THE mighty monarch, in theatric sack,
> Carries his whole regalia at his back;
> His royal consort heads the female band,
> And leads the heir-apparent in her hand;
> The pannier'd ass creeps on with conscious pride,
> Bearing a future prince on either side.   (212-17)

The "pannier'd ass" which is creeping on with "conscious pride" seems to be a correlative of the burdened "monarch." Although Churchill derides strolling players, he does not consider them to be pernicious as long as they accept the limitations of their condition. Elaborating upon his picture of such players with the same skillful use of antithesis as in the above lines, he writes:

> In shabby state they strut, and tatter'd robe;
> The scene a blanket, and a barn the globe.
> No high conceits their mod'rate wishes raise,
> Content with humble profit, humble praise.
> Let dowdies simper, and let bumpkins stare,
> The strolling pageant heroe treads in air:
> Pleas'd for his hour he to mankind gives law,
> And snores the next out on a truss of straw. (236-43)

It is not, then, the strolling monarch who is content to rule for his hour that Churchill finds a proper subject for satire but the strolling player who, having become successful on the glamorous London stage, begins to confuse himself with his role. The object of Churchill's satire is the player who "scorns the dunghill where he first was bred" (249) and is "Taught by Mock Honours Real Pride t'assume" (253). Churchill finds the esthetic arrogance of the deluded players most annoying when they "Presume . . . / To rule in Letters and preside in Taste" (258-59), establishing themselves as sole "ARBITERS of Wit" (261).

Criticism of the players comes to a climax in the verse paragraph that attacks Garrick as a "Vain Tyrant" who is guarded by "puny GREEN-ROOM Wits and Venal Bards" who have sold their freedom for free admission to the theater (266-69). Churchill, who had lavishly praised Garrick himself several months earlier in *The Rosciad,* dissociates himself from these sycophants with a characteristic assertion of independence. Abruptly reducing the tyrant (whose aim as a player is to please) to a slave, he concludes the passage: "Ne'er will I flatter, cringe, or bend the knee / To those who, Slaves to ALL, are Slaves to ME" (274-75).

The sudden shift in Churchill's attitude toward Garrick is rather curious. At least part of the explanation seems to lie in that actor's reaction to *The Rosciad,* for Churchill's praise of the new Roscius virtually at the expense of most of the other players would certainly have placed Garrick in an uncomfortable position. If that position had forced Garrick to pretend disapproval of the poem, Churchill no doubt would have been informed of the ingratitude and acted

accordingly. At any rate, this explanation is one that Davies gives.[20] But whatever the cause, Garrick became the "Vain Tyrant" of *The Apology,* the actor who has forgotten his place. It is actors like him who have confused their roles with reality that the satirist, as the agent of truth, must disabuse:

> And, if o'er-weening of their little skill,
> When they have left the Stage they're Actors still;
> If to the subject world they still give laws,
> With paper crowns, and sceptres made of straws;
> If they in cellar or in garret roar,
> And Kings one night, are Kings for evermore;
> Shall not bold Truth, e'en there, pursue her theme,
> And wake the Coxcomb from his golden dream?   (278-85)

The deluded actor, blurring distinctions, becomes an apt subject for Churchill in his characteristically eighteenth century concern with the discrepancy between appearance and essence.

The third part of *The Apology* centers upon Churchill's defense of his versification, which he claims is modelled upon the vigorous lines of Dryden rather than upon the more polished verse of Pope. Calling to mind Pope's famous passage on sound echoing sense in *An Essay on Criticism,* Churchill attacks what he sees as the contemporary emphasis upon smoothness at the expense of vigor and sense:

> Verses must run, to charm a modern ear,
> From all harsh, rugged interruptions clear:
> Soft let them breathe, as Zephyr's balmy breeze;
> Smooth let their current flow as summer seas;
> Perfect then only deem'd when they dispense
> A happy tuneful vacancy of sense.   (340-45)

Condemning those who "mangle vigour for the sake of sound" (349), he describes his own verse in terms of the "gen'rous roughness of a nervous line" (355).

Churchill's characteristic iconoclasm appears to be submerged for the moment as he projects himself into the historical development of the neo-Classical heroic couplet. The seventeenth century English poet Edmund Waller is praised as the "Parent of harmony in English verse" who "In couplets first taught straggling sense to close" (363-65). Skipping from Waller to Pope, Churchill admits that the latter is unrivaled in "polish'd numbers" and "majestic sound" (366-67).

But Pope's verse lacks variety, and "E'en excellence, unvary'd, tedious grows" (369).[21] Thus, Churchill will return to Dryden for his inspiration:

> HERE let me bend, great DRYDEN, at thy shrine
> Thou dearest name to all the tuneful nine.
> What if some dull lines in cold order creep,
> And with his theme the poet seems to sleep?
> Still when his subject rises proud to view,
> With equal strength the poet rises too.
> With strong invention, noblest vigour fraught,
> Thought still springs up and rises out of thought;
> Numbers, ennobling numbers in their course,
> In varied sweetness flow, in varied force;
> The pow'rs of Genius and of Judgment join,
> And the Whole Art of Poetry is Thine.   (376-87)

Churchill's preference for Dryden's vigor over Pope's correctness anticipates by some twenty years Dr. Johnson's well-known comparison: "If the flights of Dryden . . . are higher, Pope continues longer on the wing. If of Dryden's fire the blaze is brighter, of Pope's the heat is more regular and constant. Dryden often surpasses expectation, and Pope never falls below it. Dryden is read with frequent astonishment, and Pope with perpetual delight."[22] Both Churchill and Johnson, while continuing the neo-Classical tradition of the heroic couplet, refuse to pay undue homage to Pope. In turning from Pope, they also turned away from Horace, who had been Pope's model, to Juvenal.[23]

The Apology ends on an even more personal note when Churchill defends not his verse style but his lifestyle. He already seems to be feeling the conflict of interests between his roles as priest and as poet that within two years he resolved by his resignation from his clerical duties. Somewhat querulously, he asks:

> What if a man delight to pass his time
> In spinning Reason into harmless Rhime;
> Or sometimes boldly venture to the Play?
> Say, Where's the Crime? . . .   (398-401)

Like the typical eighteenth century rationalist, he will determine his future course according to reason: "If REASON's for me, GOD is for me too" (421). While of interest biographically, the conclusion of

The Apology tends to weaken the poem from an esthetic point of view. We are inclined to be sympathetic with the Critical Reviewer who remarked that Churchill "complains . . . of being censured as a clergyman for having indulged in the idlenesses of poetry; surely this complaint cannot affect the reviewer, who never enquired whether he was a priest or a publican, a curate or a cobler."[24]

III *A Defense of Individualism*

Night, published in November 1761, can be regarded as a natural outgrowth of *The Apology*. Formally, it is another verse epistle in heroic couplets; thematically, it focusses upon individualism, a significant motif in the earlier poem. More important, however, is the confessional aspect of both poems; for, while Churchill's defense of his extra-clerical activities is only an appendage to *The Apology*, it is central in *Night*.

Night, addressed to Churchill's friend Lloyd, is the most interesting and effective of his early poems.[25] Subject probably to growing criticism of his night life, Churchill defends it by viewing his personal habits in a universalized context of moral, philosophical, and social polarities. He opposes frank libertinism to hypocrisy, individual reason to opinion, and the individual to society. The individual is a son of night, and his solace lies in wine, women, and old friends. An outsider, he has withdrawn from the occupations of day, the pursuit of wealth and power. The sons of day are soulless automatons, masked players on the stage of life, ridiculous armchair politicians. Churchill rejects their "prudence" and opinion for personal integrity.

The contrast between the sons of day and those of night emerges early in the poem:

> LET slaves to business, bodies without soul,
> Important blanks in Nature's mighty roll,
> Solemnize nonsense in the day's broad glare,
> We NIGHT prefer, which heals or hides our care.   (7-10)

Churchill expands his portrait of the daylight man by elaborating upon his habit of conforming:

> THE Wretch bred up in Method's drowsy school,
> Whose only merit is to err by rule,
> Who ne'er thro' heat of blood was tripping caught,

> Nor guilty deem'd of one eccentric thought,
> Whose soul directed to no use is seen
> Unless to move the body's dull Machine;
> Which, clock-work like, with the same equal pace,
> Still travels on thro' life's insipid space . . . (19-26)

The conflict of lifestyles that is suggested leads to the question of "good hours." As in *The Apology*, Churchill is guided in this matter by reason, which he prefers to arbitrary, vulgar opinion:

> Reason, collected in herself, disdains
> The slavish yoke of arbitrary chains,
> Steady and true each circumstance she weighs,
> Nor to bare *words* inglorious tribute pays.
> Men of sense live exempt from vulgar awe,
> And Reason to herself alone is law.
> That freedom she enjoys with lib'ral mind
> Which she as freely grants to all mankind. (45-52)

In defending his disregard of the conventional interpretation of "good hours," Churchill resorts to a characteristically neo-Classical appeal to reason. But his reason is neither the right reason of Dr. Johnson nor the common sense of Swift; Churchill's sense is not common but individual. Reason, for him, is not a restraining force, but a handmaid of freedom.

After justifying his choice of night over day, Churchill describes his nocturnal pursuits. Night represents an escape for him, an escape from the evils of the daylight world. He welcomes hyperbolically the "oblivion" induced by alcohol (85), but he clearly prefers even more his midnight conversations with Lloyd when they spend time reminiscing about their days at Westminster School. Night is not simply a time to escape into conviviality; it is also the occasion for serious reflection. Paradoxically reversing the traditional connotations of light and darkness, Churchill states that things that can be seen plainly "beneath NIGHT's honest shade" (153) are "through a false medium . . . shewn by day" (139). Night is the occasion when,

> Impatient of restraint, the active mind,
> No more by servile prejudice confin'd,
> Leaps from her seat, as wak'ned from a trance,
> And darts through Nature at a single glance.
> Then we our friends, our foes, ourselves, survey,
> And see by NIGHT what fools we are by DAY. (117-22)

Churchill, who masqueraded as curate of St. John the Evangelist
during the day, does not exclude himself from the satire. His suggestion that the day-man and the night-man are not distinct but different sides of the same personality gives his satire added psychological depth. Assuming again the role of the outsider, Churchill demonstrates
the necessity of his withdrawal from the daylight world. The self-
seeking inhabitant of that world must be a flatterer: "To Nature
dead he must adopt vile art, / And wear a smile, with anguish in his
heart" (165-66). The openness of the satirist's personality prevents
him from dissembling; and, characterizing himself as a plain dealer,
he prays:

> Foe to restraint, unpractis'd in deceit,
> Too resolute, from Nature's active heat,
> To brook affronts, and tamely pass them by;
> Too proud to flatter, too sincere to lie,
> Too plain to please, too honest to be great;
> Give me, kind Heaven, an humbler, happier state:
> Far from the place where men with pride deceive,
> . . . .
> Calm, independent, let me steal thro' life.   (179-88)

The frankness Churchill emphasizes is not only that of the satirist
but also that of the confessing libertine.

Withdrawn from the pursuit of either "greatness" or "riches," the
outsider can better perceive the vanity of the daylight world: "Spectators only on this bustling stage, / We see what vain designs
mankind engage" (195-96). From the perspective of nighttime,
political activity in the form of military conquest appears
meaningless:

> Squirrels for nuts contend, and, wrong or right,
> For the world's empire kings ambitious fight.
> What odds? — to us 'tis all the self-same thing,
> A Nut, a World, a Squirrel, and a King.   (203-06)

His satiric levelling almost worthy of Pope, Churchill reduces the
Seven Years' War to absurdity. The prolonged war was giving rise to
new taxes and to new governments, and thus it had made the
English more than usually conscious of politics. A great deal of un-
intentional irony is involved as Churchill, who would soon be

engaged with Wilkes in editing the political journal *The North Briton*, mocks this nation of statesmen:

> All would be deem'd e'en from the cradle fit
> To rule in politics as well as wit.
> The grave, the gay, the fopling, and the dunce,
> Start up (God bless us!) statesmen all at once.   (215-18)

Even the women have become politically conscious. As Joseph Addison had done half a century earlier,[26] Churchill ridicules them for this indecorous behavior: "From nymph to nymph the state infection flies, / Swells in her breast, and sparkles in her eyes" (227-28). But the political nymph is no more ridiculous than the shopkeeper-turned-statesman who is comically preoccupied with establishing a favorable balance of power:

> Fearfully wise, he shakes his empty head,
> And deals out empires as he deals out thread.
> His useless scales are in a corner flung,
> And Europe's balance hangs upon his tongue.   (251-54)

In contrast to the politically involved sons of day, the outsider can even be indifferent to such things as the prospect of new taxes; for "No tribute's laid on *Castles* in the *Air*" (274).

The poem attains a climax as Churchill defiantly presents his libertine values. To a picture of nocturnal conviviality similar to the one described earlier, he adds female companions:

> THUS have we liv'd, and whilst the fates afford
> Plain Plenty to supply the frugal board,
> Whilst MIRTH, with DECENCY his lovely bride,
> And Wine's gay GOD, with TEMP'RANCE by his side,
> Their welcome visit pay; whilst HEALTH attends
> The narrow circle of our chosen Friends,
> Whilst frank GOOD-HUMOUR consecrates the treat,
> And [WOMAN] makes society complete,[27]
> Thus WILL we live, tho' in our teeth are hurl'd
> Those *Hackney Strumpets*, PRUDENCE and the WORLD.   (287-96)

The picture of Churchill's night life is balanced and ceremonial. "Plain Plenty" balances "frugal board"; "Mirth," "Decency"; Bacchus, "Temperance." The emphasis is on restraint, and the

ceremonial nature of the passage enhances that attitude. Personifica-
tions and mythical figures people the scene, mix with the "chosen
Friends," and all partake of a communion-like feast that has been
"consecrated" by libertine-priest "Good-Humour." The marriage
ceremony is also suggested when the poet refers to "Decency" as the
"bride" of "Mirth." "Woman" appears as another abstraction, and
perhaps Churchill is suggesting that Woman (even though of easy
virtue), who "makes society complete," modifies Man in the same
way that decency modifies mirth — as he does later in *The Times*. At
any rate, while defying convention in the concluding couplet of this
passage, he has made an effort to present a subdued and even
dignified picture of his night life.

In his rejection of Prudence and the World, Churchill implies that
his critics are not so much concerned about his moral integrity as
they are about his open violation of a decorum endorsed by the masses. Prudence has become equivalent to hypocrisy — the meaning it
has for the earl of Bute who addresses the future King George III:

> Should raging passions drive thee to a whore,
> Let Prudence lead thee to a *postern* door;
> Stay out all night, but take especial care
> That Prudence bring thee back to early prayer.
> As one with watching and with study faint,
> Reel in a drunkard, and reel out a saint.   (319-24)

In a world in which wisdom is no more than "lukewarm caution"
and in which goodness is no more than a "demeanour grave" (331-
32), Churchill rejects the role of the prudent man. To the suggestion
that "*You* must be wrong, the World is in the right" (352), he responds with his definition of the world as "many fools in same opinions join'd" (358). A ringing defense of the morally convinced individual against mere numerical authority concludes the poem:

> Steadfast and true to virtue's sacred laws,
> Unmov'd by vulgar censure or applause,
> Let the World talk, my Friend; that World, we know,
> Which calls us guilty, cannot make us so.
> Unaw'd by numbers, follow Nature's plan,
> Assert the rights, or quit the name of man.
> Consider well, weigh strictly right and wrong;
> Resolve not quick, but once resolv'd be strong.
> . . . .
> If to thyself thou canst thyself acquit,

Rather stand up assur'd with conscious pride
Alone, than err with millions on thy side.   (371-82)

As Churchill did earlier when opposing private reason to public
opinion, he defends his libertine ways by appealing to the rights of
the individual. His expression of individualism, more characteristic
of a Byron than a Swift, looks forward to the Romantic rather than
reflects the neo-Classical mood. A wide gap exists between Churchill
and men like Dryden, Swift, and Pope with their faith in normalcy
and their intolerance of aberration. These men, generally inimical to
social or political disruption, highly valued order and, consequently,
decorum. Dryden speaks for them all when he says: *"Common quiet
is Mankind's concern."*[28] Churchill scorns conformity; for him, a
man is a "wretch" who "ne'er thro' heat of blood was tripping
caught, / Nor guilty deem'd of one eccentric thought" (21-22).

IV   *The Cock Lane Ghost*

The Ghost began as light-hearted ridicule of popular superstition,
then turned into a burlesque of the recent Cock Lane Ghost incident, and finally developed into a political satire against Chief
Justice Mansfield. The Cock Lane "ghost" was purportedly that of
one Fanny Lynes, who lived with her deceased sister's husband,
William Kent, before her own death from smallpox in 1760. The two
resided a while on Cock Lane in London at the home of a Richard
Parsons, whom Kent was forced to sue for repayment of a loan. Two
years after Fanny's burial, Parsons reported that her ghost was in
communication with him through the medium of his eleven-year-old
daughter, Elizabeth; upon interrogation, the ghost accused Kent of
murder. Seances with Fanny's ghost had become a form of public
entertainment before a committee of investigation was appointed.
Its report, composed by Dr. Johnson, labelled the ghost a fraud.
Parsons and his accomplices were tried before Lord Mansfield and
convicted of conspiracy.[29]

The first of *The Ghost's* four books was written, reportedly, at
South Cadbury under the title of "The Fortune Teller."[30] The Cock
Lane Ghost affair, which came to the public eye in January 1762,
gave Churchill and other writers a popular, topical point of departure.[31] He added some lines to the first book, wrote a second, had the
two books published a few months later, and followed with the third
book in October of the same year. In the interval of over a year
between the publication of the third and fourth books, the test of

strength between Wilkes and the administration was nearing a climax. Thus, in the fourth book (November 1763), Churchill's main target is the administration's chief jurist, Mansfield, whose professional integrity he hopes to publicly discredit.

Book I of *The Ghost,* a capsule history of credulity, is notable mainly for its lengthy satiric portrait of William Talbot, lord steward of the household, who had fought a duel with Wilkes after the latter had ridiculed him in *The North Briton.* Book II presents a burlesque account of an investigation of the "ghost" by a committee that had included Dr. Johnson. Book III continues the tale insofar as it recounts the investigators' arrival at the home of the lord mayor, Sir Samuel Fludyer ("Dullman"); they wish his aid to prevent Fame crying their ridiculous behavior about the London streets. In talking with his chaplain, Lewis Bruce ("Sir Crape"), the mayor decides to label the affair a plot and to call a citizens' assembly. After a lengthy discourse on the respective merits of reason and fancy, Book IV shows the politically cautious mayor deciding to send his chaplain as a proxy to the citizens' assembly. A stylized description of the procession to the convocation concludes with a portrait of Mansfield.

As can be seen, very little of the 4500 line poem concerns the Cock Lane Ghost, which is all but lost in a tangle of disgression. Churchill uses the ghost story in somewhat the way that Sterne was using the life of Tristram Shandy[32] — it is the nucleus for a virtual miscellaney of parody and satire held together by a web of associations. There is, however, a certain amount of unity as Churchill rings changes on the theme of deception. As unreal as Fanny's ghost, the poem's unifying symbol, are Talbot's courage and Mansfield's justice.

To the modern reader, the poem is primarily of interest for Churchill's playful wit and for his references to his better-remembered contemporaries, Dr. Johnson and Sterne. The poet scorns the first and praises, as well as occasionally imitates, the second. Churchill's playful wit sometimes takes the form of Hudibrastics that often rival those of his predecessor Butler. A good example of his skill in this area is his description of the first English fortunetellers:

> MATRONS, who toss the Cup, and see
> The grounds of Fate in grounds of Tea,
> Who vers'd in ev'ry modest lore,
> Can a lost Maidenhead restore,
> Or if their Pupils rather chuse it
> Can shew the readiest way to lose it.   (I, 117-22)

The delightfully awkward feminine rhyme of the last couplet provides a rhythmic climax to the passage and underlines the comic reversal in the pupils' choice.

Equally playful is Churchill's sketchy treatment of the ghost story. His dramatization of the seance that Fanny holds for the official investigators begins:

> Hark! something creeps about the house!
> Is IT a *Spirit*, or a *Mouse?*
> HARK! something *scratches* round the room!
> A *Cat*, a *Rat*, a *stubb'd Birch-broom.*
> HARK! on the wainscote now IT knocks!   (II, 303-07)

To prove its existence, the ghost is asked to perform a test that consists of knocking a certain number of times. After the investigators decide with wonderful pedantry that three knocks, if repeated three times, are more sacred than nine, the ghost responds accordingly: "THRICE She *knock'd*, and THRICE, and THRICE" (II, 328).

When Churchill describes the investigators' midnight venture to the churchyard vault, he playfully parodies the so-called "graveyard" school of poetry. Mocking the school's efforts to achieve sublimity through the evocation of terror, he writes:

> The Church-yard teem'd — th' unsettled ground,
> As in an Ague, shook around;
> While in some *dreary vault* confin'd,
> Or riding on the *Hollow Wind*,
> HORROR, which turns the heart to stone,
> In dreadful sounds was heard to groan.   (II, 711-16)

Churchill portrays the investigators as terrified: "All staring, wild, and out of breath" (II, 717). Mock solemnity, together with a brevity that gives a note of anticlimax to the suspense-filled action, characterizes the actual investigation: "SILENT ALL THREE WENT IN, ABOUT / ALL THREE TURN D SILENT AND CAME OUT" (II, 807-08).

While Churchill develops the action of his fable only sketchily, he is more thorough in his portraits, especially those of Dr. Johnson, who appears here and again in Book III. Already a formidable figure in English literary society, Johnson is ridiculed for his vocabulary, for his unpleasant appearance, and for his apparent duplicity. It is ironic that one of the most morally aware men of the age should become, in Churchill's poem, another example of man's decep-

tiveness. In giving Johnson the name "Pomposo," the satirist suggests among other things his subject's fondness for multisyllabic
words, a store of which his work on the *Dictionary* (1755) helped
provide him. His learned vocabulary is a virtual weapon:

> [Pomposo] to increase his native strength,
> Draws words, six syllables in length,
> With which, assisted with a frown
> By way of Club, he knocks us down.   (II, 673-76)

We think immediately of Boswell's biography which amply
demonstrates Johnson's rather formidable style as a conver-
sationalist.

While we may smile here, we are more likely to wince as Churchill
mercilessly ridicules his subject's unprepossessing appearance.
When Pomposo smiles to encourage his frightened fellow investigators, his smile is "ghastly": "Features so horrid, were it light, /
Would put the Devil himself to flight" (II, 686-88). Later, he appears "Horrid, *unwieldy, without Form* / . . . Of *size prodigious* (III,
793-95) and "form'd on *doubtful* plan, / Not quite a *Beast,* nor quite
a *Man*" (III, 827-28). While these particular satiric thrusts equally
violate Churchill's implicit strictures against those who "draw
humour out of Nature's fault" (*The Rosciad,* 402),[33] they are not so
cruel as his allusion to Johnson's partial blindness when Churchill
scorns the great critic's failure of vision that is evident in his support
of the false plagiarism charges against John Milton. Churchill gives
Johnson the name of the Cyclops that Odysseus blinded by referring
to him as "*our Letter'd* POLYPHEME" (II, 230).

Churchill does not stop with Johnson's manner and appearance,
for he also attacks his character when, in Book III, he indicts him for
violating his personal integrity. One example of apparent duplicity
was Johnson's recent acceptance of a pension from the king after his
Dictionary had cynically observed: "In England it [a pension] is
generally understood to mean pay given to a state hireling for
treason to his country." Thus, Pomposo "damns the *Pension* which
he takes / And loves the STUART he forsakes" (III, 819-20). What
seemed to be another lapse of integrity was Johnson's apparent
failure to produce his edition of Shakespeare's plays for which he
had already taken money from the subscribers. Thus, Pomposo "for
Subscribers baits his hook, / And takes their cash — but where's the
Book?" (iii, 801-02).[34] Churchill's attempt to vilify his innocent sub-

ject is more amusing than anything else, but the portraits in general are valuable as a kind of minority report.

What motivated the attack? Johnson himself thought that his un-favorable criticism of Churchill's poetry had sufficiently irritated the satirist.[35] While plausible, this explanation ignores the obvious comic discrepancy between the rather formidable Samuel Johnson, "Whose very name inspires an awe" (II, 655), and the somewhat far-cical nature of the Cock Lane Ghost affair in which he became in-volved. Perhaps Churchill would have exploited this incongruity if Johnson had said nothing about his poetry.

In contrast to his scorn of Johnson is the satirist's admiration for Sterne. He reveals a deep sympathy with the newly triumphant author of *Tristram Shandy*, whose genius he openly acknowledges and whose manner, as we have observed, he sometimes consciously imitates. For Churchill, the novelist's genius lay in his ability as a comic artist and in his skill in handling digressions. Churchill's first mention of Sterne occurs in his ironic invocation of Truth, here the verity of the comic vision. When he calls upon the Goddess Truth, Churchill places himself in the great tradition of European comedy by naming as his masters Rabelais, Cervantes, Swift, and the "neophyte" Sterne (who was then travelling on the Continent):

> But come not with that easy mien,
> By which you won the *lively Dean* [Swift],
> Nor yet assume that Strumpet air,
> Which RABELAIS taught Thee first to wear,
> Nor yet that arch ambiguous face,
> Which with CERVANTES gave thee grace,
> But come in sacred vesture clad,
> Solemnly dull, and truly sad!
>
> Far from thy seemly Matron train
> Be Idiot MIRTH, and LAUGHTER vain!
> For WIT and HUMOUR, which pretend
> At once to please us and amend,
> *They* are not for my present turn,
> Let them remain in *France* with STERNE.   (II, 161-74)

In *The Dunciad*, Pope had already set a precedent for including Swift with Rabelais and Cervantes,[36] but Churchill's association of the fairly recently published Sterne with these great comic artists was even bolder and more astute.

Both Churchill and Sterne were fond of digression. While the novelist's ramblings seldom violate the essential organic unity of his work, the poet's often do so. Acknowledging Sterne's superiority in this area, Churchill pauses after one of the poem's many digressions to pay a second tribute to the novelist:

> Could I, whilst *Humour* held the Quill,
> Could I *digress* with half that skill,
> Could I with half that skill return,
> Which we so much admire in STERNE,
> Where each *Digression*, seeming vain,
> And only fit to entertain,
> Is found, on better recollection,
> To have a just and nice Connection,
> To help the whole with wond'rous art,
> Whence it seems idly to depart;
> Then should our readers ne'er accuse
> These wild excursions of the Muse,
> Ne'er backward turn dull Pages o'er
> To recollect what went before . . .   (III, 967-80)

Churchill is not only praising Sterne but also imitating him as he takes the reader into his confidence as the narrative artist who points out the difficulty he faces in returning to his subject. Throughout the second half of *The Ghost,* Churchill occasionally dons a Sterne-like mask of the self-conscious, playful narrator who inserts himself *as narrator* into his work as he speaks directly to the reader with whom he is pretending to share the secrets of his craft.

Like Sterne's, Churchill's imagined readers include the prudish; and he shows an awareness of this characteristic and even has consideration for them:

> To higher subjects now SHE [Fame] soars,
> And talks of *Politics* and *Whores,*
> (If to your nice and chaster ears
> That term *indelicate* appears,
> SCRIPTURE *politely* shall refine,
> And melt it into *Concubine*) . . .   (III, 281-86)

Both Sterne and Churchill, burlesquing the criterion of temporal probability, carefully point out to their readers the correspondence between reading and narrative time. Sterne shows that the servant Obadiah could actually have fetched Dr. Slop in the "two minutes,

thirteen seconds, and three fifths" of reading time between the sum-
moning of Obadiah and Dr. Slop's arrival, even though the latter
lived eight miles from Shandy-Hall.[37] In a similar way, Churchill explains to his readers how the Goddess Fame spent her time while he,
describing her flight, had stopped to digress:

> But tho' to Poets we allow,
> No matter when acquir'd or how,
> From Truth unbounded deviation,
> Which custom calls *Imagination*,
> Yet can't they be suppos'd to lie
> One half so fast as FAME can fly.
> Therefore (to solve this *Gordian* knot,
> A point we almost had forgot)
> To courteous Readers be it known
> That fond of verse and falshood grown,
> Whilst we in sweet digression sung,
> FAME check'd her flight, and held her tongue.   (III, 503-14)

Churchill, like Sterne, is not only fond of digressing but likes to
play with his readers' fears that he is unable to control his material.
Sterne, after giving an account of a long conversation pursued by the
Shandy brothers while they were going down stairs, playfully
cautioned the reader: "Is it not a shame to make two chapters of
what passed in going down one pair of stairs? for we are got no farther
yet than to the first landing, and there are fifteen more steps down to
the bottom; and for aught I know, as my father and my uncle *Toby*
are in a talking humour, there may be as many chapters as steps; —
let that be as it will, Sir, I can no more help it than my destiny. . . ."[38]

Churchill displays a similar attitude. After *The Monthly Review*
had dismissed the first three books of *The Ghost* as a "digressive, in-
coherent production,"[39] he wrote 776 lines in Book IV before even
mentioning his supposed subject. At this point, he inserted a brief
exchange between himself and "some Critic Post" (perhaps the
Monthly Reviewer), which calls attention to the fact that he has not
learned his lesson and states that his material is out of his control:

> For instance now — this book — the GHOST —
> Methinks I hear some Critic Post
> Remark most gravely — 'The first word
> Which we about the Ghost have heard.'
> Peace my good Sir — not quite so fast —
> What is the first, may be the last,

> Which is a point, all must agree,
> Cannot depend on You or Me. (IV, 777-84)

The pretense is carried on in the next three verse paragraphs, all of which begin with the phrase "But to return —" before the poet introduces still another digression. Finally, only "Blind Chance" leads Churchill back to his topic; the subject of his last digression "happens" to be related to his central subject. Burlesquing the use of the associative process as an organizational device, he writes:

> Thanks to my Stars — I now see shore —
> Of Courtiers, and of Courts no more —
> Thus stumbling on my City Friends,
> Blind Chance my guide, my purpose bends
> In line direct, and shall pursue
> The point which I had first in view,
> Nor more shall with the Reader sport
> Till I have seen him safe in port.   (IV, 963-70)

In this manner, Churchill moves from incidental political satire ("Courtiers" and "Courts") to his fable (the action of his "City Friends"), which has become a means for political satire on a grander scale, with the lord mayor and lord chief justice its targets.

If there is any unity to *The Ghost*, it is thematic in nature; for Churchill is developing in various ways the concept of man's deceptiveness. Highly relevant to the theme of deception is the ironic digression that functions as a kind of preface to Book IV. The passage, delightfully paradoxical, examines the eighteenth-century assumption that reason is superior to fancy. Both are shown to be, in a sense, unreal: reason is unreal insofar as it is opposed to sensation: fancy has a great deal of psychological reality. Churchill, who appealed to the authority of reason when he attempted to justify his nonconformity in *The Apology* and *Night*, now equates reason with tyranny.[40] Reason is a tyrant over the senses, and a life of reason is a stoic's life: "True Members of the *Stoic* weal, / [We] Must learn to think, and cease to feel" (IV, 159-60). Similarly, the satirist equates wisdom with wretchedness and states that the delusion of happiness is second only to happiness itself; "For next . . . / To *being* happy here below, / Is to *believe* that we are so" (285-88). The man whose joy is one of fancy "Mocks boasted vain *Reality*, / And *Is*, whate'er he wants to Be" (IV, 309-10). No irony is involved as Churchill

points out how his own impoverished, hopeless life was saved by
fancy in the form of poetry:

> FANCY, in richest robes array'd,
> Came smiling forth, and brought me aid,
> Came smiling o'er that dreadful time,
> And, more to bless me, came in *Rhime*.   (IV, 343-46)

In the manner of Swift, Churchill makes an abrupt, unsignalled
shift in tone. He is suddenly satirical as he shows how fancy
"comprehends Mankind" (IV, 348). Looking forward to the conclusion, he points out that the power of fancy is evident in processions.
On such occasions, the cowardly knight is transformed into a hero.
The knight,

> Who could not suffer for his life
> A Point to sword, or Edge to knife,
> And always fainted at the sight
> Of blood . . .
> . . . .
> Grac'd with those ensigns, which were meant
> To further Honour's dread intent,
> The Minds of Warriors to inflame,
> And spur them on to deeds of Fame,
> With little Sword, large Spurs, high Feather,
> . . . .
> A Hero all at once became.   (IV, 441-65)

Similarly, fancy has the power of turning back the clock so that the
aging woman can see herself again as a girl: "Quite alter'd was the
whole machine, / And Lady —— was fifteen" (IV, 625-26). Fancy,
a means of salvation for the poet, is suddenly reduced to being a
source of ridiculous delusions; and Churchill's essay in psychology
trails off into a satiric miscellany.

We can view these portraits as variations on the theme of deception. A similar tension between appearance and reality is manifest in
Churchill's treatment of Talbot, Fludyer, and Mansfield. In Talbot's
portrait, which appeared in the 1763 edition after his bloodless duel
with Wilkes, Churchill presents this amateur boxer and newly
created earl as a coward masquerading as a bully. This "Hero" is the
type who

> Would be deem'd ready, when you list,
> With sword and pistol, stick and fist,
> Careless of points, balls, bruises, knocks,
> At once to fence, fire, cudgel, box,
> But at the same time bears about,
> Within himself, some touch of doubt,
> Of *prudent* doubt, which hints — that fame
> Is nothing but an empty name;
> That life is rightly understood
> By all to be a real good;
> That, even in a *Hero's* heart,
> *Discretion* is the better part.   (I, 223-34)

Like Shakespeare's Falstaff, Talbot knows that "honor" is but "air"
and that "the better part of valor is discretion."[41]
   Just as "prudent" is Fludyer, or "Dullman." The politically
cautious lord mayor is not simply content to support (or to appear to
be supporting) those presently in power; he does not want to dis-
please those out of power either. His problem is how to take part in
the procession of London citizens without really doing so, and his
solution is to manipulate appearances by sending a proxy:

> That's your true Plan — to obligate
> The present Ministers of State,
> My *Shadow* shall our Court approach,
> And bear my pow'r, and have my *coach,*
> . . . .
> *To curry favour, and the grace*
> *Obtain, of those who're out of place,*
> *In the mean time I* — that's to say —
> *I proper, I myself* — *here* stay.   (IV, 1441-50)

The split between appearance and essence attains a dizzying new
dimension here.
   A different kind of split marks Churchill's presentation of the lord
chief justice, and the tension between seeming and being generated
throughout the poem now reaches a climax. Dramatically contrasting the real with the ideal Mansfield, Churchill first introduces
into the citizens' procession that concludes the poem a nameless
jurist whose doubtful loyalty and questionable professional integrity
are intended to remind the reader of the chief justice. The satirist attempts to revive the old charge of Jacobitism, of which the Scottish

judge had been cleared ten years earlier,[42] when he accuses the nameless jurist of being "for Rebellion fully ripe (IV, 1841):

> Faithful to JAMES he still remains,
> Tho' he the friend to GEORGE appear:
> *Dissimulation's Virtue here.*   (IV, 1848-50)

Churchill also accuses this judge of perverting the law: he "Puzzles the cause he can't maintain, / . . . And, where he can't convince, confounds" (IV, 1872-74).

The portrait concluded, this "monster," who filled the citizens with horror, is suddenly displaced by an idealized jurist named Mansfield:

> Abash'd the Monster hung his head,
> And, like an empty Vision, fled.
> . . . .
> LOYALTY, LIBERTY, and LAW,
> Impatient of the galling chain,
> And Yoke of pow'r, resum'd their reign;
> And, burning with the glorious flame
> Of Public Virtue, MANSFIELD came.   (IV, 1923-34)

The ultimate triumph of fancy is the transformation of Mansfield into an idealized public servant. Such a Mansfield can only be a figment of the public's fancy.

The Ghost has been neglected by critics in the past. Professor Brown, who omitted an analysis of it from his critical biography of Churchill, dismisses it as a "potboiler": "Despite its detailed topical interest and occasional flashes of poetry, *The Ghost* as a poetic whole must be pronounced a potboiler, and it is regrettable that selections from it are so often included in anthologies as representative of Churchill's work."[43] Undeniably topical and digressive, *The Ghost* is characteristic of Churchill in another, more significant way. It reflects his wonderful exuberance, which the poet, in defiance of his critics, gave reign to here and elsewhere even though it often led to excess. It is this exuberance and Churchill's skillful use of comic verse that, at least to some extent, redeem the poem.

CHAPTER 3

Early Political Satire:
The North Briton, *Poetry of 1763*

D URING the spring of 1762 and shortly after publication of the
first two books of *The Ghost*, Churchill became acquainted
with Wilkes, who had asked for his aid in producing *The North
Briton*, an opposition journal aimed at the earl of Bute, who had just
assumed leadership of the ministry. Churchill found himself in the
middle of the political controversy of the time which focussed on the
peace negotiations to end the Seven Years' War. In *The North
Briton*, Wilkes and Churchill attacked Bute and his fellow Scots, the
conduct of the war, and the articles of peace. The only complete
poem that Churchill published during the year of his editorship was
The Prophecy of Famine, which complemented the attack in prose
against not only the first minister but also the land of his birth.

After the "libelous" forty-fifth number of *The North Briton* terminated the periodical in April 1763, Churchill continued to write
political satire in verse. His defense of Wilkes, whose prosecution
had already been initiated by the administration, is the common
denominator for this satire. *An Epistle to William Hogarth* accuses
the artist, who had published a caricature of Wilkes, of being willing
to sacrifice liberty to satisfy his envy; for an attack against Wilkes is
an attack to Churchill against liberty. In *The Conference*, Churchill
opposes a reverence for truth to self-interest in justifying his role: he
is a political satirist who defends his friend at the expense of the
good will of the establishment. Finally, *The Author* attacks the party
hacks of the day, focussing on John Kidgell, the Anglican divine who
played an active part against Wilkes in the controversy over *An Essay on Women*.

In its form, this early political satire in verse is somewhat
derivative from the poems that preceded it. All four of the works are
composed of heroic couplets. *The Prophecy of Famine* is parodic like
The Rosciad, though it is mock-pastoral rather than mock-epic. *An*

Epistle to William Hogarth is, as its title suggests, in the tradition of
the verse epistle, as were *The Apology* and *Night*. In his attack
against Hogarth and again in *The Conference,* Churchill uses
dialogue as a formal device. The essays for *The North Briton* represent Churchill's only excursion into prose for satiric purposes.

I *Prose Satire:* The North Briton

The irony of having a Scot, Smollett, support an administration
headed by another Scot, Bute, in a weekly called *The Briton* did not
go unnoticed by the Englishman Wilkes who named his antiadministration periodical *The North Briton.* In the first number,
published on June 5, 1762, Wilkes remarked in his new persona:
"Though I am a NORTH BRITON, I will endeavour to write *plain
English,* and to avoid the numerous *Scotticisms* the BRITON abounds
with; and then, as the world is apt to mistake, he may be taken for a
Scotsman, and I shall pass for an *Englishman.*"[1] The persona, which
was impossible to sustain, did provide a ready source of irony that
could be tapped for individual numbers. Churchill uses this ironic
mask very effectively in Number 10, for example, which discusses
the best measures that Scots might adopt to subvert the Church of
England. From a literary point of view, the numbers that employ the
persona tend to be the most interesting.

The North Briton was published almost every Saturday from June
1762 through April 1763,[2] with Wilkes writing most of the essays.
While Churchill may have written, in whole or in part, as many as
fifteen, only five complete issues can be attributed to him with any
certainty. They are numbers 8, 10, 18, 27, and 42.[3] Although the essays are of no considerable literary merit in themselves, they do add
to an understanding of Churchill the political satirist and his times.

Churchill's first essay, Number 8, is an attack against Bute as a
"favourite." With indirection, the satirist sets about to vindicate
three contemporary statesman to whom the term "favourite" was
currently being applied by various political periodicals. Churchill
praises Bute's predecessors, the duke of Newcastle and William Pitt,
who had shared the leadership of the previous, Whig administration.
Turning to Bute, who is not named, the satirist writes with an insinuating doubleness: "As to the third person, his services are of
such a nature, that — but lest I should be suspected of partiality I
shall drop this point . . . " (45). Instead of attacking Bute directly,
Churchill uses an historical analogy. By implication, he compares
Bute to Henry VI's favorite, the earl of Suffolk, who was finally

given up to "the resentment of an exasperated people" (46). The contest, Churchill would have it, is between the chief minister and the English people.

More important from a literary point of view is Number 10. Its inspiration was Swift's *Letter Concerning the Sacramental Test*, which predicts that one of the less desirable consequences of any repeal of the Test Act would be the eventual establishment of Scottish Presbyterianism as the national religion of England. As Churchill will do once more in *The Prophecy of Famine*, he follows Swift's example of appealing to the prejudices and fears of the English to accomplish a political end. The number begins with a letter to the North Briton from a fellow countryman, who signs himself "Presbyter." Assuming that the Scots already control the state, Presbyter recommends that they seize power in the church to ensure the continuance of that control: ". . . then might we lord it with security, and, the terrors of the church co-operating with the secular arm, our power would be *universal, absolute,* and *perpetual*" (54). The rest of the issue consists of the North Briton's reply.

As a persona, the North Briton is in the tradition of Swift's Modest Proposer, who functions doubly as both object and means of satire. As object, Churchill's persona reveals himself to be a shrewd opportunist who is to be scorned as well as feared. As means of satire, he incidentally attacks the materialism of the English clergy:

But if you would destroy, or lessen the rights of *churchmen,* if you would controvert their claims, supplant them in their preferments, and make encroachments on their power, then must you expect a general cry, the whole spiritual body will be up in arms, the thunders of the church will be levelled against you, and the populace must be taught that religion is struck at, and the church in danger. Safer indeed will our nation always find it to attack a *Saviour* than a *surplice,* to rase out the *four evangelists,* than to shew an inclination for plucking *one spiritual ear of English corn.* (56)

The North Briton concludes by quoting Swift ("our arch enemy"), who predicts Presbyterian domination in his *Letter Concerning the Sacramental Test.* Swift's fears, the North Briton hopes, are "in the spirit of *prophecy*" (57).

The persona functions more like the ingenuous Gulliver than the Modest Proposer in Number 18, as he ironically justifies Bute's conduct of the war and expresses confidence that "our great patron" (110) will make a good peace. As for the conduct of the war, Churchill presents the administration's failure to pursue the war,

once negotiations for peace have commenced, as a shrewdly designed plan to convince the enemy of England's superior confidence and power. Thus, "to let our fleets lie rotting in port, to suffer our men to be enervated with sloth, and to dissolve in inactivity, to squander away our treasures, and to send out, merely by way of amusement and to take the air, our bravest admirals and our strongest fleets, at a time when we are engaged in a war with France and Spain, these are instances of such a confident and well-grounded superiority, as must strike terror into our enemies . . . " (109).

Churchill discards the persona, though not the indirection of irony, in Number 27. By this time, criticizing the administration was becoming dangerous: some of the writers for the opposition weekly *The Monitor* were arrested in November and then released on bail, and a warrant for the arrest of those involved in the publication of *The North Briton* was issued but never served. As a result of these proceedings, Wilkes and Churchill had some difficulty in getting their periodical printed. The atmosphere of fear that prevailed is reflected in the opening of Number 27: "Almost every man I meet looks strangely on me — some industriously avoid me — others pass me silent — stare — and shake their heads. — Those few, those very few, who are not afraid to take a lover of his country by the hand, congratulate me on my being alive and at liberty — They advise circumspection — for, they do not know — they cannot tell — but — the times — Liberty is precious — fines — imprisonment — pillory — not indeed that they themselves — but — then in truth — God only knows. — " (167).

Dissociating himself from the timid, Churchill attacks the administration for its action against *The Monitor* and for its peace preliminaries. Although he does not speak in the persona of the North Briton, he applies the indirection of irony. Taking up the question of *The Monitor,* he observes that he himself found nothing in the periodical that would warrant the arrests. Nevertheless, he will have faith in the judgment of the administration since no government would be foolish enough to do what it has been accused of. "The particulars of that procedure [the action against *The Monitor*] have not, indeed, transpired; but, till the contrary appears, it is a justice we owe to every administration, to suppose they have some reason for what they do" (169).

Discussing further the legality and wisdom of the proceedings against the writers for *The Monitor,* Churchill pretends to relate the gossip of the "abettors of faction" (169). They would have it that one of the reasons for the arrests was the periodical's criticism of the

peace preliminaries. However, since each citizen has the right to criticize such things, this cannot be the case. For his part, unable to believe that the preliminaries currently being circulated are authentic, he will withhold commentary until he is satisfied on this point. Nevertheless, he manages to make the point that these preliminaries are inadequate in that they allow for the return of too much conquered territory to the French. Behind this screen of indirection, Churchill boldly insists upon the individual's right to freedom of expression.

In Number 42, not only is the mask of the North Briton dropped, but no attempt is made at sustained irony of any sort. The satire is aimed mainly at the discrepancy between the administration's superficial devotion to economy, necessitated by the expenses of the war, and its essential prodigality, manifested especially in various forms of bribery. Bute, the essay charges, "is for ever retailing the *word* [economy] to us, even when he is practising the most unbounded prodigality" (279). To restore a regiment's full complement of officers just before it was disbanded and, thus, to swell the half-pay lists[4] was one example of prodigality. The awarding of commissions in such circumstances, Churchill suggests, can be a form of bribery: "I beg to know how many weeks Mr. *Gilbert Elliot's* son has had a captain's commission, and if he is yet *ten* years old?" (280). The chief example of ministerial graft was a new government loan, financed by subscriptions that were limited, the essayist claimed, to ministerial "creatures" and "tools." Unusually favorable to the privileged subscribers were the terms of the new loan; Churchill refers to the interest payments as "the most enormous sum ever divided in so short a time among any set of men" (281). These and similar allegations lead to the observation: "For the future, whenever I hear of *Scottish œconomy*, I shall conclude, that in private and household concerns it means *sordidness;* in public matters, *profusion, corruption,* and *extravagance*" (287). Although it may be dense with topical allusions, Churchill's last attempt at prose satire does contain some political truths that give it a certain timelessness.

Churchill's prose satire was highly praised, on occasion, by his collaborator on *The North Briton.* After publication of the poet's first essay, Number 8, Wilkes wrote to him: "I admir'd exceedingly what I read last saturday. Are you determin'd to have the palm of prose, as well as poetry?"[5] He also praised Number 21, which Churchill had

probably not written entirely but had extensively revised. Referring to that number, which defended Wilkes against the charge that he had spoken harshly to Bute's son in a bookseller's shop, Churchill's friend wrote: "You have manag'd the North Briton incomparably; you ride that fierce steed with the truest spirit and judgment."[6] It would, of course, be a mistake to take these statements for anything more than what they are: the profusive Wilkes's encouragement of his friend upon publication of his first essay and, again, upon publication of an essay in which he assisted Wilkes's defense against the accusations of young Bute. Whatever Churchill's merits in writing prose may have been, he seems to have preferred poetry as a vehicle for satire. In the middle of his career on *The North Briton*, he published the first of his many political satires in verse.

II   *Verse Satire:* The Prophecy of Famine

Growing from Churchill's sketch for a *North Briton* essay, *The Prophecy of Famine* carries on the attack against the administration by attempting to focus the widespread prejudices against Scotland on the Scottish earl of Bute. This "Scots Pastoral," as it was sub-titled, plays upon English prejudices by painting a dismal picture of an impoverished, hungry Scotland and by detailing the history of Scottish "perfidy" as the background for the Highland goddess Famine to prophesy a peaceful conquest of England — a conquest already begun under the authority of Bute. Without seriously over-stating the case, *The Critical Review* reported: "Every passage which history could furnish, that insinuated anything, either true or false, to her [Scotland's] prejudice, is artfully interwoven, every public prejudice against her heightened and inflamed, and nothing omitted that might contribute to *hang her up to scorn* . . . and brand her name to all posterity."[7]

In the first half of *The Prophecy of Famine*, a preface to the actual "Scots Pastoral," Churchill states his preference for nature over art (the simple pastoral over the artificial) before announcing his intent to make poetic amends for his past mistreatment of the Scots in *The North Briton*. In the form of the "Scots Pastoral," the "amends" let the Goddess Famine console the shepherds Jockey and Sawney, depicted as survivors of the Battle of Culloden, with the prophecy of a Scottish conquest of England.

The ironic vision of *The North Briton* essays is present in the first part of the poem, where Churchill pretends to be sympathetic with

the Scots. Echoing the bastard Edmund in Shakespeare's *King Lear*,[8] he proclaims himself a devotee of Nature who will follow her to her natural habitat — Scotland:

> Thou, NATURE, art *my* goddess — to thy law
> Myself I dedicate — *hence* slavish awe
> Which bends to fashion, and obeys the rules,
> Impos'd at first, and since oberv'd by fools.[9]
> *Hence* those vile tricks which mar fair NATURE's hue,
> And bring the sober matron forth to view,
> With all that artificial tawdry glare,
> Which virtue scorns, and none but strumpets wear.   (93-100)

Churchill's irony is rather complex here. Basically, art is opposed to nature. At first, "art" refers to the artificial and corrupt and is associated with servitude, while "nature" refers to the pure and real and is associated with freedom.

The echoing of Edmund's "Thou, Nature, art my goddess . . ." should alert the reader to the probability of the ambiguity involved in Churchill's seemingly simple contrast of art with nature. For Edmund, Nature was the goddess of a world that was ruled not by natural law but by the law of the jungle, a world where the illegitimate child was more "natural" than the legitimate. Churchill's Nature takes on some of the connotations of Edmund's a few lines later when the poet points to the goddess's kingdom, Scotland: "Where undisturb'd by Art's *rebellious* plan, / She rules the *loyal Laird*, and *faithful Clan*" (109-10). Art, in the sense of order ("Art's . . . plan"), now has become positive and, thus, "rebellious" to the lawlessness of Nature; the perfidious, rebellious laird and clan are "loyal" and "faithful" only to Nature.

In this way Churchill introduces the subject of his poem, Scotland. The satire is rather mild as he continues his ironic praise of that land by elaborating England's "indebtedness" to her northern neighbor. After reciting Scottish literary contributions, the satirist expresses a desire to be bathed in the river Tweed, which becomes a second river Lethe:

> . . . slowly winding the dull waters creep,
> And seem themselves to own the power of sleep,
> . . . on the surface Lead, like feathers, swims. . . .   (141-43)

Further reduced, Nature's kingdom has some features of Hades or of Pope's *Dunciad*.[10]

This prefatory ironic satire against the Scots becomes more intense, though still comparatively mild, when Churchill addresses his friend Wilkes. After alluding to Wilkes's friendship with the Scottish duke of Argyll[11] and praising his honesty and generosity, the satirist pretends to dissociate Wilkes from *The North Briton's* anti-Scottish policy:

> Oft have I heard thee mourn the wretched lot
> Of the poor, mean, despis'd, insulted *Scot*,
> . . . .
> When *Scriblers*, to the charge by int'rest led,
> The fierce *North-Briton* foaming at their head,
> Pour forth invectives, deaf to candour's [kindliness's] call,
> And, injur'd by one alien, rail at all;
> . . . .
> Thy gen'rous soul condemns the frantic rage,
> And hates the faithful, but ill-natur'd, page. (179-94)

While the passage seems to be defending the Scots against the invective of antiadministration periodicals, it contains some damaging assertions. The Scots, after all, are "poor, mean, despis'd, insulted" and, despite the Act of Union, "aliens"; Bute ("one alien") has, indeed, "injured" the English; and *The North Briton*, while "ill-natur'd," is "faithful" to the truth.

The satire becomes more abusive when Churchill moves from ironic preface to mock pastoral, where he furthers his ridicule of the Scots by depicting them as poor, defeated, and rapacious. The pastoral introduces two musical shepherds, Jockey and Sawney, and their Scottish environment which is characterized by its barrenness: "The plague of Locusts they secure defy, / For in three hours a grasshopper must die" (297-98). When a storm sends the boys for shelter to Famine's cave, the satirist emphasizes this theme further:

> *There* webs were spread of more than common size,
> And half-starv'd spiders prey'd on half-starv'd flies;
> In quest of food, Efts strove in vain to crawl;
> Slugs, pinch'd with hunger, smear'd the slimy wall. (327-30)

This scene is the backdrop for the shepherds' dialogue which develops into a mock pastoral lament for the Scots' defeat at Culloden. Reducing the Scottish soldiers to bandits and herders, Churchill implies that they were hopelessly outclassed by the English:

> Five brothers there I lost, in manhood's pride,
> Two in the field, and three on gibbets died;
> *Ah!* silly swains, to follow war's alarms,
> *Ah!* what hath shepherd's life to do with arms!   (391-94)

More than a designation of the pastoral role of Jockey and Sawney, the term *shepherd* becomes in the last line an epithet for the Scottish people.

The satire grows harsher as the Goddess Famine interrupts the despairing shepherds with her hopeful vision of the future. Intended as encouragement by the goddess, the prophecy begins with some of the strongest invective levelled at the Scots in the poem:

> Pent in this barren corner of the isle,
> Where partial fortune never deign'd to smile;
> Like nature's bastards, reeping for our share
> What was rejected by the lawful heir;
> Unknown among the nations of the earth,
> Or only known to raise contempt and mirth;
> Long free, because the race of Roman braves
> Thought it not worth their while to make us slaves;
> Then into bondage by that nation brought,
> Whose ruin we for ages vainly sought,
> Whom still with unslack'd hate we view, and still,
> The pow'r of mischief lost, retain the will;
> Consider'd as the refuse of mankind,
> A mass till the last moment left behind,
> Which frugal nature doubted, as it lay,
> Whether to stamp with life, or throw away . . .   (423-38)

If these northern neighbors were only contemptible in their poverty and impotence, there would be nothing to fear; Churchill also wants to present them as a serious threat.

Churchill's Scots become less contemptible and more threatening when their Goddess Famine prophesizes that their future glory lies in ravishing England, not forcefully but cunningly. To give his myth a pseudohistorical basis, the satirist briefly traces, from Roman times to the Rebellion of 1745, what he projects as Scotland's treacherous past. Interpreting more recent events to substantiate his myth, Churchill has the goddess point out that the fulfillment of her prophecy has already begun under the banner, as it were, of another Stuart — John Stuart, earl of Bute, "whose nature [is] royal as his name" (533).

Churchill also plays upon the prejudices of his readers by comparing the Scots with Jews and the Scottish migration into England with the Israelite invasion of Canaan. The Biblical allusions that function to amplify Famine's prophecy compare the Scots to Israelites; England, to the Promised Land; Bute, to the Messiah.[12] The Goddess Famine, then, becomes a Hebrew prophet predicting the advent of Christ — or anti-Christ, as it turns out to be.

The parallel, which occurs in the second part of the poem, is anticipated in the introductory section by some scattered references to the Old Testament. When Churchill expresses his wish to be purified in the River Tweed, he compares himself to the Syrian captain Naaman, whose leprosy was cured when the Hebrew prophet Elisha had him bathe in the River Jordan: "There let me bathe my yet unhallow'd limbs, / As once a SYRIAN bath'd in JORDAN's flood" (144-45). The terms of the parallel may seem contradicted when the satirist compares, though ironically, Scotland to the Promised Land in a subsequent allusion which identifies the antiadministration journalists, who are surveying Scotland, with Moses, who viewed the Holy Land just before his death from Mount Pisgah: "On *Northern Pisgah* . . . they take their stand, / To mark the weakness of that *Holy Land*" (189-90). Later, pretending to repent his role as co-editor of *The North Briton,* Churchill refers to the Scots as "the chosen race": "Once, be the hour accurs'd, accurs'd be the place, / I ventur'd to blaspheme the chosen race" (217-18).

In the description of Scotland that begins the actual "Scots Pastoral," the poet evokes the Egyptian captivity of the Israelites by mentioning a "plague of Locusts" (297). The significance of this Old Testament image, as well as the earlier allusions, becomes apparent when the Goddess Famine uses the language of Exodus to prophesy a Scottish takeover of England:

> But times of happier note are now at hand,
> And the full promise of a better land:
> *There,* like the *Sons of Israel,* having trod,
> For the fix'd term of years ordain'd by God,
> A barren desart, we shall seize rich plains
> Where milk with honey flows, and plenty reigns.   (445-50)

Seen as a reenactment of the Israelite invasion of Canaan, the Scottish migration takes on a more ominous aspect.

Equally ominous is the projection, through Biblical allusion, of the earl of Bute as a kind of political anti-Christ when the Goddess

Famine, like a Hebrew prophet foretelling the coming of the Messiah, predicts the triumph of her noble son:

> That Son, whose nature, royal as his name,
> Is destin'd to redeem our race from shame.
> His boundless pow'r, beyond example great,
> Shall make the rough way smooth, the crooked straight,
> Shall for our ease the raging floods restrain,
> And sink the mountain level to the plain.   (533-38)

Opposed to Bute, the true (English) "Savior" is the hero of the Battle of Culloden, the duke of Cumberland, whom the goddess refers to in the next verse paragraph (555-56).[13] But he, like Christ, will be rejected by his people.

Churchill's abuse of the Scots, not to mention the anti-Semitism involved in his utilization of a Biblical parallel, all in the name of liberty, is difficult to understand if we are not aware that proponents of liberty have usually been exclusive. Even if we disregard the abusiveness as Churchill's Scottish admirer James Boswell did, we must disagree with the biographer's high opinion of the poem.[14] Of no great literary merit in itself, *The Prophecy of Famine* is valuable from the point of view of Churchill's development in the art of indirection.

III   *A Caricaturist Caricatured*

In September 1762, William Hogarth became involved in the political controversy surrounding the earl of Bute's attempt to end the Seven Years' War when he attacked Lord Temple, one of the opposition leaders, and his propagandists, Wilkes and Churchill, in a cartoon entitled "The Times."[15] Wilkes's response was immediate. "Hogarth," he informed Churchill, "has begun the attack today — I shall attack him in hobbling prose, you will I hope in smooth-pac'd verse —"[16] Before the end of the month, Wilkes had carried out his part of the counterattack in *North Briton* 17. Although Churchill's *An Epistle to William Hogarth* did not appear until the following summer, he was just as enthusiastic as Wilkes about punishing the famous artist. He now had not simply another opportunity to lash the enemies of liberty but a foe whose extraordinary stature helped make him an ideal subject for satire. As Churchill wrote to Garrick: "I am happy to find that he [Hogarth] hath at last declar'd himself, for there is no credit to be got by breaking flies upon a Wheel, But Hogarths are Subjects worthy of an Englishman's pen."[17]

A month before Churchill's poem appeared, Hogarth retaliated for the *North Briton* 17 attack by publishing a caricature of Wilkes. Drawn during the hearing that followed Wilkes's arrest for involvement in the publication of the "seditious" *North Briton* 45, it shows a grinning, cross-eyed, gap-toothed Wilkes who sits leaning forward in a chair and supports on the end of a staff, just above his head, an upturned vessel, labelled "LIBERTY" — his liberty cap. The "cap" can be seen as a kind of halo ironically contrasting with the suggestion of horns made by Wilkes's wig.[18] Near him is a desk on which lie copies of *North Briton* 17 and 45. This derisive cartoon induced Churchill to complete his *Epistle*, which he made to focus now on Hogarth's attack against the champion of liberty.

Churchill's animosity toward Hogarth, as well as his delight at returning to versification since his duties with *The North Briton* were terminated, appears in a letter written to Wilkes shortly after publication of Hogarth's caricature: "My head is full of Hogarth, and as I like not his Company I believe I shall get him on Paper, not so much to please the Public, not so much for the sake of Justice, as for my own ease — a motive ever powerful with indolent minds. I have begun already — and seem to like the Subject. I have been so long out of Verse, that it appears like a new World. And has acquired fresh charms from disuse. I have laid in a great stock of gall, and I do not intend to spare it on this occasion — he shall be welcome to every drop of it."[19]

An Epistle to William Hogarth was published before the end of June 1763. Its rather harsh treatment of the aging artist prompted Garrick to write the following to George Colman: ". . . let me know how the Town speaks of our Friend Churchill's Epistle — it is the most bloody performance that has been publish'd in my time — I am very desirous to know the opinion of People, for I am really much, very much hurt at it — his description of his Age & infirmities is surely too shocking & barbarous — is Hogarth really ill, or does he meditate revenge?"[20] Hogarth *was* meditating revenge, and it appeared about a month later in the form of another caricature — this one of Churchill as "The Bruiser."[21]

One of Churchill's more carefully structured poems, the *Epistle* falls into two major parts: a dialogue between Candour (kindliness) and the satirist, and the attack against Hogarth. The dialogue is, in part, a debate between the plain-dealing poet and the advocate of prudence. More than the simple antagonist of the dialogue, Candour functions as a vehicle for irony. As an ingénue, she unwittingly supports the poet's position and unintentionally goads him into

action by filling him with righteous indignation that finally forces him to expose the great Hogarth in all his "meanness." The second part of the poem is a lengthy portrait of the painter, whom Churchill addresses directly as he reminds him of his limitations both as man and as artist.

The dialogue, with its dramatic and ironic tension, contains some of Churchill's best writing. Candour sometimes praises the satirist while seeming to rebuke him; at other times, she unknowingly gives credence to his negative view of the world. In both cases, she functions to substantiate the satirist's assumed position of personal integrity that is opposed to the corruption of the world. The reader does not have to rely on the poet's personal defense of his satiric art; his outspoken antagonist indirectly confirms the rectitude of his position in her very criticism. Upbraiding the poet for writing satire instead of panegyric, Candour reminds him:

> WHEN Poverty, the Poet's constant crime,
> Compell'd thee, all unfit, to trade in rime,
> Had not Romantic notions turn'd thy head,
> Had'st Thou not valued Honour more than bread,
> Had Int'rest, pliant Int'rest been thy guide,
> And had not Prudence been debauch'd by Pride,
> In flatt'ry's stream Thou would'st have dipp'd thy pen,
> Applied to great, and not to honest men,
> Nor should Conviction have seduc'd thy heart
> To take the weaker, tho' the better part.   (89-98)

Candour, here, is quite right in her opinion. The irony lies in the dichotomy between two conflicting standards of values: Candour's and the poet's. To her, pride (personal integrity) is something that debauches; conviction, something that seduces. Obviously, her values, despite her good intentions, have become distorted; and we are quick to side with the poet.

The ironic antagonist also supports the poet indirectly when she attempts to show him the perversity of his outlook upon the world. Candour, echoing the irresolute Hamlet,[22] points out that the satirist's estimate of man as incorrigible in his envy

> Sicklies our hopes with the pale hue of Fear;
> Tells us that all our labours are in vain,
> That what we seek, we never can obtain,
> That, dead to Virtue, lost to Nature's plan,
> ENVY possesses the whole race of man,

>   That Worth is criminal, and Danger lies,
>   Danger extreme, in being good and wise.   (244-50)

Again, Candour is right. Again, it is a question of values. The satirist, unlike his antagonist, insists upon seeing things as they are.

Besides supporting the satirist's view of man, the ironic antagonist effects the climax of the poem by intensifying the satirist's righteous rage until it explodes in a diatribe against Hogarth. Gradually pressing the poet to the wall, Candour first accuses him of being misguided. She then says he is dangerous to man's peace of mind. Finally, she accuses him of being malignantly deceptive. His view of man is false — so false that there exists no one man who would fit into the general picture. Candour challenges him to show her just one man as bad as he had painted mankind in general; if he can, she will withdraw her accusation. The poet has no choice. To illustrate the ubiquity of envy, he immediately seizes upon Hogarth.

In this manner, Churchill effects the transition into the second main part of the poem, a portrait of Hogarth. While the indirect statement of the first part shifts to direct satire, the dramatic quality inherent in the dialogue between Candour and the satirist is preserved when the satirist addresses Hogarth. The drama involved is intensified at the beginning of the portrait when Churchill presents a courtroom scene with Candour as the judge, the satirist as the king's counsel, and Hogarth as the defendant. The scene is initially set when Candour challenges the poet to "Produce one proof" in "Truth's sacred court" (297-99). The satirist, in the role of king's counsel, replies:

>   HOGARTH — I take thee, CANDOUR, at thy word,
>   Accept thy proffer'd terms, and will be heard;
>   Thee have I heard with virulence declaim,
>   Nothing retain'd of Candour but the name;
>   By Thee have I been charg'd in angry strains
>   With that mean falshood which my soul disdains —
>   HOGARTH stand forth — Nay hang not thus aloof —
>   Now, CANDOUR, now Thou shall receive such proof,
>   Such damning proof, that henceforth Thou shalt fear
>   To tax my wrath, and own my conduct clear —
>   HOGARTH stand forth — I dare thee to be tried
>   In that great Court, where Conscience must preside;
>   At that most solemn bar hold up thy hand;
>   Think before whom on what account you stand —

> Speak, but consider well — from first to last
> Review thy life, weigh ev'ry action past —
> Nay, you shall have no reason to complain —
> Take longer time, and view them o'er again —
> Canst Thou remember from thy earliest youth,
> And as thy God must judge Thee, speak the truth,
> A single instance where, *Self* laid aside,
> And Justice taking place of fear and pride,
> Thou with an equal eye did'st GENIUS view,
> And give to Merit what was Merit's due?   (309-32)

Churchill has heightened the drama in the *Epistle* with action, dialogue, and an appropriate shift in style. Suggested by the dialogue is a brief scene played by Candour, the satirist, and Hogarth. The satirist, standing between Candour and Hogarth, turns emotionally from one to the other; and Hogarth hesitantly enters, raises his right hand to take the oath, opens his mouth as if to complain that he is being pushed too quickly, and finally listens mutely to the accusation.

Though still highly rhetorical, this passage has a strong flavor of the colloquial which sets it off from the rest of the poem. This flavor is largely achieved by simulation of the relative incoherence of unmeditated speech. Breaks in thought occur as the satirist, while calling forth Hogarth, parenthetically addresses Candour at the same time. A particular reaction on the part of the defendant causes the poet to jump without transition from one idea to another:

> Review thy life, weigh ev'ry action past —
> Nay, you shall have no reason to complain —
> Take longer time, and view them over again —
> Canst Thou remember from thy earliest youth . . .

Behind the colloquial effect, the style is still highly rhetorical and controlled. One of Churchill's favorite rhetorical devices is anaphora, used sometimes for emphasis though more often to tighten the structure of the verse paragraph. Here, anaphora occurs when the satirist three times calls forth the defendant. This device is not only structurally effective, framing as it does the parenthetical asides to Candour; it also gives a sense of urgency to the passage and, more importantly, helps to establish the colloquial tone and dramatic effect that Churchill is trying to achieve.

The attack against Hogarth, thematically established in the first

part of the poem, centers upon his alleged envy, a sin common to "great" men. Reminiscent of Pope's adverse judgment of Addison in his famous portrait of Atticus[23] is Churchill's accusation that Hogarth cannot abide any serious competition in his own field. But Hogarth, according to the poet, has gone one step farther than other "great" men in that he resents excellence in *any* individual. This trait, the satirist concludes, is the reason for Hogarth's antipathy toward the champion of freedom. Envy has grown so powerful in the artist that he is willing to sacrifice English liberty, if this be necessary, to gratify his personal resentment. Hogarth's sentiment is: "Let Freedom perish, if, to Freedom true, / In the same ruin WILKES may perish too" (417-18).

This distortion of values, this blindly selfish passion in the artist so enrages the satirist that he shifts to what seems almost pure invective, as he turns from Hogarth's moral weakness, which might be corrected, to his physical weakness, old age, a natural and universal disability. Callously amplifying this physical weakness, Churchill points out the paradox of living malice in a dying man:

> WITH all the symptoms of assur'd decay,
> With age and sickness pinch'd, and worn away,
> Pale quiv'ring lips, lank cheeks, and falt'ring tongue,
> The Spirits out of tune, the Nerves unstrung,
> Thy Body shrivell'd up, thy dim eyes sunk
> Within their sockets deep, thy weak hams shrunk
> The body's weight unable to sustain,
> The stream of life scarce trembling thro' the vein,
>
> . . . .
> Can'st thou, e'en thus, thy thoughts to vengeance give,
> And, dead to all things else, to Malice live?   (419-30)

When Garrick, somewhat theatrically, termed the poem "barbarous," he was overlooking the rhetorical function of lines such as these. As much a portrait of old age as of aging Hogarth, they satirically diminish the poem's subject to a figure of harmless impotence. Moreover, their apparent brutality is a kind of objective correlative of the satirist's wrath, its intensity an index of the heinous nature of Hogarth's offense.

Churchill elaborates the theme of envy by pointing out that Hogarth is envious not only of living competitors but of dead rivals. After he reminds the artist of his dismal failure to outrival the ancients with his painting of the grieving Sigismunda, which was re-

jected by the individual who had commissioned it,[24] the satirist has
the opportunity of giving his portrait an aura of objectivity. He
praises the painter's comic genius:

> In Comedy, thy nat'ral road to fame,
> Nor let me call it by a meaner name,
> Where a beginning, middle, and an end
> Are aptly joined; where parts on parts depend,
> Each made for each, as bodies for their soul,
> So as to form one true and perfect whole,
> Where a plain story to the eye is told,
> Which we conceive the moment we behold,
> HOGARTH unrivall'd stands . . .   (559-67)

But Churchill's praise is so faint as to become, like that of Pope's Atticus, damning. Comedy, something "natural" to Hogarth, could
easily be called by a "meaner name." He has not violated the critical
commonplaces, and the result is something rather superficial: "a
plain story to the eye is told, / Which we conceive the moment we
behold." The tone of the passage is ironic; what appears to be unqualified praise is actually highly qualified — to the point that it
becomes something less than praise, preserving the general negative
portrait of Hogarth. Again, the devil's advocate functions, as in the
case of Candour, as the satirist's ironic spokesman.

Similarly, the satirist appears to compliment, in a backhanded
way, the aged artist when, at the end of the poem, he points out the
"universal truth" that the best decay most quickly:

> SURE 'tis a curse which angry Fates impose,
> To mortify man's arrogance, that Those
> Who're fashion'd of some better sort of clay,
> Much sooner than the common herd decay.   (629-32)

Jonathan Swift and Sir Richard Steele, both of whom suffered
serious disabilities before their deaths, come to the satirist's mind
most immediately as examples.[25] By evoking these literary stalwarts
of the previous age, Churchill seems to be equating Hogarth's artistic stature with theirs. But, once more, the poet undercuts his apparent praise with irony: "The greatest GENIUS to this Fate may
bow; / REYNOLDS, in time, may be like HOGARTH now" (653-54). On
the surface, Churchill is saying that Hogarth's present deficiencies
are simply the result of his superior genius. But the phrase "the

greatest genius" is linked by the logic of the heroic couplet to a younger painter of considerable reputation, Sir Joshua Reynolds. Thus, Churchill is really saying that Hogarth may be great, but Reynolds is the greatest; moreover, while Reynolds *may* decay, Hogarth has already done so.

The poem ends, then, with Churchill's emphasizing not simply the aging Hogarth's infirmities but implying that the artist, like Steele and Swift, has suffered serious deterioration. Thus, this prominent supporter of the administration and critic of Wilkes is reduced in stature from a great artist to a man "sunk, deep sunk, in second Childhood's night" (638). While Churchill's performance may be "barbarous," it is something far superior to simple invective. His skillful use of indirection, anticipating his memorable "Dedication" to the *Sermons*, raises it to the level of art.

IV   *The Libertine Redeemed*

"The [Carr] family are in the gratest distress, and you are universally condemn'd for having made a worthy family unhappy," Wilkes wrote to Churchill early in November 1763 to let him know the public's reaction to the poet's recent elopement with the adolescent Elizabeth Carr.[26] Churchill's pursuit of pleasure may have been about to interfere seriously with his political mission at this point, for how could he go on assuming the pose of the righteous satirist who was serving virtue when men like Boswell's friend Temple were referring to him as a "monster"?[27] Since some sort of public apology was needed, Churchill's *The Conference* not only apologizes but shows that in his public life the satirist is incorruptible and even noble.

The poem pits patriot against peer. In an attempt to silence the patriot poet, a cynical peer, convinced that self-interest basically motivates all men, first tries to appeal to that instinct in the poet. When he asks the poet whether his self-interest has never triumphed over his virtue, the latter admits to some pangs of conscience which readers have generally attributed to remorse arising from the Carr affair.[28] Admitting to selfish behavior in his private life, the patriot poet points out that his public life is beyond reproach. When he sees that the satirist cannot be convinced, the peer tries to frighten him with the suggestion of prosecution; but his threat only serves as an opportunity for the satirist to make the heroic announcement that he is ready to die for his ideals.

Like the first part of *An Epistle to William Hogarth*, *The*

Conference is a dramatic dialogue; but it is more realistic and immediate than the earlier poem because Churchill's interlocutor is not an abstraction like Candour but a believable proadministration lord who, understandably, is trying to silence Wilkes's most articulate defender. The poem's setting is in no way allegorical, but direct and naturalistic: the satirist finds himself alone at a dinner table with his noble host, for the hostess and other guests (including the king himself) have withdrawn. Churchill sets the scene with unusual economy by immediately placing in opposition "the proud Landlord" and "his threadbare guest" (4). The former appears bored, uncouth, overconfident:

> My Lord, in usual taste, began to yawn,
> And lolling backward in his Elbow-chair,
> With an insipid kind of stupid stare,
> Picking his teeth, twirling his seals about —   (6-9)

The lord's aggressive gestures indicate that the attack has already begun; he does not waste any time on pleasantries but gets to the point at once: "CHURCHILL, You have a Poem coming out. / . . . I really fear / Your Muse in general is too severe" (10-12).

After this brief introduction, the narrator disappears, leaving the stage to his antagonists. In the course of the agon (or struggle), the peer emerges as shrewd, cynical, amoral. He has accepted the Hobbesian view of man as a creature fundamentally motivated by Self, which the lord virtually deifies as "Our first great Mover, and our last great End" (176). It is his basic philosophy of life which, despite his astuteness, blinds him to the possibility of altruism and, therefore, to the real nature of the satirist. Patriotism, to him, is only a political stance, adopted for self-serving ends:

> To feign a red-hot zeal for freedom's cause,
> To mouth aloud for liberties and laws,
> For Public good to bellow all abroad,
> Serves well the purposes of private fraud.   (153-56)

While the peer's judgment indicates the limitations of his cynical outlook, it also reflects the kind of criticism of his own political career that Churchill's enemies could have been making in real life; and it is a bold stroke on the poet's part to say of himself the worst that could be said.

The cynical, self-serving peer functions as a foil to the patriot poet

whose character is that of the righteous, independent satirist. Churchill's persona, who is somewhat similar to that of Pope in *An Epistle to Dr. Arbuthnot,* serves virtue and rejects demeaning patronage. With a humility uncharacteristic of his creator, he attributes his economic success to his readers: "A gen'rous PUBLIC made me what I Am" (150).[29] His humility is also evident when he acknowledges his indebtedness to the generosity of Dr. Pierson Lloyd, who had rescued him from debtor's prison. Imaging Lloyd as Christ and himself as Peter, Churchill describes the incident in terms of the apostle's attempt to walk on water, in order to give a religious aura to his righteous satirist:

> Sinking beneath the storm, my Spirits fail'd
> Like PETER's faith, 'till One, a Friend indeed,
> . . . .
> Image of him whom Christians should adore,
> Stretch'd forth his hand, and brought me safe to shore.   (112-18)

In the course of the agon between poet and peer, Churchill unobtrusively and dramatically introduces his apology, the raison d'être for the poem. Rather than damaging him, this admission of guilt strengthens the character of his righteous persona. Instead of a libertine, he appears as a humble, frank, repentant sinner. Moreover, the antagonism of his bullying inquisitor adds to our sympathy for him. Finally, his blemished private life sets off to advantage his untarnished public career; and one of Churchill's telling points is his distinction between the two spheres. "Ah! what, my Lord, hath private life to do / With things of public Nature?" (213-14) he asks with some exasperation before making his confession.[30] Churchill is (and rightly so) not at all explicit about his "sin," which he refers to in terms of "those scenes,"

> Which, without pain and horror to behold,
> Must speak me something more, or less than man;
> Which friends may pardon, but I never can.   (215-18)

Cleverly, he at once diminishes his "crime" (friends may pardon it) and inflates his remorse (he will never be able to forgive himself). The "horror" that he refers to becomes "tragic horror" a little later as Churchill continues to amplify hyperbolically his patriot poet's remorse. He claims that the scandal involved ("the babbling of a busy world" [221]) is nothing; it is his conscience that pains:

> Free and at large might their [the world's] wild curses roam,
> If All, if All alas! were well at home.
> No — 'tis the tale which angry Conscience tells,
> When She with more than tragic horror swells
> Each circumstance of guilt . . .   (225-29)

We should be aware, of course, that the persona is speaking and not the libertine Churchill.

Churchill does not stop with this public confession but uses the personal scandal to establish his unblemished public career. To prove his altruism in the public sphere, the patriot poet rejects the peer's attempt to manipulate him; and, in doing so, he displays not only his personal integrity but also his courage. Churchill has the peer threaten the poet with the possibility of prosecution by the government so that he can demonstrate the depth of the poet's courage. Virtually challenging the administration to do its worst, the poet asks the "GOD of *Truth*" (375) for strength to give his life, if necessary, to defend his freedom:

> Let Me, as hitherto, still draw my breath,
> In love with life, but not in fear of death,
> And, if oppression brings me to the grave,
> And marks him dead, She ne'er shall mark a slave.   (381-84)

Because Churchill's verse is weak here, he cannot support the heroic sentiment he is trying to express; and the fearless patriot is ultimately not convincing. Nevertheless, Churchill has succeeded in shifting his reader's critical judgment from himself to his enemies. The subject of public scandal emerges a victim of political tyranny.

Churchill's skill lies in the way that he has taken the strategy of the satiric apologia and used it to redeem his injured reputation and to attack his political enemies, all in defense of his friend John Wilkes. The dramatic dialogue allows him to satirize the administration indirectly by letting the peer, presented as a typical member of the king's party, reveal himself to be cynical, self-serving, devious, unscrupulous, threatening. More important, the dialogic method also allows him to "prove" his own essential incorruptibility by resisting the lord's attempts to sway him. The reader sees, as it were, the poet's virtue in action.

Finally, we have to admire Churchill's boldness. Something more than mere rhetoric is involved in his challenge to the administration; Churchill *is* taking a risk. The ministry had already displayed its

power when it silenced *The North Briton* by arresting Wilkes. Although he was released and was later successful in his lawsuit against those responsible for his arrest, Wilkes's (and Churchill's) contest with the administration over freedom of the press was far from over. In the same month that *The Conference* appeared, the ministry began proceedings against Wilkes for reissuing *North Briton* 45 and for printing *An Essay on Women*.

V   *The Satirist versus the Party Hack*

Instrumental in the attempt to blacken Wilkes's character was John Kidgell, the clergyman who assisted in bribing Wilkes's printers to obtain a copy of *An Essay on Women* for presentation to the members of the House of Lords. Kidgell immediately capitalized upon the situation by publishing in November 1763 *A Genuine and Succinct Narrative of a scandalous, obscene, and exceedingly profane libel, entitled, An Essay on Women*, which explained how he had managed to obtain a copy of the poem; and, in the course of condemning it, he described in detail the obscene passages.[31] A satirical portrait of this hypocritical priest, who "Most lusciously declaims 'gainst luscious themes" (389), functions as the climax of Churchill's *The Author*. Published a month after *The Conference*, the poem continues Churchill's projection of himself as the courageous patriot poet by indirectly contrasting himself with the party hack who is presented in a series of satirical portraits as mercenary, hypocritical, and treacherous.

The Author's surface contrasts Briton's slavish modern writers with the heroic writers of her past who were the defenders of English liberty. The poem opens with an ironic lament for the literate man in eighteenth century England where learning is no longer rewarded. That this is the country where the "hardy Poet . . . Bade Pow'r turn pale" (88-91) is difficult to believe. In a long, formal digression, Churchill emphasizes both the power of satire and the fact that satire is no respecter of rank. While lamenting the current state of letters, he indirectly shows that the heroic writer still exists — himself. Opposed to such heroic writers are the slavish party hacks, a number of whom Churchill presents in a gallery of satiric portraits that concludes the poem.

The general structure of the poem is based on contrast but not one of a simple kind. Churchill's characteristic indirection comes into play as he more or less explicitly contrasts himself as an ex-clergyman with Kidgell and another clerical pamphleteer, Philip

Francis, who mask their basic treachery in priestly garb and who
make the satirist, whatever the reader might think about his defection from the priesthood, look honest — if only an honest libertine.
More important is the way in which Churchill implicitly contrasts
himself with the political hirelings. He does this in a long "digression" which is really an integral part of the poem in that it presents
the satiric norm or positive, not in the kind of static portrait that
Churchill draws of himself as a reluctant clergyman near the end of
the poem but in a more dramatic one. As in the previous poem, we
see the satirist in action — courageously warning potential enemies
of Wilkes that he does not respect parliamentary privilege, that a
peerage will not protect its guilty holder from his satire, that even a
king is not beyond his reach.

The "digression" is introduced when the poet, contrasting the
slavish present with the heroic past, recalls the enormous power once
wielded by the satirist: he "Bade Pow'r turn pale, kept mighty
rogues in awe, / And made them fear the Muse, who fear'd not
Law" (91-92). "How do I laugh," he explodes, suddenly inter-
rupting his train of thought to consider the role of satire in the context of various ridiculous responses to it. This introjection prefaces
each response to form a rhetorical pattern that eventually becomes
typical of Churchill — a pattern that unifies and intensifies the passage.

As in the two previous poems, *An Epistle to William Hogarth* and
The Conference, the satirist is given an antagonist, here several of
them, to achieve the dramatic effect that Churchill wants. One is
Publius (perhaps Smollett),[32] who tells the poet: "All sacred is the
name and pow'r of Kings" and "Statesmen . . . / Were never made
for Poets to controul" (123-26), and who thereby implies that some
subjects are superior to satire. In response, the satirist uses a religious
analogy to give a kind of sacerdotal aura to his profession; Churchill
has found a new priesthood in his role as patriot poet:

> The blessed Saints above in numbers speak
> The praise of God, tho' there all praise is weak;
> In Numbers here below the Bard shall teach
> Virtue to soar beyond the Villain's reach;
> Shall tear his lab'ring lungs, strain his hoarse throat,
> And raise his voice beyond the trumpet's note,
> Should an afflicted Country, aw'd by men
> Of slavish principles, demand his pen.   (133-40)

Another antagonist is an unidentified lord who feels that his rank should give him immunity from satire, especially by someone not his peer:

> What, shall a reptile Bard, a wretch unknown,
> Without one badge of merit, but his own,
> Great Nobles lash, and *Lords*, like common men,
> Smart from the vengeance of a Scribbler's pen? (153-56)

This speech gives Churchill a chance to display his impartiality and courage. Indeed, he is seen to represent that very heroic past, the loss of which he has just been lamenting. Boldly, he tells his antagonist that, if he acts like a nobleman, he will be treated like one; if not, he will be exposed — even if he happens to be the king:

> Tho' God in vengeance had made Thee a King,
> Taking on Virtue's wing her daring flight,
> The Muse should drag thee trembling to the light,
> Probe thy foul wounds, and lay thy bosom bare
> To the keen question of the searching air. (180-84)

No idle threats these. Churchill concludes his digression with an attack, though a somewhat guarded one, against not the king but one of his ministers, the earl of Sandwich, secretary of state for the southern department, who had betrayed his friend Wilkes when he spoke against *An Essay on Women* before the House of Lords.

This particular nobleman, whom Churchill would expose more thoroughly in later works, *The Duellist* and The *Candidate*, appears in *The Author* as a specific example to support the poet's claim for the power of satire. Earlier, another antagonist, who had referred to satire as a "harmless dart," had prompted the poet to declare that satire is not only effective but that its effects linger on after the subject's death:

> When in the tomb thy pamper'd flesh shall rot,
> And e'en by friends thy mem'ry be forgot,
> Still shalt Thou live, recorded for thy crimes,
> Live in her [Satire's] page and stink to after-times. (221-24)

As a specific example of the power of satire, he evokes Sandwich,[33] "who, from the moment of his birth, / Made human Nature a reproach on earth" (227-28). Even he "Would blush should he be

told, by Truth and Wit, / Those actions, which he blush'd not to commit" (231-32).

In such a way does Churchill dramatize himself, or more precisely his persona, that he emerges by the end of the digression as the courageous satirist — as "the author" who, rather than sell his pen to a repressive government, uses it, as did his spiritual ancestor Andrew Marvell, to attack the government. In contrast to this righteous, courageous satirist are the administration hirelings: two editors of newspapers that had supported the Bute ministry, Arthur Murphy and John Shebbeare (Shebbeare edited *The Moderator*); an historian who had put his literary talent at the disposition of the ministry, William Guthrie; and the two pampleteering clergymen already mentioned, Philip Francis and John Kidgell. A more overt, specific contrast occurs with the clergymen, who in their hypocrisy and treachery make Churchill, who earlier that year surrendered his gown, look good. With his satiric portraits, Churchill also, more obviously, intends to discredit these Tory propagandists.

First in this gallery is Arthur Murphy, who "shifts his sails, and catches ev'ry wind" (260). Churchill underscores the mercenary nature of the party hack in the portrait of this former editor of *The Auditor* who threatened to expose his employers because he felt insufficiently rewarded:[34]

> Pay him but well, and MURPHY is thy friend.
> He, He shall ready stand with venal rimes
> To varnish guilt, and consecrate thy crimes,
> To make corruption in false colours shine,
> And damn his own good name, to rescue thine.

> But, if thy niggard hands their gifts with-hold,
> And Vice no longer rains down show'rs of gold,
> Expect no mercy; facts, well grounded, teach,
> MURPHY, if not rewarded, will impeach.   (276-84)

Murphy appears not only venal but completely unreliable.

Of less importance are the political writer John Shebbeare and the historian William Guthrie. The Jacobite (and thus "seditious") inclination of Shebbeare is stressed, but Guthrie is ridiculed for the gross factual errors of his recently published *Complete History of the English Peerage* in which he "Makes Women bring forth after they are dead" and "on a curious, new, and happy plan, / In *Wedlock*'s sacred bands joins Man to Man" (320-22). Churchill does not have

to explain how Guthrie's knack for presenting the impossible as historical fact made him a natural for the ministry.

After this comic interlude, the portraits become darker as Churchill turns to the two clergymen who are more truly the objects of his satire than the bungling historian. Since one of them, Philip Francis, had acted as an agent for the Tory leader Henry Fox, Churchill associates him with the alleged double-dealing involved in the execution of Fox's steward, John Ayliffe, whom a false promise of pardon supposedly kept from incriminating his master.[35] Alluding to these circumstances, Churchill writes:

> Dost Thou contrive, for some base private end,
> Some selfish view, to hang a trusting friend,
> To lure him on, e'en to his parting breath,
> And promise life, to work him surer death?   (331-34)

If so, Francis is the man: "The Atheist Chaplain of an Aetheist Lord" (340).

Sandwiched between his portraits of such hypocritical clergymen as Francis and Kidgell is Churchill's apologia for his recent defection from the priesthood. Churchill is concerned, as he was in *The Conference,* with his image as a righteous satirist. He begins his defense by emphasizing the fact that he had never freely chosen the life of a parson: "Bred to the Church, and for the gown decreed, / 'Ere it was known that I should learn to read . . ." (341-42). He also reminds his readers of the incredibly low income of the average "working priest" when he refers with more than a trace of bitterness to "pomp of *rev'rend begg'ry*" and to being "Condemn'd . . . / To pray, and starve on forty pounds a year" (349-52). These are indeed extenuating circumstances, but the defection can be viewed as something more than forgiveable. When we consider that the treacherous, hypocritical Francis is a priest, Churchill's resignation becomes even virtuous: "Virtue to my conduct witness bears / In throwing off that gown, which FRANCIS wears" (355-56). Only at this climactic point does Churchill actually identify the "Aetheist Chaplain" of the preceding portrait.

Having made his point, Churchill does not repeat it. Instead of dissociating himself from corrupt, hypocritical clergymen as he did with Francis, he ironically identifies with Kidgell. But Churchill identifies with the name only after he has condemned the person in this final and most vigorous sketch of modern authors. As he had

done in the previous portrait, he withholds the name of his subject until the sketch is completed.

That Churchill, who shared Juvenal's contempt for the homosexual, which would be articulated soon in *The Times*, should most immediately be concerned with his subject's effeminacy is no surprise. "Suffice it that the wretch from SODOM came" (366). Connected with that is Kidgell's double life (which in its doubleness was not much different from the life Churchill himself had led until recently):

> The Preacher is a Christian, dull but true;
> But when the hallow'd hour of preaching's o'er,
> That plan of doctrine's never thought of more;
> CHRIST is laid by neglected on the shelf,
> And the vile Priest is Gospel to himself.   (378-82)

It is his subject's hypocrisy that Churchill stresses most. That trait of Kidgell is most apparent when, in exploiting *An Essay on Women*, this alleged student of John Cleland (author of the pornographic *Fanny Hill*) "Most lusciously declaims 'gainst luscious themes, / And, whilst he rails at blasphemy, blasphemes" (389-90).

A startling ironic reversal occurs when Churchill, at the end of his anonymous portrait, identifies with Kidgell, who like himself, is superior to the anonymous clergyman just ridiculed. Taking up again the problem of self-seeking among the clergy, he holds up Kidgell and himself as satiric norms:

> Such be their Arts, whom Interest controuls;
> KIDGELL and *I* have free and honest souls.
> We scorn Preferment which is gain'd by Sin,
> And will, tho' poor without, have peace within.   (395-98)

The reversal is complicated even further as Churchill pretends (as he does again in the "Dedication" to his *Sermons*) that he is still an impoverished clergyman.

By setting off his own career against those of Francis and Kidgell, Churchill cleverly takes what some might consider a personal fault — his resignation from the priesthood — and turns it into a virtue in much the same way that he had earlier turned the shame attached to his elopement to his advantage. Not only as a fearless critic of his times but as a master of indirection has Churchill proven himself "the author."

CHAPTER 4

Later Political Satire: Poetry of 1764

DURING the first eight months of 1764, Churchill published four major poems; and each one evolved from the political conflict in which he and Wilkes were engaged. With the exception of *Gotham*, each of these political satires was occasional, exploiting a suspicious move made by Wilkes's enemies in the administration. In *The Duellist*, Churchill tried to show that the duel in which Samuel Martin, joint secretary to the treasury, seriously wounded Wilkes was an attempt at assassination planned by his friend's political enemies. The candidacy of the earl of Sandwich for high steward at Cambridge gave Churchill the opportunity to portray in *The Candidate* one of the men who had been instrumental in the attempted character assassination of Wilkes as an incompetent scoundrel. In *The Farewell*, Churchill uses Robert Clive's sailing for India as newly appointed governor of Bengal to suggest that the administration's support of Clive and the East India Company might not be in the nation's best interests. Meanwhile, he was commenting more generally and more indirectly on the political situation by presenting negative and positive pictures of monarchy in *Gotham* that was published serially during this eight-month period.

Dominant themes in these poems are liberty and patriotism. *The Duellist*, which equates legal and physical attacks against Wilkes with ones against freedom, suggests that death is preferable to life without liberty. Churchill's advocacy of freedom is even stronger in *Gotham* in which, referring to the Glorious Revolution, he parenthetically proposes revolution as a universal political alternative: "thro' ev'ry age, in ev'ry land, / Written in gold let REVOLUTION stand" (II, 675-76). *The Candidate*, recognizing that loyalty can sink to servility and that freedom can run into license, suggests a reasoned balance between loyalty and liberty as the norm. Patriotism is the central theme of *The Farewell*, which opposes the patriot with the citizen of the world.

In regard to prosody and satiric technique, these poems tend to employ forms that Churchill had used previously. *The Duellist* is his third and last experiment with the octosyllabic couplet. Dialogue as a structural device, which was previously used in *An Epistle to William Hogarth* and in *The Conference*, functions less successfully in *The Farewell;* but the ironic eulogy of *The Prophecy of Famine* is used more effectively against the earl of Sandwich in *The Candidate*. The lyric mode, evident in *The Prophecy of Famine*, surfaces again in *Gotham*, a new experiment in indirection.

I   *An Assassin Exposed*

On November 15, 1763, John Wilkes was under fire in both houses of Parliament. In the House of Lords, the earl of Sandwich and Bishop Warburton attacked his character in their denunciation of *An Essay on Woman*. In the House of Commons, Sir Fletcher Norton, the attorney general, helped initiate more serious charges against him when he succeeded in getting *North Briton* 45 voted seditious. A potentially more dangerous attack against Wilkes was made on the same day in the House of Commons by Samuel Martin, who insultingly denounced the author of *North Briton* 40, which referred with something less than respect to Martin's appointment as joint secretary to the treasury.[1] The confrontation seemed intended to provoke a duel, for which Martin proved to be well prepared. Horace Walpole probably reflected the opinion of many of his contemporaries when he wrote: "I shall not be thought to have used too hard an expression, when I called this [the duel] a plot against the life of Wilkes."[2]

Martin's attempt upon Wilkes's life fitted into an emerging pattern of related situations. Less than fourteen months earlier, Wilkes had exchanged shots with William Talbot, who became the "hero" of *The Ghost*, Book I, for his efforts. Ten months after this duel, Wilkes was challenged in August 1763 to another duel in Paris by the Scots Captain John Forbes. Churchill, in a letter of advice to his friend, expressed agreement with Wilkes's designation of the duel, which never materialized, as an attempted assassination: "Forbes and you had no legitimate cause of combat, I mean no cause which could be deem'd legitimate even in a Court of Honour. The ground on which he call'd you out was the most unreasonable in the world,[3] nor should I scruple to say, what I am certain I could prove, that however fair his Subsequent proceedings might have been, yet his principles were faulty, and he was rather in your own very proper

and forcible words to be consider'd as an Assassin than as a Gentleman."[4]

A month after the duel with Martin, another Scotsman, Alexander Dunn, threatened to kill Wilkes but was arrested before he was able to attempt to fulfill his threat. According to Walpole, the "mob" was of the opinion that Dunn was in the employ of the earl of Sandwich.[5] The name "Dunn," as well as "Forbes," becomes a synonym for "assassin" in *The Duellist* (617) in which Churchill's purpose is to promote the idea that Wilkes was the target of political assassination. In an attempt to discredit his friend's political enemies, *The Duellist* depicts Warburton, Sandwich, and Norton as conspiring against Wilkes, using Martin as their tool.

The Duellist is in the tradition of *The Ghost*, the fourth book of which had been published two months earlier in November 1763. As he did in the earlier poem, Churchill uses octosyllabic couplets, occasionally reminiscent of *Hudibras*. Mock-heroic elements, while not so apparent as in *The Ghost*, occur most notably in Book III with its mock visit to the underworld, with the intervention of the supernatural in the form of the Goddess Fraud, and with the mock-heroic presentation of the speeches. The mock-heroic elements, plus the Hudibrastic note that occasionally enters the meter, tend to give the poem a burlesque tone that may be appropriate enough for a conspirator's portrait but that inappropriately puts the attempted assassination (although it is not actually presented in the poem) in a ridiculous light. The gravity of the situation, as Churchill saw it, is diminished. What would Wilkes have to fear from a mid-eighteenth century Hudibras?[6]

Churchill's revelation of the "plot" behind the Wilkes-Martin duel fills three books. As a long introduction, the first book contrasts the patriot Wilkes with the statesman Fox, suggests a threat to Wilkes and liberty, and indirectly presents Martin as a hired assassin. The second book gives a historical matrix to the poem with an allegorical presentation of recent events — Bute's rise to power, the appearance of *The North Briton*, the arrest of the printers, the libel judgment against *North Briton* 45 — and all of them lead to the usurpation of Liberty's throne by Statecraft. Dramatizing the allegory's final phase, the third book presents the conspiratorial trio — Norton, Sandwich, and Warburton — which is seeking the means of destroying Wilkes until Fraud comes to their aid with an offer of her eldest son, Samuel Martin, the assassin-duellist.

The most notable things about *The Duellist* are Churchill's use of

indirection and his satiric portraits. The best examples of indirection are the introductions of Fox and Martin. Fox functions, in the first book, as a foil to Wilkes in *The Duellist*'s central polarity between politician and patriot — a polarity that is allegorized in the second by Statecraft's triumph over Liberty and that is dramatized in the third by the secret midnight tryst of conspirators. Fox made himself eligible for this role by promoting with extensive bribery the Peace of Paris, which Churchill considered a betrayal of national interest.

To establish a mood of treachery, Churchill calls up personi- fications of various vicious types, including the "Noble Gamester," who, playing fast and loose with British possessions, "with the mo- tion of a die, / Dost make a mighty Island fly" (81-82). These denizens of sleepless night, "on whose lids / That worm, which never dies, forbids / Sweet Sleep to fall" (121-23), are called to witness sleeping Innocence, a bedfellow of no other than Henry Fox, Lord Holland. Startling us with such an ironic reversal (one heightened by rhetorical climax), the satirist calls these sleepless vil- lains to "that holy bed, / Where PEACE her full dominion keeps, / And INNOCENCE with HOLLAND sleeps" (126-28). To heighten the irony, Churchill gives Fox as guardian angel the spirit of the statesman's former steward John Ayliffe, whom Fox was thought to have betrayed on the eve of his execution to preserve himself. No matter what happens "to make night hideous,"

> Still is thy sleep, Thou Virtuous Man,
> . . . .
> Still shall thy AYLIFF, taught, tho' late,
> Thy friendly justice in his fate,
> Turn'd to a guardian Angel, spread
> Sweet dreams of comfort round thy head.   (139-46)

More than simple ironic reversal is involved; the satirist is suggesting that Fox is so hardened in crime that he is invulnerable even to Ayliffe's ghost.

In contrast to the hardened politician is the vulnerable patriot Wilkes whose very existence is threatened by the dark night which shelters those who plot against him. A threat to Wilkes is a threat to liberty in Churchill's eyes; he hints at a "deed" that "Might tear up Freedom by the root, / Destroy a WILKES, and fix a BUTE" (151-52). Casting about for an appropriate curse to wither any villain who could be bribed to attack the champion of liberty, Churchill comes

up with the epithet "Martin," as if the latter's name were already synonomous with "assassin," the way Quisling's became a synonym for "traitor" during World War II:

> May He, — but words are all too weak
> The feelings of my heart to speak —
> May He — O for a noble curse
> Which might his very marrow pierce —
> The general contempt engage,
> And be the MARTIN of his age.   (243-48)

This offhand mention of the ur-assassin ironically functions as the climax of the first book and nicely prepares for the actual appearance of the duellist at the climax of the third (and of the poem as a whole): following Mother Fraud's generous offer of his services, "straight the portals open flew, / And, clad in armour, to their view / M[ARTIN], the *Duellist*, came forth" (1011-13).

Although he makes an appearance of sorts at the climax of the opening and closing books, mock-hero Martin is less the object of Churchill's satire here than his conspiring "brothers"; lengthy portraits of each of them make up the bulk of Book III. Norton, who was attacked earlier in *The Ghost* and in *An Epistle to William Hogarth*, is presented as completely unscrupulous in his practice of law:

> How often, in contempt of Laws,
> To sound the bottom of a cause,
> To search out ev'ry rotten part,
> And worm into its very heart,
> Hath he ta'en briefs on false pretence,
> And undertaken the defence
> Of trusting Fools, whom in the end
> He meant to ruin, not defend?   (839-46)

In such manner, Churchill attempts to cast doubt upon the integrity of the man who condemned the last number of *The North Briton* as a seditious libel.

The earl of Sandwich, who has already been referred to in *The Author* and who was to become the antihero of *The Candidate*, is presented as he was known — as a libertine; and Churchill indirectly underlines the ridiculous hypocrisy involved in Sandwich's denunciation of *An Essay on Woman*. The licentious nature of Sandwich is reflected in this list of his capabilities:

> To run a horse, to make a match,
> To revel deep, to roar a catch,
> To knock a tott'ring watchman down,
> To sweat a woman of the Town,
> By fits to keep the Peace, or break it,   ·.
> In turn to give a Pox, or take it . . .   (917-22)

The forty-five-year-old minister appears as a sort of glorified juvenile delinquent who is engaged in adolescent, morally undifferentiated, frenzied action.

The best and most interesting of the portraits is that of Bishop Warburton, who had seconded Sandwich's denunciation of *An Essay on Woman* in the House of Lords. Notable in its own right, the portrait is of added significance in that it looks forward to Churchill's ironic "Dedication" to Warburton, published posthumously a year later. The bishop of Gloucester is portrayed as an ambitious, hypocritical opportunist, whose pride is equalled only by his servility:

> . . . so proud, that should he meet
> The Twelve Apostles in the street,
> He'd turn his nose up at them all,
> And shove his Savior from the wall;

and "so mean"

> That he would cringe, and creep, be civil,
> And hold a stirrup for the Devil,
> If in a journey to his mind,
> He'd let him mount, and ride behind.   (671-80)

Churchill portrays Warburton as having deliberately attempted to raise himself above his humble origins ("To make himself a Gentleman" [694]) by becoming a parson with the ambition of attaining a bishopric. Warburton is shown as coming up to London "from the plow / And Pulpit" (719-20); and, striving to be accepted as a wit, he becomes "the Poets' Parasite" (722). Since Warburton's ambition makes him behave in ways that are violently antithetical to his profession, Churchill seems to be insinuating the hypocrisy involved in the Bishop's denunciation of *An Essay on Woman:*

> He, in the highest reign of noon,
> Bawl'd bawdry songs to a Psalm Tune,

> Liv'd with Men infamous and vile,
> Truck'd his salvation for a smile,
> To catch their humour caught their plan,
> And laugh'd at God to laugh with Man. (731-36)

Churchill also ridicules Warburton's ambitions as a theologian and as a critic. In the former role, "He in defence of Scripture wrote; / So long he wrote, and long about it, / That e'en Believers 'gan to doubt it" (742-44). The bishop's career as a critic can be seen as another example of unpriestly behavior. Alluding to his editions of the works of Pope and Shakespeare, Churchill deflates at once the critical and theological pretentions of Warburton: "He wrote, t'advance his Maker's praise, / Comments on rhimes, and notes on plays" (755-56).

As he had done in his character of Hogarth, Churchill ironically assumes the stance of an objective observer by acknowledging any virtue that his subject might possess. In Warburton's case, it is chastity, but that characteristic proves to be but a metaphor for sexual impotence as Churchill relays the gossip that the bishop's only son (born, incidentally, in Warburton's fifty-eighth year) was fathered by the assumed author of *An Essay on Woman,* the deceased politician Thomas Potter (775-84). This rather scurrilous attack is not uncharacteristic of "The Bruiser" who had previously used Johnson's partial blindness and the physical infirmities of Hogarth for satiric purposes.

A summary in the form of a series of epigrammatic antitheses, reminiscent of Pope's method in his portrait of Addison,[7] concludes the sketch of Warbarton:

> A Man, without a manly mind;
> No Husband, tho' he's truly wed;
> Tho' on his knees a child is bred,
> No Father; injur'd, without end
> A Foe; and, tho' oblig'd, no Friend;
> . . . .
> A Judge of Genius, tho' confest
> With not one spark of Genius blest;
> Amongst the first of Critics plac'd,
> Tho' free from ev'ry taint of Taste;
> . . . .
> A great Divine, as Lords agree,
> Without the least Divinity;
> To crown all, in declining age,

> Enflam'd with Church and Party-rage,
> Behold him, full and perfect quite,
> A false Saint, and true Hypocrite.   (788-810)

Rhetorically underscored by antithesis and oxymoron, the generalized epithet "hypocrite" sums up the various particular charges against Warburton, while giving the portrait a sense of unity and completion. *The Duellist*, not one of Churchill's more memorable works, does mark an advance in his skill at portraiture.

That the enemies of Wilkes felt the sting of Churchill's satirical lash is evident in the following lines from a letter by Wilkes that was written several months after the publication of the poem: " . . . I have suffer'd much from the reports spread here about the *Duellist*, and the anger of Lords, Bishops, &c. I only mean from the vexatious circumstances of forcing you to herd with solicitors, attornies, &c. any other resentment you despise; and as to my Lord of Gloucester [Warburton], his will always be as impotent as his lust."[8] Threat of legal action, which Wilkes alludes to, was apparently not taken very seriously by Churchill. His attacks against the government in general and against Sandwich and Warburton in particular were to become even stronger in the months that followed the publication of *The Duellist*.

II   *The Gray Lothario*

In the spring of 1764, the earl of Sandwich actively campaigned for the office of high steward, an important administrative post at the University of Cambridge, one that for many years had been governed by leaders of the Whig party. Churchill helped frustrate Sandwich's efforts by publishing *The Candidate*[9] which emphasized the earl's reputation as a libertine. The poem also discredited Sandwich as a potential university administrator by attributing to him the responsibility for what Churchill saw as the failures of the Grenville ministry.

Published at the beginning of May, Churchill's poem opens with a characteristically long introduction in which the poet ironically announces with much rhetoric his conversion from satire to panegyric. Sandwich, who is chosen as object of his new mode of versification, is at first ironically contrasted with the fictitious rake Lothario;[10] however, the portrait of Lothario is no less than an exaggerated, generalized character of Sandwich himself. The mock panegyric then becomes more topical as Churchill, listing the earl's ministerial

"triumphs," indirectly blames Sandwich for the economic ills of the nation. With these accomplishments, the earl is now proffering his services to the cause of higher education. After cataloguing Sandwich's Cambridge supporters in a mock-heroic vein, Churchill suggests Oxford as an alternative to Cambridge. The poem concludes with an attack against Oxford where, at the Encaenia held the previous year, Wilkes (and indirectly Churchill) had been publicly insulted.[11]

Perhaps more interesting to today's reader than the portrait of Sandwich is the autobiographical passage in the introduction of the poem. Churchill does not present himself as the satiric norm, as he did in *The Author;* rather, he introduces the passage in a catalogue of his previous topics — actors, authors, critics, Scotland, states, patriots, Wilkes, self, satire — that he intends to discard in favor of "panegyric." His rejection of the topic *self* is a kind of last will and testament in which he spurns his literary heirs, expresses a longing for immortality through his verse, and writes his libertine epitaph. Afraid that "posthumous nonsense" will be published in his name, he proclaims: "*Know all the World,* no greedy heir shall find, / Die when I will, one couplet left behind" (137-38).[12] The passage ends with Churchill's rather charmingly expressed vision of literary immortality from which his epitaph was later taken:

> Let one poor sprig of Bay around my head
> Bloom whilst I live, and point me out when dead;
> Let It (may Heav'n indulgent grant that pray'r)
> Be planted on my grave, nor wither there;
> And when, on travel bound, some riming guest[13]
> Roams thro' the Church-yard, whilst his Dinner's dress'd,
> Let It hold up this Comment to his eyes;
> Life to the last enjoy'd, *here* Churchill lies;
> Whilst (O, what joy that pleasing flatt'ry gives)
> Reading my Works, he cries — *here* Churchill lives. (145-54)

Six months later Churchill was dead; his executors inscribed his headstone in the Dover churchyard with the verse "Life to the last enjoy'd, *here* Churchill lies." The flippant nature of the epitaph tends to emphasize the negative, adolescent aspects of Churchill's individualism, but it also obscures both the courage and industry evident in his hard-hitting satiric attack against the enemies of Wilkes. Just as Swift's *saeva indignatio* was partly a mask, so in part was Churchill's hedonism; and, while Swift's early critics often

failed to respond to the comedy in his work, Churchill's critics have been sometimes inclined to pass him off too lightly.

While interesting in itself, this intrusion of the author does not especially add to the poem's total impact in that Churchill establishes no fundamental connection between the satirist and his victim as he did in *The Author*. The dramatic contrast here, though only an apparent one, is, as we have observed, between the ironically eulogized Sandwich and the fictitious Lothario, who is really a mirror of the earl. In the portrait of Sandwich, mock panegyric blends with mock heroic to diminish with grotesque comparisons this alleged enemy of English liberty. Churchill holds up the earl against Shakespeare's Macbeth and Prince Hal. When the satirist hails the earl at the beginning of his portrait (271-75), the reader recalls the witches' hailing of Macbeth before leading him to his ruin with visions of grandeur. A little later, Churchill echoes Vernon's description of Prince Hal mounting his horse to recall the upsurge of Sandwich's political career after Bute's resignation: "like a MARS . . . / We saw Thee nimbly vault . . . / Into the seat of pow'r, at one bold leap" (283-85).[14]

Churchill gives an interesting twist to his mock-heroic treatment of Sandwich in the portrait of the gay Lothario, an ironic foil to the mock hero. The negative portrait, which turns out to be a mirror image of Sandwich himself, is introduced with intentional ambiguity. Except for a shift in pronouns, from second to third person, there is no indication that the negative characteristics attributed to Lothario do not apply to the earl until the seventh line of the Lothario portrait, where the fictitious name is introduced. The portrait builds from a list of follies to one of vices, all of which are applicable to Sandwich. The catalogue of follies, reminiscent of an earlier sketch of the earl in *The Duellist*, has the effect of presenting Sandwich as an adolescent, thereby making his candidacy for an administrative position in the halls of higher education appear thoroughly ridiculous. A series of infinitives underlines the misdirected, adolescent energy of the gray Lothario:

> To whip a Top, to knuckle down at Taw,
> To swing upon a gate, to ride a straw,
> To play at Push-Pin with dull brother Peers,
> To belch out Catches in a Porter's ears,
>
> . . . .
> With midnight howl to bay th' affrighted Moon,

> To walk with torches thro' the streets at noon,
> ....
> To coin new-fangled wagers, and to lay 'em,
> Laying to lose, and losing not to pay 'em . . .   (325-44)

The portrait concludes with an ironic contrast of the vicious Lothario with the subject of Churchill's mock panegyric, Sandwich. Nature, the poet explains, "having brought LOTHARIO forth to view, / To save her credit, brought forth SANDWICH too" (413-14). Churchill's technique here is one that he used twice before with notable effectiveness: first in his portrait of the earl of Mansfield, which concludes *The Ghost;* later in his character of John Kidgell, which ends *The Author.* The effect of an optical illusion, a kind of double vision, is achieved in the juxtaposition of the real with the ideal — in this case, the evil Lothario with the "noble" Sandwich.[15]

Not content simply to diminish the candidate, Churchill holds up to scorn Sandwich's chief supporters at Cambridge in a series of satiric miniatures; and he goes even further afield in his attempt to avenge an insult against Wilkes and himself by adding portraits of some members of the Oxford faculty, including a few former Jacobites. What saves this section from diffuseness is its thematic unity with the rest of the poem. The dominant, apparently contradictory motifs in this mock-academic procession of actual and potential supporters of Sandwich are gaiety and profundity. The former, arising from licentious images and allusions, indirectly supports the portrait of Lothario presented earlier, not allowing the reader to forget the adolescent character of this academic imposter. The apparently contradictory note is in the mock-profound vein of Pope's *Dunciad;* the dull, grave pedantry to be found in higher education is suggested and Sandwich is shown, at the end of the poem, to be in harmony with it — the perfect candidate in this respect.

To underscore the gay, or licentious, nature of the candidate, Churchill alludes on two occasions rather directly to Sandwich's sexual promiscuity. One reference is to the earl's affair with the niece of the provost of King's College, Cambridge, John Sumner. Labelled "Pandarus," Sumner marches in the burlesque academic procession "without his Niece":

> Her, wretched Maid! committed to his trust,
> To a rank Letcher's coarse and bloated lust,
> The Arch, old, hoary Hypocrite had sold,
> And thought himself and her well damn'd for gold.[16]   (625-28)

The second allusion is to Sandwich's membership in the Hell Fire Club, which met at Medmenham Abbey, where Sir Francis Dashwood, Bute's chancellor of the exchequer, gathered his brother and sister "Franciscans" for their sacrilegious orgies:

> Whilst Womanhood, in habit of a Nun,
> At M[EDMENHAM] lies, by backward Monks undone;
> . . . .
> [DASHWOOD] shall pour, from a Communion Cup,
> Libations to the Goddess without eyes.   (695-701)

The theme of Sandwich's sexual promiscuity is developed on the metaphorical level at the beginning and conclusion of Churchill's satire against Oxford which is personified as a whore for that purpose. Suggesting the licentiousness of the earl, as well as the former Jacobitism of the university's chancellor, the earl of Litchfield, Churchill in the first instance depicts the welcome that Oxford would give Sandwich if he should give up his candidacy at Cambridge. Pretending to comfort the candidate, Churchill asks:

> Is there not OXFORD? She with open arms
> Shall meet thy wish, and yield up all her charms,
> Shall for thy love her former loves resign.
> And jilt the banish'd STUARTS to be thine.   (659-62)

The poem ends on a similar note. Sandwich's exploitation of women for sexual gratification becomes a striking metaphor for any future relationship between him and the academy. The profligacy of the candidate is associated again with his academic ambitions when the Goddess Science is called upon to carry the earl to Oxford: "Hither then wing thy flight, here fix thy stand, / Nor fail to bring thy SANDWICH in thy hand" (673-74). Playing upon the etymology of the word "sandwich," Churchill indirectly evokes a picture of the earl strolling toward the university, as if toward a gaming room, holding in his hand some cold beef between two slices of toast.[17]

Apparently but not actually antithetical to this motif of licentiousness is the mock profundity of Churchill's academic procession. The latter motif is anticipated early in the poem when the satirist, rejecting writers as the subject of further versification, proclaims: "Sleep let them all, with DULLNESS on her throne, / Secure from any malice, but their own" (45-46). The procession is led by Cambridge

academicians dressed in "black, the liv'ry of their trade"; they are a "grave, grave troop" (616-18). Prominent among the Oxonians are Joseph Browne, vice-chancellor of the university, and William Blackstone, the famous jurist. A rather abusive portrait of the aging Browne, who was to suffer a severe stroke the following year, develops the sleep motif introduced earlier:

> BROWNE comes — behold how cautiously he creeps —
> How slow he walks, and yet how fast he sleeps —
> But to thy [Sandwich's] praise in sleep he shall agree;
> He cannot wake, but he shall dream of Thee.[18]   (741-44)

The procession's *center* of gravity is the "scowling" Blackstone, whose famous *Commentaries on the Laws of England* would be published during the next five years. His lectures, the source of the *Commentaries*, were apparently already known for their subtlety and profundity. It is these qualities that Churchill expands upon in his satiric portrait of the conservative jurist:

> So deep in knowledge that few lines can sound,
> And plumb the bottom of that vast profound,
> Few grave ones with such gravity can think,
> Or follow half so fast as he can sink,
> With nice distinctions glossing o'er the text,
> Obscure with meaning, and in words perplext,
> With subtleties on subtleties refin'd,
> Meant to divide, and subdivide the mind,
> Keeping the forwardness of Youth in awe,
> The Scowling BLACKSTONE bears the train of LAW.   (753-62)

The best of the miniature portraits in *The Candidate*, this sketch owes something to Pope — most obviously in its echoing of *The Dunciad*.[19] While the periodicity (which here withholds the victim's name till the final line) had already come to be a hallmark of Churchill's style, it was a rhetorical device that Pope had employed quite effectively too, most memorably in his portrait of Atticus.

Following the appearance of Law, Churchill introduces two more ironically appropriate personified abstractions, Divinity and Loyalty; and the latter is no longer alien to the university in its inclination toward the dubious current ministry. Churchill's tone is momentarily straightforward when he balances in a brief digression loyalty with freedom —

> LOYALTY without FREEDOM is a chain
> Which Men of lib'ral notice can't sustain,
> And FREEDOM without LOYALTY, a name
> Which nothing means, or means licentious shame.   (787-90) —

before ironically suggesting that the union of loyalty and liberty will
be fostered at Oxford by the licentious and treacherous earl.[20]

In the concluding picture of Sandwich, he is reclining vacant-
mindedly beneath his "plant of Union" (793) while Oxford graces
his brows with wreathes that once crowned the Stuarts. This scene
effectively merges the antithetical themes that characterize this section of the poem — frivolity and profundity are revealed as two sides
of the same coin. In a mock-heroic vein, the satirist addresses his
subject:

> . . . Wisdom's happy son, but not her slave,
> Gay with the gay, and with the grave ones grave,
> Free from the dull impertinence of thought,
> Beneath that shade, which thy own labours wrought,
> And fashion'd into strength, shalt Thou repose,
> Secure of lib'ral praise, since Isis flows,
> True to her TAME, as duty hath decreed,
> Nor longer, like a harlot, lust for TWEED,
> And those old wreaths, which OXFORD once dar'd twine,
> To grace a STUART brow, she plants on thine.   (797-806)

Churchill's rhetorical antithesis and his balance of "gay" and
"grave" signal the resolution of the poem's recurring paradox, and
the explanation for this balance is Sandwich's freedom from "the
dull impertinence of thought." The image of the River Isis's lust for
the River Tweed suggests the character of Sandwich's gaiety and
picks up the image of Oxford as the whore presented earlier. As
before, Oxford's sexual unfaithfulness is also a metaphor for the
political betrayal that Churchill suggests in the final couplet. The
deliberate ambiguity of these lines raises the question whether the
Oxford Jacobites have accepted the House of Hanover, as
represented by George III, or whether the king's ministers,
represented by Sandwich, share in a sense the reactionary political
view of the Oxonians. While this gray Lothario, who can be gay or
grave as the occasion warrants, is a figure of ridicule, he is at the
same time in his essential thoughtlessness, his lack of any real con-
victions, a potential threat. In any case, Sandwich is definitely not

the man for the job; and the satirist has made his point well. Although Churchill's self-indulgence as an artist, which is manifested in the lengthy, rather irrelevant introduction that interests us now for reasons other than the poem itself, weakens the overall effectiveness of his satire, *The Candidate* does present evidence of a general improvement in his craft, particularly in his use of irony and thematic imagery.

III A *"Conspiracy"* Exposed

Expanding upon the theme of loyalty, Churchill turned from the academic world to that of commerce in his next poem, *The Farewell*, which was published in June 1764, a month after *The Candidate*. Again he points an accusing finger at the ministry by suggesting that its support of Robert Clive and the East India Company might not be in the nation's best interests. The occasion for the poem was Clive's setting sail for India after the directors of the East India Company had confirmed his jaghire[21] and reappointed him governor of Bengal. Clive, reputed to be the wealthiest man in Britain when he returned from India in 1760, had at this time the political support of George Grenville, the king's chief minister.[22]

Like *The Conference*, *The Farewell* is a dialogue between the poet (P.) and his antagonist who is, in this case, an anonymous friend (F.). Considerably more than half the poem is devoted to the theme of patriotism, which Churchill develops by contrasting the poet's love for his country with his friend's internationalism. Once the rightness of patriotism has been established, Churchill questions, in the latter part of the poem, the loyalty of the political-economic establishment as he indirectly suggests a conspiracy among the "titled upstarts" (362) that formed a potential political aristocracy. Churchill's purpose is not only to expose what he sees as collusion but to contrast the rapacity of England's leaders with what he projects as his own altruism. As a result, he subjects the quality of patriotism, the basis of his stance as patriot-poet, to rigorous scrutiny. There is no question as to the reality of the poet's altruism; it is assumed. Questioned, instead, is the rightness of patriotism. Is it a virtue or a mere prejudice? Is it an obstacle to a more universal love?

Churchill creates for this Platonic dialogue an antagonist who is a rationalist with an international perspective. To him, patriotism is a prejudice. He cannot accept the poet's insistence upon the "naturalness" of the patriotic passion, emphasizing as he does the rational aspect of the "natural." For him, nature cannot contradict

sense. In this "enlight'ned age," he is unable to believe that "this grand Master Passion, this brave rage, / Which flames out for thy country, was imprest, / And fix'd by Nature in the human breast" (169-72). As far as the poet is concerned, patriotism is so "natural" that it is beyond the rational, beyond good and evil:

> Whether this Love's of good, or evil growth,
> A Vice, a Virtue, or a spice of both,
> Let men of nicer argument decide;
> If it is virtuous, soothe an honest pride
> With lib'ral praise; if vicious, be content,
> It is a Vice I never can repent;
> A Vice which, weigh'd in Heav'n, shall more avail
> Than ten cold virtues in the other scale.   (235-42)

But is such devotion to one's country compatible with an enlightened altruism of international scope? Isn't it an obstacle to that "nobler Love which comprehends the whole" (250)? The rational antagonist contends:

> The gen'rous Soul, by Nature taught to soar,
> Her strength confirm'd in Philosophic lore,
> At one grand view takes in a world with ease,
> And, seeing all mankind, loves all he sees.   (255-58)

Although the poet considers this attitude "barren speculation at the best" (270), he points out that there is no real contradiction between love of country and love of mankind. In arriving at this conclusion, Churchill echoes Pope's attempt in *An Essay on Man* to reconcile the Hobbesian doctrine of self-interest with the Shaftesburian theory of natural benevolence in the concept that self-love leads to social love:[23]

> That spring of Love, which in the human mind,
> Founded on self, flows narrow and confin'd,
> Enlarges as it rolls, and comprehends
> The social Charities of blood, and friends,
> Till smaller streams included, not o'erpast,
> It rises to our Country's love at last,
> And He, with lib'ral and enlarged mind,
> Who loves his Country, cannot hate mankind.   (293-300)

Proving, as it were, the possibility of an expansive altruism, even though one based on self-love, Churchill uses it to set off what he

sees to be a limited self-serving rapacity of the members of England's political-economic establishment.

The occasion for this dialogue is the patriot-poet's impending departure for India, the fictional matrix of *The Farewell*. That the poet should feel that expatriotism is his only course of action is intended to underscore Churchill's suggestion of domestic political corruption. Things have gotten so bad that the patriot-poet has to leave; he cannot stand by, powerless, to witness the rape of his country. No more than a son could calmly witness "his honour'd Mother forc'd"

> Could I with patience, by the worst of Men,
> Behold my Country plunder'd, beggar'd, lost
> Beyond Redemption, all her glories cross'd
> E'en when Occasion made them ripe, her fame
> Fled like a dream, while She awakes to shame.   (310-14)

The situation is so bad indeed that Churchill, looking into the future, suggests that England is threatened by the emergence of a political aristocracy. He points to this danger when he prays:

> Let not a Mob of Tyrants seize the helm,
> Nor titled upstarts league to rob the realm,
> Let not, whatever other ills assail,
> A damned ARISTOCRACY prevail.   (361-64)

More subtle is the way in which Churchill lets the poet's antagonist make, though indirectly, the accusation of ministerial collusion. Much like Candour in *An Epistle to William Hogarth*, the poet's friend presses him to be more specific: "Shew us our danger" (377). Echoing a charge made earlier, the poet again hints at a conspiracy; he points darkly to those who "Breed doubts between the People and the Throne," while they "Themselves pass unsuspected in disguise, / And 'gainst our real danger seal our eyes" (388-92). Convinced that a conspiracy may indeed exist, the previously skeptical friend insists that the poet "mark" the conspirators "and let their names recorded stand / On Shame's black role, and stink thro' all the land" (393-94). He is told that to do so would be courageous but rather imprudent because of the corruption of the nation's judicial system.

The dialogue seems to take a different tack as the friend, conceding the argument, questions the poet's decision to leave England for India. Won't Europe satisfy his "vast wrath": "Cannot thy mis-

begotten Muse lay bare / Her brawny arm, and play the Butcher there?'' (426-28). Will India serve the satirist's purpose better? What can he use for a subject that won't be foreign to his English readers? Casually, Churchill has circled back to his target: "the [East India] Company" (472) is the poet's reply. When the friend asks that the company, whose "sores which never might endure the air" have already been "laid bare" (475-76),[24] be spared, he assumes the role of ingénu. In the same vein, he presents unwittingly Churchill's personal objection to the inordinate power of the East India Company[25] whose apparent collusion with the ministry is concrete evidence of an emerging aristocracy. Speaking for Churchill, the friend indirectly indicts the government:

> From their [company directors'] first rise e'en to
>   the present hour
> Have They not prov'd their abuse of pow'r,
> Made it impossible, if fairly view'd,
> Ever to have that dang'rous pow'r renew'd,
> Whilst, unseduc'd by Ministers, the throne
> Regards our Interests, and knows its own.   (479-84)

Despite the fact that the East India Company has proved its abuse of power, that power has not been restricted, and the implication is that the king has been seduced by his ministers to disregard both the people's interest and his own. The idea that the king was a basically innocent puppet of his ministry was, of course, a fiction that Churchill and Wilkes exploited in *The North Briton* and elsewhere.

After suggesting collusion between the ministry and the East India Company, Churchill concludes the poem by naming one of the men that the poet, because of prudence, had refused to mention earlier. He does so in the rather casual way that is in keeping with the general indirection of this part of the poem when he refers again to the company as a possible topic of satire:

> P. Should ev'ry other subject chance to fail,
> Those who have sail'd, and those who wish'd to sail
> In the last Fleet, afford an ample field
> Which must beyond my hopes a harvest yield.
>
> F. On such vile food Satire can never thrive.
>
> P. She cannot starve, if there was only CLIVE.   (485-90)

Churchill mentions offhandedly the name of the man reputed to be the wealthiest individual in Britain as if this stalwart of the political-economic establishment were the last resort for an impoverished satirist. With ironic nonchalance, the satirist marks his victim and lets his name "recorded stand / On Shame's black role, and stink thro' all the land."

But the indirection of this poem is not so effective as it has been elsewhere; in fact, it tends to dissipate the satire's force in anticlimax — real anticlimax, not just the ironic anticlimax that Churchill is trying to achieve. This lack of thrust, together with the poem's failure to transcend its topicality, helps make *The Farewell* one of Churchill's less successful pieces.

IV   *A Mirror for the King*

Churchill's satire against the British political establishment is less topical than in his other political satires and is more fundamental in *Gotham*,[26] which deals with the question of kingship. Published in three books over a six-month period, the poem centers upon the fiction that Churchill is the newly crowned patriot-king of an island, Gotham, that he has just discovered. Book I, published in February 1764, which presents the poet in a playful mood, is a politically innocuous panegyric of the new king in a mock-lyric vein. There follow two contrasting views of kingship, one historical and the other Utopian: the historical view occupies Book II, published in March 1764, which traces the decline and fall of the nonpatriotic Stuarts; Book III, August 1764, explores the duties of a patriot-king, the chief of which is to redress his subjects' grievances.

Gotham opens with an attack against colonialism that serves to introduce both Churchill's fiction of the patriot-king and his central theme of tyranny. In a passage reminiscent of Swift's expression of antiimperialism in the Fourth Voyage of *Gulliver's Travels*,[27] Churchill equates colonialism to enslavement as he points out the paradoxical nature of the cross as the symbol of both Christianity and European imperialism. Christ died to save man; the cross is planted in newly discovered lands to enslave him:

> Cast by a tempest on the savage coast,
> Some roving Buccaneer set up a Post;
> A Beam, in proper form transversely laid,
> Of his Redeemer's Cross the figure made,
> Of that Redeemer, with whose laws his life,

> From first to last, has been one scene of strife;
> His royal master's name thereon engrav'd,
> Without more process, the whole race enslav'd,
> Cut off that Charter they from Nature drew,
> And made them Slaves to men they never knew.   (I, 13-22)

Churchill further develops the paradoxes involved in the economic exploitation of India and America by Christian Europe ("EUROPE took their *Gold,* and gave them *Grace,*" [I, 68]) before he ironically offers as the basis of his claim to Gotham the precedent of Europe's claim to India: "I plead Possession, and till one more bold / Shall drive me out, will that Possession hold" (I, 107-08).

The bulk of the first book of *Gotham* is a kind of ode in which the island kingdom celebrates the reign of its patriot-king. In response to the exhortation "Rejoice, Ye happy GOTHAMITES, rejoice," the refrain of Book I, Gotham sings and the various singers are systematically catalogued. An orchestra of musical instruments is followed by a chorus of the ages of man, where childhood

> His trembling lash suspended in the air,
> Half-bent, and stroking back his long, lank hair,
> Shall to his mates look up with eager glee,
> And let his Top go down to prate of Me;   (I, 181-84)

and old age "Shall for a moment, from himself set free, / Lean on his Crutch, and pipe forth praise to Me" (I, 235-36). This chorus is accompanied by all of nature, from the flowers of the earth to the orbs of the sky, and even by time in the form of the months and the seasons. Waxing more lyric than satiric, Churchill applies the lash but occasionally and even playfully as when, in his catalogue of trees, he opposes the Scotch fir to the English oak (I, 298-304).

There is something of an Old Testament cadence to Churchill's ode which has specific allusions to the Song of Songs and the Psalms. Gotham becomes Israel; Churchill, the Old Testament God:

> Shall CHURCHILL reign, and shall not GOTHAM sing?
>
> The *Show'rs,* which make the young hills, like young Lambs,
> Bound and rebound, the old Hills, like old Rams,
> Unwieldy, jump for you . . .   (1, 312-15)

The Old Testament "mountains"[28] are "old hills," jumping "unwieldy" like "old rams": the picture is slightly grotesque. This

grotesque exuberence can also be seen when the biblical allusions
merge with images of sexual potency as the poet mentions the
"*Cedar*, whose top mates the highest cloud, / Whilst his old Father
LEBANON grows proud / Of such a child" (I, 299-301).[29] Similar,
though with a change of sex, is the poet's description of the
sunflower,

> Who, madly rushing to the Sun's embrace,
> O'ertops her fellows with aspiring aim,
> Demands his wedded Love, and bears his name.   (I, 268-70)

These fleeting fantasies of sexual potency are indeed appropriate to
the libertine Churchill's attempt to express the feelings he has as the
beloved patriot-king of Gotham.

While generally delightful in its playful lyricism, this prefatory
book is more self-indulgent than relevant — so much so that the
poet finds it necessary to serve notice that the subsequent books will
be more serious and to the point. He will dare to speak, he boasts,
what others "scarce dare to Think" (I, 500). But, unrelated to the
subject of kingship, a lengthy digression about the art of poetry
functions as an introduction to Book II. The digression is more
valuable for what Churchill says about his own practice as a poet
than for any critical observations that he makes since his are rather
traditional neo-Classical views. Regarding the place of ornament
and sense in poetry, he advises, in a Horatian vein, that, "if You
mean to profit, learn to please" (II, 88). But only a few can achieve
the "golden mean" between "sense" and "grace," the essentials of
good poetry: "SENSE perfects GRACE, and GRACE enlivens SENSE" (II,
156).[30] Churchill himself is not one of those few. Expressing a
characteristically hedonistic sentiment, he explains in a digressive
apologia:

> Had I the pow'r, I could not have the time,
> Whilst spirits flow, and Life is in her prime,
> Without a sin 'gainst Pleasure, to design
> A plan, to methodize each thought, each line
> Highly to finish . . .   (II, 165-69)

Moreover, the quality of Churchill's verse is conditioned by the fact
that he has an almost psychological compulsion to write. With comic
exaggeration, he confesses:

Nothing of Books, and little known of men,
When the mad fit comes on, I seize the pen,
Rough as they run, the rapid thoughts set down,
Rough as they run, discharge them on the Town.[31]   (II, 171-74)

Though these lines contain a measure of truth, Churchill is also posturing again as he juxtaposes this expression of flippancy with his serious political satire.

Churchill's main concern in *Gotham* is political power, its use and abuse. More specifically, he sets off his vision of a patriot-king with sketches of Stuart kings, all of whom he presents as tyrants. Conducive to tyranny is the concept of the divine right of kings that Churchill condemns when he writes of James I, the first of the Stuarts, as "Leaving behind, a curse to all his line, / The bloody Legacy of RIGHT DIVINE" (II, 419-20). The satirist is also concerned with a related issue — the bad influence of ministers upon the monarch. In recalling the reign of Charles II, he comments: "Bad counsels he [Charles] embrac'd thro' indolence" (II, 609). More at fault, in this respect, was his predecessor Charles I, who was executed in 1649: "Tutor'd to see with ministerial eyes; / Forbid to hear a loyal Nation's cries" (II, 469-70). Churchill speaks of the ministers as "seducing" the king, as he does in *The Farewell* when he refers to the relationship between George III and his cabinet. Evoking the execution of George's unfortunate predecessor, he writes:

> Unhappy Stuart! harshly tho' that name
> Grates on my ear, I should have died with shame,
> To see my King before his subjects stand,
> And at their bar hold up his royal hand,
> At their commands to hear the monarch plead,
> By their decrees to see that Monarch bleed.
> What tho' thy faults were many, and were great,
> What tho' they shook the basis of the state,
> In Royalty secure thy Person stood,
> And sacred was the fountain of thy blood.
> Vile Ministers, who dar'd abuse their trust,
> Who dar'd seduce a King to be unjust,
> Vengeance, with Justice leagu'd, with pow'r made strong,
> Had nobly crush'd; *the King could do no wrong.*   (II, 523-36)

Churchill ironically undercuts his expression of sympathy for the executed monarch when he concludes with "*the King could do no*

wrong," a principle of the British constitution that had long since, as this excerpt makes clear, proved to be a fiction in practice. At the same time, he wishes to separate the king from his ministers in keeping with his pretense that George III is not responsible for the misdeeds of his ministry.[32] But it is the bloody fate suffered by his Stuart predecessor that Churchill is holding up as an exemplum to George III.

Churchill is more direct when he relates the fate of the last Stuart tyrant, James II, for there is no talk about the sacredness of kingship here. Interweaving wish with history, the poet evokes the Glorious Revolution that expelled him in 1688 thus:

> [England] sent him in despair to beg his bread,
> Whilst she (may ev'ry State in such distress
> Dare with such zeal, and meet with such success)
> Whilst She (may GOTHAM, should my abject mind
> Chuse to enslave, rather than free mankind,
> Pursue her steps, tear the proud Tyrant down,
> Nor let me wear if I abuse the crown)
> Whilst She (thro' ev'ry age, in ev'ry land,
> Written in gold let REVOLUTION stand)
> Whilst She, secur'd in *Liberty* and *Law,*
> Found what She sought, a Saviour in NASSAU.   (II, 668-78)

The satire reaches a climax at the end of the second book as Churchill rhetorically heightens the intensity of the passage with parenthetical asides that suggest barely controlled emotion. The parentheses, as well as the fiction of his personal sovereignty, allow him to present the relationship between past and present with a desired indirection as he offers revolution as a viable political alternative.

Book III of *Gotham* presents another "mirror" for George III, by giving him a positive picture of the patriot-king that contrasts with the negative composite picture of the Stuarts. Churchill emphasizes the independence and accessibility of his ideal monarch. Unlike the Stuarts, the patriot-king will be free from ministerial control; he will refuse to be a mere puppet:

> Shall I, true puppet-like, be mock'd with State,
> Have nothing but the Name of being great,
> Attend at councils, which I must not weigh,
> Do what they bid, and what they dictate, say,

> Enrob'd, and hoisted up into my chair,
> Only to be a royal Cypher there? (III, 255-60)

Independence can only be achieved through knowledge; therefore, the patriot-king's "first, great duty is — To KNOW" (III, 328) rather than to accept things on trust from his ministers. Gotham's monarch will devote himself to the study of history and law: he will

> Examine well on what my Pow'r depends,
> What are the gen'ral Principles, and Ends
> Of Government, how Empire first began,
> And wherefore Man was rais'd to reign o'er Man;   (III, 535-38)

and he will "Dive to the very bottom of the Law," separating the "dead letter" from the "Spirit" until he finds the "*Constitution*'s very Soul" (III, 606-10).

As patriot-king, Churchill will always be accessible to his subjects and ready to redress their grievances. Thus, he tells them:

> And thou, where e'er thou art, thou wretched Thing,
> Who art afraid to look up to a King,
> Lay by thy fears — make thy grievance plain,
> And, if I not redress thee, may my Reign
> Close up that very Moment —   (III, 653-57)

These lines, published five days after the convicted Wilkes was publicly summoned for sentencing, can be read as a kind of threat against George III.[33] As he did at the end of Book II, Churchill is suggesting revolution as a means of coping with political injustice. In so doing, he is fulfilling the promise he made at the end of Book I to speak what his less courageous fellows were afraid to think; but his message is guarded here by characteristic indirection and not nearly as direct as it would be a few months later in *Independence*, where he challenges the ministry to do its worst: "I dare to suffer All [the ministry] dares to do" (527).

CHAPTER 5

Later, Miscellaneous Satire: Poetry of 1764 (continued), Posthumous Verse

W ITH one exception, Churchill's poetry of this period reflects
the themes and techniques that have already been noted in his
earlier verse. *The Journey* is an expression of individualism — more
precisely, artistic individualism; *Independence* combines an attack
on the aristocracy with a plea for liberty; the "Dedication" to the
Sermons is a personal satire against a political enemy of Wilkes,
Bishop Warburton, in the form of an ironic eulogy. The anomaly
here, at least in terms of subject, is *The Times,* which expresses
Churchill's moral indignation against homosexuality. As for the
relative merit of these four works, the unfinished *Journey* is perhaps
Churchill's least significant endeavor, and the "Dedication" is commonly considered to contain his best satiric verse.

I *Artistic Individualism*

It is highly appropriate that the uninhibited Churchill began and
ended a literary career devoted to the cause of political freedom on a
note of individual freedom. In *Night* (November 1761), he had
defended the idiosyncratic nature of his personal habits; in the
posthumously published *The Journey* (April 1765), which not sur-
prisingly alludes to the earlier poem,[1] he defends the uniqueness of
his art. It is Churchill's individualism that seems to have given rise to
his solicitation for political freedom — self-love leads to social love,
as he argues (after Pope) in *The Farewell.*

When Churchill claims that the Muses have temporarily abandoned him, the reader is unfortunately inclined to nod his agreement: *The Journey* lacks inspiration. Churchill doesn't seem to have
anything to write about; he attacks incidentally people like the
actor-dramatist Samuel Foote and Arthur Murphy, whom he lashed
earlier in *The Rosciad.* The chief object of his attack is the Scottish
poet-physician John Armstrong, whom Wilkes alienated with *The*

North Briton.[2] These English and Scottish writers are played off
against the poet himself who, despite his barrenness, considers his
simplicity superior to their artificiality.

The "journey" is a metaphor for Churchill's poetic career, which
he travels by himself: "I on my Journey all alone proceed" is the
rather uninspired final line of the poem's refrain. More specifically,
the present poem is "A plain, unlabour'd journey of a Day" (86).
"*Pegasus* turn'd into a common hack, / Alone I jog, and keep the
beaten track" (89-90). He travels alone because he has been abandoned by the Muses — he has temporarily written himself out, even
as his false friends had warned:

> Genius himself (nor here let Genius frown)
> Must, to ensure his vigour, be laid down,
> And fallow'd well; had CHURCHILL known but this,
> . . . .
> He might have flourish'd twenty years, or more,
> Tho' now *alas*! poor Man! worn out in four.   (25-30)

These lines have acquired an ominous note unintended by Churchill; for, already reduced to a "noble ruin" (the phrase is Garrick's[3])
by overwork, as well as by self-indulgence, he would be dead within
a few weeks.

Much as he did in *Gotham,* Churchill confesses to an inner compulsion to write. He knows that he would be better off to let his
mind lie fallow for a while, to "Apply myself once more to Books,
and Men" (36); but the lines keep coming despite his good intentions:

> . . . Whether I will, or no,
> Such as they are, my thoughts in measure flow.
> Convinc'd, determin'd, I in prose begin,
> But e're I write one sentence, Verse creeps in,
> And taints me thro' and thro'; by this good light
> In verse I talk by day, I dream by night;
> If now and then I curse, my curses chime,
> Nor can I pray, unless I pray in rime.
> E'en now I err, in spite of Common Sense,
> And my Confession doubles my offence.   (45-54)

This "compulsion" to rhyme is part of the poem's fiction, of course;
but in this case fiction probably corresponds somewhat to fact: dur-

ing the past year, Churchill had published a long poem each month. His "compulsive" writing is part of the general profligacy that is burning him out.

Even though the muses have abandoned him, Churchill regards himself as superior to his English and Scottish contemporaries because, as we have noted, he thinks that his simplicity is superior to their art. In his refrain, Churchill dismisses these "great" men as food for laughter:

> Thus, or in any better way They please,
> With these great Men, or with great Men like these,
> Let Them [the Muses] their appetite for laughter feed;
> I on my Journey all Alone proceed.   (115-18)

The isolation of the poet assumes more than the simple meaning of his temporary abandonment by the muses; it is a sign of his superior merit. More than that, his isolation can be taken as a metaphor for his individualism — in this case, his artistic integrity, his refusal to conform to the "rules." Finally, the journey itself hints at Churchill's approaching death, and the rather flat refrain takes on a prophetic quality and a certain pathos. But neither the metaphoric nor the prophetic level of the refrain saves the poem from its essential banality.

II   *Moral Indignation*

"I hope you have lash'd the rogues well in the *Times*. Pray give them one stroke for me," Wilkes wrote to Churchill, echoing Swift's famous letter to Pope.[4] These "rogues," curiously enough, were not political enemies but the homosexuals of eighteenth century London. To paint a picture of English decadence, Churchill more obviously than elsewhere turned for a model to Juvenal, that fierce critic of decadent Rome.[5] Wilkes thought that this satire, published in September 1764, two months before the poet's fatal visit to Boulogne, was one of Churchill's best and "greatly excell'd *Juvenal* in his own manner."[6]

Churchill prefaces his attack against "unnatural lust" with a sweeping condemnation of what he sees as the general shameless decadence of "the times" — an age of luxury, vanity, idleness, and dissipation. In the economic sphere, "Debts are an Honour; Payment a disgrace" (48); and typical of those mean noblemen who do not pay their bills is "Faber," whose portrait occupies the first part

of the poem. More importantly, the times are characterized by new
vices that have been imported from the Continent and especially the
"soft luxurious EAST" (255). While Italy sends her *castrati* (castrated
opera singers) and lascivious dancers to England, the East is the
source of "Sins of the blackest character" (260), including the sin of
the aging, decadent nobleman "Apicius," whose lust for his youthful
serving man "Corydon" is skillfully dramatized by Churchill in the
second part of the poem. He then generalizes his satire by warning
first the boy and then English mothers: no man is safe — "*Saint*
SOCRATES is still a Goat, tho' grey" (480).

Whether *The Times* is an exercise in imitation or a real expression
of moral indignation is not so important as the fact that it represents
a brief hiatus in Churchill's career as a political satirist. This does not
mean, however, that the poem is completely apolitical or that its
strikes against the government are merely incidental as in *The
Rosciad*. For one thing, in Churchill's evocation of Juvenal's Rome,
particularly in his portrait of Apicius, he is implicitly making a
general comparison between the decadent Rome of Nero and Domi-
tian and the England of George III.[7] More explicitly, he is attacking
the English aristocracy; both Faber and Apicius are lords, and
sodomy appears as the vice mainly of "Brutes of rank and fortune"
(347). To this privilege, or, more specifically, abuse of privilege, of
the nobility, Churchill rather bitterly objects. This view of privilege
is the really vital connection between the two main parts of the
poem.

Faber abuses the aristocracy's privilege of immunity from arrest in
civil suits when he neglects to pay his bills and, thus, helps to
bankrupt unprotected shopkeepers.

> What is't to FABER? he stands safe and clear
> Heav'n can commence no legal action here,
> And on his breast a mighty plate he wears,
> A plate more firm than triple brass, which bears
> The name of PRIVILEGE, 'gainst vulgar awe;
> He feels no Conscience, and he fears no Law.   (71-76)

Immune not only from arrest but from richly deserved contempt as
well, "FABER seems to stand / A mighty Pillar in a guilty land" (93-
94). In fact, "He might in time be Minister of State" (102). Indeed,
one of the secretaries of state at the time was the profligate
Sandwich (John Montague), whom Churchill later holds up as an

embodiment of the times when he refers to him as an offspring of the era's Meanness and Impudence: "Fate, to make them more sincerely one, / Hath crown'd their loves with MOUNTAGUE [*sic*] their son" (169-70).

Abuse of privilege emerges as a theme again in the heart of the satire, Churchill's attack against homosexuals. Observing how these shameless, fearless creatures "brave it in our streets" (287), he complains that, no matter where we go, "SODOM confronts, and stares us in the face" (294). This brazenness is attributable to privilege:

> Those who are mean high Paramours secure,
> And the rich guilty screen the guilty poor;
> The Sin too proud to feel from Reason awe,
> And Those, who practice it, too great for Law.   (297-300)

More telling is his remark to the young serving boy Corydon, when the satirist warns him about "the horrors of a rape": "Nor think thyself in Law secure and firm— / Thy Master is a Lord, and Thou a Worm, /. . . [who] Must serve his lusts" (455, 465-66).

But the attack against privilege is ultimately muted by Churchill's portrait of English decadence in general and of sexual abuses in particular. While Samuel Johnson carefully excluded from his imitations of Juvenal his model's characteristic carnality, Churchill has no such scruples. Particularly Juvenalian, though not as explicit, is his attack against the vices imported from Italy in the form of *castrati* and lewd dancers:

> *Half*-Men, whom many a rich and *noble* Dame,
> To serve her lust, and yet secure her fame,
> Keeps on high diet, as We Capons feed,
> To glut our appetites at last decreed,
> *Women*, who dance, in postures so obscene,
> They might awaken shame in ARETINE,
> Who, when, retir'd from the day's piercing light,
> They celebrate the mysteries of night,
> Might make the Muses, in a corner plac'd
> To view their monstrous lusts, deem SAPPHO chaste.   (237-46)

The wives of the English nobility (as well as the imported women) come in for abuse here as Churchill echoes one of Juvenal's themes — the insatiable lust of women (Satire VI).

A personification of English decadence, the portrait of Apicius is

also decidedly Roman in tone — something that would not be out of place in Juvenal or in the *Satyricon* of his predecessor Petronius. This aging "pamper'd glutton" (382) is found mourning in the midst of one of his sumptuous dinner parties where, "whilst he carves / For ev'ry guest, the Landlord sits and starves" (353-54). The satirist explores the possible causes of Apicius's sadness with a series of probing questions that begins:

> Why mourns APICIUS thus? why runs his eye,
> Heedless, o'er delicates, which from the sky
> Might call down Jove? Where now his gen'rous wish
> That, to invent a new and better dish,
> The World might burn, and all mankind expire,
> So he might roast a Phœnix at the fire.
> Why swims that eye in tears, which, thro' a race
> Of sixty years, ne'er shew'd one sign of grace?   (373-80)

Has his wife returned, a bill been collected, his cook ruined a dish? Each possible cause of Apicius's grief is examined and then rejected. The source of the old glutton's tearful distraction finally turns out to be his servant Corydon, a "Smooth, Smug Stripling in life's fairest prime" (421). Instead of the "sparkling Cross" which Pope's Belinda wore on her "white breast,"[8] he is "deck'd with a Solitaire / Which on his bare breast glitt'ring play'd" (418-19). The sketch ends with the satirist warning the serving boy to beware rape. Choice of detail, wit, irony, and suspense help make this little drama the most readable part of the satire.

Churchill's satire against homosexuality (an all but exclusively masculine phenomenon in this poem) seems to be more than an exercise and more than an expression of traditional prejudice like the underlying anti-Semitism of *The Prophecy of Famine*. His moral outrage occasionally seems to border on hysteria: "Sins worse / Than . . . plagues, which truly to unfold / Would make the best blood in my veins run cold, / And strike all Manhood dead" (260-63); "Distending wide her jaws, let Hell prepare / For those who thus offend amongst Mankind, / A fire more fierce, and tortures more refin'd (276-78); "should I sit tamely down, / Suppress my rage, and saunter thro' the town / As One who knew not, or who shar'd these crimes?" (659-61); "I must speak, or burst" (680). Although there are echoes of Juvenal (Satire I), this tirade seems to be something more than the traditional hyperbole of the outraged Juvenalian satirist; indeed, Churchill may have unconsciously

recognized in these aberrant men his own shadow-self. Professor George Sherburn has gone so far as to suggest that *The Times* "was an unsavory depiction of the vices of the day with emphasis at times on vices to which Churchill himself was perhaps not a stranger."[9]

Be this as it may, heterosexual love emerges as the satiric norm in *The Times*. Lamenting that women are "out of date" (319), Churchill interrupts his attack against homosexuality to include a brief panegyric about the opposite sex — "the pride and happiness of Man"; "by all the Loves and Graces taught, / With softest arts . . . / To humanize, and mould us to her will"; "formed . . . / With the persuasive language of a tear / To melt the rugged temper of our Isle, / Or win us to her purpose with a smile"; "the quickest spur . . . / The fairest, best reward of ev'ry deed" (301-12). The panegyric becomes quite sensual as he describes the raptures of physical love:

> No more the Heart, that seat where Love resides,
> Each Breath drawn quick and short, in fuller tides
> Life posting thro' the veins, each pulse on fire,
> And the whole body tingling with desire,
> Pants for those charms, which Virtue might engage
> To break his vow, and thaw the frost of age,
> Bidding each trembling nerve, each muscle strain,
> And giving pleasure which is almost pain. (323-30)

The phrase "giving pleasure" is indicative of the satirist's general attitude toward women; expressed rather bluntly here, it manifests itself more indirectly elsewhere as in the lines previously quoted. While valued highly, women are not valued in themselves but only in their relationship to men; Churchill shares here, as he does in his repugnance for homosexuality, the prejudices of his age.

Although we might not applaud the sentiments of *The Times* — the intolerance of divergent modes of sexual behavior and the somewhat condescending attitude toward women — we might admire the boldness of Churchill who, so much of a product of his age, was yet able to defy the mores of his society when he felt that it was necessary to do so to implement his satire. The extent to which he was defying contemporary conventions in his open treatment of a tabooed topic (Wilkes mentioned the "boldness" of his descriptions) is evident not only in the fact that he felt it necessary to conclude *The Times* with an apology[10] but also in the critical response to his poem. "We do not remember," solemnly begins an essay in *The Critical Review*, "during the course of our undertaking, to have

entered upon the review of any work with so much reluctance, as
upon the performance before us: however, we shall endeavour to preserve that decency from which its author has too often deviated."[11]

III   *A Declaration of Independence*

Churchill returned to his role of patriot-poet within a few weeks
when, early in October, he published his final and strongest assertion of independence. Developing themes previously introduced in
The Author, Independence opposes lord and bard and attacks the
system of patronage that made the poet dependent upon the
aristocrat. The poem moves from a demonstration of the bard's
superiority to the lord, to consideration of the demeaning nature of
patronage, to a declaration of independence, to a call to arms to the
vocal, patriotic minority. Though Churchill's boldest political satire,
the poem tends to be mediocre from an esthetic point of view. In its
relative lack of subtlety and inventiveness, it differs sharply from his
"Dedication" to the *Sermons*, also written during these last few
months of Churchill's life.

Not content with simple independence, Churchill here insists
upon a society in which merit (as opposed to hereditary social
position) is the only thing that can elevate one man over another.
Merit is natural; titles, artificial. Thus, "Bards may be Lords, but 'tis
not in the cards, / Play how we will, to turn Lords into Bards" (91-
92). We suspect that Churchill, who had achieved independence
and even distinction as a poet, was rankled (as was Wilkes in
somewhat similar circumstances) because he was forever excluded
by birth from the "artificial" peerage.[12] In a barely disguised plea
for acceptance, he has Reason cry out: "Those must Honour *Them*
[Bards], who honour *Me*, / They . . . / In their own right,
Precedence shall obtain, / *Merit* rules here [heaven]" (206-09).
Elsewhere,

> Titles, with Me, are vain, and nothing worth,
> I rev'rence Virtue, but I laugh at Birth.
> Give me a Lord, that's honest, frank, and brave,
> I am his friend, but cannot be his slave.
> . . . .
> I love his Virtues, and will make them known,
> Confess his rank, but can't forget my own.
> Give me a Lord, who, to a Title born,
> Boasts nothing else, I'll pay him scorn with scorn.   (265-74)

To "demonstrate" the actual superiority of an independent bard to an hereditary lord, Churchill introduces the fiction of a heavenly synod where the two titles are literally weighed, one against the other, and where the title *lord* is found lighter than air. For the typical modern lord, Churchill chose the patron of poets George Lyttelton (allegedly a model for Fielding's Squire Allworthy) who, in the proceedings against Wilkes in the House of Lords, had openly expressed his shock upon hearing excerpts read from *An Essay on Woman*.[13] Churchill caricatures Lyttelton's physical appearance to point out the paradoxical combination of weakness and pride that characterizes the lord. The portrait emphasizes the baron's gaunt face and his unusual height that is supported by precariously thin legs. After describing his virtual facelessness, the satirist depicts Lyttelton's towering weakness:

> With Legs, which we might well conceive that Fate
> Meant only to support a spider's weight,
> Firmly he strove to tread, and with a stride
> Which shew'd at once his weakness and his pride,
> Shaking himself to pieces, seem'd to cry,
> Observe good People, how I shake the sky.   (129-34)

The bard, Churchill himself, while symbolically weightier than the lord, is almost as ridiculous in appearance. The difference is that, in his case, there is some essential worth beneath the appearance:

> Vast were his Bones, his Muscles twisted strong,
> His Face was short, but broader than 'twas long,
> His Features, tho' by Nature they were large,
> Contentment had contriv'd to overcharge
> And bury meaning, save that we might spy
> Sense low'ring on the penthouse of his eye;
> His Arms were two twin Oakes, his Legs so stout
> That they might bear a Mansion House about.   (157-64)

As they had laughed at Lyttelton, the gods now laugh at the bard. With Churchill's characteristic boldness, the satirist "join'd their mirth, nor shall the Gods condemn / If whilst They laugh'd at him, he laugh'd at them" (185-86). Able to penetrate appearances, Reason "Look'd thro' his soul, and quite forgot his face" (188). When the two titles are placed on Reason's scale, the bard's merit outweighs the lord's birth: "*Merit* rules here [heaven], Be it enough

that *Birth* / Intoxicates, and sways the fools of earth" (209-10). In such manner, Churchill tries to indicate the essential injustice of social hierarchies.

At a time when many writers seemed to be prostituting themselves to political patrons as party hacks, Churchill had to distinguish between independent and patronized bards. Holding the latter up to ridicule, he lets a patron reduce his poet to a spaniel:

> I've kept a *Bard* myself *this* twenty years,
>
> . . . .
> He, like a thorough true-bred Spaniel, licks
> The hand which cuffs him, and the foot which kicks,
> He fetches, and he carries, blacks my shoes,
>
> . . . .
> He wears my colours, yellow or true Blue,
> Just as I wear them; 'tis all one to him,
> Whether I change thro' conscience, or thro' whim.   (325-34)

Churchill curses poets like this, "who not themselves alone expose, / But *Me*, but *All*, and make the very name / By which They're call'd, a standing mark of shame" (342-44).

That independence was Churchill's highest value is especially evident when he associates it with life itself. Before going on to suggest an unwillingness to live without it, he speaks of his first taste of freedom as a rebirth and recalls, in an apostrophe to Independence, the liberation that his success as a poet had brought him: "Bow'd down, and almost crush'd, *Thou* cam'st, tho' late, / *Thou* cam'st upon me, like a second birth, / And made me know what life was truly worth" (514-16). The connection between Churchill's love of independence and his role as a political satirist becomes very clear when he moves abruptly from the personal to the political sphere. His fiction is to suggest a political threat; the lord as minister threatens the bard as patriot. When the bard naively boasts of his independent "Cot," where "PEACE dwells within, and LAW shall guard the door" (522), he is interrupted by a threatening voice, which begins: "O'erweening Bard! LAW guard thy door, what LAW? The LAW of ENGLAND—" (523-24). Churchill leaves the sentence unfinished to announce the dramatic arrival of the personification Administration: "To controul, and awe / Those saucy hopes, to strike that Spirit dumb, / Behold, in State, ADMINISTRATION come" (524-26).

The bard as patriot challenges the lord as minister when Churchill virtually defies the administration to do its worse. On the eve of the outlawing of his convicted fellow-patriot Wilkes, he boldly has the satirist reply:

> Why let Her [Administration] come, in all her
>   terrors too;
> I dare to suffer all She dares to do.
> I know her malice well, and know her pride,
> I know her strength, but will not change my side.
> This melting mass of flesh She may controul
> With iron ribs, She cannot chain my Soul.   (527-32)

Referring to the action that had been taken against Wilkes, Churchill continues:

> Where is this Minister? where is the band
> Of ready slaves, who at his elbow stand
> To hear, and to perform his wicked will?
> Why, for the first time, are they slow to ill?
> When some grand act 'gainst Law is to be done,
> Doth [Mansfield] sleep . . .   (535-40)

After this display of courage, Churchill exhorts the minority of "loyal patriots" (563) to whom the poem is addressed: the poem concludes as he calls upon those "brave few" (573) to come to the defense of their imploring country. There are only two alternatives, the poem states — liberty or death. Imploring England, "Seeming to breathe her last in ev'ry breath, / . . . kneels for Freedom, or She begs for Death" (579-80). Had things gone differently, Churchill's defiant political rhetoric may have captured the imagination of future generations as did the well-known challenge of the American patriot Patrick Henry who was soon to echo him.

Churchill, as it turned out, was greatly exaggerating the threat of the administration of George III to English liberty. Historians have shown that the king had no intention of attempting to close his eyes to the Revolution of 1688 and its guaranty of civil liberties.[14] The fact remains, however, that Churchill suspected foul play on the part of the government and that his suspicions seemed to be supported by the administration's deliberate and temporarily successful efforts to silence one of its shriller critics, John Wilkes. The significant thing

is not what we can see retrospectively as Churchill's misreading of current events but the courage of that political satirist who did not allow himself to be intimidated by the fate of his friend.

IV   A Sermon for Bishop Warburton

Churchill's greatest literary achievement is the ironic "Dedication" to his Sermons, published posthumously in February 1765.[15] Dedicated to William Warburton, the sermons themselves are ten undistinguished discourses on prayer, eight of them on the Lord's Prayer. The Critical Review found them "tolerable, but not extraordinary productions. The thread of the author's discourse is generally trite, and the whole seems to be more calculated for the edification of an ordinary congregation, than the entertainment or instruction of a judicious reader."[16] While Tooke claimed that the sermons were written by Churchill, it is recorded elsewhere that the satirist "used laughingly to say they were none of his: whose name they were, the public, if they could, might find out." The informant adds: "I always suspected them to have been compilations, and compilations of his father's: for he himself, I am persuaded, would not have submitted to that kind of drudgery."[17] Whatever the case, it is appropriate that the satirist was dedicating to the bishop of Gloucester nothing of artistic merit but a collection of pious clichés — the "sacred Dullness" he refers to in the poem (83).

The "Dedication," while based on the same material that Churchill used in his satiric portrait of Warburton in The Duellist, is superior to that work because it treats its subject with ironic indirection and manages to give the material focus.[18] The subtle irony of the poem arises partly from the satirist's employment of the mock panegyric, a mode he had experimented with less successfully in his attack against Sandwich in The Candidate. Further tension is generated by an ironic contrast, which runs throughout the "Dedication," of the "great" bishop with the "unknown" Churchill; and this ironic contrast gives the poem its focus.

The main parallels between the satirist and his subject are their humble origins, their service in the Church of England, and their literary careers. While Warburton seems to have transcended those origins, Churchill does not. The religious devotion of the bishop, who gave up a legal career for the church, seems just the opposite to the worldliness of the satirist, who left the church for poetry. Warburton, who had established himself as a critic with his editions of Shakespeare and Pope, might have been Churchill's literary foster father, guiding him in those days when he could have used a guide,

but the bishop was too busy, the satirist ironically assumes, with spiritual matters. It is along these lines that Churchill, as ingénu, sets himself up as a foil to the "great" bishop.

The ironic contrast is immediately apparent in the mocking toast (the libertine poet toasts the respected bishop) that opens the poem:

> HEALTH to great GLOSTER — from a man unknown,
> Who holds thy health as dearly as his own,
> Accept this greeting — nor let modest fear
> Call up one maiden blush — I mean not here
> To wound with flatt'ry — 'tis a Villain's art,
> And suits not with the frankness of my heart.
> Truth best becomes an *Orthodox* Divine,
> And, spite of hell, that Character is mine;
> To speak e'en bitter truths I cannot fear;
> But truth, *my Lord*, is panegyric here. (1-10)

The "anonymity" of the dedicator seems, at first, to be the result of simple ironic reversal; Churchill not only was the greatest living satirist in England but was known particularly to Warburton whom he had mercilessly ridiculed in *The Duellist*. The dedicator is "unknown" in that he is not "great" like the bishop.[19]

Churchill's insistence that he is an "orthodox" divine seems, again, to be an example of simple ironic reversal; later in the poem he refers to the fact that he had already thrown off the clerical gown. As the italics in this passage indicate, he is amplifying the poem's central contrast between himself and Warburton by opposing "an *Orthodox* Divine" to "*my Lord* [Bishop]." The quality of an "orthodox" divine singled out here is truthfulness. In opposing "truth" to "flattery," Churchill may be opposing his "Dedication" to Warburton's prefatory eulogy of Pitt that was published not long before the bishop, in a sense, betrayed that statesman.[20]

Churchill measures himself against Warburton again when the dedicator lets the bishop know that he is not impressed by "pomp" and "power":

> Think not, a Thought unworthy thy great soul,
> Which pomps of this world never could controul,
> Which never offer'd up at Pow'r's vain shrine,
> Think not that Pomp and Pow'r can work on mine. (29-32)

Elaborating upon the superficial aspects of the bishop, such as his name and mitre, that have not impressed him, Churchill ironically

includes Warburton's ancestry: "'Tis not thy Birth — for that is low as mine, / Around our heads no lineal glories shine" (55-56). This common denominator will be insisted upon again at the end of the "Dedication" with a more devestating effect when Churchill pulls this upstart's ladder from under him.

Summarizing his distinction between appearances and essence, the dedicator ironically advises the bishop: "Thy Virtue, not thy Rank, demands my lays; / 'Tis not the Bishop, but the Saint I praise" (69-70). Churchill seems to praise Warburton not simply for something that he lacked but for something that he disapproved — the "sanctity" (that is, religious enthusiasm) of the evangelical Methodists.[21] Similarly, he refers to the bishop's "fiery zeal" (136) when presenting Warburton's condemnation of *An Essay on Woman* as an example of the influence of "Grace" (128).

Warburton becomes a kind of mock father figure as Churchill mentions the death of his real father in the context of his earlier, unfulfilled desire for the friendship of the great critic. In an autobiographical passage, reminiscent of the negative view of clerical life presented in *The Author*, the dedicator laments:

> Much did I wish, e'en whilst I kept those sheep,
> Which, for my curse, I was ordain'd to keep;
> Ordain'd, alas! to keep thro' need, not choice,
>
> . . . .
>
> Those sheep, which my good Father (on his bier
> Let filial duty drop the pious tear)
> Kept well, yet starv'd himself, e'en at that time,
> Whilst I was pure, and innocent of rime,
> Whilst, sacred Dullness ever in my view,
> Sleep at my bidding crept from pew to pew,
> Much did I wish, tho' little could I hope,
> A Friend in him, who was the Friend of POPE.   (73-86)

The sleep image, reminiscent of *The Dunciad*, is followed by an ironic tribute to Pope in an heroic couplet skillfully phrased in the manner of that despised master.[22] On the surface, the couplet states that the poet had ardently wished without much hope for the friendship of Warburton, who earlier had been friends with another poet, the famous Pope. The second halves of the two lines have a certain equivalence in that they both qualify what has gone before — as if the reason for the lack of hope were Warburton's friendship with Pope. An opposition has been established here between the

satirist and his predecessor. Churchill is indirectly stating his poetic inferiority to Pope, but his humility is a mock humility — the tone of the poem in general.

What the dedicator had hoped to gain from the bishop was a modicum of his critical insight, which Churchill ironically praises:

> Rais'd 'bove the slavery of common rules,
> Of Common-sense, of modern, antient schools,
> Those feelings banish'd, which mislead us all,
> Fools as we are, and which we Nature call,
> He, by his great example, might impart
> A better something, and baptize it Art.   (97-102)

Immediately striking is the shift in meaning of the word "common" from "common rules" to "Common-sense"; the bishop's uniqueness is seen not as genius but a snobbish eccentricity. Thus, the thing that Warburton, as a cleric, can "baptize" as "art" is a perversion rather than a refinement of nature. Concluding this survey of Warburton's role as a critic with a direct reference to his function as an ironic foster father, the dedicator recalls the youthful wish that the famous editor "Might, like himself, teach his adopted Son, / 'Gainst all the world, to quote a WARBURTON" (111-12).

But the dedicator knows now that he had been a fool for expecting that the bishop's deep concern for the salvation of man would permit him to waste his time on "toys like mine" (119). Rising to a pitch in his ironic defense of Warburton's religious devotion, he brings in a specific example of it. At this point, the poem assumes a mock-heroic tone as Churchill recounts Warburton's ridiculous condemnation of *An Essay on Woman* in the House of Lords. The picture we get of the bishop is that of a zealous evangelical preacher, a type that Warburton would have been likely to disapprove:

> . . . Methinks I now
> See stern Rebuke enthroned on his brow,
> And arm'd with tenfold terrours — from his tongue
> Where fiery zeal, and Christian fury hung,
> Methinks I hear the deep-ton'd thunders roll,
> And chill with horrour ev'ry sinner's soul —
> In vain They strive to fly — flight cannot save,
> And POTTER trembles even in his grave —
> With all the conscious pride of innocence,
> Methinks I hear him, in his own defence,

> Bear witness to himself, whilst all Men knew,
> By Gospel-rules, his witness to be true.   (133-44)

"With all the conscious pride of innocence," Warburton (innocent in more than a legal sense, though ultimately guilty) denies having fathered the salacious annotations to Potter's *Essay*. Implicit, perhaps, is the denial that he fathered his only son, whom gossip attributed to the same Potter — if "Gospel-rules" refers to the precept about knowing the tree by its fruit.

Further ironic contrast occurs when the dedicator points out the "superiority" of the bishop, who gave up the law for the church, to himself, who gave up the church for poetry. Playing on the meanings of "shadow" and "substance," Churchill writes:

> I, like an idle Truant, fond of play,
> Doting on toys, and throwing gems away,
> Grasping at shadows, let the substance slip;
> But you, *my Lord*, renounc'd Attorneyship
> With better purpose, and more noble aim,
> And wisely played a more substantial game.   (155-60)

The game imagery here suggests that Churchill was naive for playing boys' games and that Warburton was wise for playing men's games. Beneath the irony, the poet is seen to be innocent and idealistic; the bishop, to be guilty and materialistic.

Churchill sustains the tension of the "Dedication" until the very end, when Warburton is pictured "to the topmost round / Of Fortune's ladder got" (166-67). Standing below, looking up with "wond'ring eye" (169) and "without envy" (170), the satirist warns him of moral giddiness:

> Let not thy Brain (as Brains less potent might)
> Dizzy, confounded, giddy with the height,
> Turn round, and lose distinction, lose her skill
> And wonted pow'rs of knowing good from ill.   (171-74)

The concluding couplet reminds the bishop again of his lowly origins; he is not to "Forget what once he was, tho' now so high; / How low, how mean, and full as poor as I" (179-80). The "low," "mean," "poor" poet in the last line of the poem is the same as the "man unknown" in the first line; and his station is to be seen as "low" only in its relationship to the bishop's "greatness."

Churchill seems to have thought the "Dedication" incomplete when he brought proofsheets of it and his unfinished *The Journey* to Wilkes at Boulogne just before his death. While it is not difficult to imagine what new directions *The Journey* might have taken if the satirist had lived, it is not at all so clear how the "Dedication" would have been additionally developed. The "fragment" as he left it seems to be a unit to most modern readers. There is a note of finality in the last couplet; moreover, those lines seem to resolve the tension that appears in the first line with its opposition of "great" and "unknown." Regardless of Churchill's intentions, it is clear that the "Dedication" represents his highest achievement as a satiric poet. Free of the sometimes wearisome digressions that characterize Churchill's poetry in general, it is sharply focussed on its subject, who is skillfully played off against the persona of the satirist, a kind of ironic foil. Moreover, there is a subtlety of tone in the "Dedication" that we do not find in his other poems — almost as if Churchill, just before his untimely death, had found his true poetic voice.

CHAPTER 6

Achievement and Significance

THE scope and quality of Charles Churchill's poetry has been largely defined in the preceding four chapters of this study, but his achievement in that peculiarly neo-Classical medium, the heroic couplet, has only been hinted. Churchill's indebtedness to his famous predecessors, Dryden and Pope, is rather obvious; but what is less obvious and deserves statement is the manner in which this satirist developed the heroic couplet as a vehicle for verse satire. What also needs recognition is the magnitude of his achievement in the context of neo-Classical political satire.

I   *The Satirist as Orator*

The English verse satirist of Churchill's day had two major distinct and fairly well-established mediums in which to work: the octosyllabic (iambic tetrameter) couplet and the heroic (iambic pentameter) couplet. Preferring the heroic couplet, which he molded into something distinctly his own, Churchill was proficient in both forms. Early in his career he had tried and then immediately discarded a third type of couplet — one composed of an anapestic rather than an iambic meter. He used this rather unusual meter in an unpublished satire against the dean, Zachary Pearce, and chapter of Westminster, "The Conclave." The first eight lines, all that remains of the endeavor, are as follows:

> The Conclave was met, and Longinus the Pope,
> Who leads a great number of fools in a rope,
> Who makes them get up, and who makes them sit still;
> Who makes them say yea or nay, just as he will;
> Who a *critic* profound does all critics defy,
> And settles the difference 'twixt *Beta* and *Pi;*
> Who forgiveness of faults preaches up to another,
> But forbids it to come near himself or his brother.[1]

An effect of the anapest is a metrical lightness, one more suitable to burlesque than to the Juvenalian tone that was to become associated with Churchill. The meter of "The Conclave" also seems more artificial than the more traditional iambic meter and particularly the iambic pentameter. Artificiality arises from the singsong effect of the anapests, and the tendency of the four-foot line is to break in the middle, as do all of the lines except the fourth in the excerpt quoted above. At any rate, Churchill was to turn in subsequent poems to the more traditional meters of the neo-Classical verse satirists.

The octosyllabic couplet had long been an established meter for nonsatiric poetry; and readily recalled are such successful experiments with it as Christopher Marlowe's "The Passionate Shepherd to His Love"[2] and Andrew Marvell's "To His Coy Mistress." Samuel Butler most memorably used this meter as a medium for satire in *Hudibras*. Influenced quite possibly by Butler, Jonathan Swift successfully made use of octosyllabic couplets as a medium for light satire in such poems as "The Beasts' Confession to the Priest" and "Verses on the Death of Dr. Swift."

No doubt influenced initially by Butler and Swift, Churchill wrote some of his earliest poems in iambic tetrameter couplets: "The Fortune Teller," which developed into Book I of *The Ghost*, and the unpublished "Bard." He used that meter only occasionally in his later verse, such as the "Epistle to R. L. L.," *The Ghost*, and *The Duellist*, and not at all in the last nine months of his short career. These couplets, however, are not often Hudibrastic; that is, they seldom have that jingling rhythm, comic rhyme, and epigrammatic thrust associated with Butler's verse. Indeed, Churchill's octosyllabic couplets show the same flexibility and individuality as his pentameter couplets which do not slavishly reflect the practice of Dryden and Pope but generally, especially in the later months of his career, show a distinct style of Churchill's own. In fact, Churchill's two favorite forms of expression are closer to each other than the one is to Butler or the other is to Dryden and Pope.

Occasionally Churchill does use, especially in the first book of *The Ghost*, comic rhyme in a manner reminiscent of *Hudibras*, as in this couplet from the history of fortune telling that introduces the poem: "At its first rise, which all agree on, / This noble Science was CHALDEAN" (I, 21-22). Similarly, Churchill's portrait of Warburton in *The Duellist* is, in part, reminiscent of the satiric portraits in *Hudibras*:

> To prove his Faith, which all admit
> Is at least equal to his Wit,
> And make himself a Man of note,
> He in defence of Scripture wrote;
> So long he wrote, and long about it,
> That e'en Believers 'gan to doubt it;
> He wrote too of the inward light,
> Tho' no one knew how he came by't,
> And of that influencing grace,
> Which in his life ne'er found a place;
> He wrote too of the Holy Ghost,
> Of whom, no more than of a Post
> He knew, nor, should an Angel shew him,
> Would He or know, or chuse to know him.   (739-52)

Although the third couplet echoes Pope,[3] the rhyme in this passage is particularly reminiscent of Butler. There is the multiple rhyme in this couplet and in the last one and the awkward rhyme in the fourth couplet in which "light" is linked to "by't," forcing an unmelodious elision and a false emphasis on the prepositional phrase. The indecorous chiming of "Holy Ghost" and "Post," rather arbitrary and meaningless, makes a sort of nonsense rhyme. In other ways, though, such as the run-on lines and the scarcity of closed couplets, this passage is more characteristic of Churchill than of Butler.

The distinctiveness of Churchill's octosyllabic couplets is perhaps best observed where he applies that medium to panegyric as he does when he praises, like Juvenal, the Old Patriots:[4]

> Hail those Old Patriots, on whose tongue
> Persuasion in the Senate hung,
> Whilst They this sacred Cause maintain'd!
> Hail those Old Chiefs, to Honour train'd,
> Who spread, when other methods fail'd,
> War's bloody banner, and prevail'd!
> Shall Men like these unmention'd sleep
> Promiscuous with the common heap,
> And (Gratitude forbid the crime)
> Be carried down the stream of time
> In Shoals, unnotic'd and forgot,
> On LETHE's stream, like flags, to rot?
> No — they shall live, and each fair name,
> Recorded in the book of fame,
> Founded on Honour's basis, fast
> As the round Earth, to ages last.
> *(The Duellist, I, 189-204)*

There is virtually no resemblance to the octosyllabic couplets of Butler and Swift in these lines which bear the imprint of that oratorical style that came to be distinctive of Churchill and that usually characterizes the verse that he wrote during the last two years of his career.

In most of his poetry, Churchill is working in a tradition that goes back to Chaucer, the first to use the heroic couplet. In the seventeenth century, the heroic couplet was significantly modified by Ben Jonson, Edmund Waller, Sir John Denham, and others into a tighter unit called the "closed couplet."[5] This neo-Classical form of the heroic couplet was perfected by Dryden and Pope who used it as a medium for their great verse satires. In Pope, whose primary value was correctness, the tradition may be said to have reached its climax.

Early in Churchill's career, he acknowledged his indebtedness to this tradition. As Pope did in his *Epistle to Augustus*,[6] he pays tribute in his *The Apology* to the harmonious Waller and to the vigorous Dryden. Like Pope, Churchill refers to that correctness, or polish, which his predecessor valued so highly; but he rejects it in favor of the unevenness of Dryden's verse.[7] Although Churchill swore allegience to Dryden rather than to Pope, an analysis of his verse shows that it resembles in different ways the poetry of both. Like Pope, he uses the triplet and Alexandrine infrequently and has a preference, stronger than Dryden's, for rhetorical devices such as balance, antithesis, repetition, and alliteration, as well as for monosyllabic words, especially verbs, as rhyme words. Like Dryden, he gives comparably more emphasis to the verse paragraph as opposed to the couplet as a structural unit; in line with this practice is his more frequent use of the run-on line, though this aspect of his versification has sometimes been exaggerated.[8]

More generally, Churchill could not, or would not, emulate the precision of Pope. He pays less attention to diction, less attention to the inner rhetoric of the couplet. As a consequence, there is less of that delightful ambiguity that is associated with the Popean couplet. To explain Churchill's practice in a less positive way, he tended to be somewhat careless; but his works are far from being the "rude, unfinish'd brats" that he cheerfully referred to in *Gotham* (II, 175). He seems to have shared that complacency that Johnson attributed to Dryden, and it would not be too much of a distortion to apply Johnson's criticism to Churchill: "he seldom struggled after supreme excellence, but snatched in haste what was within his reach; and when he could content others, was himself contented. He did not keep present to his mind an idea of pure perfection; nor compare his

works, such as they were, with what they might be made. . . . from
his contemporaries he was in no danger. Standing therefore in the
highest place, he had no care to rise by contending with himsef; but,
while there was no name above his own, was willing to enjoy fame
on the easiest terms."[9]

When judging Churchill's verse in the context of that of his great
predecessors, to describe it only in terms of its deviation from and
tendency toward the practices of Dryden and Pope is to un-
deremphasize, if not miss completely, the fact of the individuality of
Churchill's style. Churchill's poetry, especially his more mature
verse, differs significantly from that of his predecessors in the tradition of the heroic couplet and manages to achieve a distinction and
relevance of its own in its highly rhetorical nature. While he may not
be so subtly rhetorical in the use of figures as some of them (especially Pope), Churchill is more intensely rhetorical than any of the
better known neo-Classical satiric poets. Churchill's is the rhetoric
of the orator more than that of the poet.[10]

One of the better descriptions of Churchill's verse is one of the
earlier descriptions that appeared in a review of Tooke's 1804 edition
of Churchill's poems, from which Tooke included excerpts in his second edition in 1844. The reviewer, one William Taylor, in commenting on *The Prophecy of Famine*, which he considers the best of
Churchill's works, states: "It has imagery and condensation, which
Churchill rarely has; and it displays that periodic structure, or poetic
paragraph, that progressive evolution and swell of the versified
sentence which elevates poetry into oratory, and which constitutes
the highest merit, peculiar to Churchill's style."[11] In comparing
Churchill's style to that of the orator and in isolating "periodic structure" as the most significant aspect of that style, Taylor suggested a
fruitful approach to Churchill's versification.

Churchill's periodic structure is particularly evident in the introduction to his caricature of Thomas Fitzpatrick which was added
to *The Rosciad* in 1763:

> With that *low* CUNNING, which in fools supplies,
> And amply too, the place of being wise,
> Which nature, kind indulgent parent, gave
> To qualify the Blockhead for a Knave;
> With that *smooth* FALSHOOD, whose appearance charms,
> And reason of each wholsome doubt disarms,
> Which to the lowest depths of guile descends,
> By vilest means pursues the vilest ends,

Wears Friendship's mask for purposes of spite,
Fawns in the day, and Butchers in the night;
With that *malignant* ENVY, which turns pale,
And sickens, even if a friend prevail,
Which merit and success pursues with hate,
And damns the worth it cannot imitate;
With the *cold* CAUTION of a coward's spleen,
Which fears not guilt, but always seeks a screen,
Which keeps this maxim ever in her view —
What's basely done, should be done safely too;
With that *dull, rooted, callous* IMPUDENCE,
Which, dead to shame, and ev'ry nicer sense,
Ne'er blush'd, unless, in spreading VICE's snares,
She blunder'd on some Virtue *unawares;*
With all these blessings, which we seldom find
Lavish'd by Nature on *one* happy mind,
A Motley Figure, of the FRIBBLE Tribe,
Which Heart can scarce conceive, or pen describe,
Came *simp'ring* on; to ascertain whose sex
Twelve sage impannell'd Matrons would perplex.   (117-44)

While the sentence is not strictly periodical, rhetorical climax is the dominant structural principle of the verbal unit. The subject, the "Motley Figure," is withheld for twenty-four lines until after five of his chief attributes, or "blessings," have each been introduced and amplified. The periodicity of this passage is only one of the markedly rhetorical devices involved; the others are anaphora and grammatical parallelism, another aspect of rhetorical repetition. Each of the subject's attributes is introduced with a prepositional phrase, each beginning with the same word, and amplified by one or more relative clauses.

The concluding verse paragraph in the satriric portrait of the "neuter" Fitzpatrick presents two other aspects of Churchill's rhetorical style. Complicating his subject's identity problems further, the satirist writes:

Nor shall the MUSE (for even there the pride
Of this *vain Nothing* shall be mortified)
Nor shall the MUSE (should Fate ordain her rhimes,
Fond pleasing thought! to live in aftertimes)
With such a Trifler's name her pages blot;
Known be the Character, the *Thing* forgot;
Let *It,* to disappoint each future aim,
Live without Sex, and die without a name!   (171-78)

The oratorical note is emphasized by the parenthesis and the imperative. Both, in this case, mark a change in the satirist's voice. Until now, Churchill has been describing in declarative sentences the entrance of Fitzpatrick ("*It smil'd, It smirk'd, It wriggled to the chair*" [162]); abruptly, his voice changes to the imperative, as he forbids his muse to name the unnameable. The use of the imperative at the conclusion of the portrait strengthens the periodic structure of the passage. The satirist's voice is also modulated in the parenthetical clauses. Whether in the nature of asides or afterthoughts, these inner statements emphasize additionally the immediacy of the speaker and, thus, the oratorical nature of Churchill's verse; by delaying completion of the sentence's main idea, they also contribute to the overall periodical structure.[12]

Another oratorical device that both emphasizes the poet as speaker and contributes to the periodic structure of the verse is the rhetorical question. This device is particularly effective when combined with anaphora, as in the series of rhetorical questions in the "Dedication" to the *Sermons* where Churchill ironically explains why Warburton, who had befriended Pope, had never done the same for him:

> Fool that I was, could I so much deceive
> My soul with lying hopes; could I believe
> That He, the servant of his Maker sworn,
> The servant of his Saviour, would be torn
> From their embrace, and leave that dear employ,
> The cure of souls, his duty and his joy,
> For toys like mine, and waste his precious time,
> On which so much depended, for a rime?
> Should He forsake the task he undertook,
> Desert his flock, and break his past'ral crook?
> Should He (forbid it Heav'n) so high in place,
> So rich in knowledge, quit the work of Grace,
> And, idly wand'ring o'er the Muses' hill,
> Let the salvation of mankind stand still?   (113-26)

As the nineteenth century reviewer Taylor suggested, periodicity goes hand in hand with the verse paragraph which Churchill employed instead of the closed couplet as his basic structural unit. The verse paragraph just quoted is composed of three independent segments of varying lengths, and only one of them (the second) is a closed couplet. The first is the longest (eight lines) and the most

fluid; it employs enjambment several times (lines 1, 2, and 4) and a heavy caesura, or almost full stop (a semicolon), within the second line, rather than at the end of it. The use of enjambment and the heavy caesura help to shift the structural emphasis away from the couplet to the verse paragraph in rhetorical passages such as this one.

Churchill's oratorical style is most effective when, like Cicero attacking the conspirator Catiline before the senate of Rome, he attacks rather directly particular enemies of Wilkes and liberty before the forum of the English citizenry. Most notable are his attacks against William Hogarth, the earl of Sandwich, and Bishop Warburton. In the second half of *An Epistle to William Hogarth*, in the central part of *The Candidate*, and throughout the "Dedication," Churchill is speaking face to face to the subject of his satire in the role of public prosecutor who increasingly assumes the pose of ironic eulogist.[13] His rhetoric — the repetition, the questions, the interjections, the commands, and the periodic structure — gives added force to his voice and, thus, to his accusations. Verse has become a club in the grasp of the "Bruiser."

The role of the satirist as public prosecutor is quite explicit in *An Epistle to William Hogarth*. Forced to defend a negative view of human nature, the satirist calls forth the man who dared to mock publicly Wilkes's role as champion of liberty:

> HOGARTH stand forth — Nay hang not thus aloof —
> Now, CANDOUR, now Thou shall receive such proof,
> Such damning proof, that henceforth Thou shalt fear
> To tax my wrath, and own my conduct clear —
> HOGARTH stand forth — I dare thee to be tried
> In that great Court, where Conscience must preside. (315-20)

More subtle and more damaging, is Churchill's public accusation of William Warburton in the ironic "Dedication" to the *Sermons*. This poem is easily the best example of Churchill's use of rhetoric (including irony) as a deadly instrument. In a voice that had become distinctively his own, Churchill brings to a forceful conclusion his ironic eulogy of the bishop thus:

> *Doctor, Dean, Bishop, Gloster*, and *My Lord*,
> If haply these high Titles may accord
> With thy meek Spirit, if the barren sound
> Of pride delights Thee, to the topmost round

Of Fortune's ladder got, despise not One,
For want of smooth hypocrisy undone,
Who, far below, turns up his wond'ring eye,
And, without envy, sees Thee plac'd so high,
Let not thy Brain (as Brains less potent might)
Dizzy, confounded, giddy with the height,
Turn round, and lose distinction, lose her skill
And wonted pow'rs of knowing good from ill,
Of sifting Truth from falshood, friends from foes;
Let GLOSTER well remember, how he rose,
Nor turn his back on men who made him great;
Let Him not, gorg'd with pow'r, and drunk with state,
Forget what once he was, tho' now so high;
How low, how mean, and full as poor as I.   (163-80)

II   An Evaluation

While Churchill has been admired by individual poets over the centuries, from William Cowper in the eighteenth to Yvor Winters in the twentieth,[14] his actual influence has been small. It was confined almost exclusively to the work of long-forgotten verse satirists in the years immediately following his death. Although short-lived and ultimately unfruitful, his influence was for those few years rather pervasive. "One might say without exaggeration," Joseph M. Beatty has observed, "that every writer of abusive verse during the decade following 1764, looked to [Churchill] as a model or was in some way affected by his spirit."[15]

Beginning his career as a verse satirist after the heroic couplet had been carried about as far as it could be in the direction of correctness, Churchill attempted to revitalize this favorite neo-Classical verse form by developing it in a new direction — or, rather, he turned back from the Horatian elegance of Pope to the Juvenalian vigor of Dryden and developed his rhetorical mode into a style uniquely his own. The fact that Churchill's experimentation with the heroic couplet bore little fruit beyond his own plentiful crabapples, as Dr. Johnson was pleased to describe the poems,[16] does not at all detract from his achievement.

Churchill's heroic couplets are also significant in that they reveal the rhetorical, as opposed to metaphorical, basis of much neo-Classical verse. Often rather topical, public, and declamatory, it intended, like oratory, to persuade an audience. The oratorical role of the eighteenth century poet is more apparent in the works of

Churchill than it is in the verse of neo-Classical poets like Dryden, Pope, and Johnson. This aspect of Churchill's style is what Taylor singled out when he referred with admiration to "that progressive evolution and swell of the versified sentence which elevates poetry into oratory."

More important than Churchill's role in the evolution of the heroic couplet is his role as a political satirist in an age renowned for its political satire. He is in the tradition of men like Dryden, who held up to scorn the earl of Shaftesbury and his fellow rebels in *Absalom and Achitophel*, and like Swift and Fielding, who defied Sir Robert Walpole, the one in his *Drapier's Letters* and the other in farces such as *The Historical Register for 1736*. Fielding was effectively silenced by Walpole with the passage of the Licensing Act (1737) much the way *The North Briton* was repressed a quarter century later by the Grenville ministry.

While Churchill's satiric verse was strongly influenced by Dryden, the two are antithetical in their political views. Dryden's *Absalom and Achitophel* supports the establishment; his highest value is order. "What Prudent men a settled Throne would shake?" he asks. "For whatsoe'r their Sufferings were before, / That Change they Covet makes them suffer more."[17] Churchill, unlike Dryden, has little concern for order; his highest value is freedom. To him, revolution is a viable political alternative. "Thro' ev'ry age, in ev'ry land," he proclaims at the end of the second book of *Gotham*, "Written in gold let REVOLUTION stand" (675-76).[18] The pendulum has swung from the conservative aftermath of the English Civil War of the 1640s to the radical prelude to the American and French revolutions.

In his political attitude, Churchill shows less of a kinship with Dryden than he does with such Romantic poets as the young William Wordsworth and Lord Byron. He also looks forward to the Romantic movement in his individualism — in his sense of self as opposed to the group, his sense of isolation, particularly evident in his last poem, *The Journey*, with its refrain, "I on my Journey all Alone proceed." Churchill, in effect, sees himself as an outsider. His individualism is something more than Swift's pose of the morally outraged misanthropist. Though Churchill does not display the self-conscious introspection of a Wordsworth or a Coleridge, he places more emphasis upon self as opposed to society than his neo-Classic predecessors did. In his individualism, Churchill can be considered a transitional figure.

While Churchill's political values tend to be antithetical to Dryden's, the two poets are quite similar in that they employ many of the same techniques to implement their political satire. Most of the elements that make *Absalom and Achitophel* an outstanding example of English political satire in verse are present in Churchill's works, and some of these elements are wit, formal dialogue, and the satiric portrait. What is most conspicuously lacking in Churchill's satire is the sort of sustained fiction that operates in *Absalom and Achitophel* in the form of the religious allegory. Although Churchill is capable of using most of Dryden's satiric techniques as effectively on occasion as his master, he has no single political satire comparable to *Absalom and Achitophel.*

Closely allied to political satire, especially in Churchill's case, is personal satire, or caricature. In this area, when the "Dedication" is compared to Dryden's *MacFlecknoe,* Churchill is seen to his best advantage. Both poems are relatively short, carefully crafted, and attain part of their effect through a continually modulated tone. Dryden chose the mock-heroic form to ridicule the comic dramatist Thomas Shadwell; Churchill used the ironic eulogy to attack the Bishop of Gloucester.[19] Dryden is treating a professional comedian in a heroic vein; Churchill, praising an elderly dignitary of the church for qualities that one of his station should possess. There is some broad humor in the earlier poem, culminating when Flecknoe's coronation speech is interrupted as he suddenly drops through a trapdoor. Churchill's poem, partially because of the basic form he has chosen, does not have this broad humor; it is more subtle and certainly more deadly, with the satirist near the end of the poem ominously warning the bishop, who has successfully climbed to the top of the ladder, to beware moral giddiness. While both poems suffer the inevitable fate of topical verse — that is, an increasing baggage of footnotes — the "Dedication" suffers less in this respect. Although Churchill obviously falls far short of Dryden in terms of overall achievement, his "Dedication" does compare quite favorably to *MacFlecknoe.*

Charles Churchill's career was a short one in which he wrote furiously and prolifically. There is no doubt that his poetry is weakened by a certain redundancy and by general carelessness; at the same time, it has an exuberance that has diminished little with time. At his best, in the "Dedication," he has made a truly signifi-

cant contribution to English poetry. Whether "such Talents with prudence had commanded the Nation"[20] is doubtful, though Garrick's estimate *is* a useful reminder of the magnitude of Churchill's unfulfilled genius.

Notes and References

Preface

1. Wallace Cable Brown, *Charles Churchill: Poet, Rake, and Rebel* (Lawrence, Kansas; 1953); Edward H. Weatherly, ed., *The Correspondence of John Wilkes and Charles Churchill* (New York, 1954); Douglas Grant, ed., *The Poetical Works of Charles Churchill* (Oxford, 1956); Yvor Winters, "The Poetry of Charles Churchill," in *Forms of Discovery* (Denver, 1967), pp. 121 - 45 (originally published in two parts in the April and May 1961 numbers of *Poetry*).

2. Brown, p. 127.

3. Winters, p. 145.

4. Johnson's antagonism toward Churchill may not have been the reason for the latter's exclusion from the *Lives;* it is more likely that, for one reason or another, Churchill's name had been omitted from the list of the booksellers for whom Johnson had undertaken the series. See Hesther Lynch Piozzi, "Anecdotes of the Late Samuel Johnson LL.D.," in *Johnsonian Miscellanies*, ed. George Birkbeck Hill (Oxford, 1897), 1, 271 - 72.

5. Louis I. Bredvold et al., ed., *Eighteenth Century Poetry & Prose* (New York, 1939, 1956); Geoffrey Tillotson et al., ed., *Eighteenth-Century English Literature* (New York, 1969).

6. Although Book IV of *The Ghost* was published in November 1763, the poem is discussed with Churchill's poetry of 1761 - 1762. *The North Briton*, published from June 1762 to April 1763, is discussed as a unit at the beginning of Chapter 3, which is devoted to Churchill's early political satire. *Gotham* is analyzed at the end of Chapter 4, despite the fact that some of the other poems treated in that chapter were not published until after Books I and II of *Gotham*. *The Journey*, although the last of Churchill's poems to be published, is discussed at the beginning, rather than the end, of Chapter 5.

Chapter One

1. The full title reads: "The Bruiser C. Churchill (once the Reverend!) in the Character of a Russian Hercules, regaling himself after having kill'd

133

the Monster *Caricatura* that so sorely galled his virtuous friend, the Heaven-sent Wilkes." See Ronald Paulson, *Hogarth: His Life, Art, and Times* (New Haven, 1971), II, 394.

2. *The Candidate*, l. 152. Included in Grant. Subsequent references to the poems in this edition are included in the text.

3. For an elaboration of the background of this incident, see below, pp. 62 - 63. For Hogarth, the club represented *The North Briton;* and Churchill was a false Hercules, a pretender to heroic virtue. See Paulson, II, 393 - 95.

4. David M. Little and George M. Kahrl, eds., *The Letters of David Garrick* (Cambridge, Massachusetts, 1963), I, 378.

5. The newly born bear cub was supposedly given a shape only when its mother licked it. See William Shakespeare, *3 Henry VI*, III. ii. 161.

6. For particulars, see below, p. 41.

7. The so-called "Fleet" marriage was one clandestinely performed by a parson imprisoned for debt in the Fleet Prison, London, in return for ten to twenty shillings or a few bottles of gin. See Thomas Burke, *The Streets of London* (London, 1940), p. 80.

8. Grant associates Churchill's marriage with his withdrawal from college (p. xii); so does Brown, who believes that the marriage took place in 1749, the year following the probable date of withdrawal (p. 17).

9. Seven years later, Oliver Goldsmith echoed the last line of this passage in *The Deserted Village*, where he described the village preacher as "passing rich with forty pounds a year." See Arthur Friedman, ed., *Collected Works of Oliver Goldsmith* (London, 1966), IV, 293.

10. Charles was born in 1754; William, in 1757; Charlotte, in 1759.

11. W. Tooke, ed., *The Poetical Works of Charles Churchill. With copious notes and a life of the author by W. Tooke* (London, 1844: 2nd ed.), I, xxxii - xxxiii. Of these two poems, all that remains today are the opening lines of "The Conclave," quoted below, p. 120.

12. *The Monthly Review*, XXV (December 1761), 451. The remark was made in a review of *Night*, published in November 1761.

13. W. S. Lewis, ed., *The Yale Edition of Horace Walpole's Correspondence* (1939; rpt. New Haven, 1961), VII, 374.

14. Frederick A. Pottle, ed., *Boswell's London Journal, 1762 - 1763* (New York, 1950), pp. 51 - 52.

15. Wilkes reminds Churchill of a meeting of the fraternity in a letter written on June 15, 1762. See *Correspondence*, p. 3. For accounts of the Hell Fire and Beefsteaks clubs, see Louis Clark Jones, *The Clubs of the Georgian Rakes* (New York, 1942).

16. *Correspondence*, p. 5.

17. *Ibid.*, pp. 73 - 74.

18. *Ibid.*, p. 75.

19. Churchill complains to Wilkes in the autumn of 1762: "What I imagined to be St. Antony's fire turns out to be St. Cytherea's." In the

spring of the following year, he writes: "I am most confoundedly bad, Confin'd to my room with an Eruptio Veneris, where I am likely to continue some days." *Ibid.*, pp. 16, 54.

20. *Ibid.*, p. 83.

21. *Ibid.*, p. 47.

22. The depth of Wilkes's personal commitment is unknown. His comment that he himself was not a Wilkite, together with his unabashed hedonism, has always made him suspect. A recent commentator may be going too far when he writes that Wilkes "probably embarked on the enterprise in order to retrieve his personal fortunes." Donald Greene, *The Age of Exuberance: Backgrounds to Eighteenth-Century English Literature* (New York, 1970), p. 80. See also, pp. 144 - 45, note 1, 2 below.

23. The fact that Wilkes was successful in his pursuit of legal action against such high-ranking government officials as a secretary and undersecretary of state tends to undercut his and Churchill's charge of tyranny.

24. *Correspondence*, pp. 68 - 69. The challenger was the Scots Captain John Forbes, who resented Wilkes's insulting treatment of Scotland.

25. The poem, a parody of Pope's *Essay on Man*, was probably written by Wilkes's late friend the politician Thomas Potter. Wilkes printed only a limited number of copies of the poem to be distributed privately among his friends.

26. Four years later, Wilkes returned to England, where he was fined and imprisoned for almost two years. He continued in his role as champion of liberty, going on to be elected lord mayor of London in 1774.

27. Quoted in Frank Brady and Frederick A. Pottle, eds., *Boswell on the Grand Tour: Italy, Corsica, and France, 1765 - 1766* (New York, 1955), pp. 71 - 72. Translated by the editors.

Chapter Two

1. Churchill's versification is discussed below, Chapter 6.

2. Churchill visited Westminster School in the autumn of 1762 for the King's Scholars' performance of Terence's *The Eunuch*. See *Boswell's London Journal, 1762 - 1763*, p. 63.

3. Davies substantiates this view to some extent in a letter to Garrick dated August 13, 1763. See J. Boaden, ed., *The Private Correspondence of David Garrick* (London, 1831), I, 165. Churchill had attacked Davies's enunciation: "He mouths a sentence, as curs mouth a bone" (322).

4. Thomas Davies, *Memoirs of the Life of David Garrick* (London, 1780), I, 306.

5. *Ibid.*

6. *Correspondence*, p. 88. Churchill referred to Woodward as "Great master in the science of grimace" (370).

7. In Dryden's *MacFlecknoe* (1678), the contemporary dramatist

Thomas Shadwell is crowned by his "father," the poetaster Richard Flecknoe.

    8. The following passages come to mind most immediately: "The mighty monarch, in theatric sack, / Carries his whole regalia at his back" (212 - 13); "The strolling pageant heroe treads in air: / Pleas'd for his hour he to mankind gives law, / And snores the next out on a truss of straw" (241 - 43).

    9. "Epistle to R.L.L.," published in *The Library* (1761), I, 152 - 55. See Grant, pp. 447 - 50. The poem is unsigned, but Grant believes that it "can be plausibly attributed to Churchill on the grounds of the style . . . the subject . . . and the person addressed — the initials probably stand for Robert Lloyd," p. 561.

    10. The first edition contained 730 lines; the eighth edition, 1090 lines.

    11. Brown, p. 43.

    12. These additions consist of lines 67 - 104, included in the seventh edition; lines 117 - 78, included in the eighth; and lines 539 - 616, in the fifth.

    13. In his letter of August 27, 1764, Wilkes suggested that Churchill supply "a few short explanatory notes" with future poems. "I have been," he explained, "so many months absent from the great theatre of London, I begin to find obscurities in your late pieces." *Correspondence*, p. 89. Today, of course, we have copious notes to the poems, thanks to the various editors and especially to the most recent one, Professor Grant.

    14. Alexander Pope, "The Dunciad Variorum: Appendix I," in John Butt, ed., *The Poems of Alexander Pope* (London, 1965), p. 433.

    15. *The Critical Review* XI (March 1761), 212. The three men, referred to as the "new triumvirate of wits," were not mentioned by name. "*Connoisseurs*," however, alludes to *The Connoiseur*, a literary magazine put out by Colman and Thornton; Lloyd is referred to as "Mr. L—".

    16. Both denied it — Murphy in the advertisement for *An Ode to the Naiads of Fleet Ditch*, a scurrilous attack against Churchill in revenge for the latter's treatment of him in *The Rosciad* (see Grant, p. 477, note to ll. 108 - 23); and Smollett in a letter to Garrick. For Smollett's letter, see Edward S. Noyes, ed., *The Letters of Tobias Smollett, M. D.* (Cambridge, Massachusetts; 1926), pp. 69 - 70.

    17. See Wilbur L. Cross, *The History of Henry Fielding* (New Haven, 1918), II, 392 - 99).

    18. See above, p. 26.

    19. See Grant, p. 479, note to ll. 206 - 11.

    20. Davies writes:

Mr. Garrick's situation, during the anxiety and uneasiness of the players, was something aukward. . . . He certainly felt all the charms of a distinction which placed him on an eminence superior to all men of his profession. Churchill had raised a magnificent colossus to him on the broken statues of his contemporaries. He, however, seemed not to approve the wantonness of that pen which had made him another Saturn, and so greedy an engrosser of praise, as to swallow, not only his own,

but that of his household too. Whether he was induced to look coldly upon his pan-egyrist, or had dropped some expressions which were officiously carried to Churchill, I know not. (p. 309.)

Garrick's production in April of Samuel Foote's comedy *Taste*, which satirized Churchill and some of his friends, also may have angered the poet. See Edward H. Weatherly, "The Personal and Literary Relationship of Charles Churchill and David Garrick," in Charles T. Prouty, ed., *Studies in Honor of A. H. R. Fairchild*, University of Missouri Studies, XXI, 1 (Columbia, Missouri; 1946), 153 - 60.

21. Earl R. Wasserman points out that Churchill's attitude toward Pope was not unique: "Throughout the second half of the eighteenth century the protests against the monotony of Pope's closed couplets come in increasing number." Some of the protesters were Joseph Warton, William Cowper, and, indirectly, Samuel Johnson. See "The Return of the Enjambed Couplet," *ELH*, VII (1940), 244 - 45.

22. Samuel Johnson, *The Lives of the English Poets* (London, 1820), III, 170.

23. Churchill was most obviously influenced by Juvenal in *The Times*. The Juvenalian influence was rather pervasive in what W. B. Carnochan distinguishes as "post-Augustan" verse satire. See "Satire, Sublimity, and Sentiment: Theory and Practice in Post-Augustan Satire," *PMLA*, LXXXV (1970), 260 - 67.

24. *The Critical Review*, XI (May 1761), 410.

25. The poem was dismissed as of little value by the early reviewers. *The Critical Review*, XII (November 1761), 370, claimed that it did "little honor to . . . [the author], considered either in the character of a clergyman or a poet."

26. Joseph Addison, *The Spectator*, No. 81 (Saturday, June 2, 1711).

27. The word "woman" was omitted from the first three editions of the poem.

28. John Dryden, "Religio Laici," in H. T. Swedenberg, Jr., ed., *The Works of John Dryden: Poems 1681 - 1684* (Berkeley, California; 1972), II, 122.

29. For further details, see Grant, pp. 483 - 85.

30. See Tooke, II, 218n.

31. See Grant, p. 485.

32. *Tristram Shandy* was published over a period of eight years, from 1760 to 1767, and, by this time, the first six volumes had appeared. In its review of *The Ghost*, I - III, *The Monthly Review*, XXVII (October 1762), 316, called the poem "a kind of *Tristram Shandy* in *verse*."

33. Churchill was criticizing the mimics of the day:

Doth a man stutter, look a-squint, or halt?
Mimics draw humour out of Nature's fault:

With personal defects their mirth adorn,
And hang misfortunes out to public scorn. (401 - 04)

The attitude that physical defects were not proper objects of ridicule was not at all new. In a letter to John Dennis written in 1695, William Congreve complained that "sometimes Characters are barbarously exposed on the Stage, ridiculing Natural Deformities, Casual Defects of the Senses, and Infirmities of Age." Republished in J. E. Spingarn, ed., *Critical Essays of the Seventeenth Century* (1908 - 1909; rpt. Bloomington, Indiana, 1957), III, 245. In the preface to *Joseph Andrews* (1742), Henry Fielding stated: "Much less than the misfortunes and calamities of life are natural imperfections the object of derision." See Maynard Mack, ed., *Joseph Andrews* (New York, 1967), pp. xxii - xxiii.

34. Boswell saw these lines as instrumental in getting Johnson to complete the edition, which was finally published in 1765. Boswell writes: ". . . we may almost conclude that the Caesarian operation was performed by the knife of Churchill, whose upbraiding satire, I dare say, made Johnson's friends urge him to dispatch." George Birkbeck Hill, ed., *Boswell's Life of Johnson* (New York, 1891), I, 370.

35. Boswell recalls the following conversation with his friend on that subject:

He [Johnson] talked very contemptuously of Churchill's poetry, observing, that 'it had a temporary currency, only from its audacity of abuse, and being filled with living names, and that it would sink into oblivion.' I ventured to hint that he was not quite a fair judge, as Churchill has attacked him violently. JOHNSON. 'Nay, Sir, I am a very fair judge. He did not attack me violently till he found out I did not like his poetry; and his attack on me shall not prevent me from continuing to say what I think of him, from an apprehension that it may be ascribed to resentment. No, Sir, I called the fellow a blockhead at first, and I will call him a blockhead still. However, I will acknowledge that I have a better opinion of him now, than I once had; for he has shewn more fertility than I expected. To be sure, he is a tree that cannot produce good fruit: he only bears crabs. But, Sir, a tree that produces a great many crabs is better than a tree which produces only a few.' (*Ibid.*, I, 485)

It is worth while noting that Boswell's opinion of Churchill's poetry is higher than Johnson's. Reflecting on the sentiment quoted above, he writes:

In this description of Churchill's poetry I could not agree with him. It is very true that the greatest part of it is upon the topicks of the day, on which account, as it brought him great fame and profit at the time, it must proportionally slide out of the publick attention as other occasional objects succeed. But Churchill had extraordinary vigour both of thought and expression. His portraits of the players will ever be valuable to the true lover of the drama; and his strong caricatures of several eminent men of his age will not be forgotten by the curious. Let me add, that there are in his works many passages which are of a general nature; and his *Prophecy of Famine* is a poem of no ordinary merit. It is, indeed, falsely injurious to Scotland, but therefore may be allowed a greater share of invention (486).

For a more thorough examination of the relationship between Johnson and Churchill, see Brown, pp. 206 - 09.

36. O Thou! whatever title please thine ear,
 Dean, Drapier, Bickerstaff, or Gulliver!
 Whether thou chuse Cervantes' serious air,
 Or laugh and shake in Rab'lais' easy chair . . . (I, 19 - 22)

Alexander Pope, "The Dunciad," in *Poems*, p. 351.

37. Laurence Sterne, *The Life and Opinions of Tristram Shandy, Gentleman*, ed. Ian Watt (Boston, 1965), p. 79.

38. *Ibid.*, p. 211.

39. *The Monthly Review*, XXVII (October 1762), 316.

40. Churchill is using the term "reason" in a more traditional way than he did in his earlier poems.

41. William Shakespeare, *I Henry IV*, V.i.136, V.iv.120.

42. See Grant, p. 509, note to ll. 1797 - 1894.

43. Brown, pp. 144 - 45.

Chapter Three

1. John Wilkes and Charles Churchill, eds., *The North Briton*, "from No. I to No. XLVI inclusive. With Several useful and explanatory Notes, not printed in any former Edition. To which is added, A copious Index to every Name and Article. Corrected and revised by A Friend To Civil And Religious Liberty" (London, c1769), p. 6. Subsequent references to this edition will appear in my text.

2. Three weeks elapsed between Numbers 44 and 45.

3. Scholars are not in agreement as to exactly what Churchill did write. In addition to the five essays mentioned above, he probably wrote an originally unpublished extraordinary for April 7, 1763, as well as prefaces to Numbers 22 and 26, which featured Lloyd's poem "The Poetry Professors," and extensively revised Numbers 21 and 44. See George Nobbe, *The North Briton: A Study in Political Propaganda* (New York, 1939), pp. 64 - 75.

4. The half-pay lists were lists of inactive commissioned officers who were entitled to an allowance of one-half (or less) the pay they got while on active duty.

5. *Correspondence*, p. 10.

6. *Ibid.*, p. 28.

7. *The Critical Review*, XV (January 1763), 61 - 62.

8. William Shakespeare, *King Lear*, I.ii.l.

9. Churchill's attitude toward the rules here is the same as it was in *The Apology* and in "An Epistle to R.R.L.".

10. Images of dullness, sleep, and lead permeate Pope's poem.

11. Touring Scotland in 1758, Wilkes visited the duke at Inveraray. Grant, p. 515, note to ll. 159 - 62.

12. Scotland, at one time, is ironically compared to the Promised Land.

13. The duke of Cumberland opposed the Bute administration in Parliament. See Grant, p. 516, note to ll. 553 - 56.

14. For Boswell's comments on the poem, see above, p. 138, note 35.

15. See Paulson, II, 358 - 60.

16. *Correspondence*, p. 15.

17. Quoted in Grant, p. 517. At this point, Churchill had published *The Rosciad*, *The Apology*, *Night*, and *The Ghost*, I - II. Among his subjects were Smollett, Garrick, and Johnson. A month after this letter, *The Critical Review*, XIV (October 1762), 306, in reviewing the first three books of *The Ghost*, criticized Churchill's choice of William Whitehead as a subject of satire by quoting the line from Pope that Churchill had alluded to in his letter: "the poor inoffensive *laureate* . . . is treated with more asperity than a character so harmless could, we think, well deserve; for, as a poet, not much more good-natur'd than Mr. Churchill, has observed, 'Who breaks a butterfly upon a wheel?' " See Alexander Pope, "An Epistle to Dr. Arbuthnot," in *Poems*, p. 608.

18. See Paulson, II, 385 - 87.

19. *Correspondence*, p. 48.

20. *The Letters of David Garrick*, I, 378.

21. See above, p. 13, for a description of the engraving. Churchill took offense at the caricature. He implies in a letter to Wilkes that an individual's private life falls outside the province of satire: "I take it for granted You have seen Hogarth's Print — was ever any thing so contemptible — I think he is fairly Felo de se . . . . he has broke into my pale of private Life, and set that example of illiberality, which I wish'd — of that kind of attack which is ungenerous in the first instance, but justice in the return. I intend an Elegy on him, supposing him dead." *Correspondence*, pp. 59 - 60. Although he never wrote the elegy, Churchill spoke of the dying Hogarth as if he were already dead in his poem *Independence* (178).

22. William Shakespeare, *Hamlet*, III. i. 85.

23. Pope, "An Epistle to Dr. Arbuthnot," in *Poems*, pp. 604 - 5.

24. See Grant, pp. 522 - 23, note to ll. 481 - 86.

25. Swift deteriorated mentally before his death; Steele suffered a disabling paralysis before his. Churchill wrongly implies that *both* men were senile.

26. See above, p. 18.

27. On November 23, 1763, Boswell's correspondent William J. Temple wrote: "He [Churchill] ran off the other day with a beautiful young lady of fifteen, but is already returned. When the afflicted father asked him when he would send back his daughter, he answered perhaps he would *have done with her* in about ten days. Such a monster!" Frederick A. Pottle, ed., *Boswell in Holland, 1763 - 1764* (New York, 1952), pp. 78 - 79.

28. This tradition was established by *The Monthly Review*, XXIX (November 1763), 385 - 89.

29. *The Critical Review*, XVI (December 1763), 444, in reference to this acknowledgment, pointed out: "We do not, indeed, remember any gentleman in the world of literature whom the public have so liberally contributed to support, or to whose decrees, how arbitrary soever, it hath so implicitly submitted, as to Mr. Churchill."

30. Churchill made the same distinction in a letter to Wilkes which condemned Hogarth's print "The Bruiser" as "ungenerous" for having broken into his "pale of private Life." *Correspondence*, p. 59.

31. See Grant, pp. 527 - 28, note to ll. 357 - 98.

32. This is Grant's conjecture, p. 526, note to ll. 107 - 26.

33. Although Churchill uses only an initial here and his description is rather general, his readers probably would have been quick to fill in the blank; Sandwich's profligateness was well known. Churchill was not to spell out the earl's name until six months later in *The Candidate*.

34. See Thomas Gray, "Notes on Churchill," *Transactions of the Royal Society for Literature*, XXXVI (1918), 14.

35. See Tooke, I, 227n.

Chapter Four

1. Wilkes referred to Martin as "the most treacherous, base, selfish, mean, abject, low-lived and dirty fellow, that ever *wriggled* himself into a secretaryship" (265).

2. Horace Walpole, *Memoirs of the Reign of King George III*, ed., G. F. R. Barker (London, 1894), I, 253.

3. Forbes had challenged Wilkes for his attacks against Scotland.

4. *Correspondence*, pp. 67 - 68.

5. Paget Toynbee, ed., *The Letters of Horace Walpole* (Oxford, 1904), 416 - 17.

6. Satire, of course, always trivializes to some degree.

7. Pope, "An Epistle to Dr. Arbuthnot," in *Poems*, pp. 604 - 5. Compare especially "A tim'rous foe, and a suspicious friend" (l. 206).

8. *Correspondence*, p. 80.

9. Churchill was not alone in his satirical attack; the prospect of Sandwich's becoming high steward of Cambridge provoked even the reticent Thomas Gray to write a short poem with the same title, published posthumously in 1777.

10. The name of the young seducer in Nicholas Rowe's *The Fair Penitent* (1703), "Lothario," had become a common noun by this time.

11. John Burton, fellow of Corpus Christi College, Oxford, attacked Wilkes in an oration at the Encaenia. His awareness that Churchill was in the audience did not at all intimidate him. See Grant, pp. 541 - 42.

12. Churchill did, of course, leave more than one couplet behind; both *The Journey* and the "Dedication" to the *Sermons* were published posthumously by Churchill's brother and executor, John Churchill.

13. One of the more notable "riming guests" was to be Lord Byron whose visit to the Dover cemetery a half-century later inspired his rather melancholic musing on this "Comet of a season" in his poem "Churchill's Grave." See Ernest Hartley Coleridge, ed, *The Works of Lord Byron* (New York 1966), IV, 45 - 46.

14. William Shakespeare, *1 Henry IV*, IV.i.104 - 10.

15. That Churchill was probably trying to avoid suit for libel in each instance does not diminish the satiric effectiveness of this technique.

16. We have Gray's assurance that Sumner, although "mean and roguish without disguise," was not at all instrumental in Sandwich's affair with his niece: "His niece professed herself a common *whore;* of course she fell in Ld. Sandwich's way, & was for a time in his keeping, but not at all by the Uncle's procurement." "Notes on Churchill," p. 177.

17. Sandwich once sustained himself with slices of cold beef and toast during a twenty-four hour gambling bout. The "sandwich" was named after him.

18. Grant suggests that "sickness may have made him [Browne] slow in his movements at the time of Churchill's visit to Oxford" for the Encaenia in 1763, p. 548, note to ll. 737 - 44.

19. See the sketch of Colley Cibber at his desk, "Sinking from thought to thought, a vast profound!" Pope, "The Dunciad," in *Poems*, p. 726.

20. For having betrayed his former friend Wilkes, Sandwich had been nicknamed "Jemmy Twitcher," after the thief who betrays Macheath in John Gay's *Beggar's Opera* (1728). See Walpole, I, 249.

21. A "jaghire" was an annuity paid by the district governed to the governor.

22. See Grant, pp. 457 - 58, note to ll. 27 - 28; pp. 544 - 45, note to ll. 447 - 56.

23. See Alexander Pope, "An Essay on Man," Epistle III, which concludes: "Thus God and Nature linked the general frame, / And bade Self-love and Social be the same." *Poems*, p. 535.

24. According to Grant, "internal dissensions" and "mismanagement" were the "sores" revealed in the official debates over Clive's appointment. See p. 549, note to ll, 473 - 84.

25. As Grant points out, "Churchill is advocating the repeal of those charters whereby the Company was granted a monopoly in the Indian trade and complete autonomy in the conduct of its affairs." See p. 549, note to ll. 479 - 84.

26. Gotham, of course, is Great Britain, and the allusion to "the wise fools of Gotham" is intended to suggest what Churchill saw as the general gullibility, especially in the political sphere, of the English. Earlier, depicting the progress of fraud in England, Churchill had written in *The Ghost*: "KNAVES starve not in the *Land of Fools*" (I, 374). Similarly, he refers to the political innocence of the English in *The Prophecy of Famine*, in which the goddess, after reciting the history of Scotland's "treachery," states:

These facts, which might, where wisdom held the sway,
Awake the very stones to bar our way,
There shall be nothing, nor one trace remain
In the dull region of an English brain.
Bless'd with that *Faith*, which mountains can remove,
First they shall *Dupes*, next *Saints*, last *Martyrs* prove. (525 - 30)

For the origin of the saying "the wise fools of Gotham," see R. Chambers, *Book of Days* (London, 1864), I, 462 - 63.

27. Jonathan Swift, *Gulliver's Travels*, ed. Herbert Davis (Oxford, 1959), p. 294.

28. Psalm CXIV.4.

29. See Song of Songs V.15.

30. Similarly, in "Epistle to R. L. L." Churchill writes:

The cinquant ring of tinsel sound,
Unto the ear is pleasing found;
But sense gives value to the whole,
Rhime is the body, sense the soul. (9 - 12)

31. As they did throughout his brief career, the lines were coming easily to Churchill. Writing to Wilkes at this time, he commented enthusiastically: "Gotham goes on swimmingly — I made forty Lines today." *Correspondence*, pp. 44 - 45. A similar determinism had been expressed by Pope:

Why did I write? what sin to me unknown
Dipped me in ink, my parents', or my own?
As yet a child, nor yet a fool to fame,
I lisped in numbers, for the numbers came.

"An Epistle to Dr. Arbuthnot," in *Poems*, p. 602.

32. This very distinction between the king and his ministry was in fact what Dr. Johnson saw as the real meaning of the maxim: "you are to consider, that in our constitution, according to its true principles, the King is the head; he is supreme; he is above every thing, and there is no power by which he can be tried. Therefore, it is, Sir, that we hold the King can do no wrong; that whatever may happen to be wrong in government may not be above our reach, by being ascribed to Majesty. Redress is always to be had against oppression, by punishing the immediate agents." *Boswell's Life of Johnson*, I, 490 - 91.

33. While *The Monthly Review*, XXXI (August 1764), 102, referred to an "insolant tendency" in Book III "which cannot be mistaken," *The Critical Review*, XVIII (August 1764), 107, refused to acknowledge Churchill's intent: "We cannot see with what propriety some of Mr. Churchill's enemies have called this a satire, nor can we think that there is in England a wretch so mean as to dream of its being a contrast."

Chapter Five

1. *The Journey*, ll. 149 ff.

2. Wilkes's abuse of the Scots forced Armstrong to part company with him. "I cannot," the physician-poet wrote to the editor of *The North Briton*, "with honour or decency associate myself with one who has distinguished himself by abusing my country." Quoted in the *Dictionary of National Biography*.

3. *The Letters of David Garrick*, I, 412. Some months later, Garrick advised his friend George Colman of Churchill's imminent death: "Churchill I hear, is at the point of death at Boulogn. This may be report only — he is certainly very ill — what a lust of publishing has possess'd him for some time past — the greatest Genius no more than the greatest Beauty, can withstand such continu'd prostitution — I am sorry, very sorry for him — such Talents with prudence had commanded the Nation —" (429 - 30).

4. *Correspondence*, p. 91. For Swift's letter, see Harold Williams, ed., *The Correspondence of Jonathan Swift* (Oxford, 1963), III, 103.

5. This is not to imply that Churchill imitated any one of Juvenal's satires (two of which dealt with the same subject) the way Samuel Johnson had earlier adapted Satires III and X in *London* (1738) and *The Vanity of Human Wishes* (1749). With Churchill, it's more a case of tone, general subject matter, and rather bold (for his time) treatment of sexual perversion — though nothing to match Juvenal's frankness. Smollett had been less bold when touching upon the same subject in his Juvenalian satire *Advice (1746)*.

6. *Correspondence*, p. 91.

7. As Morris Golden has observed, the homosexuality of *The Times* functions as "a flourishing symbol of England's decay." "Sterility and Eminence in the Poetry of Charles Churchill," *JEGP*, LXVI (1967), 343.

8. Alexander Pope, "The Rape of the Lock," in *Poems*, p. 223.

9. George Sherburn, "Mid-Century Poets," in Albert C. Baugh et al, ed., *A Literary History of England* (New York, 1948), p. 1020.

10. "Your apology to the fair at the end saves all," Wilkes wrote, "and will leave the modestest virgin unhurt by the boldness of some of the descriptions." *Correspondence*, p. 91. Wilkes may have had in mind the following lines, which portray the homosexual as disgusted with female sexuality:

> A Maidenhead, which, twenty years ago,
> In mid December, the rank Fly would blow
> Tho' closely kept, *now*, when the Dog-Star's heat
> Enflames the marrow, in the very street
> May lie untouch'd, left for the worms, by Those
> Who daintily pass by, and hold their nose. (565 - 70)

11. *The Critical Review*, XVIII (September 1764), 198 - 99.

12. The historian J. H. Plumb points out that "the English aristocracy of the 18th-century had an arrogant contempt for any male who did not belong

by birth to their world. They could be gracious; they could be friendly; they could accept working alliances; what they could not suppress was the social contempt which repeatedly broke through. And the hard core of this attitude was to be found at Court, in the House of Lords, and the great ministers who became Wilkes's *bêtes noires*." In a review of *The Extraordinary Mr. Wilkes: His Life and Times* by Louis Kronenberger, *The New York Times Book Review*, February 10, 1974, p. 4.

13. See Walpole, I, 247.

14. See J. Steven Watson, *The Reign of George III, 1760 - 1815* (Oxford, 1960), chs. I, IV.

15. Brown judges the "Dedication" as "unequalled in English poetic satire" (p. 144). Yvor Winters goes even further when he claims it "the greatest English poem of the eighteenth century and one of the great poems in our language" (p. 145).

16. *The Critical Review*, XIX (February 1765), 117-18. Churchill may have been following the example of Sterne who four years earlier, capitalizing on the fame of *Tristram Shandy*, published *The Sermons of Mr. Yorick*. This is not to ignore the frequency of sermon publishing at the time. In a six month period from July to December 1762, in addition to volumes XIII and XIV of *The Works of Swift*, which included four sermons, there were five collections and nineteen separate sermons noted in *The Monthly Review*.

17. Tooke, III, 319; R. B. Peake, *Memoirs of the Colman Family* (London, 1841), I, 155 - 56. The informant was Churchill's friend Richard Shepherd.

18. The fact that Churchill probably intended to develop the poem further does not mean that what he had already written cannot stand as a unit.

19. The term "great" had been frequently applied in a sarcastic manner to George II's chief minister, Sir Robert Walpole, who had managed to amass a huge fortune while in office. John Gay had this in mind when he mentioned the "statesman . . . so great" in the opening song of *The Beggar's Opera* (1728), where he links Walpole to the treacherous Peachum. See John Gay, *The Beggar's Opera and Companion Pieces*, ed. C. F. Burgess (Northbrook, Illinois; 1966), p. 5. Fielding had explicitly dissociated greatness from goodness in *Jonathan Wild* (1743), where the benevolent Thomas Heartfree is opposed to the "great" criminal, Wild.

20. The eulogy is contained in the "Advertisement" to Warburton's *The Doctrine of Grace* (1763). The bishop's later congratulatory address on the Treaty of Paris, composed in the name of the clerics under his jurisdiction, was a blow to Pitt. See William Stanhope Taylor and John Henry Pringle, eds., *The Correspondence of William Pitt, Earl of Chatham* (London, 1838), II, 253 - 57.

21. Warburton had attacked the Methodists as fanatics in *The Doctrine of Grace: or, the Office and Operations of the Holy Spirit vindicated from the Insults of Infidelity and the Abuses of Fanaticism* (1763). As Grant has pointed out (p. 533, note to 11. 745 - 52), Churchill had already alluded to this work in *The Duellist*. See p. 122 above. In the "Dedication," Churchill

asks rhetorically whether the bishop should "quit the work of Grace" (124), before introducing Warburton's zealous attack against *An Essay on Woman*.
    22. Churchill's attitude toward Pope may have been partly influenced by his antagonism toward the latter's friend and literary executor, William Warburton. This point has also been made by Professor Sherburn. See "Mid-Century Poets," p. 1020. At any rate it seems that Churchill's hostility was more than simply a reaction against Pope's verse, which actually influenced his own in many ways. See Edward H. Weatherly, "Churchill's Literary Indebtedness to Pope," *Studies in Philology*, XLIII (1946), 56 - 69. The extent of Churchill's scornful and rivalrous feelings toward Pope, as well as his soaring confidence, is suggested by Davies, who mentions that Churchill "held Pope so cheap, that one of his most intimate friends assured me, that he had some thoughts of attacking his poetry; and another gentlemen informed me, that in a convivial hour he wished the bard of Twickenham was alive, that he might have an opportunity to make him bring forth all his art of poetry, for he would certainly have a struggle with him for pre-eminence." Davies, I, 318.

Chapter Six

    1. Grant, p. 447. Quoted in Tooke, II, 275. "Longinus" is identified by Tooke as Zachary Pearce, dean of Westminster (I, xxxiii).
    2. Marlowe has grouped the couplets into stanzas of four lines each.
    3. In Book IV of *The Dunciad*, Richard Bentley, master of Trinity College, Cambridge, tells the Goddess Dulness: "For thee [we] explain a thing till all men doubt it, / And write about it, Goddess, and about it." *Poems*, p. 780.
    4. See Satire VIII.
    5. A strict closed couplet consists of a sentence or an independent sentence unit.

    6. Waller was smooth; but Dryden taught to join
        The varying verse, the full-resounding line,
        The long majestic March, and Energy divine.
    . . . .
        Late, very late, correctness grew our care . . .

Alexander Pope, "The First Epistle of the Second Book of Horace Imitated: To Augustus," in *Poems*, pp. 644 - 45.
    7. See above, pp. 34 - 35.
    8. See Wallace Cable Brown, *The Triumph of Form: A Study of the Later Masters of the Heroic Couplet* (Chapel Hill, North Carolina; 1948), pp. 87 - 102. For other more detailed comparisons of Churchill's verse to that of Dryden and Pope, see Joseph M. Beatty, "Charles Churchill's Treatment of the Couplet," *PMLA*, XXVII (1919), 60 - 69; and Weatherly, "Churchill's Literary Indebtedness to Pope."

9. Johnson, I, 427.

10. The oratorical nature of Churchill's verse reflects the Juvenalian influence on "post-Augustan" verse satire. See Carnochan.

11. Tooke, I, xiv-xv. Taylor's attitude toward oratory reflects the values of the latter half of the eighteenth century.

12. At its worst, the parenthesis was a mannerism with Churchill who sometimes overused it. Aware of this tendency, he comments ironically in *The Ghost:* "Our drift (Parenthesis For once apart) is briefly this," IV, 123 - 24.

13. Churchill speaks as ironic eulogist only briefly in *An Epistle to William Hogarth* when he discusses Hogarth's achievement as comic artist, ll. 547 - 68.

14. See William Cowper, "Table Talk," in *The Poetical Works of William Cowper*, ed. H. S. Milford (London, 1967: 4th ed., repr.), p. 15; and Winters, "The Poetry of Charles Churchill."

15. Joseph M. Beatty, "Churchill's Influence on Minor Eighteenth Century Satirists," *PMLA*, XLII (1927), 170.

16. For Johnson's opinion, see note 35, p. 138.

17. John Dryden, "Absalom and Achitophel," in *Poems*, p. 29.

18. Of fundamental importance, however, is the fact that both men supported the British political institution of constitutional monarchy.

19. It should be understood, of course, that these genres are not mutually exclusive. Ironic eulogy, for example, is evident in *MacFlecknoe* in Flecknoe's ironic praise of Shadwell.

20. See above, note 3, p. 144.

Selected Bibliography

PRIMARY SOURCES

The Correspondence of John Wilkes and Charles Churchill. Ed., Edward H. Weatherly. New York: Columbia University Press, 1954. Contains an introduction with pertinent biographical and historical facts and also a comprehensive bibliography of background material to the political campaign of *The North Briton*.

The North Briton, "from No. I to No. XLVI inclusive. With Several useful and explanatory Notes, not printed in any former Edition. To which is added, A copious Index to every Name and Article. Corrected and revised by A Friend To Civil and Religious Liberty." Ed., John Wilkes and Charles Churchill. London, c1769. For an account of Churchill's contribution to this periodical, see above, p. 53.

The Poetical Works of Charles Churchill. Ed., Douglas Grant. Oxford: Oxford University Press, 1956. This most recent and authoritative edition of Churchill's poetry contains a well-documented biography, helpful preliminary notes with the historical background to the individual poems, abundant footnotes, and an appendix discussing poems attributed wrongly or with inconclusive evidence to Churchill.

Sermons. London: W. Griffin, 1765. The authorship is questionable; see above, p. 114.

SECONDARY SOURCES

BARRON, JOSEPH M. "Stylistic Development in the Poetry of Charles Churchill" (Ph.D. dissertation, Case Western Reserve University, 1969). Stylistic analysis of "representative" early, middle, and late poems (*The Apology, An Epistle to William Hogarth, The Author, The Candidate,* and the "Dedication") in terms of audience, meter, rhetoric, imagery, and metaphor.

BEATTY, JOSEPH M. "The Battle of the Players and Poets, 1761-1776." *Modern Language Notes*, XXXV (1919), 449-62. Presents the literary-historical context of *The Rosciad*.

———. "Charles Churchill's Treatment of the Couplet." *Publications of the Modern Language Association,* XXVII (1919), 60-69. Examination of Churchill's versification.

———. "The Political Satires of Charles Churchill." *Studies in Philology,* XVI (1919), 303-33. Discussion of *The Prophecy of Famine, An Epistle to William Hogarth,* and *The Duellist* in the context of the political scene of 1763.

BLANTON, RAYMOND EUGENE. "Charles Churchill: Eighteenth-Century Literature in Transition" (Ph.D. dissertation, University of South Carolina, 1971). Examination of Churchill's life, style, satiric devices, ideas, and poetry in terms of his individualism and love of freedom, with emphasis on Churchill as a transitional figure anticipating the Romantic movement.

BROWN, WALLACE CABLE. "Charles Churchill and Criticism in Transition." *Journal of English and Germanic Philology,* XLIII (1944), 163-69. Survey of Churchill's critical views as reflected in his poetry.

———. *Charles Churchill: Poet, Rake, and Rebel.* Lawrence, Kansas: University of Kansas Press, 1953. Most complete and authoritative biography of Churchill; includes chapter discussing most of Churchill's major poems.

———. *The Triumph of Form: A Study of the Later Masters of the Heroic Couplet.* Chapel Hill, North Carolina: The University of North Carolina Press, 1948. Includes chapter on Churchill; contains, in addition to some of the critical analyses of individual poems included in the item listed immediately above, an examination of the influence of Dryden and Pope on Churchill's versification.

CARNOCHAN, WALTER BLISS. "Charles Churchill: A Critical Study" (Ph.D. dissertation, Harvard University, 1960). Study of Churchill's character, as reflected in his verse; his satiric theory; his poetry, in terms of structure, form, style, and language; his utilization of personification and allusion; and his reputation during the eighteenth century.

———. "Satire, Sublimity, and Sentiment: Theory and Practice in Post-Augustan Satire," *PMLA,* LXXXV (1970), 260-67. Includes a discussion of Churchill's "Dedication" as an exception to the typical "pseudo-Juvenalian" satire of the second part of the eighteenth century.

CUNNINGHAM, WILLIAM FRANCIS, JR. "Charles Churchill and the Satiric Portrait." In *Essays and Studies in Language and Literature,* ed. Herbert H. Petit, pp. 110-32. Pittsburgh: Duquesne University Press, Duquesne Studies, Philological Series, V, 1964. Examination of Churchill's role in the "breakdown" of the formal verse portrait.

———. "The Satire of Charles Churchill" (Ph.D. dissertation, University of Pittsburgh, 1961). Comprehensive study of the major poems in terms of literary, political, moral, and self-revealing satire; also an examination of Churchill's satiric technique.

DATZ, HYMAN HERBERT. "The Satire of Charles Churchill: A Critical Study" (Ph.D. dissertation, Columbia University, 1961). Fairly comprehensive analysis of the major poems; focus on Churchill's satiric persona.

FISHER, ALAN S. "The Stretching of Augustan Satire: Charles Churchill's 'Dedication' to Warburton." *Journal of English and Germanic Philology*, LXXII (1973), 360-77. Discusses Churchill's modification of Pope's satiric mode and examines the "Dedication" as the poem in which Churchill solved the problems that his "aesthetics of literalism" had created for him.

GOLDEN, MORRIS. "Sterility and Eminence in the Poetry of Charles Churchill." *Journal of English and Germanic Philology*, LXVI (1967), 333-46. Discusses Churchill's poetry in terms of structuring images of superiority and sterility.

HOPKINS, KENNETH. *Portraits in Satire*. London: Barrie Books Ltd., 1958. Contains a biography of Churchill, which includes brief discussions of most of his major poems.

LEE, DWIGHT AUGUSTUS. "Charles Churchill as a Political Writer" (Ph.D. dissertation, University of Missouri, 1952). Includes study of Churchill's political thought as reflected in both his prose and verse.

LOCKWOOD, THOMAS F. "Charles Churchill's Satire" (Ph.D. dissertation, Rice University, 1967). Focusses on Churchill's manipulation of the satiric persona.

NOBBE, GEORGE. *The North Briton: A Study in Political Propaganda*. New York: Columbia University Press, 1939. Comprehensive study of the career of *The North Briton*, with biographies of Churchill and Wilkes and discussions of the political background, the question of authorship, and the individual numbers.

PIPER, WILLIAM BOWMAN. *The Heroic Couplet*. Cleveland: The Press of Case Western Reserve University, 1969. Contains analysis of Churchill's use of the heroic couplet.

SIMON, IRÈNE. "An Eighteenth-Century Satirist: Charles Churchill." *Revue belge de philologie et d'historie*, XXXVII (1959), 645-82. Examination of Yvor Winters' high evaluation of Churchill (see below); focusses upon *An Epistle to William Hogarth, The Candidate*, and the "Dedication."

WALDHORN, ARTHUR. *Charles Churchill, Conservative Rebel*. New York: New York University Press, 1955. Abridgment of a Ph.D. dissertation on Churchill's political views.

WEATHERLY, EDWARD H. "Churchill's Literary Indebtedness to Pope." *Studies in Philology*, XLIII (1946), 56-69. Survey of similarities between the works of the two poets.

WINTERS, YVOR. *Forms of Discovery: Critical and Historical Essays on the Forms of the Short Poem in English*. Denver: Alan Swallow, 1967. Includes a critical study of Churchill's poetry with a thorough analysis of the "Dedication."

Index

153

101396

DATE DUE

Contents

part of India, even before 1947. Then, they say, the subcontinent was "British India," "undivided India," "pre-partition India," or the "Indo-Pakistani subcontinent." "South Asia" seems much simpler.

With any English language discussion of a people who write in a non-Roman script, transliteration of words creates annoying problems. There are several systems for spelling in English the words of Urdu or Bengali. The Middle East scholar usually draws on traditions for transliterating Arabic. The Asian scholar follows British practice, which reflects British accent in speaking. The author has generally tried to use the style most commonly used by Pakistanis.

A word of warning should be given regarding statistics. Few of them are as accurate as those from Western countries. In any country with a high illiteracy rate and with underdeveloped techniques of gathering data, figures are at best only approximate. Averages, too, are sometimes misleading in a society in which extremes—of wealth and poverty, of desert and jungle, educated and illiterate—are so common. Above all, there is no "average" Pakistani any more than there is an "average" American.

The author, who must take the responsibility for the statements and opinions in the book, nevertheless has had the help of several talented friends in preparing these few pages about Pakistan. Stephen Oren was most helpful in corroborating the facts and figures from his extensive and recent studies of Pakistan. Edward Metcalf, and particularly Ava Weekes, assisted immeasurably in editing the manuscript, reducing academic jargon and hopefully making the book more readable.

RICHARD V. WEEKES

June 1964

viii

Foreword

To anyone who has visited Pakistan for even a day, this book will seem incomplete. The people who live there are so varied in dress, language, and ways of living that no single description in less than several thousand pages can hope to do them justice. Perhaps this is just as well. The reader can more easily embellish the lines that follow from his own experiences. After all, no person's generalizations about people are much better than anyone else's, whether about Pakistanis or Americans.

For those who have not visited Pakistan, this book is meant to convey a brief idea of the nature of the country and its people. Hopefully, it will encourage them to look further and peer more deeply into the various subjects which follow. There are many scholarly books about Pakistan covering history, religion, politics, economics, and anthropology. They expand greatly on the complexities of Pakistan which here may seem oversimplified.

Throughout the book, Pakistan is called a "South Asian" country. This is a wholly arbitrary designation on the author's part, although there is increasing use of the term in the United States. South Asia refers to the countries of Afghanistan, Pakistan, India, Ceylon, Nepal, Bhutan and Sikkim, which have also been placed in the "Indian subcontinent," a term no Pakistani would use. Educated West Pakistanis like to think of their country as part of the Middle East. Educated East Pakistanis call themselves Asians. Neither considers Pakistan

For the first traveler in the family,

MY FATHER

D. VAN NOSTRAND COMPANY, INC.

120 Alexander St., Princeton, New Jersey (*Principal office*)
24 West 40th Street, New York 18, New York

D. VAN NOSTRAND COMPANY, LTD.
358, Kensington High Street, London, W.14, England

D. VAN NOSTRAND COMPANY (Canada), LTD.
25 Hollinger Road, Toronto 16, Canada

Published simultaneously in Canada by
D. VAN NOSTRAND COMPANY (Canada), LTD. 1964.

This book is one of the volumes in *The Asia Library*, a
series initiated by The Asia Society, Inc., a non-profit, non-
political, membership association whose purpose is to help
bring the people of America and Asia closer together in
their appreciation of each other and each other's way of life.

PRINTED IN THE UNITED STATES OF AMERICA
BY LANCASTER PRESS, INC., LANCASTER, PA.

PAKISTAN

*Birth and Growth
of a Muslim Nation*

by
RICHARD V. WEEKES

MAP BY DOROTHY DE FONTAINE

D. VAN NOSTRAND COMPANY, INC.
Princeton, New Jersey
Toronto · London · New York

The Asia Library

THAILAND: An Introduction to Modern Siam—2nd Ed.
by Noel F. Busch

CEYLON: An Introduction to the "Resplendent Land"
by Argus John Tresidder

INDONESIA: A Profile
by Jeanne S. Mintz

THE PHILIPPINES: A Young Republic on the Move
by Albert Ravenholt

AFGHANISTAN: Land in Transition
by Mary Bradley Watkins

PAKISTAN: Birth and Growth of a Muslim Nation
by Richard V. Weekes

The Asia Library is published in cooperation with The Asia Society, New York. Additional volumes in preparation

PAKISTAN

Birth and Growth
of a Muslim Nation

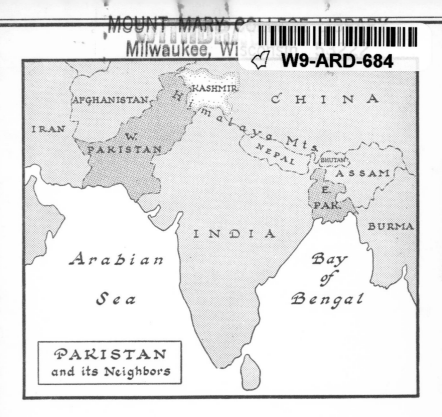

AFGHANISTAN

IRAN

KASHMIR

W. PAKISTAN

Himalaya Mts.

C H I N A

NEPAL

BHUTAN

A S S A M

E. PAK.

BURMA

I N D I A

Arabian

Sea

Bay

of

Bengal

PAKISTAN
and its Neighbors

Rangpur

Brahmaputra R.

A S S A M

Bogra

Mymensingh Sylhet

Rajshahi

Ganges R. Dacca

Comilla

Chittagong

0   100

EAST PAKISTAN

Dorothy deFontaine

INNOVATION IN THE SOCIAL STUDIES

Teachers Speak for Themselves

EDITED BY

DALE L. BRUBAKER

UNIVERSITY OF CALIFORNIA
SANTA BARBARA

THOMAS Y. CROWELL COMPANY
NEW YORK, ESTABLISHED 1834

300.712
B886

To George S. Counts

SCHOLAR AND INNOVATOR

FOREWORD

In a world shrunken by instant communication systems and supersonic transportation, when the day-to-day business of understanding our peers and the age in which we live is of critical importance, the discipline of the social studies takes on an importance and urgency as never before. So it is appropriate that today in our secondary schools there is a trend toward a more creative and more challenging interpretation of the place and meaning of the social studies curriculum. The "new social studies," like its earlier counterpart "the new math," is a fresh and innovative revision of some very traditional material. Many of these changes were brought about by curriculum studies at our larger universities. Perhaps an even greater number were suggested by teachers themselves in their attempts to involve students in a more rewarding investigation of United States and world history, civics, and, increasingly, economics, at the junior high and high school levels.

Innovation in the Social Studies is an account of some of their efforts. Written by teachers themselves, the chapters are enthusiastic, creative, imaginative, but realistic. Both the encouraging successes and the revealing less-than-successes are presented in the awareness that the teacher can learn equally from each, and that new ideas can be tested only through experimentation.

In an era when it is no longer enough—if, indeed, it ever was—for a teacher to "know how" to teach, when he must not only be more knowledgeable in his subject field, but also be more sympathetic to the interests, needs, and responses of his students, his community, and his country,

Dale Brubaker's book is an important step toward a necessary reinterpretation of the purposes and content of the
social studies curriculum. I recommend *Innovation in the
Social Studies* to all present and prospective teachers, administrators, and school board members who look back with
a certain amount of discomfort to the days when they
struggled through "the old social studies" by memorizing
Wilson's Fourteen Points and the terms of the Treaty of
Prague. This volume has something more to offer, much
more.

JAMES C. STONE

PREFACE

The phrase "the new social studies" is currently in vogue in a way which is reminiscent of "the new math" of a few years ago. The attention now being given to social studies by teachers, administrators, professors, textbook publishers, professional and philanthropic organizations, and state and federal governments indicates the concern presently held for the social studies. With concern comes controversy and ferment concerning objectives, procedures to reach desired objectives, and evaluation procedures.

The problem recognized by all those who are interested in social studies innovation is that research pertinent to particular treatments and sequences of different treatments is in its infancy. Therefore, at present we must rely more on intuition than on hard empirical data. But what is the social studies teacher in our schools and the future social studies teacher in our teacher education classrooms to do *right now?* Of course, he can keep informed about innovations being carried on at university-run centers, but these centers usually disseminate newly developed materials on a limited experimental basis.

There is, however, a good deal more innovation presently going on in secondary social studies than the observer might imagine. Teachers enter a school system, find themselves dissatisfied with traditional approaches, and proceed to experiment on their own. This book offers accounts of particular innovative approaches which have been written by the teachers who introduced such approaches. The sophisticated academician may well find much in these chapters with which to quarrel. The reader should likewise critically appraise each chapter for its merits and shortcomings.

The writers have been asked to consider some of the following points in writing their chapters: (1) a description of the school population in general and the particular class discussed in the chapter; (2) barriers to change which were advocated and those things which facilitated change; (3) a description of the approach employed, including those sources which were found to be most helpful; and (4) a description of some of those things which happened as a result of their approach with concrete examples to demonstrate their ideas. Some chapters did not lend themselves to this outline but necessarily entailed a different context in which the writer wrote his account.

Most of the approaches discussed in this book took place within commonly named social studies courses. As a point of information it might be well to specify the common secondary social studies curriculum:

Grade Seven:	The Old World—Eastern Hemisphere Geography and History or World Geography
Grade Eight:	United States History
Grade Nine:	Civics
Grade Ten:	World History
Grade Eleven:	United States History
Grade Twelve:	Problems of Democracy or Government and Economics *

Within the context of the secondary social studies curriculum, each innovator has instigated his approach. Almost all of the approaches discussed in this book may be used at any grade level of the secondary social studies curriculum. For this reason it is encumbent on you, the reader, to sift through the writer's ideas to discover that which may be relevant to your own situation.

D. L. B.

* "Grade Placement of Social Studies Topics in the Schools of the United States." Paper of the Rand McNally Company in the editor's possession. Received in the winter of 1965.

ACKNOWLEDGMENTS

The editor wishes to express his appreciation to the contributors who have enthusiastically received the idea for this book; the selections they have written bear the imprint of this enthusiasm.

The editor also wishes to express his appreciation to the editors of *Social Education* for permission to publish the following articles, which originally appeared in that journal: "Teaching World History on Television" and "A Course in Problems of American Democracy," by Gerald Leinwand; "Current Events and the American History Course" and "Using Documents in Junior High School," by Muriel Moulton; and "An Independent Study Course in Russian History," by James M. Haught.

Finally, the editor owes a great debt of gratitude to Theresa Champ for her secretarial assistance.

CONTENTS

xiii

CONTRIBUTORS

DALE L. BRUBAKER Mr. Brubaker formerly taught at Okemos High School, Okemos, Michigan. He is now Assistant Professor of Social Science Education at the University of California, Santa Barbara.

GEORGE FRAKES The chapter written by Mr. Frakes is based on his previous experience as a teacher at San Marcos High School, Santa Barbara, California. He presently teaches at Santa Barbara City College.

W. EUGENE HEDLEY Mr. Hedley taught at Morongo Unified School District in California. He is now an Assistant Professor of Education in the area of Philosophy of Education at the University of California, Santa Barbara.

JAMES HAUGHT Mr. Haught is presently completing a doctorate at Syracuse University. His chapter describes his teaching experience at Shaker High School, Latham, New York.

MARILYN KOURILSKY Mrs. Kourilsky is now completing her doctorate at the University of California, Los Angeles. Her chapter is based on her teaching experience in California.

GERALD LEINWAND Mr. Leinwand was formerly a social studies teacher at Forest Hills High School in New York. He is presently an Associate Professor of Education and Assistant Dean in the School of Education at the City College of the City University of New York.

RONALD MOTT Mr. Mott was formerly a teacher at Okemos High School, Okemos, Michigan. He is now completing doctoral work at Michigan State University.

MURIEL MOULTON Mrs. Moulton formerly taught at the University of Chicago Laboratory School. She presently teaches at the Francis W. Parker School, Chicago, Illinois.

JOHN NELSON Mr. Nelson is the Head of Teacher Education at the University of California, Santa Barbara. He formerly taught in secondary schools in California.

NEAL ROSENBERG   Mr. Rosenberg is presently a doctoral candidate at the University of California, Berkeley. His chapter describes an approach he instigated while a teacher at Santa Barbara Junior High School, Santa Barbara, California.

MICHAEL SAUNDERS   Mr. Saunders teaches at La Cumbre Junior High School, Santa Barbara, California. He is also the Chairman of the Social Studies Department.

HARRY SIMS   Mr. Sims is a teacher at La Cumbre Junior High School, Santa Barbara, California.

DENNIS L. SONNENBURG   Mr. Sonnenburg's chapter on the "slow learner" is based on his experience at Santa Barbara High School, Santa Barbara, California. His chapter on junior high school social studies was written while in his present position as a teacher at La Cumbre Junior High School, Santa Barbara, California.

DAVID YOUNT and PAUL DE KOCK   Both Mr. Yount and Mr. DeKock teach at El Capitain High School, Lakeside, California.

COMPETITIVE DEBATE IN EIGHTH GRADE SOCIAL STUDIES

W. EUGENE HEDLEY

How can the social studies teacher interest his students in the social studies and at the same time teach and have his students learn in an intellectually honest way? The following selection discusses competitive debate as a teaching approach which stimulates interest while still developing the intellectual capacities of the students and the teacher. The central theme dealt with in an eighth grade social studies class was the American Presidency. Although the author of the selection does not advocate this approach for any great length of time, he does see value in using such an approach on a short-term basis.

The eighth grade social studies curriculum in California schools usually calls for the teaching of United States history and the Constitution. The problems confronting the social studies teacher are numerous, especially concerning means of creating enthusiasm and interest on the part of the students. But, so too are the opportunities. The possible ways of approaching and presenting the subject matter of United States history are great, indeed. What is presented in this chapter is one more approach; it is presented in the belief that there can never be too many techniques available for the teacher concerned with the continual improvement of teaching methods.

In an effort to generate some interest in a non-grouped, eighth grade social studies class of thirty-two students, the teacher decided to focus upon the theme of the American Presidency. The use of such a theme was a real challenge in that it was certainly a "shop-worn" approach, thoroughly familiar to the students. My effort was directed toward getting the students to look beyond the biographical dimension with which they were so familiar and to consider the Presidents of the United States in the light of their actual performance as presidents.

It was soon evident that the students lacked any non-biographical criteria by which to determine or evaluate the performance-in-office of the American presidents. However, this proved to be an opportunity rather than an obstacle. Using as our guide Clinton Rossiter's work *The American Presidency*,[1] we were able through class discussions to evolve a working set of criteria which were understood and "usable" by the class. But this was only the beginning, for the criteria alone did not provide the kind and level of interest that teachers most desire.

It was at this point that our junior high speech teacher suggested to me the use of competitive debate. We gladly accepted the suggestion in the hope that competition would provide the needed interest and enthusiasm to encourage the students to carefully and thoroughly apply the criteria. The speech teacher provided us with George Musgrave's

[1] Clinton L. Rossiter, *The American Presidency* (New York: Harcourt Brace and World, 1956).

work *Competitive Debate: Rules and Techniques,*[2] from which the speech teacher and the writer were able to distill a set of rules that would be appropriate to and manageable by an eighth grade class. Thus, following the development of the set of criteria by the class, the students were provided with the competitive debate rules along with the necessary explanation.

The next step of the procedure was to assign to each student an American president for whom he was to apply the criteria for the purpose of determining the positive achievements of his administration. For this and the following step, students were provided with some research materials in the classroom such as encyclopedias and some of my college texts and paperbacks. The students were also provided with several hours to make use of the school library, and many students extended their search to the public library.

Next the students were paired-off (with some regard for matching abilities) and "exchanged" presidents. However, the time allowed at this point was only about one-half that of the previous step. The procedure of this step followed that of the previous one with the major exception that the students now applied their criteria to discover the weaknesses of the administration of the president under study.

Now the class was prepared to begin a series of debates— all based on the topic: "Resolved that President 'X' was a better president than President 'Y'." A toss-of-the-coin decided which of the two students debating would take the affirmative; thus, the president that he first studied would be substituted for President 'X.' Incidentally, some consideration was given to pairing the presidents on the basis of some comparable achievements.

Clearly, time was an important factor in carrying out this

[2] George McCoy Musgrave, *Competitive Debate: Rules and Techniques,* 3d ed. (New York: H. W. Wilson Company, 1957).

activity. It proved necessary to impose strict time limits on the debaters. This initial series of debates put a time limit of two minutes for each opening statement (affirmative and negative) and one minute for the rebuttals (one each). The class as a whole—armed with their abbreviated debate rules and standards—judged each debate, declared the winner, and were allowed a minute or two for comments on the debate. Thus, it was possible to complete the debates within a week.

Following this activity the class decided that they would like more extensive debates. With class suggestions, the teacher therefore organized eight debate "teams." These teams were composed of three speakers (opening, rebuttal, and concluding), four researchers, and a coach. Two of the researchers prepared the "case" for their president while the other two prepared the "case" against the opposing team's president. Four pairs of presidents were selected on the basis of contrasting positions, similar amounts of influence in the subsequent direction of national affairs, and the number of positive accomplishments of their administrations. All this, of course, is an extremely subjective determination. However, such pairs as Jefferson and Jackson, Theodore and Franklin Roosevelt, John Adams and John Quincy Adams, and Madison and Monroe do serve to emphasize certain important and informative periods of our history.

This more extensive form of debate was again judged by the students while the teacher served as timekeeper and referee. Time limits for this series of debates were allotted as follows: five minutes for opening statements, three minutes for rebuttals, and two minutes for concluding statements—a total of twenty minutes per debate. These time limits permitted two debates to be held per class period. The research time allowed prior to the debates was considerably less than that allowed previously, primarily because the students had become more familiar with the sources of information and also because they had become more skilled "researchers," being more aware of *what* they were looking for in terms of information.

During the course of the debates the class received a challenge from another eighth grade social studies class to pit our best debaters against theirs. So, following our series of debates, the class selected the three best speakers, the four best researchers, and the best coach to form a debate team to represent our class. The team was given one week to prepare to debate upon the topic of "Resolved that Andrew Jackson was a better president than Thomas Jefferson." While the team prepared itself, the class returned to the more standard curriculum. Neither team knew in advance who would be taking the affirmative side of the question.

This final debate was allowed additional time through the addition of a second rebuttal with the first speaker for each team also giving the summation at the end. The speech teacher was invited to serve as the judge of the debate while the other social studies teacher and myself served as timekeepers. With three classes sitting as an audience, the competitive spirit ran high. Following the debate, the speech teacher explained in detail the basis upon which he had judged the contest.

Certain impressions emerged from this venture into the use of competitive debate in connection with eighth grade social studies: First, the use of debates clearly achieved the initial purpose of providing increased incentive for the students to engage in nonbiographical depth studies of the American presidents and their administrations. Second, the students seemed to become aware for the first time of the necessity of having some criteria in mind before beginning any study; that is to say, to have some idea of what you're looking for before you begin is a valuable tool in research. Third, the students received some initial training in research. By "research" the writer refers to the ability to collect and compile information from multiple sources. Finally, the debate activities had the virtue of involving the entire class both as participants and as judges, thus commanding a rather high level of attention and the resultant educational "profit" from the shared information derived from the "listening" to the debaters.

In connection with this particular class it was interesting to note that while the more "academically talented" generally proved to be the most able "researchers," it did not follow that they made the best debaters or coaches. Many of the "below average" students emerged as exceedingly able debaters and coaches. It would seem that the technique of competitive debate provides an opportunity for many students to receive recognition and success who would otherwise remain "undiscovered" and "uninspired" during the more "normal" procedures of eighth grade social studies.

By way of conclusion, a word of warning is offered. Interest in competitive debate is not long-lasting at the eighth grade level. It does appear, however, to be a good technique for a single unit with a duration of from four to six weeks.

Questions for Discussion

1. Is competitive debate limited to the eighth grade or could it be used effectively at other levels of the curriculum? Explain.

2. What subjects for competitive debate are as appropriate or more appropriate than the subject of the American Presidency?

3. What sources would you use in dealing with the subjects advocated in your answer to Question 2?

4. What problems would you encounter in employing the approach advocated by the writer?

5. Should this approach be used mainly for students who are "fast learners"?

2

DEBATING THE PAST

Moral Judgments and the Teaching of Social Studies

NEAL ROSENBERG

The treatment of controversial issues in secondary social studies classes is a major concern of those interested in social studies education. Mr. Rosenberg suggests that students too often debate moral issues on the basis of ignorance rather than knowledge. He suggests that students might best begin their inquiry into moral issues by developing critical or logical thinking in dealing with issues about which they have fewer definite opinions. Therefore, students might well begin by debating historical rather than current issues. As each student learns to make intelligent decisions about moral issues he will be fulfilling his purpose as a student of the social studies.

Thirty-eight students in thirty-eight desks, and among them were the brightest students in the eighth grade. They were too many to be divided into groups, too restless to spend day after day in lecture, and too intelligent to waste their

7

time on busy work. Seventh period U.S. history needed a
lift. Three months of innovation had borne no fruit until
one afternoon the writer challenged the class with a new
type of question.

The class was studying the Westward Movement and, in
particular, the founding of the Lone Star Republic. Despite
the writer's enthusiasm for this period of our republic's history, classes were as dry as the West Texas Plain. The day
before the class had read the chapter in their textbook explaining why the Texans had revolted and how victory was
achieved. The writer began by asking the class if they felt
that Texas had the moral right to secede from Mexico. Were
the Texans justified in their actions? The writer explained
to the class that citizens often choose to consider the moral
implications of military and political decisions, that many
feel that the ends do not justify the means. And that, as
students, they might find it profitable to practice the art of
thinking on such matters by debating questions from history.
Perhaps, the writer suggested, by considering issues about
which we have very few definite opinions, we will learn
more about thinking about moral issues than if we were to
start by arguing the questions of Vietnam or civil rights.

The class was given fifteen minutes to re-read the section
on the events leading up to and the "causes" of the rebellion. Each student was required to outline his ideas roughly
for his own reference during the period; this outline was to
be turned in at the end of the period as a disciplinary
encouragement to those who were suffering from seventh-
perioditis. Fifteen minutes later the discussion began:

INSTRUCTOR: Before I let you loose on the question, I want to
               remind you of the ground rules. First, no rioting.
               Second, I want you to make a decision, pro or
               con, about the action of Texas. You can change
               your mind at any time, but I want you to force
               yourself to have an opinion. Now, if the last per-
               son who has just spoken was pro-Texan, then I

ROY:
want only to see hands from the people who disagree with the Texan position and vice versa. In this way, both sides will get equal amounts of time to present their cases.

Those are the rules; I'll write the question on the board. (The instructor writes, "Did the Texans have the moral right to secede from Mexico?") Who starts?

ROY: Well, it's pretty obvious who's right. The book says that the Mexicans wouldn't let any more Americans into Texas, and that they wouldn't let them keep their slaves, and stuff like that. The Mexicans were pushing the Texans around so the Texans had the right to get out and take their land with them.

MARK: The Texans didn't own the land. Mexico did. If the Texans didn't like it, they could move.

SHARON: I guess Mark doesn't believe in the Declaration of Independence. It says that when a people are misruled they have the right to have their own country. So Mark's idea is wrong.

(Sharon's remark temporarily slows the opposition.)

INSTRUCTOR: Think for a moment. How might the Mexicans have looked at what the Texans were doing?

JEFF: I've got the answer. I think Mark and Sharon both missed the point. Roy says the book says that Mexico wouldn't let the Texans keep their slaves. Does anybody in this room believe in slavery? So who was wrong? The Mexicans or the Texans? The Texans, of course.

JOY: But that was back in the 1830s, and . . .

So it went. Discussion was spirited; students became involved. Which side won the day? Neither. By the end of the discussion there were a few more pro-Mexicans than pro-Texans, and the pro-Texans had lost a few adherents; but the purpose of the instructor had not been the planned acceptance of a common opinion. *The benefits of free de-*

*bate are not confined to the side that wins the most ad-
herents, but to the entire system.* Debate not only changes
opinions, it also develops and clarifies them.

The lesson that day frankly had been an experiment. As
a method for studying the factual content of history, it
proved successful. Students needed the information found
in the text to develop and defend their points of view.
During the debate several students turned back to their
text to take another look at the facts, presumably to see if
they might bear re-interpretation. And, as a method of
invigorating classroom atmosphere, the lesson had proved
successful. The students had debated with earnestness and
ardor.

But the experiment served still another purpose. It suggested a course objective and a teaching strategy to implement it. In the opinion of the writer, the theme of morality
is one of the essential features of American politics today,
and it can be discerned in both domestic and foreign policy.
School integration and American involvement in Vietnam
are commonly justified in moral terms. Not all statesmen
are moralists, nor are all voters idealists, but few public
officials would try to rationalize political action in blunt
terms of power realities. The generalized, undefined value
of political moralism is in danger of joining other equally
amorphous "American way" values of freedom, democracy,
individualism, and equality.

If this is so, then a natural course objective would be for
students to learn to consider, debate, and make decisions
with reference to the moral implications of those issues.
Such an objective is not a demand for the teaching of any
specific or generalized set of values. Nor does it call for a
course entitled "Introduction to Axiology" to be incorporated into the curriculum. But an occasional lesson with this
objective in mind does seem appropriate.

Open discussion, with the instructor encouraging rather
than directing debate, seems to the writer the most appro-

priate way to help students understand how an issue can be studied in terms of questions of morality. The writer has seen some students turn to him for an "acceptable" decision rather than face the task and consequence of making up their own minds. Deciding for oneself, the writer contends, is a difficult but necessary process to the well-being of a functioning democratic system. The pre-planned conclusion of a teacher-led discussion is not representative of this process.

Present day political and moral issues (e.g., the unionization of agricultural workers or "The War on Poverty") quite naturally provide the fuel for debate. But there are problems in their use. Students tend to debate from ignorance unless the instructor has done considerable work to gather materials for their study. Moreover, students may bring to the room a preconception of the problem which interferes with the decision-making process. Often, though not always, such an entrenched position has been inherited from parents without rational reappraisal. Whatever the pedigree of the idea, the final consequence of open discussion may be to reinforce practices of defending the students' own views rather than to teach the value of inquiry through open democratic debate. And finally, if students are allowed to discuss freely a political or social issue and pursue, either individually or collectively, their own ideas, then it is likely that sometimes they will come to conclusions which may incite outside pressure groups to bring unfair criticism upon the school and individuals within the school. Such risks are of individual concern, but the teacher should be cognizant of the fact that they do exist.

Thus we return to the experiment. By debating a historical issue, we avoid the problems of ignorance, pre-commitment, and controversy. The information required to give discussion a factual footing is in the classroom materials. (If it is not, your school needs new study materials.) Quite properly, your students need to study those materials.

Offer your students a diet of historical controversy. When studying Rome, open debate with "Were the assassins of Julius Caesar justified in killing this popular leader?" A more general topic in the same area of history would be "Did the commerce and peace brought to the Mediterranean world by the Romans justify the existence of the Empire?" Students studying revolutionary America might be roused with "Were the Loyalists fairly treated?" or "Did Britain have the legal and moral right to tax the colonies?"

Topics are not hard to find for this type of discussion. History by nature is commonly the record of the controversies of man, and thus possible questions should abound within the covers of any history text.

What should be the results of the teaching strategy here outlined? Clearly, whatever the outcomes, in actual decision-making situations they will be inextricably bound together. Separation is artificial; and it is only for the purposes of explanation and evaluation that the hypothesized consequences are categorized. Through practice, then, students are predicted to achieve development in the following three areas:

1. Thinking critically—Each discussion is preceded by the reading of and written organization of the facts. This, when combined with teacher guidance concerning the values of viewing events in historical context and realizing that an issue becomes such because of the existence of at least two popular contrary opinions, should enhance the students' abilities to organize and weigh information and ideas on matters of controversy.

2. Expressing oneself—To make their opinions known, students necessarily must volunteer to speak to the group. In this situation their actual oratorical skill is of minimum importance; of maximum importance, rather, is the logic and strength of their brief presentations. All of this practice is gained within the dynamic changing context of open debate where motivation is high and embarrassments are few.

3. Developing attitudes—As in any carefully constructed class discussion of political and moral issues (present or past), there should be the imperceptible but valuable development of student attitudes toward the importance of searching for answers to problems which have no easy answers. This particular strategy of debating the issues of the past should also yield a greater appreciation for the guidance value of history.

Thus, the utilization of this teaching strategy logically should aid in developing student skills of critical thinking and self-expression and should effect positive student attitudes toward thinking for oneself, decision-making, and the value of history.

Questions for Discussion

1. Are moral judgments a proper consideration for social studies classes?

2. Should you, as the writer suggests, start with less controversial issues and move to more controversial issues?

3. Do you favor the kind of debate advocated by the writer?

4. Does increased understanding of an opposite view necessarily mean you will have more respect for the view you initially opposed?

5. What are the advantages and disadvantages of the approach advocated by the writer?

3

A CROSS-CULTURAL APPROACH TO THE TEACHING OF CIVICS AND VOCATIONAL GUIDANCE

DALE L. BRUBAKER

The comparative cultures or cross-cultural approach to the teaching of social studies frequently lacks the degree of sophistication necessary for the most effective teaching and learning. One main reason for this is that social studies teachers are not as well versed in the behavioral sciences as they might be. The following selection describes the anthropological approach adopted by a teacher whose work in the behavioral sciences will be readily apparent. It is especially interesting to note that the cross-cultural approach was used in a ninth grade class of civics and vocational guidance.

INTRODUCTION

Secondary school social studies courses in American schools have been primarily history oriented. Social studies teachers usually have a major or minor in history and consider themselves history teachers.[1] Although in recent years the behavioral sciences have made small inroads into the social studies curriculum area, obstacles to such efforts are many, including lack of teacher preparation in the behavioral sciences.

Ninth grade civics courses usually emphasize the structural study of local, state, and federal government. The three branches of government are studied within the context of American history so that the Constitution, for example, is seen in light of historical events leading to its adoption. Problems of interpretation and implementation of the Constitution are also studied in historical perspective.

In the case of the ninth grade vocational guidance course, psychological testing and studies of particular occupations are aimed at helping the student understand himself so that he can make intelligent decisions concerning his future. Members of counseling departments frequently teach these courses so that the orientation to such courses might well be labeled psychological.

The difficulties encountered in acquiring a qualified teacher to teach both a semester of vocational guidance and a semester of civics are many. Counselors may or may not have a background in history and political science whereas teachers of civics are not likely to have a counseling background. Semester vocational guidance courses are frequently taught by counselors having a guidance orientation while semester civics courses are taught by teachers with a history orientation. However, compromises are frequently made in the hiring and placement of teachers so that a teacher or counselor might well find himself teaching both civics and guidance, thereby slighting the area in which he is ill-prepared. For, although it does not logically follow that the teacher with adequate training in an area will

[1] Richard Gross and William Badger, "Social Studies," *Encyclopedia of Educational Research*, ed. Chester Harris (New York: Macmillan, 1960), pp. 1296–1313.

teach that which he has learned, it does logically follow that the teacher without adequate training in an area cannot teach that which he has not learned.

It is only natural then that the ninth grade social studies area frequently becomes the battleground where dissatisfaction and discontent culminate in controversies between teachers and counselors, teachers and teachers, teachers and administrators, and counselors and administrators. On one point, however, all involved seem to agree: vocational guidance and citizenship education to assist youth in becoming active and participating members of society are responsibilities of the public school system. However, proposed changes are met by many different interest groups, with some wanting to retain the status quo, others wanting to make slight changes, and still others wanting to adopt an entirely different approach.

This selection describes an approach adopted by an innovative teacher who had both an excellent background in the behavioral sciences and the courage to implement her ideas in a public school system.[2]

Two ninth grade classes at Pattengill Junior High School, Lansing, Michigan, were involved in the experimental program. These students had an average seventh and eighth grade point average of D+ to C— in their four main courses (English, mathematics, science, and social studies); they similarly had the same grade point average for the same period of time in social studies classes. They had an average intelligence quotient score of 108.23.

[2] The teacher, Mrs. Kay Howell, was unable to write this selection herself because of other demands on her time, viz., her simultaneous responsibilities as mother, Ph.D. candidate, and research assistant in Michigan State University's Social Science Teaching Institute.

The writer · carefully studied Mrs. Howell's classes during the 1964–65 academic year and felt the reader would profit from an account of her most interesting approach to civics and vocational guidance.

THE CROSS-CULTURAL APPROACH

The basic approach employed in the experimental classes at Pattengill Junior High School was anthropological.[3] The comparative cultures approach was used only after the students were introduced to basic social science terms, e.g., culture. The first culture studied was that of the Hopi Indians. The teacher interested the students by showing an excellent movie, "Hopi Indian." For the study of Eskimo culture the movie "Nanook of the North" was used.

After interest was stimulated, the students were guided to materials which provided more background. All of the students read about the Hopi Indians in an interesting paperback entitled *Four Ways of Being Human* by Gene Lisitzky. Appropriate television programs were recommended by the teacher when such programs were available, as were magazines containing relevant information. Students were urged to understand that there is no definitive source on a particular culture. Each Friday the students used class time to work on a project of their own choosing concerning the particular culture being studied. They then shared their findings with other students.

When the teacher felt that the students were fairly well-

---

[3] The comparative cultures approach was first used by the anthropologist E. G. Taylor, who presented a paper, "On a Method of Investigating the Development of Institutions; Applied to Laws of Marriage and Descent," at the Royal Anthropological Institute of Great Britain. John W. M. Whiting, "The Cross-Cultural Method," *Handbook of Social Psychology*, ed. Gardner Lindzey (Cambridge, Mass.: L. Addison-Wesley, 1954), Vol. I, p. 523.

Although the comparative cultures method has been used by university anthropologists since 1889, its use in other academic disciplines at the university level can be described as limited. The use of the comparative cultures approach in public schools in any systematic manner has been virtually nonexistent. One can therefore see the innovative nature of the experimental ninth grade social studies course at Pattengill Junior High School.

18 DALE L. BRUBAKER

acquainted with the first culture, she gave them the following summary sheet to complete individually:

CULTURE

I. GEOGRAPHICAL ENVIRONMENT
   A. Location:
   B. Climate:
   C. Condition of Soil:
   D. Terrain:
   E. Precipitation:
   F. Other Important Factors:

II. ECONOMY (How the material needs are met)
   A. Food:
   B. Clothing:
   C. Shelter:
   D. Tools and Weapons:
   E. Division of Work (inside and outside family):
   F. Is there specialization in production? If so, how is it exchanged between producers and consumers?
   G. Is there a lack of or an abundance of wealth? What effects does this have on the over-all culture?

III. FAMILY ORGANIZATION
   A. What practices regulate marriage which establishes the family unit? (Who may marry and what is involved in the ceremony?)
   B. Who makes up the family unit?
   C. How are family groups related to each other?
   D. Who is head of the household?
   E. What practices regulate divorce?
   F. When is a child in the family considered an adult?

IV. LANGUAGE
   A. How do they communicate with each other?
   B. What means of communication is used other than the spoken word? For example, drums, smoke signals, newspaper, etc.
   C. Is there a special vocabulary in their language for things most important in the culture? For example,

the Eskimos have many words for different kinds of snow.

V. RELIGION

A. How do they explain the origin of man?
B. How do they explain death and life after death if any?
C. What are the basic or most important rituals used in religious practices?
D. Does the geography affect their religion in any way?
E. What are some of the major or most important beliefs in their religion?
F. What religious ceremonies are used to recognize the important stages of life?

VI. RULES FOR LIVING TOGETHER (Code of conduct)

A. What are the rules of conduct between various members of the family?
B. What are the things that give people prestige in the society?
C. Are some groups more important than others? If so, which are the most important groups?
D. Do they have a government to organize *who the leaders will be* and *how members of the society will be controlled?* If no government, how are leaders chosen and how are people controlled?
E. Is religion involved in the *code of conduct?* If so, how?

VII. AESTHETICS (Artistic expression)

A. What means are used for personal expression—dance, decoration of body, clothing, utensils, music, etc.?
B. Does religion have any effect on their artistic expression? If so, how?
C. Do the various means of aesthetic expression serve any purpose other than pleasure?
D. If you like, show illustrations of art forms.

Note: Please include any other information you would like concerning the culture.

Many students had trouble filling out the summary sheet the first time, but by following this same procedure for other cultures throughout the year, they became much more proficient. The point to be made is that the comparative cultures method was not used to any great extent until the students first had a good understanding of the particular culture they were studying.

When the teacher discussed a culture, e.g., the Eskimos, she made frequent comparisons with American culture. As more cultures were studied the comparisons became much more interesting. The students had learned to use social science concepts, e.g., culture, groups, status, and role, cross-culturally. The following summary of a class period suggests how such concepts were explored.

TEACHER: Do all cultures provide for differences in status for their members?

STUDENTS: Yes. We can't think of any exception.

TEACHER: Different societies determine what will determine status and what will give its members prestige. One's status dictates the role he is supposed to play. Isn't it true that you are expected to play a certain role as a member of your family?

STUDENTS: Yes.

TEACHER: What is the role and how does it differ according to whether or not you are a boy or girl?

GIRL: As a girl I am expected to help my mom with the dishes.

BOY: I'm expected to help my dad with work around the yard.

TEACHER: True. And in your homes certain people have more prestige than others. For example, who in your home has the most prestige?

STUDENT: My dad. (One boy said his mother.)

TEACHER: In our school we all play certain roles and these roles give us certain status and prestige. The teacher, the custodian, the principal, and you students have certain status because of the roles we play. There is a hierarchy of prestige. My status is higher than that of the custodian and the principal's status is higher than mine. What happens when we step out of our roles? What would happen, for example, if I acted in the role of the principal and told other teachers how they should act?

STUDENT: You would be fired.

STUDENT: There would be a lot of conflict.

TEACHER: True. We are expected to stay within our roles. This leads me to the next question. What determines status in our society? What gives one prestige?

STUDENT: Money.

TEACHER: What else gives one prestige?

STUDENT: Education.

TEACHER: What determines status and gives prestige to the Eskimo man?

STUDENT: To be a good hunter.

STUDENT: To be a good fisherman.

TEACHER: What determines status and gives prestige to the Eskimo woman?

STUDENT: To have her teeth worn down. This means that she chews her husband's boots well so that they are soft and keep out the water.

TEACHER: What do we think in the United States if a woman has wrinkled hands?

STUDENT: Dishpan hands.

TEACHER: What do we think in the United States if a woman looks old?

STUDENT: It's bad. Women use dye to keep their hair dark. In the United States it is better to be young than old.

TEACHER: I believe that you now understand how status and role are related and how prestige is greater in some roles than in others. An important idea that I want you to write down is that prestige is based on what is valued in a culture and different cultures value different things.

Throughout the academic year, the teacher and students explored the advantages and disadvantages or problems in using the comparative cultures approach. The teacher tried to make the students aware of the fact that the knowledge they acquired was not definitive but a starting point from which they could study more extensively in the future, in many cases in a particular college discipline.

Students also learned that the comparative cultures scholar should always be precise and discuss the material he has abstracted in relation to the context from which it has been abstracted. For example, the students were discussing whistling as a form of behavior practiced at American football games and at Spanish bullfights. Whistling at a football game in the United States is complimentary but at a bullfight it is a form of denunciation. To use the comparative cultures approach students learned that one must first know what a particular act, e.g., whistling, means in a particular context and then relate the act to the context from which it came in communicating about this behavior to other people.

The teacher and her students were faced with the problem of deciding which accounts of behavior were most reliable. It might well be argued that a secondary school student is not capable of making such difficult decisions. One might further argue that students have not been allowed to make such intellectual decisions previously and therefore are not prepared to make such decisions now. It is precisely at this point that the teacher had the sensitivity of an artist, for she helped students learn to be discriminating and make wise decisions. "In a society of free men, the proper aim of education is to prepare the individual to make wise decisions." [4] The teacher had an excellent subject matter background so that she could recommend certain sources which the student might use. The teacher also had the spirit of the learner and was a serious scholar herself. Such a spirit was contagious.

[4] Paul Woodring, *A Fourth of a Nation* (New York: McGraw-Hill, 1957), p. 111.

The teacher did an excellent job in encouraging the formulation of hypotheses and attempts to test them.[5] This stimulated student interest, for students were naturally inquisitive about people in other cultures who live in ways quite different from their own.

The students learned to search through the various social science disciplines for answers. In short, the comparative cultures approach acted as a catalyst in whetting the intellectual appetites of the students.

The comparative cultures approach gave the students a wider perspective, thus making them less provincial. After watching a movie on Eskimo culture, many questions were raised comparing the Eskimo's way of life to the American way of life. One boy asked, "Why is it that Americans are so odor conscious?" Another student asked, "Does the cold weather make the Eskimo more industrious?" Students learned that that which is different is not necessarily laughable. At the first of the year many of the students in the ninth grade experimental classes snickered when members of an African society were lightly clad in a movie they were watching. With time, it was observed that differences in dress habits were accepted without snickering. The students had reached a more objective vantage point and learned to be at least tolerant if not appreciative of the idiosyncrasies of people in other cultures. They also became more aware of their own idiosyncrasies.

Experimental group students learned to identify the similarities between cultures as well as the differences. Rather than being bound to a single culture, the student's findings related to human behavior in general. Students learned that all men have certain needs in common, e.g., food, although they meet these needs in different ways. They also found that the species *homo sapiens* is unique from other forms of life because of similarities which *all men*

[5] Victor Barnouw, *Culture and Personality* (Homewood, Ill.: Dorsey Press, 1963), p. 525.

have in common. For example, man has learned to communicate via language.[6] In this he is distinct from other forms of life.

In summary, the comparative cultures approach served as a useful supplement to the intensive study of particular cultures.

Questions for Discussion

1. Do you feel that you have a sufficient background in the behavioral sciences to employ an approach similar to the one described in this selection?

2. How would you initially appraise this approach for ninth grade students?

3. What barriers would exist for you if you wanted to adopt the cross-cultural approach?

4. Would you try to emphasize the similarities rather than the differences between cultures in the interest of international understanding? Would this be good social science?

[6] Leslie A. White, "Culturological vs. Psychological Interpretations of Human Behavior," *The Bobbs-Merrill Reprint Series in the Social Sciences,* Number 309.

SIMULATIONS AND THE SOCIAL STUDIES

The Use of Game Theory in Teaching U. S. History

DAVID YOUNT and PAUL DEKOCK

The use of game theory as a simulation device in social studies is most intriguing to social studies educators. Social scientists, especially behavioral scientists, have demonstrated strong interest in game theory and await the results of research in this area. The following selection should capture the imagination of the reader and point to one direction social studies innovation may take.

INTRODUCTION

After team teaching U.S. History to eleventh graders for several years, we were still wrestling with too many lethargic and uninterested students. How could we involve them in history so that they would care, know, decide, and act? We wondered whether our problem had been inherent in our approach: when we *stand over* our classes and *teach* history (rather than *sit among* students *learning* history), aren't we trying to teach democratic principles in an authoritarian manner?

To find answers to such questions we went to the Western Behavioral Sciences Institute of La Jolla, California, where we discovered the fascinating world of educational simulations. Even though we agreed with many of the educational principles of game theory as recommended by the institute, at first we hesitated to use them, for they seemed to require too great an upheaval of the normal school routine and too many administrative headaches. However, after studying the principles and the available facilities, we adapted and originated simulations which we believe allow any teacher in any classroom situation to use game theory without disrupting the normal school routine. The following paragraphs illustrate how we integrated various game principles into our history instruction, how we organized the classroom to facilitate and control game play, and how a specific game we created—Disunia—was developed and used in our high school, El Capitan, a suburban southern California high school of fourteen hundred students who represent a relatively typical cross section of American youth.

SIMULATION PRINCIPLES IN DISUNIA

One of the basic principles of simulations is *allowing students as much freedom* from domination by the teacher as possible in order that a truly democratic classroom atmosphere can develop. To overcome the strong tendency to dominate and dictate that even the best teachers have, we organized our classroom into action areas and replaced the usual desks with tables and chairs. (Chair desks can be used just as well if they are not bolted on runners.) Then we grouped our students, who are a blend of all ability levels, and assigned each group a particular "home base" area for both group and individual activities. In the Disunia game each of our seventy students became a member of one of the thirteen colonies which had been established on the planet Edonia (i.e., the classroom) by refugees fleeing an atomic holocaust that had enveloped the earth. We re-inforced this setting by having the refugees call their new nation Disunia, a perhaps too-obvious prophecy of how each colony would jealously hug its sovereignty. As teachers, we deliberately paralleled the Articles of Con-federation period, for we wished our students to simulate the frustrations faced by concerned Americans during the crisis of 1781–89.

Once the above setting was established, the students were ready for *interaction through involvement,* the second basic principle of simulations. In general, this interaction can be brought about by giving the groups conflicting goals and the individuals goals which conflict both with group goals and with other individuals' goals. In order to create a setting wherein these conflicts could occur and to direct this interaction into the usual substance of the high school American history curriculum concerning the Articles of Confederation period, we gave our Disunians differing amounts of industrial and agricultural wealth points, differ-ing geographical advantages and disadvantages, and dif-fering populations—all factors corresponding approximately to the historical circumstances of the first states. (See our map of Disunia, p. 28.) We explained to our students that in order to survive, colonies had to trade with other colonies to reach the best balance possible between industrial and agricultural production and consumption and that they had to overcome various geographical barriers through negotia-tion. Another stimulus to interaction was provided by using an overhead projector upon which we placed various "pres-sure factors" from time to time. For example, an announce-

DISUNIA

American Studies Simulation

Aortic Ocean

Waite Mts

Mussets

ADOBECK MTS.

Wendon Pond

Theos R.

Nova

Hire

Rhine Ibid

Cannonut

Nova Yuk

A N D R E A N   MTS.

the GREAT VALLEY

Thoreau R.

Nova Jory

Doflore

Anteleer Ocean

Pandea

Silky Mts

Cumberley Gap

Messerland

Vespa

Noah Coah

Mint Julep Mts.

Soah Coah

Gumma

Gulf of Mantico

28

ment was made that a neighboring planet, Thoratus, was threatening to invade and capture all of the colonies of Edonia. Since none of the colonies had thought of external threats as much of a problem until this announcement, considerable interaction occurred when the Disunians established an assembly. A place for the assembly to meet (a conference room off the classroom) was provided and the assemblymen were allowed to solve the foreign threat however they thought best. As might be expected, the assembly voted to raise an army and support it through taxation. However, this solution was not as easily formed into action as the assemblymen had anticipated, for they discovered that a number of their constituents frowned upon taxes. Most Disunians were hesitant about giving up their wealth points as taxes to a national government, since such action lessened both their group and individual point accumulations. (We had told them that these point accumulations would affect their unit grade.) "Make the big, rich colonies pay for the army!" cried the smaller states. "Oh no! Make all colonies pay equally," countered the bigger states. Of course, from the teachers' standpoint, these conflicts were fine, because they produced democratic interaction, considerable involvement, and a good, if not perfectly accurate, parallel with the actual historical situation.

A third basic principle upon which simulations are based is *competition* keyed to vibrant interaction among people, rather than to sterile interaction of student and textbook or student and teacher. Reward comes immediately from accumulated points representing power directly useful in the educational game, rather than from letter grades useful mainly as instruments to mollify parents and teachers. To accomplish this type of competition and reward, simulations require various types of point systems. In Disunia we set up a "money" system consisting of mimeographed CGS's (Consumer Goods and Services) bills. We awarded this play money to students for performing specific tasks which we integrated into the simulation. The CGS's we divided into two categories: Blue, which represented "Industrial" wealth, and Green, which represented "agricultural" wealth. Each group was designated as primarily an industrial or agricultural colony; an individual in an industrial colony was "paid" in Blue CGS's, an individual in an agricultural, in Green. Students were told that the object was to have their colonies reach a favorable balance between Blue and Green CGS's by the end of each playing period and that part of their reward (i.e., grade for the unit) would depend on how well their group accomplished this objective. Therefore, in Disunia, a student worked not only for himself but also for his group. Thus, competition, the third principle, fostered the second, interaction through involvement.

Another basic principle of simulations in our view is the *inclusion of the factual knowledge* normally presented in a high school social studies course. Freedom, interaction-involvement, competition—all these principles are fine, but we wanted our students to grasp history as well as appreciate how human beings encounter one another in groups. To insure knowledge of history, we organized the simulation so that each student performed a number of *basic* assignments. If the student accomplished each satisfactorily, he then had the opportunity to do *depth* assignments involving individual research. In Disunia we assigned eight basic assignments (the two paragraphs and six brief tests were explained to the students in advance in behavioral terms, spelling out the exact expected performances with material dealing with American history, 1781–89). We also made available optional depth work for those students demonstrating the ability and desire to pursue it (e.g., "Hamilton's Contributions to the Formation and Adoption of the Constitution of 1787").

Having been given the assignments for the unit, students were then free to practice another basic principle of simulation construction: *decision-making*. Both individuals and groups had decisions to make. Each individual could decide to work or not work, do only basic work, or do the basic work and proceed to depth work. In addition, the simulation forced individuals in each colony not only to decide how to solve mutual problems but also to act on their decisions. The unit was organized, therefore, so time was available for both individual and group decision-making. In Disunia we alternated individual and group working periods. Since individuals raced through or plodded around in the basic assignments, we set up an audio-visual room containing taped lectures and overlay transparencies on the background of each of the assignments. The students were free to use these A-V materials whenever they felt they needed them, and teachers were free to tutor the slower students. Group decision-making was controlled by requiring each group to turn in each day a Decision Form showing its decisions in the areas of trade, government, and military affairs. The individual work and the group Decision Forms were collected each day, graded, analyzed, and returned the next day. These results were then translated into a Group Standing Chart and posted for all to see. This action brought considerable peer group pressure to bear on students who were not working. Consequently, a number of students assumed leadership roles they likely never would have assumed under normal classroom conditions.

However, providing opportunities for decision-making is not enough. Simulations must also provide the opportunity for *commitment*; that is, time and place for students to act on the basis of strong feelings about a decision they have made. In Disunia, students were not only given the opportunity of writing their own constitution; they were also given the individual right of voting to accept or reject it. Since one of the "pressure factors" we had introduced into the game was the fact that three of the colonies had succeeded in capturing and taming certain man-like creatures, the Appletans, and had then integrated them into their economy, when the question of representation came up in the constitutional ratification convention, the question of how to count the Appletans disturbed the delegates. Heated indeed were the subsequent economic and moral arguments over whether or not these creatures were indeed people. At least a dozen students made impassioned speeches from the convention floor for the abolition of slavery; an equal number, perhaps more, argued that each colony should have the right to make up its own mind on this issue. Explosively, the convention broke up when three colonies left to form their own slave-free nation. Unfortunately for them, however, the thirteen colonies' economic welfare was so interwoven that the three seceding colonies could not survive independently. The only answer was compromise. And though some were so committed as to be willing to take an "F" group grade (which they would have received had their colony failed economically), rationality prevailed, and the constitution was saved by having all the colonies contribute an equal sum for the purchase of the freedom and the education of the Appletans.

The reader should note carefully a concluding simulation principle: the *change of role for the teacher* using simulations. The teacher no longer tells or dictates knowledge; he simply provides an organizational structure allowing the student to discover knowledge. The teacher no longer demands that students learn; he simply provides a stimulating environment where learning has immediate impact. Finally, the teacher no longer dominates, standing over his students as though he were their lord and master; he simply starts them on their way, steps to the periphery of the action, and there arbitrates disputes when necessary, gives tutorial help to the floundering, acts as a resource for the fast, and, in general, merely facilitates learning.

SUCCESSES

The basic reason for the success of our Disunia game was that most students could not help getting involved. From the game's beginning, interaction took place because both individuals and groups had to make decisions as represented by the following student reactions: "Whom are we going to send to the Assembly of Disunia?" "How should our representative vote?" "Should we trade with that bigger colony?" "Since we're a landlocked colony, how are we going to get our goods to the sea?" "What can we do about Joe, who isn't doing his basic assignments and is holding back our colony's growth?" "What should we do about the Appletans?" "If we want to free them, how are we going to raise the CGS's to pay off their worth?" Once the constitutional convention began, other decisions had to be made rapidly and regularly under considerable pressure, for each colony felt it had to have some influence upon the new constitution.

This involvement through interaction cannot help but be a memorable experience for many of our students. During the constitutional convention, about one half of our seventy students spoke several times on many subjects. A violent debate on the future of the Appletans broke out when their citizenship had to be defined in the new constitution. Thus, many students learned to care, for they had committed themselves to a stand on a historical issue. As mentioned above, three of the thirteen colonies, incensed when the other ten colonies refused to either free the Appletans or return them to the Great Valley, stormed out of the convention and temporarily set up a new nation in an adjoining room. When one of the teachers went in to keep order, he was summarily told to leave: "We're capable of ruling ourselves," they said. After the teacher left, the

Potentianians—the name they chose for themselves—elected a leader and took steps to use their economic power to try to force Disunia into agreeing to "a fairer treatment of the Appletans, who are just as human as you are."

Back in the convention rabble-rousers began crying for war (the game allows war, though waging it is extremely costly to a colony's wealth and, therefore, to a student's grade). One intellectual girl suddenly had had enough. She had been waiting impatiently for a day and a half to amend the constituion on other issues she felt to be more important than those then disrupting the convention. Striding to the microphone, she attacked with a vengeance: "You fathead boys yelling for war don't realize what it'll cost us." Saner voices finally arranged a summit meeting held during a lunch break. (One average-ability girl gave up a social club responsibility to represent her colony.) The two countries, without help from either teacher, decided to unite again after finding the workable compromise discussed earlier.

As we sat in the back of the room and let students have the freedom to run their convention as they wanted to run it (*they* were making the decisions, we weren't), we remarked to one another: "Isn't it marvelous how we'll be able to bring up this economic-moral dilemma they've worked themselves into when we study the Civil War and slavery during Unit IV?"

Other successes marked our experiences with Disunia. Most students decided to try all basic assignments. Previously we had had trouble getting all students to care enough to try. Receiving play money as reward as well as grades and being disapproved of by fellow colony members if they were not contributing to their colony's growth pressured most students into trying. Brighter students also were freed to suceed. Able rapidly to complete the basic assignments, they had time for research in the school library. Their knowledge of *The Federalist Papers* and the contributions of certain founding fathers occasionally popped up during the convention in the key speeches these capable students made. By thus using knowledge as power in their lives, these able students no longer thought of historical knowledge as a dead thing embalmed on paper which would only interest a teacher.

On multiple choice tests on knowledge of 1781–89, students showed no significant increase over students taught by the traditional lecture-discussion methods we had used in the past. However, in essay tests and in comments to their teachers, students at various ability levels showed understanding of concepts not usually understood by high school history students: how men set in motion forces over which they lose control; how change is inevitable; how important historical change is often shaped by those who have the least to lose; how men get imprisoned by ideas and emotions and how they are willing to sacrifice everything for them; and how dramatically parallel Disunia proved to be with *The Lord of the Flies,* a novel many of the students had read.

PROBLEMS

We encountered several problems in our Disunia simulation. First, some students sat and did nothing but waste time. They refused to get involved, regardless of the interaction boiling in the classroom. At first this worried us. "How in the world can they sit there and do nothing?" we asked one another. But then we realized that in simulations the laziness that students often hide behind a book or a bland expression is quite evident to the teacher who is not in front of the class talking all the time, but is free to walk around and observe. Some students failed to involve themselves in the game as well as we felt they should because they disliked the game. "We're not used to so much free-dom," one sharp girl told us. "And look at those characters over there staring at the wall. You should be telling them what to do, not letting them waste time. And we should be getting lectures on the historical period, not playing a game." (Obviously many dull and bright students must be conditioned to the relationship between freedom and learning.)

Second, problems bubbled to the surface in Disunia, be-cause, in creating the game, we had not anticipated them: trouble with the complexity of economic trading; fuzzy directions on how taxation was to take place; faulty esti-mation of the time necessary to finish basic assignments; insufficient usage of "pressure factors" on the overhead projector. However, we have already decided how to elimi-nate these four problems when we rewrite the game's procedures, and we expect these particular problems to plague us no more.

The third and final cluster of problems, we believe, are inherent in using the democratic process in the classroom. Brighter students came to us perturbed—as we were per-turbed—because "some of those dumbbells are dominating our group with their popularity, and they're making the wrong decisions." We replied, "You'll have to reason with them. Win them over in some way. After all, you live in a democracy. One man's ideas are supposed to get a hearing equal to another's." We also flinched when we saw the convention floor swept by torrents of emotion rather than shafts of cold, calculating reason. For example, a perfect Piggy from *The Lord of the Flies,* whom we were in-wardly cheering for his perceptive oration, was soundly booed back to his seat. Again, democracy in action. We just felt that an experience in democracy and constitution writing as vivid and memorable as this far outweighed the "errors" our judgment told us our students were making.

FINAL COMMENTS

Social studies teachers courageous enough to abandon their traditional classroom domination for the exhilaration possible in education simulations should carefully think through the principles we have been discussing. They must first decide how much classroom freedom they will feel comfortable in allowing. Next, by following the simulation principles, they can plan simulations which will fit their own social studies courses. Careful, *extremely detailed* planning must precede the first run-through of a simulation, for inevitably problems appear that were not anticipated. (For example, we estimate that creating Disunia took at least thirty-five man-hours of planning—and this was the fourth simulation we had created and the seventh we had played with our students. Nevertheless, we made organizational errors which lessened the game's effectiveness and which more careful planning most probably could have eliminated.) But interested teachers should not let such remarks lessen their desire to innovate with game theory instruction. Remember that from early childhood we human beings have loved to play. For play not only adds zest to the grayness of life, it also teaches us much about what it means to be a human being.

ORGANIZING SIMULATIONS IN THE CLASSROOM

Principles	*Organization Steps*
FREEDOM Eliminates typical teacher-dominated class — democratic organization replaces authoritarian organization	Arrange classroom into activity areas Divide students into groups

Principles	Organization Steps

INTERACTION THROUGH INVOLVEMENT
 	
    Group to group
    Individual to group
    Individual to individual
	Give groups conflicting goals
	Give individuals goals which conflict with groups and other individuals

COMPETITION Emphasis upon extrinsic reward designed to create/cause intrinsic reward	Establish point system where individuals and groups receive points representing power and intensifying interaction Intertwine individual and group grades
KNOWLEDGE Basic information necessary for understanding the unit being studied	Organize knowledge into specific behavioral performances explained to students in beginning of game Design depth assignments for more capable students

DECISION-MAKING
 	
    By individuals
    By groups
	Give student responsibility for deciding how hard he'll work and when he'll do his work
	Allot sufficient class time for all students to succeed in basic assignments
	Allot sufficient class time for group meetings for group decisions

COMMITMENT Individual learning to care enough to overcome fear of consequences of his actions	Plan culminating experience allowing students opportunities to commit themselves to action Subtly plan stepping-stone experiences which move the game to the culminating experience

Principles	Organization Steps
TEACHER ROLE Organizes Facilitates Acts as resource	Plan the game with extreme care Arbitrate disputes by interpreting game rules Stimulate game movement to culminating experience by using "pressure factors" to insure interaction Help individual students Keep out of way—let students make own decisions

Questions for Discussion

1. Should classrooms in the social studies be quiet or noisy? When? Why? What variables are involved?

2. Do you see any relationship between poor student performance in the social studies in acquiring knowledge and the traditional method many social studies teachers follow in organizing basic assignments, tests, and classroom activities?

3. Which is the more effective pressure on reluctant students, that coming from teacher or from peer group? What are the advantages and dangers in using each?

4. Should students be given the freedom to make "wrong" and inaccurate decisions in social studies classes when the teacher knows that he will never be able to "correct" them?

5. Should a social studies teacher allow his students time to act on their commitments?

6. How far into the background should a social studies teacher fade in the classroom?

7. What is your reaction to the following statement? "Social studies teachers should stop organizing their classrooms so that they are *teaching* most of the time; instead, they should organize their classrooms so that their students are *learning* all of the time."

8. Should a portion of a student's grade be determined by a group's success or failure?

9. Which of the principles of educational simulations do you agree with? Not agree with? Why in each case?

10. Can you make a list of areas, problems, and periods in history which you feel could be used to create effective simulations for social studies classes?

5

MAKING GEOGRAPHY RELEVANT FOR STUDENTS IN BASIC SOCIAL STUDIES CLASSES

MICHAEL SAUNDERS

Geography classes frequently become a place into which slow learners are counseled. Counselors, teachers, and students know this so that the teacher has an especially difficult time in teaching these geography classes. The teacher frequently completely reevaluates his objectives, procedures for reaching such objectives, and evaluation procedures. This happened in the case of the author of the following selection. Recognizing the fact that his students had a very low self-concept, he decided to structure his class in such a way that he could try to improve his students' self-concepts. All readers will recognize the problem posed by this selection; not all readers will agree with the writer's approach. It should be recognized, however, how representative this class is of many geography classes in the United States.

"There is not a fiercer hell than the failure in a great object."

JOHN KEATS

41

Many students in the writer's ninth grade world geography class found school their "fierce hell." They were junior high school pupils in a school of twelve hundred students, which was located in a lower middle class neighborhood with most of the students of similar background. Failure was common to this group of twenty students; they were in the slowest ability group of the ninth grade class. All had poor reading abilities, most of them scoring lower than the tenth percentile on the SCAT and STEP verbal scales. Many had no overt aspirations to complete high school. A known 60 per cent had serious extracurricular problems with their peers, parents, or police.

World geography, a required subject, came at the beginning of the second semester; the first semester had been a study of American government. Attention was given to physical and cultural geography during the twelve-week course.

After assessing the first semester in terms of the pupils' learning experience and the teacher's satisfaction, a complete revision was realized. The program was designed to provide the student with successful experiences at all times. To implement such an undertaking the teacher had to dispense with a number of traditional concepts and techniques. The three areas of success incentives, curriculum organization and implementation, and classroom atmosphere were modified.

SUCCESS INCENTIVES

To prevent the students from having feelings of failure, no tests for grading purposes were given. Testing existed only for self-evaluation. In order to find success on self-tests, students were encouraged to use notes taken in class and at home.

Each student selected a partner, preferably someone with whom he could communicate, to work with on daily assignments and on a research paper. Students found success and motivation through mutual reinforcement. In several cases the most capable readers were placed with near non-readers to keep the groups balanced.

Each student compiled a notebook with the aid of his partner. Notebooks furnished the objective basis for the grade. Assignments going into the notebook were corrected by each student's partner. Each student had a chance to and was encouraged to make corrections and completions before the notebook was graded. In this way each pupil was able to compile a notebook which was well done.

In order to insure success, the teacher had to structure the teaching progression, beginning with the most basic information.

CURRICULUM ORGANIZATION AND IMPLEMENTATION

Basic geographic concepts were arranged from simple to complex. The teacher felt the conceptual approach was well within the grasp of the group and would provide a lasting educational experience not cluttered by geographic trivia. No more than one concept was initiated daily; no more than four concepts were presented weekly.

A five-part classroom routine was established to provide feelings of security. "Structure lessons," dittoed sheets presenting a geographic concept, were distributed daily. No longer than one page, double-spaced, the structure lesson emphasized anecdotes and examples of the concept. Structure lessons were incorporated in the notebook along with other materials. A cumulative vocabulary list was built with two to four words learned per day. Although quite traditional in approach, basic vocabulary exercises had to be implemented in order to understand the structure lessons. Oral interplay was used daily to give students a chance to use their newly acquired knowledge. Oral interplay consisted of situation questions, informal debate, or a defense or attack of a statement. Short themes emphasizing practical experiences and relying upon the student's own limited background were given with each structure lesson. Daily work sheets were used to aid understanding. Work sheet emphasis was on other than written skills wherever applicable. Work sheet success was attained through co-operative effort with one's partner.

CLASSROOM ATMOSPHERE

Informal interpersonal relations were essential. The teacher had the role of the friendly helper. During discussions, the teacher frequently sat among the students to enhance a relaxed atmosphere. Weekly competition on a group basis was established to boost morale. Competition was in the form of quiz games, bulletin board contests, or debates. Though relaxed and informal, an orderly classroom was maintained.

The structure lesson provided the heart of the conceptual approach. Valuable sources for geographic anecdotes and examples, along with structure lesson concepts, were found in the following volumes:

Lewis M. Alexander, *World Political Patterns* (Rand McNally, 1963).
John J. Bradley, *World Geography* (Ginn and Company, 1957).
Henrick Deleeuw, *Crossroads of the Mediterranean* (Garden City Books, 1954).
Eva Knox Evans, *Why We Live Where We Live* (Little, Brown, 1963).
Norton Ginsburg (ed.), *The Pattern of Asia* (Prentice-Hall, 1958).
M. Hammondsworth, *Geography of World Affairs* (Penguin Books, 1959).
Sol Holt, *World Geography and You* (Van Nostrand, 1965).

Norman Pounds, *The Earth and You* (Rand McNally, 1962).
Wheeler, Kostbade, and Thomas, *Regional Geography of the
World* (Henry Holt and Company, 1957).

APPRAISAL

Frequently when something new is attempted, the response
is favorable, not because it is a better way of achieving the
task, but because it is a novelty. The writer was unable to
ascertain the influence of this effect. As a result of the new
approach, enthusiasm was high initially, and morale remained significantly above that experienced in previous
years with similar groups. For example, students arrived
early for the class rather than sneaking in at the last minute;
some students also stayed after class to discuss ideas with
the teacher whereas such students usually did not demonstrate this kind of initiative in their classes. Disciplinary
confrontations became a thing of the past. Student concern
was not about how to outsmart the teacher, but was about
how to help each other. Through no design of the instructor,
students requested help before school and at noon. The
help was not requested for "apple polishing" purposes but
was of a genuine desire for knowledge. Two girls, for example, requested to come to school a half hour early each
day in order to work on a project on nationalism. The
project was based on popular magazines such as *Life* and
National Geographic.

Group pressures were exerted by the peer group on
students reluctant to accept the new situation. Several
students became outcasts during the initial adjustment
period. Personal antagonisms toward partners and feelings
of being treated like small children were objections voiced
by the outcasts. Some of the students, for example, moved
their chairs apart from each other and frequently made
snide remarks in order to needle each other. Time and the
security of success seemed to blanket the rebellion.

The emergence of new class leaders was an unexpected result of the new approach. Several previously introverted boys suddenly became authorities on everything. Some of the isolates, especially those with physical disabilities, appeared to have higher prestige because of their new status. One boy in the process of studying emerging nations learned all the names of every country in Africa. He also learned the names of the colonial powers which formerly controlled the nations. He constantly talked about these emerging nations; "the new nation of Botswana" was his favorite phrase. Oral interplay sessions seemed to become contests as the new leaders vied to break into the established intellectual hierarchy of the class.

The idea of performing to please the teacher or to achieve a good grade appeared to be of little concern to most students. Mild animosity, however, was directed toward the instructor when a concept was unclear or when a student was confused. "Are you trying to confuse me on purpose?" one student queried. Another student asked, "Are you trying to push me this hard because I'm slow?" These reactions became signs indicating a need to reteach or review the lesson.

PROBLEMS

Although advised of evaluative criteria and procedures, several students felt they had earned better grades than they had been given. Explanation of abilities and course content did little to soothe these dissatisfied students. In each case a telephone call was made to a parent explaining the situation. Without exception, parents felt the grades were of little consequence and were well satisfied with their child's progress.

As might be expected with reluctant, slow learners, school attendance was a problem. Irregular attendance severely hampered the geographic sequence. Frequently students were out for extended periods of time. When these long-term absentees returned, they had to be completely reoriented to the program. The partner arrangement proved to be unreliable, especially when pupils switched partners as a result of absenteeism.

The problems of class organization and administration were minor in comparison to other tasks faced by the innovator. As with anything new, preparation, both research and clerical, was extremely time-consuming. The fact that the experimental class was one of the writer's six classes compounded the problem. Teachers' aides were frequently used to ease the clerical load.

The writer has concluded that slow learners can find success in the geography class. Although far from satisfied with the program, the writer did find new interests, desires to learn, and social relationships in his conceptual-success-oriented world geography program.

Questions for Discussion

1. Do you agree with the writer's major goal for this class, that is, to provide his students with successful classroom experiences?

2. Do you agree that no tests should have been given for grading purposes?

3. What is your impression of the partner arrangement device used by the teacher?

4. Do you believe that it would be possible for you to adopt the role of teacher as friendly helper and still maintain proper discipline?

5. What is your opinion of competition as a teaching device as used by the writer?

6. What sources would you add to those the writer used?

7. How would you attempt to deal with the problems discussed in the latter part of this selection?

REACHING THE SLOW LEARNER

DENNIS L. SONNENBURG

When a beginning teacher encounters his first class of slow learners he is often shocked. It is easy to give up, but the courageous young teacher will work all the harder to find new methods, new materials of instruction, and perhaps even new objectives. This was the case with Mr. Sonnenburg. As he readily admits in the selection, there are many unsolved problems in the approach which he adopted, but he was forced to deal with the situation as it was at the time he taught the basic class in social studies. The reader cannot help but admire the energy and devotion of the teacher as he tries to reach the slow learner.

INTRODUCTION

A teaching experience has a different meaning for different teachers. To some it is an opportunity to direct young minds; others find it a source of mental stimulation; to many it is a source of authority and power. And there are those who feel it is a task—pleasant or unpleasant—which needs to be done. On separate occasions teaching may assume contrariety. The following teaching experience, for the purpose of this report, may be called an experiment, not because a hypothesis was set up at the beginning of the semester and subsequently tested, but rather because the observations and evaluations used throughout this experience have influenced classroom methods of teaching and the instructional materials used. The experience set forth is intended to present a description of the teaching situation, the students' skills problems, the methods incorporated to reach "basic" students,[1] and some conjecturing on notions concerning teaching and the school which will merit more thought and discussion among educators.

It was apparent that most members of the class [2] had never found much pleasure in doing schoolwork or in learning. Evidence of this is found in their overt behavior. Their entire classroom manner revolved around creating or capitalizing on distractions which might detain them from their studies. Various techniques, from "visiting" to sharpening pencils, were employed to avoid the painful process of reading, writing, or discussing the history lesson at hand. It was evident that they had practiced this behavior for so long that it had become habit with them, actually hinder-

[1] The basic student in this case is a slow reader. Most students in this program, although in the sophomore year in high school, have between fifth and eighth grade reading ability, and are placed here as a result of the score achieved on a test taken by all students in junior high school. Students are usually removed from this remedial program by teachers when student ability greatly exceeds test scores. These students typically lack motivation to read and study.

[2] This was a tenth grade world history class and was composed of twenty students: one student was a Negro, thirteen had Mexican-American backgrounds, and six were of various other backgrounds. There were ten boys and ten girls: three were age fifteen, thirteen were sixteen, and four were seventeen. Fathers were generally blue-collar laborers with a couple being white-collar workers. Most mothers were housewives and several were nurses and store clerks. Nearly all students lived with both parents. The school population, based on an enrollment of approximately twenty-four hundred students, was recently evaluated: 1 per cent was Oriental, 4 per cent Negro, 20 per cent Mexican-American, and 75 per cent was "other whites."

ing the probability of their becoming interested in learning, books, or teachers. This lack of interest was a tremendous handicap to overcome. Later evidence showed that the traditional approach to teaching history continued—even reinforced—the setting in which these patterns were born and nurtured. The classroom environment had to be changed somehow, so that poor student behavior patterns could in turn be altered rather than be perpetuated.

As long as school and learning were painful, or at least unpleasant, little could be accomplished other than negative reinforcement. The first requisite, then, was to create a comfortable atmosphere for the students. They needed to feel free to express themselves in front of their peers and the teacher. To establish rapport, frequent desk visits were made during class working assignments; an attempt was made to cultivate a sensitivity to their feelings, while at the same time trying to develop in them a sensitivity to the teacher's goals and wishes. During the semester six students were counseled outside of class for twenty minutes to an hour each.[3] At this time praise and encouragement were given for efforts at expression, both oral and written. Most of the students felt that the teacher liked them and wanted to help them, but in many cases their classroom behavior habits were so well ingrained that the rapport which had been established had little meaning when the time came to concentrate and work.

[3] Prior to each counseling session, time was spent studying the student's accumulated folder of progress, which contained report cards dating back through junior high and elementary school, various test results, notes concerning disciplinary problems, and various other papers. The counseling sessions were directed toward exposing student attitudes which might have prompted their classroom behavior. Counseling was not attempted until midway through the semester, after a good student-teacher rapport had been established. The counseling sessions were quite informative and the students appeared comfortable and open. The teacher felt that this type of counseling, if done regularly with each individual by the classroom teacher, could be quite effective in discovering and changing established attitudes.

The main goal for the semester was merely to get students to think conceptually and, hopefully, to write and speak in the form of complete expressions of thought. Nearly every class member had difficulty expressing himself in complete thoughts. It was reasonable to assume that in most of these cases self-protective attitudes lay behind poor performance. In order to get students to conceptualize it was necessary to get at these attitudes which defended them like the strongest shields against attempts to provoke certain kinds of thinking.

This, of course, posed the problem of how class time should be spent. Was it justifiable to spend much of the class time using various methods [4] to break through the barrier of attitudes when the class was primarily one in world history? It could not be justified if learning in this class meant that a set of designated facts were to be placed in the students' minds. However, it *could* be justified if a history class were taken to be a part of a larger, more general education and if education were seen in its

[4] In order to find out students' attitudes it was necessary for the teacher to encourage expression. This meant that a teacher could not set himself up as a hard and fast disciplinarian who demanded an absolutely quiet room. Such conditions could never create an atmosphere in which students might feel free to express attitudes. This teacher did not, however, let students have a free reign. At first they wasted some time. Those who least liked to study soon revealed themselves. Considerable class time was spent discussing issues the students might bring up—issues which did not relate directly to the history text. Some of the topics we discussed were flying saucers, mass transportation, perception, planned cities, school rules, responsibility, and attitudes in general. As the semester progressed, the teacher observed that some of the students, those who were less inclined to concentrate than the others, were not putting any effort into their classwork, and were wasting a great deal of time "visiting." It became necessary to clamp down on these students, to become more demanding and intolerant of unnecessary visiting of any sort. This resulted in their producing more work. It seems that these students could never be very productive people unless they became internally motivated rather than externally motivated. The goal, then, must be to work for self-directedness, and not other-directedness, on the part of these students.

truest sense—the fostering of a healthy attitude toward learning, thinking, and the application of facts and ideas.

What good comes of teaching or learning history if it is associated only with the classroom and connotes only certain events? It is thus always separate from the rest of life: it is only an hour in each day, five days each week. And it can be even less if the student can manage to be absent a couple of times each week. History does not influence him outside of the classroom. As a matter of fact, he thinks his life would be a little more bearable without it.

I decided that the best way to get at attitudes was to begin with the history text [5] and just get the feel of the class. Frequent complaints of "why do we have to study this?" gave opportunities to probe more deeply into students' attitudes and to encourage their finding reasons which would satisfy them. The concepts of analogy or cause-and-effect were too abstract or too vague to justify studying history. That these concepts enable us to understand man

[5] The text material available for the course was especially written for the remedial reading program: Jack Abramowitz, Ph.D., *World History Study Lessons* (Chicago: Follett Publishing Co., 1962). It is composed of nine units (subtitled booklets); for example:

    Unit 1: The Ancient World and the Middle Ages
    Unit 2: From the Middle Ages to Modern Times
    Unit 3: The Rise of Democracy
    etc.

Each unit is in turn broken into lessons; for example:

    Unit 6: The Expansion of Democracy
        Lesson 1: Reform in England
        Lesson 2: France Again Becomes a Republic
        Lesson 3: The Rise of Unionism
        etc.

The lessons are composed of from three hundred to five hundred words each. They are designed to emphasize vocabulary building and building and relating concepts. The questioning technique at the end of each lesson emphasizes selecting from multiple choice answers and true and false questions also. Occasionally there are essay questions which the students and this teacher found generally uninteresting. Dr. Abramowitz has done a fine job in designing the reading material and emphasizing concepts. However, the same cannot be said for the questioning technique he has selected.

and his institutions, or to be able to make predictions, or just to have them stimulate the mind meant nothing to almost all of these students.

Because the students had such an extreme lack of interest in the subject, they were easily distracted. This cannot be overstated. They virtually jumped at the opportunity to be distracted. At times, quelling distractions and channeling energies was the teacher's constant occupation. This was a draining experience, and a normal teaching load of five periods or so would wear the patience of any teacher, thus possibly affecting his rapport with the class, and perhaps also his health.

SKILLS PROBLEMS

It should be kept constantly in mind just what kinds of skills problems these students have. The assignment to the basic program was done not on the basis of I.Q., but on the basis of scores achieved on a reading test. The reading test was one of a number of tests given in a two- or three-day series to students at the junior high level. A certain range of low scores qualified a student for the basic program, which involves special classes with special material designed to increase appropriate skills. The I.Q. range varied within the class (I.Q. is a difficult thing to measure when academic skills are so poorly developed). Most of the students in the class were suspected to be of average intelligence; perhaps a few below average. This indicated that most were very capable of thinking and working productively and of formulating concepts and interrelationships which might be somewhat complex. In short, they had the equipment, but they did not know how to use it.

It became obvious through oral reading that there was definitely a vocabulary problem: polysyllabic words presented difficulties in pronunciation. They lacked the skill required to take a word apart, pronounce it syllable by syllable, and then put it back together again. This frustrated and disturbed them, and it was a major reason why reading lacked appeal for them. They had not learned that they could master this skill and thereby diminish the problem. Most of the students tended to see the difficulty as never-ending, and thus they had formed the attitude that reading would never be any fun. Reading which was complex only strengthened this attitude.[6]

Examples of words which proved to be stumbling blocks are: unsanitary, dominated, unity, frequently, underdeveloped, legislation, economic, confederation, democratic, etc. The list is almost endless. A change in the form of a word—e.g., democracy to democratic, unite to unity, or legislate to legislation—nearly always threw them. It was also found that although they could say a word, they might have much difficulty either in spelling it or in using it in a manner that reflected a working conceptual grasp of the idea with which the word was associated. This is not to say that these students could not conceptualize well. It is merely to say that they could not understand the words with which they had been asked to conceptualize. The following are several examples of questions they were asked on the blackboard and the responses they gave:

QUESTION: Why can't the underdeveloped countries today help solve their problems by imperialism or colonization of other lands?

STUDENT RESPONSE: Why ca'nt [7] the undeveloped countris to-

[6] It is going to be necessary that each student learn to identify a skills problem, work at correcting it, see his own progress, and come to view himself as a person who can overcome difficulties. He must see that he has the capability of changing his own behavior to a way which can be rewarding. Until these students come to see themselves as people who can overcome difficulties by hard work, there will probably be little progress. This is getting at the attitude which inhibits performance.

[7] Grammar, spelling, and punctuation are presented here exactly as they appeared on student papers.

> day help sole their problems by impeialism
> or colanzation of other lands? because most
> of the underdeveloped countris don't have
> anything to trade for what they get.

In discussions all week long it had been emphasized that
lands were generally no longer available to colonize. It is
obvious that this student has conceptualized what underdeveloped countries are, but not what imperialism or
colonization are.

QUESTION: How did the Industrial Revolution influence imperialism?

STUDENT RESPONSE: The country that had the industrial revolution thought themselfs superior so try to
take over other countries.

It had been emphasized during the week that raw materials and a market for goods were needed. The student
has conceptualized the idea that the Industrial Revolution
had put a country in a superior power position, but she had
not realized what economic needs had developed.

QUESTION: Give one good reason for and give one
good reason against nationalism.

STUDENT RESPONSE: Give one good reason *for* well it because
to prevent the spread of democratic ideas
and the spirit of nationalism. give one good
reason against nation . . . well it because
some people think as themselves as Americans' and loyalty is to one country the
U.S. of America.

The second part of this student's answer sounds as though
he has probably conceptualized the idea of the narrow-
mindedness that might grow out of a feeling of nationalism.

QUESTION: List any idea of life in which you or your
parents may not benefit from democratic

ways. If this could be changed or improved, tell how.

STUDENT RESPONSE: I think that they benifit from it all people should have a benifit from it because there is so much to it. Democracy really helpes us to stay what we are our Country. I think that it benifits everybody really.

This is a girl who was thinking in terms of concepts, but who has generalized to the point of danger. Her grammar hinders her expression.[8]

At times students displayed good conceptual ability:

QUESTION: How might a poor underdeveloped country try to obtain natural resources of food from elsewhere? Give a reasonable answer.

STUDENT RESPONSE: make a tready, or a trade tready with other countries and if they ar to poor thy'll have to morgage something of value that will pay for what they have borrowed.

This had been talked about in class discussion previously.

QUESTION: Give a good example of how democratic growth in each of these three areas (this refers to a previous answer) has reached you or your parents.

STUDENT RESPONSE: 1 Economie–Better and faster was of producing things. 2 Political–more rights say in government. 3 Social–the people were better organized and familer with each others country. Better education.

[8] The fact that any expression or communication at all was taking place here was of the utmost importance. It was regretted, however, that more time was not taken to work with individuals on certain skills, such as grammar or spelling, with which students may have had trouble. This type of assistance is going to have to be given to each individual consistently if he is going to improve his skills and gain confidence in overcoming difficulties. In this class, improvements have been mainly in the area of attempts at expression and conceptualization, and not in the grammar skills area.

This reply gives evidence that this girl had conceptualized a working framework. Such well organized thoughts were quite rare and too often the questions were left with no answer or only several words in a halfhearted attempt. It is not unreasonable to suspect that their poor grammar skills and their lack of self-confidence and interest, not a lack of ability to conceptualize, caused such demonstrations. All of the above questions were developed as a result of facts and ideas that had been emphasized in the class reading and discussions.[9]

Perhaps the method of questioning, designed to provoke thinking, does not appear much more satisfactory than the multiple choice type of question if one is after definite and clear responses. However, too many teachers have preferred the clear response (for grading purposes and to expedite the teacher's time) to the true and muddled thinking of these students. Because they were handed easy-to-grade questions, these students could conceivably pass from room to room and year to year with their inadequacies being tolerated by their teachers and themselves. Perhaps it is because nearly everyone else had given up on them that they gave up on themselves. They have had little or no proof that they could work on skills and improve them, so why try?[10]

The technique used identified some of the skills problems which specific students had. It was also an attempt to develop skills at the conceptual level. (It is difficult to say how much progress is possible here without a lot of

[9] Absenteeism from this class was frequent and may have affected performance in answering questions. However, the answers point out the skills problems that existed.

[10] Evaluation is, indeed, a problem—especially when a teacher's goals are far above what the students will achieve. Progress is barely seen. It takes a keen sense and a flexibility of standards to see it. Its form may be disguised or it may be so slow or slight as to be unnoticeable. Not seeing the improvement makes rewarding well nigh impossible and thus, perhaps, student efforts are stifled for lack of a reward.

work in other skills, mainly because the self-confidence needed in conceptualizing is denied the students because of their poor grammar skills.)

From the time these students enter the history class until the time they leave, they are confronted with a demand to perform using skills they either lack or use poorly. How can anyone have the desire to perform when he feels inadequate? These students are no exception. To reverse the situation, would an English teacher who had not developed any athletic skills or a delicate sense of coordination like to perform daily for an hour in a gymnastics or other class requiring physical skill? Probably not too well, but then the teacher has an advantage, for he is skillful in the use of words and conceptualizing, which means he has the advantage of being able to analyze the problem symbolically and conceptualizing a rationalization for his inadequacies. The student who is poorly skilled in conceptualizing has trouble conjuring up an adequate rationale other than those attitudes we see expressed by defiance, belligerence, apathy, or avoidance.

CLASSROOM METHODS

Since history had little or no meaning to nearly all of these students, several approaches were decided upon to make the subject more meaningful and to give the students some interest and understanding, as well as to encourage thought processes. The tool of analogy offered the best opportunity for staying within the law [11] (that is, using the text appropriated for the course) and also creating interest. The recent Watts riot was compared to the French Revolution. Similarities and differences in causes and results—especially

[11] California, *Education Code* (1963), sec. 13556 reads: Every teacher in the public schools shall enforce the course of study, the use of legally authorized textbooks, and the rules and regulations prescribed for schools.

immediate causes as opposed to underlying causes—were discussed. Then, the McCone Commission, which was a follow-up to the Watts Riot, was compared to the Congress of Vienna, which followed the French Revolution.[12]

By the time this method of teaching had been decided upon, the class was in the middle of the subject area and there was little time to acquire or gather enough resource information for twenty students, let alone gather material at the appropriate reading level. Therefore, the teacher presented information on Watts orally and attempted to draw students into discussion. Since there was little reading material [13] made available to them (and assigning extra reading on their own would have been a vain expectation), it was necessary to proceed with little real knowledge at the students' fingertips. They had little to offer other than attitudes which were usually quite generalized and un-original, e.g., "The Negroes don't know how well off they are," or "The Negroes are being discriminated against." Nevertheless, their attitudes were respected and information was offered which might point out the complexity of

[12] There are potential difficulties with this approach: (1) the teacher can easily gather resource information on current events, but obtaining enough material to supply twenty or thirty students is quite another story. This led to our approach of lecture and discussion. (2) Reading material, even if obtainable on current events in quantity, must be of the appropriate reading level to meet student skills. (3) There is the problem of presenting controversial issues: (a) selecting editorials or news from various sources can result in a touchy situation with administrators and parents unless done with tact and skill, e.g., selecting several dominant points of view; (b) some teachers find it difficult to present controversial issues because they are not capable of releasing their teaching methods from their own biases and/or they feel a good deal of discomfort in presenting issues like the Watts riot in a racially mixed class. (4) There are probably teachers who would rather not be bothered with using anything other than standard textbook material.

[13] A Report by the Governor's Commission on the Los Angeles Riots, *Violence in the City—An End or a Beginning* (December 2, 1965), was made available and several students spent time browsing through it with much interest.

the problem and thus help to undermine their set attitudes.[14]

Student interest in this subject definitely surpassed that of the routine history lesson. In a student's own words, "This is something that is happening now." Their world of distractions still existed, but to a lesser degree, thus encouraging the teacher that these behavior patterns could at least be threatened, if not changed.[15]

In studying the Industrial Revolution, the recent bracero problem in California was referred to and again information was presented by the teacher. Several aspects of the bracero problem were compared to the Industrial Revolution, e.g., job opportunities, machines and mass production, the replacement of men by machines, the need for child labor laws, sanitation problems in factories and housing, and so on. Again interest was evoked—particularly when the job opportunities for the unskilled were discussed. Many students had thought that the braceros' expulsion was beneficial for high school dropouts and unskilled laborers, as they could now have these jobs. They were shocked to find out how effectively machines were designed to replace the braceros, that agricultural production probably increased with machine use, and that jobs were not available except temporarily until machines were designed.

The technique for drawing students into discussion was

[14] A high degree of sophistication in techniques of presenting material, controlling discussions, challenging attitudes, or building concepts requires much skill and is difficult to achieve with the first attempt. A teacher should not feel subdued by failure in an early attempt, but he must work to develop these skills.

[15] The author felt that an opportunity to present many concepts and ideas and to have stimulated even more interest was lost for want of more preparation and experience. This semester would have been a good time to study concepts of migration, ghettos, the culture of poverty, civil disobedience, violence, and many other areas which lend themselves to history and give it some emotional appeal.

based on the observation that nearly no one was going to volunteer to speak.[16] The teacher would "toss out" a question, idea, or piece of information and then ask for comments, but often the only "response" would be numerous side conversations and "projects," such as magazine reading, sleeping, and the like. When no one answered the teacher's challenge, a specific person would be asked to contribute. If this student did not respond, he would be asked another question, and another, until he said something (even if he were merely asked what he had had for breakfast). Once the student made some response, the teacher would work back in the other direction, trying to cultivate a series of responses which would create an idea, opinion, or bit of information. This approach did not always work, but it did keep the class attentive. Next, the teacher would go elsewhere with a question, using the same technique, and moving around the room in order to confront the students physically as well as mentally. Some days were better than others for keeping students' attention.

To see how the students would react if they could study anything they wanted, the teacher decided to ask them to choose a subject for study. Narcotics, Vietnam, and parent-

---

[16] The author suspected that these students during pre-high school years had never been the "talkers" in group discussions. A few attempts were not sufficiently rewarded, probably, to encourage further attempts. It was interesting to note in this class that peers were quick to criticize and laugh at many attempts by certain students at discussion. This, of course, had a negative reinforcing effect. An attempt was made to overcome the atmosphere of ridicule by pointing out to those who laughed and criticized that ignorance was something we all shared and yet we all had things we knew, too; that we should work to share our knowledge, or at least make our ignorance known so that we might be informed by someone who knows; that we should never be ashamed to speak up and inform others of our knowledge or lack of knowledge. I pointed out many things of which I had little knowledge, yet hoped to learn. Everything possible was done to encourage discussion, or at least to voice ideas (even if wrong).

teenager relationships were suggested. For lack of time, only narcotics, which had provoked the most enthusiasm, was investigated.

Before a discussion of narcotics could be undertaken, the teacher decided that everyone in the class would have to do some reading. The purpose here, of course, was to give some background. Much class time was spent discussing how to obtain information from the library. Three girls compiled a bibliography of recent magazine articles from the *Reader's Guide to Periodical Literature* and obtained a subscription list from the library. The bibliography was organized so that each person had two assigned readings in recent periodicals. After several days it became obvious that most of them had no intention of reading on their own. (Several students did read from magazines and books at home. Two students even purchased a special issue of a magazine which they had observed the teacher using.)

It was arranged, therefore, for the students to spend a class period reading in the library. Magazines listed in the bibliography were obtained from the librarian and distributed to the students. I insisted that they take notes. Most of them did not know what was important or what they should write down; they required individual assistance in these efforts. It was apparent that the magazines were generally too technical and difficult for most of them to understand, although several of the "faster" students managed the reading and note-taking with some competency. The students who were most easily distracted during class discussions continued to be distracted during this reading period, even though they were dealing with material in which they had previously claimed an interest. In most cases their reading skills had not been developed to the point of enabling them to understand the magazine articles. It became obvious, too, that their participation in distractions was a pattern of behavior to which they readily turned when other skills failed them. This established pattern was their biggest handicap, for it was even preventing them from working on their skills problems.

The writer must point out again that the students did not view themselves as *being able* to alter and improve their skills. Instead, they thought of themselves as pulling a "D" grade so that they could stay in school and eventually receive a diploma. "D's" are something they have always gotten and will always get. This has been a reinforcement system which has convinced them that they have not improved, are not improving, and will never improve. However, it is this low self-concept which must be changed, and it can be changed only by diligent work with each individual toward improvement in grammar, reading, spelling, and oral skills, so that he can see his own definite progress.

Following the trip to the library, students spent the next three class sessions in listening to the teacher read from an article in *The Drug Takers*.[17] The article was about John and Karen, who were heroin addicts in an eastern city in the United States. The students responded with eagerness and enthusiasm, and they often interrupted the reading to make comments, now and then prodding the teacher to continue reading. (If only we could have had twenty copies, so that the students might have read for themselves!) The article generated the most interest and personal involvement seen all semester. Their reaction served to strengthen this teacher's point of view that these students must have the kind of material that gets them involved. This is the type of subject matter that must be used; it is a prerequisite for working on skills.

For several reasons the topic of narcotics had to be dropped upon completion of the John and Karen story. An entire week passed, during which text material relating to World War I was covered. At the end of the week the

---

[17] This was a Special Report by *Life* and *Time* written by James Mills, "Karen and John: Two Young Lives Lost to Heroin," *The Drug Takers* (New York, 1965); pp. 6–29.

students were asked to write a half-page description of the life of a narcotics addict. It was astounding to find out how much they had remembered and how well they expressed it. All but two students turned in descriptions. Of those who turned in work, many filled one complete side of a sheet of standard-size notebook paper. The following are two examples of papers written by boys who had taken little interest or done little work up to the time we began discussing narcotics. The first essay was written by the only Negro boy in class, a boy who had displayed extreme interest while the narcotics story was being read. It should be added that a time limit was put on the essays, and many students were still writing at the end of the period and probably would have written more if given more time. (As in previous quotations from student papers, punctuation, spelling, and word usage have not been changed.)

The life of a narcotic addict is a very lousy life. They dont care about anything. They go around steeling money and goods.

The addict does not like his habbit but he can't help it his body is built up to it and he can't do without it. He doens't care about himself he only cares about where he is going to get his stuff.

Most of the addicts go to needle park to wait for there pusher. The police hardly ever do anything about it but when they can get them with the drugs on them the have got them.

When it is costing the addict to much money he will turn him self into a hospital so when he comes out his habbit wont be so expensive and he wont have to take so much.

The other student wrote:

It's pretty hard when your a narcotic wondering where your going to get the money to buy stuff who your going to rob or what your going to rob.

Then you got to worry about getting caught with it on you. When your an addict it's really a sloppy life Because they hon't even clean the neddle or take a bath or change cloath.

The following, written by a girl, is one of the longer essays:

Well to start off with before they go to bed they have to go out and find some herione for when they wake up in the morning. Its really a terrible life to live and I no that I would never take the stuff and I would try to stop anyone I saw taking it. Well the girl usually becomes a prositiute and the robs and steals and thing he gets his hands, They usually need about 10 to 15 to 20 dollars a day it depends upon how much he needes. They really are dirty people the girl usually if she hasn't have any she doesn't feel like doing anything she doesn't take baths wash her hair but when she has a date going on she gets real slicted up. When they don't have any stuff they go to the hospital go get some and when when they get out they don't need as much money. They all use the same needle and can you emaghen how dirty it is it most carry a lot of germs. They sleep where ever they find a place park benches, brake into cars and sleep there. Then when they get the stuff they dont no if its good or bad and if its bad they lose maybe 10 to 20 dollars. Well I no I wouldn't give up the life I live for a life like that. you just cantn't believe the things they do. Now days you don't know what this world is coming to.

It is apparent that not only were these students interested enough to remember some facts and ideas but they also took some pride in their form of expression. This was true of all the papers. Both of the boys wrote with more skill than either had previously demonstrated. Sentence and paragraph structure as well as spelling reflect a good deal of concentration.

On the same day of this test another student, who had recently been in much trouble because of truancy, turned in a four-page report on the subject of LSD. The report was done on her own initiative and she was self-motivated to do the research for it. It was well written and she was quite proud of it.

It was unfortunate that the semester ended at this point. If only there had been more time, this interest might have generated even more enthusiasm and concentration. Since the students now took pride in their written expression, it would have been an opportune time to persuade them to correct their spelling and sentence structure as well as the organization of their paragraphs. What improvement might have been seen in a semester or a year if they could have been kept consistently interested in writing, correcting, and improving their form of expression!

To speculate, if the semester had continued, what might we have done? We could have discussed the narcotics traffic of the world and traced routes from where the "stuff" is grown to where it is refined and how it is smuggled from one location to another. This opens the door to world geography and commerce, international law and cooperation, and organized crime. Next, we could have discussed law enforcement and the apprehension and prosecution of addicts and people dealing in narcotics. This might have led to civil liberties and civil rights; the use of search warrants and wiretapping. From here an interest could be generated in the Constitution, the courts, and the enforcement system. Would this not be an ideal time to discuss police states and tyranny? Also, we could have discussed relevant laws—how they were passed, during what period, by whom, and the possibility of the existence of congressional investigations at the time. Then cures could have been investigated, and the social problems behind drug addiction discussed: What is currently known about cures? What are different states doing? What is the federal government doing? Are private groups concerned? An investigation of this problem and its cures in other countries would be in order. From this the students might have learned that developed and underdeveloped countries face these problems quite differently. The teacher could have pointed out the relationship between narcotics addiction and programs for curing it and the political situations in different countries.

If a curriculum were well coordinated, students like these might spend their science period studying the physiology of drug addiction, which could well lead them into a discussion of the nervous system and the circulatory system. The math period might be spent figuring out the dollars and cents spent on drugs, law enforcement, transportation, crime, and numerous other factors. The students might be taught what statistics are, their accuracy, and how to use them.[18]

Of course, what we are really doing here is capitalizing on the students' interests; getting them emotionally involved so that they willingly (because they are self-motivated) work to build skills and concepts. The interest does not have to be narcotics, and in some student groups other topics would work far more effectively. Yet they could be used in the same manner to lead the students with their cooperation through many doors.

CONJECTURE

There is, of course, the possibility of approaching these students' problems by trying to assess what has caused their undesirable behavior patterns to develop. The causation, however, is not always readily assessed, and, even if assessed, the mere assessment does not necessarily effect a cure. The thing we are interested in here is not particularly

---

[18] Other questions which were asked on their test: (1) If Karen gets $20 a "trick" (customer) for her career in prostitution, how many "tricks" must she get to support a $100 per day habit? (a) per day? (b) per month? (c) per year? (2) If Karen "picked up" venereal disease from her 125th customer, how many men could she pass the disease to in that year? The students were shocked at their figures and they did the math willingly.

what has caused the behavior to develop, but rather how to deal with the problems at hand.[19]

In order to build skills and correct poor habits one must have the cooperation of the student. If he has no desire to correct them, it is quite likely that attempts to force him to correct them can be only inefficient at their best, for the student would feel pushed and frustrated, and the teacher would feel frustrated and pushy.

Enlisting student cooperation has its problems. A big barrier is a curriculum setup wherein it is expected that certain material will be covered from this or that textbook, particularly as a preparation for the next year's course. This sort of setup tends to emphasize the importance of the material rather than the learning it might bring about. Plainly these students have little interest in history as it is presented traditionally.[20] This teacher is convinced that the learning process was inadequate enough in the class to justify questioning the value of using the traditional approach on this type of student group. The traditional course makes no sense to such students: it does not help them in their lives in any way that they can see.[21]

[19] It might be added that what originally caused such skills problems to develop may no longer be the cause. Feedback and reinforcement mechanisms may have become so imbedded as to assume the role of cause, and thus the result could become quite complex.

[20] Students were asked if they liked to read. Nearly all of them said yes. When asked if they liked to read our textbook, nearly all of them said no. They said that they would prefer reading magazines or books which interested them. They also indicated that the text was not difficult for them to read—a fact which was substantiated by their oral reading from it in class. Perhaps if text material were presented differently, these students could be interested in it and would be more willing to read it.

[21] The teacher has had to ask himself what value is inherent in history. For what reason do these students have to know specific historical events? What is the net effect of history, as traditionally taught, upon their perspectives? It seems that history has value if it stimulates the mind to see relationships, or causes and effects, or to formulate concepts, or if it simply gives a mind pleasure in its ponderance. It does not seem (to this teacher) that any given historical

Another complication confronting the teacher is what goes on the other twenty-three hours in each day of these students' lives. How much of what the teacher tries to build up is torn down at home and elsewhere, or even in the very next period? How many times has a teacher told one of these students, "I don't care what you do or think about outside of this room, but when you are in here you are going to do and think as I want you to." What could be a more effective attitude in convincing a student to divorce classroom learning from his extracurricular life? This attitude, in turn, has implications for the school as a social system: those who want to build the school on the idea that it should educate in the total sense—fostering responsibility, creating healthy attitudes toward living, integrating classroom learning into students' lives, and teaching creative enjoyment—must be concerned for the basic student who lives a marginal or peripheral life at school as well as in the larger community, for this is the student who does not normally get involved with his school or with his community.

What effect does our grading system and teacher and administrative personnel attitudes (which are too often entirely college directed) have on these students? The students' sense of importance and belonging is wounded and the students become somewhat rebellious. But the real damage is in the attitudes and behavior patterns into which we have helped force these students. We have tried to change them through negative sanctions or logic. The negative sanctions have taken the form of bad marks both in subject areas and in citizenship. Teacher attitudes and comments toward them are also often aimed at shaming or degrading behavior. All of them have a past record of poor

event is important of itself. It is important only if the mind can take something from it. The net effect upon these students is rarely that of conceptualizing relationships which may have value in explaining something else; neither does it often work to foster a positive attitude toward further conceptualizations, learning, or thinking.

marks. Such marks have done nothing to build a sense of pride around schoolwork and, instead, have acted as stigmas which force the students to build their own defenses. In these defenses we see manifested their attitudes towards learning. These students will tell you how little incentive they gain from a citizenship grade based upon demerits. (Under this system any undesirable conduct results in points or demerits being subtracted from one hundred points or merits. If a student acquires enough demerits he fails in citizenship, possibly preventing graduation.) Students' efforts become centered on how far they can push the teacher before he gives out demerits. This is an amusement which suits and encourages disruptive classroom habits. The writer believes that such a negative system puts the burden of the quality of behavior upon the teacher, and not upon the student, since it is a matter of how much he will let the students get away with that "draws the line." It would be better for the student to learn to evaluate and sanction his own behavior; to learn where he should "draw the line." Motivation must be internalized if these people are expected to be responsible citizens when there is no teacher standing over them. How such self-direction can best be achieved is uncertain in this teacher's mind. Perhaps it is more effective to question students about their behavior and to help them to discover for themselves why they behave as they do, then lead them to suggest other, more desirable conduct. However, in a situation such as this, a teacher should not expect immediate results.

Most of the students show concern about "failing" by working for a "D," since this means they can stay in school.[22] However, just as with college-bound students the grade often gains importance over the learning, so it does with the basic student. His concern is for the "D" so

[22] Personal counseling sessions revealed that most students are staying in school because a close relative or friend is encouraging the maintaining of a "D" level.

that he can stay in school long enough to receive his diploma. Learning is generally unimportant. The "D" certainly carries ambivalent meaning for the basic student. While it is a symbol of sufficient achievement to continue in school, it is also a stigma. There is really no prestige attached to this grade. If anything, "D" stands for "dumb." This teacher would be in favor of doing away with any grades for the basic student. Under the present system the student performs to get his "D." If this "goal" were taken away perhaps the student could think beyond the grade and see that the classroom serves a function other than grading: it can be a place of learning—and learning can be accepted when one is not going to be penalized for making an effort. Perhaps learning could become identified as a pleasure and filled with the rewards of self-content gained in the contemplation of ideas.

And how effective has logic ever been in changing anyone's behavior? Many great men have been driven by compassion or compulsion to work long and hard at a task, even to the extent of physically taxing experiments. Yet, would the logic that their work could be ruinous to their health have changed their behavior patterns? We have tried to convince these students that they should study our version of history—we have practically forced them to study it— yet they neither see its importance nor show any interest. They have instead searched for things which capture their interest. These are the distractions which we teachers fight. Still we go on with our traditional approach to teaching history (this approach may be nothing but a bad habit), and the students continue looking for distractions, thus causing their behavior patterns to become more deeply ingrained. This is how they learn to hate school and learning of any kind.

Perhaps we should consider changing *our* ideas. Perhaps history is not necessary—at least not the way it is taught now. Perhaps we could redesign our curricula to better accomplish the desired ends. At least we might come up with something that interests, excites, and gives a sense of value to these students. One consequence might be that they would become more useful and productive citizens. We are not headed in this direction now. Students learn little because they see little importance in what we ask them to learn. They find the subject matter generally uninteresting, and it has become their habit not to care.

We need to find a presentation of history that will influence these students' lives. We must make history live for them, both in the classroom and out, so that they will see how history has influenced their lives and how history can tell them much about themselves. History must come to mean any and every thing that has happened in the past: the discipline of history must come to mean a study of any significant past events of any person, family, community, state, nation, or world and even beyond this. We must be willing to admit that many significant events (e.g., the French Revolution, the growth of nationalism in Europe, or the development of transportation and communication in the nineteenth century) which may loom important for the teacher or curriculum consultant may not assume importance for the basic student—and we must be willing to look for importance on their level.

These students get excited about studying things that seem important to them—things like narcotics, Vietnam, parent-teenager relationships, and other areas. But even with these topics they seem to have trouble concentrating because of the bad classroom habits they have developed. History courses developed around such topics could aid in getting students emotionally involved in the material, thus taking the first step toward developing new behavior patterns. These topics could lead to improved reading, writing, and discussion skills, and could help them see the importance and applicability of history to their own daily lives. Once the students become personally involved, interests in a broader perspective and perhaps the consideration of other historical events (even the traditionally important ones!) could very well continue to build their interests, perspectives, attitudes, habits, and the application of learning to their daily lives.

Questions for Discussion

1. What should be the goal of education in dealing with basic students?

2. If poor attitudes hinder student performance in many cases, how should the teachers and administrators be confronting this problem? At what grade levels?

3. Do authoritarian teachers and quiet classrooms reflect healthy attitudes toward learning and behaving?

4. Do lenient teachers and a noisy classroom reflect healthy attitudes toward learning and behaving?

5. Are our grading systems unintentionally reinforcing undesired attitudes?

6. To what extent do attitudes influence learning or its application?

7. If classroom textbooks are inadequate to provoke interest and learning what should be done?

8. Is there a need for a service to provide current and interesting material for various levels of classroom work?

9. Is the traditional approach to teaching history necessary or valuable?

10. Is there a need for teachers who work with basic students to have special training? What type of training?

TEACHING WORLD HISTORY ON TELEVISION

GERALD LEINWAND

*The use of television to teach social studies is certainly
controversial in the minds of many social studies teachers. In
the following selection, Mr. Leinwand describes his first attempt to program a course in world history. Although he
found the experience rewarding, his description of problems
encountered is most forthright and honest. This article is not
only interesting for the social studies teacher in particular
but also for those interested in educational television in
general.*

Early in the spring of 1962, I received a call from the high
school division of the Board of Education of the City of
New York asking if I would be interested in participating in
a television audition for the purpose of selecting a television teacher for a high school world history course. This
course was to be presented as part of the School Television
Service of the Board of Education using the facilities of

New York's new educational television station WNDT, Channel 13. The opportunity to explore at first hand the much discussed educational potential of television, and the challenge such an opportunity afforded, encouraged an affirmative reply.

When finally I was asked to give the course, an indication that I had won (or lost, depending upon how you look at it) the turn of the "wheel of fortune," I discovered that my troubles and problems had just begun, troubles and problems which never seemed to end but only multiplied until my "tour of duty" was finally completed. In this article I should like to say something of our aims and plans, my television experiences, and to provide an evaluation of television as an educational medium for high school social studies in the light of those experiences.

AIMS AND PLANS

During the late spring of 1962, a group of social studies chairmen and I met rather frequently to draw up a series of fifteen programs for the proposed world history course which was scheduled to be given from September, 1962, through January, 1963. The fifteen programs as finally agreed upon, which were to make up the series to be known as "Highlights of World History" were as follows:

Reconstructing the Beginnings of Western Civilization
The China of Marco Polo
Medieval Man
Islam and the Crusades
Leonardo da Vinci—Man of the Renaissance
Captains Courageous—The Age of Exploration
The World Columbus Found—The Indians of Spanish America
The Mighty and the Meek—European Society Under Absolutism
The French Revolution—A Case Study
Napoleon—Man and Legend

Machines and Men—The Impact of the Industrial Revolution
From Elizabeth I to Elizabeth II—The March of Democracy
   in England
The Faces of Nationalism—Emotion, Unity, Frenzy
Giants of Science
The Story of a Year—1871

These topics were selected because they seemed to be
best suited to carry out in substantial measure the aims we
had in mind. These may be briefly enumerated as follows:

   To enrich the course of study by discussing selected aspects of
      world history sometimes overlooked in the traditional treat-
      ments of the subject.
   To stimulate interest in world history among students and
      teachers.
   To add "spice" to the world history course by providing
      teachers with an additional audio-visual medium of instruc-
      tion.
   To encourage experimentation among teachers in new tech-
      niques in their approach to world history teaching.
   To broaden the course of study so that it incorporates more
      than the customary West European orientation.
   To dramatize and crystallize significant episodes, eras, or
      individuals.
   To provide a point of departure for stimulating class discus-
      sions.
   To explore the opportunities and limitations offered by tele-
      vision instruction insofar as they apply to the social studies.

In order to achieve maximum viewing by high school
students and effective utilization by teachers, substantial
publicity was given to the proposed series. The programs,
together with a brief synopsis of each, some suggested
readings, and some questions and activities were listed in
the WNDT *Secondary School Television Guide* and made
available to each social studies department. In addition,
individual departments often mimeographed the topics and
distributed them to individual teachers. The *Bulletin* of

the Association of Teachers of Social Studies of the City of New York likewise carried a listing of the topics.

Each television program was to be twenty minutes in length and was to be produced on tape two weeks ahead of the viewing date. The program was to be presented three times on a single day (Thursday) so that classes unable to view the program at one hour might be able to do so later in the day. Eventually it was decided to kinescope the series; that is, to place the programs on film so that they would be available through the Bureau of Audio-Visual Instruction in subsequent terms.

Within this framework, I, as television teacher for the course, was free to select those points of emphasis I chose and to make use of whatever methods, materials, and guests my ingenuity could uncover. For the wide latitude and freedom to experiment with television that I was given, I am most grateful. But this freedom carried with it the responsibility to make the wisest choices of content, to select the best materials available, and to make the most forthright presentation possible.

PROBLEMS AND EXPERIENCES

To the beginner, the problems of appearing before the eye of the television camera are formidable indeed. However, a very fine five-day orientation program which included on-camera practice, make-up advice, and evaluation of the studio's resources helped overcome the initial feeling of panic and stage fright. Although this feeling never entirely left me (nor any of the other broadcasters, I later discovered), it was sufficiently brought under control so that I could concentrate on attempting to put together effective programs.

At our planning sessions it seemed as if we had a world of materials at our fingertips—films, filmstrips, slides, pictures, guests, and technical equipment of all kinds—resources we had but to tap and each of these would come to do our bidding. But it soon became evident that this was not to be the case. Limitations of space in which to work and time in which to prepare the programs, of funds with which to buy or rent necessary materials and props, of equipment with which to present maps or other data in dramatic form were hurdles to be overcome if the effectiveness of the series was to be assured. Aggravating these problems was the fact that the School Television Service functioned within the framework of a new educational television station which was itself still groping with its own problems of mustering financial support and community acceptance.

Complicating problems for the television teacher is the fact that all films, filmstrips, slides, illustrations, books, music, and guests must be "cleared for television" in one way or another before they can be used. "Is it cleared for television?" became a question that I learned to ask early and often. Locating materials cleared for TV not only involved a vast amount of time, "leg work," as well as clerical work, but clearance requirements effectively limited the materials that could be shown as well.

For understandable reasons valuable commercially produced films and pictures were not available for television use, as producers were fearful that by making their films or pictures available for television, particularly for a series that was being kinescoped, their future sales of the films or pictures would be curtailed. Adding to my frustrations was the fact that some films that were both available and cleared for television had to be shown in their entirety. On a twenty-minute program it was rare that any show had more than two or three minutes' worth of film. Often, too, films that we would have liked to use were simply too expensive for us. Since there are approximately seventy running feet of film in a two-minute segment, even the special educational television rate of about $2.50 a running foot of film was for us prohibitive in cost.

Museums and art galleries are truly treasure chests of information and materials. But making such materials available for television showing was generally difficult and often impossible. For one thing, museums understandably would not allow items from their precious collections to be taken to the television studio without a representative of the museum standing by. This costs money, money which our budget simply did not provide. We tried, sometimes successfully, to get around this by inviting a representative of the museum to be the guest on the program on which his materials were to be used, but this rarely worked more than once.

All sorts of irritating developments and limitations on what we had hoped to do arose out of conflicts growing out of the contracts governing the work rules under which the unions and the studio had agreed to abide. On one occasion, because models of Leonardo da Vinci's inventions, which had been loaned to us by the International Business Machines Corporation, were delivered in a truck rented by I.B.M. rather than by a theatrical hauler, the prop men refused to handle the models. Only extreme persuasion and "as a special favor" to me "for this one time only" were the men prevailed upon to unload the props and arrange the set. In another case, after I had located a suit of armor, the studio did not allow it to be delivered because, so they said, the prop men "did not have time" to bring the suit of armor from the sidewalk to the studio. On another occasion, the art department had made a model of a guillotine but once again the prop men had to be coaxed into setting it up in its proper place because to them it should have been made in the wood-working shop, not the art shop.

For the program on the French Revolution, two professional announcers regularly employed at WNYE, the Board of Education's radio station, were to play the roles of "defense" and "prosecuting" attorneys at the "trial" of Louis XVI before the National Convention. The announcers were to appear in the costumes of the day. The costumes were rented and we looked forward to a fine program, but at the last minute the use of the costumes was vetoed for fear that costumed announcers would be regarded as actors and so aggravate the already tense relation between WNDT and the television actors' associations. These episodes would have been genuinely humorous were it not for the near calamity with which several of the programs were faced as a result.

EVALUATION AND SUMMARY

One of the most rewarding experiences of my teaching career was the opportunity to teach on television. My eyes were opened to a new dimension in education, to a new medium of instruction, and to a new industry in general. But what of television as a medium of instruction in the social studies?

As used in New York City, television served to enrich and supplement the teaching of world history. No teacher was replaced, viewing was voluntary and generally within a classroom situation. Effort was made to have the television content enrich and enliven the world history classroom, not serve as a substitute for it. However, while potential for growth is enormous and television teaching is here to stay, the fact is that viewing among high school classes was extremely limited.

The problem for high school viewing of school TV programs grew largely out of the programing difficulties within the high schools themselves. Often teachers who would have liked to have utilized the programs were not meeting their classes when the programs were offered; or, when they did meet their classes no world history program was being aired. Aggravating matters was the fact that an insufficient number of television receivers was available and getting them moved into a classroom sometimes presented difficulty and tended to discourage the use of television. Moreover, in classes I observed, and judging from reports of colleagues, TV reception left much to be desired. Sometimes it suffered from technical difficulties. More frequently, however, the difficulties grew out of a lack of window shades with which to darken a room or inadequate care and maintenance of the television receiver itself.

Another obstacle to the effective use of television in high school social studies was the fact that after the novelty wore off teachers had to be cajoled into making use of the medium. In the elementary school, teachers who themselves may not be experts in art, music, or science may look forward to a television lesson to supplement their own activities. On the high school level teachers consider themselves subject specialists, and are inclined to doubt that a television program can provide any enrichment that they themselves cannot provide. And, given some of the limitations on the use of materials previously suggested, in some cases they are right. It is ironical that a film or filmstrip that can, under ordinary circumstances, be used by a classroom teacher is not readily available to a television teacher.

Nevertheless, teachers should be encouraged to use television because the very nature of the medium provides a built-in motivation for further study. Moreover, it should be remembered, that few teachers, even the very best, can take the time to preview pictures and edit films and exercise the care that goes into the make-up and presentation of a television program.

Technical "know-how" makes possible the production of a host of varied and informative television programs, but often the same technical facilities available to commercial channels or even to the evening offerings of the educational channels are not available to the high school television teacher. To make such technical equipment and skill available to secondary school television teachers is one of the big tasks ahead for school television.

In view of the nature of the high school student, the specialist capacity of the high school teacher, the program difficulties in the high school, as well as the limited number of sets available, efforts should be made to present high school programs after school hours when programs can be viewed at home. In this way, teachers could direct the attention of the students to coming programs, assign suitable homework, encourage family discussion, and provide for follow-up the next day.

Presenting high school programs during and after school hours with a degree of sophistication that would enable them to compete more successfully with the informative programs offered on the commercial networks requires a high degree of sympathetic understanding by the management of educational television. In the School Television Service all in-school programs from kindergarten to twelfth grade were lumped together. In such an arrangement the secondary school is at a disadvantage since preparing programs to meet the learning needs of the more advanced and critical student requires approximately the same consideration lavished on the evening educational offerings.

Forward-looking management of educational television stations must also cooperate more effectively in bringing about "break throughs" that will enable school television services to make programs more exciting. The rules governing the use of films and other illustrative materials may be reasonable for commercial television but they require considerable modification in the area of educational television. Here management of educational television channels should assume the leadership in prevailing upon commercial channels, film producers, and publishers to make their materials more readily and inexpensively available for educational and in-school television broadcasting.

In a similar vein, forward-looking representatives of

management and labor both have to review their practices and demands so that the rules under which television personnel work do not strangle educational television in their web. At the present time, in-school television, by no means a "wasteland," seems to be a vast "no man's land" to which the commercial restraints and procedures applied to the use of materials and personnel do not seem to fit but in which no new set of equitable procedures has as yet been found. On more than one occasion, those who would have been eager to make materials available to me found that their hands were tied in that they simply had no precedent or guidelines they could easily follow.

Closely associated with these problems is the question of compensation for the television teacher. Much has been said and written about this subject and its ramifications are many and deep. It seems to me that because programs of the television teacher are likely to be re-used in subsequent years some form of additional compensation is entirely in order. Wherever I went in my effort to secure guests or materials for the planned programs this question came up and the sentiment in favor of some form of additional payment for re-use of programs was universal. In all fairness, a fund for modest honorariums to guests should be provided.

In the course of my term of service as a television teacher I had the opportunity of associating with talented colleagues, skillful producers, and magnificent directors. In the course of gathering materials for the programs I had the opportunity of meeting a host of prominent men and women in education, industry, and diplomacy. All of these people were uniformly courteous and helpful in substantial measure. By and large, in all fairness it must be said that the large private corporations were by far the most cooperative in making displays, props, films, and guest experts available to me. Their help was of enormous value and was offered willingly and with "no strings" attached.

The experience to me was particularly rewarding because

the School Television Service of which I was a part was part of WNDT and I was able to be an "eyewitness" to many of the birth pangs of a new educational television channel. And, hopefully, signs of change and progress are in the air. In response to repeated urging that kinescopes of "Highlights of World History" be made available on an evening hour so that the series might be made assigned viewing, this was finally agreed upon for the spring term (1963). Although an early evening hour (5:40 to 6:00 P.M.) on Saturday night is hardly "prime time" even for a high school program, nevertheless it represents a start. While much remains to be done in many areas of producing the programs, utilizing the programs effectively, and making fair and appropriate rules governing the use of copyrights, residual payments, and labor-management relations—rules which meet the peculiar needs of educational television —there is evidence that educational television in general and school television in particular will mature enough to make a significant contribution to the education of youth.

Questions for Discussion

1. Are the facilities for television instruction available in the community where you teach or where you would like to teach?

2. If such facilities do exist how do you see yourself as a participant in educational television? What role or roles would you be able to play?

3. Of the problems cited in this chapter which do you feel would be hardest for you to solve?

4. What would your solutions be to some of the problems posed in this chapter?

5. Do you feel that the value of teaching social studies on television would outweigh the disadvantages involved?

8

A STRATEGY FOR TEACHING GIFTED STUDENTS HIGH SCHOOL SOCIAL STUDIES

GEORGE FRAKES

The beginning teacher is often shocked by the wide range of abilities of his social studies students. A few students may not be able to read whereas others may be more academically advanced than the teacher. A real challenge to the social studies teacher is to meet the many and diverse interests of the most capable or gifted students in such a way that they do not simply receive more assignments but assignments of a more sophisticated quality.

The following selection describes a teacher's approach in meeting the challenge of the gifted student. It is a candid description of the advantages and disadvantages of the particular strategy he used.

A problem which concerns many social studies instructors is how to stimulate the diverse interests of gifted students while maintaining high standards of academic quality. To solve this problem demands above all else a thorough knowledge of the subject that is taught. It is little wonder that students grow tired of the superficiality that is so common in many social studies classes. Teachers of able students must also be able to organize their instructional strategies so to relate their subject to the individual student's interests.

Such an approach to teaching is a challenge to the most able and experienced instructor. It is known that far too often the traditional teaching techniques or strategies for high school history or social studies (lectures, written assignments prepared in class, recitation, periodic tests and quizzes, and written homework assignments drawn from a textbook) do not stimulate or tax the intellectual ability of gifted students. Indeed many "so-called" gifted programs mean merely more unimaginative assignments of the traditional type. As a result of the prevailing secondary school technique of history teaching, by the time of their high school graduation, the able students often indicate a dislike of the tedium and lockstep they endured fifty minutes a day. The problem of unimaginative social studies teaching is well known to perceptive teachers at every level of education. The crucial question which instructors should ask is what can be done to improve the level of instruction in our field.

A partial answer to this problem came in the 1960s when a host of new social studies and history programs, sources of curricular materials, bibliographical information, paperback texts, and new resource facilities were developed to assist the teacher who desires to upgrade his teaching. Academic and educational bodies such as the American Historical Association, the National Council for the Social Studies and its local councils, the Service Center for the Teachers of History, the Educational Testing Service Advanced Placement program, the Council for Basic Education, the United States Office of Education, and the Organization of American Historians have recently taken a more active interest in secondary school history and social studies. Yet the magnitude of the flood of teaching materials from these and other organizations now available presents certain new problems to the classroom teacher of gifted students. How can the wealth of these materials be incorporated in the teacher's already bulging lesson plans without making honors courses into a disjointed "grab bag" of unrelated information?

Of course there is no easy answer to this question. It really depends upon the teacher's objectives for the course and his skill in presenting the material. Hundreds of possible or actual successful solutions to the problem of teaching social studies have been developed based upon the variables of individual personality, capabilities of the instructor, and the idiosyncrasies of particular school situations. What the writer suggests as a possible solution to the problem of developing a strategy or technique of teaching the gifted student is clearly not the only or the "best" method, but can be recommended as an approach which worked well in his experience.

To gain an understanding of this teaching strategy, the writer suggests an examination of a four-week assignment in American history. This case study is a unit which was assigned to public high school students in an honors section. The unit began with an introduction by the teacher of the work that would follow during the next four weeks. The introduction was presented in such a manner as to clarify the objectives considered important, to give a preview of the high points of the subject matter to be studied, and to illustrate sources of information for possible research concerning the period.

During the course of the first meeting in the unit the teacher normally distributed a unit syllabus for the students' use. The syllabus was an attempt to present an outline of the key points to be covered in lecture and discussion during the class meetings. It also contained a statement of objectives, certain required assignments for all students, and a description of the manner in which students would be evaluated. The required material in the assignment section was brief and intended to give all the members of the honors section a common background of the most important historical concepts of the period. The final aspect of the syllabus was the inclusion of certain suggestions for independent research or general topics which could be further defined by the student and teacher. The student who elected to attempt independent research, however, was not limited by the teacher's suggestions.

There were other responsibilities for the teacher beyond the writing of the syllabus and orientation of the students in his class. The instructor using this teaching strategy had to plan certain days for directed library research. He also led discussions about certain questions which arose from the students' reading and research. However, the emphasis placed upon research did not mean that the traditional methods were overlooked; considerable time in class was spent in lectures and class discussion. Lecturing to gifted students in this method of teaching meant more than breaking down the information in college textbooks to the high school level. Instead, the lecture was an attempt to interpret major concepts in American history. This was done in many cases by "postholing" or examining certain key events, ideas, persons, or historic trends in some depth and linking the "posthole" topics with lectures which surveyed the less significant factors in American history. Indeed it was discovered that few teaching approaches fail to interest gifted students more than a shallow rehash of material they can read in their high school textbook. Conversely, the coming to grips with important issues in considerable depth excites the interest of bright eleventh graders.

The teacher, when not lecturing, spent the remaining class periods in a variety of ways. One was the introduction of guest speakers and later the guidance of class discussions concerned with the guest speakers' remarks. Assisting students with research was another responsibility of the instructor. The teacher also moderated occasional debates between class members or related student projects to the major objectives of the unit and historical period studied. Of course some class periods were spent giving unit quizzes or examinations.

Besides such activity by the teacher, the instructor working with gifted students would attempt to learn the nature of students' research and periodically discuss how their work was progressing. Since not all students were working at the same project (indeed, the assignments were based upon a "contractual" agreement with each student determining what he or she wanted to attempt), personal contact in the first few weeks of the year was very important.

A brief explanation is necessary about the nature of the contract approach to student evaluation. After a few years of teaching, the writer became well aware that the level of enthusiasm for history among gifted students varied widely. Some able students loved the subject, others tolerated it but were diligent in completing assignments in order to receive a college recommending grade, while still others disliked history and relied upon their superior intelligence and recall to merely float through the class with a passing grade. Since this pattern of student response was often the case, it was felt that those gifted students who were content with only receiving a passing grade on written assignments should be required to complete a brief written minimal assignment covering the most significant historical concepts. However, such students were required to maintain a high standard of quality in their work to receive minimum credit. For those students who wished to receive higher than average credit for their work, a contract was established between the student and the instructor. A student who wished to receive a "B" grade, for example, would do the minimum assignment and select a research topic or project which would demand about the same amount of effort as a "B" effort in a traditional textbook assignment for an honors class. However, under the individualized assignment pattern, the student could select an assignment to his liking as long as it was related to the historical period and pursue it for four weeks and complete the project prior to the end of the unit. An "A" student's level of performance and amount of research were expected to be higher than those of a "B" student, and possible assignments prepared by the teacher made provision for this gradation. In the case of all students a half-executed or sloppily done assignment would not bring about the fulfillment of the contract. Instead, the student had to perform at a level commensurate with his ability to receive the grade he sought.

Besides the student's responsibility for an adequate performance in his written assignment, he or she also had a reading assignment for every unit. Prior to the widespread use of paperbacks, the writer used either a lower division college textbook or superior high school text supplemented with additional readings assigned in anthologies of primary sources or certain applicable monographs placed on reserve at the school library. Since the advent of low-cost paperbacks, unit-texts, and problem books, the teacher has a wealth of materials from which to choose. The instructor who uses the approach of multiple texts may select one paperback for each historic period or indicate several sources which might be suitable. The latter approach creates a slight problem of a lack of uniformity of background, but is offset by the introduction of a variety of historical interpretations which stimulates class discussion and critical thought.

Dependent upon the type of written assignments and amount of required reading, an additional requirement of approximately six critical book reviews a year was established. In satisfying this requirement, bibliographical lists were written to aid the student in book selection. Works selected were always present in the high school or public libraries or were available in a low-cost paperback edition at local book stores.

Thus it can be seen that the heart of this recommended teaching approach or strategy was the attempt to stimulate the student's interest in history by the use of an individual approach to student assignments and a wide range of different reading materials. Such an approach, when thoughtfully used, could and did bring variety and diversity of interpretation to the standard high school history class. This approach improves class discussion and encourages a critical, insightful attitude toward the awesome authority of the textbook if one is used. The use of individualized assignments in history can have the added advantage of linking students' interests in a variety of modern fields thus giving a greater understanding of the past as well as a clearer insight to modern events. Examples of commonly held current interests of gifted students which have historical significance are: minority group problems, civil rights, war and military strategy, science and technology, art, music, social values, and religion.

Implementation of this teaching strategy of individualized assignments and reading demands some ingenuity on the part of the teacher. Obviously for such a method to succeed, the teacher would have to know a great deal about the students in his class. He must be aware of their academic strengths and weaknesses, school interests, and even possibly their extracurricular activities. This takes some time, but can be a rewarding experience when the instructor can see the enthusiasm of his students in their approach to their historical study.

Other aspects of the teacher's ingenuity are related to the problem of working closely with school officials. For example, school librarians and in some cases local public librarians and nearby college library officials should be contacted to make arrangements prior to the start of the semester. The teacher and librarians should select appropriate books for student reading lists, to plan when the works would be needed, and to establish procedures to place the books on reserve. The high school history teacher using such an approach to his teaching of a gifted class often has to coordinate his plan of teaching with school administrators who can be upset or confused when instructors vary from traditional methods.

Teachers who attempt such a teaching strategy have to take care in watching the progress of their students. Some boys and girls, even though very bright, procrastinate and have difficulties in adjusting to the freedom from not turning in the "even numbered questions in the middle of the next chapter" every other day. Instructors using this method can help the occasional gifted student who has trouble in developing individual initiative by carefully noting his participation in class discussion and by making a practice of individually discussing the progress of the student's unit assignments a week or two prior to the completion date. Those students who continue to experience difficulty can be aided by the instructor, who can suggest sources to read or require a preliminary outline or statement of progress prior to the deadline established in the unit instructions. If difficulties persist, some students can be helped by members of the counseling staff. In the case of some under-achieving students, the only course of action is to transfer the student to another history section where more conventional methods are used.

There are other aspects of this approach to teaching history that present a challenge to the teacher of honors students. One of these is the nature of gifted students' thirst for reading materials which are related to the unit of study. Hopefully these books should include primary materials as well as secondary works and general reference works. The teacher should be aware of the bibliography of his teaching field and be able to suggest sources suited to the student's subject and ability. Another instructional problem is that of relating the teacher's lectures, class discussion, audio-visual teaching aids, and unit examinations to the needs and interests of the different members of each year's honors class in history.

Besides the aspects of proper sources and student involvement in the teacher's curriculum, the instructor must consider the problem of which students should be admitted to an honors class. Indeed, the selection of gifted students is one of the most crucial factors in determining the success of this teaching strategy. Generally speaking, most successful honors programs rely upon other social studies teachers' recommendations, previous grades in history and social studies, and standardized aptitude and intelligence test results. Besides the problem of the quality of the students in the honors class, there is also the consideration of the total number of students to be enrolled. A desirable class size would normally be between ten and twenty students.

A final related administrative consideration is that of the honors teacher's overall instructional load. It is obvious that such an instructional strategy is very demanding of a teacher's time. In many progressive, enlightened districts the honors instructor's remaining load is reduced.

Even if proper administrative considerations are made, there remain certain responsibilities which must be accepted by the teacher. One of the most significant is the selection of instructional materials. Some teachers using this method of teaching supplement a relatively brief "core" textbook with inexpensive paperbacks, often biographies or studies of a particular period or theme. Other supplementary works are the previously mentioned anthologies of primary sources, monographs on reserve, primary sources, problem approaches to events or periods such as the Amherst or Holt pamphlet series, or the wealth of new primary casebooks. Still other teachers allow greater freedom in allowing students to read works in related disciplines such as historical geography, American literature, economics, sociology, political science, or even historical fiction.

A related instructional challenge to the flexibility of student reading assignments is the problem of fairly evaluating the students' progress when they are reading various sources. In the writer's experience, this difficulty was resolved by basing students' grades on a variety of different measures. Grades would be determined by students' progress in writing about their research or reading, class discussion, as well as tests. Tests would be used less often than the daily quiz which is so common in many traditional classes. In the four week period of a unit, normally only one quiz and a fifty-minute period examination at the conclusion of the unit would be assigned. Examinations in this method of teaching stressed students' understanding of basic historical concepts and other important instructional objectives emphasized in lecture, discussion, or in research assignments required of all students. Students' research and reading would be evaluated by a critical reading of the short papers which the boys and girls presented to the teacher near the conclusion of the unit of study as well as class oral recitation or discussion.

The evaluation of the course reflects only part of the teacher's work. In this teaching strategy, the emphasis is upon the instructor being the central resource in the high school history instructional program. In this role, the instructor revises the program rather than relying upon a textbook, an instructor's manual, or an outdated curriculum guide. The teacher is almost forced to rethink his teaching program and lesson plans each year as he considers the character and interest of his class. This reexamination of teaching approach does not mean that the teacher has to start "from scratch" in rebuilding his lesson plans each year. For example, lecture notes, bibliography and research reading assignments, certain discussion topics, and selected examination questions can be retained and periodically used for years. After a few years of improvisation, the teacher can reuse assignments to meet recurring individual requirements. The advantage of this reuse comes in the gradual elimination of unsuitable teaching approaches and satisfaction in observing the effect of the upgrading of your work.

The ingenuity of the teacher in planning his teaching strategy can bring a further rich reward of teaching to an alert, highly motivated class of gifted students who are actively involved and deeply interested in their subject. The instructor also can profit from the diverse interests of a class of high school gifted students, who can certainly present a continuing source of new information to practically force the teacher to improve his own fund of knowledge about his subject. The teacher who uses this instructional approach states that the level of student knowledge of traditional subject matter is far higher than those of matched students taught under the older method of following the lead of a dry, encyclopedic textbook. In fact, students who have had the opportunity of examining several sources of information often provide a real stimulus for both the teacher and other class members by their class discussion.

This strategy of teaching high school history or social studies provides an excellent opportunity for the instructor who is not content to perpetuate the traditional textbook-centered approach. By individualizing assignments and requiring a variety of reading, the teacher can stimulate the diversity of interests present in any class of gifted students. Even though there are certain problems in adopting this method of teaching, the advantages connected with this teaching strategy can be recommended to far outweigh the disadvantages. Perhaps the most rewarding aspect in this approach to teaching is the growth of both students' and the teacher's knowledge.

UNIT II

America's Colonial Age, 1607–1763
Honors Class

UNIT OBJECTIVES

Knowledge and Understanding:
1. The origin of American political, constitutional, social, legal, intellectual, and religious institutions.
2. The transition of Western European and particularly British tradition to North America.
3. The importance of geographic factors in early American history.
4. The growth and development of colonial society and thought during this 156-year period.
5. The importance of British colonial policy, international politics, and inter-colonial wars in shaping American colonial development.
6. The importance of the frontier and the origin of sectionalism in American history.
7. The colonial background for the American Revolution.

Attitudes, Skills, and Values:
1. An appreciation for the accomplishments of colonial Americans.
2. An awareness of the influence of pre-revolutionary Americans in shaping the institutions of the United States in many fields.
3. Realization of the problems of this period and an ability to relate events of this age to those of modern America and the newly developing nations of the twentieth century.
4. An ability to understand the forces which cause political, social, and intellectual change, reform, and revolution.
5. The ability to read primary and secondary materials critically and insightfully.
6. An interest in American literature, historical geography, and biography.
7. An ability to use the library for research.
8. An ability to draw generalization from data, and then present material clearly in written or oral form.

Textbooks:

Wright, ver Steeg, Nye, Link, Degler, *et al., The Democratic Experience* (Dem. Exp.)

Starr, Todd, and Curti, *Living American Documents* (Documents)

Craven, Johnson, and Dunn, *A Documentary History of the American People* (C,J,&D)

Turner, *The Frontier in American History* (Turner), Reserve Book Desk

UNIT SYLLABUS

(* = Assignment due or test)

Dates	Lecture and Discussion Topic	Reading Assignment
September 27 (40 min.)	Introduce the unit; discuss objectives, grading standards, and research projects; lecture: The European background for exploration and colonization.	Dem. Exp. 2-25 C,J,&D 3-58, 61-66 Documents 2-8
September 29 (80 min.)	Lecture: Early British colonization, geographic and Indian influences, and the nature of seventeenth-century society; discussion of the problems of historical research and bibliography in this period.	"
October 1 (80 min.)	40 minute period: Library orientation and research. 40 minute period: Lecture and discussion: Seventeenth-century colonial thought, religion, political and constitutional institutions.	Documents 9-25 Dem. Exp. 46-54
*October 4 (40 min.)	Turn in subjects for investigational exercises and research topics for students who wish to attempt them. Lecture: The rise of New France and the origin of Anglo-French rivalry; discussion of the "Old" British colo-	Documents 36-38

Dates	*Lecture and Discussion Topic*	*Reading Assignment*
	nial system and the early growth of American political and constitutional independence.	
October 6 (80 min.)	Lecture: Colonial economic growth, 20 minutes. Class divides into two groups of eight students. Group I, library research for thirty minutes, then discussion of reading assignments and research projects. Group II, discussion first, then library research.	C,J,&D 89-110
*October 8 (80 min.)	20 minute quiz. Two films, Colonial Williamsburg series. Lecture: Immigration and the colonial frontier. Student-teacher conferences about student's research.	Turner 1-38
October 11 (40 min.)	Lecture: The eighteenth-century colonial mind; discussion of outside reading, and individual conferences about research.	C,J,&D 75-88, 111-120 Dem. Exp. 54-59 Documents 26-29
October 13 (80 min.)	Lecture and discussion: The British colonies as a part of world politics and the impact of the French and Indian wars. Discussion and criticism of preliminary reports of research projects (students whose surnames start with "A" to "L").	Documents 30-35 C,J,&D 121-133
October 15 (80 min.)	Lecture: 1763, a turning point in colonial history. Discussion of outside reading, remaining preliminary research reports.	"

Dates	Lecture and Discussion Topic	Reading Assignment

*October 18 (40 min.) — Turn in unit notebook (required outline of basic questions, and when applicable, investigational exercises and research projects). Unit examination, 40 minutes.   ″

ASSIGNMENTS AND GRADING STANDARDS FOR THE UNIT

1. In order to pass, all students will answer the required questions in the "Outline of Basic Questions" and complete the required map exercise. The answers will be turned in to the teacher the last day of the unit (October 18). Students should be prepared to discuss the questions in class.

2. Students who desire a "B" grade or higher should complete two of the investigational exercises.

3. Students desiring an "A" grade should complete the two investigational exercises and one of the advanced research projects.

4. How you will be graded: 5 per cent of the total grade for this three-week period is determined by class discussion, 10 per cent by the quiz, 50 per cent by the required work and optional exercises and research, and 35 per cent by the unit examination.

5. In order for a student to receive full credit for his homework and research, all work must be clearly written and indicate thorough and careful preparation.

OUTLINE OF BASIC QUESTIONS
(Required of all students)

A. Colonial Foundations. (Answer the questions in sentences and paragraphs)

   1. Explain the most important factors in Europe during the fifteenth and sixteenth centuries which caused the beginnings of exploration and colonization.

   2. Why did the English colonies have such different political characteristics? Comment upon (a) Virginia, (b) the New England Colonies, (c) Maryland, (d) Pennsylvania, and (e) South Carolina.

3. Discuss the different major religious denominations in colonial America.

(a) Why did different religious sects tend to be most important in different sections of colonial America?

(b) What was the religious "Great Awakening" of the eighteenth century and why was it considered to be a reaction against the enlightenment?

(c) What contributions did colonial religion make to the establment of American democratic ideals and modern religious toleration and pluralism?

4. Discuss the impact of geography upon the colonists by commenting upon the following:

a. The Appalachian Mountains
b. The Tidewater
c. The Frontier
d. The Piedmont
e. The Fall line
f. Climatic factors
g. Soils
h. Native crops and raw materials

i. Please locate the following on a map: Boston, New York, Philadelphia, Williamsburg, Newport, Charleston, Montreal, Quebec, Louisbourg, the New England Colonies, the Middle Colonies, the Southern Colonies, the Ohio River Valley, the Kentucky country, important Indian tribal areas, and a,b,d, and e above.

5. Describe the importance of the French, Spaniards, and Indians in shaping the American colonial character. Also comment upon the following:

a. Intercolonial wars.
b. Foreign forces caused the colonists to be dependent upon the British crown for support.
c. As a force in developing frontier independence and ingenuity.

6. What forces caused the colonists and the Mother Country to grow apart by 1763?

INVESTIGATIONAL EXERCISES
(For those students who desire a "B" or "A" grade)

Select two of the following:

1. Construct a comprehensive time-line on butcher paper indicating important persons, events, discoveries, founding of colonies, military and diplomatic matters, and historical trends

from 1607 to 1680 or 1680–1730 or 1730–1763. (Select one out of the three possibilities.)

2. Draw a series of historical maps showing the following: (a) the advancing colonial frontier in 1620, 1700, 1740, and 1763; (b) the location of important military battles and campaigns; (c) the location of the centers of colonial slavery; and (d) important colonial trade routes and commercial centers.

3. Discuss the importance of the frontier as a safety valve and source of economic wealth for colonial Americans.

4. Sketch a series of pictures indicating colonial homes in different regions. Write a brief description telling why the homes were different. Also comment upon how colonial homes reflected the character of American society at that time.

5. Describe three important incidents in colonial America prior to 1763 which indicated the growing spirit of independence. (Examples are Bacon's Rebellion, the John Zenger Case, etc.)

6. Outline the required two chapters in the *Democratic Experience* and analyze three selections from C,J,&D.

7. Describe the origin of Negro slavery in the colonies. To what extent are modern attributes toward Negroes influenced by the colonial tradition?

8. Draw portraits of four colonial leaders and write a brief one page biography of each.

9. Comment upon the growth of transportation in the colonies in the eighteenth century.

10. Prepare a short oral report (approximately five minutes) or written paper four pages in length about one of the following subjects:

Sir William Shirley	Sir William Johnson	William Byrd
Nathaniel Bacon	William Penn	Peace of Paris 1763
Benjamin Franklin	The colonial newspaper	King William's War
Jonathan Edwards	Moravian settlements	Quakers
The Turner Thesis	John Peter Zenger Case	Colonial Government

11. Draw a graph showing the growth of colonial science and technology in the eighteenth century. Indicate, if possible, the

invention, the scientific discovery, the technological innovation, and the date and person responsible.

12. Prepare a chart indicating the colonial social structure in each of the four geographic sections (New England, Middle Colonies, the South, and the Frontier).

13. Work out another topic with the teacher.

ADVANCED RESEARCH ACTIVITIES
(For students who desire an "A" grade)

1. Some authorities claim that the growing discontent which caused the American Revolution was due to economic and political developments prior to 1763. Write an essay which either defends or rejects this thesis. (Limit your essay to ten pages or less.)

2. Prepare a debate with other students on the following topic: "Resolved that British salutary neglect was the greatest influence which shaped American principles of independence and political individualism."

3. Comment upon the aspects of present-day American constitutional development which can be traced to the colonial period. Which of these developments were British and which were colonial innovations?

4. Write a critical review of two related books on a similar subject. In your review, consider the two authors' interpretation of the same subject; their style, sources, documentation, and theses. You may select biographies, monographs, treatises, or surveys of some facet of colonial history. If you wish, you may compare a well-written historical novel with nonfiction on the same general subject.

5. Describe the importance of sectionalism in colonial life. To what extent does modern American sectionalism reflect the earlier colonial image? What were the causes of sectionalism in the colonial period? What were some of the effects of sectionalism?

6. Compare and contrast "everyday life" in the northern and southern colonies. Also consider the differences in colonial society with that of mid-twentieth-century America.

7. Work out a research project with the instructor.

BIBLIOGRAPHY OF SECONDARY MATERIALS
IN THE SCHOOL LIBRARY

Research Materials

Charles M. Andrews, *The Colonial Period in American History*, 4 volumes.

Herbert L. Osgood, *The American Colonies in the Seventeenth Century*, 3 volumes.

————, *The American Colonies in the Eighteenth Century*, 4 volumes.

Lawrence Henry Gipson, *The British Empire before the American Revolution*, 11 volumes, first 8.

Wilbur R. Jacobs, *Diplomacy and Indian Gifts.*

Daniel Boorstin, *The Americans: The Colonial Experience.*

Ray A. Billington, *Westward Expansion.*

Louis B. Wright, *The Cultural Life of the American Colonies, 1607–1763.*

William W. Sweet, *Religion in the Development of American Culture.*

Merle Curti, *The Growth of American Thought.*

Jack P. Greene, *The Quest for Power.*

Richard Morris, *The Encyclopedia of American History.*

Also check the following books in the library for sources of information: The works of Francis Parkman, The New American Nation Series, the University of Chicago series, the Yale Chronicles of America series, the bibliography on pages 59 and 60 in the *National Experience*, the *Harvard Guide to American History,* and the pamphlets of the Service Center for the Teachers of History.

Enjoyment:

There is a vast amount of historical fiction and biography for this period. If a student wants to read historical fiction for credit, please bring your book and discuss it with the teacher. A few authors for your consideration are: James Fenimore Cooper, *The Last of the Mohicans,* and his other Leatherstocking Tales; Catherine Drinker Bowen, W. D. Edmonds, Esther Forbes, Nathaniel Hawthorne, Mary Johnson, Washington Irving, Bruce Lancaster, F. van Wyck Mason, Kenneth Roberts, and William Gilmore Simms.

Questions for Discussion

1. Critically appraise the contractual approach adopted by the teacher. Would you adopt such an approach? If so, what variations would you add to his basic thesis on this subject?

2. The writer advocates a very individualized approach in dealing with gifted students. What problems do you feel might keep you from employing such an approach?

3. The writer states, "A problem which concerns many social studies instructors is how to stimulate the diverse interests of gifted students while maintaining high standards of academic quality. *To solve this problem demands above all else a thorough knowledge of the subject that is taught."* Would you agree with the writer on this point?

4. The selection of students for an honors class is very important. What suggestions do you have for selection procedures?

5. What evaluation procedures would you use in dealing with gifted students?

6. Do you feel that you are qualified to teach an honors section in any or all areas of the social studies curriculum?

9

A SCIENTIFIC APPROACH TO THE TEACHING OF ECONOMICS

MARILYN KOURILSKY

In the opinion of the writer of the following selection, "Economics is unlike history and U.S. government (and other social studies courses) in that most of its subject matter is not institutional but rather conceptual." Her remark is both interesting and timely: a major effort is now being made in many social studies projects to identify key concepts from the various social sciences and history. The reader should find the discussion about economics as a science and what the student should know about economics to be of interest and value.

The purpose of this paper is mainly to describe an approach to the teaching of economics that proved successful. First, I will discuss my observations concerning the state of teaching economics in the high school. Second, I will explain my approach to the teaching of economics. Third, I will describe the student population concerned. Fourth, I will discuss what I believe the student should know about economics, and last I will describe the results of my approach.

THE STATE OF TEACHING ECONOMICS IN THE SECONDARY SCHOOLS

On the basis of my observations, the teaching of economics at the secondary school level leaves much to be desired. The underlying assumption of most secondary public school instructors is that anyone with a general secondary teaching credential is qualified to teach economics. This assumption is erroneous in that not only are most holders of general secondary credentials unqualified to teach economics but many college majors in social studies holding credentials have inadequate backgrounds in economics. Economics is unlike history and U.S. Government (and other social studies courses) in that most of its subject matter is not institutional but rather conceptual. An individual who wishes to teach economics needs not only instruction in these concepts but training in how to apply these concepts to the experiences of the high school student. (For example, in teaching the student the effect of the government's setting a price ceiling on a product which is below the equilibrium price, a teacher may find that he can use the example of World War II rent controls in a college class but will have more success at the high school level if he uses first the hypothetical example of a price ceiling on box-boy services.)

Many high school instructors and administrators also hold misconceptions about the nature of the subject matter of economics. Economics is not the same as business administration; it is not the study of consumer finance, and it is not a course in how to buy stock and bonds. Its principles apply to all of these and more but it does not restrict itself to any one of them. The study of economics will not guarantee that one will get rich in business although it should develop principles that may be used by a businessman. The study of economics will not guarantee the creation of an all-wise consumer, a man with a high income, a stock market expert, or a full and useful life for every person. Its principles, however, may help one as a businessman, a consumer, or an investor. In other words, a grasp of the principles of economics does not guarantee that a man will be kept out of the bread line but it will give him a good idea of why and how he got there.

Few individuals who teach economics appear to be aware that it is a social science that studies the behavior of people in relation to their environment—that it develops *principles* useful to any individual or group that has to make decisions, and this, of course, includes everyone.

Rather, the course in economics, as it is now being taught, can easily become a vehicle by which to imbue the students with the instructor's personal preferences. Thus, if the student is attending a class taught by a conservative individual, he is more likely to learn the disadvantages of both government spending and the Keynesian approach to economics. On the other hand, if he is attending a class taught by a liberal, he is likely to learn the advantages of social legislation, WPA programs, and government regulation of industry. At best, the student is faced with the ordeal of memorizing a barrage of terms and institutions —e.g., the number of members of the Federal Reserve Board of Governors, the definition of bimetallism, prime beef, etc.

A course in economics should not have to degenerate into the pattern I have described. Potentially, it can supply the student with the tool—an analytical framework—he can apply to the solution of problems, based on his value system. In other words it can provide him with the "scientific habit of mind."

The economics teacher's role in the classroom is analogous to the role of the scientist in policy-making. The scientist explains to the public (as should the teacher to his students) what his assessment is of the goal they want to achieve based on his *science* (and not his value judgment), the possibility of achieving the goal, the possible ways to achieve the goal, and the consequences of certain courses of action. The student, like the public, must learn to assess these consequences and make the decisions involved.

What this really means is that the scientist in public policy and the teacher in the classroom can explain what the consequences may be if one does certain things, but he should not attempt to make the decision as to what one should do. The medical scientist, for example, can make known to the public what he knows about the effects of smoking on the human system; he cannot, however, say that smoking in and of itself is either "good" or "bad." Whether it is good or bad is a matter of personal and public values and goals. One can, for example, imagine situations in which smoking would be "bad" but one can also imagine situations in which it would be "good." Most of us would not deny the condemned man a last cigarette.

The point is that the medical scientist can assist people in making intelligent decisions about smoking by explaining to them what he knows about the effects of smoking. As a result, the individual and the society may change their goals—the individual may quit smoking and/or the society may outlaw it. Similarly the high school teacher with the "scientific attitude" or "approach" may, for example, describe the economic effects of socialized medicine, based on his knowledge of his discipline, but he should not and must not make a value judgment as to whether this policy is "good" or "bad." Having given the student the tools with which to analyze this issue and other issues, such as foreign aid, federal aid to education, national defense, aid to the aged, the farm problem, big unions, big business, minimum wage laws, and unemployment, he should then *encourage* them to make their own *decisions*.

A SCIENTIFIC APPROACH TO THE TEACHING OF ECONOMICS

I teach economics as a social science that studies the process of making decisions. Economics can be approached as a science in that it deals with some fairly well defined subject matter; it has a general body of knowledge about this subject matter; and it has some standard analytical tools or reasoning devices that are used by economists to solve problems within the general area of its subject matter.

Because of the nature of man and his environment, individuals, organizations, and societies are constantly involved in activities which necessitate decision-making. It is this process that the subject of economics studies. Economics has developed a general body of knowledge about this aspect of human behavior, and it has developed some "good" principles of decision-making, principles that I attempt to teach my class.

It is true that the social sciences are less exact than the physical sciences, primarily because they deal with a subject that is in many ways more complex than the subject matter of the physical sciences. In addition, the social scientist cannot conduct the same sort of controlled experiments that the physical scientist can. Nevertheless, there is a general core of knowledge about the decision-making process that has been developed in economics and that has been verified by repeated observation of people in similar circumstances at different times.

It is often brought out in the study of economics that

economists agree on the facts and tools of their discipline but disagree on how to use these tools—policy decisions—because "policy," the goals that an individual ought to pursue, is subjective and non-scientific. The fact that economists, as scientists, are in general agreement on the facts of their science, but disagree among themselves on questions concerning how this knowledge ought to be used, is no more a criticism of economists and economics than it is of physicists and physics. For example, in the 1940s there was general agreement among scientists to the effect that the proximity of two elements would release enough energy to destroy large numbers of people and devastate large geographical areas. They were also agreed that if this energy were to be released over a Japanese city it would destroy many people and major portions of the city.

However, given this scientific agreement on the basic tools of their discipline, there arose the question of policy concerning the *use* of this knowledge—"Should we drop the bomb?" On this question there was much disagreement because non-scientific factors were involved—religion, training, politics, and so on—which influence an individual's beliefs and values. When it comes to policy—courses of actions—experts, scientists (whatever one wants to call them) are just as subject to personal values as anyone of us. This includes experts in all fields, physics, economics, chemistry. It is more noticeable in economics because its experts so often disagree (because of different values and preferences) on how to use the knowledge of their discipline.

I believe that the course in economics should be one in which the teacher instructs the students in the tools of the discipline and not one in which the instructor indoctrinates the students in what he thinks ought to be. For example, if I were discussing policy regarding recession and inflation, I might bring out that recessions and unemployment in our society develop because of insufficient spending power on goods and services, that an increase in spending on goods and services would thus tend to increase employment, and that any one of many possible government actions (policies) would tend to increase the spending on goods and services: (1) an increase in the amount of government spending balanced by an equal increase in taxes; (2) an increase in the amount of government spending not balanced by taxes, or deficit spending; (3) deficit spending brought about by an increase in government spending, but by a decrease in taxes; (4) an "easy money" policy on the part of the government designed to make borrowing by businessmen and consumers easier and less costly.

It is my function as the instructor to describe these alternative anti-recessionary policies and show how each of these policies *could* achieve the desired result: increased employment. However, if I mention which *specific* policy the government *should* employ at a given time—what ought to be—I am using my position of authority as a vehicle to inbue the students with my own preferences. For example, if I personally believe that government spending is, by itself, undesirable, it is not my proper function to point out that I do not favor policies 1 and 2. Rather, it is my function to explain the alternative policies and let each individual in the class make up his own mind on which policy is best at a given time. One effective way to deal with these controversial topics is to schedule a formal debate on the issue, thus allowing the advantages and disadvantages of each policy to emanate from the class (e.g., "Resolved that fiscal policy in the form of higher taxes should be enacted to curb the present inflationary spiral").

In sum, what I am advocating is a "scientific approach" to the teaching of economics, an approach that can be employed whether one believes that economics is a science, a discipline, a knack, or an art.

THE STUDENT POPULATION

The school in which I taught was what is commonly termed a comprehensive high school, one of many in a large urban community. It is located in a lower-middle-class business and residential area serving a preponderantly Jewish population and has a student body numbering of approximately twenty-seven hundred.

The economics course is offered as an elective to twelfth grade students who have completed one and a half years of study of United States history and government.

In this particular school, the course was originally offered to students of average and above-average ability, but it was eventually offered to students of three ability levels: honors classes (students with recorded I.Q.'s of 130 and above), academically enriched classes (students with recorded I.Q.'s of 110 to 129), and average classes (students with recorded I.Q.'s of 90-109).

Although the same topics were taught to all of the classes, variations in methods and the level of application were employed depending upon the sophistication of the group. It should be added that the students as a whole were very responsive and the brighter ones in particular were highly motivated. This, in part, can be attributed to the supportive-enthusiastic attitude of the parents.

WHAT THE STUDENT SHOULD KNOW
ABOUT ECONOMICS

On the basis of a twenty-week semester I divide my course into five parts. During the first week of the class I teach the fundamentals of debate and give the student the outline which is included at the end of this section (pp. 126–29).

I shall describe what I attempt to teach in each of the

five units of the course (assuming the reader has some acquaintance with the principles of economics). I shall also include examples of the procedures, activities, and materials I employ.

In *Part One* of the course I deal with economics as a science, the central economic problem, the relation between resource ownership and the form a society's economy takes, general principles of the operation of a market economy, and a comparison between the free enterprise economy and the centrally planned economy.

A. *Economics as a Social Science:* The purpose of this section of the course is to explain to the student the general nature of the subject matter of economics—to develop some general ideas concerning what economics is and what it is not, and what the capabilities and limitations of economics and economists are.

B. *Scarcity—The Universal Fact of Life:* In this section I use the principle of abstraction which I have discussed with the class earlier to bring out the nature of the basic and universal economic fact of life. It is this fact of life and its implications with which the science of economics is concerned, and it is this fact of life that is the cause of all of the economic problems that any individual or any society faces. What I hope the student has learned at the end of this section is something about each of the following: (1) although individuals differ from each other in an almost infinite number of ways, they have in common the characteristic that each of them has wants. The actual satisfaction of any want requires the use of something in the individual's environment—the use of "resources"; (2) while the environments of individuals and societies differ in that they are made up of different types and amounts of resources, they will have in common the fact that whatever is available to them (their resources) is limited in amount in relation to the uses to which they may be applied; (3)

thus every individual and every society is faced with the condition the economist calls "scarcity"—the existence of scarcity means that every society has to "solve" the same basic problems; and (4) the device, or organization, or social mechanism that solves a society's economic problems is the society's "economy." Different societies have different types of economies, and it is largely meaningless to compare the efficiency with which the economies of different societies perform.

C. *The Form of Resource Ownership and the Manner in Which a Society's Economy Solves the Problems of What, How, and for Whom:* There are two conceptually extreme types of economies, the centrally planned or directed economy and the market exchange (free enterprise) economy. Both types perform the functions of allocating resources and distributing income—solving the problems of "what, how, and for whom"—but they accomplish these ends by different methods. All real world economies are combinations of these conceptual extremes, but they can be classified as being predominantly either "directed" or "free." To understand the real world economies, it is necessary to understand the principles upon which each type operates.

Members of a society can choose between two types of resource ownership—social ownership and private ownership. If the members of a society choose to honor social ownership, the automatic result is a centrally planned or directed economy. If they choose to honor private ownership, the automatic result is a market exchange economy. While real world economies contain elements of these two extreme forms, a society that honors the vital elements of private ownership will have a market exchange economy.

Essentially, a "valuable" or "good" use of resources in a directed economy is whatever the planners say. In a market exchange economy, a "valuable" or "good" use of resources is whatever the individual owners wish to use them for. This will be a "profitable" use.

What I hope the student has learned at the end of this section is (1) the meaning of ownership, (2) how and why collective ownership results in a directed economy, (3) how and why private ownership results in a market exchange economy, and (4) a comparison of the two types of economies.

D. *Principles upon Which a Market Economy Operates to Allocate Resources and Distribute Income:* In a market exchange economy the problems of what to produce, how to produce, and for whom to produce are solved through the activities of resource owners who are interested in profit (gain). In a completely free system a valuable or efficient use of resources is a use that is profitable to resource owners. In a system in which complete freedom does not exist —in which the society places restrictions on the freedom of resource owners—profit is still the criterion of what is a valuable or efficient use of resources. So long as resource owners have the freedom to choose among the alternative uses for their resources that *are* available to them, resources will be devoted to uses that are profitable. Social interferences with the freedom of resource owners do not alter the principles upon which a market economy operates so long as any freedom of choice is allowed.

What I hope the student has learned at the end of this section is an understanding of (1) the solution of the individual problems of what, how, and for whom, (2) the interrelations of the solutions of the problems of what, how, and for whom, (3) the real world modifications of the free market, (4) the meaning of valuable or efficient use of resources in a market economy, and (5) the advantages of exchange or trade.

E. *The Free Enterprise Economy and the Centrally Planned Economy Compared:* The student may believe that a free market economy depends for its operation on, and emphasizes, the "baser" motives of man, while the centrally planned economy relies on, and fosters, the "good" in mankind. He may also believe that the centrally planned economy can somehow avoid the problems associated with scarcity.

It is not "cooperation" or any natural harmony of interests that resolves the problems of what, how, and for whom in any economy, but "coordination." Regardless of the societal arrangement under which they live, all individuals have a desire for self-betterment. Those who favor a free economy believe that coordination is best achieved by channeling these desires through inducements rather than by central direction or force.

What I hope the student has learned at the end of this section is that (1) the fact of scarcity cannot be eliminated by the manner in which an economy is organized, (2) both systems must provide incentives for their members, and (3) neither system is "pure."

At the end of the unit the class discusses and analyzes such questions and problems as: (1) with the advance of atomic science and other fields of technology, the productive powers of our economy may grow until we have an economy of real abundance; (2) by resolving "the economic problem" the free-enterprise economy will assure each individual an equal share in the goods and services he helps to produce; (3) although economists usually agree on economic theory, they should be ready and willing to tell society how the world "ought" to be; (4) if a society chooses to honor private ownership of resources (private property), a market mechanism will result; (5) the solution to the "what" problem in a free enterprise system is directly related to the solution of the "for whom" problem; (6) if people wanted for others rather than for themselves, scarcity would be eliminated; (7) the institution of "free trade" (willing exchange) increases the total output that is available from given resources.

As already noted most (4) of these statements are false. It may also be noticed that these statements not only make excellent discussion questions to discover whether the student is getting a "feel" for economics, but they also make good test questions.

At this point the main idea the teacher is trying to get across is that regardless of how altruistic a society may be or how affluent it may become, as long as the wants of society—the uses to which resources may be put—are greater than the available resources, scarcity will exist; and it is scarcity with which the study of economics concerns itself.

In addition, the teacher is trying to establish the "scientific habit of mind" (question 3), and to stimulate the students to examine their understanding of the workings of a free-enterprise economy (questions 2, 4, and 5). Question 7 examines their understanding of the advantages of exchange and trade. There are many other questions of a similar nature that can be employed by the teacher, questions that examine the student's ability to apply rather than to memorize concepts.

After this unit it may be worthwhile to schedule a panel discussion on "What Should Be the Economic Goals of a Democratic Society?" and a formal debate on "Resolved that power resources should be developed by private as opposed to state enterprise." The instructor might suggest selected readings in Shelley M. Mark and Daniel M. Slate (eds.), *Economics in Action* (Belmont, Calif.: Wadsworth, 1962) and Campbell R. McConnell (ed.), *Economic Issues* (New York: McGraw-Hill, 1966).

In *Part Two* I attempt to teach the principles of the market mechanism, the functions performed by the price mechanism, and the effects of interferences with the price mechanism.

A. *Principles upon Which a Market Economy Operates to Allocate Resources and Distribute Income:* In a market economy prices play a major role in the solution of the problems of what, how, and for whom, i.e., they allocate resources and distribute income. To understand the operation of a market economy one must understand the principles upon which the price mechanism operates. Prices are established by the forces of supply and demand, and an understanding of the price mechanism requires an understanding of these forces. While the demand for and supply of different products differ in many respects, they have in common certain abstract characteristics. What the teacher wants the student to learn is (1) the concept of demand and the characteristic that all demands have in common, mainly that the attitude of people toward all economic goods is the same in that more of a good will be purchased at lower prices than at higher prices; (2) the concept of supply, which at this point is sufficient to understand that the basic characteristic of supply is that more will be offered at higher prices than at lower prices; and (3) equilibrium price, that is, given the attitudes of buyers and sellers about a good and its price (demand and supply), there is a (conceptual) equilibrium price that will reconcile these conflicting attitudes.

To teach the concepts and characteristics of demand and supply the instructor can choose five to ten students (who like to eat chocolate) and ask them how many bars of a given description of chocolate each would be willing to buy at various prices. The instructor and class will notice that at higher prices fewer of the candy bars are demanded than at lower prices. He can then ask the class if this is a coincidence. Some will of course say yes, but there is always someone (regardless of the level of the class) who will point out that at lower prices one can bring in new uses for the good. For example, one boy who was running for boys' league president stated that at "high" prices he would buy only enough to eat himself, but at one cent per bar he would buy "enough to give to his friends and future constituents." The student is illustrating the main characteristic of demand, stated geometrically, the law of downward sloping demand. If the class is average or above average the instructor can illustrate the concept with a demand curve that ⌐‿‿‿ᵒ slopes downward to the right. The instructor can use the same example (candy bars) to show the characteristics of supply and the way the equilibrium (market) price is established.

B. *The Functions of Market Price:* Market prices perform two basic functions. They "ration" the goods and services in existence at any one time among the possible uses and users for those goods and services, and they "allocate" resources into their possible uses over a period of time, that is, they bring about "change" in the system. What the teacher wants the student to learn is: (1) *the rationing function of price.* There are many possible ways of performing this rationing function, each method containing an implicit or explicit standard for determining what and whose wants are to be satisfied. No particular method is the best *per se.* Market price is *one* way of rationing goods among their possible uses. The standard involved in this method is the ability to pay and the willingness to pay for the goods. It is an "impersonal" method of rationing goods (the teacher can use the example of Rose Bowl tickets to show other ways of rationing a good). (2) *The allocation function of price.* A market economy relies on the search for gain (profit) on the part of resource owners to accomplish this end, the desire to achieve profit and avoid loss. Profits and losses are the result of two sets of prices, the price the firm receives for its products and the price it pays for resources used to produce what it sells (its costs). The "price" of a product reflects the value that demanders place on those resources in *other* uses.

At this point the instructor can discuss the often misunderstood economic principles of (1) profit as a cost, (2) the meaning of "economic" profit and loss, and (3) economic profits and losses and allocation.

C. *Interferences with the Price Mechanism:* Interferences with the price mechanism can take many forms, either public or private. Such interferences may or may not be desirable, but they do have certain predictable results. What the instructor wants the student to learn is (1) the effects of price ceilings and price floors on the rationing function of price, (2) the effects of price ceilings, price floors, and private interferences on the allocation functions of price, and (3) alternatives to establishing price ceilings and price floors.

At the end of this unit the student will have learned concepts that enable him to discuss and analyze such issues as (1) alternative methods to solving the California water shortage, (2) alternative solutions to the farm problem, and (3) the effects of minimum wage legislation. There are many other problems and issues to which the student can apply the tools of supply and demand. What is important is that the instructor has not told the students what he thinks ought to be but rather has given them the tools they can use to come to their own conclusions.

At the end of this unit the teacher might schedule a debate on "Resolved that 90 per cent of parity should be established" or "Resolved that direct payments to farmers should be eliminated"; or "Resolved that the federal government should pass a 'right-to-work' law." A panel discussion might also be scheduled to observe how the class utilizes the principles they have learned in analyzing the question: —Is automation a threat to employment in the long run?

I would advise assigning readings in the books of readings by Mark and Slate (*Economics in Action*) and McConnell (*Economic Issues*).

In *Part Three* I attempt to teach the principles of the operation of different types of markets, the economic scientists' models of markets, and the principles of rational decision-making.

A. *General Principles of the Operation of Different Types of Markets:* Markets can be classified as "competitive" and "non-competitive." Most real world markets are non-competitive in the strict sense of the word, but it is useful to understand the abstract characteristics of each type separately and the manner in which these market types perform the functions of allocation and distribution. What the instructor hopes the student will understand at the end of this section of the course is the essence of competitive and non-competitive markets and the sources of non-competitive (monopoly) power.

B. *Specific Models of Market Performance—Long-run Analysis:* As part of his set of analytical tools, the economist has developed rigorous models of the different types of markets. These abstract models are not exactly like the real world, but they do provide the economist with a means of analyzing and predicting real world events. The models contain the abstract characteristics common to individual suppliers (firms) and the abstract characteristics common to industries made up of these firms. Four basic industry types are used, two of the polar-extreme types and two of the "in between" (more realistic) types. What the teacher wants the student to learn is (1) the model of the individual supplier—the firm and its costs including the concept of fixed costs, variable costs, and the general effect of costs on decisions, and (2) models of performance of industry types—perfect competition, (perfect) monopoly, monopolistic competition, and oligopoly.

C. *The Principles of Rational Decision-making:* In order to complete the models of firm and industry performance, it is necessary to develop the concept of marginalism, to relate marginal to average, and to explain the universal principles of maximizing behavior. What the instructor wants the student to learn is (1) the meaning of marginal, (2) the relation between marginal and average, (3) the universal principle of maximization, (4) firm behavior and maximization, and (5) a synthesis of the model of maximization of the perfectly competitive firm and the long-run behavior of the perfectly competitive industry.

At the end of this unit the students have learned concepts that will enable them to discuss such issues as the effects of different kinds of taxes on different market structures, government regulation of monopoly, the role of administered prices in our economy, the effects of advertising on economic efficiency, and an analysis of price wars.

After this unit it may be worthwhile to schedule a panel discussion on whether corporate concentration is compatible with a free society. The instructor might also have a debate on "Resolved that labor unions should be subject to anti-trust laws."

In *Part Four* I attempt to teach the meaning and functions of money, the monetary system, and the principles of commercial and central banking.

A. *Money—Its Nature and Functions:* "Money" can be and has been almost anything. It is important to understand the basic nature of money, the factors that make it money, and the role it plays in the functioning of the economy. The principles and ideas the teacher hopes his students will learn include (1) real and money wealth, (2) the evolution of money, and (3) the role of money in the economic process, that is, how money permits increased specialization but can lead to instability.

B. *The Principle of Commercial Banking:* The money supply of the United States consists of two types: something people call "cash" and something known as checking accounts or "demand deposits." Assuming the existence of some form of "cash"—hard money or government issued currency—a firm known as a "bank" comes into existence. This firm will have assets and liabilities (things it owns or controls and things it owes). The bank will attract "primary" deposits of cash. It can lend this cash or, as will happen, it can lend demand deposits. When it does this it "creates" money—it assumes the "commercial banking function." The *use* of this money by individuals transfers ownership of the demand deposits. Repayment of loans "destroys" money (demand deposits). Three basic factors operate to limit the ability of banks to create demand deposits: the "cash drain," the "reserve requirement," and the existence of more than one bank in the economy. The latter factor limits only the ability of the single bank to expand, not the ability of the banking *system* to expand. What the teacher wants the student to understand at the end of this section is (1) the evolution of demand deposits as money and (2) the limits to expansion of demand deposits.

C. *The Central Banking Principle:* Most if not all of the "difficulties" the student sees with commercial banks "creating" money are solved by the introduction of a "central" bank. The relationship between the central bank and the commercial banking system can be illustrated by examining the structure and activities of the United States' central bank—the Federal Reserve System. What the teacher wants the student to learn is (1) the reasons for the evolution of the Federal Reserve System and (2) the relation of the Federal Reserve System to the commercial banking system (the mechanics of issuance and return of cash, the mechanics of the issuance of reserves, and the mechanics of monetary control).

At the end of this unit the student may attempt to evaluate historically the performance of the Federal Reserve System, the alternative monetary policies aimed at controlling inflation and deflation, and whether monetary policy really works. The instructor might schedule a debate or discussion on whether "tight" money is stifling our economic growth.

In *Part Five* I attempt to teach the determinants of the level of national income, production and employment, and the principles of international trade.

A. *National Income and Employment:* Whereas in Part Three I was concerned with the principles upon which a market economy solves the problems of what to produce, how to produce, and for whom to produce—the composition of national output—in this section I am concerned with the factors that affect the level or amount of production and employment that takes place in a market economy. What the instructor may attempt to teach is (1) the meaning of income, output, and employment; (2) the factors affecting the level of income and employment (including definitions of the types of demand and of saving and the general factors influencing each type of demand); and (3) the importance of investment—the condition of equilibrium, fluctuations in employment and production, and investment, saving, and growth.

In discussing income or employment theory the instructor is concerned with analyzing the factors that influence the level of aggregate demand; thus he must analyze the factors that affect each of the components of aggregate demand. This includes consumption spending, investment spending, government spending, and foreign spending. He can utilize these components to explain the process of inflation, deflation, and Keynes' multiplier.

B. *The Economist's Analytical Models of Income, Employment, Saving, and Investment:* This section I teach only in the honors class. It employs more precise and involved models than those used in the previous section to analyze the factors that affect the level of income, employment, and output, and to explain and analyze the effects of saving and investment.

C. *The Principles of International Trade:* The reasons for international trade are essentially the same as the reasons for trade between regions within a country and between individuals in a country. The main "complication" that arises in international trade does so because more than one type or means of payment is involved. Two countries can benefit from trade even though one has an absolute advantage in producing everything, if the other country has a comparative advantage in producing anything. Exchange can increase the total output that is available.

Ultimately payment must take place in the form of goods and services, but proximately it takes place in "money." Trade creates a demand for the currency of the selling country and a supply of the currency of the buying country. Foreign exchange rates are the result of this demand and supply. The balance of payments of a nation indicates how it "stands" relative to the rest of the world. Various factors operate to adjust one nation's trade relations with the rest of the world: the market mechanism in the form of exchange rates, internal price levels, and national income, as well as discriminatory policies in the form of exchange (price) controls.

What the teacher wants the student to understand in this particular section is (1) the principles of absolute and comparative advantage and (2) the means of payment.

At the end of this unit the students will have learned concepts that will enable them to discuss (1) the different kinds of inflation (e.g., wage induced and seller inflation), (2) alternative government policies to combat inflation, (3) the question of whether the business cycle has been or will be conquered, (4) whether tax policy should stimulate consumption or investment, (5) gold and the United States' balance of payments, and (6) the advantages and disadvantages of flexible exchange rates. The teacher might schedule a discussion on whether deficit spending can cure our economic ailments and/or a discussion on the relative merits of monetary versus fiscal policy in promoting economic growth and combating inflation. The instructor might also schedule a debate on "Resolved that an international system of flexible exchange rates should be established." *Economics in Action* by Mark and Slate will also prove useful during this section.

FUNDAMENTALS OF DEBATE

I. PURPOSE OR OBJECTIVE

A. General purpose of debate

B. *Objective of affirmative* (burden of proof)
   1. Must present a prima facie (on first appearance) case.
   2. Must show that status quo is undesirable, inefficient, etc., indicating a need for change.
   3. If affirmative fails to present a prima facie case, the debate can stop there—the negative has won the debate before it has said a word.
   4. After affirmative has shown there is a need for a change, they must present a plan.
      a. The plan must be practical and practicable.
      b. They must show how their plan will alleviate the evils they have presented.
   5. If the negative admits that a problem exists but shows that the affirmative's plan will not solve that problem, the negative has won.
   6. Must show that the negative is not solving the problem and that it cannot under the status quo.

C. Objective of negative
   1. Must merely refute those arguments presented by the affirmative.
      a. Show that the evidence is inadequate, the reasoning illogical, or

    b. Show that the affirmative has not identified the real issues in the debate.

2. Can show that the status quo is sufficient, i.e., no need for a change.
3. Can show that the real need is for a modification of the status quo and not the type of radical change that would be brought about by the affirmative's plan.
4. Can admit there is a need for a change, but present a counterproposal (in which case they now assume the burden of proof).

II. HOW TO PRESENT A PRIMA FACIE CASE

A. Must identify the real issues (inherent in topic).

B. Must establish contentions (should contain or relate to issues).

C. Must substantiate contentions.
   1. Via evidence
     a. Fact
       1. Statistics
       2. Observed phenomena
     b. Opinion
       1. Expert
       2. Lay (weak evidence)
       3. Personal (weak evidence)
   2. Via logic
     a. Inductive
     b. Deductive
     c. Causal
     d. Analogy

III. HOW THE NEGATIVE REFUTES A PRIMA FACIE CASE

A. Show that the affirmative has not established a clearcut (prima facie) need for a change in the status quo.

B. Show that the disadvantages of the affirmative plan would outweigh any of the advantages.

C. Negative has two methods.
   1. Hit the affirmative at the foundation or crux of its arguments by disproving its contentions.

2. If not, refute each sub-point of each contention until the contentions fall.

D. Negative has two weapons.
 1. Refute affirmative's use of evidence as inadequate.
    a. Is it reliable?
    b. Is it based on sufficient samples?
    c. Is it quantitative as well as qualitative?
    d. Is it relevant?
    e. Is it honest?
 2. Refute affirmative's use of logic.
    a. Does the logic support the contentions?
    b. Does it lead to the conclusions advocated?

E. Negative defends the status quo.
 1. Show that the status quo is working.
 2. Show that with certain modifications it could work.
 3. Show that the difficulties presented by the affirmative are not inherent in the status quo.
 4. Show that even if these difficulties did exist, the status quo is still better than the affirmative's program.

IV. MECHANICS OR PROCEDURE OF DEBATE (formal rules govern these procedures).

A. Constructive speeches (8 minutes each).
 1. First speech is always given by affirmative; it is the only prepared speech.
    a. Introduces topic.
    b. Defines terms.
    c. States contentions of affirmative and supports them.
    d. Tells what his colleague will do.
 2. First Negative.
    a. Accepts or rejects the terms as defined by the affirmative.
    b. Refutes need established by affirmative.
    c. Supports his own case for the status quo.
 3. Second Affirmative.
    a. Reconstructs affirmative case for need.

        b. Refutes negative case.

        c. Presents a plan.

    4. Second Negative.

        a. Refutes affirmative case.

        b. Resubstantiates negative case.

B. Rebuttal speeches (4 minutes each; no new contentions).

    1. First Negative.

        a. Continues to refute what his partner has missed.

        b. Shows how affirmative has failed to support a prima facie case for a change according to its plan.

    2. First Affirmative.

        a. Reconstructs (resubstantiates) affirmative case by picking out the *real issues* and shows how the Affirmative has successfully dealt with the need it established.

    3. Second Negative.

        a. Has the affirmative really identified the crucial issues? Shows how the affirmative has failed to do this.

        b. Summarizes negative case.

    4. Second Affirmative.

        a. Summarizes case.

        b. Shows how case still stands and why Affirmative has won.

RESULTS OF A SCIENTIFIC APPROACH TO THE TEACHING OF ECONOMICS

The main outcome of this approach was an increase in the responsiveness of the students. The average and the gifted students were challenged and at first frightened by the prospect of having to apply rather than regurgitate what they had learned. In the beginning many had difficulties in answering questions they really knew. They would parrot back some section of a lecture that had nothing to do with the question asked. By the fifth week most of them had gotten the knack of not being afraid to think and were really gratified to find that they could put together concepts in analyzing a problem.

It is interesting to note that several students who were temporarily suspended from school for one reason or another (often obstreperous behavior) made an effort to be on school grounds and at the windows of the classroom during the regular class period in order that they would not miss a class session. I would attribute this not so much to any other type of motivation than that the students felt flattered at having their thoughts and views considered sufficiently important and valued to be solicited.

Since my senior year in college I have firmly believed that economics could and should be taught in the high school, and my experiences in the teaching of economics have reinforced this attitude.

I helped make up the tests that one professor administered to his U.C.L.A. sophomore class which contained more than two hundred students. I also administered these tests to my own students (some essay tests and some objective tests) and the results of the high school as compared to the college students were as follows: The high school class with average students came out approximately the same as the U.C.L.A. students although the average high school class had a lower percentage of "A's." The academically enriched and the honor students had approximately the same percentage of "A's" as the U.C.L.A. students but had a larger percentage of "B's" and no "D's" or "F's."

I think teaching economics in the high school is an exciting and exhilarating experience partly because of the immediate feedback from the students. If they do not understand, they grimace and make faces of agony whereas the college student has developed more sophistication and will usually smile no matter how baffled he may be. The high school student through his responses inadvertently teaches the teacher how to teach.

Questions for Discussion

1. Do you agree with the writer's statement that " . . . the teaching of economics at the secondary level leaves much to be desired" or are you more optimistic about the present state of the subject?

2. If you agree with the writer as quoted in question 1, why do you feel that we face the problems we do in the subject of economics as taught at the secondary level?

3. Do you agree with the writer in advocating a "scientific approach" to the teaching of economics?

4. If you agree, what do you see as the characteristics of a scientific approach to the teaching of economics?

5. Do you think economics as a subject-matter field should be an elective area of the social studies curriculum? How would you defend the point of view that it should be required?

6. Do you feel that economics should be taught according to the interdisciplinary or multidisciplinary approach?

10

INQUIRY AS A PROCESS IN THE LEARNING OF ECONOMICS

JOHN A. NELSON

Economics has been at best the most misunderstood area in the social studies curriculum. This is ironic in view of each individual's almost complete involvement in economic decisions and structure from the "cradle to the grave." The problem appears to be three dimensional: economics as a field of study is not well understood by teachers and curriculum experts; the nature and extent of the mutual interdependence dictated by the nation's socioeconomic organization is largely unrecognized; and thus few citizens are being offered an opportunity to grasp the economic concepts and trends necessary for survival during an era of dynamic change. Dr. Nelson provides valuable insight into a teaching methodology that should contribute greatly to the solution of this problem.

If one reviews the secondary school curriculum over the last several decades he will find periods of emphasis on the teaching of economics and at other times an apparent neglect of the subject as such. A closer look at the content and teaching procedures of such courses reveals a lack of a sustained success in teaching this field. It should be pointed out that while the problems involved in the teaching of economics are not peculiar to that subject but are common to all the social studies, they are more obvious in courses such as economics which are not required courses and where student dissatisfaction is demonstrated by a lack of enrollment.

The attempt to make high school students professional economists rather than economic literates at the secondary school level has led to courses that include content typified by complicated, theoretical marginal cost curves and procedures that ignore human motivations which might spark the interest of students. There has been a reluctance on the part of the teacher to utilize the excellent experiences of the students for fear that it will appear to be other than a "solid" course. We have taught economics with a seeming ignorance of the psychological and sociological factors related to learning. Another reason for the cyclical lack of success in the teaching of economics is exemplified by those who misunderstand the concept of "relevance" and teach economics in a manner which includes little of a substantive nature. Such approaches, in reality, are referred to as "Consumer Economics," thereby containing only areas such as the preparation of the family budget. This is not to say that such an area is not important, but it does not belong in a substantive course in economics.

It is important for teachers of economics to recognize that they need not change the basic content of a course in economics to make it overly complicated in order to "impress" or overly simplified to the extent that it removes the very heart of the subject.

Further complicating the problem is the fact that poor methodology is combined with the use of texts that give inadequate basic concepts and facts.

In a recent study made by the Textbook Committee of the Committee on Economic Education of the American Economic Association (1963)[1], professional economists assessed the economic content of twenty-four widely used high school textbooks in the social sciences and concluded "that the high school student whose knowledge of economics has been acquired through courses circumscribed by . . . [these] . . . textbooks . . . would be quite unprepared to cope understandingly with most problems of economic policy." More specifically, they found that ". . . (1) the emphasis is on understanding consumer economics rather than on understanding the functions of an economic system; (2) much that is significant is omitted, much that is included is relatively unimportant; (3) routine descriptions of how the economic system operates are more common than analysis of cause and effect relations, etc.; (4) when value judgments are made, they are not identified or examined as such; and (5) some errors of fact and analysis are present. In sum, descriptive and narrative material dominated the textbooks to such an extent that little opportunity was given for critical thinking, understanding, or the developing and testing of hypotheses."[2] There is very little reason to believe that these economists feel that all high school students should read in toto *Prosperity and Depression* by Gottfried Haberler or *Readings in the Theory of Income Distribution* by Howard Ellis (although some students could certainly benefit if they were directed toward certain sections of these and similar books).

In contrast to poor text materials is the series prepared

[1] Textbook Committee of the Committee on Economic Education of the American Economic Association, "Economics in the Schools," *American Economic Review,* LIII, No. 1, Part 2, Supplement (1963), pp. 1–27.
[2] B. G. Massialas and F. R. Smith, *New Challenges in the Social Studies* (Belmont, Calif.: Wadsworth, 1965).

by the Council for the Advancement of Secondary Education.[3]

In sum, the above is a plea for a recognition of the extent and limits of students' experiences and for the use of materials and methodology that will allow the discipline of economics to be understood. Perhaps the foregoing discussion has painted an overly discouraging picture. It should be pointed out, therefore, even though they are not too prevalent, some teachers of high school economics have sparked students to the excitement of the subject. Their success has been the result of several significant beliefs: (1) students can be trusted to develop correct answers for themselves; (2) learning is an internal process; (3) a teacher's role is that of a guider of learning who, at appropriate times, presents possible sources of information and alternative paths toward solutions of problems; (4) a teacher should be a sufficiently secure human being who is not threatened by, but, rather, enjoys seeing students arrive at solutions without the "expert" giving him the correct answer or the exact way to arrive at this end; (5) a teacher has a responsibility to capitalize on students' past experiences and to expose them to new experiences; and (6) a teacher must recognize and not be threatened by the fact that the inductive approach may well produce learners who will go beyond him in the development of economic concepts. These ideas are not new. In fact much has been written in this area by such outstanding educators as Clements and Fielder.[4] They are, however, apparently ignored as demonstrated by the unsophisticated level of the teaching of economics.

The above judgmental statements are not useful unless some specific examples of how economics might be taught

[3] See C.A.S.E. Economic Literacy Series (McGraw-Hill Book Company, 1960–1962). A revision of this series is currently in preparation.

[4] H. Millard Clements and William R. Fielder, "Social Studies: Design and Deception," *The Elementary School Journal,* Vol. 65, No. 2, 1964.

are given. The following discussion is based on the writer's experience as a teacher of economics in California schools. If a teacher selects *Changes in the American Economic System* as one area of economics to be studied, he must, at the outset, realize that he will not be doing justice to the subject if he gives merely an overly simplified explanation such as conditions changed throughout history, and as a result, the economic system changed. First of all, this is a very effective way of convincing students that the subject is boring. It is vital to develop an intrinsic interest on the part of students. There is no way to directly relate what happened historically to the lives of students today. The writer found that his students became interested when they recognized there were throughout history real live human beings who acted in certain ways as a result of particular physical and human factors. Being more specific, the writer generalized about the fact that the environment in which capitalism developed was greatly different from that in which we now live. He also generalized about how our present system originated in the Industrial Revolutions in Europe and the United States. Another generalization was that no single factor was responsible for the economic changes throughout history. All too often the above generalizations are expounded by the teacher, students are tested, and, if they can regurgitate them, there is an assumption that students understand the changes that have taken place in our economic system. What has actually happened is that students are not given the opportunity to intrinsically enjoy economics but rather they learn that it is an uninteresting area. If the teacher exposes students, through reading and discussion, to the actual events and conditions that made up the environment and injects human elements into the subject, he is doing economics some justice, but he is still falling short of the real possibilities.

The teacher who develops with students the motivations of human beings that resulted in their actions, and encourages students to discuss freely the same issues that were considered by people years ago will come closer to helping students really understand the subject. The development of economic studies which were the outgrowth of man's attempt to discover "natural laws" that govern the operation of society need not be an obscure approach. If one were consistent with the position taken above concerning an effective teacher, he would encourage and give every opportunity to students to discuss their feelings about such "natural laws." Students will then have some empathy with the economists of the classical school and, as a result, will learn about classical economics. If students really became involved in attempting to seek explanations of the European Industrial Revolution and its impact on society, they would be ready to read the writings of Ricardo, Mill, Malthus, Bentham, and other major classical economists. This procedure is quite different from having students exposed to the writings of these men without the necessary student involvement with the same factors the historical characters were concerned about.

Another mistake too often made is to have students exposed to, but *not really learn about,* the organized system of thought that was useful to the classical economists. If students are not allowed to relive the problems of the day as much as is possible, how can they possibly appreciate and really know the systems of thought that were developed by the classicists?

To expound to students that classical economists developed the concept that capitalism is based on the institution of private property which each person should be free to obtain to the extent of his ability and that protection is necessary to preserve life, liberty, and property could well end up as an empty and quickly forgotten concept. Even though you cannot place students in a time machine so they could easily relive those days, we can allow them to inductively realize how logical the position was for the classicists.

If we do not permit students to have this experience, we are only fooling ourselves if we think they can understand the emergence of the institutionalists or "nonclassical" economists.

If students have a real understanding of the environment of the classical period and the resulting beliefs and actions of human beings, they can come inductively to many of the conclusions of the institutionalists who faced a changing environment.

The writer found that students who really shared the feeling of the classicists and recognized the reasons for their conclusions could, when presented with the facts of increased specialization, concentration of economic power and interdependence, inductively develop the position of Veblen, Commons, and Mitchell.

Another area of economics that might be considered is the dealing with *determination of levels of economic activity in our system.* On the surface this would appear to be a topic that logically should not be considered by secondary school students because it is not a direct concern of theirs and should be left to those beings trained to be professional economists. To the extent that this is true or not would depend on the degree of involvement of students. The writer found it uncommon to find students who were not concerned with levels of economic activity, although they understand these levels in terms that may seem selfish or socially unsophisticated. Even if there is no apparent direct relationship to their level, there is no reason why a teacher cannot capture the imagination of students in the apparently theoretical problem and they in turn can realize an intrinsic excitement and enjoyment of becoming intellectually involved in a dynamic system. This can occur only if the necessary link to the student is made. One could make the generalization that the price level is related to the quantity of money, how fast it is spent, and the quantity of good available and exchanged. If not handled correctly this could appear to be a sterile, uninteresting statement. However, if one developed, with the students, the idea that the price they pay for something is related to how much money they have and how much of the item is available, there is a better chance that he will have an interest and appreciation for the concept involved. There is a still more effective way to teach the concept. The writer tried to inductively teach the concept by allowing considerable discussion based on student experiences, reinforced with appropriate readings from which students could develop the concept for themselves. The concept became theirs and was defended by them as something important. This approach is quite different from the first approach suggested.

Exploration of another area of economics may be useful in explaining the approach that has been strongly recommended in this selection. Within that area of economics known as Money and Banking, there is an almost inevitable consideration of price level and the value of money. Perhaps the easiest way to handle the topic would be to give students conclusions in the form of generalizations and then furnish them with the equation of exchange ($MV = PT$). From this the students might be able deductively to show that the generalizations are correct and the equation is operational. Have the students really learned about price level and the value of money? It is doubtful. They could probably repeat what was said, but a more thorough investigation would show the knowledge is still with the teacher and the text and does not really belong to the student. It is difficult to understand why we are so compelled to give students the "correct" conclusions instead of having the students develop them for themselves, thus giving a much greater assurance that they have learned, which is, by necessity, an internal operation. A teacher cannot "learn" a student about price levels and value of money. If a student learns he will be able to inductively arrive at the conclusions that we are so compelled to give him. Perhaps a more specific example will explain this position. Students are aware that there is a given stock of money (M), that money is spent a number of times over a given period, that goods and services have a price (P), and that there is a given quantity of goods and services. Through discussion the writer discovered that students were able to verbalize these obvious factors and give examples from their own experiences. This process must, however, be done developmentally. It is not difficult to motivate students to explain from their own experiences that there seems to be a relationship between the price level and the value of money. There might be a fear on the part of the teacher that the students might arrive at the overly simplified formula M = P. During this inductive process it should be an exciting thing to see students develop, from their discussion, that there is a strong relationship between M and P. Granted, we do not want the student to stop here and have an overly simplified idea of the relationship. It will, however, disturb the inductive process to have the teacher "fill in" the rest of the equation for the students. Intelligently handled, the process will be that in which students, through reading and discussion, recognize the inadequacy of the overly simplified idea that M = P. Once they recognize that it is inadequate and does not satisfy them as a sufficient explanation, they then are ready to explore, reason, and find those other elements that make the conclusion more reasonable. It does not take much suggesting on the part of the teacher for students to realize that the stock of money (M) is not really static, but rather is somewhat larger since it changes hands and is spent a number of times. Students will reap considerable satisfaction from having "discovered" the sophistication that adding the V gives to the concept of the quantity of money. The same kind of process can be employed, having students develop inductively the idea that price (P) alone does not explain enough, but that one must consider the number of goods and services sold (T) if the general concept of the average price (PT) is to have meaning.

It should not bother a teacher that students use terms not found in typical college economics texts. In fact, it would prove how inductively they have learned if they can explain the concept of MV = PT in terms unique to their ways of expressing things. The greatest test of the success of this inductive process would be to see the break-through where students find new conclusions with greater sophistication. To the extent that students come up with ideas concerning additional refinements that go beyond those which the teacher has considered, the teacher has been a success. All too often teachers are bothered by students who learn through the process of discovery rather than allowing the teacher to be the fountain of knowledge.

An assumption in the above discussion has been that students should develop concepts inductively, using the resources the teacher can furnish while basically relying on the students' abilities to reason. A student is going to reason within his present realm of experience. Unfortunately, we do not see often enough that concepts do not have to be crammed down students' throats but are reasonable within their perspective. An example is the concept of *liquidity in relationship to the equation of exchange.* The teacher could give a formal definition of liquidity in an economic context, explain that a desire for liquidity would be the number of times a dollar is spent (V) and would therefore play a role in a new balance between MV and PT. This would take a very short time to explain and students could be asked to read a good explanation in any economics text-book. Once this is done there might be the mistaken assumption that students understand the concept. There is a good chance that they haven't really learned the concept but have accepted the teacher's and text's expert explanation. It will take longer, but there is a much better chance that the student will have learned the concept if the teacher would allow him the opportunity to discuss within his own experiences his encounters with the choice between having his wealth in a form in which he can get his hands on it (high liquidity) or in a form that he may have to wait for it for a while (low liquidity). He then will understand the human motivations involved with V and consequently with all the elements in the equation of exchange. The same process could be productively used for each of the other elements, M, P, and T.

Somewhat parenthetically, but not without importance, a comment should be made concerning the appropriateness of the approaches discussed in this article to "slow," "average," and "fast" students. There is no reason why a teacher who recognizes the specific methods appropriate for students with different learning rates cannot use the suggested approach with any student who is educable. There is the unfortunate tendency to reject this approach because of several myths. One of these is that slower students need specifics, which, stated another way, means teaching them deductively. Slower students can reason and receive the same satisfactions from an inductive process as can faster students. On the other hand, the approach may be rejected for fast-learning students on the basis that they need to get into more complex economic concepts and, therefore, should not waste their time in an inductive approach. It is true that they should not be held back and this does not need to happen. They can move more rapidly toward *their* conclusions than slower students and consequently no time needs to be wasted.

In summary, the broad objective of this selection was to raise some issues about the approaches to teaching economics. There was deliberately no attempt to discuss appropriateness of areas in economics to be taught or exact methodology to be used. Assuming the teacher of economics has had good preparation in the subject, his decisions as to which areas to emphasize and which to de-emphasize should not be of too great a concern. Also, assuming intelligence and inventiveness, the exact particular methods to be used need not be of great concern. The crucial question is: what approach will make the content and methods most effective? The position taken in this paper has been that if we practice what we know about learning, we, as teachers, will guide a student toward certain directions, and that effective learning will be realized only if it takes place inductively. This approach can be accepted readily by some but this writer is fearful that it may be a threat to the teacher who feels he does not have time to allow such a process or that the approach will not allow him to show students that he knows in advance what students will eventually learn for themselves through his guidance. It could also be a threat to that teacher who cannot tolerate students possibly arriving at concepts that go beyond those which he himself has not considered. To the extent that we realize the study of economics is not an end in itself, but is a tool that may allow students to gain some intrinsic enjoyment of knowledge and as a tool of inquiry, it is essential that the inductive approach be seriously considered as an effective way to accomplish these goals.

Questions for Discussion

1. What do you see as the relationship in economics between substantive content and teaching methodology?

2. Do you consider the approach that this teacher used achievable?

3. What reservations do you personally have about implementing the writer's approach?

4. Would you prefer to teach a class in economics or would you rather incorporate economic concepts within the broad area of social studies? What implications does the writer give on this subject?

5. Evaluate the relevance of the writer's approach for the future professional economist compared to the person not going into this area.

6. How would *you* implement economic concepts advocated by the writer?

A COURSE IN PROBLEMS OF AMERICAN DEMOCRACY

GERALD LEINWAND

The problem-solving approach to the teaching of social studies is best realized in the Problems of Democracy course usually taught at the twelfth grade level of the social studies curriculum. Mr. Leinwand suggests that students should generate their own group of significant problems in American democracy. These problems might then be investigated through the use of committees. Methods of critically appraising sources could then be developed and finally realized in individual term papers. The course is aimed at helping the student acquire ". . . a greater awareness of the current national and international political, social, and economic problems America faces."

A Problems of American Democracy course was offered for the first time in our school in February, 1961. It consisted of a single class, largely experimental in nature, in which a trial-and-error procedure was adopted to determine the most satisfactory techniques for such a course. With a term's experience to guide us, and with the cooperation of the department chairman and the school administration, a vastly improved program consisting of two classes was offered in February, 1962.

Eligible for the senior course in Problems of American Democracy were those twelfth-grade students who had already completed the final term of required social studies (in our school it is American History II) and who had passed the regents in American History and World Backgrounds III. The course is a full major, but is not an honor class. It may be elected by competent but not necessarily outstanding social studies students.

AIMS OF THE COURSE

The Problems of American Democracy course aims to provide students with a greater awareness of the current national and international political, social, and economic problems America faces. It seeks to provide opportunities for more thorough investigation into the origin, background, and current status of these problems as well as to develop techniques of research in original and secondary sources that may help to provide greater insight into them. The course also aims to provide pre-college experiences in such areas as research techniques, and in independent readings based on a bibliography of pertinent materials available in our library and prepared by our librarian.

PROCEDURES AND TECHNIQUES

Early in the term, beginning with the second or third sessions of the classes, the students were asked to select a group of significant problems in American democracy about which they thought they should know more. All suggestions were listed on the board and later mimeographed and distributed. With a copy of the tentative list of topics in the hands of each student, the problems were reworded, refined, combined, or deleted as necessary, and finally the following problems for the term's work were selected:

Is the United Nations doomed to failure?
Has enough progress been made in Civil Rights and Civil Liberties?
How should America respond to the Common Market?
What road to international peace should America take?
Can capitalism survive the challenge of communism?
What major problems are faced by American labor today?
How successful is America's foreign policy?
Do we need a department of urban affairs?
Is there an educational crisis?
Do we need an expansion of Federal social services?
Do extreme right-wing societies threaten American democracy?
How good is American scientific progress?
What effect do modern methods of communication have on American youth?

It was recognized that probably not all of these topics could be covered with the same degree of thoroughness. However, it was decided to keep the list reasonably large so that flexibility might be maintained throughout the term and so that there would be a choice of topics during the term as well as at the beginning.

The students, organized into five committees, chose those five problems on which they preferred to work first. This depended not only on their own interests, but also on what was considered to be most vital in terms of current developments. An attempt was made to permit students to select those areas in which they preferred to work, but in some cases, to make the committees optimum in size and to distribute talent and opportunities for leadership more equitably, students were simply assigned to those topics where they were needed. Generally, they accepted the assignments without complaint.

The committees were told that the object of their report to the class was to summarize and crystallize the topics which they had chosen. The reports were to show evidence of an active and spontaneous exchange of ideas based on substantial planning, reading, and study rather than a series of individual reports. Frequent meetings were held with the first committee to report in order to set a good example for the others. While the committees were preparing their oral contributions, formal lessons relating to each of the problem areas were presented.

During the course of the term, many of the committees presented their reports in interesting ways. The U.N. committee interviewed an official of that body. The committee on education interviewed a number of students whose past schooling had been in Europe, India, or the Far East.

The first unit, which lasted about two weeks, was devoted to consideration of research techniques and the nature of historical criticism. Students were taught that "in historical studies doubt is the beginning of wisdom." [1] Elementary forms of criticism were developed and the precautions to be taken in using such sources as diaries, memoirs, government documents, and public speeches were considered.

In subsequent class lessons students were taught how to sift the more scholarly sources of information from the more superficial ones. They were given illustrations of correct and incorrect documentation, shown the use and application of footnotes, and the form for bibliographical entries. Students were taught to take notes and to outline, and group and individual guidance was given in the choice of topics for term papers. Before the final presentation of

[1] Allen Johnson, *The Historian and Historical Evidence* (New York: Scribner's, 1928), p. 50.

the term papers, each student was required to submit an annotated bibliography and an outline of the proposed study.

Although a text was provided each student, greater reliance was placed on related outside reading and on *The New York Times* and its supplements. The newspaper was delivered daily to each student and each Monday was set aside as a current-affairs day. The topic for the day was agreed upon a week ahead of time, and the assignment was to be attentive to newspaper and editorial accounts on that topic.

In this way, the class considered such topics as United States policy toward Cuba, the need for an Urban Affairs Department, the question of the resumption of atmospheric atomic testing, the prospects for peace between France and Algeria, the Geneva disarmament conference, to mention but a few. Sometimes these lessons were teacher led, sometimes student led. On other occasions a single editorial on the assigned topic was evaluated, while occasionally a tape recording of a television or radio program was replayed for the groups and evaluated by them.

Each Friday of the week was library day. The classes and teacher met in the library where the committees scheduled to report planned their work and made use of the library facilities in so doing. Others spent their time working on term papers, reading generally on the problems under consideration, or doing their committee studies. Teacher help, when and where needed by the students, was always available. The students appeared to welcome the opportunity of using the library since during those periods it was used exclusively by the "problems" classes. Students particularly welcomed individual conferences on troublesome problems involving methods of working on term papers, evaluating sources of information, presenting committee reports, or on obscure points made during the lessons. To keep "boon-doggling" to a minimum, students were required to submit an annotated reading list, by date, of what they had read or worked on during each of the library periods.

Since an attempt was made to probe at greater depth and at greater length than is done in regular classes, where often similar but not identical topics are considered, the informal lecture was found to be the most effective device for imparting background data not easily or quickly mastered by the students. These lectures, carefully prepared, often reinforced with illustrative material in the forms of charts and graphs presented with the use of the overhead projector, and enthusiastically delivered, found a receptive audience. After an informal presentation of about fifteen or twenty minutes, the students were usually full of questions, contributions, contradictions, and objections, and a lively and informed discussion followed. These discussions usually suggested further avenues of investigation and further opportunities for committee activity.

Following these procedures and using these techniques, the Problems of American Democracy classes became a rewarding and informative experience for the entire group.

Questions for Discussion

1. Do you feel that the social studies curriculum should include a Problems of Democracy course or does such a course overemphasize the negative aspects of our form of government?

2. Do you feel that a Problems of Democracy course should be taught at the twelfth grade level or at another level of the curriculum?

3. Do you think the students should generate the problems they want to discuss or should this matter be left to the teacher's judgment?

4. Appraise the list of problems listed by the writer as to which problems you feel should be added and which should be excluded.

5. Would you use committees in the way the writer used them? Would you use committees at all?

6. What instructional materials would you use which the writer did not mention in this selection?

12

CURRENT EVENTS AND THE AMERICAN HISTORY COURSE

MURIEL MOULTON

The relationship between the teaching of current events and the teaching of history is both crucial and controversial. Some historians feel secondary school students should understand history in order to deal with current events; other historians feel the learning of history has intrinsic value and, therefore, they make no claim as to the value of learning history in order to better understand and operate in today's world. The following article should help the reader resolve this conflict for himself.

Teachers of American history are often asked to teach current events. It is difficult, however, to integrate into our study of the American past the events of the American present. All too often the "daily history" of which we are a part is seen as something quite separate from the study of American history. Added to an already overloaded schedule, current historical developments easily become a Friday-afternoon recitation unrelated to the study of American history. But is seems to me that current events could be used to help students understand what happened in the past. Conversely, an understanding of what happened in the past can be decisive in developing a mature view of the world that is whirling around them. If events taking place today could be related to what we study in school, American history as well as current events might achieve a new dimension.

In my eleventh-grade classes this year, I tried to develop some means of establishing those links between the past and the present which might give a new perspective to American history as well as to current events. In the earliest weeks of the course, I concentrated on using current events to clarify a basic historical problem: federalism. With a reasonably successful beginning, we could later move on to a more sophisticated integration of past and present events.

We began the semester with a consideration of the problems which existed in the relationship between Great Britain and the American colonies. It took two class periods to isolate the question: "How can the advantages of centralized power and local autonomy both be preserved?" In other words, the students were confronted with the problem of distinguishing between matters of local concern and those of national concern. The recurrence of various forms of this problem from colonial times right up to the present "states' rights" arguments was to form a focal point for the correlation of the past with current events, so careful foundations had to be laid.

The students read pertinent sections from *The Pocket History of the United States* by Allan Nevins and Henry Steele Commager, and *A Documentary History of the United States* by Richard Heffner, in addition to excerpts from the writings of John C. Miller, Merrill Jensen, Andrew C. McLaughlin, Alfred H. Kelly, and Winfred A. Harbison. The discussions accompanying these readings centered around the problem of distinguishing between local and central jurisdiction as expressed in the events surrounding the Declaration of Independence and the Articles of Confederation.

At the time of our study there were many news items and editorials in the press about the conflict between federal and local jurisdiction in the context of the civil rights effort and the amendatory efforts. Some of the more perceptive students began to mention some points of similarity between the newspaper stories and our study of the early federal question. The current situation gradually became a point of comparison in the discussions of the more remote issue of federalism in colonial and early American times. It was noteworthy that some of the chronically disinterested students responded with enthusiasm to this approach to history.

Pedagogically, this approach was particularly useful in helping the students to understand the implications of the federal problem. Charts and diagrams of the relationship between England and her American colonies, colorful examples like the Stamp Act and the Boston Tea Party, do not transmit the implications of the federal problem as effectively as the newspaper accounts of the clash between former Governor Wallace of Alabama and the late President Kennedy.

An example of using present-day news events to help develop a deeper historical insight can be seen in regard to the period surrounding the adoption of the Constitution of 1787. I have found that students are inclined to favor the democratic Jeffersonians and to look with distrust upon the aristocratic Hamiltonians. Students quickly work themselves into a superficial sympathy with the proponents of a position which they do not really understand. The vividness and contrast of the personalities of the protagonists obscure for too many students the import of the dispute. Without a more sound and practical understanding, it is folly to urge a "fair consideration of both sets of principles in view of the difference of the American society at the end of the eighteenth century." Students tend to like Jefferson, they tend to resist Hamilton. Yet it was democratic, egalitarian Jefferson who urged principles of decentralization. Today these principles are most generally associated with the conservative section of our society. The principles can be studied directly in contemporary context. The implications of Jefferson's and of Hamilton's position in regard to state and central power are too easily obscured by labels and by romanticism. Viewed in a contemporary setting whose reality is at times shockingly stark, the question of state and central jurisdiction is not so blithely answered.

I found that when I used current events in my American history courses, both to clarify a historical understanding as well as to increase understanding of some important modern affairs, it was necessary to alter my lesson plans drastically and often in order to take advantage of unanticipated opportunities. For example, we had made considerable progress on the exposition of the federal question. It had been my plan to proceed chronologically to the Louisiana Purchase, which I saw as a logical next focal point. However, on a Monday morning, several students brought in copies of a lengthy but well-written article which dealt with some proposed amendments to the Constitution. One of the proposed amendments would affect judicial review; another, apportionment. It seemed that an opportunity had arisen to study some important aspects of our government, as well as to familiarize ourselves with some current events. I had never met the author of the article, a professor of political science at a university in our city. After a brief phone conversation in which I explained to him what I was trying to do, he agreed to appear before each of my three classes in seminar sessions to discuss the article.

My students were impressed and flattered that a college professor would agree to spend a whole morning with them.

Almost all of them readily began the preparations for his visit. In Heffner and in Nevins and Commager we read about *Marbury* v. *Madison,* with special attention to the emergence of the policy of judicial review. We added to that some excerpts from *A Constitutional History of the United States* by Kelly and Harbison. It was like walking through sand for some of the more reluctant scholars, but I limited our preparations to three intensive days. The students' own feeling of responsibility to be "up" to the impending visit carried us through it without major casualty.

The actual sessions with our professor seem to have been well worth the effort. Obvious means of evaluation such as attentiveness, the tone and quality of the questions, "sitting in" on an extra session if a study hall coincided with a seminar session, and extending the question period into the lunch hour, all seemed to indicate that the episode was a valuable one. However, perhaps more significant was the recurring reference to "the article" or "the professor" in class discussions weeks and months later. In addition, of course, the students achieved a view of the amendatory procedure, described in the Constitution, as something which really happens; and most of them became cognizant of the judicial review as an active policy with a highly controversial background as well as a hotly contested future.

About mid-year I found an opportunity to use current events to infuse excitment into a historical situation which has usually seemed intolerably dull and remote to students. The relationship between the past and the present in this particular situation was reciprocal, as a matter of fact, because in this case a knowledge of what had happened in the past served to illumine a confusing series of recent events. The situation was the development of American political and strategic interests in the Pacific at the turn of the century. This, it seemed to me, could be considered the supreme test of the efficacy of bringing current events into the body of my American history course. I wished the students to understand some of the reasons for the development of American foreign policy at the turn of the century. I also wished them to be able to look at the current explosive situations in Cuba and Panama with some depth of understanding. That, of course, is a great deal to expect from fifteen-year-olds. I aimed for at least a knowledge of the vulnerability of our coastline before the Panama Canal was built, of the need for fueling stations in the Pacific, the role of American business interests, and of the conditions under which the *now* much disputed treaties with Cuba and Panama were consummated.

The Panama crisis developed while we were studying the economic philosophy of Andrew Carnegie. That was to lead into a broader study of the early twentieth century. It was the "right time" for Panama, though I hadn't planned to spend much time on the Pacific this year. I had planned to try to use the Cuban situation a little later, and let it go at that. However, this was an opportunity too good to miss. Since the situation had excitement inherent in it, I decided to provide a minimum of class time for it, presenting it instead, as a "special assignment." While "special assignments" often mean they will have to put in more work, students usually greet them with interest and enthusiasm. A "special assignment" usually means that there will be virtually no routine home work assignments, the possibility of group work, and probably some "released time" during the day for special research and group meetings.

Three categories of topics were established: "Samoa and Hawaii: Imperialist Beginnings"; "Cuba and the Philippine Islands"; and "Panama." Students in each class simply signed up to work on the topic in which they were most interested. In an attempt to insure practical grouping and to prevent unwieldy groups, I stipulated that no group have more than six members. I said that if more than six people signed up for any group, I would arbitrarily reassign them. I encouraged them to talk it over with their friends and to try to spread themselves more or less evenly. Each of my three classes was thus divided into three groups. Each group was to present a thirty-minute oral report and a written version of the oral report, not more than two type-written pages in length. Students were told that the oral report must be interesting as well as informative. Neither "gimmicky" materials nor mere statistics would be acceptable. It was suggested that they might think of the written reports in terms of what they would like the other group to write out to make it easier for them to evaluate the situation described in the reports. Students were also informed that written reports must be typed on a ditto master and handed in two days before the group's oral presentation. It was also required that the written report be in proper form, well written, and include a bibliography of the sources upon which both the oral and written reports were based.

The instructions for the special assignment also specified that the reports must deal with the following types of information: strategic significance of location; change in U.S. foreign policy reflected in relation to the country; general change in U.S. foreign policy and outlook; results of this new policy in the past and in recent events; economic interests involved; relation of the past to the present.

Students reacted in various ways to the requirement that in addition to their research in the microfilm library and in the *Readers' Guide to Periodical Literature* they must also spend some time discussing their topic with an "expert." I felt free to include this stipulation because our city has several excellent universities which harbor not only generous, cooperative teachers, but an abundance of capable graduate students. The latter are almost always willing to spend half an hour with a couple of enthusiastic teen-agers. Another reason for including interviews in the required research is that it adds excitement. Current periodicals and microfilmed newspapers are interesting and fun, of course, but none of these can compare with the excitement of a twenty- or thirty-minute chat with a graduate student who is devoted to the importance of his field of specialty. Academicians often tend to be proselytizers. They seem to be unable to resist the urge to convince all comers of the urgent importance of their particular phase of historical study. I have found it beneficial to expose my students to them.

The results of the project were encouraging. Of the nine groups (among the three classes) the work of five could easily be ranked as excellent; three as uneven, but generally well done; and one as quite poor. Three main criteria were used in judging the reports, both oral and written: (1) clarity of links between past and present; (2) accuracy and selection of historical and current factual material; and (3) organization.

That the students enjoyed and profited from the research they did was evident from the high academic quality of the reports and the good-humored fun with which they were presented. Bibliographies included magazines such as *Newsweek, The Reader's Digest, Time,* and others dating back to the 1930's; *The Outlook, The Review of Reviews,* dating back to the 1900's; *The Congressional Record, The Wall Street Journal,* and others of 1898, and a great variety of contemporary newspapers and magazines. The latter, supplying the current events and a good deal of interpretation, presented a new version of a familiar problem: conflicting information. We had met and dealt with conflicting information in other parts of the course, but had never confronted it in a modern setting. The students could understand without pain that older methods of news gathering were less reliable, or that the conflicting interpretations of the disputes between Andrew Johnson and the Radical Republicans must be viewed objectively. But it seemed quite difficult for many of them to accept that, even today, experts really do disagree about what is happening. The interviews proved especially useful in that regard. It would be unrealistic to expect that even the most highly motivated fifteen-year-old could produce an analysis of the Cuban or the Panamanian situations—with or without historical links! However, having flopped around in old and current publications for a while, they were able to bring some sensible questions to their interviews. Students were left almost completely on their own to find a suitable person to interview. My suggestions were limited to methods and procedure. Among the people interviewed by my students were college professors of American history, the dean of a college, a graduate student from Panama, and a former official of Castro's government, now teaching in a nearby college.

It seems evident that the projects themselves were a success. The students learned what they needed to learn to fulfill the requirements. They went considerably further than that, however. In general, they became interested in the development and conflicts presented in their topics, and, impelled by the urgency of the daily headlines, they seem to have brought to their reports a degree of enthusiasm and interest which, however desirable, can never be required—only hoped for.

A description of an attempt to include current events in the school year 1963–1964 cannot be complete without some mention of the tragic event—the assassination of President Kennedy on Friday, November 22, 1963. Any consideration of *using* this event in the ordinary sense of the word was out of the question. But I was not able to ignore it. We had all been together when it happened—crowded into the small Senior Room, stricken and silent as the television confirmed the news. I had seen "my" girls crying, "my" boys white-faced, all of them as frightened as I was. We had, indeed, shared a moment of tragedy. When we returned to school the following week, and I stood before my first class in the morning, I felt more clearly than I ever had before the urgent importance of my profession. They would soon lose their constraint, I knew. The stifling depression which had settled upon the nation would be thrown off by them first. But there would remain their question, and my responsibility to help them learn to find an answer, not only to the past, but more especially to the present.

Questions for Discussion

1. Do you feel that the teaching of current events is an appropriate part of any secondary social studies course?

2. If you answer number 1 in the affirmative, how would you relate the teaching of current events to the teaching of history? How would you relate the teaching of current events to the teaching of the social sciences?

3. What sources would you use to implement your approach to the teaching of current events?

4. What community resources would you like to use in implementing your approach to the teaching of current events?

5. What barriers do you feel may exist if you wish to implement the approach adopted by the writer?

13

A SOCIAL STUDIES SEMINAR FOR TWELFTH GRADE STUDENTS

DALE L. BRUBAKER

Although there are many extracurricular activities in the secondary school curriculum, few of these activities are designed for the intellectual life of the student. The following selection describes a social studies seminar held on a monthly basis in the homes of the teacher and his students. Paperback books were used and authors of such books were guests when possible. Although problems were encountered in holding the seminars, the writer is convinced that this approach is a much needed one in the social studies.

The social studies teacher fresh from his alma mater is frequently convinced that he has a new or unique approach which will make him a special kind of social studies teacher. Our beginning teacher needs to feel that his contribution will be important; so ego-building, fact or fancy, serves an important purpose. This is not to say that our new teacher lacks a certain apprehensiveness, a kind of anxiety that increases during the long summer before the first real teaching experience occurs.

This article describes the "unique" approach the writer introduced at Okemos High School, Okemos, Michigan. The sample treated—or mistreated—consisted of approximately one hundred high school seniors per year. The socio-economic background of the students was primarily upper middle class, with 80 to 90 per cent likely to enroll in college the following year. These students were members of a required government class. They were randomly assigned to the class since the school did not practice "ability grouping" in its social studies program.

In the fall of 1961 the teacher introduced a monthly seminar based on the following ground rules:

1. Seminars will be held at students' and the teacher's homes and will last from approximately 7:30 to 10:30 P.M.
2. Any high school senior is welcome and should feel free to attend with or without a date. Students should feel free to attend or not attend. No teacher pressure should be applied.
3. Seminar topics will be closely coordinated with the topical outline followed in the regular course. Whenever possible, authors of assigned paperbacks and articles will be guests.
4. Students should feel the seminars are theirs and the teacher should stay in the background.
5. There should be ample time during the seminar for students to ask questions and support their own ideas.
6. On two occasions there will be a Hyde Park Corner Night when a student may stand up, say anything he wants to say, and then support his stand in front of fellow students. The floor will be his until another student succeeds in acquiring it.

A seminar schedule was established and followed each year. The following assigned readings and corresponding guest list indicate topics covered during the 1963–64 academic year:

Assigned Readings	*Seminar Guests*
The Republic by Plato	Dr. Paul Coburn, Professor of American Thought and Language, Michigan State University
The Prince by Machiavelli *The "Higher Law" Background of American Constitutional Law* by E. S. Corwin	
"Politics and the Human Covenant" by John F. A. Taylor, *The Centennial Review,* Winter 1962 *Foundations of American Constitutionalism* by Andrew McLaughlin	Dr. John F. A. Taylor, M.S.U., Professor of Philosophy
Second Treatise of Government by John Locke *Letters from an American Farmer* by Crevecoeur *The American Character* by D. W. Brogan *American Capitalism* by Louis Hacker *The United States Political System and How It Works* by David C. Coyle	Hyde Park Corner Night
The Rights of Man in America by Gilman Ostrander	Dr. Gilman Ostrander, M.S.U., Historian
The Worldly Philosophers by Robert Heilbroner	Dr. Maurice Perkins, M.S.U., Economist
Communism by A. G. Meyer	Dr. Alfred Meyer, M.S.U., Political Scientist
American Diplomacy by George Kennan	Dr. Wesley Fishel, M.S.U., Political Scientist

Assigned Readings	*Seminar Guests*
Freedom and Responsibility and the American Way of Life by Carl Becker	Hyde Park Corner Night

The reader might well ask, What really happened to the students as a result of the seminars? Although the effects of the seminars were not measured in any sophisticated manner, the following appraisal by the teacher might be of interest and value to the reader.

TEACHER'S APPRAISAL

Large attendance demonstrated that students valued the seminars: between fifty and seventy-five students attended each seminar. Student and parent interest was also evidenced by the fact that they were eager to have seminars in their homes. Seminar sessions were treated by students as a time for serious listening, discussion, and thinking, but they were also considered important as an opportunity to meet with fellow students and adults in an informal way. A rather interesting pattern developed at each seminar, not by design, but naturally. Students questioned the guest professor and each other in a large group situation for an hour or an hour and a quarter, and then small groups formed spontaneously to pursue previously raised questions or points of contention. As the evening progressed, students often moved from group to group. The only person who appeared to be incidental to the whole process was the classroom teacher.

There was no monolithic response to seminar guests, for at the end of the year each student had his favorite professor, i.e., the guest he liked best. There was little agreement as to which professor did the best job. Students did agree, however, that there was great value while still in high school in meeting college professors in an informal situation.

After several of the seminars, students seemed alienated for a brief period of time from the regular classroom sessions and the teacher. The students appeared to be more detached, less secure, and more independent. This was understandable, for at the seminars students asked questions of the speakers which would elicit answers that substantiated or contradicted the teacher's classroom ideas. Frequently the teacher's classroom "gems" were not substantiated by the seminar guest. New points of view disturbed a few students to such an extent that they could see little value in entertaining more points of view. One student blurted out in class, "I think we young people have no right to question the ideas of older people. We shouldn't try to 'get at' our guest's ideas." However, other students were satisfied with proximate answers and found questioning and discussion rewarding and even novel.

Most students reacted favorably to the coordination of seminar topics with the topical organization followed in classroom meetings. They felt that the assignment of special books to be read for seminar sessions would have demanded time from their already full assigned-reading schedule. In fact the concurrency of class work and seminars frequently caused students to reread books because of what speakers had said at the seminars.

Not only the students were challenged by the seminars: the teacher still retains vivid memories of the long rides home in the car, ideas swirling through his mind. Something exciting had happened that evening.

Guests were often reluctant, at first, to meet with the students; but as the evening progressed they relaxed and enjoyed the session. They were then eager to return the following year. As one guest professor remarked, "You have an enviable situation here; one which we seldom have with our undergraduate students at the university."

PROBLEMS ENCOUNTERED

The picture presented thus far is quite "rosy," but as any innovator knows, there are problems involved in introducing and conducting a new program. The very idea of substituting paperbacks for the traditional textbook was an immediate problem. The school policy stated that teachers could recommend paperbacks but could not force students to buy them, since a portion of the students' textbook fees had already been spent on a social studies text. Fortunately, the school librarian had previously seen the value of paperbacks for high school students, and as a result, she had an excellent selection of paperbacks for sale in the library. To "get around" the school policy, the librarian and teacher collaborated: students could purchase a book for their own personal libraries at home or they could borrow a book from the "social studies library" established by the librarian and teacher. In each case, when a book was recommended approximately ninety students purchased the book and ten students borrowed the book. This solution was, of course, not satisfactory to all; compromises seldom are. At first it was a status symbol to carry a paperback on the high school campus. It was also considered a good insurance policy to read a number of paperbacks, for college was just ahead for the seniors involved.

Instigating the seminar was comparatively easy, for students and parents were ready for a more academic approach to the teaching of social studies. The administration, who no doubt felt the pulse of parents and students, also gave the seminars their full support. It must be stated honestly that there were few active supporters of the seminars among fellow staff members. This is understandable, for especially in the social studies area are other teachers' approaches to teaching challenged. (The reader must re-

member that the seminars were instigated during the first
year of the writer's teaching career.) However, at the
same time the writer probably exaggerated in his own mind
the amount of antagonism on the part of colleagues.

A problem soon encountered at the seminars was whether or not students should be able to smoke. The teacher
had mixed feelings on the subject. The students resolved
this among themselves by suggesting that this be left up to
the host or hostess at the home where the seminar was to be
held; most parents allowed the students to smoke. The
rather interesting result was that the first couple of seminars
were like the "smoke-filled back room" of political lore. It
was "in" to smoke; many new smokers performed with
buffoonery unequaled by the zeal of Don Quixote as he
charged his windmills. After a couple of seminars the
majority of the students saw how ridiculous the whole thing
was becoming and therefore curbed each other's smoking
so that the speaker could once again be seen.

A potential problem involved transportation to and from
seminars. When an administrator's daughter was involved
in a minor accident in front of the teacher's house, it appeared that seminars might have to be discontinued. There
was no difficulty, however, as the administrator proved to
be one of the strongest supporters of the seminars.

In closing, the writer must admit that although there
were problems involved, the holding of seminars made
high school teaching much more exciting and interesting
than it otherwise would have been. Overall, it was worth
the time and effort involved.

Questions for Discussion

1. Are seminars in the social studies valuable only for high
school seniors? Are they valuable only for college-bound students? Are they most advantageously employed in suburban
schools?

2. Evaluate the ground rules adopted for the social studies seminar described in this selection.

3. Do you see any special problems arising from a Hyde Park Corner Night?

4. Evaluate the assigned reading list as to its appropriateness for the student population involved.

5. What do you see as the main limitations to your adopting a social studies seminar program?

6. What do you see as the main value in holding social studies seminars? How do you think your students would react to such a program?

7. What community resources, e.g., speakers or guests, could you use for your seminars?

8. How would you react to the question of whether or not students should be able to smoke at seminar sessions?

9. Was the teacher premature in trying to instigate seminars during his first year of teaching?

10. Where would the main opposition be if you tried to adopt social studies seminars?

11. How could you alter the seminar program discussed in this chapter to meet your particular needs as a teacher in Community X?

14

AN INDEPENDENT STUDY COURSE IN RUSSIAN HISTORY

JAMES HAUGHT

It is the feeling of some social studies educators that both the "fast learner" and the "slow learner" have received too little attention. In the following chapter, Mr. Haught describes an exciting course in Russian history for bright and capable social studies students. His reading list, objectives, and teaching methods are most impressive given the group of students with whom he worked.

Although several high schools in the United States are now offering courses in Russian history, Shaker High School, Latham, New York, launched a program for its 1963–64 term that might prove to be new in many ways. The format of this Russian history course places an emphasis on independent work. One of the primary aims of the course is to bridge the gap between high school and college in terms of materials and methods of instruction by accustoming the student to taking a greater responsibility for his own achievement. In an effort to achieve this primary purpose, the student is allowed to spend four periods each week in the school library working on an independent research project of his own choosing. Taking advantage of a unique six-year program of instruction in the Russian language, the students are able to do part of their research in materials written in Russian.

Another unusual aspect of this Russian history course is the use of visiting lecturers from the surrounding colleges and universities. There are eight colleges and universities located within a twenty-five-mile radius of Shaker High School which offer programs in Russian studies. Drawing on the personnel in these programs, the high school has been able to give the students an opportunity to participate in seminar discussions with college and university professors, who are both informative and challenging in their special fields of Russian studies. Topics considered were many and varied, including, among others, Ivan the IV, The 1917 Revolution, Nineteenth-century Russian Literature, Religion and the Church in Russia, Soviet Economic Progress, and The Government in the Soviet Union. The students have been impressed by the contrast in teaching techniques used by college professors and those used by high school instructors.

Like most courses in Russian history, this course aims to help students gain an insight into the background and realities of the problems encountered in the Cold War with the U.S.S.R. Another objective is to teach the students the techniques of historical research and to encourage them to seek greater scope in historical analysis.

In order that the students might become fully aware of the wide range of Russian history before they selected their specialized research topics, the course opened with a three-week survey of Russian history. During these first three weeks, the students met together daily with the instructor. During the remainder of the year, however, they met only once a week as a group. These meetings featured lecturers, outstanding films or filmstrips, and group discussions in an attempt to give direction to the activities of the group. A schedule was set up whereby each student could meet privately with the instructor once each week for the purpose of reporting and discussing the progress of his independent study. In these private conferences, the instructor encouraged the student to develop his topic as fully as possible by creating an extensive bibliography and scanning all available resources. In creating the bibliography, the students were encouraged to use not only the facilities of the school's library, but the surrounding college libraries as well, and to make frequent use of such reference materials as the *Reader's Guide* and *The New York Times Index*. To further assist in the preparation of the research papers, the school library rented and placed at the students' disposal a microfilm machine for viewing back issues of newspapers.

Since the Russian history students spent four periods a week in the library, a special section was set aside for their use. All the library's resources on Russian studies were placed in this section and a table and locker were assigned to each student. An honor pass to the library was issued to each member of the course to facilitate the use of study hall periods.

During the course of the year the students were expected to read eight books dealing with specific topics of Russian studies. A different topic was emphasized each month, and the students were assigned a paperback to read and upon which to make a brief report. The following topics were assigned:

Current foreign policy with emphasis on postwar developments.
Geography and its effect upon the history and people of Russia.
History in the seventeenth through the twentieth centuries with emphasis on the 1917 Revolution.

Literature from the eighteenth century to the present.

Economics: Emphasis on statistical evidence of the economic achievements and failures of Russian communism.

Influence of history on the art of Russia from the Byzantine period to the present.

Influence of religion on the history of Russia.

Relationship between the party and government including the theoretical structure of both and the actual location of power.

The paperbacks were carefully selected on the basis of content, price, and suitability for the reading abilities of high school seniors. The following were selected for the course:

J. A. Armstrong, *Ideology, Politics and Government in the Soviet Union*. New York: Frederick A. Praeger, 1962.

R. W. Campbell, *Soviet Economic Power: Its Organization and Challenge*. Boston: Houghton Mifflin, 1960.

George F. Kennan, *Russia and the West under Lenin and Stalin*. Boston: Little, Brown and Company, 1960.

Hans Kohn, *Basic History of Modern Russia*. Princeton, N.J. D. Van Nostrand Company, 1957.

Emil Lengyel, *The Soviet Union: The Land and Its People*. New York: Oxford Book Company, 1961.

P. Miliukov, *Architecture, Painting and Music in Russia*. New York: A. S. Barnes, 1960.

P. Miliukov, *Religion and the Church in Russia*. New York: A. S Barnes, 1960.

Bernard Pares, *Russia: Past and Present*. New York: Mentor Books, 1949.

Marc Slonim, *An Outline of Russian Literature*. New York: Oxford University Press, 1958.

The topics selected by the students for their research papers were varied and comprehensive in content. Considerations of available resources, involvement of time, and student interest led to some topics being changed during the first semester, but the early enthusiasm with which the students worked resulted in satisfactory reports and bibliographies before the first semester came to a close. The following are examples of the topics selected:

"The Reign of Nicholas II and the Influence of Rasputin"

"Development of the Political Structure of the Soviet Government and Its Influence on Marxism"

"The Liberation of the Serf in Russia: A Comparison with the Liberation of the American Negro Slave"

"Dostoevski: His Reflection on the History of His Time"

This senior course in Russian history was offered in place of the regularly scheduled economics course in the twelfth grade and fulfilled the credit requirements of twelfth-grade social studies. Although several students preferred to select the alternate course in economics, the general demand for Russian history made competitive selection necessary. Eligible for the course were those students who had satisfactorily passed the regents test in one year of American history and world history and who, in addition, had shown exceptional ability and maturity in their eleventh-year course in American history.

Of paramount importance to students, parents, and administrators, as well as to the future of the Russian history course, was the philosophy used in marking the students. In view of the fact that each participant in the course had been selected because of the record of his past achievements, and assuming that each student would continue to strive for greater achievement, a three-grade marking procedure was adopted. During the course of the year, if any student failed to meet the minimum grade requirement, he was given an opportunity to move to a senior course in economics where the requirements were not so intensive. The Russian history course was meant to have high standards, but in no way was it intended as "punishment" for those who took it. Marks were based on monthly written reports, student participation in seminar discussions, a mid-term oral examination, and the final research paper.

It would be ridiculous for any high school to attempt such a course in Russian history without the full cooperation of the administrators, instructors, and the students who took the course. The administrator must be willing to risk the chance of community resistance toward such a course. He must be willing to provide time in the school schedule, funds for speakers and materials, and tolerance of the student independence demanded by such a course. The instructors must be willing to give extra time and effort in working with each student independently and in preparing the group seminars, as well as in correcting the students' work. The instructors must avoid the temptation to regulate the students' research work too closely. The librarian must be willing to prepare adequate resources for the students and to see that they are able to use the library facilities correctly. The students themselves must be willing to accept a greater amount of responsibility in order to produce more than would normally be expected of them in a high school history course, and to produce this work under conditions of relative independence. Given the full cooperation of these three groups, the Russian history course could not complete a fully successful term without the cooperative interest of the surrounding colleges and universities in providing lecturers and needed materials.

The impressive contrast between the teaching techniques used by college professors and high school instructors has already been noted, and it is hoped that this contrast will help the student to adjust more rapidly to his first year in college. The self-discipline demanded by independent work is not easily acquired by a high school student. Even a bright and capable high school student has much to learn in this area. However, it is hoped that the format of the independent study course in Russian history at Shaker

High School will do much to help students obtain a higher level of educational maturity.

It is the feeling of the writer that such educational maturity was achieved by most of the students. In one class discussion, talk centered on the two types of Soviet farms: the rigid collective farm or *kohloz*, on which the farmer lives and works only a small portion for himself; and the more liberal state farm that operates like a factory, hiring farmers for wages. One student commented that the Soviet government is moving toward a more universal state farm system. "I guess they're becoming more capitalistic and we're becoming more socialistic," related the student. "What's another capitalistic trend in the Soviet Union?" queried the teacher. "Lotteries," quipped the student. "That's an example of our supply and demand law," retorted another student.

One of the girls in the class studied Catherine II with the feeling that Catherine should have concentrated more on the serfs than on territorial expansion. "I have come across three volumes of Catherine that must have been written by someone friendly to the court," the student commented, "for the account given is very biased in Catherine's favor."

If educational maturity is to discover and then question your discovery in light of more extensive research, then these students were well on their way to such educational maturity.

Questions for Discussion

1. Would it be possible to teach a course such as the writer describes in a secondary school which does not have courses in the Russian language?

2. Could adjustments be made in the course described so that average students could benefit from such an approach?

3. What sources would you include and exclude if you were to teach this course?

4. Could you teach a course like the one described in this chapter? What kind of background in Russian studies is required on the part of the teacher?

5. Do you feel this course is too specialized for a secondary social studies curriculum?

15

USING DOCUMENTS IN JUNIOR HIGH SCHOOL

MURIEL MOULTON

A recent trend in social studies education is the emphasis on historiography and social science methodology. The following writer's use of primary sources for junior high school students is most interesting in light of this recent trend. Students learned to discover for themselves the importance of historical problems while at the same time developing research techniques.

The study of American history through the documents of each period is usually reserved for senior high school or college students. This year I attempted to use that approach with my seventh-grade American history classes. To seventh graders, the study of history is too often the study of devitalized events—events which bear no relation to real people, least of all to themselves.

Today's twelve-year-olds, we must remember, never knew a world in which there were no jet planes. A natural sky, free of man's beeping and blinking instruments, is at most a vague memory to them. Even World War II is known to them mainly through the "B-minus" movies they see on television. The fact that their own parents may have served in that conflict or can remember hearing Franklin Roosevelt's Fireside Chats doesn't bring those events any nearer—it only proves how old their parents are.

Born into the Atomic Age and whirling dizzily through the Hydrogen Age into who-knows-what unbelievable future—to these children then, how unreal must seem the American Revolution, the Civil War, or even World War I with its primitive gas masks. How can we bring into the focus of reality the American past?

Teachers today face the immediate and continuing problem of finding ways to transmit a conceptually abstract past to a generation concerned with other problems. I decided to try using a series of documents with my students because I felt that one way to make past events seem more real was to bring the students as close as possible to the events. In other words, to have them discover the events through some of the very words in which they were originally described.

A more pedantic reason was that students need to lose their fear of imposing-looking documents. They need to learn a technique for approaching complicated or unfamiliar types of material. They also need to know that there are many different kinds of historical sources.

Whenever possible, I employed a problem-solving method, trying to put the students in the position of articulating and working through some particular historical problem. The goal of this method is twofold: to develop in the students an emotional as well as a rational commitment to the importance of certain problems and their solutions; and to provide exercise in the development of elementary techniques in research.

The first document to which I exposed my students was the Constitution of the United States. This was the first and simplest of the exercises. For this I used a standard textbook edition of the Constitution: the original wording in a broad column on the left, and explanations in the right-hand column. Even with the document so annotated, many students resisted exploration, and some tried to "wait it out" until we got to something easier.

Without mentioning the Constitution itself, I introduced this segment of the course—after a brief examination of the colonial and revolutionary periods—by posing the question: What does a country do *after* a revolution?

Talk turned for a while to the new nations of Africa, which at that time were going through their birth throes. In a short time we had on the blackboard a list of problems which a country might face at its inception. We narrowed the list down to those problems which probably confronted the early leaders of the thirteen states. Some of the problems suggested by the students were: organizing a central government, taxation, uniform money, relations with other countries.

Using what they already knew from earlier readings, the students were able to suggest some attitudes toward government which were probably held by people in those days. The students pointed out experiences during the colonial period which resulted in fear of a strong central government. I quickly turned attention to that point and, using suggestions from the class, we constructed what amounted to the Articles of Confederation as the logical reaction of the people at that time. Once these articles were set up, it was simple to see some of the difficulties the nation faced under that kind of organization. Then came the obvious question: What did they do about these problems? I resisted the pat answer offered by several students, who declared simply that the solution was that the Constitution was written.

Pointing to the list of problems they had placed on the blackboard, I asked: What did they do about this particular problem, or that one? The more conscientious students were perplexed, some were frankly anxious, many were uncomfortable. They didn't know the answers and they weren't sure that they weren't expected to know them. Finally someone asked: "Well, can we look in the Constitution?"

It was quickly discovered that their textbook had the Constitution in an appendix. They found it, and most of them promptly fell in and were swamped, despite the explanatory notes.

After several minutes of floundering, one of the quicker students said: "Here's something about what the President is allowed to do." Another found something about the rights of the states, and another about the powers of Congress.

From that beginning, and using the problems which they had stated earlier, it was an easy task to find out what actually had been done to solve them, and in the process to make the first big step in the use of documents.

Most documents are not presented with explanatory notes, nor would it be desirable to limit the students to documents which had been so altered. Therefore, when we took up the settling of the near-West, I used a variety of the vivid and lively accounts of that period. Shortly, however, we found ourselves on the verge of war with Mexico over the acquisition of Texas and the Southwest. At this point I found virtually nothing appropriate to the junior high school level which was not simplified to the point of inaccuracy. The most exciting questions surrounding that period were obscured. In an attempt to bring life and a sense of the reality of those times into our modern city classroom, I turned to the documents of the period.

I sketched briefly a profile of Mexico, its deserts, its isolating mountains, its jungles, and its three hundred years of subjugation under Spanish colonial rule. With the chaotic birth of the Republic of Mexico, we began our study of the period from 1820 to 1845. With Polk's War Message to Congress and the Sumner Resolution opposing the war with Mexico, we concluded it.

These two documents, written after all for the ears of the layman, exemplify both the emotions and the logic on which was based the conflict of opinion. The speeches themselves posed the problem. The students were given duplicated copies without explanatory notes. Quickly we went through them together, defining words. Then I asked which paragraphs the students didn't understand. One student didn't understand the third paragraph of the Sumner Resolution. Another student volunteered to explain the third paragraph, and still others criticized or clarified the explanation. Inevitably the criticisms and explanations became partisan. Students were either for Polk or for Sumner. As the end of the class session approached, I suggested that since they felt so strongly about the matter, they might have an informal debate the next day. They seemed very pleased at the suggestion and only a little subdued by the qualification that they should read at least one reference book about the Mexican War, making careful notes of pertinent facts. Excitement mounted again when one of these students observed that since each student had a copy of *both* speeches, each side could scrutinize the opposing speech for weaknesses and use the opponent's own words against him.

There is no precise way of assessing which or how many of the students found a reference book and read it, made notes, or so much as glanced over the speeches outside of class. I suspect that some students probably did make the suggested preparation, but found it impossible to venture into the heat of a rough-and-tumble debate among their peers. Others may have been too young or too resistant or too involved in other affairs to become interested.

That many did identify some of the main problems facing the nation in 1845, and became warmly aware of

various attempts at solutions to those problems is unde-
niable. Tape recordings which I made at the time of these
debates, and which I studied afterward, reveal evidence of
that fact. The tapes reveal that more than the usual few,
articulate, leading students participated constructively.
The tapes also show that not only did the students rather
proudly use direct quotations from the speeches to support
or demolish an argument, but they were able to state the
issues in their own vehement words in response to challenges thrown at them by "the other side."

An additional advantage of this kind of approach is the
very positive pleasure of the students in the accomplish-
ment of the task itself. As some of them said to me at the
end of that class session: "That was fun!"

With the expansion to the Pacific and the settling of the
territories, the questions of slavery, secession, and the Civil
War became topics of discussion. Everyone, of course, knew
about the Civil War, and no one was in favor of slavery.
This segment of the course promised to be dull and virtually
without challenge to the students. Again I found the materials for the junior high school level oversimplified and
inclined to side-step the most stimulating issues of the
period.

The students reflected an almost total lack of awareness
of the long and painful discussions in and out of Congress
on the legality and morality of slavery and secession—discussions in which both Northerners and Southerners ear-
nestly tried to find an answer short of war. Also I found
the students ignorant of the Constitution-based arguments
of the secessionists.

One of the sources I used was a recording of the last
speech in Congress of Robert Toombs, Senator from Geor-
gia. In this speech Toombs expressed the Southern position
as it was based, not only on emotion, but on the Dred Scott
decision, and on an interpretation of the Constitution.
Read by Melvin Douglas, I believe the students were

impressed more deeply than they would have been by any more pedantically conventional method of presentation.

The problems of using a document in this form are different from those one faces in presenting printed material. In this form I found it necessary to give students some advance practice in taking quick notes. With careful preparation, I was able to point out in advance some main ideas to listen for without giving the whole thing away, and thus making it pointless for them to listen at all.

There are certainly many other and perhaps better documents than the ones I chose to use. The results of this limited venture proved successful enough to warrant further investigation leading to a broader application of the approach described here.

Questions for Discussion

1. Would you feel qualified to teach a course like the one described in this selection?

2. What sources would you include which the writer did not use?

3. Do you feel this kind of course is premature for junior high school students?

4. What barriers do you think would deter you from adopting this approach?

5. What implication does the Space Age have for a course such as the one described in this selection?

16

SEVENTH GRADE WORLD HISTORY

A New Definition of the Roles of Teachers and Students

DENNIS L. SONNENBURG

World history is a course that has baffled the best of teachers. The scope of the subject alone is enough to perplex the teacher. The following chapter describes one teacher's attempt to organize the subject matter of the course; the most controversial part of the chapter, however, is his thesis that the students should "teach the course" under the guidance of the teacher. The reader will find this thesis most thought-provoking.

This essay will describe how this teacher, after beginning his seventh grade world history class in a traditional fashion with the development of civilization in Egypt, decided to organize the remainder of his school year in a rather unorthodox fashion: he decided to give the students an opportunity to teach the class.

Some of the key thoughts that led to this decision were: (1) The traditional approach to teaching world history, which involves a neat chronology of the development of a select sequence of civilizations (with some being ignored), seemed terribly sterile and limiting.[1] (2) The fact that the bulk of knowledge that is available cannot be taught or learned in the time span allotted for this course forces three issues: (a) the need to set limits on what will be taught, (b) the need to produce a good cross section or give breadth to world history so that the student can know generally what has happened where, so that he may study it at his need or convenience, (c) the need to develop research and communicative skills so that information can be obtained and utilized at his will.[2] (3) The ever-present

[1] The most generally accepted approach to teaching world history it seems is to follow a state prescribed textbook; this is understandable since this is the reading matter legally appropriated for the course and often the only reading material available. Nearly all state texts have with the same unoriginality defined world history functionally as a study beginning with the Egyptian civilization and progressing through the Greek and Roman civilizations and culminating in the growth and development of the European world up to the time of the exploration of the New World. It is not unusual to find that the civilizations of the Far East have been neglected as has that part of Africa which lies south of the Sahara.

[2] We need to admit that keeping abreast of current knowledge in all fields has become increasingly problematic over the years, and this trend seems destined to continue. So rapid is this accumulation of knowledge that man has had to depend increasingly on computers to deal with the quantity. Man, himself, has not been able to significantly increase his natural ability to cope with such huge amounts of information. Man is physically incapable of reading and absorbing such great bulks of literature as recorded in such diverse jargons and different languages. All signs indicate that knowledge shall continue to increase, both in quality and quantity and at rapid rates. *Homo sapiens,* however, shall continue to face physical limitations with little change and probably shall rely more and more upon developing a technology which will assist him in coping with the enormous task of organizing the world's knowledge, so that he might withdraw it as needed at any particular time. The point to be made here is that teachers and students must recognize the limitations of the individual mind and work within these limits. We must admit to specialization

circumstance in mass education that the opportunity for dialogue (which is particularly a stimulus for the thought processes) is decreasing as the ratio of students per teaching personnel increases. This seems to press for the development of a technique in a classroom whereby the students have the opportunity to develop oral skills—particularly of dialogue.[3] (4) It seems essential that we prepare our students to teach one another to offset the trend to rely upon designated teaching personnel or units for information, and thus leave out the wide range of interpretation to which information should be subjected. The teaching situation should be one of dialogue and not monologue for a maximum understanding of knowledge.[4]

---

as not only being practical but necessary. Having a broad general perspective of world history is also important so that specialized skills might be used in any area if desired and so that interrelationships can be seen. Also essential is the confidence that the student might hopefully gain in knowing that he can seek out and evaluate information on his own. (What better training could there be for living in a democratic society?)

[3] Educators must accept the challenge of mass education and work to develop more effective methods of communication. Many excellent electronic devices such as instant feedback circuits, television, and video tapes are now being used in some schools. There is, however, another need that is not satisfied with mass media: it seems every teacher is faced with explaining material in many ways to try to make it meaningful for each student sitting in front of him. This is a chore which becomes more burdensome with the increasing numbers of students. It seems that each student deserves an opportunity to come to grips with an idea or piece of information. This writer maintains that we have not called upon our chief resource to face this situation—the students, themselves. Many capable students might well be taught to be teachers as well as students. They might learn valuable research skills, organizing skills, and communicative skills, which could direct them toward becoming educators in an informal sense, thus performing a vital function for education.

[4] History is too often presented as a book of orderly rationalized facts. We have not only taken the emotional, irrational, and humorous aspects of history and diminished their significance in the making of history, but we have passed off the more acceptable interpretations of history as truth. We need to introduce a working concept of historical interpretation in the classroom. After all, what went on before

METHOD AND ORGANIZATION

Each class member spent the first six weeks of the year doing research and writing two short reports on various selected topics on the subject of Egyptian history.[5] It was toward the end of the oral reports on the Egyptian topics that the teacher decided to organize the rest of the course so that the students might have an opportunity to develop skills important in teaching. The class was quite agreeable to the suggestion that they each do research and teach the class on a given topic.

It was decided that countries offered neat and easily conceptualized entities which could also be assigned with the idea of doing equal justice to the continents of Europe, Africa, and Asia. However, there were too many countries to assign all of them and expect each student to organize a teaching unit around five countries. This teacher selected a sample from each continent, and students then chose from these countries for their teaching unit.[6]

---

us isn't nearly as important as what we think occurred. Giving information to large numbers of students is far less a problem than getting them to find meaning in it by thinking it over and having good discussions. In effect, what is needed is a sharing of experiences and the development of good communicative skills. If we are to teach for education in the truest sense we need to teach these students to communicate and find meaning among themselves. They must become teachers to each other, thereby sharing experiences and values.

[5] This class was ranked third from the top within a system that groups its students into sixteen homogenous levels based on STEP and SCAT tests and past classroom performance. There were twenty-eight members in this world history class. The class met with the teacher the last period each day. This group was quite vocal and carried on a discussion almost endlessly. They were not cautious about voicing dissenting opinions. Grammar and spelling skills were very underdeveloped in this group. The school has an enrollment of about thirteen hundred students and draws from the middle and lower socioeconomic strata.

[6] The following countries were eventually decided upon: *Africa—* Nigeria, Morocco, Algeria, Ethiopia, Republic of the Congo (Evolu-

The next step in organizing the course was planning the schedule for teaching presentations. After the countries which gave an adequate representation of each continent were drafted, the students were asked to choose the country on which they would like most to report. In most cases the students were satisfied with their assignments. Those who were adamant in their dissatisfaction were allowed to select another country with the approval of the teacher.

One student volunteered to be the first to teach the class. This, in effect, established the continent of Africa for the first group of presentations. Arbitrarily it was decided that the Middle Eastern, European, and the Far Eastern countries would follow in that order with an occasional exception.

It was also arbitrarily decided that two class periods— carried out over two days (about thirty-five minutes' teaching time each period)—would be appropriated for each student to teach the class about his country. A schedule was worked out to accommodate six students during the first three weeks, with one student per week scheduled for

---

tion of Man), Republic of South Africa, and Ivory Coast; *Europe*— Greece, Italy, France, Switzerland, Hungary, United Kingdom, Sweden, Finland, and U.S.S.R.; *Asia*—Israel, Turkey, Iran, China, India, Japan, Philippines, Indonesia, and Vietnam. One exception to this was one unit or report on the "Evolution of Man." This was designed to fill the gap that most texts leave at the beginning of the history of mankind. For some unexplained reason the students are expected to understand man's development and progress in the world by tuning in on him quite late rather than at his origin and without reference to what went on before his creation. Perhaps there should be a place for some discussion in world history on the relation of physics—the origin of the universe and the nature of matter and energy, biology— the process of natural selection and evolution of life, and theology— the science of religion. The differing degrees of complexity and organization of structures along with interrelationships of all the processes should be emphasized. This would tie much subject matter together for the students and perhaps give them a perspective linking the natural sciences to the social sciences. It seems this would present a good opportunity for team teaching between various departments at school.

the remainder of the year.[7] With this type of schedule the first three weeks were expected to be cramped; after that there would be class time available each week for supplementary material to be presented by the teacher and for discussions on technical questions regarding the teaching units or on assigned reading.[8]

To get the students started a four-page dittoed instruction paper, explaining the nature of the assignment and how to begin the research, was distributed. The first page of this paper was designed to inspire as well as explain:

The Pleasure of Teaching

For the last eleven years or so you have been experiencing the *pleasures of learning* about the world in which you live. Now you have the opportunity to add to your pleasures: for in addition to learning about your world, *you are going to experience the satisfaction of having taught someone else* about a small part of it.

As you learn from each other about certain areas of the world, you are going to feel a *sense of pride* in the information you have been able to give, as well as that which you have received from others.

Your *success* in the study of world history shall be determined by the *quality of information* you give your classmates

[7] It was decided that the first person would need at least a month to get organized, so the calendar of scheduled teaching dates began a month hence. This teacher volunteered to present a "model" for them to follow. He selected Afghanistan and met all the requirements he asked them to meet in preparation for teaching. This presentation was given one week prior to the first student report. This teacher believes the "model" eliminated much confusion.

[8] Each student was assigned a textbook for the year: Kenneth S. Cooper, Clarence W. Sorensen, Lewis Paul Todd, *The Changing Old World*. (California State Department of Education, 1964.) The students were given reading assignments in this text which generally corresponded with the teaching unit at hand. Occasional tests were given on the reading assignments. This text was very well written and covered the continents of Africa, Europe, and Asia most adequately.

as well as by the *ability with which you receive information from them* and *from other sources.*

It is important for you and your classmates to *understand what you read, hear, or see.* Probably the *most important tool* which will generate understanding is *Organization.* You will continually collect information (for your report and from other reports). It is essential that you *continually organize* material so that you understand its relationship to other material.[9]

The next two pages were directions for getting the students started on their research: where to begin looking for information, how to take notes, and the organizing of material. The last page was a calendar of the assigned teaching dates for individuals.

Several days after the above paper was given out another set of ditto pages was given, this time explaining the exact requirements of the teaching unit. In brief form the requirements were:

I. Write a well-organized report on the history of "your" country.[10]

II. Draw a large colorful map of the country on posterboard, which will be used during your oral presentation. Utilize the reverse side of the posterboard for imaginative illustrations.

III. Include designated information on three master ditto sheets. These will be run off and you will distribute this information to the class members:

[9] This teacher would rewrite this and place an emphasis on understanding ideas behind the information and relating facts to ideas to give their meaning rather than vaguely emphasizing the quality of information.

[10] This should be at least five pages long and should emphasize: (a) the importance of the country's geography in its history; (b) a description of the people's way of life who have been involved in that history; (c) a description of any particularly important civilization that grew in this country.

Page 1:   Top ½—Diagram your country as part of its continent, note the bordering countries.

Bottom ½—Diagram your country with important geographical features and landmarks listed.

Page 2:   Top ⅔—Develop an outline from your written report using complete sentences. Use major topics, subtopics, and specific facts.

Bottom ⅓—Draw a time line and list a few important events in the history of your country; make time gaps equivalent distances apart if possible.

Page 3:   Top ½—Develop a concise written summary of your country's history, relating it to geography.

Bottom ½—Develop a concise paragraph telling the importance of this history to you, to us, to the people of the country, or to the world.

IV. Devise a short but fair test to administer to the class during the last fifteen minutes of your teaching.[11]

V. Submit to the teacher an outline of your plan for teaching. This should cover your use of time during two class periods.

VI. The use of teaching aids is recommended as they add interest and usually increase learning.[12]

---

[11] Specific details regarding the nature of testing were also listed. It was completely up to the person teaching the unit as to what type of test he wished to administer. This teacher strongly encouraged open-note tests to motivate note-taking and utilizing the testing situation as a learning situation. The test questions were to be given orally and the class members were to write their responses on paper. Grading of the exams was left to the person giving the exams, as was the assigning of grades. These grades were entered in the teacher's grade book and went toward the final class grade.

[12] These included: motion pictures, slides, "outside" speakers, records, tapes, costumes, artifacts, literature from the country, etc.

VII. Prepare to meet certain due dates the week prior to and up through your teaching.[13]

WEEK PREVIOUS TO YOUR TEACHING

Mon.	*Tues.*	*Wed.*	*Thurs.*	*Fri.*
1. Order slide projector, phonograph, etc.	1. Poster-board map due	1. Written report due 2. Written outline of what will be on dittos due	You will receive: 1. Master dittos 2. Report 3. Outline	1. Outline of teaching plan due

WEEK OF YOUR SCHEDULED TEACHING

Mon.	*Tues.*	*Wed.*	*Thurs.*	*Fri.*
1. Master dittos must be given to teacher ready to duplicate	1. Distribute dittos to class 2. TEACHING PRESENTATION	1. TEACHING PRESENTATION	1. Return tests 2. Give grades to teacher 3. Resubmit written report 4. Submit copy of test*	1. Class evaluation of the teaching presentation *

* These were added after the first presentation had been given.
[13] The first series of preparations were, of course, given some leeway in meeting these due dates and adjustments were made for allowing two presentations per week for the first few weeks.

Class periods for the several weeks prior to the initial presentation consisted of research both in the library and classroom. Many explanations were given regarding technical aspects of doing research, the organizing of material, and the nature of the assignment.

AN EVALUATION

Since this teacher is striving for a certain amount of growth and maturity in student presentations and for the class to become more receptive to each new "teacher" as the year progresses, he feels that an accurate evaluation in terms of the overall success or failure of such an experiment in the classroom cannot be assessed at this time.[14]

To this date five students have taught the class and if this program were to be evaluated at this time only in terms of how much good information (pointing out cause and effect relationships rather than just giving names, dates, and places with few meaningful relationships)[15] has been ex-

[14] There are also characteristics unique to a given class, which many teachers might call the "class personality," which influences technique. For instance, this class had much individual rivalry for status within the group which was expressed in terms of sarcastic and impatient remarks by some class members toward others. This served to undermine the rapport certain students needed to present the teaching unit effectively. This item was brought to the attention of the class several times during the five presentations. This is definitely one area in which the teacher is hoping for class maturity and which could affect the success of this program.

[15] So far this year this teacher has constantly emphasized the importance of ideas and relationships over the memorizing of unrelated facts. In the reports to date (oral and written) there seems to have been an emphasis on presenting isolated facts. This it seems may have several explanations: (1) these facts are immediately tangible, they involve passing new information, and they seem important; (2) these students have been conditioned to a factual type of information exchange as being the essence of history and knowledge, thus explaining why they seem important; (3) ideas of interrelationships are neither tangible nor important because this has not been the conditioning of these students.

changed—as was suggested for success in "The Pleasure of Teaching"—it would tend to be a failure as this teacher sees it. However, the writer believes several things which will not allow him to be so harsh: (1) The value in this technique lies in the individual experience of researching, organizing, fulfilling requirements, presenting material to a group, attempting to engage in dialogue with a class which at this point may be no more than an awkward first step, evaluating a class, evaluating himself, being evaluated by the class and teacher,[16] receiving information from many other people, and attempting to evaluate its meaning and importance; (2) the quality of information exchanged as the year passes will improve as the class matures and relaxes (since one report per week will be the pace for the remainder of the year and this will allow for time each week to evaluate what we are doing as a class and give opportunity for growth in the proper direction; and (3) specific changes made in the technique could allow for the exchange of better information.

There have been specific items evaluated in the mechanics of this experiment that the teacher would alter. These conclusions are based on the individuals who have performed thus far and the class reaction to them.

[16] Following each teaching unit presentation each member of the class was asked to evaluate the person's performance as a teacher. They were asked to list several strong points and weak points in the presentation and assign a letter grade. (The evaluations were generally very honest and forward; while letter grades assigned tended to be very high.) This teacher collected these evaluations, and after reading them he arrived at an average letter grade mathematically derived from these evaluations. This letter grade, in addition to eight other letter grades assigned by this teacher, made up the evaluation given each student upon completion of his teaching presentation. The evaluation form has the following items: (1) written report, (2) use of aids, (3) content and neatness of dittos, (4) content and neatness of poster map, (5) oral material presented, (6) oral poise and effectiveness, (7) quality of test, (8) class evaluation of you, and (9) meeting due dates.

A major concern to the teacher was the concept his students had of history—dates, names, and places with a few relationships shown. The students' generally sterile presentation of facts cannot be blamed on their lack of knowledge or inability at this age to consider ideas generalized from facts. The teacher has had enough discussions with this group to realize that they are capable of seeing ideas very clearly, especially if they are pointed out, e.g., we had a good discussion after finding that witchcraft was outlawed in a certain African country on whether this reflected a wish of the majority of Africans in this country or whether a minority was imposing its will upon a majority. And if this is so, how is this justified—on the basis of education, race, or what? They, of course, needed to know both the fact that a white minority ruled the country plus our concept of majority rule to make a connection here. This, itself, was an example of their ability to work with both a fact and an idea and to make a connection which provoked much thinking. The point is that they need to be taught to look for relationships in addition to being taught facts. It seems that this could be worked for in the primary grades so that this type of thinking might become a conditioned response.

It is all too apparent that these students have the facts available yet lack that ingredient which pushes them to their capabilities in conceptualizing relationships. In an attempt to overcome such a deficit this teacher would modify his program in several ways: first, he would spend the first few weeks of the year teaching for a focus on ideas and interrelationships between ideas and facts as a method in studying, teaching, and understanding history (this might be done by demonstrating numerous historical interrelationships with the use of facts and ideas); second, he would not overload the first few weeks with presentations, but instead would allow for a great deal of discussion following each presentation on information that was brought up in the unit. This might give the class a better feeling of what was wanted or where to head in future presentations; third, it would be ideal if each student could have the opportunity to teach the class on more than one occasion so that definite improvement might be worked for within the year (time is so limiting that it probably would not be possible to have several assignments involving as much work as this one, but it is possible that a less involved assignment with a focus on students learning to reach for ideas and interrelationships could be satisfactorily worked out to accommodate more reports per person); fourth, the teacher would change the nature of the specific information which is required on the master dittos (he would (a) delete the second map on the first page as the space could be better used to give information, (b) do away with the outline as it places an emphasis on factual information rather than on ideas and interrelationships, (c) incorporate the last page plus the space now available into two pages of dittoed summary of the written information [report] gathered on the country by the student. This would make more written information available to the class and the relationships of factual information to ideas could be more easily expressed); fifth, the teacher would require that each student in the process of teaching involve the class in a discussion over some issue related to his topic in order to give practice to voicing ideas and engaging in dialogue in a group situation; and sixth, to follow through on this emphasis of relating facts and ideas, this teacher would require that an essay question be included on each test given by a student (this would encourage both written expression of ideas for those taking the test and the interpretation of this expression and understanding of the ideas for the reader of the exams).

CONCLUSION

In conclusion the teacher would like to suggest that those concerned for our educational product should: evaluate the traditional material presented in world history classes; work for teaching specialized skills so that the students might take these and find, evaluate, and utilize knowledge at their convenience; call upon students as a resource available and ready to be trained for contributing to teaching and education in general; admit that historical interpretation is not only real but essential for gaining an understanding of knowledge. It is the writer's feeling that this can only take place through dialogue—the exchange of ideas and facts with all aspects of interrelationships considered.

Questions for Discussion

1. Would you be willing to adopt an approach similar to the one prescribed by the writer?

2. How does the academic level of the students involved relate to the writer's thesis?

3. How would you define the approach advocated by the writer of this selection?

4. What sources would you recommend to implement the approach used by the teacher?

5. What problems can you identify in the approach used by the teacher?

17

WRITING IN THE SOCIAL STUDIES

Suggested Innovations

HARRY SIMS

Teachers sometimes view the research paper as an all-purpose assignment which requires a minimum of effort on the teacher's part and yields a rich harvest of student thought. Mr. Sims argues that the research paper should be a precise instrument that requires a sophisticated and precise introduction to students. If this means too much time taken from other activities, then another type of assignment is clearly called for, according to the writer. He furthermore feels that a haphazard approach to the research paper can only result in a superficial level of thinking among students.

At one time or another every social studies teacher is confronted with the question of whether or not to include a research paper[1] in his course requirements. After a recent

---

[1] "Research paper" as used here and afterward will refer to any extended assignment in which the student is expected to devote the majority of his time for the paper to the collection and analysis of primary and secondary data. An example of such an assignment might be the following: "Discuss the economic causes of the Civil War."

and brief analysis of student papers, the present writer was willing to settle this question for himself with an unqualified "No!" Witness the following quotation from a student's paper:

> The soldier home from the war found something new in America. Johnny found his American Beauty drifting away from the prim morality of the pre-1914 world even faster than the Model T would carry her. The girl who had kissed him at the depot on his departing, with her skirt dragging in the dust, had been working harder and harder on the "new freedom" in his absence. When he got home she wanted to be more like the "Mademoiselle from Armentieres."

Even an untrained observer can sense the journalistic flavor of this passage and realize that it is not characteristic of high school student writing. It was in fact "lifted" almost entirely from a library reference text; and to illustrate the extent of this student's plagiarism, the original source is quoted in full:

> Johnny found his American Beauty drifting away from the prim morality of the pre-1914 world even faster than Henry Ford's Model T would carry her. The girl who kissed him demurely at the depot, while her skirt swept the dusty floor, had been working harder and harder on the New Freedom in his absence. When he got home she wanted to be more like the Mademoiselle from Armentieres.[2]

Another more subtle form of plagiarism occurs when the student paraphrases another source into his own words but neglects to acknowledge the other writer's significant ideas. Such would appear to be the case in the following quotation from a student's paper.

> [William Jennings] Bryan was a son of the Middle Border, and he became the prophet of its faith. To some, particularly eastern businessmen and industralists, he may have appeared as the agent of Lucifer. Whatever Bryan may have been to his

2 Paul Sann, *The Lawless Decade* (New York: Crown, 1957), p. 19.

contemporaries, devil, saint, or simply a product of the Middle West; his ethical and religious ideas, together with their social, economic, and political implications do much to account for his prominence and power.

Whether or not the student has completely paraphrased these thoughts into his own words is not known. By considering this question, however, one avoids asking a far more important question: Of what real value is the well-paraphrased paper? Ultimately, it is the student's *ideas* which the teacher wishes to evaluate, and for a student to "lift" ideas is just as reprehensible and self-defeating as outright plagiarism.

Unfortunately, evidence of plagiarism as cited in these two examples was found to be prevalent in an alarming number of students' papers. Furthermore, there is no reason to suspect that these papers are not characteristic of the work done by a large segment of social studies students throughout the country. Who is to blame for this: student or teacher? This is a difficult question to answer, but probably the major portion of the blame must go to the latter. Certainly one point is clear: serious problems of student writing in the social studies do exist, and such problems suggest that the several teaching objectives underlying the use of written assignments are in need of a major reassessment.

Perhaps the root of the research paper problem lies in a teacher's frequent "all or nothing" approach to written assignments. In other words, he considered only two alternatives: either his students write an extended research paper or they write no paper at all. Such an attitude, of course, ignores a host of other writing alternatives. In the following pages the writer will (1) discuss several difficulties surrounding the traditional research paper assignment and (2) suggest a few alternatives to the research paper which may eliminate these difficulties. If there is to be any one underlying thesis for this discussion, it is simply this: *all*

social studies writing assignments can be justified only on
the grounds that they elicit *some* genuinely individual and
creative thought from the student.

THE STUDENT RESEARCH PAPER

Quite possibly, the largest single source of difficulty connected with the student research paper originates with its
introduction by the instructor. From a variety of sources [3]
it seems apparent that many teachers either neglect to
make such an introduction or, when they do, they fail to
make some crucial distinctions clear to students. The in-
variable result is the familiar "paste and scissors" response.

One reason for this response is frequently a confusion in
the teacher's mind between "skills of applied technique"
and "skills of mental application." Borrowing an overworked statement from ethics: It is a confusion of means
and ends. Skills of applied technique are often referred to
in educational journals as "library skills" or "investigative
skills." They include such abilities as knowledge in the use
of periodical indexes, card catalogues, reference books, and
encyclopedias. The problem is that many teachers assume
that a firm foundation in these more superficial skills is all
that is required to stimulate original and critical thought in
their students.

Evidence that some teachers do confuse the nature of
these two types of skills is supplied by an assignment sheet
recently given to an eighth grade class in a well-to-do suburban school district. The assignment's introduction (seven
pages long!) is entitled "Paper Preparation: The Essentials."
These "Essentials" include details similar to the above-
mentioned skills of applied technique and the elements of
proper manuscript form; yet nowhere does the introduction
even so much as mention the role of the individual stu-

[3] Such sources include materials from teachers, research paper outlines, articles from educational journals, and personal experiences.

dent's own thinking. The teacher haphazardly assumes that the student will bridge the gap between the conclusions of his sources and the positing of his own conclusions. Thus, what appears on paper to be a very complete introduction to the research paper largely ignores the primary purpose of the assignment: the encouragement of the student's own thought.

A second misconception which should be dealt with in an introduction to the research paper stems from the one first mentioned. Not only are the skills of applied technique overemphasized at the expense of the skills of mental application, but, very often, the former are being used indiscriminately as well. Important differences between the various applied skills are not being considered. The result, therefore, is the unconscious encouragement of undisciplined investigative procedures among students.

An illustration of how these important distinctions have been glossed over is provided by the frequently heard phrase "materials center" in reference to school libraries. In a very general sense the term can be an apt label. Current usage, as evidenced by articles in several educational journals, implies, however, that the various "materials" are of equal value for use in a student's paper—i.e., that material gained through the use of one skill is just as important as material gained from another.[4] Obviously, the authors who use the phrase assume that teachers will be sophisticated enough to make the necessary distinctions. Yet if the teachers, administrators, and professors of education who write these articles fail to make these distinctions explicit, then it seems reasonable to assume that a large number of teachers

[4] In particular, articles by Helen Carpenter, "Study Skills: Treasure Hunt for Information," *Instructor* (January, 1965); Frederick Cyphert, "The Junior High School Library Develops Investigative Skills," *Clearing House*, XXXIII (October, 1958); and Marilyn Robbins, "Teaching Library Skills to Junior High Honor Students," *The Science Teacher*, XXXII (February, 1965) fail to make any discriminations between these various skills.

likewise fail to make these distinctions clear to their students.

Perhaps the two main distinctions to be pointed out to students are (1) the differences between fact and opinion and (2) the differences between primary and secondary sources. A good deal of controversy continues to surround the first distinction, and this is particularly true in the social sciences and history. Such controversy, however, is hardly a legitimate excuse for sidestepping the issue.

Edward Hallet Carr, a historian, presents one of the best discussions on the first distinction. In his view, "The historian is necessarily selective. The belief in a hard core of historical facts existing independently of the interpretation of the historian is a preposterous fallacy, but one which it is very hard to eradicate." [5] Nevertheless, this view should not be taken to mean that there are no different *degrees* of objectivity among historical facts. As Hunt and Metcalf point out, all facts have a higher or lesser probability of approximating the truth.[6] Thus, the role of the teacher is to clarify these subtle and often elusive distinctions and to present history to the student as "a continuous process of interaction between the historian and his facts." [7]

One definite advantage of clarifying the role of facts and opinions to students is that it allows them a greater measure of flexibility in their writing. Having an awareness of the reciprocal nature of fact and interpretation allows the student to perceive more clearly the role of his own contribution to the paper. In a sense he can "get on top" of his material, ask his own questions, and tentatively suggest his own answers. Clements and Fielder, two educationists who

[5] Edward Hallet Carr, *What Is History?* (New York: Knopf, 1964), p. 10.

[6] Maurice P. Hunt and Lawrence E. Metcalf, *Teaching High School Social Studies* (New York: Harper and Brothers, 1955), p. 78. The authors go on to suggest the use of a "fact-value continuum" as a means of graphically demonstrating the relative position of facts in relation to the approximate truth.

[7] E. H. Carr, *op. cit.*, p. 35.

have written extensively in this field, would certainly support this position. They believe that study ". . . consists of formulating and answering a series of questions that are not directed toward authorities but toward oneself." [8]

Once the teacher has properly introduced the respective roles of fact and interpretation, the second major distinction—primary versus secondary sources—becomes much easier for the student to grasp. Another historian, Louis Gottschalk, explains the differences between these two succinctly: "A primary source is the testimony of an eyewitness, or of a witness by any other of the senses, or of a mechanical device like the Dictaphone. . . . A secondary source is the testimony of anyone who is not an eyewitness." [9] To be sure, both primary and secondary sources will vary in quality—a fact which should also be pointed out to students.

While Gottschalk's definitions make the distinction between the two types of sources appear very obvious, it is one that is not always made—even by the most distinguished historians. Robert Brown in his critical analysis of Charles Beard's economic interpretation of the Constitution points out numerous instances of such an indiscriminate use of sources:

> He [Beard] . . . proceeded on the assumption that a valid interpretation could be built on secondary writings whose authors had likewise failed to collect the evidence. If we accept Beard's own maxim "no evidence, no history" and his own admission that the data had never been collected, the answer to whether he used historical method properly is self-evident.[10]

[8] H. Millard Clements, William R. Fielder, and B. Robert Tabachnick, *Social Study: Inquiry in Elementary Classrooms* (New York: Bobbs-Merrill, 1966), p. 20.

[9] Louis Gottschalk, *Understanding History* (New York: Knopf, 1965), p. 53.

[10] Robert Brown, *Charles Beard and the Constitution* (New York: W. W. Norton, Inc., 1956), pp. 194–95.

Very often school libraries contain a preponderance of predigested materials and have little in the way of primary materials. Under these circumstances students would be placed in an unfair position. On the one hand, they would be asked to utilize both fact and interpretation, while on the other hand no primary sources would be easily available to them. Past experience suggests at least two immediate solutions. One is to be found in the number of excellent books which contain collections of historical documents that are neither predigested nor prejudged for the student.[11] Another is to be found in the large number of free or inexpensive materials printed by the Federal government and easily available to any teacher. The Government Printing Office is the world's largest publishing concern, and among the thousands of articles it publishes annually are materials which may be adapted to almost any grade level.[12] Moreover, state governments and Federal and state congressmen are usually eager to send materials to teachers or students upon request. While these sources of data by no means solve the problem, they do provide a good starting point.

Once the teacher has properly introduced the research paper to students as outlined above, he still faces the universal problem of plagiarism. Regardless of the instructor's

[11] Henry Steele Commager, *Documents of American History*, 6th ed. (New York: Appleton-Century-Crofts, 1958) and *Fifty Basic Civil War Documents* (Princeton, N.J.: Van Nostrand, 1965); Norman F. Cantor, *The Medieval World 300–1300* (New York: Macmillan, 1963); Benjamin Keen, *Readings in Latin-American Civilization* (Boston: Houghton Mifflin, 1955); Leonard W. Levy and Merrill Peterson, *Major Crises in American History I* (New York: Harcourt, Brace and World, 1962).

[12] In particular, two free Government Printing Office publications are recommended. They are (a) the bi-weekly list of "Selected United States Government Publications" and (b) the various "Price Lists" containing the publications under different categories including history, labor, geography and explorations, tariff, political science, and foreign relations. Both of these may be obtained by writing the Government Printing Office, Washington, D.C., 20402.

threats or pleas for honesty, there will always be some students who will copy outright or alter only slightly the work of others and call it their own. At best, then, the research paper is a calculated risk. Teachers must accept the originality of students' papers on faith, because they simply do not have time to check on the relative honesty of each student.

If the research paper requires a lengthy introduction and if it inevitably encourages plagiarism among some students, can it still be a valuable teaching device? The answer is a qualified "yes." The key to the question is, of course: "What does the teacher expect to accomplish through the assignment?" If he expects a lengthy display of the student's own thinking, then he should restructure the assignment. Perhaps the *maj*or point in favor of the student research paper lies in its development of organizational skills. This in itself can be of great value in teaching students to write, for it requires each student to construct his own unique synthesis of the materials at hand. Even papers with dozens of footnotes still reflect this organizational creativity. In accordance with the nature of the course and the time allotted, therefore, the research paper can serve a valuable purpose.

ALTERNATIVES TO THE RESEARCH PAPER

Since organizational skills reflect only one aspect of writing in the social studies, a major shift in emphasis would clearly seem desirable. Additional objectives that can best be accomplished by means other than the traditional research assignment demand greater attention. Such objectives include opportunities for persuasive writing. While there are doubtless other objectives, the importance of these three cannot be denied. Consequently, the following paragraphs will offer three term paper assignments embodying these objectives as alternatives to the research paper assignment.

The first assignment attempts to offer the student an opportunity to work in an area within the social studies relatively free from prior discussion and interpretation. The entire area of county and municipal elections is one such example. The potential for student creativity and individual interpretation and criticism in this area appears virtually limitless. Aside from local newspaper editorials, students are faced with as much "primary material" as they wish to consider. A more specific example of an assignment is the following: During the course of a local political campaign students would be asked to choose two opposing candidates and collect as much information as possible about each one; then, *on the basis of this data,* they would decide which candidate was the better of the two. The local League of Women Voters always presents summary statements made by each candidate, and such a publication could be a good point from which to begin.

It need hardly be said that there are tremendous supplementary benefits from such an assignment. Here is a list of the more important ones: (1) there is an immediate increase of student political awareness at the local level; (2) students are encouraged to see the candidates in person or at least hear them speak; (3) distinctions between fact and opinion and between primary and secondary sources become more meaningful; and (4) the usual forms of plagiarism are practically eliminated.

While this assignment outwardly resembles the traditional research assignment described earlier, it differs in the most fundamental respect. Emphasis is shifted almost completely toward the role of the student's own thinking. Removing the opportunity for the student to appeal to higher authorities allows him to develop a measure of confidence in the possible validity of his own interpretations. Certainly this assignment could not be used in all social studies courses; but surely it would be readily adaptable to any course in government and for some junior and senior high school United States history courses as well. In fact, the *type* of assignment would have applications for any social studies course.

The second alternative term paper assignment attempts to combine the study of a particular subject with an exploration and clarification of one's own values and perspectives.[13] Raths, Harmin, and Simon in their book *Values and Teaching* argue that the "valuing process" is one of the most neglected areas in education. Further, they add that

> . . . the pace and complexity of modern life has so exacerbated the problem of deciding what is good and what is right and what is worthy and what is desirable that large numbers of children are finding it increasingly bewildering, even overwhelming, to decide what is worth valuing. . . .[14]

Hopefully, the assignment outlined here would provide at least one occasion for the student to examine his own values critically.

The example given is in the form of a cross-cultural comparison. The teacher begins by asking the students to choose from a selected list one country with which they would like to compare some aspect of life in the United States. Once the students have committed themselves to a country, the teacher informs them that they are to reverse the expected basis of the comparison and evaluate life in the United States through the eyes of a foreigner. By reversing the usual ordering of the comparison, the teacher challenges the student to evaluate himself from a more objective standpoint. As a specific example, the teacher might have the individual evaluate the typical American high school student as his Soviet counterpart would see him. Unlike the first alternative, a comparative type of

[13] See Neal Rosenberg, "Debating the Past: Moral Judgments and the Teaching of Social Studies," pp. 7–13, in this volume.

[14] Louis Raths, Merrill Harmin, and Sidney Simon, *Values and Teaching* (Columbus, Ohio: Charles E. Merrill Books, 1966), p. 7.

question must rely heavily on secondary sources; nevertheless, in the present example the primary emphasis would still be on the individual student's own thinking.

The third alternative assignment challenges the student to combine his persuasive writing abilities with the available resources. In this example the teacher deliberately presents to the class controversial evidence which appears to contradict a cherished value or belief. The student's task, then, is to refute or defend the evidence as best he can. In essence a "problem" is created, and students are expected to "solve" it. The instructor, of course, must be careful not to make the evidence appear too absurd or too easily refuted; also, he must keep the nature of the problem from becoming too abstract, e.g., "Do we still have freedom of speech in the United States?" By no means should the teacher convey the idea that there is *necessarily* any one right or wrong answer. Indeed, he may wish to suggest that there is perhaps no answer. One example of a cherished belief would be that the majority of Americans are "decent, law-abiding people." After stating this belief, the teacher would then cite statistics revealing that over 90 per cent of all adults have at one or another time committed crimes "for which they could have received a jail or prison sentence." [15] Such a thought-provoking statement as this cannot fail to elicit varied and intriguing student responses.

CONCLUSION

In considering this discussion as a whole there is perhaps one unifying generalization which will draw together the various ideas: no one type of written assignment can individually achieve all the objectives related to writing in the social studies. Once aware of this fact, each teacher should

---

[15] Edwin H. Sutherland and Donald Cressey, *Principles of Criminology*, 6th ed. (Philadelphia: Lippincott, 1960), p. 39.

include within his "repertoire" a variety of written assignments with a full cognizance of their respective strengths and weaknesses. By thus pairing his teaching objectives with his written assignments, the teacher can structure his curriculum accordingly. Both the instructor and the student will begin then to work more effectively.

Questions for Discussion

1. Should the research paper ever be assigned to "below-average" students?

2. Under what conditions could the social studies teacher give his students a choice of written assignments?

3. Should a research paper assignment be given to junior high school students?

4. When should the social studies teacher work in cooperation with his school's English department?

5. What is the role of the school librarian in relation to writing in the social studies?

6. Under what circumstances would a series of short essays be preferable to a research paper, and vice versa?

7. At what point in the semester should the teacher require a research paper to be written?

8. Three alternatives to the standard research paper assignment have been suggested in this chapter. What are some other alternatives?

18

N.D.E.A. INSTITUTE IN AMERICAN HISTORY

A New Frontier in Teacher Education

RONALD MOTT

The great amount of ferment in the social studies is due in large part to the efforts of the Federal government in general and the 1958 National Defense Education Act in particular. Secondary social studies teachers and university professors are meeting across the country in an effort to update the substantive content and teaching methodologies used in secondary social studies classes. A key assumption is that the teacher is probably the most important variable in the classroom situation and therefore his level of intellectual sophistication must be raised. It is because of the role of the Federal government in the New Social Studies that this selection on an N.D.E.A. Institute is included in this book. The writer's discussion of what the institute did for him and his list of subjects and source materials should be of value to the reader.

The plight of the secondary social studies teacher was vividly portrayed by Dr. Van R. Halsey, Assistant Professor of History at Amherst College, Amherst, Massachu-

212

setts, when he said, "lack of funds for diversified historical material; economy-minded school boards which promote the purchase of a large hard-covered text; overworked and many times poorly prepared social studies teachers; a grueling schedule of five classes a day, five days a week, which prevents any considerable amount of innovation on the part of the teacher; the necessity for most teachers to work during the summer rather than develop new approaches to their own courses—all these things force the average history teacher to stick to the familiar textbook-coverage approach in his history course." [1]

Strategies to liberate social studies from the above "cultural lag" have come from numerous quarters. One substantial quarter was provided with the enactment of the National Defense Education Act in 1958. Expansion of this act to include social studies provided funds for numerous institutes around the country. This article is concerned only with the five-week N.D.E.A. American History Institute held at Michigan State University from June 21 to July 30, 1965.

The purpose of this article is to provide prospective American history teachers with a description of a particular history institute and to analyze some of the institute's outcomes. The reader should be reminded that this is only one participant's perception and appraisal and the conclusions arrived at should not necessarily be generalized for others. In addition, a content outline for the institute is printed at the end of this selection and should be referred to while reading the article.

The institute was staffed by three professors from the history department of Michigan State University: Dr. Charles Cumberland, Dr. Justin Kestenbaum, and Dr. Alan Schaffer. The major goal of these professors was to improve the quality of history teaching by the participants

[1] Van R. Halsey, "American History—A New High School Course" (Amherst, Mass.: Amherst College, 1960).

in our public and private secondary schools. Their intermediate objectives toward the realization of this goal were:

1. To develop the ability to recognize, understand, and use a thematic approach in the study of history.
2. To demonstrate the importance of meaningful discussions and written book critiques in historical inquiry.
3. To demonstrate to the participants the value of historical biographies.
4. To demonstrate what the social sciences have to offer to historical inquiry.
5. To apprise history teachers of selective literature in American studies, especially those that are in inexpensive paperbound editions.
6. To apprise the participants of the various research agencies, especially journal publications, which are readily available.
7. To provide a forum for a cross-regional exchange, among the participants, as to how history is studied in their respective regions.

Thirty-five participants representing every region in the United States attended the institute. The requirements of the participants for the five-week session were: (1) to purchase and read twenty paperbacks, (2) to come prepared to class each day to discuss the material read, and (3) to write and submit book critiques on those books designated by the professors.

A typical day at the institute would run as follows. One of the three professors (refer to content outline) would lead a discussion for an hour and a half on the different interpretations of the theme for the week. The professors, during these sessions, wanted the participants to analyze different interpretations verbally by utilizing the fund of information contained in their reading. Hence, the theme for the week acted as a hypothesis around which the stuff of history could be organized.

After a short break, the total group was divided into three groups. Each group went to a separate classroom and, led by one of the three professors, discussed the books read for the theme of the week. Any questions concerning the previous total group discussion, the books read, the written book critiques, and the methodological problems in teaching history on the secondary level were discussed in these smaller group sessions. It must be noted here that if someone was looking for ready-made answers in these discussion sessions, he did not find them, but did find additional questions to be asked.

Evaluation procedures consisted of written book critiques and mid-term and final essay exams.

As to the significant outcomes of the institute, these should be in direct correlation to how well the objectives were accomplished. It must be noted that the institute is not a panacea for the teacher in American history. It does not give him a "bag of tricks" to take back to the classroom. But one of the significant results of the institute is the recognition that the teacher is probably one of the most important variables in bringing about innovation in the study of history in the secondary schools. Hence, the institute is more of a recommendation of how to study history rather than teaching him history, per se.[2] It is an attempt to transfuse new blood into an old system, by recommending a thematic approach to historical inquiry. This does not mean that the thematic approach is the only remedy, but it is a better method than most in promoting critical thinking. It is also recognized that the recommendation is futile unless the teacher is committed to a life of quality historical study. Implicit in this commitment is that the history teacher becomes an agent of change to help liquidate the "cultural lag" noted by Dr. Van R. Halsey.

[2] W. H. Cartwright and R. L. Watson, *Interpreting and Teaching American History*, 31st Yearbook (Washington, D.C.: National Council for Social Studies, 1961), p. 4.

It is the opinion of this writer that the institute accomplished its objectives. One, it introduced the writer to the thematic approach to historical inquiry. Two, the institute provided the writer with the opportunity to develop a particular thesis and attempt to maintain it by thoughtful discussion. Three, it taught the writer that the teaching of history is not jamming a packaged fund of information down students' throats. Remember, students are not empty containers to be promptly filled up; they have to have time to think about what they are reading. As one historian remarks, "Surely, for the teacher of history, it should be clear that to develop the skill of critical thinking in students is a prerequisite to any other values that spring from a study of history." [3] This means we must be more selective in our choice of content and methods, instead of just covering ground. Four, I became more aware of the important contributions of socio-psychology in the study of history, i.e., studies by David Riesman, Seymour Martin Lipset, Samuel Lubell, Daniel Bell, Richard Hofstadter, and David Potter. Five, by purchasing the twenty paperbacks, I now have the beginnings of a library of American studies. Six, the institute provided me with the inexpensive opportunity to become a subscriber to the *Journal of American History*. And last, the institute gave me the opportunity to discuss with other participants from California to New York to Alabama, different substantive and methodological approaches to the study of American History.

It is the writer's recommendation that more institutes should be provided so that many more teachers of history can have this liberating experience.

[3] *Ibid.*, p. 4.

SCOPE AND SEQUENCE OF THE
MICHIGAN STATE UNIVERSITY N.D.E.A. HISTORY INSTITUTE

Theme I: "The American Mind"—June 21–25. Professor Schaffer.

PROBLEM	ACTIVITIES	BIBLIOGRAPHY
1. Is there a unique American mind?	1. Dr. Alan Schaffer led total group in discussion of Theme I for an hour and a half each day.	Carl Degler, *Out of Our Past* (New York: Harper Colophon Books, 1962).
2. What were the differences between the colonists and the Englishmen who stayed in England?	2. Later, the total group was divided into three groups. Each group went to a separate classroom and, led by one of the three professors, discussed the books read for Theme I. Written book critiques were due on specified books from the bibliography each session.	Albert Jay Nock, *Jefferson* (New York: Hill and Wang, 1956).
3. What was the colonial mind? Were there separate Northern and Southern colonial minds?		Henry Steele Commager, *The American Mind* (Yale University Press, 1950).
4. Was the American Revolution a unique accomplishment?		Daniel Boorstin, *The Americans: The Colonial Experience* (New York: Vintage, 1958).
5. Did capitalism come over on the first ship?		
6. Has there been a continuity or change in the American mind?		

Theme II: "The American Constitutional System"–June 28–July 2. Professor Kestenbaum.

1. What is the nature of the Union?
2. What kind of a document is the American Constitution?
3. What is the role of the Court?
4. What policies did the Court adopt?
5. What is the difference between procedural and substantive due process?
6. Is the Union a government of men or laws?
7. Is the Constitution a political and/or economic document?
8. What has been the Court's record on civil liberties?

1. Dr. Justin Kestenbaum led total group in discussion on Theme II.
2. Later, group divided into separate sections for discussion of books read and critiques written.

Carl B. Swisher, *The Growth of Constitutional Power in the United States* (Chicago: Phoenix edition, 1963).
Robert H. Jackson, *The Struggle for Judicial Supremacy* (New York: Vintage, 1964).
Alexander Bickel, *The Least Dangerous Branch* (New York: Bobbs-Merrill, 1962).

Theme III: "The American Frontier"–July 6–9. Professor Cumberland.

1. Did the frontier create democratic institutions?
2. What motivated the English

1. Dr. Charles Cumberland led total group in discussion of Theme III.

Frederick Jackson Turner, *The Frontier in American History* (New York: Holt, Rinehart &

to go into the interior?

3. The safety-valve theory—symbol or myth?

4. Who went west, the urban masses or the urban affluent?

Theme IV: "The American Economic System"–July 12–16. Professor Schaffer.

1. What is meant by economic growth?

2. What is meant by economic determinism?

3. Is there a correlation between Protestantism and the profit motive?

4. Did the Navigation Acts have a restraining effect upon surplus accumulation in the colonies?

5. Was 1783–1789 a critical period in U.S. history or is this a phony issue?

6. Is the concept of free enterprise reality or myth?

2. Separate group discussions of books read and critiques written.

1. Dr. Alan Schaffer led total group in discussion of Theme IV.

2. Dr. Stuart Bruchey led a discussion on the findings of his new book.

3. Separate group discussions of books read and critiques written.

Winston, 1963).

Henry Nash Smith, *Virgin Land* (New York: Vintage, 1950).

Louis B. Wright, *Culture on the Moving Frontier* (New York: Harper Torchbook, 1955).

Thomas C. Cochran, *The American Business System, 1900–1955: A Historical Perspective* (New York: Harper Torchbooks, 1957).

Stuart Bruchey, *The Roots of American Economic Growth* (New York: Harper & Row, 1965).

Samuel P. Hays, *The Response to Industrialism* (University of Chicago Press, 1957).

Jeannette Mirskey and Allan Nevins, *The World of Eli Whitney* (New York: Collier Books, 1962).

Theme V: "America and the World"—July 19–23. Professor Kestenbaum.

1. Has foreign policy been America's number one problem?
2. Are there continuities in U.S. foreign policy?
3. Is the concept of isolationism symbol or myth?
4. What is the public philosophy and its effect on foreign policy?
5. Have we implemented a legalistic-moralistic approach to solving problems in foreign policy?
6. Are there fundamental incompatibilities between American and Communist foreign policy?
7. Who was responsible for Pearl Harbor?
8. The decision to drop the atomic bomb and its consequences for the world.

1. Dr. Justin Kestenbaum led total group in discussion of Theme V.
2. Separate group discussion of books read and written critiques.

George Kennan, *American Diplomacy, 1900–1950* (New York: Mentor, 1950).

Arthur S. Link, *Wilson the Diplomatist* (Chicago: Quadrangle Press, 1965).

Selig Adler, *The Isolationist Impulse* (New York: Collier Books, 1961).

Should we follow a policy of liberation from or coexistence with communism?
10. Is Moscow still the monolithic source of power for the communist movement?

Theme VI: "Reform in America"—July 26-30. Professor Cumberland.

1. What is a reform movement? What is a radical movement?
2. Is the labor movement a reform movement?
3. Progressive reform—symbol or myth?
4. "Was Progressive reform an agrarian crusade against big business?" [4]
5. "Was Progressive reform a struggle by the middle class against corporate power?" [5]

1. Dr. Charles Cumberland led total group in discussion of Theme VI.
2. Separate group discussions of books read and written critiques.

Alice Felt Tyler, *Freedom's Ferment* (New York: Harper Torchbooks, 1962).
Richard Hofstadter, *The Age of Reform* (New York: Vintage, 1955).
John Higham, *Strangers in the Land* (New York: Atheneum, 1963).

4 David M. Potter and Curtis R. Grant, *Eight Issues in Amercan History* (Palo Alto, Calif.: Scott Foresman and Company, 1966), Issue 6, pp. 100–119.
5 *Ibid.*

221

Theme VI: "*Reform in America*"—*July 26–30. Professor Cumberland* (cont.)

6. "Was Progressive reform nothing more than business domination?" [6]

7. Are communism and socialism within the American reform tradition?

8. The New Deal–sharp break with the past or continuity?

[6] *Ibid.*

Questions for Discussion

1. What is your opinion of the barriers to change discussed by Professor Van R. Halsey? Would you agree that such barriers often lead to the "familiar textbook-coverage approach"?

2. Evaluate the intermediate objectives for this particular institute in light of your objectives in attending such an institute.

3. Do you feel that the institute overemphasized either teaching methodology or substantive content?

4. Do you feel that the institute underemphasized either teaching methodology or substantive content?

5. What is your opinion of the themes, activities, and sources used in the institute?